Banking Structures in Major Countries

Innovations in Financial Markets and Institutions

Editors:

Robert A. Eisenbeis and Richard W. McEnally
University of North Carolina at Chapel Hill
Chapel Hill, North Carolina, U.S.A.

Other books in the series:

England, C. and Huertas, T.:
THE FINANCIAL SERVICES REVOLUTION

Gup, B.:
BANK MERGERS: CURRENT ISSUES AND PERSPECTIVES

Kormendi, R., Bernard, V., Pirrong, S., and Snyder, E.:
CRISIS RESOLUTION IN THE THRIFT INDUSTRY

Hancock, D.:
A THEORY OF PRODUCTION FOR THE FINANCIAL FIRM

Banking Structures in Major Countries

Edited by
George G. Kaufman
Loyola University of Chicago

Kluwer Academic Publishers
Boston/Dordrecht/London

Distributors for North America:
Kluwer Academic Publishers
101 Philip Drive
Assinippi Park
Norwell, Massachusetts 02061 USA

Distributors for all other countries:
Kluwer Academic Publishers Group
Distribution Centre
Post Office Box 322
3300 AH Dordrecht, THE NETHERLANDS

Library of Congress Cataloging-in-Publication Data
Banking structures in major countries/edited
  by George G. Kaufman.
    p.   cm.—(Innovations in financial markets and
  institutions) Includes bibliographical references and
  index.
  ISBN 0-7923-9136-5
    1. Banks and banking—Europe.   2. Banks and banking
  —United States.   3. Banks and banking—Canada.
  4. Banks and banking—Japan.   5. Banks and banking—
  China.   I. Kaufman, George G.   II. Series.
  HG2974.B36   1991
  332.1—dc20   90-6621
                                                          CIP

Copyright © 1992 by Kluwer Academic Publishers

All rights reserved. No part of this publication may be reproduced,
stored in a retrieval system or transmitted in any form or by any means,
mechanical, photocopying, recording, or otherwise, without the prior
written permission of the publisher, Kluwer Academic Publishers, 101
Philip Drive, Assinippi Park, Norwell, Massachusetts 02061.

Printed on acid-free paper.

Printed in the United States of America

Contents

About the Authors	vii
Preface	xiii

1   1
Bank Structure in Canada
Lawrence Kryzanowski and Gordon S. Roberts

2   59
Bank Structure in Chile
Sergio de la Cuadra and Salvador Valdés-Prieto

3   113
Banking Structure of China
Zhou Lin

4   155
Banking in the European Economic Community: Structure, Competition, and Public Policy
Joseph Bisignano

5   245
The French Financial System
L. Beduc, F. Ducruezet, and P. Papadacci

6   293
The Structure of the Italian Financial System
G.P. Szegö and V.S. Szegö

7   333
The Evolution of Japanese Banking and Finance
Thomas F. Cargill and Shoichi Royama

8 Bank Structure in Switzerland Urs W. Birchler and Georg Rich	389
9 The British Financial System David T. Llewellyn	429
10 The United States Financial System Herbert L. Baer and Larry R. Mote	469
11 Bank Structure in West Germany Randall Johnston Pozdena and Volbert Alexander	555
Index	595

About the Authors

George G. Kaufman is the John F. Smith Jr. Professor of Finance and Economics at Loyola University of Chicago. He previously taught at the University of Oregon and was an economist at the Federal Reserve Bank of Chicago. He has been a visiting professor at Stanford University and the University of California at Berkeley, a visiting scholar at the Federal Reserve Bank of San Francisco and the Comptroller of the Currency, and also served as the deputy to the assistant secretary for economic policy at the U.S. Treasury Department. He is a member of the board of directors of the Rochester (NY) Community Savings Bank and was an elected trustee of the College Retirement Equities Fund.

Professor Kaufman has published widely in professional journals and authored/edited many books including; *The U.S. Financial System* (Prentice-Hall, 4th edition, 1989), *Restructuring the American Financial System* (Kluwer, 1990), *Perspectives on Safe and Sound Banking* (MIT Press, 1986), and *Deregulating Financial Services* (Ballinger, 1986). He is a co-editor of the *Journal of Financial Services Research* and an associate editor of the *Journal of Money, Credit, and Banking*, the *Financial Review*, and *The Journal of Financial Research*. He has testified numerous times before Congress. He has been honored by his peers by being elected president of both the Western Finance and the Midwest Finance Associations. Kaufman is co-chair of the Shadow Financial Regulatory Committee.

Volbert Alexander is professor of economics at the Justus-Liebig-University Giessen (West Germany). He formerly was professor of economics at the University of Siegen. He obtained his Ph.D. in economics and a postdoctoral degree in economics from the University of Konstanz. His main fields of interest are monetary macroeconomics, monetary and fiscal policy and monetary theory.

Herbert L. Baer, Jr. is an assistant vice president and senior economist at the Federal Reserve Bank of Chicago where he studies the regulation of the financial services industry. He holds a Ph.D. in economics from Northwestern University. He has published studies on the S&L industry, regulatory taxes, international banking, the control of systemic risk in financial markets and regulatory reform in a number of journals and has also published in several books and conference volumes.

Louis Beduc graduated from the Institute of Political Studies in Paris and received his masters in economics from the University of Paris. He has been an executive at the Bank of France since 1988 and works in the monetary statistics and studies division where he focuses on flow of funds statistics, financial forecasts, and public finance.

Urs Birchler has a Ph.D. in economics from Zurich University in 1980. He is head of the banking studies section of the Swiss National Bank in Zurich.

Joseph Bisignano is assistant manager of the monetary and economic department at the Bank for International Settlements (BIS) in Basel, Switzerland. He has a B.A. from the University of Buffalo, M.B.A. from Columbia University, and Ph.D. from Stanford. He previously was senior vice president and director of research at the Federal Reserve Bank of San Francisco and has taught economics at Rutgers and Stanford Universities.

Thomas F. Cargill received his Ph.D. from the University of California at Davis and teaches at the University of Nevada, Reno. He has published extensively in the areas of financial markets and monetary policy and has been a visiting scholar at several major regulatory agencies in both the United States and Japan. His latest book is *Central Book Independence and Regulatory Responsibilities: The Bank of Japan and the Federal Reserve*.

Sergio de la Cuadra received his M.A. and Ph.D. from the University of Chicago. He is currently the president of Sergio de la Cuadra y Asociados S.A.; chairman of the Board Distribution Chilectra Metropolitana S.A. and member of the Board Bolsa de Valores de Chile. He previously served as Governor of the Central Bank of Chile, Minister of Finance, member of the board of Banco de Chile and of several other corporations and as professor at the Catholic University of Chile.

Francoise Ducruezet graduated from the Institute of Political Studies in Paris and received her law degree from the University of Paris. She has been an executive at the Bank of France since 1977 and worked in the banking supervision department until 1986. Since 1986, she has worked in the monetary statistics and studies division, concentrating on financial national accounts.

Lawrence Kryzanowski is professor of finance of Concordia University (Canada). He received his B.A. from the University of Calgary and his Ph.D. from the University of British Columbia and has visited the University of British Columbia, the University of Rochester and the Canadian Federal Department of Finance. He is the co-author of a major Canada finance textbook, the author of a number of other books and has published widely in leading journals in finance and economics. He is also a former co-editor of the *Canadian Journal of Administrative Sciences*.

Zhou Lin received his B.A. in economics from Northeastern University of China and an M.A. from Southwest Union University in China. He also received an M.A. in economics from the University of Wisconsin at Madison. He was a division chief and department head at the Bank of China and visiting professor at California State University at Northridge. He is currently research fellow and professor at the Research Institute of Finance and Banking of the People's Bank of China and counsellor at the State Council of the People's Republic of China.

David Llewellyn is professor of money and banking and chairman of the Loughborough University Banking Centre. He has formerly held economics posts at the British Treasury, the International Monetary Fund, and Nottingham University. He has written extensively in the areas of international finance, U.K. financial markets and institutions and regulation in finance, and has served as a consultant to several financial institutions and regulatory agencies in various countries.

Larry R. Mote is an economic adviser and vice president at the Federal Reserve Bank of Chicago. He is a graduate of the University of Maryland and was Fulbright Scholar at the University of Cologne, before doing graduate work in economics at Cornell University. He has been a visiting professor of finance at the University of Oregon and is currently a visiting scholar with the Congressional Budget Office. He has published extensively on issues on banking structure and the Glass-Steagall Act.

Randall Johnston Pozdena is vice president in charge of finance, banking and regional research at the Federal Reserve Bank of San Francisco. Before assuming his present position, he was a professor of economics and a management consultant. He holds an undergraduate degree in economics from Dartmouth College and a PhD in economics from the University of California, Berkeley. He has written articles on a wide variety of topics, including bond market behavior, international banking, the payments system, and corporate financial structure and is the author of a book on housing.

Salvador Valdes Prieto received his Ph.D. in economics from the Massachusetts Institute of Technology. He currently is assistant professor of economics at University Catolica de Chile. His main areas of interest are financial systems, industrial organization and macroeconomics. He has written a number of articles on these topics in scholarly journals. He has worked in Chile as assistant to the Minister of Economics and as a consultant to the Superintendence of Banks, the Central Bank and the Finance Legislative Committee.

Georg Rich is chief economist and a director of the Swiss National Bank in Zurich. After completing his undergraduate studies at the University of Zurich, he obtained a Ph.D. in economics from Brown University in 1969. Until 1977, he taught at Carleton University in Ottawa (Canada) and served as chairman of the economics department from 1972 to 1974. He is author of a book and numerous scholarly articles.

Gordon Roberts is the Bank of Montreal Professor of Finance at Dalhousie University (Canada). He received his B.A. from Oberlin College and his Ph.D. from Boston College. He has been a visiting faculty member at the University of Arizona, the University of Victoria, the University of Zimbabwe and Xiamen University (China). He has published widely in finance and economic journals and serves on the editorial board of three journals.

Shoichi Royama is professor of money and banking at Osaka University. He attended Tokyo University and received his Ph.D. from Osaka University. He has been a scholar at the Bank of Japan and has been involved in a number of research projects for the Ministry of Finance regarding the future structure of Japanese banking. He has published extensively in Japanese and English. His most recent publication in English is *The Transition of Finance in Japan and the United States: A Comparative Perspective*.

Pierre Papadacci Stephanopoli graduated in economics from the Universite d'Aix-Marseille. He has been an executive at the Bank of France since 1977 and worked in the electronic data processing department until 1986. Since 1986, he has worked in the monetary statistics and studies division, concentrating on monetary and banking statistics.

Giorgio Szegö is professor of banking and finance at the University La Sapienza in Rome and director of the Post Graduate School in Banking Policy and Law at the same university. He previously taught at the Universities of Bergamo, Venice and Milano and was rector of the University of Bergamo for nine years. He has been visiting professor at

Massachusetts Institute of Technology, New York University, Case-Western Reserve and Purdue. He has been a consultant to the I.M.F. and the World Bank. Professor Szego has published widely in professional journals and authored/edited many books including: *Portfolio Theory*, *Mercati Finanziari ed Attivita' Bancaria Internazionale*. He is co-editor of the *Journal of Banking and Finance*.

Vittoria Szegö is employed at IMI (Istituto Mobiliare Italiano) in the capital markets Division. She previously was a financial analyst at CREDIPAR (Rome) and a research assistant at CERBAF (Research Institute for Banking and Finance). She has published in professional journals on the subject of mergers and acquisitions in the Italian banking system.

Preface

The ongoing globalization of financial markets has increased the importance to users of financial services, policy-makers and financial analysts of understanding the structure and operation of banking systems in other countries as well as that in their own country. This volume contributes to such an understanding. The structure and operation of the banking system are described for 10 important countries, plus the European Economic Community, under one cover. The contributing authors are knowledgable and widely respected experts. The author, or at least one of the coauthors, of each chapter is a resident of the country described. Each chapter follows a broadly similar outline, although the attention devoted to any particular area varies substantially according to authors' perceptions of its relative importance in the particular country. The chapters spotlight the similarities and differences among the structures. The volume should serve as both a handy and authoritative reference guide for practitioners, regulators and students of international banking.

An early benefit of the book was an international conference held in Chicago in the fall of 1989 on the world integration of financial markets. A number of the authors of the chapters presented brief versions of their papers. The conference was sponsored jointly by the Federal Reserve Bank of Chicago and the MidAmerica Institute. The audience was primarily senior officers and regulators of financial institutions in the midwest. The conference generated considerable interest in both the subject matter and the contents of this book.

Brief biographical sketches of the contributing authors are shown at the end of the book.

Banking Structures in Major Countries

1 BANK STRUCTURE IN CANADA
Lawrence Kryzanowski and Gordon S. Roberts

1. Description of the Current Structure of Financial Institutions and Markets

About 800 depository institutions (banks, trust and finance companies, and credit unions) and nondepository institutions (insurance companies and investment dealers) operated in Canada during 1987. The Canadian financial services industry employed 600,000 people and produced about 15% of Canada's gross domestic product during 1987 (Falconer, 1988). A summary of the powers and types of businesses conducted by various types of financial institutions, along with the responsibilities of their major regulators, is presented in table 1-1.

The assets of selected private institutions, and their relative shares of total assets and GNP, are presented in table 1-2. Although the relative shares of total assets of the chartered banks and of the trust and mortgage loan companies increased from 1967 to 1981 and then decreased from 1981 to 1986, the relative shares of total assets of the pension funds increased from 1967 to 1981 and from 1981 to 1986.

Some descriptive statistics for the 25 largest financial institutions in Canada in terms of total assets for 1988 are given in table 1-3. Although

Table 1-1. Regulatory Differences Among the Various Types of Financial Institutions in Canada for Various Characteristics

	Banks	Credit Unions and Caisses Populaires	Trust Companies	Loan Companies	Life Insurance Companies	General Insurance Companies	Investment Dealers
Deposits	Allowed	Allowed	Allowed	Allowed	Can provide only depositlike short-term deferred annuities	Not allowed	Deposits accepted in form of cash management accounts
Statutory reserves Primary (non-interest bearing)	10% on demand deposits 2% on notice deposits up to $500 million 3% on notice deposits over $500 million 3% on foreign-currency deposits of Canadian residents	Not required	Not required	Not required	Not required	Not applicable	Not required
Secondary	Required as set by Bank of Canada	Not required	Not required	Not required	Not required	Not applicable	Not required
Deposit insurance	CDIC coverage	Covered by RADQ in Quebec; OSDIC in Ontario; protected by stabilization funds in other provinces	CDIC coverage, except RADQ for provincial companies in Quebec; some companies not covered	CDIC coverage, except RADQ for provincial companies in Quebec; some companies not covered	None	Not applicable	Industry contingency fund

BANK STRUCTURE IN CANADA

Activity							
Mortgage lending	Allowed	Allowed	Allowed	Allowed	Allowed	Allowed	Allowed
Commercial lending	Allowed	Allowed	Restricted to inclusion in basket (varies, depending on incorporation)	Restricted to inclusion in basket (varies, depending on incorporation)	Not allowed	Not allowed	Not allowed
Personal lending	Allowed	Allowed	Restricted to inclusion in basket (varies, depending on incorporation)	Restricted to inclusion in basket (varies, depending on incorporation)	Can only offer policy loans	Not allowed	Can extend credit on margin accounts
Corporate securities underwriting	Allowed through subsidiaries	Not allowed	Not allowed	Not allowed	Not allowed	Not allowed	Allowed
Securities distribution	Allowed through subsidiaries	Allowed	Allowed	Not allowed	Not allowed	Not allowed	Allowed
Investment counseling	Not allowed domestically	Not allowed	Allowed	Not allowed	Allowed	Allowed	Allowed
Portfolio management	Restricted to nondiscretionary funds domestically	Not allowed	Allowed	Restricted to acting as agency	Allowed	Allowed	Allowed
Trustee services	Not allowed, discretionary services	Not allowed	Allowed	Not allowed	Not allowed, except for provincially incorporated companies in Quebec	Not allowed, except for provincially incorporated companies in Quebec	Not allowed

Source: Update of Economic Council of Canada (1987).

Table 1-2. Domestic Assets of Selected Financial Institutions Issuing Claims to the General Public: Selected Years, 1870–1986[a]

Private Financial Institution	1870 Millions of Dollars	1870 Percentage of: Total Assets	1870 Percentage of: GNP	1967 Millions of Dollars	1967 Percentage of: Total Assets	1967 Percentage of: GNP	1981 Millions of Dollars	1981 Percentage of: Total Assets	1981 Percentage of: GNP	1986 Millions of Dollars	1986 Percentage of: Total Assets	1986 Percentage of: GNP
Chartered banks	131	92.2	28.5	22,889	38.0	34.8	182,157	46.29	55.48	245,212	40.74	50.82
Trust and mortgage loan companies	—	—	—	6,733	11.2	10.2	59,186	15.04	18.03	76,440	12.70	15.84
Credit unions and caisses populaires	—	—	—	3,113	5.2	4.7	31,331	7.96	9.54	45,090	7.49	9.34
Quebec savings banks	7	4.7	1.5	458	0.8	0.7	1,786	0.45	0.54	6,482	1.08	1.34
Life insurance companies	4	3.1	1	12,323	20.5	18.8	39,070	9.93	11.90	68,474	11.38	14.19
Consumer loan and sales finance companies	—	—	—	4,437	7.4	6.8	14,252	3.62	4.34	17,949	2.98	3.72
Mutual funds	—	—	—	1,993	3.3	2.9	4,234	1.08	1.29	14,962	2.49	3.10
Pension funds	—	—	—	8,273	13.7	12.6	61,514	15.63	18.74	127,336	21.15	26.39
Total assets of selected private institutions	142	100.0	31.0	60,219	100.0	91.6	393,530	100.00	119.87	601,945	100.00	124.75

[a] As of March 31.

Sources: Neufeld (1972) for 1870. Economic Council of Canada, *Efficiency and Regulation: A Study of Deposit Institutions* (Ottawa: Supply and Services Canada, 1976) for 1967. Bank of Canada Review, Report of the Superintendent of Insurance for Canada, Statistics Canada and Quarterly Estimates of Trusteed Pension Funds for 1981 and 1986.

the chartered banks occupy the first five ranks and six of the top ten ranks, the ranking contains a cross section of the types of financial institutions that are found in Canada and are discussed below.

1.1. Commercial (Chartered) Banks

Chartered banks are depository institutions with federal charters. Although some near banks in Canada come under federal supervision (federally chartered trust companies) and others are licensed by the provinces (credit unions and some trust companies), only chartered banks are required to hold primary reserves in noninterest-bearing assets.[1]

Chartered banks in Canada are allowed to take deposits of all kinds, to issue demand, term, and mortgage loans to both individuals and companies, and to invest in securities (with some limitations on their equity holdings), and to underwrite and distribute government securities. Through wholly owned subsidiaries, the chartered banks are permitted to engage in certain kinds of financial leasing, factoring, venture capital investments, and the corporate underwriting, brokerage, and distribution of securities. The chartered banks are specifically prohibited from offering discretionary (trust) services, and are generally prohibited from insurance brokerage and domestic portfolio management or investment counseling.

In some cases, the federal government has ignored bank practices that appear to violate the spirit of the law. While the Bank Act prohibits banks from selling insurance, most of the major banks have offshore reinsurance subsidiaries that indirectly insure most mortgage and consumer loans for their bank clients. Some banks have also begun to market insurance products to their credit card customers (McNish, 1989a). During 1988, the Canadian banks launched a vigorous campaign to be allowed to sell insurance to the public through their branches. The insurance companies provided stiff opposition to the entry of the banks into this lucrative market ($10.9 billion in property and casualty premiums and $12.3 billion in life and health premiums in 1987). The upcoming federal legislation probably will not give the banks the right to offer insurance company products through their branch networks. But the banks probably will be able to incorporate subsidiaries that will be able to promote their own products through their own branches (Horvitch, 1989b).

At the end of 1988, 7 Schedule One and 59 Schedule Two banks operated in Canada (Canadian Bankers Association, 1989). Schedule

Table 1-3. The Top 25 Financial Institutions in Canada Based on Total Assets for 1988

Rank by assets 1988	Rank by assets 1987	Assets (in thousands)	Company (Head Office)	Rank by Revenue	Revenue (in thousands)
1	1	$110,054,340	Royal Bank of Canada (Montreal), October 1988	1	$10,594,976
2	2	94,687,528	Canadian Imperial Bank of Commerce (Toronto), October 1988	3	9,157,580
3	3	78,908,911	Bank of Montreal (Montreal), October 1988	2	9,180,181
4	4	74,674,837	Bank of Nova Scotia (Halifax), October 1988	4	7,032,561
5	5	59,285,378	Toronto Dominion Bank (Toronto), October 1988	5	5,862,035
6	7	34,246,830[a]	La confederation des caisses populaires Desjardins du Quebec (Quebec)	7	3,531,851
7	9	31,825,000[b]	Trilon Financial Corp. (Toronto)	6	3,883,000
8	8	31,798,000	Caisse de depot et placement du Quebec (Quebec City)	10	2,633,000
9	6	30,922,587	National Bank of Canada (Montreal), October 1988	9	3,097,613
10	10	29,219,217[c]	CT Financial Services Inc. (London, Ont.)	8	3,264,964
11	11	16,026,238[d]	Central Capital Corporation (Halifax)	12	1,758,471
12	12	12,191,557	National Trustco Inc.[e] (Stratford, Ont.), October 1988	13	1,262,673
13	15	10,202,891[f]	Montreal Trustco Inc. (Montreal)	14	1,106,832

Rank by net income	Net income (in thousands)	Return on Assets %	Return on Shareholders Equity %	Employees	Foreign Ownership %	Major Shareholders
1	$712,318	0.67%	15.07%	46,096		Wide distribution
3	591,030	0.65%	13.34%	36,194		Wide distribution
4	553,352	0.68%	15.27%	34,115		Wide distribution
5	506,647	0.69%	16.91%	29,113	3	Wide distribution
2	667,776	1.17%	18.49%	22,853		Wide distribution
8	205,078	0.64%	13.09%	26,939		Member federations
10	169,000	0.57%	12.34%	25,000	1	Brascan 46%, Olympia and York 14%
n.a.	n.a.	n.a.	n.a.	222		Quebec government 100%
7	226,298	0.74%	15.12%	13,126		Wide distribution
6	231,978	0.85%	19.12%	11,504		Imasco 99%
14	63,301	0.44%	7.14%	5,400	1	L. Ellen, H.R. Cohen 65% combined
13	68,743	0.59%	12.79%	4,451		NVG Holdings 22%, E-L Financial 18%
15	61,595	0.69%	14.46%	3,018	1	Power Financial 64%

Table 1-3. (Continued)

Rank by assets 1988	Rank by assets 1987	Assets (in thousands)	Company (Head Office)	Rank by Revenue	Revenue (in thousands)
14	13	9,821,657[g]	Laurentian Group Corp. (Montreal)	11	2,152,800
15	14	9,300,000	Canada Mortgage and Housing Corporation (Ottawa)	15	925,000
16	17	7,172,809	General Motors Acceptance Corp. of Canada (Toronto)	16	828,756
17	16	6,522,400	Export Development Corp. (Ottawa)	19	619,000
18	18	6,153,041	Province of Alberta Treasury Branches (Edmonton), March 1988	21	594,992
19	*	5,164,000[h]	Alliance-Industrial Financial Corp. (Montreal)	18	693,000
20	19	5,145,847	Lloyds Bank Canada (Toronto), October 1988	23	507,127
21	22	4,971,451[i]	First City Financial Corp. (Vancouver)	17	734,873
22	28	4,832,290[j]	Hongkong Bank of Canada (Vancouver), October 1988	26	400,376
23	24	4,398,303	Ford Credit Canada Ltd. (Oakville, Ontario)	22	552,756

Rank by net income	Net income (in thousands)	Return on Assets %	Return on Shareholders Equity %	Employees	Foreign Ownership %	Major Shareholders
26	22,872	0.23%	3.97%	7,500	20	Group Victoire, France 18%, Laurentian Life 63%, Eaton's 11%
17	50,000	0.53%	100.00%	3,069		Federal government 100%
16	52,782	0.78%	15.06%	620	100	General Motors Acceptance, Detroit
54	4,200	0.06%	0.47%	503		Federal government 100%
96	(24,816)	n.a.	n.a.	2,946		Alberta government 100%
32	10,905	0.23%	3.99%	2,450		Industrial Alliance Life 100%
69	2,168	0.04%	0.73%	1,468	100	Lloyds Bank, Britain
19	40,276	0.83%	11.94%	900	2	Belzberg family 72%
27	20,837	0.50%	7.67%	1,400	100	Hongkong and Shanghai Banking, Hong Kong
20	39,856	0.95%	16.96%	471	100	Ford Motor Credit, Dearborn, Mich.

Table 1-3. (Continued)

Rank by assets 1988	Rank by assets 1987	Assets (in thousands)	Company (Head Office)	Rank by Revenue	Revenue (in thousands)
24	27	4,330,167	Hees International Bancorp Inc. (Toronto)	24	477,654
25	20	4,307,191	Farm Credit Corp. (Ottawa), March 1988	27	384,018

Notes: For banks, shareholders equity includes appropriations for contingencies. For trust companies, assets do not include estate, trust, and agency business.

* Not on last year's list.

n.a. Not available/not applicable.

^a Includes assets of caisses populaires, member federations, and Caisse Centrale Desjardins, but excludes those of Trustco Desjardins Inc.

^b Consolidates results of Royal Trustco. Assets at year-end were $28.5 billion.

^c Consolidates results of Canada Trustco. Assets figure not available.

^d Consolidates results of Guaranty Trust (assets at year-end $5.8 billion), Central Trust (assets at year-end $4.9 billion), Central and Guaranty Trust (name change from Financial

One banks, which include the "Big Six" domestically owned banks, are subject to a 10% limit on ownership by any one party. Schedule Two banks, which can be wholly owned subsidiaries, are limited as a group to 12% of the assets of the banking system. With one exception (the Laurentian Bank), the Schedule Two banks are foreign owned (Financial Post, 1989). The ten largest chartered banks in term of total assets for 1988, and their relative rankings in terms of all financial institutions, are given in table 1-4. While Canada's major banks are growing, other financial institutions are gaining ground on the banks. For instance, although the National Bank still ranks as the sixth largest bank, it has been overtaken in terms of assets by the federation of Quebec credit unions (the Confederation caisses populaires Desjardins), by a pension fund (Caisse de Depot et Placement du Quebec), and by a holding company (Trilon Financial, which is the parent of the trust company Royal Trustco).

Unrestricted branching has long been a key feature of the Canadian

Rank by net income	Net income (in thousands)	Return on Assets %	Return on Shareholders Equity %	Employees	Foreign Ownership %	Major Shareholders
9	190,959	4.68%	12.48%	20	2	Edper Enterprises 41%, Canadian Express 14%
98	(511,838)	n.a.	n.a.	560		Federal government 100%

Trust, assets at year-end $1.2 billion), and Yorkshire Trust (assets at year-end $790 million).

[e] Name changed from National Victoria and Grey Trustco.

[f] Results not consolidated with parent company. At press time, BCE Inc. had made an offer to acquire all outstanding shares.

[g] Consolidates results of Laurentian Bank. Assets at year-end were $4.8 billion.

[h] Consolidates results of General Trustco of Canada. Assets at year-end were $4.9 billion.

[i] Consolidates results of First City Trust. Assets at year-end were $3.6 billion.

[j] Includes results of Midland Bank Canada acquired in 1988.

Source: *The Financial Post 500* (1989): 162–163.

banking system. As a result, Canada has developed a highly concentrated banking system dominated by six large banks. In 1988, these six banks ranged in asset size from US$ 25.6 billion to US$ 91.3 billion. Table 1-5 shows that the top six banks accounted for over 80% of all bank assets at the end of 1987. This level of concentration has been in place (with some fluctuation) since 1930.

Selected data on these Big Six Schedule One banks are presented in table 1-6. Although these banks are quite profitable, they have rather lackluster market/book-value ratios and price-earnings ratios relative to other companies listed on the Toronto Stock Exchange. Canada's Big Six banks are highly internationalized. For example, the Royal Bank of Canada has consistently ranked as one of the top 20 banks in foreign exchange in *Euromoney's* poll of corporate treasurers (specifically, ninth, third, and fifth in 1987, 1988, and 1989, respectively) (*Euromoney*, 1989). The Bank of Montreal (eighth) and the Royal Bank (tenth) were ranked in the top ten banks for investors and other nonfinancial institutions in a

Table 1-4. The Biggest Banks, Trusts, and Credit Unions in Canada Based on Total Assets for 1988

BIGGEST BANKS

Rank	Rank in Top 100 1988	Assets (in thousands)	Company
1	1	$110,054,340	Royal Bank of Canada
2	2	94,687,528	Canadian Imperial Bank of Commerce (CIBC)
3	3	78,908,911	Bank of Montreal (BOM)
4	4	74,674,837	Bank of Nova Scotia (BNS)
5	5	59,285,378	Toronto Dominion Bank (TD)
6	9	30,922,587	National Bank of Canada
7	20	5,145,847	Lloyds Bank Canada
8	*	4,844,000	Laurentian Bank
9	22	4,832,290[a]	Hongkong Bank of Canada
10	26	4,142,127	Citibank Canada

* Consolidated under parent's results in our list of top 100 financial institutions.
[a] Includes assets of Midland Bank Canada acquired in 1988.

BIGGEST TRUST COMPANIES

Rank	Rank in Top 100 1988	Assets (in thousands)	Company
1	*	$28,500,000[a]	Royal Trustco
2	12	12,191,557	National Trustco
3	*	11,600,000[b]	Central Guaranty Trust
4	13	10,202,891	Montreal Trustco
5	*	4,900,000	General Trustco
6	*	3,600,000	First City Trustco
7	28	2,678,069	Trustco Desjardins
8	41	1,596,695	Standard Trustco
9	*	1,500,000	Counsel Trust
10	63	862,355	Co-operative Trust

* Consolidated under parent's results in our list of top 100 financial institutions.
[a] Canada Trustco would vie with Royal Trustco for the number one spot, but the parent CT Financial declined to provide figures.
[b] Consolidates four subsidiaries of Central Capital Corp.: Central Trust, Guaranty Trust, Yorkshire Trust, and Nova Scotia Savings & Loan. Central Capital Subsidiary Central & Guaranty Trust (the new name for Financial Trustco) is not included in the figures.

Table 1-4. (Continued)

BIGGEST CREDITS UNIONS

Rank	Rank in Top 100 1988	Assets (in thousands)	Company
1	6	$34,246,830	Confederation caisses populaires Desjardins
2	36	1,735,678	Vancouver City Savings Credit Union
3	44	1,441,890	Credit Union Central of Saskatchewan
4	46	1,347,487	British Columbia Central Credit Union
5	60	932,187	Canadian Co-operative Credit Society
6	61	929,882	Ontario Credit Union League
7	74	655,980	Surrey Credit Union
8	75	648,888	Pacific Coast Savings Credit Union
9	77	608,869	Civil Service Co-operative Credit Society
10	78	604,500	Capital City Savings & Credit Union

Source: *The Financial Post 500* (1989): 175.

Euromoney poll for 1989. Furthermore, in the *Euromoney* ranking of the top 500 banks based on the dollar value of equity for 1987, five of the Big Six Canadian banks ranked in the top 100. Their rankings are as follows: Royal Bank (35), Canadian Imperial Bank of Commerce (46), Bank of Montreal (50), Toronto-Dominion Bank (54), and Bank of Nova Scotia (53). In a current round of deregulation, the chartered banks are lobbying for increased powers in the domestic market, where their main competitors are the trust companies.

1.2. Other Depository Institutions

1.2.1. Trust Companies. When regulation of chartered banks was made a federal responsibility under Confederation in 1867, their powers were specified in the first Bank Act. The Act followed past practice in denying banks the power to act in a fiduciary capacity as trustees for individuals and corporations. As a result, the first trust company was incorporated in Ontario in 1872 under provincial authority.[2] This distinction between banks and trust companies is unlike U.S. practice. However, the difference between banks and trust companies in Canada is becoming increasingly blurred.

Table 1-5. The Relative Size of Individual Chartered Banks, 1870–1987 (Selected Years)

Dec. 31st	1880 %	1920 %	1930 %	1970 %	1980 %	1987 %
Bank of Montreal	22.49	18.19	25.68	19.55	13.58	17.32
Royal Bank of Canada	1.53	18.79	27.29	25.17	18.34	21.01
Canadian Bank of Commerce[a]	12.28	15.27	19.77	22.76	16.35	18.17
Imperial Bank of Canada[a]	2.55	4.34	4.23	22.76	16.35	18.17
Bank of Nova Scotia	2.24	7.86	8.46	13.64	12.40	14.69
Bank of Toronto[b]	3.57	3.23	3.92	12.03	10.03	11.26
Dominion Bank[b]	3.16	4.65	4.54	12.03	10.03	11.26
Banque Provinciale du Canada[c]	.92	1.41	1.61	2.21	5.50	6.16
Banque Canadienne Nationale[c]	.71	2.42	4.65	4.32	5.50	6.16
Other	51.0	24.3	(.2)	(.6)	23.80	11.44
Number in "other" category	(27)	(9)	(2)	(2)	(5)	(62)
TOTAL (%)	100	100	100	100	100	100
$millions	193	3,057	3,144	47,307	281,244	486,384
Two largest (%)	34.6	36.8	52.8	47.8	34.69	39.18
Five largest (%)	43.7	64.4	85.5	92.9	70.70	82.40

[a] Canadian Imperial Bank of Commerce after 1960.
[b] Toronto-Dominion Bank after 1955.
[c] National Bank of Canada after 1979.

Source: "Monthly Returns of the Chartered Banks," *Canada Gazette* (Ottawa: Queen's Printer) and C.A. Curtis, "Statistics of Banking," *Statistical Contributions to Canadian Economic History* Vol. 1 (The Macmillan Company of Canada Ltd., 1931).

Table 1-6. Selected Data on Canada's "Big Six" Banks, 1988, Ranked by Assets

Data	Royal Bank	Canadian Imperial Bank of Commerce	Bank of Montreal	Bank of Nova Scotia	Toronto Dominion	National Bank
Return on average common equity	22.18%	17.25%	20.64%	26.85%	24.01%	25.31%
Return on average assets	0.87%	0.76%	0.88%	1.04%	1.38%	1.06%
Dividend payout ratio[a]	32.6%	29.7%	33.8%	19.3%	20.5%	25.5%
Net interest margin	3.11%	2.86%	3.27%	2.95%	3.53%	2.94%
Year-end assets in US$ (millions)[b]	$91,345	$78,591	$65,494	$61,980	$49,207	$25,666
Average asset leverage	28.2x	24.6x	25.2x	26.7x	18.1x	25.9x
Common equity/assets	3.62%	4.16%	4.10%	3.79%	5.57%	3.89%
Base capital/gross assets	4.14%	4.84%	4.29%	4.00%	5.58%	4.60%
Loss experience ratios	0.54%	0.45%	0.28%	0.11%	(0.13)%	0.30%
Nonperforming loans ratio	1.55%	2.39%	3.29%	1.13%	1.77%	1.57%
Market/book value	1.03x	0.99x	0.91x	0.90x	1.45x	0.98x
Price/trailing earnings (before LDC reservations)	5.68x	6.76x	4.98x	4.05x	7.10x	4.57x

[a] All ratios on a before-LDC-reservations basis, averages of quarterly figures.
[b] $1 CDN = .83 US$.

Source: Wood Gundy, Investment Research, reports of various banks, December 1988.

Like the banks, the trust companies are characterized by a large concentration of assets in the largest firms. For example, in 1984, the Big Six banks and the four largest trust companies accounted for 86% of all deposits covered by Canada Deposit Insurance. The other 14% of deposits was accounted for by 143 other institutions (Wyman, 1985). The ten largest trust companies in 1988 are listed in table 1-4. Mortgages represent the largest asset class on the balance sheets of trust companies, which also invest significantly in government and corporate bonds. With their deposits covered by the Canada Deposit Insurance Corporation up to $60,000, trust companies are able to compete for core deposits through a system of brokered deposits similar in concept to the U.S. system, but smaller in scale (Wyman, 1985).

To exceed 20 times leverage, trust companies must comply with additional specific portfolio requirements, and meet certain earnings, cash-flow, and liquidity requirements. For example, at least two thirds of their assets must be invested in government securities, residential mortgages, commercial mortgages (if insured or meet certain quality tests), and commercial paper of issuers that meet certain earnings tests.

Trust company regulations evolved in the early 1900s so that, in addition to their fiduciary activities, these institutions could be allowed to act as near banks accepting deposits in the form of noncheckable trust certificates. In the 1970s, trust companies began to offer checkable deposits with clearing arrangements through a chartered bank. Unlike banks, trust companies are not required to hold noninterest-bearing, primary reserves with the Bank of Canada. Trust companies incorporated in Ontario must hold 20% reserves in the form of liquid assets.[3] Their leverage is restricted to 20 times equity. Trust companies were also permitted to write mortgages and to make other types of secured loans.

After World War II (and particularly in the early 1960s), the assets of trust companies grew rapidly as they introduced new products, such as pooled pension funds and mutual funds. Trust companies, like credit unions, offered longer branch hours and more attractive savings instruments than the chartered banks. Prior to the 1967 Bank Act revision, banks faced an interest rate ceiling of 6% on deposits (similar to Regulation Q in the U.S.). However, trust companies were not governed by this restriction.

By abolishing the interest-rate ceiling and allowing banks to make mortgages, the 1967 Bank Act reduced the competitive advantage of trust companies. The 1980 Bank Act revision enhanced these powers for the banks but retained the differential reserve requirements between the banks and the trust companies. The latter are scheduled to be phased out in 1990. Until the current round of deregulation, cross-ownership between banks and trust companies was restricted to 10% of voting shares.

1.2.2. Savings Banks. Government ownership of banks and near banks began in the 1830s when the Governments of Newfoundland and Nova Scotia established savings banks. The reason was apparently the underdevelopment of private savings institutions. The savings banks in these provinces were taken over by the federal government in 1867. In 1929, they were absorbed into the Post Office Savings Bank, which had been established in Ontario and Quebec by the federal government after confederation. In 1968, the Post Office Savings Bank was abolished.

The Governments of Ontario (1920), Manitoba (1920–1930), and Alberta (1938) also ventured into the savings bank area. Government-owned savings banks remain in operation in Ontario and Alberta. While the Ontario Savings Offices simply lend their funds to the Ontario Government for general spending purposes, the Alberta Treasury branches directly compete with other deposit-taking institutions across a wide range of deposit, lending, and financial services.

1.2.3. Credit Unions. Credit unions are chartered under provincial legislation. Provincial supervision consists of the required filing of financial statements with the appropriate provincial regulatory authority, the imposition of certain liquidity tests and certain minimum reserves, the requirement to belong to a provincial deposit protection fund, examination by provincial government and/or deposit protection fund examiners, and the restriction of the type and amounts of loans and investments that can be made (CICA, 1984).

Some credit unions have become financial supermarkets that compete with the banks. These credit unions allow their members to deposit money, invest in term deposits, use a variety of personal checking accounts that pay interest, purchase tax-deferred savings plan contracts, obtain personal and mortgage loans, and purchase insurance (CICA, 1984). The ten largest credit unions are listed in table 1-4.

During the late 1800s, Canadian banks accepted savings from all groups and lent money only to some (particularly merchants and industrialists). Since farmers, fishermen, tradesmen, and laborers had no access to other credit-granting institutions, they borrowed from money lenders who often charged usurious interest rates.

In 1900, Alphonse Desjardins established the first caisse populaire in Lévis, Quebec. The caisse populaire operated within the geographic boundaries of the parish, where people would be prepared to be of mutual assistance to those they knew. Because members had limited liability, nonmembers were reluctant to lend funds to the caisse. In the period before World War I and in the 1920s, Desjardins and his supporters were unsuccessful in their attempts to place credit unions under federal legislation.

In the 1920s, Desjardins assisted the organization of credit unions in the United States. The U.S. credit unions differed from the Quebec caisses populaires in two respects. First, their members were usually linked by a social or occupational bond and not a parish bond. Second, they were prepared to lend to a wider constituency.

In 1928, St. Francis Xavier University in Antigonish, Nova Scotia began a program of cooperative education through study groups in small communities. Community credit unions evolved from these study groups and were based on similarity of needs. These cooperatives lent to individual members, businesses, and other cooperatives.

In the 1920s, Western Canada was still in the relatively early stages of economic development. Farmers and fishermen required short-term credit for working capital and long-term credit to purchase fixed assets. Since the lending policies of the banks did not meet these needs, the need for locally based and locally responsive money sources was evident. Thus, in the spirit of cooperation, the forerunner of the present western-based credit union system was developed.

Prior to the 1967 revision of the Bank Act, which opened up personal loans and mortgages to chartered banks, credit unions experienced asset growth faster than the growth rate of the population. Credit unions utilized their affinity ties with their customers to compete very effectively with finance companies for consumer loan business, and with banks and trust companies for retail deposits.

Since 1967, credit unions lost market share in the battle for intermediation business, although some credit unions (such as the Caisse Populaire Desjardins) are comparable in size to the large banks and trust companies. In the 1970s, credit unions began to purchase shares in banks and insurance companies and began to expand into insurance, banking, and trust activities (Neave, 1981).

The credit unions in the western provinces retrenched during 1984–1986, and grew again in 1987–1988. Consolidation shrunk the number of credit unions in British Columbia to 118 (with 280 branches) in early 1989 from 136 (with 314 branches) five years earlier (Schreiner 1989).[4] During 1988, the Quebec government passed legislation that allowed the Caisse Populaires Desjardins to sell insurance directly to the public through its branches.

1.3. Investment Dealers and Merchant Bankers

1.3.1. Investment Dealers. Investment banking in Canada has traditionally been conducted by investment dealers who assist in new security issues, buy and sell securities for their own inventory, and act as agents for their clients. The inventory of Canadian investment dealers consists primarily of Treasury bills, commercial paper, banker's acceptances, and client loans and receivables. The largest 15 investment dealers are identified in table 1-7. Three of the top fifteen firms are U.S. controlled.

Investment dealers rely heavily on short-term loans to finance their inventory. Since 1953, a subset of investment dealers has obtained purchase/resale agreements under which the Bank of Canada is prepared to purchase Government of Canada securities from the dealer and to resell them to the dealer at some future date at a fixed price. Since 1980, the rate charged on such "lender-of-last-resort" arrangements has been the bank rate.

Investment dealers also obtain "day" loans from the chartered banks, which are collateralized with Government of Canada securities and can be continually renewed. The maximum dollar value of such loans equals the value specified in the purchase-and-resale agreements with the Bank of Canada. Investment dealers also obtain "special-call" loans from the chartered banks, which are callable on short notice but cannot be used by the banks as secondary reserves. The largest source of short-term financing of investment dealers is call loans provided by nonbanks. These loans vary in rates, collateral conditions, and currency of denomination.

Among the four pillars of the Canadian financial institutions (i.e., banks, trusts, insurance companies, and investment dealers), the investment dealers were the real conglomeraters during the 1970s and early 1980s. Through their money market operations, they encroached on the banks through the commercial paper market. They operated on an agency spread of $1/8\%$ to $1/4\%$. Even with a flexible prime rate, the banks could not match this spread due to the interest-cost effect of reserve requirements. Through their margin accounts, the investment dealers encroached on the bank's consumer loan business. Their financial innovations included cash-management accounts and credit cards. Through discretionary accounts and investment-management divisions, the investment dealers encroached on the fiduciary business of the trust companies. Simultaneously, the investment dealers were, until quite recently, successful in excluding nonindustry investors and foreigners from the investment industry with arguments appealing to the protection of the "national interest."

Table 1-7. Top 15 Investment Dealers

Total capital (in thousands) 1988	Company (Head Office)	Revenue (in thousands)	Earnings (in thousands)	Employees	Major Shareholder
$285,980	Burns Fry Holdings Corp. (Toronto)	$164,331	$13,541	1,450	Security Pacific (U.S.) 30%
270,422	RBC Dominion Securities Inc. (Toronto)	279,142	44,806	2,224	Royal Bank of Canada 67%
234,353	Gordon Capital Corp. (Toronto)	n.a.	n.a.	n.a.	Employees
221,387[a]	Wood Gundy Inc. (Toronto)	n.a.	n.a.	1,929	C.I.B.C. 62%
183,800	Scotia McLeod Inc. (Toronto)	n.a.	n.a.	n.a.	Bank of Nova Scotia 100%
175,049	Nesbitt Thomson Deacon Inc. (Toronto)	n.a.	11,809	n.a.	Bank of Montreal 75%
127,461	First Marathon Inc. (Toronto)	64,005	25,938	320	Publicly traded
113,470	Richardson Greenshields of Canada Ltd.	n.a.	n.a.	1,829	James Richardson & Sons 75%
79,579	Midland Doherty Financial Corp. (Toronto)	113,301	(8,976)	1,874	Union Enterprises 34%

73,412	Merill Lynch Canada Inc. (Toronto)	n.a.	1,154	Merill Lynch & Co. (U.S.) 100%
64,240	Pemberton Houston Willoughby Investment Corp. (Vancouver)	n.a.	n.a.	Publicly traded
63,427	Levesque Beaubien & Co. (Montreal)[b]	89,935	(6,900)	National Bank of Canada 68%
50,021	Loewen, Ondaatje, McCutcheon Inc. (Toronto)	23,469	(10,372)	Publicly traded
39,356	Walwyn Inc. (Toronto)	62,455	(11,124)	3,722	Fairfax Financial Holdings, Confederation Life[d]
3,527	Prudential-Bache Securities Canada Ltd.	54,653	(26,012)	740	Prudential-Bache Securities (U.S.) 80%

Notes: Earnings are pretax and preshareholder distribution. Canarim Investment Corp. and Geoffrion Leclerc declined to participate in the survey. In 1989, the former merged with Gordon Capital Corp. and the latter merged with Levesque Beaubien & Co.
[a] Includes standby subordinated loans.
[b] Plans to merge with Geoffrion Leclerc May 1, 1989.
[c] Excludes unusual and extraordinary items.
[d] Together they hold 51% on a fully diluted basis.
n.a. Not available.
Source: The Financial Post 500 (1989), 171.

In June 1987, a coordinated change in regulations at both the federal and provincial level (Ontario) allowed the banks to acquire investment dealers. As a result, all the major banks now have investment banking arms. There is no Canadian counterpart to the Glass–Steagall separation of functions in the United States. Since the Schedule Two banks and foreign-owned investment banks are also allowed to undertake investment banking activities, competition has intensified. Because the takeovers contravened the U.S. Glass–Steagall Act, the Canadian banks were forced to sell the U.S. operations of their newly acquired subsidiaries. In late 1989, the Canadian Imperial Bank of Commerce and the Royal Bank of Canada asked the U.S. Federal Reserve Board for permission to establish securities subsidiaries in the United States to compete with the U.S. banks. In September of 1989, the Federal Reserve had increased the amount of corporate securities underwriting authorized for U.S. banks to 10% (from 5%) of the total revenues of the banks' securities subsidiaries.

Based on their dominance of automated transaction technology, banks are expected to take over most of the operations now controlled by their brokerage subsidiaries. Brokerage subsidiaries will be confined to research, creativity-oriented mergers and acquisitions, liability trading, and possibly equity distribution (Whyte, 1989).

1.3.2. Merchant Banking. Merchant banking is a highly entrepreneurial branch of corporate finance. It involves management advisory services, the arrangement of financing, and equity or equity-related investment. Canadian banks have until recently not been active in this field. Leading Canadian merchant banks controlled by nonfinancial interests include Hees International Corp. (a specialist in turnarounds that includes such partners as Brascan Ltd.), Unicorp Capital Corp., and Roy-L Merchant Group Ltd. Canadian merchant banks, which are owned totally or partially by subsidiaries of nonbank financial institutions (primarily trust companies), include First City Capital Markets Ltd. and Terra Con Capital Corp. The nonbank financial institutions use their merchant banking subsidiaries to generate business by completing their product offerings. For example, Terra Con provides investment opportunities for its parent's (Counsel Capital's) real estate arm and lending opportunities for Counsel Capital's parent's (Counsel Corp.'s) trust companies. Unlike the commercial banks, these merchant banks are not constrained by limits on their investments in nonfinancial companies.

Recently, the banks have entered into this field. The Canadian Imperial Bank of Commerce was the first to enter by venturing with

Gordon Capital Corp. in 1988 to form Gordon Investment Corp. (GIC). With initial capital of $400 million, GIC plans to participate in deals worldwide and to make investments in domestic and foreign investment companies. The National Bank and Claridge Investments Ltd. formed National Claridge Inc. in 1988. In this 50:50 partnership, the National Bank will hold only 10% of the voting stock in order to comply with the limit set by the Federal Superintendent of Financial Institutions.

The Canadian banks perceive merchant banking as a vehicle for increasing their product range and for participating in a business with high expected returns. Due to fierce competition, the traditional corporate business of the banks has declined (especially in terms of profit margins). Detractors argue that merchant banking is not a business that can be run institutionally.

1.4. Insurance Companies and Pension Funds

1.4.1. Insurance Companies. In 1985, 156 life and health insurance companies and 244 property and casualty insurance companies operated in Canada (Canadian Bankers Association, 1987). The 25 largest life insurance companies in Canada in 1988 are listed in table 1-8.

Life insurance companies are generally confined to underwriting insurance and selling annuities. Although they are not permitted to take deposits, they issue annuities that are close substitutes for term deposits. They have not been granted powers to underwrite securities or to conduct other fiduciary services. They are permitted to manage funds, including pension funds, on behalf of customers via segregated funds. Like trust and mortgage loan companies, life insurance companies may invest in mortgages, real estate, government securities, secured corporate debt, unsecured corporate debt, and equity. Maximum investment limits apply to common shares and real estate investments. Although a significant portion of the industry consists of mutual companies, most insurance companies are shareholder owned.

As reflected in table 1-2, the assets of life companies grew from insignificance in 1870 to second place behind the chartered banks by the 1930s. This growth was largely based on sales of individual whole-life policies to a population whose numbers and income were growing. In the post-Depression period, new sales came more from term policies. An emphasis on group insurance led to slower asset growth. While life companies remained the second largest group in 1967, their relative share began to decline. After the stock market crash of 1987, a flight to

Table 1-8. The Top 25 Life Insurers in Canada Based on Total Assets for 1988

Rank by Assets 1988	Assets (in thousands)	Company (Head Office)	Status[a]	Premium income (in thousands)	Revenue (in thousands)	Net Income (in thousands)	Employees
1	$23,888,315	Manufacturers Life Insurance Co. (Toronto)	C/M	$3,762,357	$6,023,936	$143,444	5,991
2	23,188,813[b]	Sun Life Assurance Co. of Canada (Toronto)	C/M	2,901,309	4,959,490	247,569	5,778
3	17,257,730	Great-West Life Assurance Co. (Winnipeg)[c]	C/S	3,413,769	4,966,459	131,305	5,566
4	13,599,085	Confederation Life Insurance Co. (Toronto)	C/M	3,107,916	4,318,107	62,471	5,126
5	11,365,518	Canada Life Assurance Co. (Toronto)	C/M	2,234,671	3,728,981	140,414	3,205
6	10,967,000	Mutual Life Assurance Co. (Waterloo, Ontario)	C/M	1,747,000	2,866,000	89,000	4,273
7	9,331,943	London Life Insurance Co. (London, Ontario)[c]	C/S	1,420,046	2,305,724	93,305	5,436
8	8,988,809	Crown Life Insurance Co. (Toronto)[c]	C/S	2,035,607	2,917,988	8,645	2,579
9	5,999,878	Imperial Life Assurance (Toronto)[c]	C/S	776,694	1,198,978	10,904	2,642
10	5,406,318	Standard Life Assurance Co. (Montreal) Nov./88	F/M	920,437	1,449,408	88,497	1,300
11	4,515,229	North American Life Assurance Co. (Toronto)	C/M	637,917	1,388,681	43,881	1,936
12	4,468,102	Metropolitan Life Insurance Co. (Ottawa)	F/M	853,873	1,336,575	17,487	1,732
13	2,998,172	Prudential Assurance Group (Kitchener, Ontario)	F/S	515,340	822,623	n.a.	638
14	2,938,900	Prudential Insurance Co. of America (Toronto)	F/M	486,555	758,080	29,649	2,735

BANK STRUCTURE IN CANADA

15	2,913,015	Industrial-Alliance Life Insurance Co. (Quebec)	C/M	489,425	747,497	29,539	1,375
16	2,012,600	Aetna Life Insurance Co. of Canada (Toronto)	F/S	457,200	642,600	22,000	950
17	1,967,189	Maritime Life Assurance Co. (Halifax)	F/S	312,565	539,119	34,295	591
18	1,794,606	Les Cooperants (Montreal)	C/M	147,799	349,535	7,085	2,500
19	1,406,449	Assurance-vie Desjardins (Quebec City)	C/M	309,417	459,295	14,678	680
20	1,140,327	La Laurentine Vie (Quebec City)	C/S	217,068	325,161	8,050	737
21	1,079,394	National Life Assurance Co. of Canada (Toronto)[c]	C/S	202,850	323,503	10,111	419
22	1,009,085	Empire Life Insurance Co. (Kingston, Ontario)[c]	C/S	157,541	245,283	13,124	563
23	923,270	New York Life Insurance Co. (Toronto)	F/M	167,395	269,968	15,865	235
24	797,411	La Savegarde Assurance sur la vie (Montreal)	C/S	143,162	196,084	(2,829)	375
25	638,547	SSQ Mutuelle d'Assurance (Quebec City)	C/M	196,463	267,937	5,132	560

Note: For multiline companies, figures exclude property and casualty business.

[a] C = Canadian; F = Foreign; S = Stock company owned by shareholders; M = Mutual company owned by policyholders.
[b] Segregated funds are included in assets but not in figures for premium income, revenue, or net income.
[c] Great-West Life is 97.4% owned by Great West Lifeco, which is 86.3% owned by Power Financial; London Life is 98% owned by Lonvest; Crown Life is 94% owned by Crownx; Imperial Life is 99.3% owned by Laurentian Group; National Life is 100% owned by Industrial Alliance Life Insurance; Empire Life is 81% owned by E-L Financial and 19% by Guardian Royal Exchange PLC.
[d] Name changed from Excelsior Life Insurance.
[e] Name changed from Laurentian Mutual Insurance.
n.a. Not available.
Source: *The Financial Post 500* (1989), 169.

safety caused a modest increase in the assets of life insurance companies. However, in 1988, they remained smaller than the trust companies.

Life companies offered annuity pension products prior to Confederation.[5] The first Canadian-owned company was Canada Life, which was founded in 1847 and is still in existence. Its major founder, Hugh C. Baker, was the manager of a branch of the Bank of Montreal. This foreshadows the current desire of bankers to get into the life insurance business (Neufeld, 1972).

According to Neufeld (1972), Canadian life companies in the pre-Confederation period were important to the development of Canadian capital markets. They invested exclusively in mortgages and other Canadian securities. Furthermore, the Canadian life companies showed greater willingness than the banks to purchase the debt of municipalities and corporations.

Confederation established that the regulation of life insurance companies was a federal responsibility.[6] Federal legislation in 1875 and 1877 established a Superintendent of Insurance with the power to examine companies' books and to ensure that insurance companies held adequate reserves. In the period before the Great Depression, legislation was introduced to control the investments eligible to be held by life companies. These restrictions did not prevent at least one company from investing heavily in common stock in the period prior to the Crash of 1929. In 1932, new legislation limited common stock investment (at book value) of insurance companies to 15% of company assets. Unlike the number of banks, the number of life insurance companies has increased over time. Mergers have been discouraged by regulatory authorities, and foreign control has been limited (Neufeld, 1972).

Starting with the 1983 reform of its legislation governing life insurance companies, Quebec has encouraged aggressive expansion of insurance companies into related areas. During 1989, the Quebec government announced new measures that would allow independent insurance brokers to sell all types of insurance and to offer other types of financial services. Not only would they be able to grant mortgages and collect deposits on behalf of financial institutions, but they would able be albe to associate in the same office with investment dealers, financial planners, and mortgage brokers.

The 52-year-old federal act that regulates insurance companies is outdated. For example, it requires insurers to keep records on paper, it does not allow boards of directors to use telephone conference calls, and asset transfers are only allowed between federal companies. As a result, the Laurentian Group had to create a federal company in order to

BANK STRUCTURE IN CANADA 27

Table 1-9. The Largest Pension Funds in Canada

Rank	Pension Fund	Assets at market value Dec. 31 ($ million) 1988	1987	% of assets managed in-house	Chief Contact
1	Ontario Municipal Employees Retirement System	10,533[a]	9,068[a]	86%	Robert Silcox, director of investments
2	Canadian National Railway	6,100	5,913	99%	Tulio Cedraschi, president, CN Investments
3	Bell Canada	5,200	4,816	100%	John Hilliker, president & CEO, Bimcor Inc.
4	Hospitals of Ontario Pension Plan	4,266	3,866	98%	E.Y. Baker, senior vice president, finance
5	Canadian Pacific	3,600	3,464	98%	G.H. Cloutier, president, CP Pension Investment Management
6	Ontario Hydro	3,564	3,302	100%	Peter de Auer, Director, pension fund
7	Hydro-Quebec	2,740	2,508	80%	Pierre Olivier, Manager, pension fund investment
8	Air Canada	2,534	2,310	73%	H.W.C. Gibbs, General Manager, pension investment
9	General Motors of Canada	2,106	1,991	nil	Hedi Kunz, Treasurer
10	Canadian Broadcasting Corp.	1,794	1,554	95%	Jerome Lapointe; pension fund manager

[a] Includes estimated market value of nonmarketable securities of $1.162 billion at year-end 1988, and $1.161 billion at year-end 1987.
Source: *The Financial Post 500* (1989): 126.

transfer its direct mail marketing business from a federally incorporated unit to its Quebec insurance company (McNish 1989a).

1.4.2. Pension Funds. Canada's pension funds consist of both public and private entities. The two types of public plans are the insurance plans, which apply to an entire population (such as the Canada and Quebec Pension Plans), and the employee-based pension plans, which cover a specific set of public employees (such as Canadian National and Air Canada prior to its privatization). A variety of plans are run by private companies, or by trust companies, insurance companies, and other investment managers for private companies.

The ten largest pension plans are listed in table 1-9. As is shown in table 1-2, pension fund assets have grown rapidly. This growth moderated after the stock market crash of 1987 because stock prices declined sharply, and this portion of pension-fund assets are "marked-to-market."

Pension fund contributions above current benefit requirements can be invested in eligible assets. These include government bonds, corporate issues that meet prescribed dividend/earnings quality tests, and real estate that meets certain quality and income tests. Investments in foreign property that exceed 10% of the total fund are subject to an onerous penalty under the Income Tax Act. Both the legal profile of pensions and the accountability of pension fund fiduciaries are increasing rapidly.

1.5. Financial Markets

In Canada, money, bonds, and some stocks trade over-the-counter, and most stocks trade on the floor of one of Canada's five organized stock exchanges. The major Canadian stock exchanges in decreasing order of traded dollar value are the Toronto Stock Exchange (TSE), the Montreal Exchange (ME), and the Vancouver Stock Exchange (VSE). Many Canadian stocks are listed on more than one Canadian stock exchange, and some stocks are interlisted on the New York and American Stock Exchanges. In Canada, regulation of securities is a provincial responsibility.

Two ongoing developments will have a pervasive impact on the structure and functioning of the Canadian financial markets. The first is the internationalization and deregulation of capital markets. This has led to negotiated commission rates, the recapitalization of investment dealers, and various mergers of investment dealers and banks, as well as of foreign and domestic investment dealers. The second development is the movement towards automated trading. This should increase the operational efficiency of Canadian financial markets.

In the early 1980s, the main growth in Canadian securities markets occurred for federal government issues. After the bull market began in 1982 and interest rates dropped, corporate financing increased through 1986. It declined in 1987 with the market crash and recovered somewhat in 1988 (Kalymon, 1989; *Bank of Canada Review*, March 1989). During the 1980s, the use of bankers' acceptances and commercial paper increased, partially reflecting the trend toward securitization.

Asset-backed securities in the form of Canada Mortgage and Housing Corporation (CMHC) mortgage-backed securities were introduced in 1985. More recently, CMHC has issued inflation-linked, mortgage-backed securities to appeal to institutional investors. Asset-backed securities are not yet popular with nongovernmental issuers (Kalymon, 1989).

Based on a survey of 33 firms in Canada in 1987–1988, Kalymon (1989) concluded that Canadian markets have been slow in adopting financial innovations. For example, although bond options and futures are both traded on the Toronto Stock Exchange Index, their use has been limited. The most commonly used Canadian futures are the Canadian dollar contracts traded on the Chicago Mercantile Exchange.

Interest rate and currency swaps are the most widely adopted innovations in Canada. According to Kalymon (1989), the players include investment dealers as arrangers, Schedule One banks running swap books, and smaller banks, trust companies, and larger nonfinancial corporations as both providers and users.

The rate of acceptance of innovations is expected to increase as a result of investment dealers merging with more internationalized chartered banks and of foreign brokerage firms entering Canada. In addition, recent changes in the rules governing institutional investors allow for a greater use of derivative securities within a more general measure of "prudence."

2. Brief History of the Development of the Current Banking Structure, Focusing on Aspects that are Unique to the Country and on More Recent Changes

Paper money, in the form of playing cards stamped with an official seal, was introduced in New France in 1685. The first bank notes appeared with the creation (pre-Confederation) of Canada's first chartered bank, the Bank of Montreal, in 1817.[7] As is evident from table 1-10, sav-

Table 1-10. Founding Dates of Various Financial Institutions and Various Other Regulatory Milestones

Fire and casualty insurance companies	1809
Chartered banks	1817
Savings banks	1819
Life insurance companies	1847
Brokerage houses	1850s
Permanent building societies or mortgage loan companies	1855
Government Note Issue	1866
Government insurance and pension account	1870
Trusteed pension plans	1874
Trust companies	1882
Caisses populaires and credit unions	1900
Closed-end investment trusts	1901
Finance companies	1916
Consumer loan companies	1928
Farm Credit Corporation (formerly Canadian Farm Loan Board)	1929
Mutual funds	1932
Bank of Canada	1935
Investment contract companies	1940
National pension plans	1965
Deposit insurance	1967
Foreign owned (Schedule Two) banks chartered[a]	1980
Ontario banks permitted to purchase brokers	1987
Size restrictions removed from U.S.-owned banks under Free Trade Act	1989
Reserve requirements phased out	1990?
Amex bank chartered—first to combine commercial interests with banking	1990

[a] Initially referred to as Schedule B banks.
Source: Adapted from Neufeld (1972).

ings banks, domestic (non-British) insurance companies, and brokerage houses were established prior to Confederation.

Based on table 1-2, the total assets of all nongovernmental financial intermediaries in Canada were equal to 31% of GNP, and the total assets of the chartered banks were equal to 28.5% of GNP in 1870. By 1967, the total assets of all private financial intermediaries were equal to 91% of GNP. The banks' relative share steadily declined from 92% to 38% of the total assets of all financial intermediaries. Although the share of the banks has increased since 1967, it has gone down from 1981 to 1986.

2.1. Chartered Banks in Perspective

Neufeld (1972) argues that public acceptance of bank liabilities (*in the form of bank notes*) as a medium of exchange was the *raison d'etre* of Canadian banks from the founding of the first bank in 1817 through the 1850s. Prior to Confederation in 1867, bank deposits slowly began to replace bank notes as the preferred medium of exchange. In 1870, "the bank deposit, both as medium of exchange and asset to hold, may in important respects still have been a relatively 'unabsorbed' financial innovation" (Neufeld, 1972, pp. 135–136). From 1870 to 1910, the number of bank branches expanded and deposits became widely accepted. In 1870, one bank branch existed for every 29,000 people. By 1910, one bank branch existed for every 3000 people (Neufeld 1972).

The number of banks grew to a peak of 48 in 1879. Since Canada followed the English and Scottish traditions, early populist fears of centralized banking were far weaker in Canada than in the United States. As a result, bank charters were granted by the federal government (not by the provinces), and their numbers were restricted. In 1871, when the first Bank Act was enacted, 36 banks operated in Canada. This number was not exceeded until 1980, when the new Bank Act permitted a new class of charters for foreign-owned banks. From 1871 through 1929, there were at least 27 direct failures, 35 amalgamations, and one addition in the banking sector.[8] The major failure of the Home Bank in 1923 is discussed further below. At the end of 1928, only ten banks operated in Canada.

From 1820 to the present, 104 banks have been active, and 47 (44%) of these banks have either failed or had their business wound up (i.e., voluntarily liquidated)! This latter figure considerably underestimates the number of insolvent banks, since a large number of banks were eliminated by merger when a "weak" bank was purchased by a "strong" bank. Neufeld (1972, p. 81) comments that "[t]he large number of failures is rather surprising in view of the Canadian banking system's reputation for solvency." This reputation is largely based on the *timing* of Canadian bank failures; namely, none occurred between 1923 and 1985. In addition to the legal and policy differences between the United States and Canada discussed below, amalgamations may have been encouraged by possible economies of scale that were present in Canada and not in the U.S. due to the much lower population density in Canada.[9]

2.2. Canadian Banks in the Great Depression

A widely held belief is that the diversification afforded by national branching gave Canadian banks more strength relative to U.S. banks during the Depression. Due to national branching, Canadian banks could draw on deposits from urban regions, which were not as badly hurt by the Depression, to cover withdrawals from rural branches. This advantage can be overemphasized as an explanation for the absence of bank failures in Canada. While the statistics cited by Benston (1986) for the U.S. suggest that failure was higher for rural, mainly unit banks, the distinction between rural and urban banks was less clear-cut in Canada.[10] According to Jamieson (1953), the entire Canadian economy in 1930 was largely resource based. Thus, geographic diversification would not necessarily have guaranteed the solvency of Canadian banks.

According to the *Canadian Encyclopedia* (1988, pp. 933–955), Canada and the U.S. were affected similarly by the Depression. Canadian GNP dropped by 42% from 1929 to 1933 versus a 33% drop for the U.S. In 1933, the Canadian unemployment rate was 30%, and 20% of the population was on government relief. When world trade collapsed, Canada was highly vulnerable since one third of its economic activity was export driven. The western, wheat-growing provinces were devastated economically. In Saskatchewan, for example, total income dropped to 10% of its pre-Depression level, and two thirds of the farm population was on relief. While Ontario and Quebec were not hit as hard because their economies included other industries, the Maritimes were already in dire economic straits before 1929.

This description suggests that diversification indeed did play a role in preventing bank failures in Canada since Canadian banks were spared from being concentrated solely in the hardest-hit, prairie provinces. But it also meant that banks were exposed in the Maritime provinces. Furthermore, the entire Canadian economy was more heavily dependent on the world economy than was the U.S. economy.

Given the similar shocks to the U.S. and Canadian economies (i.e., a loss of about one third of GNP), Canadian banks were probably only economically solvent at *long-run* asset values.[11] With an implicit system of 100% deposit insurance in place, the government provided a floor value when the market values of the banks fell below their book values. Due to this system of forbearance, financially insolvent banks were allowed to remain in business. These banks avoided firesale insolvency, which occurs when bank assets must be liquidated quickly at "firesale prices" (see Benston and Kaufman, 1986).

While diversification did not keep Canadian banks from economic insolvency, it did control the extent of insolvency. To prevent firesale insolvency triggered by runs, the Canadian government provided liquidity to banks under the Finance Act in a more generous manner than did the Federal Reserve in the United States. This was facilitated greatly by having only ten banks to deal with. Furthermore, to keep their money in the banks, depositors required some assurance that the Canadian banks would be tided over.

With a small number of relatively large banks, regulators and governments consider allowing a bank to fail and impose losses on uninsured depositors as being unacceptable. The Canadian government provided an implicit guarantee to the public that no chartered bank would be allowed to fail with depositor losses. This guarantee was *implicit* because it was never formally embodied in law, and it was equivalent to 100% deposit insurance.[12] Beckhart (1929) documents that the government policy was to arrange forced mergers for insolvent banks. Beckhart (1929, pp. 196–197) concludes that such mergers were not unique to Canada: "... the tendency to fewer banks is world-wide and *is not a phenomenon whose appearance is due to the type of banking system existing here* [emphasis in original]." He argues that the impetus for mergers came primarily from smaller banks near failure and from government, and not from larger banks seeking to expand. Primary evidence for the existence of such a public policy comes from parliamentary documents and the popular press during the 1920s. Both a former and serving Minister of Finance stated government policy in favor of forced mergers to avoid failures.[13]

2.3. Canadian Banks in the Post-World-War-II Period

During the 1950s, the pace of change in banking accelerated. The 1954 Bank Act revision permitted the funding of National Housing Act mortgages by the banks. This mortgage business grew until the mid-1960s, when a 6% interest-rate ceiling was placed on time deposits (similar to the U.S. Regulation Q). The banks' mortgage business grew again after 1967, when the interest-rate ceiling was removed.

During this period, the banks diversified their assets by increasing their foreign currency assets and by establishing subsidiaries in mortgages, venture capital, and mutual funds. This represented an early round in the merging of the traditional "four pillars" of Canadian finance. In the 1960s, like the American banks, the Canadian banks introduced credit cards and new instruments of liability management, such as negotiable certificates of deposit, bankers' acceptances, debentures, and personal checking accounts. The 1967 Bank Act revision reinforced these trends by removing prohibitions on mortgage lending, reducing reserve requirements, and abolishing interest-rate ceilings (which had hampered effective competition by banks in the field of consumer loans).

Between 1967 and 1981, these changes generated growth in the market share of banks relative to finance companies and life insurance companies (see table 1-2). Trust companies experienced dramatic growth by being first in the introduction of new products, aggressive marketing, and having longer hours of service, in order to capture a larger share of the retail banking market. By 1980, trust companies had become the main competition for banks. The 1980 Bank Act strengthened the competitive position of trust companies (and credit unions) by granting them access to check-clearing facilities through the Canada Payments system (ECC, 1986).

In accordance with the regulatory dialectic (Kane, 1987), banks argued for Bank Act changes in the 1980 revision that would strengthen their ability to compete, while trust companies, which were under provincial regulation, sought to maintain the status quo. The 1980 Bank Act revision made a sweeping change in response to globalization of banking. It allowed foreign banks to incorporate banking subsidiaries in Canada as Schedule Two banks.

Many foreign banks already had subsidiaries operating in wholesale banking, where they could not accept deposits. Since they were not allowed to call themselves banks, they were unregulated. Under the 1980 Bank Act, foreign banks were restricted to a 20:1 leverage ratio, and their aggregate total assets were limited to 8% of aggregate total domestic assets (Ellert, 1988). Since foreign-owned banks grew quickly, the limit was raised to 16% of total bank assets. With the Canada/U.S. free trade agreement, U.S. banks were exempted from the total asset ceiling and the remaining foreign-owned banks were subjected to a 12% ceiling as of January 1, 1989. During July of 1989, the non-U.S. foreign-owned banks were petitioning the federal government to remove the ceiling (Horvitch, 1989d).

The 1980 Bank Act modified past practice of leaving the decision on what constituted appropriate leverage of Canadian banks to their managements. It empowered the Inspector General (IG) of Banks (now the Superintendent of Financial Institutions) to set maximum leverage ratios. However, the IG did not use this authority until 1983 to set a desired range of 20:1 to 25:1 of assets to capital. In 1985, the IG moved to the lower limit (Estey, 1986).

In 1982 (the year prior to the year the IG used his power to set maximum leverage ratios), the average leverage multiplier for Canadian-owned banks was 30:1. This high level of leverage was reached due to high real (and nominal) asset growth during the late 1970s and the low price–earnings ratios of banks, which discouraged their managements from issuing new equity capital. The existence of explicit and implicit deposit insurance allowed the banks to substitute public capital for bank capital, and, thus, helps to explain the increase in leverage.

The 1980 Bank Act addressed the need to strengthen bank capital by authorizing a new class of secondary capital in the form of subordinated debentures and preferred shares. In the early 1980s, the Big Six Schedule One banks accessed these sources of secondary capital. They subsequently refinanced with new common equity as stock prices rose.

Until the 1980 Bank Act revision, the chartered banks were permitted to deal in the corporate underwriting, brokerage and distribution of securities. Although they were not active in this area, the 1980 Bank Act prohibited banks from underwriting corporate securities. Although they were allowed to be a part of a selling group that is distributing corporate securities, banks had not typically been invited by investment dealers to so participate. The 1980 Bank Act also prohibited banks from first-hand brokerage in securities, although they were permitted to buy and sell securities through brokers on behalf of their clients.

The 1980 Bank Act made only small adjustments to other aspects of this outdated system, such as reserve requirements, deposit insurance, and business-activity restrictions. Major changes would have affected both the federally regulated banks and their main competitors, the trust companies, who were under joint federal–provincial regulation.[14] During the revision period, a major federal–provincial battle was underway on constitutional reform. This caused the federal government to defer changes to those provisions until the 1990 Bank Act.

3. Current Regulation and Supervision

From 1980 through 1986, 22 financial institutions failed in Canada. The failures included two western banks, fourteen trust and loan companies (ten chartered at the federal level), five insurance companies, and one other financial institution (ECC, 1986).

Other fundamental changes included disintermediation (particularly, the securitization of credit), the rapid growth of financial innovations (such as swaps), and markets for derivative securities (such as options and futures). Securitization in Canada has concentrated on residential mortgages (over $2 billion at beginning of 1989) and bankers' acceptances. In Canada, derivative securities are traded on the TransCanada Options Exchange, the Toronto Futures Exchange, and the Montreal Exchange.

In 1985, the federal government released a discussion paper, *The Regulation of Canadian Financial Institutions: Proposals for Discussion* (the Green Paper), and published a report on reforming the deposit insurance system (the Wyman Report). Some federal legislation followed, and a Blue Paper outlining proposed legislation was published in 1986. The Estey Commission report, which studied the failures of the two western banks in 1985, added some new recommendations.

Table 1-11. Legislation Regulating Selected Canadian Financial Institutions

Institutions	*Acts*
Chartered banks	Federal Bank Act
Life insurance companies, segregated funds property, and casualty insurance companies	Federal Canadian and British Insurance Companies Act, the Foreign Insurance Companies Act, or a corresponding provincial Act
Trust companies	Federal Trust Companies Act and corresponding provincial legislation
Mortgage loan companies	Federal Loan Companies Act and corresponding provincial legislation
Local and central credit unions, and caisses populaires	Incorporated or registered under a provincial credit union Act; federal Cooperative Credit Associations Act
Investment dealers	Regulated under provincial jurisdiction—e.g., in Ontario, the Ontario Securities Commission; also self-regulated under the Investment Dealers Association
Trusteed pensions	Federal Pension Benefits Standards Act and corresponding provincial legislation (e.g., Ontario Pension Benefits Act, pioneering provincial legislation)
Financial corporations	Federal Small Loans Act and the Investment Companies Act
Investment companies	Federal Investment Companies Act

Source: Economic Council of Canada (1987).

BANK STRUCTURE IN CANADA 37

From 1981 through 1986, the total assets of all Canadian financial institutions grew only slightly as a percentage of GNP (see table 1-2). The compound annual growth rate for the five years ending in 1986 was only 8.87%. With developments in computer technology, a full range of services can be delivered by one institution (i.e., a financial holding company for common ownership of trust companies, life insurance companies, and real estate firms). Thus, during the period since the last Bank Act revision, competition has centered on the shifting of existing business towards nondepository intermediaries.[15] The lone exception is Quebec Savings Banks, which benefited from the faster deregulation of such banks in Quebec.

According to Kane's (1987) regulatory dialectic, regulators compete with each other for "regulatory business," while financial services firms seek the most lax regulatory environment. As is summarized in table 1-11, the regulatory maze of competing jurisdictions in the current system is based on regulation by pillar, and not by function. Apparent differences exist among the different jurisdictions. While the various regulators appear to agree on "expansion of powers, cross-pillar ownership [e.g., the ownership of investment dealers by banks], increased disclosure, and increased reporting requirements" (Porter, 1989), they disagree on a number of other key issues, which are summarized in table 1-12. Such competition facilitates avoidance of regulation, and the threat of successful avoidance leads to relaxation of regulations.

Table 1-12. Federal and Provincial Views on Regulatory Change

Issues	Federal	Quebec	Ontario	BC
Selected foreign ownership limits	Support	Support	Support	Oppose
Restrictions on commercial links	Support	Oppose	Oppose	Oppose
Total ban on related party transactions	Support	Support	Support	Oppose
Size limits on acquisitions	Support	Oppose	Oppose	Oppose
Extraterritorial provisions	Oppose	Oppose	Support	Oppose
Restrictions on networking of insurance	Support	Oppose	Oppose	Support

Notes: Regulatory differences between levels of government make the creation of new regulations more complicated in a period of rapid change. The following summary, provided by Ann Lamont, director of Policy Support of the Office of the Superintendent of Financial Institutions in her conference presentation, highlights areas of agreement and disagreement among the federal and provincial regulators on issues common to all industry sectors.

Federal, Ontario, Quebec, and British Columbia regulators all agree on the expansion of powers, cross-pillar ownership, increased disclosure, and increased reporting requirements.

Source: Porter (1989).

A domestic Canadian example is the ongoing contest between the Quebec and federal governments over the regulation of Canada's financial institutions.[16] While Quebec has effectively led the way for financial reforms by rapidly introducing new rules, the federal government has spent five years reviewing proposals for new laws.

The new rules enabled Quebec's financial institutions to enter or acquire each other's (including cross-pillar) businesses, and to broaden their power to raise capital. No limits exist on the ownership of Quebec-based institutions. Recently, the province proposed that Quebec insurance companies be allowed to acquire industrial companies to aid in the repatriation of major corporations.

Quebec's swift deregulation has greatly aided the growth of its institutions. At the end of 1987, Quebec financial institutions had lent $8.4 billion (or 34%) of the province's business loans as compared to $679 million (or 6%) in 1981. By the second quarter of 1988, Quebec companies held $41.1 billion (or 49%) of the province's deposits as compared to $17 billion (or 36%) in 1981.

By threatening to relocate their business to Quebec, some federal companies outside of Quebec successfully used the province's liberal regulations as a lever to win more powers in their own jurisdictions. British Columbia recently proposed financial reforms that closely parallel Quebec's, and the federal government is moving towards Quebec's financial reforms.

Ottawa remained passive as a number of federal insurance and trust companies switched or threatened to convert their charters to Quebec. However, when the Bank of Nova Scotia launched a Quebec securities dealer in 1987, the federal government acted quickly. Afraid that the banks would effectively remove part of their business out from under federal control by using Quebec to enter the brokerage industry, the federal (and Ontario) government moved within months to expand the banks' powers to enter the securities industry (the "Little Bang in 1987").[17]

More recently, Quebec pressured the federal government into reversing its long-standing opposition to linkages between financial and commercial companies. Most of Quebec's financial companies are owned by or affiliated with commercial companies. The federal government has opposed commercial-company takeovers of financial institutions because savings deposits could be misused to finance nonfinancial, controlled businesses, and such takeovers could lead to an undue concentration of power. Such abuses contributed to the failure of two western banks and at least four Ontario trust and loan companies since 1981. The chartered banks had also argued that purchases of this type would create an environment more conducive to "credit deprivation" (i.e., the refusal of financial firms to lend money to direct competitors of the lender's commercial company parent or affiliate).

In 1986, Imasco Ltd., a conglomerate with wide nonbanking interests, acquired control of Canada's largest trust company, Canada Trustco Mortgage Co. In 1989, BCE Inc., Canada's largest holding company, agreed to purchase Montreal Trustco Inc. The status of both purchases under federal legislation still remains unclear.

Various financial institutions have continued to push the regulators for regulatory relaxation. In early 1989, Royal Trustco Ltd. was forced to close its year-old financial boutiques in six department stores because the British Columbia government banned insurance sales where other financial services are offered. Montreal Trustco Ltd. is still waiting to expand its commercial lending by offering commercial letters of credit. Although corporate IOUs were recently allowed for trust companies in Quebec, they are prohibited in Ontario.

After three major policy proposals, one set of draft legislation, and at least five national studies, the federal government proposed still another regulatory framework during the spring of 1989. While only a part of the package has been enacted, the remainder may become law during 1990. What follows describes the legislative package. Comments on the controversial aspects of the proposed legislation will be provided with the understanding that modifications may be introduced before passage of the proposed legislation.

3.1. Major Regulatory Agencies

A Superintendent of Financial Institutions will have the combined power to regulate banks, federally regulated trust companies, life insurance companies, financial cooperatives (federally registered credit unions), and investment companies. The Canada Deposit Insurance Corporation (CDIC) and the central bank (Bank of Canada) will retain their independent status. These institutions are required to cooperate closely with provincial authorities, primarily Ontario and Quebec.

3.2. Types of Regulation

Currently, no restrictions exist on interest rates (other than usury laws) or on geographic location. However, with the increased emphasis placed on service charges by the banks,[18] the federal government has been increasingly active in monitoring the use of bank service fees. In 1988, a federal interdepartmental committee recommended new rules governing how and when banks notify their customers of any change in service charges, the appointment of an ombudsman in the federal superintendent's office to deal with complaints of bank customers, and restrictions on what banks can charge for their services. As discussed earlier, the large chartered banks have long been diversified nationally. Recently, regional trust companies have sought wider geographic diversification through mergers with trusts in other regions.

In principle, entry restrictions have been eliminated through allowing "common ownership of regulated financial institutions" and the entrance of foreign financial institutions. In practice, constraints exist in order to maintain the separation between different types of financial institutions while allowing cross-ownership of financial institutions, and to restrict ownership of financial institutions by commercial interests and ownership concentration. Economic concentration has been a secondary concern. The primary concerns include the need in some cases for a branch system to serve the public, which imposes very heavy start-up costs on new entrants, and the requirement for regulatory approval before winding up operations and surrendering a charter, which is a barrier to exit.

Banks with capital over $750 million must be widely held in that no shareholdings of more than 10% are permitted. The rules are more lenient for similarly sized trust companies in order to reflect the ownership pattern now in place. Nonbank financial corporations seeking to convert to a bank must commit to move towards no more than 10% ownership. A ceiling of 65% was placed on the cross-ownership of financial and nonfinancial assets by one group.

Foreign-owned firms seeking to expand into Canada's financial markets are required to create new firms rather than to buy existing ones. An exception is created in the case of foreign-owned firms seeking to buy Canadian securities dealers. This was a policy concession designed to recapitalize the industry.

The new regulations remove restrictions on institutions forming affiliations with other financial institutions through holding companies. Furthermore, except for selling insurance, institutions are permitted to establish networks to cross-sell products. In addition, direct powers to conduct certain lines of business, once restricted to a class of institutions, are now open to all, including commercial lending (formerly for banks only), consumer loans (formerly restricted for nonbanks), investment advice and portfolio management, and fiduciary powers (formerly prohibited for banks and insurance companies).[19]

Regulators recognize that the removal of the separation between types of financial institutions may heighten the risk of conflicts of interest and self-dealing. Specific restrictions seek to control non-arm's-length and interaffiliate transactions. Enhanced disclosure rules respond to criticisms advanced after a recent failure of a major group of investment funds. Directors and auditors are given greater powers to control management.

3.3. Government Deposit Insurance (De Jure and De Facto)[20]

The Canada Deposit Insurance Corporation (CDIC) insures deposits up to a maximum of $60,000. The CDIC covers savings and checking accounts, term deposits, and deposit receipts. It does not cover Guaranteed Investment Certificates (GICs) with terms of more than five years or U.S. dollar accounts. The CDIC was established only in 1967 in response to the failure of several trust companies. Because limits are established by account names, individual depositors may have insured deposits well beyond the limit. Membership of the CDIC is limited to about 175 banks and federally and provincially incorporated trust and loan companies. Although the CDIC has emergency powers to provide assistance as lender of last resort, these powers have not been used. The CDIC charges a flat-rate insurance premium of $\frac{1}{10}$ of 1% (i.e., 0.001) of net insurable deposits. There is no risk adjustment in the assessment of the deposit insurance fees.

In the 1985 failure of two banks in western Canada, the Bank of Canada and the IG (not the CDIC) played the major role in the unsuccessful bailout effort. After the failure, the CDIC (following the example of the FDIC in the Continental Illinois failure in 1984) went beyond its de jure limits to cover the losses of all the uninsured depositors. As a result, the CDIC incurred a substantial deficit.

For a number of years, the banking industry has advocated some minimal level of market discipline through deposit coinsurance by individual depositors on deposits exceeding $20,000. Regulatory rejection of this proposal has argued that individual depositors cannot assess the credit and insurance risks inherent in a bank's assets. The banks have questioned whether the regulators have superior ability in assessing these risks (Korthals, 1989).

Under the proposed legislation referred to earlier, the CDIC has been given additional powers to discipline institutions for unsound financial practices. These include the imposition of penalty fees, and the revocation of insurance coverage. The CDIC has the power to request an inspection of a questionable member. Monitoring of member institutions is a responsibility of the Superintendent and will be discussed below.

3.4. Role of the Central Bank, Particularly as a Lender of Last Resort

The responsibilities of the Bank of Canada include advising the government on financial matters and formulating the national monetary policy. The Bank lends overnight funds to chartered banks with unexpected, temporary shortfalls in their reserve positions, either in voluntary reserves held against fluctuations in settlement or against required reserves with the Bank. As lender of last resort, the Bank may make extraordinary advances to chartered banks for renewable periods up to six months. According to Estey (1986, p. 57), extraordinary advances are intended "to prevent the failure of the particular institution which is *illiquid but still solvent* [our emphasis], and to preserve confidence in other deposit-taking institutions and the financial system." Like the CDIC, the Bank has no information-gathering functions. It relies on the Superintendent's Office for its information.

3.5. Insolvency Regulation

The Canadian approach to insolvency resolution is based on the U.K. model of voluntary self-regulation. However, in response to recent crises, the Canadian regulations are moving towards the U.S. approach of active regulation (Bartholomew, 1989). The main responsibility for supervising banks lies with the Superintendent of Financial Institutions.[21] The Superintendent has the authority to enforce Bank Act restrictions on banks and to make additional, "voluntary" guidelines. In addition to the leverage restrictions mentioned earlier, the guidelines limit to 50% the percentage of a bank's capital that may be lent to any one borrower. The Superintendent also sets guidelines on reporting, loan loss provisioning, and accounting for sovereign loans. In 1987, an increase in provisions was required that caused five of Canada's Big Six banks to report a loss for the year. During 1989, several banks voluntarily increased these provisions for Third World Debt. Nonperforming loans, exposure to financing leveraged buyouts, and other data have been added to the preinspection questionnaires and other reports that banks must file with the Superintendent.

Each bank in Canada is inspected annually.[22] Inspectors go over the preinspection report focusing on the CAMEL criteria: Capital adequacy, Asset quality, Management quality, Earnings, and Liquidity. This analysis was computerized in 1985. A team of inspectors then visits the head office of the bank, typically for one to four days. The team carries on discussions with senior management and the bank's external auditors (chartered accountancy firms). The inspectors also have the power to review minutes of directors' meetings. In some cases, retired bankers, working under contract for the Superintendent, conduct spot checks of loans in the bank's portfolio.

The inspection system came under heavy criticism after it failed to provide timely warning of the impending failure of two western banks in 1985. The Northland Bank, for example, had a portfolio of bad loans resulting from rapid growth of "risky" loans prior to and during a severe recession in western Canada. Management engaged in "survival tactics" by retaining questionable loans on accrual status, and by taking insufficient loss provisions. The Estey Commission faulted the bank's external auditors for accepting management's overly optimistic views and criticized the inspectors for believing the auditors.[23] The Commission (Estey, 1986, p. 5) noted that:

> It is clear that management did succeed in maintaining an appearance of financial health by its tactics. The financial statements became gold fillings covering cavities in the assets and in the earnings of the bank. By conventional standards of banking and bank accounting the bank would have been shown as short on assets and earnings.

Although the Superintendent's inspection staff has been increased, the external auditors remain the main source of information. Given the size of the Canadian banks and the level of resources available to the Superintendent, the inspection process must by necessity rely on information provided by management and certified by the external auditors.

In 1988, the federal government introduced capital guidelines which relate to the minimum level of capital required to credit-risk-adjust assets and off-balance-sheet items. For example, common share capital must equal 4% of business loans. Since this ratio does not depend upon the credit rating of the borrower, bankers (Korthals, 1989, p. 12) feel that the use of a fixed ratio "will drive the system toward higher risk credits to make the desired return on the mandated capital."

3.6. Standardization of Cross-Border Regulations

Some progress has been made in the standardization of cross-border regulations of the banking industry. For example, the committee charged with this task under the Bank for International Settlements (BIS) in Basel has agreed to introduce uniform risk-adjusted capital adequacy rules. Accordingly, total capital must be 7.25% of a bank's risk-adjusted assets by the end of 1990 and 8% by the end of 1992. Of the total capital, at least 50% must represent core capital (common equity) and the remainder can be supplementary capital (preferred shares and debentures). Although the treatment of off-balance-sheet items (such as unused lines of credit, bank guarantees, and currency and interest-rate swaps) has been resolved, Canadian banks and regulations may have problems with goodwill and real estate values. The BIS rules stipulate that capital should exclude any goodwill paid for acquired companies (sizeable amounts were paid for the purchase of investment dealers by the banks), and allow for discretion in the case of unrealized gains on a bank's real estate holdings (which are sizeable for the Canadian Big Six banks).

4. Major Current Domestic and International Operating and Regulatory Problems, with Particular Emphasis on Problems of Safety and Competitive Equilibrium[24]

As long as the Bank of Canada stands ready to lend to solvent institutions facing temporary illiquidity, deposit insurance is not needed to prevent bank runs based on irrational grounds (Kane, 1987; Benston and Kaufman, 1986). Furthermore, as long as runs are not systemwide (and this has been the recent experience), they simply result in the shifting of funds among institutions, and, thus, have little economic impact. If regulators can close or merge troubled financial institutions while they are still solvent at long-run economic values, then deposit insurance is not required. As argued earlier, a major reason for the stability of Canadian banks in the 1930s was the public's belief that regulators had and would exercise this ability.

Although deposit insurance is redundant on the macroeconomic level, it serves a useful microeconomic function. It saves the individual depositor the search costs associated with monitoring the financial strength of depository institutions. These benefits are paid for by taxpayers when insurance is invoked.

From our perspective, the expanded information-gathering powers of the Superintendent do not appear to be sufficient, given the expansion in the business activities of Canadian financial institutions. By continuing to rely on auditors, Canadian regulators will still lack the independent means to detect improper and possibly fraudulent practices.

Furthermore, auditors may be applying the wrong principles. Banking scholars (such as Kane, 1987) recommend the implementation of a market-value accounting system to provide better information on a bank's financial condition. Canadian regulators have made some changes in this direction. For example, they have eliminated the five-year averaging provision for loan losses, and engaged retired bankers to audit loan portfolios. However, more sweeping changes are needed. For example, most chartered banks report rate-sensitivity gaps so that investors can monitor the interest-rate risk inherent in their balance sheets. While this is an improvement over the prior practice of not reporting gaps, duration gaps are a superior measure. With the increasingly important roles of securities and insurance activities, the advantage of the duration measure is enhanced.

The proposed reforms to the CDIC do not eliminate the incentives for excessive risk-taking that are inherent in the current insurance system, although the dangers of incentive-incompatible systems of deposit insurance are well known.[25] The Canadian Bankers Association's proposal for risk-rated deposit insurance premiums could be further refined by reducing the basic coverage to $10,000 and allowing institutions the right to offer higher coverages on an optional basis. Thus, managers could signal their beliefs about the risk of their institutions, while further market discipline is introduced through coinsurance.[26] A related proposal, which was discussed earlier, would require riskier institutions to maintain higher capital levels. Since these proposals are all ex ante adjustments, they depend on the availability of better information in order to determine risk levels accurately.

The new regulations do give the CDIC expanded powers to discipline excessively risky institutions ex post. Such powers include penalty premiums and revocation of insurance. While these powers are useful, will the CDIC have the political will to use them? The 1985 experience with expanded de facto insurance limits suggests that the new regulations should include a specific prohibition against reimbursing uninsured depositors. This would force regulators to act more forcefully to prevent failures.[27]

Ownership restrictions in the proposed legislation have generated resistance from those who think the restrictions are too tight. The unpopularity of these ownership restrictions is reportedly the reason why the junior minister responsible for the implementation of the legislation was shifted to another portfolio. The press has speculated that the rule restricting ownership in banks to 10% may be removed so that Canadian banks could be controlled by domestic or U.S. interests (*Macleans*, March 6, 1989, page 9). This issue caused dissent among the board members of the Economic Council of Canada. Its recent recommendation to broaden the 10% rule to all deposit-taking institutions was not unanimous (EEC, 1989).

Canadian regulators have also proposed the imposition of "Chinese Walls" between different areas in a holding company. Unlike the "firewalls" proposed in the United States, the Chinese walls are aimed primarily at preventing the flow of insider information. However, Chinese history suggests that invaders breached the Great Wall by bribing sentries, and through other "insider" deals! Such an interpretation is consistent with the regulatory dialectic presented earlier.

A corollary of the regulatory dialectic states that financial institutions adjust their organizational structures to extract the maximum benefit from the regulatory environment. An unintended benefit for the newly authorized financial holding companies could be the flexibility to locate banking business in unregulated subsidiaries, while simultaneously procuring cheaper funds for the holding company through affiliated companies that are covered by deposit insurance. Kane (1985) gives two reasons why regulations against self-dealing are unlikely to be effective in controlling this problem, namely,

> Restrictions on interaffiliate transactions tend to be circumvented because they tend to reduce precisely the benefits of combination that a holding company is set up to exploit, and in a world of rapid changes in technology and in macroeconomic environment, holding-company managers receive more timely information about evolving ways of circumventing inherited regulations than government regulators do.

Canadian regulators sometimes claim that their system of regulating each entity in a holding company is superior to the American focus on the holding company level. They argue that such superiority obviates the problem of interaffiliate transactions. Our disagreement with this line of argument is supported by the following statement by the Economic Council (1986, p. 78):

> The complete ban on all non-arm's-length transactions that would be imposed by the Green paper would, however, negate most of the benefits to be gained from diversification.

In summary, given the shortfall of supervisory staff, granting wider powers for cross-selling of products and cross-ownership to financial institutions, along with the proposed regulatory changes, is like teaching circus acrobats a new series of tricks after removing their safety nets![28]

5. Implications of Globalization

5.1. For Domestic Banking Structure[29]

As stated above, with the enactment of the Bank Act in December 1980, foreign banks formally entered into the Canadian banking system. Although foreign-owned banks had previously operated subsidiaries under the Canadian Business Corporations Act or provincial legislation, these entities escaped many banking regulations (such as mandatory reserve requirements) because of their "nonbank" status. These entities funded corporate loans using parental guarantees for money market investments.

The Bank Act was designed to extend Canadian control and dominance in the banking industry, to stimulate greater domestic competition, and to accommodate the perceived need for reciprocal banking relationships between Canada and other countries.[30] It required foreign (Schedule Two) banks to operate in Canada as separate corporate entities and not as branches. This deviation from normal international banking arrangements was introduced to assist in the enforcement of regulatory controls by updating regulatory records of the level of capital assets and profits of the foreign banks operating in Canada. Foreign banks have to seek permission from the Superintendent before opening any new branches in Canada.

The foreign banks are required to fund at least 50% of their Canadian dollar assets with Canadian dollar liabilities to control the level of Canadian dollar business funded by foreign currency liabilities. Although these liabilities are fully hedged against foreign exchange risk, the Superintendent felt that they could represent a (unspecified) longer-term funding risk (Metcalfe, 1984).

Before granting a Canadian charter to a foreign bank, the Superintendent conducts a test of reciprocity to determine whether the Canadian banks feel that they are being treated fairly in the applicant's country. The applicant and its foreign supervisory authority must also provide evidence of reciprocity in their home country (Metcalfe, 1984).

Prior to the 1980 Bank Act, Canadian banks had been unable to operate full branches in Japan because Japanese banks were not given reciprocal privileges in Canada. Initially, each country permitted five new banking subsidiaries to operate in each other's country. Although Canada's Big 5 were allowed to enter the Japanese market, they grew slowly in this liquid market. According to the President of the Royal Bank, his Bank's activities were not restricted by regulatory barriers, but by cultural and language barriers, strong domestic competition, and strong customer loyalties (Metcalfe, 1984).

As noted earlier, the Free Trade Agreement between Canada and the United States in 1989 extends domestic bank status to American-owned banks in Canada. Thus, the expansion of American banks in Canada is no longer restricted by the asset ceiling imposed by the Bank Act.

During 1989, the federal government announced that the application by the American Express Co. to operate as a foreign bank in Canada would formally be approved, the start-up would be delayed for one year, and the company would be allowed to continue to operate its travel and insurance businesses. Although this is in violation of the Bank Act because commercial companies are not allowed to own banks, the federal government argued that the decision was consistent with its policy to expand and diversify banking in Canada. It also argued that it was using legislative flexibility to cover any special circumstances such as the Amex decision, and that several precedents existed whereby foreign banks had been grandfathered to conduct separate, nonbank businesses in Canada. However, unlike the parents of Canada's 57 other foreign banking subsidiaries, the parent of Amex Bank of Canada would not be fully regulated in its U.S. home jurisdiction.

During early 1990, federal government policy appeared to be stalled. Merrill Lynch Canada moved in the opposite direction of American Express by selling off its retail brokerage arm. Commentators conjectured that this action by Merrill Lynch resulted from word that it would not be given a Canadian bank charter (Corcoran, 1990).

Thus, as discussed above, globalization of financial markets pressured regulators to move quickly to ensure that banking institutions were neither precluded from competing in other jurisdictions nor moved to other, more lenient jurisdictions. Our critique of reregulation to date, while accepting this implication of the regulatory dialectic argues for deposit insurance reform as the *sine qua non* of this process.

5.2. For Participation of Domestic Banks in Other Countries[31]

As was discussed above, Canadian banks have long had significant international business interests. Since the international debt crisis, the six largest Canadian banks have radically pruned their business interests outside North America. This retrenchment process occurred because local financial institutions had become too competitive, and the Canadian banks wanted to raise their returns from their international operations to the level of their returns from Canadian retail banking operations.

The extent of the retrenchment in international operations has varied by bank. At one extreme, the Bank of Montreal, the Toronto Dominion Bank, and the National Bank of Canada are striving to become almost exclusively North American businesses, with the exception of the Far East. At the other extreme, the Bank of Nova Scotia (BNS) still operates in 44 countries and has recently expanded in Dominica, India, and Malaysia. In the middle, the Royal Bank of Canada and the Canadian Imperial Bank of Commerce (CIBC) are not global banks in scope but have a strong presence in some designated markets.

Although the Canadian banks (especially the BNS, Royal, and CIBC) have had a strong retail banking presence in the Caribbean for more than a century, the Royal has closed and sold businesses in Haiti, Dominion Republic, Trinidad, Guyana, and Belize, and is expanding in the Bahamas and Barbados. In contrast, the BNS has not altered its 21-nation Caribbean network. The Canadian banks' continuing business in Latin America no longer includes public finance, and consists mainly of trade finance.

Because of the exceptional growth of the local economies and the prospects of trade finance in the Asia/Pacific countries, the Canadian banks are not retrenching in these markets. This is also the case in Japan, although Canadian and other foreign players complain about the difficulty of being profitable in that market. In this region, the Canadian banks are concentrating on trade finance, investment/corporate banking, foreign-exchange and money market operations, and selectively in private banking.

5.3. Particular Emphasis on 1992 European Economic Community (EEC) Integration[32]

Most of the Canadian banks have undergone a radical retrenchment in Europe. During the past few years, the Bank of Montreal closed its Frankfurt branch and representative offices in Milan and Madrid; BNS closed its operations in Brussels and Rotterdam; and TD closed all its operations in Continental Europe. During May of 1989, the Royal Bank sold its Belgian subsidiary and part of its banking interests in France and

West Germany. The Royal plans to concentrate its West European business on private banking for wealthy individuals and on services to companies with North American links. Nevertheless, the Royal and CIBC will still have the largest and second largest European networks of the major Canadian banks, respectively.

The Royal, CIBC, BNS, and BOM retain large operations in London, which concentrate on corporate/investment banking. These London offices are at different stages of integration with the banks' Canadian investment dealer subsidiaries, which were acquired since mid-1987.

Canada's main life insurers (Sun Life, Manufacturers Life, Canada Life, Confederation Life, Crown Life, and others) are strong forces in the British market. They sell not only life insurance but also trust units (mutual funds), mortgages, and portfolio management. Unlike the banks, the Canadian life insurance companies are starting to assess the single European market of 320 million consumers that will emerge after 1992. With their substantial British operations as a base, they are talking to local life insurers and studying the various national markets in Continental Europe. The EEC is proposing to remove national barriers to the sale of life insurance. This should allow a life insurance company, which is approved to conduct business in one EEC country, to establish branches and sell services in the other 11 countries without encountering additional national regulations.

The EEC should offer some potential for Canadian insurance firms. The fragmented national markets have fostered wide variations in product pricing. For example, consumers in countries such as Italy, Belgium, Spain, and France pay much higher life insurance premiums than those in Britain and the Netherlands. Also, the EEC's principle of reciprocity in financial services should not be a problem, because the Canadian life insurance market is fairly open and many of Canada's major life companies are already in the EEC through Britain.

6. Brief Outlook for Health, Competitive Efficiency, and Structure, Particularly in a Global Environment

Despite the rise in domestic interest rates and the ongoing struggle with Third-World loans, Canada's major chartered banks had a reasonable performance during 1989 due to improved asset quality and domestic operations. Net income per $100 of average assets reached 92 cents versus 66 cents for the previous year, excluding the effects of LDC provisions and unusual items.

This performance was due to the improved quality of non-Third-World loans (mainly corporate), which allowed for a moderate reduction in provisions for loan losses in this category. Also, the banks' income tax rate has dropped due to federal tax reform. Based on net income per $100 of average assets (ROA), the Big Six banks rank as follows: TD with 121 cents, National with 100 cents, Royal with 87 cents, BOM with 81 cents, CIBC with 78 cents, and Nova Scotia with 77 cents.

The Big Six banks had total Third-World loan-loss reserves and provisions covering approximately two thirds of all loans outstanding as of the close of fiscal 1989 on October 31. In addition, their total dollar exposure has been reduced by selling off loans (Philip, 1989).[33] According to its Senior Vice President of Finance, the Third World will be a "bonafide discontinued business by year end" 1989 for the TD (Horvitch, 1989c, p. 42). Venezuela, which owes Canadian banks about $1.9 billion, recently stopped paying interest to its bankers. The banks quickly classified their Venezuela loans as nonaccrual loans. This involves $600 and $203 million in loans for the Royal and CIBC, respectively.[34]

In brief, Canadian banks are large, reasonably profitable, and internationalized. They are making reasonable progress towards resolving their LDC exposures. As discussed, strategies vary for coping with environmental shifts. An important wild-card factor is the outcome of the present round of deregulation. Nevertheless, in late 1989, investors were concerned about Canadian bank exposure from financing LDC debt, leveraged buyouts, other corporate restructurings, and real estate in troubled regions of the United States (McNish 1989d).

Due to deregulation (and subsequent reregulation), technological advances, and the globalization of financial markets, Canadian banks will continue to shift away from their historical role as intermediaries between depositors and borrowers. They will continue to diversify their range of financial products. Their deposit base will continue to be under attack as consumers become more sophisticated about investing their savings. Banks will increasingly have to respond by selling a growing array of corporate and government securities through their branches, and by raising a greater proportion of their funds through the capital (primarily, money) markets. Due to the greater variability of such financings, additional regulations may be required to protect the liquidity of individual banks.

The banks' traditional corporate business will continue to change. Many of the bank's traditional clients will continue to bypass the banks by issuing commercial paper at a price that is superior to that for bank loans. Thus, corporate bankers will spend increasing amounts of time competing to underwrite the commercial paper of corporate clients, arranging foreign-denominated debt issues, structuring interest and currency swaps, and providing financial advice on business combinations and reorganizations.

Acknowledgments

The authors benefited greatly from comments by the editor. Linda Hendry and Andrew Munn provided capable research assistance. Lillian Brown expertly prepared the manuscript. This research was supported by the Social Sciences and Humanities Research Council of Canada (SSHRC) and the Centre for International Business Studies, Dalhousie University.

Notes

1. Primary reserves were reduced in the most recent Bank Act revision in 1980. Legislation to phase out primary reserves is likely to be enacted in 1990.
2. Trust companies are permitted to seek federal incorporation.
3. These are equivalent to the secondary reserves held by the chartered banks.
4. Canada's second largest credit union, Van City, has $1.7 billion in assets (see table 1-4).
5. An early example of pension payments was the practice of granting Crown land in Canada to retired soldiers after the Napoleonic Wars. Among the soldiers receiving land in this way were the Hessian regiments, whose defeat when Washington crossed the Delaware is well known to U.S. school children. Less well known is the fact that, in order to preserve the peace, these soldiers were granted land in areas surrounded by farms owned by earlier civilian settlers. The resulting patchwork of landholding is referred to as "bordered Hessian."
6. Although a number of provincially chartered life companies exist, they compose only a minor segment of the industry.
7. This discussion draws importantly on Neufeld (1972) and Jamieson (1953).
8. These numbers are from Kryzanowski and Roberts (1989b). They correct those reported in Beckhart (1929).
9. This argument was advanced by a bank president testifying before a Parliamentary Committee in 1923. Beckhart (1929) questions its validity. Neave (1981) reports constant returns to scale.
10. Also, see Warburton (1966).
11. Preliminary analysis by Kryzanowski and Roberts (1989b) suggests that insolvency in this period would follow if it is assumed that the market value of bank assets was less than 80% of book value.
12. A close analogy exists between this policy and the current-day implicit guarantee of the FSLIC in the United States. This "too-large-to-fail" policy was first suggested to the authors by George Kaufman. Our analysis draws on Kryzanowski and Roberts (1989a,b).

13. Specifically, a former Minister of Finance stated the Government's policy as follows:

> If I had believed that the Home Bank at that time was in danger of failing, closing its doors, was insolvent, I should have gone to the Canadian Bankers' Association and told them to take over that bank. Either to one bank or more banks. . . . I would have made them do it. (McKeown Commission, April 25, 1924, Vol. 6, p. 359).

Our interpretation of the historical evidence is also supported by Neufeld (1972, p. 98) as follows:

> The dilemma of a Minister of Finance in deciding whether he should permit mergers and face increased concentration, or should prohibit them and see confidence in the banking system shaken through a possible bank failure, has been present for many decades. So far [starting *after* the Home Bank failure in 1923], he has always chosen the first alternative, thereby confirming that in practice there has been no effective anti-merger influence from government.

14. In 1984, 34 trust companies were under federal regulation, and 64 were under provincial regulation.
15. In the case of pension and mutual funds, this growth was fueled by the stock market growth. Depository institutions are again growing faster since the stock market crash in 1987.
16. Much of the remainder of this section draws heavily on McNish (1989b, B4).
17. This was stated by the Federal Minister of State for Finance as follows:

> Our policy recognizes that the financial system worldwide is evolving in a manner that will allow financial institutions in any one of the traditional four pillars to provide a full range of financial services. It protects the capacity of Canadian institutions to be effective, well-skilled participants, by bringing financial services in Canada into step with the needs and realities of the market, at home and throughout the world. [Hon. Thomas Hockin, Minister of State for Finance, Speech in the House of Commons (December 1986)].

18. For example, during the past three years, fee income has risen from 18% to 25% of the total revenues of the Bank of Nova Scotia.
19. In addition to the prohibition on insurance sales by banks as mentioned earlier, the proposed legislation still restricts banks from leasing personally owned vehicles through their branch networks. Banks will be allowed to conduct data processing and real estate activities through subsidiaries only. The Canadian Bankers Association (1989) argues for giving banks the choice of whether or not to use the branch network. In most cases, this is probably the lower-cost alternative.
20. This section draws on Estey (1986, Chapter 3) and Hockin (1986).
21. Until recently, the Superintendent's banking responsibilities were undertaken by the IG of Banks. Although much of our discussion draws on Estey (1986) on the role of the IG in the failures of two banks, we use the term Superintendent throughout to avoid confusion.
22. Our discussion of the inspection process draws on Estey (1986).
23. Giammarino, Schwartz, and Zechner (1989) demonstrate that stock market investors were better informed. They conclude that ". . . market data provided evidence that the Northland Bank was in considerable difficulty well before the bank collapsed" (p. 126).
24. This section draws on Kane (1985). It expands on his discussion by applying relevant aspects of various critiques of the U.S. system to Canada. Our major conclusions also reinforce those of Neave (1989).

25. For a complete discussion, see Kane (1989). In particular, see the sections on the current failure of FSLIC, and on the 1985 failures of the Ohio Deposit Guarantee Fund and the Maryland Savings Share Insurance Corporation. These incentives are well documented in a Canadian context in Wyman (1985, p. 25).

26. Giammarino, Schwartz, and Zechner (1989) also argue for the theoretical superiority of risk-adjusted premiums. Wyman (1985, p. 27) considers risk-related premiums a "highly desirable tool to enforce market discipline." However, he foresees a number of practical problems with implementing such a plan. Dowd (1988) suggests that these difficulties be resolved by introducing private deposit insurance.

27. As recognized in Wyman (1985, p. 30), such a prohibition is needed to make coinsurance credible.

28. For a detailed discussion of this viewpoint in the context of reforms of deposit insurance, see Todd (1988).

29. Part of this section is based on Metcalfe (1984).

30. Based on a review of regulations in France, West Germany, Italy, Japan, Switzerland, and the United Kingdom, the House of Commons Standing Committee found that only Italy had more restrictive regulations for foreign banks than domestic banks.

31. Much of this discussion draws on Horvitch (1989a, p. 8).

32. Much of this discussion draws on Horvitch (1989a, p. 8) and Pitts (1989, p. 8).

33. Like their U.S. counterparts, Canadian banks are declining government overtures to lend more to LDCs (Philip, 1989).

34. Since April 30, 1989, the CIBC has sold some of these loans to reduce its exposure to $106 million.

References

"Annual Foreign Exchange Review," *Euromoney* (May 1989), 79–80.

Arshadi, Nasser. "Capital Structure, Agency Problems and the Deposit Insurance in Banking Firms," *Financial Review* 24 (February 1989), 31–52.

Bartholomew, Philip F. "Recent Developments for Canadian 'Near Banks'," *Housing Finance International* 4 (August 1989), 28–31.

Beckhart, B.H. *The Banking System of Canada*. New York: Holt, 1929.

Benson, John N. *Provincial Government Banks: A Case Study of Regional Responses to National Institutions*. Vancouver: The Fraser Institute, 1978.

Benston, George J. "Federal Regulation of Banking: An Historical Overview," in George G. Kaufman and Roger C. Kormendi (eds.), *Deregulating Financial Services*. Cambridge, MA: Ballinger, 1986.

Benston, George J. and George G. Kaufman. "Risks and Failures in Banking: Overview, History and Evaluation," in George G. Kaufman and Roger C. Kormendi (eds.), *Deregulating Financial Services*. Cambridge, MA: Ballinger, 1986.

Bierwag, Gerald O. "Deregulation of the Financial Services Industry and Depository Institutions," *Advances in the Study of Entrepreneurship, Innovation and Economic Growth Vol. 2*. Greenwich, CT: JAI Press, 1988, 193–219.

Canada, Parliament, House of Commons Committee on Finance, Trade and

Economic Affairs. *Minutes and Proceedings of Evidence*. Ottawa: Government of Canada, October 6, 1983.
Canadian Encyclopedia. Edmonton: Hurtig Publishers, 1988.
CICA. *Financial Reporting for Credit Unions*. Toronto: The Canadian Institute of Chartered Accountants, 1984.
Corcoran, Terence. "Ottawa's Approach to Deregulation is to Let the Banks in First," *The Globe and Mail*, January 4, 1990, B2.
Crawford, Bradley. *Banking and Bills of Exchange, Vol. 2*. Toronto: Canada Law Book Inc., 1986.
DOF (Department of Finance). *The Regulation of Canadian Financial Institutions: Proposals for Discussion*. Ottawa: Supply and Services Canada, 1985.
Dowd, Kevin. "Some Lessons from the Recent Canadian Bank Failures," in George G. Kaufman (ed.), *Research in Financial Services*. Greenwich, CT: JAI Press, 1989.
ECC (Economic Councial of Canada). *Competition and Solvency: A Framework for Financial Regulation*. Ottawa: Supply and Services Canada, 1986.
ECC (Economic Councial of Canada). *A New Frontier: Globalization and Canada's Financial Markets*. Ottawa: Supply and Services Canada, 1989.
Eisenbeis, Robert A. "Risk as a Criterion for Expanding Banking Activities," in George G. Kaufman and Roger C. Kormendi (eds.), *Deregulating Financial Services*. Cambridge, MA: Ballinger, 1986.
Ellert, James C. "The Business of Banking," in *Bank Financial Management*. Montreal: Institute of Canadian Bankers, 1988.
Estey, Willard Z. *Report of the Inquiry into the Collapse of the CCB and the Northland Bank*. Ottawa: Canadian Government Publishing Centre, 1986.
Falconer, Kirk. *Financial Deregulation in Canada* (New Democratic Party Research Groups, June 2, 1988).
Farlinger, Brian. "Transition in Banking," Speech, Canadian Bankers Association, Toronto, November 3, 1987.
Financial Post. *Moneywise*, November 1989.
Francis, Diane. "Into the Hands of the Powerful," *Maclean's*, March 6, 1989, 9.
Giammarino, Ronald, Eduardo Schwartz, and Josef Zechner. "Market Valuation of Bank Assets and Deposit Insurance in Canada," *Canadian Journal of Economics* 22 (February 1989), 109–126.
Hockin, Thomas. "New Directions for the Financial Sector," Ottawa: Government of Canada, December 1986.
Horvitch, Sonita. "Big Six Banks Fine-Tuning Foreign Plans," *The Financial Post*, May 29, 1989a, 8.
Horvitch, Sonita. "Bill will Put Reins on Banks' Insurance Sales: Blenkarn," *The Financial Post*, May 30, 1989b, 3.
Horvitch, Sonita. "Banks Enjoy a Strong First Half, "*The Financial Post*, June 5, 1989c, 42.
Horvitch, Sonita. "Non-U.S. foreign banks call for asset exemption," *The Financial Post*, July 19, 1989d, 3.
House of Commons Standing Committee on Trade, Finance and Economic Affairs, *Twenty-Fourth Report*. Ottawa: Government of Canada, October 1983.

Jamieson, A.B. *Chartered Banking in Canada.* Toronto: Ryerson Press, 1953.

Kalymon, Basil A. *Global Innovation and the Impact on Canada's Financial Markets.* Toronto: John Wiley, 1989.

Kane, Edward J. "Testimony Before the Parliament of Canada's Standing Committee on Finance, Trade and Economic Affairs on The Regulation of Canadian Financial Institutions," July 10, 1985.

Kane, Edward J. "No Room for Weak Links in the Chain of Deposit-Insurance Reform," *Journal of Financial Services Research* 1 (1987), 77–111.

Kane, Edward J. "Confronting Incentive Problems in U.S. Deposit Insurance: The Range of Alternative Solutions," in George G. Kaufman and Roger C. Kormendi (eds.), *Deregulating Financial Services.* Cambridge, MA: Ballinger, 1986.

Kane, Edward J. *The S & L Insurance Mess: How Did it Happen.* Washington, DC: Urban Institute, 1989.

Korthals, Robert. "Regulations Lack Direction," *The Financial Post*, January 25, 1989, 12.

Kryzanowski, Lawrence and Gordon S. Roberts. "The Performance of the Canadian Banking System, 1920–1940," forthcoming in *Bank Structure Conference Proceedings 1989*, Federal Reserve Bank of Chicago, 1989a.

Kryzanowski, Lawrence and Gordon S. Robert. "The Solvency of the Canadian Banking System, 1920–1940," paper presented at the Northern Finance Association Meeting, Ottawa, September 23–24, 1989b.

McNish, Jacquie. "Financial Deregulation Turns into Corporate Anarchy," *The Globe and Mail*, March 20, 1989a, B1 and B2.

McNish, Jacquie. "Parizeau Embodied in Quebec Reforms," *The Globe and Mail*, March 21, 1989b, B1 and B4.

McNish, Jacquie. "Capital 'Double Count' Urged in Quebec," *The Globe and Mail*, May 25, 1989c, B4.

McNish, Jacquie. "U.S. Realty Woes Sink TSE Bank Stocks," *The Globe and Mail*, December 20, 1989d, B1 and B4.

Metcalfe, H.B.W. *Foreign Banks in Canada—A Survey Report.* Ottawa: Queen's Printer, May 1984.

Nagy, P. *The International Business of Canadian Banks.* Montreal: Centre for International Business Studies, Ecole des Hautes Etudes Commerciales, 1983.

Neave, Edwin H. *Canada's Financial System.* Toronto: John Wiley, 1981.

Neave, Edwin H. "Canada's Approach to Financial Regulation," *Canadian Public Policy* 15 (1989), 1–11.

Neufeld, E.P. *Money and Banking in Canada.* Toronto: McClelland and Stewart, 1964.

Neufeld, E.P. *The Financial System of Canada.* Toronto: Macmillan, 1972.

Philip, Margaret. "Scotiabank Raises Reserves by $800 Million," *The Globe and ail*, November 15, 1989, B1.

 Gordon, "Canadian Insurers Eye Opening European Market," *The nancial Post*, May 29, 1989, 8.

Porter, Tony. "Regulation and Innovation," *Canadian Banker* (May–June 1989), 28–29.

Schreiner, John. "Credit Unions Giving Banks Run for Money," *The Financial Post*, May 22, 1989, 24.

Schwartz, Anna J. "The Lender of Last Resort and the Federal Safety Net," *Journal of Financial Services Research* 1 (1987), 1–17.

Solomon, Hyman. "Amex Can Enter Insurance, Travel," *The Financial Post*, May 25, 1989, 3.

Todd, Walker F. "No Conspiracy, but a Convenient Forgetting: Dr. Pangloss Visits the World of Deposit Insurance," working paper, Federal Reserve Bank of Cleveland, November 1988.

Warburton, Clark. *Depression, Inflation and Monetary Policy, Selected Papers: 1945–53*. Baltimore: Johns Hopkins Press, 1966.

Whyte, Heather D. "How Brokers Will Adapt to Major Changes Ahead," *The Financial Post*, October 2, 1989, 8.

Wyman Commission Report. *Final Report of the Working Committee on the Canada Deposit Insurance Corporation (CDIC)*. Ottawa: Supply and Services Canada, 1985.

2 BANK STRUCTURE IN CHILE

Sergio de la Cuadra and Salvador Valdés-Prieto

Although the Chilean financial system is not large in absolute terms, it exhibits some features that are of general interest. The first one is that it belongs to the only country[1] in Latin America that has recovered from the international debt crisis of the 1980s. In addition, Chile has been growing at over 5% in annual terms since 1986, and the rise of the investment/GDP ratio has allowed even faster growth recently. This turns the Chilean financial system into one of the emerging markets of the developing world.

The second feature of interest is that the Chilean financial system is the product of financial liberalization policies adopted in 1974–1981. These policies were unprecedented in the developing world, where financial repression is the leading policy, and in some areas even anticipated similar reforms that the OECD countries adopted or discussed in the 1980s. The Chilean capital market is open to foreign investment, so new investors are using it as the natural foothold from which to prepare participation in the investment boom that the country is experiencing.

However, the Chilean financial liberalization was weak in prudential regulatory aspects. This, plus the acute recession brought by the debt crisis (GDP fell 14.1% in 1982) led to a spate of financial intermediary insolvencies in which over 60% of the banking system by deposits had to be taken over by the government. It is possible that the rehabilitation procedures followed in Chile may be found useful in other countries.

Most interesting, in our view, are the 1986–1989 reforms to the banking law, which created novel mechanisms for insolvency resolution of financial intermediaries moving towards greater reliance on creditors' funds. In addition, deposit insurance was redefined, restricting 100% coverage to direct money substitutes, without individual account limits. Because of this third feature, the Chilean financial system will continue attracting widespread attention in the next years.

1. Current Structure of Financial Institutions and Markets

1.1. General Overview

A wide variety of financial institutions and products compete in the Chilean capital market. Commercial banks participate in money, short-term credit, and foreign currency markets. Although these markets continue to be dominated by commercial banks, they are being challenged by obligatory pension funds, which started operations only in 1981. Market-oriented policies, which were implemented in the second half of the 1970s and which deregulated the financial market, promoted the appearance of new services and pushed traditional institutions to modernize. As a result, financial markets grew rapidly. The growth was temporarily interrupted by the internal and external debt crisis of 1981–1983. Two years later, growth resumed both in the economy and in the capital market. Although the recovery from the crisis has taken a long time, it has been used beneficially to modernize and improve the norms for prudential regulation of financial institutions and the capital market in general.

The life insurance companies are the third largest segment of the capital market. They received a big boost by the 1981 privatization of the administration of some pieces of the obligatory social security system. Competing with banks on the lending side are the leasing companies and on the funding side are the mutual funds and the *agencias de valores*. Agencias de Valores are firms that are allowed to trade in the securities markets both as brokers and as market makers. Another group of bank competitors are the *financieras*; they specialize in consumer credit and differ from banks in that they cannot offer checking accounts, or engage in foreign trade financing and foreign currency operations. Lastly, there are casualty insurance companies and health insurance companies. The latter are quite new in the market, since they were first allowed to operate in 1981.

The secondary market for financial instruments operates primarily at the Bolsa de Comercio (stock exchange) of Santiago. The largest volume of trade is in fixed-income instruments, and a minor proportion is in stocks. There is also a second stock exchange at Valparaiso, the main port of the country, but this market place has declined in importance and is insignificant. A third stock exchange, named Bolsa de Valores de Chile, started operations in the second semester of 1989. It uses an electronic transaction mode and trades most of the instruments currently traded at the Bolsa de Santiago. These markets do not currently trade sophisticated instruments like options, foreign-exchange, futures, and interest-rate futures, but will do so in the near future. Also, a project for offering custody and clearing services is in process of development. Currently, such services exist in large scale only for the pension funds and are operated by the Central Bank.

The large and rapid accumulation of obligatory savings at the pension funds, together with the restrictive portfolio requirements, has created a shortage of investment possibilities for these funds. This has made necessary the introduction of legislation permitting new investment possibilities, such as shares in real estate investment corporations, shares in venture capital corporations, and shares in investment corporations similar to closed mutual funds.

1.2. Current Structure

To describe the current structure of the Chilean financial system, we will concentrate on the banking system, which is the largest industry in the sector. For the rest of the financial services, we will just give a general view through indicators of their relative size.

1.2.1. Monetization and Financial Deepening. Absolute and relative measures of the money supply and all financial assets are shown in tables 2-1 and 2-2. For monetization, we have used the value and structure of liabilities issued by the banking system, distinguishing between those issued to the private and to the public sector. To the sum of the banking system, we add Treasury bills, corporate bonds, commercial paper, and equity to reach a magnitude for financial deepening.

At year-end 1988, total financial assets sum up to 5098 billion pesos or to US$ 20.5 billion, which is equivalent to 94% of GDP (gross domestic product). One half of this amount consists of commercial banks' liabilities issued to the private sector. The degree of bank intermediation in relation to GDP is higher than in many other developing countries with an income

Table 2-1. Monetization and Financial Deepening (As of December 1988; Millions of Pesos)

I. Banking System Financial Assets	
1. Currency	181,536
2. Demand deposits	182,490
3. Time deposits	1,064,120
4. Repurchase agreements	161,448
5. Passbook savings accounts	352,869
6. M1 (1 + 2)	364,026
7. M2 (6 + 3)	1,428,146
8. M3 (7 + 5)	1,781,015
9. Foreign currency demand deposits	47,493
10. Foreign currency time deposits	246,976
11. M_1^* (6 + 9)	411,519
12. M_2^* (7 + 10)	1,675,122
13. M_3^* (12 + 5)	2,027,991
14. Mortgage-backed bonds (letras de crédito)	341,281
15. Total commercial banks (4 + 13 + 14)	2,530,720
16. Financieras funds raised	55,786
17. Saving bank funds raised	8,416
18. Central bank promissory notes	429,000
19. Total private-sector banking assets holdings (15 + 16 + 17 + 18)	3,023,922
20. Public-sector demand deposits	175,986
21. Total banking (19 + 20)	3,199,908
II. Treasury Bills	51,635
III. Corporate Bonds and Commercial Paper	124,216
IV. Equity	1,722,774
V. TOTAL (I + II + III + IV)	5,098,533

Notes: Exchange rate: 249.1 pesos to a U.S. dollar; December 1988 daily average.
Source: Banco Central de Chile, Boletín Mensual No 733, March 1989.

level similar to Chile, but it is still much lower than in industrialized nations. The outstanding value of publicly traded equity, US$ 6.9 billion or 32% of GDP, represents a significant fraction of the total physical assets of the economy, which are estimated to be about three times GDP.

Other features of the Chilean financial structure that may be observed from table 2-1 are the following:

1. Money defined as M1 is an unusually small fraction of GDP, only 6.7%. This ratio has been traditionally small due to the Chilean

Table 2-2. Financial Assets to Gross Domestic Product, Ratios (1988: Percentages)

Ratio	Percentage
1. M1/GDP	6.7
2. M2/GDP	26.4
3. M3/GDP	32.9
4. Total commercial banks/GDP[a]	46.8
5. Total private-sector banking assets holdings/GDP[b]	55.9
6. Total banking/GDP[c]	59.1
7. Equity/GDP	31.8
8. Total assets/GDP[d]	94.2

[a] From line 15, table 1.
[b] From line 19, table 1.
[c] From line 21, table 1.
[d] From line V, table 1.
Note: GDP (1988): 5,411,025 million pesos; 22,086 million dollars. Exchange rate: 245 pesos to a U.S. dollar, 1988 average.
Source: Same as table 2–1.

inflationary environment and because interest payments on demand deposits are not allowed. Yearly average inflation for the period 1930–1988 was 35% reaching the highest rates in the decades of the 1950s and 1970s. During the decade of the 1980s, the average inflation rate declined to 19%. Despite the reduction in inflation, the demand for cash balances has fallen from a historical average of 10% of GDP, to the current 6.7%. This can be explained by the increasing competition from interest-paying money substitutes, mainly repurchase agreements and mutual funds, both of which offer positive returns for funds with one-day liquidity.

The outstanding stock of repurchase agreements (as of December 31st, 1988) was similar to the stock of demand deposits, and as a percentage of GDP they were 3.9%. By adding up M1 and this near substitute, we get 10.6% of GDP, which is very near the historical M1 ratio. Mutual funds, most of which compete directly with demand deposits, were 1.3% of GDP. Also competing with M1 is the secondary market for time deposits, which has become quite efficient.

2. Time deposits have been growing substantially since interest rates were liberalized in 1975. As of December last year, they represented 20% of GDP, and passbook accounts another 6.5%.
3. There is a significant amount of foreign currency deposits (demand

and time)—slightly over US$ 1.2 billion, representing 21% of M2 in domestic currency.
4. Saving banks are the remains of the savings and loans industry (SINAP), which failed in 1975. They were finished off in 1989, when the remaining SINAP portfolio was auctioned and acquired by some commercial banks.[2,3]
5. The financieras that survived the banking crisis of 1981–1983 are very small relative to commercial banks (only 2.2% in terms of liabilities).
6. During this decade the Central Bank has been very active floating its own debt (promissory notes) in the market. The stock of Central Bank debt in the market is very substantial, due in part to subsidies paid during the debt crisis. This paper is also used for repurchase agreement transactions, with the commercial banks and Agencias de Valores as the market-makers. The Central Bank uses also these securities to conduct open-market operations.
7. Treasury bills are a small fraction of aggregate financial assets. This is a result of fiscal reforms in 1975, the budgetary discipline of the last 13 years, and a very effcient tax collection system. Except for the recession years 1982–1985, when the central government ran deficits that rose to 6.3% of GDP in 1985, there has been a balanced or surplus[4] budget in every year since 1986.

1.2.2. The Banking Industry. Table 2-3 shows a profile of the Chilean banking system as of December 31st, 1988.

Although foreign banks outnumber Chilean banks, assetwise they represent only 16.5%. Among Chilean banks there is one state-owned commercial bank (Banco del Estado), which accounts for 19.5% of the total assets of the industry.

Total bank assets are 110% of GDP. Assets are substantially higher than total loans because of large investments in Central Bank securities, for two reasons. First, large chunks of nonperforming loans were sold to the Central Bank in 1982 and 1983, and the Central Bank paid with interest-bearing paper. Second, another large amount of Central Bank paper was obtained in the domestic debt restructurings that took place during the 1983–1985 recession, as a way of compensating the banks for the forbearance granted to bank debtors.[5]

Nonperforming loans currently represent 2% of total loans; they must be provisioned according to the rules explained in section 3. The current level of these loans excludes the 1982 and 1983 sales of nonperforming loans to the Central Bank. Loans at risk estimated according to portfolio

Table 2-3. Banking System Profile

1. Number of banks	37
1.1 Chilean	15
1.2 Foreign	22
2. Total assets*	5,967,578
3. Total loans*	3,185,463
3.1. Performing*	3,121,169
3.2. Nonperforming*	64,294
4. Loans at risk*[a]	151,205
(% of loans)	4.75
5. Loan loss provisions/loans at risk (%)	103.63
6. Leverage[b]	12.14
7. Return on assets (%)	1.65
8. Return on equity (%)	23.03
9. Personnel and other administrative costs/assets (%)	2.33

* Million pesos.

[a] The volume of loans at risk comes from the loan classification scheme run by the Superintendency of Banks. It is the sum of 1% of B loans plus 20% of B$^-$ loans plus 60% of C loans plus 90% of D loans. See section 3.2.2.4.

[b] Leverage is defined as liabilities/net worth. An average leverage of 12.14 is equivalent to a ratio of net worth to assets of 7.61%.

Note: GDP (1988): 5,411,025 million pesos.
Exchange rate: 249.1 pesos to a U.S. dollar; December 1988 daily average.
Source: Superintendencia de Bancose Instituciones Financieras. Processed from balance sheets published by banks.

classification (see section 3) amount to 4.75% of total loans. They are fully provisioned as shown in line 5 of table 2-3.

Returns obtained during 1988 are significantly influenced by transitory income obtained from foreign debt conversion, but even after excluding this income, return or equity was greater than 10%.

The ratio of personnel and other administrative costs/assets (2.33%) is lower than that for banks in other developing countries,[6] and it is also below the U.S. ratio.

The above indicators show that the Chilean banking system is well advanced in the recovery from the crisis it suffered a few years ago, which is described later. The recovery occurred in some measure because of the mechanism used to restructure bank loans, the recapitalization by the Central Bank, and the improvements in bank supervision that are described in sections 2 and 3. In addition, the resumption of economic growth in 1984 made a critical contribution.

1.2.3. Other Institutions of the Financial Sector.

1.2.3.1. Pension Funds. Since 1981, private Pension Funds Management Corporations (Administradoras de Fondos de Pensiones: AFP) manage mandatory contributions on an individual account basis. The former pension system was operated by the government, and it paid pensions out of the social security taxes collected in the same period. Benefits included a large redistribution component, administrative costs and evasion were excessive, and a growing deficit was accumulating because of the aging of the population. The new system shifts redistribution to the tax system by subjecting pensions to the progressive income tax and financing a minimum guaranteed pension through general funds.

The impressive improvement of the fiscal budget in the late 1970s made this reform possible. The government became able to stop receiving contributions but continued to service those already pensioned. The new system is based on the capitalization of savings in individual accounts, with a mandatary minimum of 10% of the salary. Because these contributions are not taxable, there is also a maximum allowable contribution, corresponding to an annual income of US$ 14,400 (Chile's per capital annual income is about US$ 1800 per year).

After eight years of operation, the number of persons contributing in the new system is above 2.0 million, compared to an employed population of 4.3 million.[7] Savings accumulated in the pension funds have been growing at a high sustained rate; in April 1989 the investment portfolio passed the 1,000,000 million pesos figure (US$ 4 billion, approximately 18% of GDP). It is estimated that when the system enters the steady state, the accumulated funds will approximate GDP.

Because pension fund investments should be long-term, the funds are generating an important demand for this type of financial assets. As a result, it is expected that they will be fundamental in the development of capital markets in Chile.

1.2.3.2. Life Insurance Industry. This industry received a big shot in the arm from the 1981 reform of the obligatory social security pension system. This reform included mandatory covering of the risks of incapacitation and death of the bread winner. In addition, most workers purchase annuities when they retire, using the funds accumulated at the AFPs. These are sold and managed by the insurance firms. The rate of growth in life insurance companies total assets in the period 1980–1988 has averaged 31% per year in real terms; as of December 1988, total assets reached almost US$ 1 billion.

This high growth is also a result of deregulation that took place in

1980; since then, prices and premia are freely determined in a competitive market. Competition has been enhanced by allowing the entry of foreign companies. However, private insurers are still banned from selling policies to cover professional diseases and work accidents.

The insurance industry is subject to a set of safety regulations focusing on risk control. This includes portfolio diversification; matching assets and liabilities according to maturity; maximum liabilities of 15 times their net worth; norms for determining the value of assets and liabilities; norms for building up reserves; and disclosure to the public and to the supervisory agency.

1.2.3.3. The Security Exchanges. Although this market has been growing since 1985, it still trades a small volume. During the last quarter of 1988, the average daily transactions were US$ 40 million, with the following compositions: commercial paper, plus promissory notes and time deposits: 55%; bonds plus *letras de crédito* and other fixed income in series issues: 43%; stocks: 2%. The small importance of traded stocks is evident (US$ 0.8 million/day). This reflects the fact that a large fraction of Chilean corporations are not public, so they are not registered on the exchange; and, of those registered only about 40 are actively traded.

1.2.3.4. Mutual Funds. Mutual funds in Chile are open-ended. However, there is a bill currently under study that will authorize close-ended funds. The bulk of mutual funds is invested in short-term debt instruments, mainly time deposits, and are offered to firms with short-term cash surpluses. The market is quite competitive, pushing down management fees to an annual rate of 1% including value-added tax (16% rate). Fees charged in mutual funds investing in stocks go up to 6%.

As of April 1989, the total investments of the mutual funds were US$ 388 million, of which 93% was invested in fixed income assets.

1.2.3.5. Agencias de Valores. The main activity of these institutions takes place at the money market; they have a portfolio of short-term debt instruments—most of them are promissory notes issued by the Central Bank—that are sold under repurchase agreements for one day or more. The market is highly competive, charging an annual fee of 0.8%.

As of April 1989, the total portfolio managed by 24 active Agencias was US$ 266 million.

1.2.3.6. Health Insurance. Entry into supply of obligatory health insurance was allowed in 1981 in Chile. The system covers medical expenses and lost working days because of sickness. The private suppliers parallel the government health insurance entity (FONASA) and compete with it. All workers have to make a mandatory contribution of 7% of their salary for health insurance, and they can choose between the private and the public options; the private option is a better alternative for middle- and higher-income people. In 1988 the number of persons covered by the private system was 567,638, which is 4.5% of the population. They paid premiums amounting to US$ 205 million. The industry has grown rapidly.

1.2.3.7. Casualty Insurance. Private casualty insurance offers a wide range of risk coverage and has been available for a long time. Premium collections were US$ 234 million in 1988. Competition in casualty insurance has been intense since 1980, when prices began to be freely determined and restrictions on the purchase of insurance and reinsurance abroad were eliminated.

2. History of the Development of the Current Banking Structure

One of the main reasons to devote a chapter to Chile is that until recently its banking system suffered more recognized insolvencies than most others in the world. In 1984, around 60% of the assets of the banking system belonged to banks that had been taken over by the Superintendency of Banks. The state-owned Banco del Estado had another 20% of the assets of the banking system. Thus, 80% of assets were controlled by the government. However, by 1987 the former 60% had been returned to the private sector through a privatization program.

The two main issues that will be discussed here are the causes for the flood of bank insolvencies, and the method followed by the authorities to rehabilitate and privatize the failed banks. A description of the reforms to the banking law that were adopted in reaction to this crisis is provided in section 3.

Since the history of the Chilean financial system is rather complex, we have prepared table 2-4 to guide the reader through the following pages.

2.1. General Background

Banking started in Chile in the 1850s, and the first Banking Law was enacted in 1860. By the 1920s, Chile had developed a significant capital

Table 2-4. The Chilean Financial System, 1952–1988 (Percentage Unless Specified Otherwise. Negative Numbers in ( ).).

Selected Year	1952	1958	1962	1970	1976	1982	1988
1. Banks and SINAP							
1.1 Banco del Estado: loans/GDP	4.1	2.2	4.7	4.3	7.0	11.4	9.4
Loan growth rate[a]	—	(6.6)	29.5	3.1	7.1	12.6	1.1
1.2 Commercial banks: loans/GDP	9.2	4.3	8.7	3.9	7.8	63.6	42.9
Loan growth rate[a]	—	(8.0)	27.0	(−5.7)	10.6	47.5	(2.2)
1.3 SINAP: loans/GDP	—	—	0.4	2.0	6.2	n.a.	n.a.
Loan growth rate[a]	—	—	—	25.9	19.1	—	—
1.4 Total loans/GDP	13.2	6.5	13.8	10.3	21.0	75.1	52.3
1.5 a) No. of commercial banks	19	28	28	27	17	39	39
b) No. of savings & loans	—	—	18	22	7	1	1
2. Central bank							
2.1 Loans to private sector non banks/GDP	1.3	0.8	1.2	0.6	0.2	0	0
2.2 % of com. bank loans financed by Central Bank	11.2	25.2	8.7	8.4	8.4	11.5	56.6[b]
2.3 Loans to public sector/GDP	2.1	2.3	11.5	9.7	33.5	4.8	5.5
2.4 Outst. issues of C. bank negotiable bonds & bills/GDP	—	—	1.9	0.6	1.7	2.5	31.9[c]
3. A.F.P. Pension Funds							
3.1 Funds/GDP	—	—	—	—	—	3.6	16.5
3.2 Indiv. accounts/labor force	—	—	—	—	—	47.6	69.9

Table 2-4. (Continued)

Selected Year	1952	1958	1962	1970	1976	1982	1988
4. Santiago Stock Exchange							
4.1 Fixed income trans./GDP[d]	0.08	0.01	0.01	0	0.03	0.28	3.11
4.2 Share transactions/GDP[d]	0.38	0.11	0.06	0.02	0.02	0.05	0.23
5. Insurance & Reinsurance							
5.1 Life: investments/GDP	n.a.	n.a.	0.04	0.04	0.71	1.3	4.2
No. of life ins. companies.	n.a.	n.a.	17	14	14	20	17
5.2 Prop. & liab.: premiums/GDP	n.a.	n.a.	0.49	0.35[e]	0.80	0.74	1.08
No. of P. & L. ins. companies	n.a.	n.a.	168	149	85	47	22
6. Health Insurance (ISAPRES)							
Premiums/GDP	—	—	—	—	—	0.55	0.95
No. of ISAPRES	—	—	—	—	—	10	30
GDP growth rate[f]	—	2.4	6.7	4.1	(1.3)	3.9	4.4

[a] Growth rates are an inflation-adjusted annual average over the period that ends in the selected year.
[b] Includes as Central Bank loans both the obligations to repurchase bad loans and the funds lent for forbearance.
[c] These securities were issued as part of the programs in note 2, and to absorb liquidity in 1983.
[d] Average monthly transaction volume in nominal terms, divided by that years' nominal GDP.
[e] The figure for this year does not include ISE, the state insurance company.
[f] Average rates shift subtantially when the period covered is modified.

Source: Elaboration from a collection of official sources, available from the authors.

market, including commercial banks, two stock exchanges, a unified foreign-currency market, a market for long-term Treasury securities and long-term mortgage bonds, and an insurance market. The degree of integration to international capital markets was higher than it is now. Commercial banks were restricted to short-term lending and borrowing, while mortgage banks operated the long end.

In 1931–1933, like most countries, Chile suffered a great depression. The government's finances ran large deficits, which were financed by money creation. Convertibility was lost and inflation soared. Bonds were not indexed to inflation, so this episode imposed a large capital loss on bondholders. In contrast to the U.S.A., no Chilean bank failed in the Great Depression, although the banks also exhibited a marked increase in their preference to invest in excess reserves.

The main heritage of the 1925–1935 period was not inflation, because that was eliminated by late 1933, but rather a substantial increase in the regulation of the capital market. Exchange controls became a permanent feature of the market, the interest-rate ceilings instituted in 1929 were consolidated, and many other types of financial regulations were tightened. The mood of that decade all over the world, which persisted in Chile until 1973, was skepticism about the ability of a private capital market to allocate savings and investment in a socially desirable way, combined with an explicit trust in the government's ability to do a better job.

Beginning in 1936, inflation began to pick up, accelerating in 1940. Over time, and especially after a sharp outburst in 1953–1954, the unpredictability of inflation severely damaged the markets in long-term bonds and life insurance policies. On the other hand, deposit interest-rate controls generated a cumulative loss of funds for the banking system. Large private firms secured access to financing and to the inflation tax paid by the remaining depositors by acquiring commercial banks. As smaller borrowers were squeezed out by the large borrowers that owned banks, politicians increased regulation by setting sectoral quotas for credit. On the other hand, the desire to reduce inflation often took the form of quantitative credit expansion limits at the individual bank level. In an attempt to absorb liquidity, marginal reserve requirements were raised above 80%, and were changed frequently and on short notice.

In 1961, the government decided to allow the use of indexation clauses in the financial system. However, this option was not offered to commercial banks. Instead, a new set of financial intermediaries, modeled on the American savings and loans, was put into place. Collectively called SINAP,[8] it was a collection of nominally not-for-profit cooperatives, and enjoyed for several years the exclusivity of indexation clauses for financial contracts. The SINAP could only lend for residential mortgage purposes and to construction companies, at fixed real interest rates.[9] After 1962, its liabilities with the depositing public began to grow. They grew substantially faster after 1965, when the government allowed SINAP to issue 60-day time deposits with an indexation clause. Because both deposit and loan real interest rates of SINAP were fixed by the government and changes in inflation were reflected in the indexed yields, this did not look dangerous at the time. However, the mismatch in the maturity structure, together with the failure to tighten capital requirements, set the stage for the insolvency of SINAP in 1975.

By 1970, the private commercial banking system had only 44% of the deposits of all banks and SINAP combined. Moreover, Banco del Estado had obtained the right to issue indexed savings passbooks in 1965, and expanded faster than the private banks. Inflation and intense competition from SINAP's and Banco del Estado's indexed deposits had almost eliminated time deposits at commercial banks. The result was that 88% of deposits at private commercial banks were held in checking accounts. In addition, the government intermediated funds and lent directly through both the Central Bank and CORFO, the state industrial holding company.

Starting in early 1971, the Allende government began to take measures to move Chile towards central planning. These included government takeover of the private capital market through the purchase of controlling interests in the commercial banks on the stock exchange through an offer for the first 50% + 1 of the shares. Afterwards, the monetary authorities attempted—and failed—to impose the regulation that each person could operate with only one bank, and hold there only one checking account. Reduced interest rates were charged on loans offered by the Central Bank to commercial banks on the condition that they were reloaned to productive companies according to specific guidelines. In a scheme invented under the previous government, the borrowing company had to project its cash-flow needs in order to get the loan, and had to submit to the conditions imposed by the bank. By requiring companies not to give or receive credit on its purchase and sales, the Allende government eliminated the independent supplier–buyer credit market, easing the way towards central planning.

By 1973, commercial banks were effectively agencies of the Central Bank, which created and directed credit. The volume of checking accounts held in the face of annual inflation rates near 500% was not as low as expected, because the companies taken over by the government in 1971–

1973 were not concerned with the inflation tax on their deposits. Households found refuge from the high inflation at SINAP and Banco del Estado indexed deposits and saving passbooks.

It is clear, then, that in 1940–1973 Chile suffered from what McKinnon and Shaw later called "financial repression," which should not be confused with excessive prudential regulation. In fact, prudential considerations were abandoned over the 1940–1973 period. Starting in late 1973, after the takeover of the government by the military, Chile underwent a process of financial liberalization. However, this liberalization process was not coordinated with the increase in supervision capabilities required by the fast-recovering Chilean capital market. The explanation of this point is the topic of the next section.

2.2. Insolvency of Intermediaries in 1974–1983

This section describes the major episodes of insolvency experienced in Chile during the financial liberalization. It will become apparent that this was attributable in part to bad luck due to the large amplitude of the business cycle from 1974 to 1985, and in part to the naiveté and unlimited trust in the efficiency of market forces exhibited by many government officials.[10]

The first liberalization steps, in 1974 and 1975, consisted in replacing credit control, both in its sectoral and quantitative dimensions, by market-oriented forms of monetary control like uniform reserve requirements. Regulatory discrimination between intermediaries was phased out through time, and the tax system was reformed to stop the taxation of the inflation component of the nominal interest rate. Meanwhile, the nominal interest rate was at first fixed at levels nearer to the inflation rate, and then freed altogether. At first indexation was disallowed for deposits of maturities shorter than one year, but then the limit was set at 90 days, in 1976. Additionally, during the second half of 1975 the government privatized the commercial banks that had been bought by the previous administration.

The liberalization was followed by two periods of large numbers of financial intermediary insolvencies. The first one (1975–1978) started with the failure of the whole of the SINAP system, continued with those of unregulated financieras and one small financial cooperative in 1976, was followed by the failure of the medium-sized commercial bank Banco Osorno y La Unión in early 1977, and spent itself with the failure of several large financial cooperatives in 1977 and 1978.

The authorities worked hard to modernize the nonbank areas of the Chilean capital market. Primary emphasis was placed on a redesign of the obligatory pension system, which was transformed in early 1981 from a state-operated pay-as-you-go system to an obligatory individual capitalization system operated by private firms. In 1980, the insurance market was allowed to issue CPI-indexed policies, and their basic law was reformed to allow for the free determination of premiums. A secondary market in commercial paper and short-term government paper was permited in 1977, and by 1981 it had been improved by a new securities law designed with the help of the U.S. SEC. Other new laws opened up the brokerage of securities to competition, allowed the existence of market-makers (Agencias de Valores), refurbished the mutual fund legislation, and reformulated the Public Companies Law. This activity finished with the reform of the Bankruptcy Law, although it came into force only in 1983, after the second series of bank failures. Foreign-exchange controls continued in place throughout the period, representing the only important area that continues to be repressed, although a move towards a freer exchange market was implemented in early 1990.

The second outburst of financial institution insolvencies started in November of 1981. Eight institutions with 8% of the deposits of the private commercial banking system were taken over by the regulators. The problems continued through 1982 as some additional small banks were taken over. The crisis reached its peak in January 1983, when several of the largest private commercial banks became insolvent. Nonperforming bank assets plus loans at risk increased to several times capital for the sytem as a whole.

If the Chilean experience is to contribute to international experience, it must provide an explanation of this dismal record. This section presents the conclusions reached by the authors in their research, which shows that the government allowed the exploitation of its implicit guarantee on bank deposits.

2.2.1. The 1975–1978 Insolvencies.

At the beginning of 1975, the following financial intermediaries were operating in Chile: 1) commercial banks, all of which continued under government control; 2) the SINAP, most of whose members were controlled by the private sector; 3) formal financieras, created during the second half of 1974, which were privately owned, free to set interest rates, and mostly unregulated; 4) informal financieras, which had been inadvertently allowed by a 1974 statute; and 5) a few unregulated financial cooperatives that operated like financieras.

During 1973 and 1974, despite a 400% annual rate of inflation, interest on SINAP long-term loans continued to be adjusted to inflation only once a year. As a result, SINAP lost most of the real income from interest in those years, while its expenses on 60-day deposits were adjusted much faster. Therefore, the private owners of SINAP had little true capital left by mid-1974.

In early 1974, the new government had announced that it would free interest rates. In fact, liberalization measures had allowed financieras to set their interest rates freely by mid-1974, and the resulting rates had been much higher than the permitted 7% above CPI on most long-term loans. Therefore, the private managers of the members of SINAP could foresee[11] that if they invested in long-term loans at fixed real rates and the high short-term rates persisted, insolvency was predictable. On the other hand, if the free real interest rate fell rapidly, SINAP would earn operating profits by investing in long-term mortgages at fixed real rates, and would recover its capital base over time.

The next ingredient for the crisis was an implicit government deposit guarantee for SINAP. Although it was not included in any statute, the heavy regulation by the government of SINAP gave rise to the belief that depositors would be bailed out. Moreover, a high government official had declared publicly in a seminar at the Central Bank in April of 1974 that

> ... foreseeing that the free real interest rate might be high, and that SINAP has a large volume of loans at low fixed real interest rates, the government will subsidize directly the SINAP for the difference, preventing its bankruptcy.[12]

In mid-1974, the SINAP started to draw on its accumulated excess reserves to invest feverishly in new housing, first financing construction companies and then engaging in long-term lending to the buyers. Since its deposits were exempt of reserve requirements, the banking multiplier allowed a 100% growth in real terms in SINAP's size during 1974. This misguided investment policy increased SINAP's exposure to high real interest rates greatly.

Our research has shown that this *was not* the result of moral hazard in risk-taking by SINAP. Rather, it was a consequence of the failure of coordination in the financial liberalization process. When SINAP was ordered to withdraw its excess reserves from the Central Bank, its only investment alternatives, as set by the statutes, were long-term loans. The alternative of returning those funds to depositors and reducing the volume of liabilities was closed because the banks could not reduce deposit interest rates without the regulator's authorization. Regulators did not favor this solution because they wanted to promote the revival of the construction industry.

In early 1975, the world price of copper, Chile's main export and the government's main source of tax revenue, fell sharply. This had two effects. First, a steep recession began, and many depositors withdrew funds to finance their needs. Second, the shock on the fiscal side put into doubt the government's resolve to live up to its guarantee. The resulting heavy withdrawal of deposits could not be accomodated by the proceeds of the sale of long-term loans and brought about the insolvency of SINAP.

The way SINAP's crisis was handled set undesirable precedents for the future. In June 1975, after many depositors had fled SINAP and only the ones that believed in official promises of guarantee remained, the government decided to freeze SINAP's 60-day deposits. In the next months, these depositors were authorized to withdraw the equivalent of only US$ 100 per month per account. The remainder could be exchanged for long-term bonds, whose price in the secondary market fluctuated between 80% and 60% of the face value. Holders of other types of SINAP liabilities, even liquid ones, were not affected. Therefore, the basic rules of precedence in a bankruptcy were not respected, signaling that the authorities considered themselves entitled to redistribute wealth arbitrarily in financial intermediary insolvencies. For intermediaries, bankruptcy risk continued to have little correlation with economic risk and high correlation with political risk.

An unexpected result of SINAP's failure was that government guarantees ceased to be credible. This allowed Chile to live a brief period similar to nineteenth-century free banking that lasted until January of 1977.

Also attributable to the severe recession[13] suffered by Chile during 1975, and concurrent with the failure of SINAP, was the failure of a number of informal and formal financieras. They had begun to operate in mid-1974 and were quite small. There was no government participation in these failures, not even in terms of facilitating the bankruptcy procedures, and depositors lost substantial figures.

The financieras were unregulated and some of them lent substantial sums to their owners, who used them to buy shares in the 11 commercial banks that were privatized in late 1975. In this privatization, the government accepted deferred payment over two years at below-market interest rates in order to get better prices. Most important, after many years of credit control and interest-rate fixing, the Superintendency of Banks had lost the ability to exercise *prudential* regulation over commercial banks. As the public ceased to believe in government guarantees on deposits after SINAP's failure, some officials began to argue that prudential regulation was not needed either. This allowed the new owners of the banks to operate with little or nonexisting capital, and to concentrate their lending on firms owned by the shareholders.

In January of 1977, the authorities changed their minds and announced the takeover by regulators of the middle-sized Banco Osorno y La Unión, recently privatized. The regulators accused the bank's owners of several criminal and civil offenses related to bad management and potential fraud. The solvency problem of Banco Osorno was apparently caused by its linkages to an informal financiera, controlled by the same group. In order to stem a general bank run, the authorities announced that the government would explicitly guarantee small deposits at all banks, financieras, and financial cooperatives, which would cover Banco Osorno, plus a formal financiera and a financial cooperative that had failed three weeks before.

The only feasible alternative, absorption of losses by other banks, was discussed in the weeks before Banco Osorno's failure. However, this required the creation of a bank cartel, which needed time to evolve. In addition, it would have implied the monopolization of the Chilean capital market.

An important aspect of this failure was that it showed the public that the government had only three alternatives when confronting a failed bank. First, the bank could be abandoned to a run by depositors. Second, it could be taken over by the regulators; however, the takeover meant that the government had the responsibility for deposits. Third, the bank could be liquidated by regulators. This was the only way to force depositors to absorb part of the loss, but according to the law, even checking accounts would be frozen in the liquidation procedure. Out of these three alternatives, the government preferred takeover by regulators. In fact, the government became so concerned about intermediary failures that it bailed out four large financial cooperatives over the next year (Sodimac, Ificoop, Creditec, and Credival) and extended the small depositor guarantee to eight more.

As a result of these actions, starting in 1977 depositors had every reason to believe that they were insured by the government. Because the preferred insolvency resolution procedure was takeover by the regulators, and because a bank could not discriminate between depositors by size unless it was being liquidated, large uninsured depositors always had some time to withdraw during the period between takeover and liquidation. Therefore, every deposit was guaranteed in practice, and all the responsibility for policing bank solvency was passed on to the regulators, with no help from the private sector.

This challenge was taken up by the regulators through improvements in the legal framework in 1977 and 1978. One important reform was to increase penalties and fines and to define new types of fraud-related crimes. At the same time, the issuance of guarantees by banks on behalf of clients was limited, and the Superintendency of Banks began to limit the types of acceptable collateral for loans, declaring bills of exchange issued by any trader unacceptable. The right to refuse a license to open a financial company was also bestowed on the regulators. In addition, the regulators obtained the right to mark down the accounting value of bank investments—although not that of loans—when they considered that that accounting value was unrealistic.

As the modernization of other segments of the Chilean capital market proceeded, commercial banks were allowed to act as development and mortgage banks, lending and borrowing at long term. A sign of regulatory sophistication was that, beginning in 1978, each new authorization began to be paired with a new solvency regulation. For example, in 1979 banks were authorized to extend long-term loans at fixed real rates, but subject to the simultaneous issuance of long-term bonds on similar terms to be sold on the stock exchange. This shifted interest-rate risk away from banks. The limit on long-term lending by banks was abolished, but the Central Bank was allowed to establish maximum limits on maturity mismatching. However, these regulations were not always careful enough, as shown by the April 1980 authorization to Chilean banks to invest in foreign banks, subject only to a once-and-for-all authorization by regulators.

The absence of new cases of insolvency of financial intermediaries lulled many people into the belief that with its new powers the Superintendency of Banks had been able to eliminate abuse. Therefore, many were happy with the combination of a government guarantee of deposits coupled with strong and sophisticated regulation.

2.2.2. The 1981–1983 Insolvencies.

To analyze the next set of major insolvencies, it is useful to point out what was not being done by the Superintendency of Banks by late 1979. Until then, it did not rate the loan portfolio of banks on an individual loan basis. Loss reserve provisions were required only when a loan went unpaid for 90 days. Therefore, if a bank renewed the unpaid loan with interest before the end of the 90-day period, it was exempt from absorbing the loss. In 1980, the Superintendency of Banks began to question the quality of the banks' loans. When it began to examine individual loans in early 1981, it realized that many of them would never be recovered.

It also became clear that the rules that required banks to diversify among debtors were ineffective. The reason was that a debtor was defined to be an individual person or organization. Therefore, any debtor that wanted more loans merely had to create a new shell company to be able to receive additional loans through the shell company without violating the law. The loans from an individual bank to the bank's shareholders were subject to the same violations. In practice, most banks lent several times their capital to their owners.

The possibility of such self-dealing sparked competition for banking licenses, and several sleepy provincial banks were bought by new owners with the purpose of financing the activities of the new owners. Moreover, the new owners did not need to put up true capital, but only to get a short-term loan to purchase the bank. As soon as they took possession of the bank, they would lend money to their shell company to pay back the original loan. By this time the Chilean banking industry was very competitive. Theory suggests that the greater is the degree of competition, the more are banks induced to exploit an unguarded deposit guarantee.

The practice of lending to the bank owners had defenders, particularly among groups that benefited from it, on the grounds that the interest rate and maturity of these loans were very similar to loans to others. They alleged that, since the loans were being invested very professionally in promising areas of the economy, there was nothing to fear. However, nothing was said about the fact that through lending to a shell company owned by the bank's owners, who would later redistribute the funds, the bank was preventing the Superintendency of Banks from examining the actual risk of the investments. Examination was made impossible through the continuous creation and liquidation of shell companies that held the loans for only a few months before passing them over to the next shell company. Although the government guaranteed bank liabilities, it could not examine the risk taken on account of its guarantee, and had to content itself with the hope of good behavior by the banks.

Realizing this, in late 1981 the regulators requested more powers from the legislative body. They obtained them through a new law, which required that the diversification limit on loans applied to any set of related companies as a group.

Using the new powers, the Superintendency of Banks required from banks a full disclusure of their loans to related parties.[14] It also announced that each bank would have to undergo "deconcentration," under which these loans would have to be reduced, until loans to the owners complied with the individual loan limit, which was 25% of capital and reserves when guarantees were offered.

Up to late 1981, the nonperforming asset situation, while bad, was not unmanageable. There was large backlog of bad loans, but the quality of supervision and examination was improving rapidly. In November 2, 1981, the Superintendency of Banks decided to take over eight minor banks and financial companies where the 1981 examination had exposed insolvency or fraud. These institutions represented 8% of outstanding peso deposits. The authorities hoped this would be the last bout of insolvencies, and that they would not recur, since examination standards had been substantially raised.

These hopes were unfounded, because the Superintendency of Banks never classified loans according to the foreign exchange and interest-rate risks of the debtor. This was in spite of widespread expectations of devaluation and allowed massive abuse of the government's deposit guarantee by all types of investors, large and small. This shortcoming of the Superintendency was in part due to the fact that the Finance Minister had promised that there would be no devaluation. Thus, the agency could not contradict its superiors by requesting loan loss provisions in proportion to exposure to currency risk. This shortcoming continues to exist in Chile in 1989.

In late 1981, Chile experienced another deep recession that would last until 1985. The recession undermined the solvency of the remaining private banks. There has been much discussion about the causes of the depth of the 1982–1985 recession, during which GDP declined 15% in real terms, and we do not intend to review it comprehensively. As Chile's foreign debt grew sharply in 1978–1982, the causes of the recession overlap with the causes of the foreign debt buildup. There is a consensus that a large part of the recession was caused by external events, like the go–stop cycle of international credit abundance, and the sharp rise in real interest rates throughout the world induced by U.S. monetary policy. There is also agreement that another important component of causes was domestic. Two of these were the backlog of bad loans brought about by the risky behavior of domestic banks over the 1976–1981 period and the tendency of some risk-prone domestic banks to indebt themselves excessively with international banks and relend these funds to clients overexposed to currency and interest-rate risk.

During 1982, the solvency of the banking sector deteriorated rapidly. In January, loans in arrears net of loan loss provisions accounted for 10.8% of the banking system capital and reserves. This percentage jumped to 19.9% in March, 27.4% in June, and 57.5% in September. In 1983 it rose to 89.5% in March, 104% in June, and 181.2% in September.[15] The reason was that the real interest rate was very high in 1981 and 1982, in the range of 40%–60% for loans. In turn, this extremely high interest rate was the result of the compounding of several factors, including the reduction in lending by foreigners, the rise in external real interest rates, the decision of Chile's Central Bank to follow a restrictive monetary policy, the risk premium charged on account of an expected devaluation of the peso, the unwillingness of banks to acknowledge their losses until the Superintendency of Banks forced them to, and the hopes of individual bank debtors for a discriminatory bailout in their favor. After the devaluations of June and August of 1982, the risk premium for expected devaluation was replaced by the realized losses on the large foreign currency exposure of many bank debtors, and real interest rates began to fall.

Chile's two largest business groups and many smaller independent investors, which operated on high leverage, went bankrupt as a result of this combination of forces. Their debts were short-term and subject to the rising real interest rates, while their assets were long-term. Thus, the shareholders' capital shrank and many went deeply into the red. This same pincer movement also impoverished other independent and smaller companies, although many of them had started from more reasonable initial leverages. In fact, the combination of the high leverage of the larger business groups and the fact that they controlled banks where they could draw on subsidized deposit insurance may explain the strange reaction of these groups when world real interest rates began to rise in 1980 and 1981. These two business groups bet that world interest rates would fall very quickly and very fast. They lost spectacularly.

In June 1982, the government decided to help banks by temporarily absorbing some of the accumulated losses. This program consisted of the purchase by the Central Bank of some nonperforming bank assets, with an obligation by the seller to repurchase those loans over time at face value. The selling bank was charged with the administration of these assets, and recoveries handed over to the Central Bank, which would reduce the obligation to repurchase by the same amount. All domestic commercial banks and financial companies supervised by the Superintendency of Banks had access to this program, including the banks owned by the two big business groups. This program was expanded in 1983. By December 1988, 14 banks and financieras were still repurchasing nonperforming loans sold earlier to the Central Bank.

In January 7, 1983, a large paper-pulp firm owned by one of the two big groups announced it could not meet its obligations. On January 13, 1983, the authorities took over eight banks, of which three were liquidated, and five continued operating under Central Bank assistance. These latter five included the two largest private commercial banks in Chile, which were owned by the two largest business groups. In addition, regulators named a Resident Inspector, who could suspend the decisions of the bank's board of directors, in two more banks. The placing of bets had come to an end.

The main purpose of these takeovers was to bring the two largest business groups under the Superintendency's control. By this time, the Superintendency had been able to reconstruct enough of the network of shell companies and to consolidate their accounts, and had found that they were insolvent at current interest rates.[16] Since the loans by all banks to these groups were not recoverable in full, their flagship banks had failed too, even when taking into account the sale of nonperforming loans to the Central Bank of June 1982. The Superintendency decided to move fast to stem the losses, which could skyrocket if the failed groups continued to manage their flagship banks under the umbrella of deposit guarantees. In order to maximize the amount recovered, the Superintendency's representatives at the banks exercised the flagship banks' right not to renew short-term credit and took control of their productive companies.

Later in 1983, the government decided to help the remaining banks with a second program of deferred absorption of additional accumulated losses. The huge real devaluation had thrown into insolvency many independent debtors, and the problem was worsened by the bottoming out of GDP at a low level, with no signs of recovery in sight. This program also consisted of the purchase by the Central Bank of nonperforming bank assets, with the obligation of the seller to repurchase these loans over time at face value. All remaining domestic commercial banks and financieras supervised by the Superintendency of Banks had access to this program. However, the banks previously owned by the big groups did not, because they had been taken over. In addition, in both 1983 and 1984 several groups of bank debtors received official subsidies in the form of long-term reschedulings of their debts at below-market interest rates. This aid indirectly helped the surviving banks.

About half of the repurchase program consisted in deferred absorption of losses only. The reason is that the Central Bank purchased around half of the bad loans with *zero percent bills*, which pay 0% interest and have no maturity date. Obviously, their economic value is zero. These bills had as their only purpose the tidying up of the losses. The 0% bills are still substantial in several Chilean banks, indicating that their true capital is smaller than book value.

There were other government subsidies as well. One of the aspects of the first foreign-debt rescheduling, in mid-1983, was that the government guaranteed the servicing of foreign debt of domestically owned banks to international banks. The last large subsidy that improved the health of bank debtors was the *preferential exchange rate*, made available by the Central Bank for repayment of debts abroad and to commercial banks that were denominated in foreign exchange; that subsidy lasted from October 1982 to June 1985. Most of these subsidies were financed with debt issued by the Central Bank, causing its current deficit.

The conclusion from this section is that the very high rate of bank failures in Chile from 1981 to 1983 was the result of the combination of 1) competition between large and small business groups to maximize the deposit insurance subsidy by taking more currency risk and 2) the severe recession suffered by Chile. However, the most important lesson is that this coincidence was not mere bad luck. The accumulation of foreign debt in 1978–1981 was all private and channeled in large part through domestic private banks engaging in risky behavior, which in turn explains a non-negligible part of the depth of the subsequent recession. The Chilean experience shows that a regulatory problem in one major industry—banking—can become large enough to affect the macroeconomic aggregates and generate feedback, worsening the situation. This experience should be taken into account by other countries.

Although the bank supervisors obtained enhanced powers in 1978 and initiated a modernization program that allowed them to find out what was happening by 1981, their speed was no match for the agile private sector. This suggests that any financial regulatory scheme that puts its trust in the action of regulators alone for its safety is bound to fail. The episode also shows that government regulators are unable to assess macroeconomic risks influenced by their superiors' policy without undermining that policy. The alternative is to rely more on the private sector. This may be done by offering a reasonable schedule of incentives: reasonable profits if the bank does not fail, and losses if the bank does fail. The critical challenge is to design a bank regulatory system that allows large losses to the private creditors if the bank fails.

2.3. 1985–1986 Rehabilitation and Privatization of the Failed Banks

This section will cover the period from 1983 to 1986, which saw the rehabilitation and recovery of the failed banks. We first describe the initial situation after the disaster, and how it exhibited growing signs of regression to financial repression. In 1985 to 1986, however, that movement was reversed, and decisive action was taken towards the privatization of the banks that had been taken over.

After the 1983 series of bank failures, Chile exhibited a movement back of financial repression. The main deposit interest rate was fixed by the authorities for more than four years,[17] so that the many banks in government hands could not pay more for deposits than a publicly announced number. The lesson is clear: when mispriced deposit insurance leads to an obviously inefficient allocation of financial resources and a recession, the situation becomes politically unstable, and powerful interests arrange a move towards financial repression in the name of "reducing the cost of credit to a level compatible with the productive activities' need to recover."

During the years of discussion about the final destiny of the failed groups' banks, the flagship banks came to participate in a large number of creditors' committees. The government decided to coordinate the administration of the bankruptcy of the two largest business groups through ad hoc Special Commitees, appointed by President Pinochet, which coordinated the actions of the representatives in each bankruptcy proceeding. The groups of creditors with better political clout obtained bailouts from the government. This happened to the shareholders of mutual funds that had invested in commercial paper issued by the non-financial companies of the two bigger failed groups. Nevertheless, the commercial paper issued by the two groups' shell companies was not bought by the government.

The final destiny of the failed flagship banks, and the associated large group of failed companies that previously belonged to the big groups, continued unresolved during the years 1983 and 1984. Some advocated permanent government ownership, in order to assure the maximum recovery of losses for the taxpayer. Others, recalling that during the Allende government state ownership had led to large operating losses, argued that the interests of the taxpayer would be best served if the companies and their banks were sold to the private sector. A third group rejected this solution on the grounds that in 1984 the Chilean private sector was almost broke and was unable to buy the banks from the government at realistic prices, while the foreign private sector would offer very low prices. This group advocated that shares in the failed banks should be given away to all Chilean taxpayers.

After many delays and cabinet reshuffles, the government made up its mind in June of 1985. It proposed a solution that combined features of all three approaches. First, the failed companies would be dealt with separately, in a case-by-case basis. Second, the big flagship banks would be sold to the private sector for a price that amounted to the full book value.

For this purpose, the Central Bank capitalized, through CORFO, substantial liquidity loans that it held against the commercial banks. However, the 0% bills were not touched, on the assumption that future profits would allow repurchase of the bad loans and the retiring of these bills. Therefore book value is larger than true economic capital, and these banks are being allowed to operate with a leverage substantially above 20, the legal maximum.

At the same time, subsidized official financing was offered to the buyers. However, in exchange for this generous financing, the new owners were required to accept a contingent liability in proportion to future profits. This liability would be extinguished once the accumulated payments fully repurchased the bad loans sold to the Central Bank in 1982 and 1983 at face value. Thus, the buyers of the failed banks assumed the obligation to channel almost 70% of the yearly dividends to the Central Bank, until the repurchase of these bad loans plus interest was completed. Basically, the Central Bank exchanged a debt liability for a participation in bank profits, so it accepted a downgrading in its claim to the banks. Old shareholders were very strongly diluted, and also excluded from dividends until the repurchase was completed.

The generous financing received by new shareholders consisted in several subsidies:

1. Investors were lent money by CORFO to buy the shares. These loans were for 15 years and carried an interest rate of 0% plus past inflation, which was subsidized in comparison to market rates near 7% plus past inflation. The loans required only a 5% down payment.
2. The only collateral for the loans was the newly issued shares, so these loans are as risky as the shares.
3. There was a 20% discount when interest was paid as scheduled.

   These subsidies implied that, effectively, buyers of new shares were paying only 30.3% of the book value of the shares,[18] which is not far off their access to only 30% of dividends. These subsidies were available only up to a small number of shares per person.
4. The government provided a tax break to new shareholders who had paid taxes in the previous two years. This feature acknowledged the fact that these taxpayers had contributed more to the solution than other taxpayers. The tax break is a credit that can be set against future income taxes for as long as the original investor holds the shares.

The government announced this complex package for sale to the public in mid-1985, and gave itself two years to complete the sale of the new rights. The public was clearly distrustful of the scheme at the outset. However, by the end of the first year of selling effort, many realized that if they bought in December, paying 5% of the nominal price, they would be able to receive dividends in April, which were projected to be around two thirds of the down payment. Adding up the tax break, the investment was attractive even if the investor attached a high probability to the event of being forced to return the shares to CORFO the next year. By the end of the second year (1986), all shares has been sold. By early 1987, after four years of government intervention, bank management and ownership had been returned to the private sector.

There existed a critical factor in the success of the placement of the new shares. Expected dividends were raised substantially when the Chilean government authorized limited prepayment of foreign debt by Chilean banks.[19] This allowed the banks to bring forth large accounting profits by taking advantage of the discount at which their debt was traded abroad. These profits were in part distributed to shareholders, so most of them reaped large profits. The perspective of earning these large profits was clear by early 1986; it also helps to explain the success of the privatization scheme. However, this maneuver reduces future profits because the substitution of domestic funds for foreign debt increased the expected financial cost of the banks. In this sense, these profits were merely brought forth to the present.

Overall, the rehabilitation and privatization of Chilean banks has been very successful, in comparison to the alternative possibilities. To evaluate the privatization procedure chosen, consider the following:

The government had to suffer the revenue loss implicit in the tax break offered to investors in these shares. The present value of this revenue loss depends on the average marginal income tax bracket, but its magnitude is near 25% of the book value of equity.[20] However, the government kept 70% of profits and obtained private management for the banks, which probably has increased the sum of total profits and consumer surplus. If private management increases profits, the government can easily be financially better off than with state ownership.

For example, if under government management bank profits are 8.06% of book value, and the profit rate increases to 10.0% due to private management, the government is indifferent from a purely financial point of view.[21] Obviously, this is a target that private management can meet easily over the long term, given the Chilean experience with state enterprise. In addition, the success of the privatization returned confidence to the private sector, explaining in part the overall economic recovery of the following four years. The new shareholders earn a contingent subsidy in the sense that if they manage the bank as badly as the government would do, say making 8.06% on book value, they still make a profit with the deal of 6.79% of book value in present-value terms. On the other hand, if the government expected to earn only 3.53% of book value by keeping the banks, then if private management earns the same, the government is financially indifferent and the new shareholders do not make any profit either.

An important side feature of the scheme was that the two largest banks (Banks of Chile and of Santiago) were sold to the public at large, with a small individual maximum amount of shares. This resulted in the atomization of ownership of these flagship banks by around 40,000 and 20,000 shareholders, respectively. This was not the case for the other two banks taken over in January 1983 that were privatized. Banco de Concepción was sold with a similar, though less favorable, scheme to the members of the Association of Private Sector Miners. The reason is that they put even less capital up front. Banco Internacional was sold on similar terms to the members of the Jewish community. Banco Colocadora Nacional de Valores was merged with Banco de Santiago before privatization.

In the flagship banks, for which ownership dilution was extreme, it became clear that the quality of its management would be subject to little effective control from shareholders. Once the first set of directors was in place, it would be difficult to displace incumbents. Therefore, the election of the first set of directors was critical to determine whether these banks would behave conservatively or not. In the first election after the flagship banks were privatized, the provisional administrators of these banks, with the blessing of the government, ran for the places in the board, together with some well-known independent bankers and economists. They won most of both boards.

2.4. 1987–1989: Stabilization of Chilean Banking

By 1987 it became apparent that the privatization scheme was vulnerable to a downturn in bank profitability, because a substantial number of shareholders might cease payments to CORFO. This would allow a hostile government to obtain a controlling share of the flagship banks. Another Achilles heel of the privatization scheme was that the obligation to repurchase bad loans had been linked to a complementary contract through which the selling bank managed the nonperforming loans for the Central Bank. This contract, which was designed in 1982 while the big groups still controlled the flagship banks and which was extended to all the other private banks who sold nonperforming loans, stipulated very strict penalties for negligent management, which included the acceleration of the obligation to repurchase.

This gave rise to fears that a future government might obtain control of the flagship banks. For example, by reducing banking's profitability through adverse regulations, it could provoke a massive return of shares to CORFO. In addition, by taking a very strict stance on the quality of management by banks of the nonperforming loans sold to the Central Bank, a hostile government could succeed in detonating the accelerating clauses and obtaining control of many privately owned banks.

These fears were addressed recently. In 1989, a new law overcame these two vulnerabilities through several mechanisms. The first mechanism failed in practice, but it is worth mentioning. The law allowed banks to purchase from CORFO the loans outstanding to the new shareholders at their market value. Then, if new shareholders stopped paying and the shares returned to the lender, i.e., the bank, the law required the bank to cancel those shares. This arrangement implied in the short term that the bank had to sell net assets (other investments) to buy these loans. Since these loans are backed by its own shares only, this would have resulted in a reduction in effective solvency. We assert this because the scheme was equivalent to the apparent increase in bank capital generated when a bank lends to purchase new shares issued by itself. The Superintendency of Banks did not force these banks to acknowledge in their accounts the effective reduction in the Capital base implied by this mechanism if they chose to adopt it, so it had implicitly bet that there would be no recession in banking during the next few years. However, the Central Bank priced CORFO loans above their market price, so no shareholder was interested in this option.

Second, the law allowed shareholders to request the end to the lien on the amount of the shares that had already been paid by servicing the loans in 1986–1989. This reduced substantially the quality of CORFO's guarantee and the risk of a forced return to state banks.

Third, the new law allowed banks to purchase from the Central Bank the nonperforming loans under their administration, at their market price (very low), while maintaining the bank's obligation to pay to the Central Bank 70% of dividends while the obligation exists. However, this obligation is reduced by the one-shot purchase of the nonperforming loans, at market value. This is exactly equivalent to the previous formula, so there is no wealth transfer. The advantage is that the sensitive managing contract is removed.

However, there might be an issue regarding the market value of the nonperforming loans. If this is set too high by the Central Bank, the bank will pay too much cash for them. It is true that there exists a counteracting effect because the bank will reduce by a greater amount its obligation to pay dividends to the Central Bank. However, the market value of a marginal reduction in the ceiling of the obligation to pay dividends to the Central Bank, when that ceiling is already very large, is much smaller than the associated cash value when the nonperforming loans are overpriced. Therefore, the government can improve its financial position by overvaluing the nonperforming loans.

Since the scheme does away with the troublesome managing contract that threatened a return to state ownership, the new shareholders may be willing to pay some premium for the nonperforming loans. In any case, this procedure became feasible only in 1989, after four years of large profits. If implemented in 1985, the government would have probably been unable to extract any premium.

To conclude, we give an overview of other segments of the Chilean capital market. In the last few years, the government has redrafted the legislation covering other capital market regulations. One of the results was a completely rewritten General Banking Law, described in the next section. Another result was the 1985 extension of the regulations that limit a bank's credit to its owners, including all their subsidiaries as one debtor, to the sensitive area of privately managed compulsory pension funds. This new law restricts the investment and purchase of inputs or sale of services by the private pension fund managers to their related companies. Because of recent experience with bearer-share societies in Panama and elsewhere, the banking law was reformed to presume that any bank's loan to a nonresident person is a loan to its owners, unless the bank proves that this is not the case.

In addition, the 1987 reform of the Insurance Companies Law extended the diversification rules applicable to the pension fund managers to the private life insurance companies, most of whose business consists of managing mandatory disability insurance and annuities. In 1989, pension fund and life insurers were allowed to make residential mortgage loans and to invest in regulated, close-ended, mutual funds that can invest in smaller nonpublic companies, commercial mortgages, and publicly traded shares.

Apart from the privatization of the flagship banks, the most important event of the last few years in the Chilean capital market has been the growth of the privately managed mandatory pension funds and life insurance companies. Established only in 1981, the pension funds have accumulated by 1989 financial claims equivalent to 17% of GDP. This number is expected to be near 40% in 1999 and to level off somewhere between 60% and 90% of GDP by 2015. The investments backing the mandatory annuities sold by the life insurance companies amount to an additional 30% of the pension funds.

These numbers show that the next years will require the securitization of Chilean assets in an unprecedented scale, in order to allow the pension funds to buy them. In fact the government obliged in 1986–1989 by putting up for sale a large number of state enterprises. The pension funds invested substantial sums in those shares and in bonds issued by them after the privatizations to finance their expansion plans. In the coming years, this balancing act will continue to be feasible only if private investment picks up and is financed through publicly traded shares or bonds to a larger extent than in the present.

3. Regulation and Supervision of Financial Markets and Institutions

3.1. Major Regulatory Agencies

The Chilean financial system is under the supervision of three governmental regulatory agencies: Superintendencia de Bancos e Instituciones Financieras (SBIF) (Superintendent of Banks and Financial Institutions); Superintendencia de Valores y Seguros (SVS) (Superintendent of Securities and Insurance); and Superintendencia de Administradora de Fondos de Pensión (SAFP) (Superintendent of Pension Fund Companies).

The SBIF is in charge of the commercial banks, financieras, and financial cooperatives. Currently the cooperatives are of little importance in the Chilean market.

The SVS exercises its supervisory powers over a wide variety of financial institutions. Among them are public corporations registered at the stock exchange market (which are called open corporations); corporations issuing debt in public offerings, even if their stocks are not publicly traded; agencias de valores; mutual funds; insurance and reinsurance companies (both casualty and life); and brokers trading on the stock exchange. It must approve the statutes and internal norms of the stock exchanges.

The SAFP was created as a specialized agency to supervise the management of the mandatory pension funds. In spite of its brief existance—it was created in 1981 when AFPs started—it has become the leader in the modernization of regulation and supervision in the Chilean capital market.

The current regulatory environment emphasizes 1) quantity and quality of the information given to the public; 2) pricing the assets of financial institutions at market prices; and 3) private rating of financial instruments being publicly offered, which is mandatory for investments by pension funds and insurance companies. In addition to these regulations, the requirements of portfolio diversification have become more stringent and efficient. They are now measured on the basis of consolidating the debt of parties related through property and of disclosing investments in assets issued by parties related to the investor through property or management.

3.2. Major Regulations of the Banking System

The law adopts the principle that banks can do only what is expressly allowed. On the other hand, the law reserves "the business of soliciting money and lending it" to the banks and financieras.

The three most important concepts embedded in current banking legislating are the following. First, most supervision is of a prudential nature. Second, liquid deposits have an explicit government guarantee and are levied a 100% reserve requirement at the margin. Third, the transfer of property rights in insolvent banks is explicitly spelled out in the law through rules that seek to preserve failing banks as going concerns and to force most of the loss on nonliquid deposit holders.

The SBIF is a government body that reports directly to the President, although in practice it works closely with the Finance Minister. The SBIF holds almost all the regulatory power over commercial banks and financieras. Some important powers are subject to either the veto of another entity, or ex post review, or both. An example of the first type is the power to decree the "intervention" or takeover of a bank, which means to legally replace the board by a SBIF appointee. This power is subject to Central Bank veto and ex post judicial review.

The SBIF's power to determine the accounting value of any bank loan can be appealed to the Superintendent of the SBIF, and then to the judiciary. Similarly, the SBIF is endowed with the power to "apply and interpret all the laws, regulations and bylaws which govern banks and financieras" (Article 12, Decree law No. 1097, of 1975). These powers reflect the trade-off between equanimity, opportunity, and effectiveness of bank supervision that is perceived by the government.

The main regulations applied to the banking system are the following:

3.2.1. Barriers to Entry.
These barriers may be defined as preventing entry of new capacity, entry of new owners, or entry of new brand names to the banking industry. In Chile, the only barrier to entry of new capacity is given by the discretionary SBIF authorization of the opening and closing of branch offices (article 31 of the Banking Law).

The only barrier to entry of new owners is the requirement that the SBIF must authorize ownership of more than 10% of a bank's shares. However, this barrier is generally acknowledged to be ineffective, since it is not defined in terms of control of the board, and does not apply to changes in the ownership of a controlling holding company. A bill that attempts to close this loophole on the ownership limit was approved recently.

Barriers to the entry of new brand names are given by article 27 of the Banking Law, which forbids the opening of a new bank without the approval of the SBIF. Currently, the SBIF bans the entrance of new brand names. This may create a rent that induces bank owners to be more risk averse. However, there are 37 bank brand names operating in Chile currently, so the actual rents may be small.

3.2.2. Regulations on Bank Assets.
The most important asset regulations are the following:

3.2.2.1. Exposure limits on loans. No *individual borrower* may borrow more than an amount equal to 5% of the bank's capital and reserves. However, the actual limit may be raised up to 25% of the bank's capital and reserves if the excess over the 5% is secured by *good enough* guarantees.

The definition of *good enough* is in article 84, No. 1 of the General Banking Law. Eligible guarantees are physical assets of a value larger than or equal to the excess over the first 5%, a value which is determined by SBIF regulations. Other eligible assets are 1) documents issued by the Central Bank, the Treasury, and other public bodies; 2) publicly traded securities classified A or B by the Pension Fund Risk Classification Commission; 3) liabilities of domestic or local banks that represent an unconditional obligation of payment; 4) documents that represents trade credit for exported merchandise; and 5) trade credit for imported merchandise, only if the local bank is empowered to dispose freely of the merchandise on arrival.

The definition of *individual borrower* is more sophisticated than in most other countries, and is spelled out in article 85 of the General Banking Law. An individual borrower includes all the corporations, partnerships, or societies of any nature where the borrower owns, directly or indirectly, more than 50% of the shares or the capital or the profits. This means that most legal loopholes are closed.

In addition, those corporations, partnerships, and other societies in which the borrower owns between 2% and 50% of shares, capital, or profits, if they get a loan from a bank, contribute the proportion of ownership times the size of the loan towards the sum of loans to that borrower. The implication is that most loopholes based on the proliferation of societies are closed too. However, this was not the case in he late 1970s and early 1980s, as described in the previous section.

Finally, obligations or liabilities held in common are considered in full for each one of the members of the community, unless it is clearly specified otherwise.

3.2.2.2. Limit on Credit to Related Parties. There is an explicit ceiling to credit to any party related to the bank through ownership or administration, which is the same as the individual borrower ceiling. Moreover, there is an additional ceiling of 100% of capital and reserves on the *sum* of loans to all parties related to the lending bank.

3.2.2.3. Equity Investments. This type of investment is basically banned. When a bank receives shares from collateral collection, it is forced to sell them in the following two years. The only exception is for investment in firms that provide specified ancillary financial services.

The authorized financial services are of two types. The first group, supervised by the Superintendency of Securities, includes mutual fund management, agencias de valores, and stockbroking. The second group is supervised by the SBIF, and include leasing, foreign banking affiliates, and networks of automatic cash dispensers.

3.2.2.4. Loan Classification. At any point in time, the banks must have classified 85% of their loan portfolio or the 400 largest debtors, whichever is the largest portfolio, in one of five categories. These are

A   Debtor that can pay without any problem on the basis of its cash flow, and in addition has pledged a solid guarantee

B   Debtor that either has enough cash flow but is risky, or has questionable cash flow but has pledged a good guarantee

B⁻ There is some evidence that the debtor will be unable either to pay fully or to pay on schedule. However, it has pledged some guarantee.

C   The debtor is in an intermediate situation where it would be able to pay between 60% and 20% of the original debt.

D   The loss will exceed 80% of the loan. Generally the debtor firm is not operating and there are no guarantees.

The SBIF suggests classification criteria, and those suggestions are backed by the power to object to the classification of any given loan. If the lending bank disagrees with the suggested classification for a given loan, it may appeal to the same SBIF, who determines which is the final accounting value of the loan.

An SBIF team makes unannounced visits to each domestic private bank an average of three times a year, and to each foreign-owned bank an average of once a year. During a visit, the SBIF team checks the classification of a random sample of loans with an average value of 20% of a bank's portfolio. Loans classified too benignly are reclassified, but loans classified too conservatively are not. The sample is not fully random because the SBIF incorporates to the sampling procedure information gathered in other banks about nonperforming borrowers.

3.2.2.5. Guidelines for loss provisioning. There are two types of provisions for loan losses: general and individual.

The general provision is calculated as the maximum between 0.75% of assets, and the number that results from requiring a 1% provision for the portfolio of B loans, plus a 20% provision for the portfolio of B-loans, plus a 60% provision for the portfolio of C loans, plus a 90% provision for the portfolio of D loans. This number is called *loans at risk*.

The individual provision is linked to the declaration of a loan as *vencido*, or nonperforming. When a loan payment has not occurred within the first 89 days after the scheduled date, the loan must be classified as *vencido* and stop accruing interest (during the first 89 days it is called *moroso*). Once the loan is declared nonperforming, the individual provision must be built up, at the rate of 1/24 of face value per month if the loan had no physical collateral, and at the rate of 1/36 of face value per month if it has physical collateral. At the end of the individual provisioning period, the loan is cancelled against the individual provision (*castigado*).

If the loan is rescheduled at any point in the provisioning period, it ceases to be nonperforming. However, the SBIF requires that rescheduling decisions be based on a written analysis or study of the cash flows of the debtor. On the other hand, the SBIF requires that when a loan is rescheduled after being declared nonperforming, the interest accrued during the period it was nonperforming must be provisioned in full immediately. In this way, that interest does not affect the statement of gains and losses unless the rescheduled loan is effectively serviced at a later time.

Finally, the SBIF reviews strictly the reschedulings that are agreed in the month that preceeds the annual balance-sheet date. This is necessary to prevent phony reschedulings, which improve the apparent solvency of the lending bank.

The general required provision is by far the most important in practice, with a current value for the system near 5% of the loan portfolio. Although the general provision is not formally linked to any individual loan, the fact that it applies only to performing loans (*vigentes*) means that switching a loan from performing to nonperforming status replaces the original general provision for the individual provision. An A loan that becomes nonperforming leads to an increase in overall provisions, while if a D loan becomes nonperforming the overall required provisions fall in the short run. However, the fact that most banks hold excess provisions means that in practice these fluctuations are smoothed out. Excess provisions for the whole banking system are over 1% as of December 1988.

Finally, there are no sectoral, geographical, or sovereign diversification regulations. Interest rates are freely determined in the market, although there is a maximum interest rate that banks can charge. This limit is set at 150% of the ongoing average interest rate in the market for each type of loan. Thus it is effectively ineffective.

3.2.3. Minimum Capital Requirements. The most important capital requirement is the one that penalizes debt/capital ratios above 20 (article 81). For this purpose, the SBIF uses what is calls *normative capital*. This is defined as beginning-of-year capital and reserves minus accumulated unprovisioned losses. If loan loss provisions exceed projected loan losses, the excess *is not* added to capital.

On the other hand, the concept of debt that is used to calculate this ratio excludes some debts to the Central Bank that were a by-product of the domestic debt reschedulings of 1983 and 1984. In these reschedulings, the Central Bank induced banks to reduce the interest rate on many outstanding loans by offering matching loans at a below-market interest rate, which had to be reinvested in the Central Bank itself at market interest rates. These transactions inflated the volume of debt issued by banks, so the SBIF excludes them from the total debt to be used when calculating the debt/capital ratio.

Another adjustment is made to exclude most liabilities with the Central Bank that correspond to the sale of nonperforming loans to the Central Bank that occurred in 1983–1985, which were required to be purchased back contingent on the realization of enough profits. These liabilities are legally a liability of bank shareholders, not of the bank, so they are excluded from the debt/equity ratio used to measure solvency.

The second most important capital requirement is the 100% reserve requirements on liquid liabilities that exceed 2.5 times capital and reserves. Liquid liabilities are the deposits and obligations that are scheduled to be payable on demand within the next ten days. This limit may severely restrict a bank's ability to capture the inflation tax on checking accounts.

Other regulations related to the banks' capital are 1) banks cannot make loans to finance the purchase of shares of the lending bank; 2) capital reductions may only be done with SBIF approval; 3) dividends cannot exceed current earnings; and 4) no provisional dividends can be distributed.

3.2.4. Contingent Liabilities. The regulation of contingent liabilities is not advanced in Chile. On the one hand, all guarantees—trade credit commitments and endorsements—are valued at 100% of their maximum value, for the purpose of the limit on debt/equity ratios. On the other hand, credit-line commitments are not monitored by the SBIF, and are taken off the balance sheet, so they do not affect the debt/equity ratio. Similarly, credit lines and guarantees in favor of a bank, as well as other contingent assets, are not set against the bank's contingent liabilities. Foreign-currency futures (yen, deutchmark, and pound sterling against the U.S. dollar) are allowed only to reduce exposure. U.S. dollar future positions are allowed subject to the restriction that the sum of the absolute value of daily net future exposures must be below 100% of capital and reserves. Foreign interest-rates futures (caps, floors, and collars) are allowed only to reduce exposure.

3.2.5. Maturity Mismatching Regulations. There are several restrictions on maturity mismatching or interest-rate risk exposure. The first is the obligation to match exactly all mortgage loans against the sale of mortgage bonds of equal maturity and payment schedule.

The second maturity mismatching regulation is set by the Central Bank. The current regulation limits the absolute value of the difference between liabilities with maturities over one year and loans with original maturity over one year to 100% of the bank's capital and reserves. But other assets and the current duration of loans are not considered. Although banks comply with this regulation, it seems to be not binding.

The third regulation on maturity mismatching, although not a SBIF regulation, is a regulation on diversification of pension fund investments. Because many banks depend on deposits from the pension funds, they must meet the criteria set by the Risk Classification Commission for the pension funds. Thus, it is binding in practice. This guideline establishes a more detailed classification of assets and liabilities according to maturity than the one required by the Central Bank. It measures mismatching according to three units of account: pesos, UF (a CPI-adjusted index), and U.S. dollars. One problem with this guideline is that it confuses the concepts of maturity mismatching and liquidity; for example, long-term bonds that trade every day are considered as having "less than one year" maturity.

The Central Bank also establishes limits to foreign currency and CPI-indexed exposures. These differ from those set by pension fund investment guidelines.

3.2.6. Interbank Loans. The law imposes a limit on loans in the domestic interbank market of 30% of capital and reserves of the lending bank. In addition, the Central Bank imposes another limit on indebtedness in the domestic interbank market, namely, 30% of capital and reserves of the borrowing bank.

3.2.7. Subordinated Debt and Pledge on Assets. In general, banks are not allowed to attach priorities nor to subordinate the debt they sell. Similarly, banks are not allowed to pledge particular assets to service particular deposits or bonds they sell, with the exception of mortgage bonds.

There are two exceptions to the general rule above. The first is subordinated debt of average maturity above ten years at the date of issue. Up to 85% of the portion that is due in two years or more will be counted as bank capital, provided that it does not surpass 20% of ordinary capital, while all of it is not counted as debt for the purpose of the limit on the debt/equity ratio. Banks and other entities supervised by the Superintendency of Banks cannot hold these securities. The second exception is for the case of a bank in trouble that is helped by other banks, treated below.

3.2.8. Taxes and Income from Nonperforming assets. The income tax and value-added laws applicable to banks is the same as for other businesses. There is a special tax on payments, which uniformly affects checks, automatic cash-dispensing machines, and credit cards. There is another tax on credit operations (loans), which amounts to 1.2% of the principal for operations with a maturity of a year or more, and a fraction thereof for shorter maturity operations, with a 0.1% minimum. This tax affects not only bank loans but most other private-sector loans that are identified by the Internal Revenue Service as a source of funds.

The tax treatment of loan loss provisions is as follows: general provisions are not considered a tax expense, while individual provisions are. This means that when a loan classification is reduced, say from A to C, and provisions must be built up, the 60% provision is considered as a reserve and cannot be subtracted from current profit for tax purposes. However, financial accounting considers those provisions as a subtraction to assets, so it produces financial losses.

On the other hand, when a loan is declared nonperforming, the individual provision that must be built up is considered expense, while the general provision that is liberated (if the classification was B or lower) is considered a once-and-for-all taxable income. This means that a bank may be exhibiting financial losses while paying taxes on its tax-accounting profits. Clearly, there is no favorable tax treatment for voluntary provisions.

The income from unpaid loans is determined as follows. While the loan is *moroso*, the accrued interest continues to be considered income, for financial and tax purposes. Once it is declared nonperforming, interest ceases to accrue and the size of the loan plus accrued and unpaid interest is frozen in pesos, so it is eroded by inflation. If the loan is rescheduled, interest begins to accrue again, according to the rescheduling terms.

3.2.9. Disclosure of Financial Information. The law forces banks to publish their financial statements in a newspaper four times a year, according to regulations of the SBIF. These regulations force banks to include both an income statement and a balance sheet, several notes regarding the degree of maturity mismatching, the volume of lending to related parties, etc., and the opinion of external auditors. In addition, the law requires the SBIF to inform the public about its own evaluation of the degree of recoverability of bank loans for each bank.

Finally, the Securities Law, which is applicable to banks that issue bonds, mortgage bonds, or which are "open" corporations, require banks to hire at least two Registered Private Risk Classifiers to classify them and to publish the outcome. The only banks that are excepted are those who have only a few owners ("closed" corporation, whose shares are not publicly traded) and do not issue bonds or mortgage bonds in the security markets.

3.2.10. Universal Banking. As emphasized above, banks cannot hold equity of other firms, except for a few exceptions related to specified financial services firms. As noted earlier, these are mutual fund managers, leasing companies, agentes de valores, and automatic cash-dispenser networks. Thus, there is no universal banking. However, nothing prevents a bank holding company from owning shares and controlling business firms directly. Nevertheless, the loans from the affiliated banks to the business affiliates will be considered related-party loans, subject to the limitations mentioned above.

3.2.11. Reserve Requirements. Reserve requirements are 10% on sight deposits, including checking accounts. Time deposits with a maturity up to one year have a reserve requirement of 4%. Bonds, mortgage bonds, other serial instruments, and deposits with a maturity over one year are exempt. These are the minimum levels, set by law, but the Central Bank may raise them. Reserves have paid zero nominal interest since January 1990, a fact that explains the observed rise in the gross margin. In addition, there is a 100% marginal reserve requirement on liquid deposits in excess over 2.5 times capital and reserves. However, this reserve can be built with interest-bearing paper issued by the Treasury or the Central Bank because its has a prudential purpose.

3.3. Deposit Insurance

Currently there are three types of explicit state guarantees on deposits. Neither of the first two requires payment of fees, so they are always taken by the beneficiaries. The deposits covered are only those issued by banks and financieras, when applicable. The third guarantee, which must be remembered in any analysis of the Chilean financial system, covers all deposits and liabilities of the state bank, Banco del Estado.

The first type of explicit fiscal guarantee covers small depositors, and covers 90% of the deposits registered on the name of each person in the entire financial system, up to 120 Unidades de Fomento (a CPI-adjusted index) per year. This means that 90% of deposits up to around, US$ 2000 per person are covered in the whole of the Chilean financial system. Deposits held by societies, partnerships, and corporations are excluded. The guarantee can be claimed only after a bank is liquidated or proposes an Agreement to Creditors. In both cases the state replaces the depositor as a creditor. The funds of the guarantee go first to cancel any obligation the depositor may have with the bank, before payment is determined. It should be noted that this definition discourages arbitrage possibilities like dividing deposits in a given bank or among several banks.

The second type of explicit guarantee covers all liquid deposits, in the cases of liquidation and proposition of an Agreement to Creditors. In both cases the Central Bank replaces the depositor as a creditor, but in addition the law grants it priority over other creditors. The law does not talk of a guarantee explicitly, because the Central Bank is constitutionally banned from guaranteeing anybody. Rather, the law says that in the cases mentioned, the Central Bank *must lend* to the failing bank, who in turn must use those funds to pay holders of liquid deposits.

Liquid deposits are defined to include checking accounts; any other deposit or obligation whose holder may legally require unconditional payment, either immediately or within the next 30 days; and all time deposits during the ten days that precede its maturity. Interbank deposits are excluded. It must be stressed that although this guarantee is offered gratis, there is a 100% reserve requirement on liquid deposits that exceed 2.5 times capital and reserves.

The maturity specifications of these regulations can be understood only in the context of other regulations. The Central Bank bans any time deposit in nominal terms for maturities shorter than 30 days, excepting interbank deposits, and CPI-indexed time deposits with maturity shorter than 90 days.

3.4. The Role of the Central Bank

The Central Bank regulatory powers are related mainly to foreign-exchange operations and to set conditions on the design of financial products that may be used by the public as substitutes for bills, coin, and reserves at the Central Bank, i.e., for the monetary base. For example, time deposits cannot be issued for less than 30 days, and raising funds for shorter periods is allowed only through repurchase agreements done with Central Bank instruments. The commercial banks are the only institutions allowed to participate in the primary market for these securities.

The Central Bank acts as a lender of last resort, and when doing so has the power to force a bank to comply with additional regulations as a condition for receiving emergency credit. This power is not diluted by the guarantee on liquid deposits, because this latter guarantee operates only after a bank has been declared insolvent.

3.5. Mechanisms to Deal with Solvency Problems

The General Banking Law endows the SBIF and the Central Bank with a number of methods for managing the transfer of property rights in failing banks, most of which attempt to keep the bank as a going concern. The methods are the following:

1. Central Bank loans, which may have strings attached, tailored to each failing bank's circumstances. These are called *normas de administración financiera*.[22]
2. Soft loans from Banco del Estado and public enterprises, which may also have strings attached. This method is not explicitly spelled out in the Banking Law, but has been used in the past.
3. Intervention or Takeover, where the SBIF names a person that legally replaces the bank's board of directors. Intervention can continue indefinitely.
4. Agreement with Creditors. This mechanism forces part of the loss on holders of nonliquid deposits.
5. Preventive Capitalization. This mechanism forces the board of a bank that is experiencing losses to call an extraordinary shareholder meeting and propose a capital increase. Shareholders are not forced to provide it.
6. Help from other banks. This mechanism allows an ailing bank to issue two-year subordinated debt and sell it to other banks. This subordinated debt is considered capital for the purposes of loan limits and the debt/equity ratio.
7. Liquidation. This is the only mechanism that halts consideration of the ailing bank as a going concern, because its license to operate as a bank is revoked. Holders of nonliquid deposits may suffer a loss and will surely suffer delay in recovering their funds.

3.6. Towards a New Approach to Bank Failures

Bailing out banks with taxpayer's money (indirectly when the Central Banks acts as lender) appears to be the worldwide system of resolving insolvency problems in the banking industry. In other words, there is a de facto or implicit insurance on all bank liabilities. In this sense, the Chilean experience has been only one more case of this type of solution. Although not satisfactory, it remains the preferred solution when a political decision is taken to support a bank. The banking problem, i.e., how to deal with insolvent banks, is an issue not yet solved anywhere. An interesting aspect of banking in Chile is that a new approach is being tried.

Even in the most free-market-oriented countries, the banking industry is as a general rule the most regulated one, and also is the one that suffers the most instability. The recent Texas experience in the United States is one example comparable to the Chilean 1981–1983 banking crisis. The most controlled market has a record of bad performance.

Why have controls been so inefficient? Why is there no market solution for the banking industry? Are the controls perverse? Henry Simons[23] saw in this weakness of the banking system a big danger for a free society. As a result, he proposed that either demand deposit banks should be subject to a 100% reserve requirement, or that they should be state owned. Simons proposed this together with a free-market, nonregulated management for the rest of the banks' operations—i.e., for term deposits and other funds managed by banks. This proposition was intended to separate the function of issuing money from fund management; the second one would be similar to a mutual fund operation.

The Chilean experience has resulted in a search for new rules of the game, under which a private solution for banks' problems could be feasible. It tries to end up with the de facto insurance, so that bank's loss becomes private. A first requisite for achieving this goal is that bank creditors become convinced that the Government or the Central Bank will not intervene when they lose. To convince them, it is necessary to have a solution for bank failures that works out economically and politically; without it, it is impossible to build up credibility in a solution that implies that the Government steps aside. An attempt to face this difficult task has been tried by the new legislation in Chile. The Chilean approach innovates in two areas: deposit insurance and bank capitalization by creditors.

3.6.1. New Deposit Insurance Scheme. Traditional deposit insurance schemes do not discriminate among types of deposits, and the coverage is limited to a maximum amount. The new Chilean scheme distinguishes between money, quasi-money, and other deposits, as follows: *money*, means banks' liabilities that, according to contract, can be called on within a period of less than 30 days; and *quasi-money* means banks' liabilities contracted for 30 days or more but expiring within the next 10 days. For these two categories there is government insurance that covers 100% of the obligation without any maximum limit.

Although there is unlimited insurance on money and quasi-money, there is a limit on the amount of these liabilities that any bank can issue. This limit has been established at 2.5 times the capital and reserves of a bank; any excess over it carries a 100% reserve requirement.

This discrimination of insurance among deposits is based on the idea that the amount of negative externalities caused by not honoring at face value a money-type liability are much higher than for other bank's liabilities. Without such a guarantee, no money-bank would ever be permitted to fail by a politically conscious government, as Chilean and worldwide experience shows.

For the other obligations, there is only small-depositor insurance, covering up to 120 U.F. (around US$ 2500). This limit applies to all the deposits in the system, not in one bank only, held by any natural person (societies and corporations are excluded). The limited insurance on term deposits is justified on the grounds that, for small depositors, information costs exceed benefits, and that there is a social benefit in permitting small depositors to channel their savings through banks.

This insurance scheme increases the feasibility of imposing losses on uninsured bank creditors. But by itself, this is not enough. It is also necessary to predetermine a set of rules that clearly define the rights of creditors in an insolvent bank and, equally important, that demonstrates that the assumption of losses by them will be politically acceptable. A scheme attempting to reach these goals was included in Chilean banking law in 1986.

3.6.2. Bank Capitalization by Creditors. When a bank faces a solvency problem, it must call its creditors (by its own initiative or mandated by the Superintendent of Banks) for a vote on an agreement proposal made by the bank. The proposition must reshape liabilities in a fashion that enables the bank to stand up by itself. The proposal must be approved by the Superintendent. The creditors must choose among three alternatives: 1) the bank's proposal; 2) a "standard agreement"; or 3) the bank's liquidation.

The standard agreement is the key element on this scheme. It should satisfy three conditions: 1) it must be, for the creditors, a better alternative than liquidation; 2) it must leave the bank in a solid financial condition; and, 3) it must be for the government a politically better solution than bailing out the creditors. If the creditors have these alternatives to choose from, the bank's proposal is forced to offer them conditions as least as good as those of the standard agreement. There are two critical elements in the standard agreement introduced in 1989 in the banking law:

1. Non-government-guaranteed debts are capitalized in an amount such that the debt/capital ratio is reduced to 14.
2. To finance the capitalization, creditors receive preferred shares. The preference stipulates that all profits go first to repurchase these shares at book value. This is an option not obligatory to the preferred shareholder.

If the creditors approve the bank's proposal or the standard agreement, the bank becomes solvent again. If it faces liquidity problems, the Central Bank can provide the funds assuming normal risks.

By mid-1989, banks were allowed to issue subordinated long-term bonds, which will be counted, with some limitations (see section 4), as capital. These instruments will be a good complement to facilitate capitalization when a creditors' agreement is needed, since they will be the first class of debt to be capitalized when insolvency threatens. And when these instruments trade in the secondary market, their prices will be an interesting gauge for the public in terms of indicating the soundness of the policies of a given bank. This would help the emergence of market-control mechanisms for limiting risk attractiveness.

These schemes are recent, and have not yet been tested in a bank failure. However, we believe their mere existence makes an important contribution to the stability of the banking system.

4. Major Current Domestic and International Operating and Regulatory Problems

One of the major current domestic problems consists of the legacy of the large number of bank insolvencies of the early 1980s. As explained in section 2, the loss was much larger than the equity of the original shareholders. Thus the government forced the new shareholders of the banks to assign a large part of future dividends to the repurchase at par value of the impaired assets sold by the banks to the Central Bank. Each repurchase allows the bank to return some 0% bills to the Central Bank, reducing the difference between book value and true capital.

As a result, a large number of Chilean banks have to channel most of their dividends to this purpose. Since 1984, only a few banks have finished repurchasing their impaired assets from the Central Bank, and some of them have been able to do so only because of an infusion of new capital by their owners. However, a substantial number of banks expect to finish repurchasing their impaired assets within the next five years. Nevertheless, the two largest private Chilean banks (Banco de Chile and Banco de Santiago) have such a large volume of impaired assets that their obligation is expected to last for somewhere between 40 years and forever.

One of the implications of this situation is to limit the growth of the rehabilitated banks' capital and reserves, because retaining earnings is virtually impossible. This is also the case for several other banks that were not taken over, but still need several years to repurchase their nonperforming loans. Although this limitation may be currently binding for many banks, in the long term it will be binding only for the two largest bank and two smaller banks.

To increase the ability of banks to raise capital funds, a proposal for allowing subordinated long-term bonds was approved in June 1989. In the proposal, 85% of the portion of the bond that has maturity over two years would be counted as capital, with a limit of 20% of the bank's true capital, if the original average maturity is ten years or more, and no prepayment or exchange options for higher priority claims are attached. Since the approval of this proposal, Chilean banks have found here an important avenue for financing growth in their effective capital base.

Another important current problem is regulation of the foreign-exchange market. Through 1989, this market has been heavily riddled by exchange control, which bans every operation unless it is explicitly authorized. However, a new Central Bank law that was recently approved inverted this principle. Some expect substantial liberalization of the Chilean foreign exchange market in the next years.

The last problem is the rapid growth of pension funds and life insurance companies. This growth requires a large sustained increase in the supply of negotiable securities for investments. This has induced regulators to undertake a search for new acceptable forms of investment, but so far there have been few successes excepting the 1986–1989 privatization of state companies. One possibility is to open the residential mortgage market to participants other than banks. This would free the expansion of the residential mortagages from the limit of banks' capital and reserves. Another is authorization for pension funds to invest in new closed-ended mutual funds that in turn invest in commercial mortgages and venture capital.

5. Implications of Globalization

Chilean banking has been exposed to the pressures of globalization for the last 15 years. As we will see, adjustment to these pressures appears to be complete now.

5.1. Implications for Domestic Bank Structure

In 1975-1976, new subsidiaries and branches of foreign banks were allowed. In addition, legislation passed in 1974 assured foreign investors in most sectors of the economy equal treatment with local investors, and foreign investment in general has been relatively large by historical standards.

During the last decade, several large foreign banks, especially some Spanish banks, have bought medium-sized local banks. Citibank has noticeably expanded its subsidiary in Chile, and its market share has grown to sixth place. These banks represent important competition for domestic banks, especially in the most profitable segments. However, during the last decade some of them have suffered large losses, and one of them decided to leave the country.

Most foreign banks maintain small branches or subsidiaries, but they have remain specialized in a given sector of business, usually multinationals, and exhibit very low growth. This second set of foreign banks do not represent an immediate competitive threat for local banks, although their high capital ratios indicate that if they wished to invest in segments of the Chilean market, capital would not be a barrier.[24]

Recently, more foreign banks have entered the Chilean market in association with local firms. This has been a response to the search by weak local financial institutions for partners that would inject new capital. The principal weakness that must be overcome is the obligation to repurchase old bad loans from the Central Bank, which drains profits and prevent expansion. In this area, globalization has opened up the mindframe of many foreign banks, which will now consider carefully an offer to participate in an emerging market such as Chile.

5.2. Participation of Chilean Banks in Other Countries

The expansion of Chilean banks abroad was first allowed in 1980. Since then, a few Chilean banks have invested abroad, most notably the BHC

Bank[25] in a Panamanian subsidiary called Banco Andino, and Banco de Chile in both a New York branch and an Uruguayan subsidary, Bank Pan de Azúcar. However, these two subsidiaries were used mainly as a means of evading Chilean regulations on credit to the bank's owners. In a typical operation, BHC would lend to Banco Andino, who would then lend to some holding company of the BHC group in Chile. Because Chilean regulators did not have authority over Banco Andino, they could not classify BHC's loans to Banco Andino appropiately.

A tightening of regulatory practices and stricter legislation, combined with the failures of Banco Andino and Banco Pan de Azúcar, has left Banco de Chile's branch in New York as the only remaining full branch abroad. The reason for this is that there are no Chilean multinationals to serve abroad, and that Chile's access to the international credit and bond markets has been limited by the fallout of the debt crisis. Therefore, Chilean banks see few reasons to invest abroad. In particular, the impact of 1992 European Economic Community financial integration is expected to be small.

6. The Outlook

Any projection of the health of the Chilean banking system must start by assessing the recovery from the 1981–1983 insolvency crisis. After the intervention by the government and the associated distribution of losses, Chilean banks emerged in a solvent position. As explained above, the debt/capital ratio of most banks was under 17 by the end of 1988, and the average ratio for all Chilean privately owned banks was 15. For international comparison purposes, it must be recalled that in Chile all contingent liabilities are booked at 100% of the maximum liability. After several years of regulatory experience, we believe that these numbers are reasonably reliable, except for the 0% bills registered as assets.

Shareholders of a large number of Chilean privately owned banks have a substantial contingent liability to the Central Bank, because they must devote a large portion of their net earnings to service debts to the Central Bank. Thus, in several banks retained earnings are not available to finance expansion.

However, there is a widely spread perception in Chilean financial circles that currently there is excess capacity in the banking industry for four reasons: first, the relative expansion of securities markets; second, the 1984 change in the company tax code that eliminated most of the previous bias in favor of debt financing for companies; third, the large capitalization with which several banks emerged from the crisis; and fourth, light supervision, which has reduced the overexpansion of banking induced by the unregulated deposit insurance subsidy. The limit on capital growth that is implied by the debt service to the Central Bank is not deemed to be important in the next few years. The authorization for the issue of subordinated bonds that may be partially counted as capital reinforces this conclusion.

Evidence of excess capacity of the banking sector may be seen most clearly in the fierce competition between banks. This is true for the corporate loan sector, where spreads are thin, and is becoming so for the consumer loan market, since branches have multiplied. The outlook is for increased competitive efficiency, expressed both in lower charges for bank services and a larger variety and availability of them. Some segments of the banking business exhibit important barriers to entry, and less competition may be expected there. This appears to be the case in the automated-cashier segment, where only two networks exist: the credit card business and the transportation of money in armored trucks.

On the other hand, foreign banks are not expected to make large inroads into the domestic banking system for two reasons. First, Chilean banking is not profitable enough, as indicated above. Second, Chile's demand for foreign loans has fallen dramatically, since most residents have chosen to reduce their foreign debt. The foreign debt of Chilean commercial banks fell by 50% in dollar terms between 1982 and 1988. Even the government has attempted to reduce the foreign public debt, although it has proceeded more slowly. However, some weak Chilean banks have been actively searching for foreign partners that would wish to inject capital and pay off the old-bad-loan repurchase agreements with the Central Bank.

The most active area of expansion in the financial business seems to be the one related to brokerage, market-making and underwriting of securities, mutual fund management, leasing, investment banking, and life insurance. Many banks have created subsidiaries to perform these and other functions, since the 1986 reform to the banking law allowed banks to enter into these businesses through subsidiaries. This area appears to be much more profitable than traditional banking, as shown by the strong entry by domestic and foreign banks and even by foreign securities houses.

As in many other countries, the outlook for bank securities activities in Chile appears complicated by the absence of a thoroughly coherent regulatory framework. In Chile, the authorities have followed the path of allowing banks to become holding companies of firms that offer security-market-related services. However, regulation is not designed at the conglomerate level and continues to be exercised at each individual business level. This creates some inconsistencies and inefficiencies. For example, although the mutual fund management subsidiary of a Chilean bank is regulated by the Superintendency of Banks, the sharing of costs with the bank is banned, and loans from the bank to the subsidiary are subject to the limit on loans to related parties. The overall regulatory scheme means that a clear-cut option between multipurpose financial conglomerates and absolute separation between commercial banking and investment banking has not been adopted in Chile. The current rule is equivalent to separation, but allows ownership ties across the wall.

Notes

1. Colombia, which is the only other Latin American country that has grown in the 1980s, never suffered a recession because of the debt crisis.
2. There are no specialized mortgage banks. Mortgage funding for housing has been undertaken by commercial banks, which issue bonds backed by the mortgages in their portfolio.
3.
4. This excludes the Central Bank's deficit.
5. Banks received an asset from the Central Bank and issued a liability to it, with a spread similar to the difference between the market cost of funds and the interest on restructured loans.
6. Europe: 2.3; U.S.: 3.0; Latin America: 6.1; See "Eficiencia y Competitividad de la Industria Bancaria Chilena," mimeo, Superintendencia de Bancos e Instituciones Financieras, Chile, August, 1988.
7. Independent workers, including providers of professional services, workers paid piece-rate, and the informal sector, are not obliged to contribute. In addition, older people are still contributing in the old pension system.
8. SINAP is the acronym for Sistema Nacional de Ahorro y Préstamo.
9. SINAP lent at an interest rate defined as past inflation plus, say 7%, where this last number was fixed by the authorities.
10. This was not universal. In 1974, the president of the Central Bank stated that liberalization was not expected to generate an increase in the flow of national savings, and that the generalization of indexation would increase the difficulty of predicting the demand for money.
11. In fact, the issue was discussed in the press from the beginning of 1974.
12. This promise was repeated by the Finance Minister in March 1975.
13. Real GDP fell 12% in 1975. This was due to the steep fall in the price of copper and the refusal of private and public foreign institutions to lend for adjustment.
14. It was found that Banco de Santiago, which fed the Cruzat-Larraín Group, had lent out 45% of its loan portfolio to its owners.
15. Starting in June 1982, the figures for loans in arrears include bad loans sold to the Central Bank.

16. The yield curve at the time exhibited very high rates for the short term. The groups claimed that their solvency had to be measured using the lower long-term rate to discount every period.

17. December 1982 to February 1987.

18. As a proportion of book value, the government receives a present value of $0.05 + (0.95/15)(1 - 0.20)/0.20$, where the last number is a 20% real discount rate, adjusted for risk. This adds up to 30.3% of book value.

19. Chapter 18 of the Foreign Exchange Control Rules.

20. Each year, 20% of the book value of the shares can be subtracted from the personal income tax base. Assuming an average marginal income tax rate of 25% among the purchasers of shares, the flow of forgone taxes is 5% of the book value of the shares. Discounting at 20% per year, we obtain the present value mentioned in the text.

21. The present value for the government, in terms of book value, is $PY_0 - \pi_0/0.20$ in the case of state management, and is $PY' = (0.70)\pi'/0.20 + 0.303 - 0.25$ with this privatization. The last two terms are the revenue from the subsidized loans and the tax revenue lost. It is easy to see that as π_0 grows, the required π' that the private sector must deliver to keep the government equally well off financially is larger.

22. This means Rules for Financial Management.

23. "Rules versus Authority in Monetary Policy," *Journal of Political Economy* 44(1), (February 1936), 1–30.

24. The following foreign banks had branches or subsidiaries in Chile in December 1988: Citibank, Chase Manhattan, Bank of Boston, Security Pacific, Amertican Express, Bank of America, Chicago Continental, Manufacturers Hanover, Morgan Bank, Republic N.B. of N.Y., Bank of Tokyo, Hong Kong & Shanghai B.C., Sudameris, Credit Lyonnaise (B. Continental), B. Exterior de España, B. de Santander (B. Español), B. Central de España (Centrobanco), B. Real, B. de Colombia, B. de la Nación Argentina, B. do Brasil, and Banco do Estado do Saõ Paulo.

25. The BHC bank was owned by the second largest Chilean business group, but was liquidated in January 1983.

References

Acevedo, Julio. "Evolucción del Sistema Financiero en 1982," Información Financiera, SBIF, January 1983.

Arellano, José Pablo. "De la Liberalización a la Intervenctión: El Mercado de Capitales en Chile: 1974–1983," *Colección Estudios CIEPLAN* 11 (December 1983), 5–50.

Barandarián, Edgardo. "La Crisis Financiera Chilena," Estudios Públicos, Santiago, October 1983.

Bosch, A.M., A. Emhart, and M. Giudice. "Concentración de Créditos en Deudores Vinculados a la Propiedad o Gestión de las Instituciones Financieras," Información Financiera, SBIF, August 1986.

Corbo, Vittorio. "Reforms with Macroeconomic Adjustment in Chile during 1974–1984," World Development, August 1985.

Dahse, Fernando. "Mapa de la Extrema Riqueza," editorial, *Aconcagua*, Santiago, 1979.

De la Cuadra, S. and S. Valdés. "Myths and Facts about Instability in Financial Liberalization in Chile: 1974-1983," mimeo, Instituto de Economía, U.C, 1989.
Díaz-Alejandro, C. "Good Bye Financial Repression, Hello Financial Crash," *Journal of Development Economics* 19:1 (1985), pp. 1-24.
Harberger, Arnold. "La Crisis Cambiaria Chilena de 1982," Cuadernos de Economía, Instituto de Economía UC, August 1984, pp. 123-136.
Harberger, Arnold. "Lessons for Debtor Country Managers and Policy Makers", in G.W. Smith and J. Cuddington (eds.), *International Debt and the Developing Countries*. Washington DC: The World Bank, 1985.
Eyzaguirre, Nicolás. "La Deuda Interna Chilena: 1975-1985", in C. Massad and R. Zahler (eds.), *Deuda Interna y Estabilidad Financiera*, Vol. II, Proyecto ECLAC/77/021. Buenos Aires: Grupo Editor Latinoamericano, 1988.
Edwards, Sebastian. "Stabilization with Liberalization: An Evaluation of Ten years of Chile's Experiment with Free Market Policies, 1973-1983," *Economic Development and Cultural Change* 1 (January 1985), pp. 223-254.
Edwards, Sebastian. "Monetarismo en Chile, 1973-1983: Algunos Dilemas Económicos," in F. Morandé and K. Schmidt-Hebbel (eds.), *Del Auge a la Crisis de 1982*. Santiago: ILADES, 1988.
Ffrench-Davis, Ricardo. *Políticas Económicas en Chile 1952-1970*. Ediciones Nueva Universidad, Universidad Católica de Chile, 1973.
Gorton, Gary. "Clearinghouses and the Origin of Central Banking in the United States," *The Journal of Economic History* 45(2) (June 1985), pp. 277-283.
Held, Günther. "Regulación y Supervisión de la banca en la experiencia de Liberalización Financiera en Chile (1974-1988)," IC/R 758, ECLAC, Santiago, Chile, May 3, 1989.
Herring, R. and P. Vankudre. "The Moral Hazard Constraint on the Pricing of Deposit Insurance," *Brookings Discussion Papers in International Economics* 40 (November 1985).
Jeftanovic, Pedro. "La evolución del SINAP durante 1974-76," in Comentarios sobre la Situación Económica, 2o Semestre, Taller de Coyuntura, Departamento de Economía, Universidad de Chile, 1976.
Lüders, Rolf. "Latin American Contrasts: Capital Markets and Development in Argentina and Chile," Universidad Católica de Chile, first Draft, May 1988.
Lüders, Rolf. "La razón de ser de la Intervención del 13 de Enero," in *Economía y Sociedad, Segunda Epoca*, (1985).
Mayer, Thomas. "A Graduated Deposit Insurance Plan," *Review of Economics and Statistics* 47 (February 1965), pp. 114-116.
Meigs, J. "Regulatory Aspects of the World Debt Problem," *Cato Journal* 4 (Spring/Summer 1984), 105.
Merton, Robert. "An Analytic Derivation of the Cost of Deposit Insurance and Loan Guarantees," *Journal of Banking and Finance* 1 (June 1977), 3.
Morcus, Alon. "Dergulation and Bank Financial Policy," *Journal of Banking and Finance* 8 (December 1984), 8.
McCarthy, Ian. "Deposit Insurance: Theory and Practice," *IMF Staff Papers* 27

(September 1980), 578.

McKinnon, Ronald. "Financial Liberalization and Economic Development: A Reassessment of Interest-Rate Policies in Asia and Latin America," Occasional Paper No. 6, International Center for Economic Growth, ICS Press, San Francisco, 1988.

Ramos, Joseph. "Auge y Caída de los mercados de capitales en Chile: 1975–1983," in F. Morandé and K. Schmidt-Hebbel (eds.), *Del Auge a la Crisis de 1982*. Santiago: ILADES, 1988.

Schmidt-Hebbel, Klaus. "Consumo e Inversión en Chile (1974–1982): Una Interpretación Real del Boom," in F. Morandé and K. Schmidt-Hebbel (eds.), *Del Auge a la Crisis de 1982*, Santiago: ILADES, 1988.

Tagle, Arturo. "Control de Operaciones Bancarias con Conglomerados de Empresas Relacionadas," Información Financiera, SBIF, July 1988.

Undurraga, Sergio. "Política de Desarrollo de un Mercado de Capitales Moderno y Eficiente para Chile," in *Estudios Monetarios III*, Banco Central de Chile, (July 1974), 41–63.

Valdés, Salvador. "Orígenes de la Crisis de la Deuda: œNos Sobreendeudamos o nos Prestaron en Exceso?" Estudios Públicos 33, Verano, 1989, 135–174.

3 BANKING STRUCTURE OF CHINA

Zhou Lin

This chapter is written generally for those who want to know about banking, banking services, and facilities, in China, for those and who want to maximize effective use of such banking services and facilities, for students in banking and commerce. For corporate executives, and for bankers themselves. An endeavor has been made to present the materials simply and concisely.

In the past ten years, the evolution of the financial system in China has been significant. The present financial system is diversified and sophisticated, and is expected to continue to make considerable progress in light of the growth of the Chinese economy.

The Chinese financial system consists of banks and nonbank financial institutions. The banking system is controlled and supervised by the Central Bank (People's Bank of China) and the Ministry of Finance. Figure 3-1 gives a clear picture of the banking system.

The nonbank financial institutions are controlled and supervised by various government departments and agencies as well as by the Central Bank. Figure 3-2 gives a clear and concise illustration of the nonbank financial institutions.

The first section of this chapter describes the current bank and non-

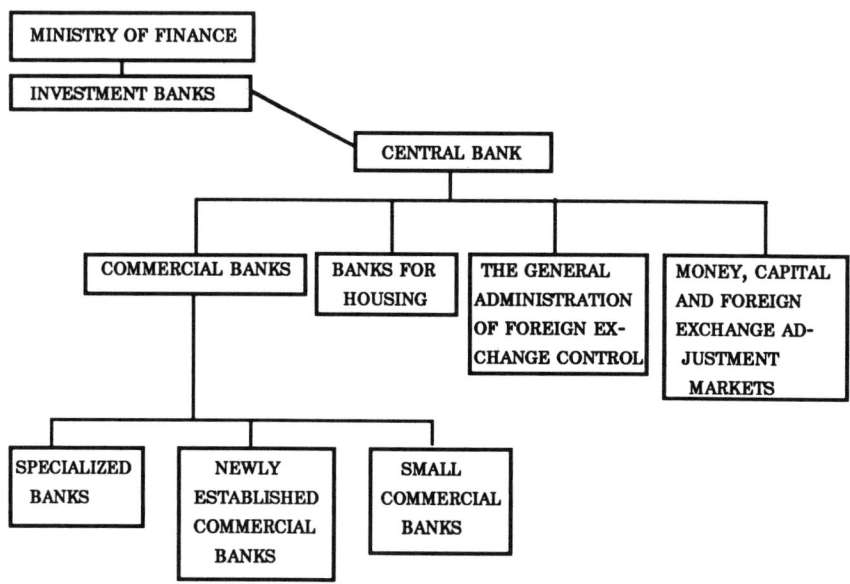

Figure 3-1. The Chinese Banking System: Subordinate Relationship in Business.

bank financial institutions in China. The second section describes briefly the evolution of China's banking structure. The third section describes the regulation and supervision that is necessary for a newly developed banking structure. This description includes the Central Bank, planning for banks, cash control by banks, supervision of commercial banks and other financial institutions, interest rates, monetary policy, and foreign-exchange control. The fourth section describes the development of principal banking operations. It reviews how the modern banking operations have been introduced to Chinese banking, including expanding short- and medium-equipment loans, loans to urban and rural collective and individual enterprises or household, the introduction of trust deposits and custodian accounts, reform of the measures of settlement of account (mode of payment), and resumption and development of bilateral clearing with socialist countries. The fifth section describes the internationalization and globalization of Chinese bank and banking. Three focuses are presented: 1) overseas Chinese financial institutions; 2) foreign financial institutions in China; and 3) China's foreign loan obligation. Abbreviations used in this chapter for China's financial institutions are given in figure 3-3.

BANKING STRUCTURE OF CHINA 115

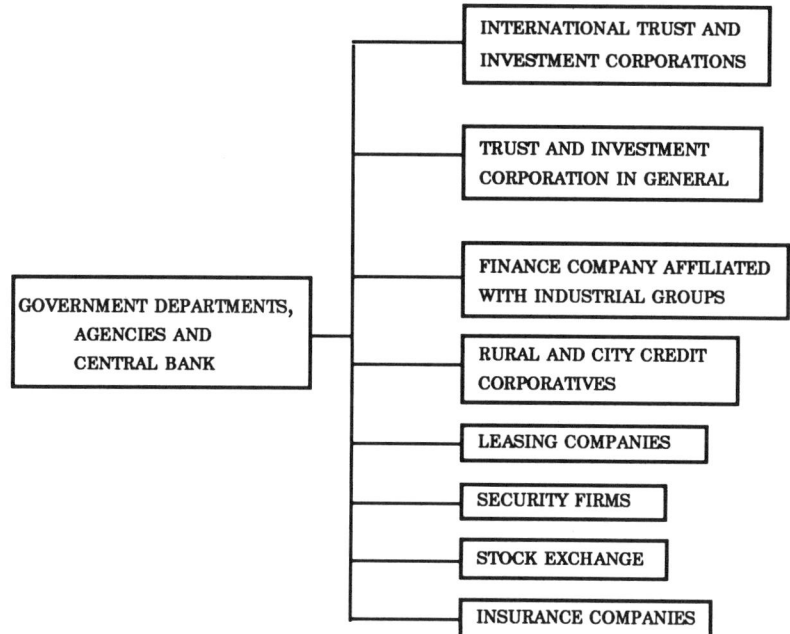

Figure 3.2. Nonbank Financial Institutions.

1. Current Bank Structure

1.1. Commercial Banks

1.1.1. Specialized Banks. The most important commercial banks in present-day China are three big commercial banks that nearly monopolize the banking transaction.

1.1.1.1. The Bank of China (BOC). The Bank of China was established in 1912. After the establishment of the People's Republic, the bank was reorganized as a state bank specializing in foreign exchange and foreign trade. It has played an important role in foreign exchange operations and international settlements and in the promotion of the country's trade and economic relations with the rest of the world. The implementation of China's open door policy has brought about a leap forward to the business development of BOC. The bank entered a new phase of business expansion with the decision by the State Council in March 1979 that the bank was to be an economic entity under its jurisdiction.

ABC—The Agricultural Bank of China	ICBC—The Industrial and Commercial Bank of China
BOC—The Bank of China	PBC—The People's Bank of China
BCC—The Bank of Communication of China	PCBC—The People's Construction Bank of China
CITIC—The Chinese International Trust and Investment Corporation	PICC—The People's Insurance Company of China
	SGAEC—State General Administration of Foreign Exchange Control
CITIC IB—CITIC Industrial Bank	
CIB—China Investment Bank	
CVIC—China Venturetech Investment Corporation	SITCO—The Shanghai Investment and Trust Corporation

Figure 3-3. Abbreviations for China's Financial Institutions.

In 1987, the Bank of China achieved considerable success by opening up new business areas under the guidance of the general policies of domestic reform as well as opening up to the rest of the world. By the end of 1987, the Bank's total assets aggregated to 441,968 billion yuan (yuan is the unit of Chinese national currency RMB (Renminbi)). The balance of the Bank's domestic foreign exchange deposits was at a record high of US$ 1.625 billion, and so was the balance of its lending and investment, amounting to US$ 12.406 billion.

1987 was also the first year in which BOC started its medium-term strategy for widening its sources of domestic funds. In order to keep up with the reform of the financial structure and obtain more Renminbi funds, BOC added another 153 branches and offices at home. By the close of 1987, the number of offices totalled 522 (exclusive of savings deposit offices) with a staff of around 30,000.

In 1987, BOC opened representative offices in Frankfurt and Panama, a subbranch in Sydney, Australia, and nine subbranches in the Hong Kong and Macao region. The year-end figure showed that the total number of BOC's overseas branches (including those of subsidiaries of the BOC Group in the region) increased to 398 with a total staff of 12,600. BOC's correspondent banks numbered 3922 located in 154 countries and regions.

1.1.1.2. The Agricultural Bank of China (ABC). This bank has the functions of managing agricultural credits, deposit taking, providing leadership for rural credit cooperatives, and training accountants for the people's communes. The objective of this institution is to strengthen the rural finance in the vast countryside where 50% to 60% of the nation's currency circulates. In so doing, it allows the PBC to concentrate on managing industrial and commercial credit in urban areas and on the coordination of overall monetary control in the country. Since the announcement of the policy of opening to the outside world, all specialized banks were allowed to handle foreign-currency operations. The ABC was restablished in February 1979 for the fourth time. Previously, three attempts to form this bank were made in 1951, 1955, and 1963. Each time it was subsequently abolished.

In 1987 ABC experienced continual progress and steady expansion. Under the guidelines of reforming the economic structure, opening to the outside world, and invigorating the domestic economy, ABC speeded up its own reform. In the process, it made new achievements in strengthening the management of loan projects, raising capital using efficiency, improving bank functions, etc. By the end of 1987, total deposits of the Agricultural Bank were 149,795 billion yuan and loans were 232,314 billion yuan. Operating offices at all levels totaled more than 44,000 with a total staff of 413,000. During 1987, ABC strove to raise more funds by adding 6183 saving offices to its operation network, improving services, and introducing new categories of deposits, pension agencies, housing savings, specialized production cost accounts, etc. By year-end, balance of ABC savings deposits had increased by 65.4%.

ABC's external businesses continued to expand. The bank obtained four credits amounting to US$ 338 million from the World Bank and International Fund for Agricultural Development to support projects for the development of farming, animal husbandry, processing, storage, and preservation, among other things. Foreign commercial loans were used to support Sino-foreign joint ventures and cooperatives that were in short supply domestically. To stimulate the development of an export-oriented economy, ABC branches in the coastal areas and special economic zones opened foreign-currency deposit and loan businesses.

1.1.1.3. The Industrial and Commercial Bank of China (ICBC). ICBC was established on January 1, 1984 in Beijing. ICBC is an economic entity under the jurisdiction of the State Council. It has taken over the business of industrial and commercial credit and savings deposits, formerly handled by the People's Bank of China (PBC). The principal tasks of ICBC are to gather funds; to strengthen the management of credit funds; to support the development of industrial production; to back the expansion of commodity circulation; to support the development of collective and individual enterprises; to advance the technical innovation of enterprises; and to play an active role in adjustment and redistribution of funds for economic construction.

The major business of the ICBC are

1. to collect savings deposits of urban citizens, deposits of industrial and commercial enterprises, institutions, schools, etc.;
2. to exercise, as authorized by PBC, unified management of the working capital of state-owned industrial and commercial enterprises;
3. to extend working-capital loans to state-owned, urban collective, and industrial and commercial enterprises;
4. to supervise technical innovation funds of industrial and commercial enterprises, and extend loans for technical innovation at the same time;
5. to do trust business as a trustee or agent, in the capacities of leasing and consultant;
6. to handle settlements of transfer accounts and cash;
7. to carry out economic investigation and provide information service; and
8. to deal with other business commissioned by PBC.

Since its founding in 1984, ICBC has established a large nationwide network of 24,000 branches and offices with 440,000 staff members. It has over 3 million corporate accounts, and over 300 million savings accounts of urban citizens. In 1987, the total assets of ICBC reached 493.9 billion yuan and total loans outstanding amounted to 444.8 billion yuan. The total deposits and loans outstanding of ICBC took up 48% and 49%, respectively, of those in the aggregate of the financial institutions of the country.

By the end of 1987, the total foreign-currency savings and deposits of ICBC had reached US$ 300 million, while foreign-currency loans outstanding were US$ 100 million. The branches engaged in foreign-exchange business have made corresponding RMB loans to clients, thus conveniencing the clients greatly and efficiently backing them. In addition, those joint-venture bank and leasing cooperations in which ICBC is involved have obtained good economic results.

1.1.2. Newly Established Commercial Banks.

1.1.2.1. The Bank of Communications of China (BCC). In 1984, former Chinese Premier Zhao Ziyang called for the establishment of a new national comprehensive bank to cope with the economic reforms, which had an equal footing with the specialized banks. The BCC was reorganized in response. First founded in 1908, BCC used to be one of the four major banks in old China. But in 1958 all its domestic business was taken over by other banks, and only its Hong Kong branch continued operation.

The reorganized BCC has four features. First, it is China's only shareowner-controlled bank, unlike other major banks in the country, which are totally state owned. The state controls the shares of the bank, and localities, enterprises, and individuals can buy their shares voluntarily, a system that can help the bank raise funds from various channels.

Second, of all major Chinese banks, the BCC is the first to seek self-balance in funds and resume sole responsibility for its profits and losses. In the past, when the egalitarian system of "sharing the same big pot" dominated, China's specialized banks relied on the central bank for funds, while enterprises relied on specialized banks. The BCC has pioneered a mode of operation that accords with the economic law while allowing enterprises to choose the bank and the bank to choose its clients. Third, the BCC is a multifunctional, comprehensive bank that can handle the business of all financial institutions, including negotiable securities and insurance. Fourth, unlike all other banks that open branches in accordance with the country's administrative setup, the BCC has set up branches only in economic centers whose business also covers their surrounding areas. Its head office is based in China's biggest industrial city, Shanghai, instead of in the capital city of Beijing.

Following the rapid expansion of business, by the end of 1987, BCC had assets totaling 44, 106, 166 yuan, total liabilities of 41, 511, 139, 899 yuan, and a net income of 884, 189, 295 yuan.

1.1.2.2. CITIC Industrial Bank (CITIC IB). CITIC IB was established in February 1987 with the approval of the PBC and the State Council, and started business in April of the same year. CITIC IB is a bank directly under and wholly owned by Chinese International Trust and Investment Corporation (CITIC). It is a state-owned enterprise involved in financial activities domestically and abroad. The bank is a comprehensive bank like the BCC.

As an independent enterprise, CITIC IB is authorized to set its own business policies and is reponsible for its profits and losses. However, its business is conducted and administrated by the PBC. The head office of CITIC IB located in Beijing. To meet the need of economic development and business expansion, it may set up branches in China and abroad with the approval of the PBC.

CITIC IB handles and is entrusted to operate the following business:

1. local and foreign currency deposits and loans;
2. export credit, arranging or participating in syndicated loans;

3. domestic and international interbank lending, borrowing, deposits, and discounts, in order to establish correspondent relationships with banks and other financial institution;
4. trade-related or non-trade-related international clearing and domestic or international remittance;
5. issuance of (or acting as an agent for issuance of) bonds and stocks in both local and foreign currencies, as well as securities trading for its own account or for the accounts of its customers;
6. foreign-exchange transactions for its customers, exchanging foreign currency for local currency, arranging swaps between foreign and local currency for its customers, and acting as an agent for selling traveler's checks and handling credit cards;
7. domestic and international financial leasing businesses;
8. trust, investment, guarantee, financial consultancy, and investment insurance business;
9. other banking business entrusted by the State Council and the PBC as well as CITIC; and
10. international financial activities with the approval from relevant authorities.

Since February 1987, there has been a rapid development in all the business lines of CITIC IB. In the first year of its operation, the Bank floated three bond issues in international markets in the name of CITIC, amounting to the equivalent of US$ 450 million. The RMB deposits in 1987 increased by 200% and foreign currency deposits by 31%, as compared with the previous year. The Bank made new loans in RMB totaling 285 million yuan, and those in foreign currencies totaling the equivalent of US$ 775 million. By the end of 1987, the Bank had a total assets amounting to 8,759, 129,678 yuan.

1.1.3. Small Local Commercial Banks. There are several small local commercial banks, such as Development Bank of Guangdong, Merchant Bank of Shenzhen (special economic zone), and Minxing Bank of Fujian province. Although those banks are small in size, they are comprehensive banks. All of them are allowed to undertake the following businesses:

1. take all kinds of deposits;
2. perform all kinds of lending activities, such as working-capital lending, fixed-asset lending, acceptance and discount bills;
3. perform settlement and remittance both at home and abroad;

4. issue, or act as an agent in the insurance of, stocks, bonds, and other securities, as well as perform security transactions;
5. Perform foreign-exchange transactions;
6. Undertake interbank lending and depositing;
7. Organize and participate in consortium loan and syndicated loan at home and abroad;
8. Undertake all kinds of trusts, investments, leases, consultancy, notarization, guarantee, real estate, and all sorts of agent services at home and abroad; and
9. Conduct other businesses permitted by PBC.

1.2. Investment Banks and Company

In China, only four banks and one corporation can be considered as investment banking institutions.

1.2.1. The People's Construction Bank of China (PCBC). PCBC was founded in 1954 as an institution specializing in handling the state's investment in capital construction. Its main tasks were to distribute funds from budgetary appropriations to various state enterprises for use as fixed capital and to ensure a smooth progress of planned capital construction. These funds were dispensed to various enterprises as nonrepayable, interest-free grants. Thus PCBC was basically a fiscal agent of the Ministry of Finance, rather than a bank.

As a part of the economic reform, PCBC underwent a significant change. The State Council of PRC decreed that, beginning in January 1981, all appropriation for capital construction to enterprises with independent accounting would be in the form of bank loans. Since then, the ability to repay the loans, with interest on time, became a criterion for judging the economic efficiency of a project. PCBC was given the authority to investigate the borrowing enterprises and to decide whether a project was feasible or not. Thus PCBC has in essence joined the banking system for the first time. Funds, however, still come from the budget. But the budgetary appropriations for capital construction will constitute a gradually diminishing portion of total capital construction. The balance thereof will be made up by bank credit. These new developments mean that PCBC was able to withhold or provide such investment funds at its discretion. In other words, PCBC could direct investment to the more efficient and productive firms.

In 1987, PCBC expanded rapidly under the guidance of the policy of reform and openess. Its total balance of deposits amounted to 82.35 billion yuan, and its total balance of loans amounted to 99.267 billion yuan. Loans appropriations from government investment amounted to 109.137 billion yuan. Total assets at the end of 1987 amounted to 277.8 billion yuan.

In 1987, PCBC established more than 3000 new savings deposit offices, received widely individual savings deposits, and enhanced the balance of savings deposits from 96 million yuan to 2327 million yuan. During this year, PCBC issued 1 billion financial bonds for the first time, to raise relatively long-term and stable credit funds. At the same time, PCBC issued construction bonds amounting to 5 billion yuan as an agent both for government and enterprises. By the end of 1987, 26 nationwide and/or regional borrowing networks for short-term funds had been established, and the total short-term borrowings amounted to 25.5 billion yuan.

In 1987, six branches of PCBC established foreign exchange operations. Shenzhen Branch received nearly US$ 100 million foreign currency deposits. Shanghai Branch successfully raised a syndicate loan of US$ 340 million for the Shanghai 300 Thousand Ton Ethylene Project. Now PCBC has established business cooperation or correspondent relationship with 22 banks all over the world.

1.2.2. China Investment Bank (CIB). The bank was established in December 1981. It serves as the intermediary to dispense loans from the World Bank and Asian Development Bank to small and medium-sized projects. For example, the World Bank began in May 1981 to implement a lending program to China of US$ 800 million. In order to increase the program's impact on Chinese economic growth, the World Bank chose to invest in smaller units rather than in large projects. Thus, a financial agency was needed to distribute the loans inside China according to the World Bank's guideline and subject to its monitoring.

Since its founding, CIB has developed rapidly. Beside loans from those international financial institutions, the bank raised foreign currency funds from overseas financial markets. The bank has business relationships with 130 foreign banks in 23 different countries.

At the end of 1987, the bank had 55 branches across the country, financing more than 700 projects, with a total loan of 5 billion yuan.

1.2.3. Two Newly Established Banks for Housing. Housing remains a crucial problem in China. Farmers in rural areas are able to build their own houses at a relatively low cost. But those who live in urban areas cannot afford to invest a big sum of money in housing. The Chinese government is encouraging certain localities to form financial institutions to take short- or long-term deposits from those who wish to buy a house and grant long-term loans to the building industry or individuals who wants to buy an apartment or house.

Under these circumstances, two banks for housing have been founded in recent years. Bank for Housing at Kifoo began to operate in December 1987 and Bank for Housing at Bengbu in May 1988. Although they are local banks and small in size, they represent a new rising force.

1.2.4. China Venturetech Investment Corporation (CVIC). CVIC was founded in early 1986, affiliating with the State Science Commission and the PBC. It is dedicated to assist research and development technological ventures by providing investment and managerial support to small and medium-sized companies and to new business. It targets small and new start-up companies, irrespective of whether they are owned by the state, collectives, or individuals. Its investment focuses are information technology, new materials, and other forms of emerging technology; it also helps existing firms to upgrade their technological level.

Utilizing venture capital investment in China is a new avenue for promoting technological innovation and its commercialization. The bank aims not only to diversify the nation's financing mechanism, but also to inject an entrepreneurial spirit into industries too timid or too financially strapped to undertake risks.

Within the past two years, with an authorized capital of 40 million yuan, CVIC's business operation increased by a big margin. Its total assets rose from 61 million yuan to 33,240 million yuan in 1987. The total investments grew from 47,735 million yuan in 1986 to 225.55 million yuan in 1987. CVIC invested in and loaned to about 85 projects, and the total portfolio investment in 1987 reached 217.9 million yuan.

1.3. Nonbank Financial Institutions

As a result of the process of economic and financial reform, nonbank financial institutions are mushrooming. They can be classified into the following groups.

1.3.1. International Trust and Investment Corporations. There are 735 trust and investment corporations mostly in big cities and coastal ports. About 80 are international trust and investment corporations. Their major functions are to facilitate the introduction of foreign investment and advanced technology into China. They also promote joint foreign and Chinese ventures and deal with various foreign investment schemes such as compensation, trade, counterpurchase agreements, and so on.

Through the activities of two big international trust and investment corporations, we can see clearly their far-reaching impact on China's economic and financial development.

1.3.1.1. The Chinese International Trust and Investment Corporation (CITIC). The CITIC was formed in October 1979 under the State Council. It undertakes economic and technological cooperation, investing, finance, and trade at home and abroad. Thus, this corporation is sometimes considered a semibanking institution. During the ten years since its inception, CITIC has grown into a conglomerate of diversified interests including production, technology, finance, trade, and services.

CITIC has invested mainly in China's eastern coastal area, which has a good infrastructure and strong technical labor force. By the end of 1987, CITIC had organized 69 Sino-foreign joint or contractual ventures and 124 domestic ventures of similar types, as well as 10 solely owned enterprises. Its business covers energy development, communications and transportation, engineering and construction, metallurgy and minerals, building materials, light and chemical industries, textiles, machinery and electric products, fishery and animal husbandry, tourism, and new technologies. CITIC has the following subsidiaries:

CITIC Industrial Bank
CITIC Travel Inc.
Sunburst Energy Development Co. Ltd.
CITIC Technology Inc.
CITIC Trading Inc.
CITIC Development Inc.
China International Economic Consultance Inc. (CIEC)
Poly Technologies Inc.
CITIC Real Estate Corporation
China Southwest Energy Resources United Development Co.

To develop its own industrial base, it established

CITIC Tianjin Industrial Development Inc.
CITIC Shanghai Inc.
CITIC Shenzhen Inc.

CITIC (Holdings) has established three exclusively owned subsidiaries in the U.S.A. Canada, and Australia, and all have reported favorable investment returns. As a result, CITIC has become a multitiered enterprise group with a registered capital of 3 billion yuan (as against the original 1.2 billion) and total assets of 14.219 billion yuan.

1.3.1.2. The Shanghai Investment and Trust Corporation (SITCO).
SITCO is a state enterprise under the direction of the Shanghai Municipal People's Government (SMPG). The SMPG has granted SITCO special right to raise funds or borrowing loans. The SMPG has received preferential treatment allowing for reduction or exemption from various duties and taxes in connection with the use of foreign capital provided by SITCO.

SITCO raises funds in both domestic and international markets by various means, including borrowings and bonds issues. The funds raised are mainly used for investment in and financing of corporations and projects in Shanghai involved in commercial construction in the region. As of the end of 1987, SITCO had received four long and medium-term foreign loans totaling approximately US$ 105 million from Japanese and Hong Kong commercial banks, and had available short-term foreign-currency credit facilities with 16 foreign banks for a total of US$ 163 million. In January 1986, SITCO sold its first overseas bond issue and issued 25 billion yen bonds in the Japanese domestic market. The proceeds were used to finance manufacturing and industrial enterprises in Shanghai. SITCO has participated in hundreds of leasing transactions with foreign and Hong Kong corporations, financial institutions, and manufacturers. Items provided include capital equipment and technology. SITCO was authorized to handle international settlement business in 1986. As of December 31, 1987, SITCO had an already established correspondent relationship with more than 77 financial institutions in 18 countries. At the end of 1987, SITCO had equity investments totaling approximately US$ 108 million in 60 ventures including 23 Sino-foreign ventures, 33 joint ventures with other Chinese partners, and 4 wholly owned subsidiaries. The other international trust and investment corporation in other cities were largely formed by using SITCO as a prototype.

1.3.2. Trust and investment Corporations in General. The other 655 trust and investment corporations conduct trust business, including trust deposit, trust loans, and trust investment; issue shares and bonds on the domestic market and handle the repayment of principal, interest, and dividends; and provide various consultancy service on economic matters.

The reason why the trust and investment corporations have developed so rapidly within such a short time period can be traced back to the 1980 reform of intergovernmental fiscal relations. Before this reform, the approach to budgetary policy, later characterized as "eating out of the big pot," undermined the revenue effort of local governments and led to waste. The reform changed this situation and a method of "separate kitchens" was instituted. The governments of different levels, even enterprises, were assigned expenditure and revenue responsibilities. Both local governments and enterprises were allowed to keep certain portions of revenue for their own expenditure. This kind of money was called extra-budgetary funds, which amounted to 180 billion yuan at the end of 1987. This huge amount of funds naturally became the source of trust business.

1.3.3. Finance Companies Affiliated with Industrial Groups. Financial companies of this type were first established in 1987. At the end of July 1988, there were only 15. They may increase more rapidly following the creation of new industrial groups in China. This kind of company can help to introduce advanced equipment and technology in China in order to support technical transformation of existing enterprises, improve the quality of products, and promote export.

In their main business scope, it is difficult to distinguish AFFILIATED FINANCE COMPANIES from trust and investment corporations. For example, the Ever Bright Finance Company, a subsidiary of the Ever Bright Holding Company, specifies its business scope as follows:

- trust deposit and loan-operations of Chinese and foreign currencies inside and outside China,
- domestic and international financial leasing operations,
- operations inside and outside China involving investment, equity joint venture, and cooperative joint venture,
- operations of borrowing foreign currencies from outside China and issuing securities of its own and for others on commission both inside and outside China,
- issuing Letters of Guarantee on foreign currencies, and
- operations of providing credit reference consultancy and all other financial operations authorized by the state or entrusted by PBC or the State General Administration of Foreign Exchange Control.

There are also 37 independent financial companies that act as the intermidiaries of interbank borrowing, rediscounting the banks' acceptance bills, etc.

1.3.4. Credit Cooperatives.
1.3.4.1. Rural Credit Cooperatives. Rural credit cooperatives were first founded in most revolutionary bases of the Red Army before the founding of the People's Republic of China. At that time, they were called *peasant's own banks*. After the founding of the P.R.C., during the period of 1950–1970, the rural credit cooperatives were gradually transformed into units of the ABC, which was not good for their further development, because their independence was restricted by ABC.

The Chinese government started to reform the rural credit cooperatives in 1981, and, at the end of 1985, more than 80% of them had been restructured. After successful reformation, their special features can now be characterized as follows:

1. Rehabilitating and strengthening the relation with the larger farmer units. At the end of 1985, the total equity shares paid by the farmers amounting to 1.16 billion yuan. About 80% of farms jointed the local rural credit cooperation. The directors of the board were elected by votes instead of appointment by the ABC branches.
2. While obtaining more autonomy in granting loans, the PBC also reduce their reserve requirement on deposit from 40% to 12%, and thus the rural credit cooperatives have more money to extend loans to the farmers and enterprises in the rural area. By the end of 1987, the total outstanding balance of both borrowing and lending reached 15.53 billion yuan.
3. The formation of a rural credit cooperative union of a country.

Table 3-1. Annual Changes in Deposits and Loans of Rural Credit Cooperative (Hundred Million Yuan)

Item	1979	1981	1983	1985	1987
Total Deposits	49.91	47.27	97.51	100	262.87
Collective deposit	4.58	7.76	−29.23	−18.01	6
Township enterprise	21.93	0.26	28.63	−8.99	13.02
Household deposit	22.76	52.52	91.79	118.21	239.6
Other deposit	0.64	−13.27	6.32	0.3	4.25
Total Loans	2.48	14.74	42.59	45.43	202.84
Collective loans	0.72	1.17	−6.53	2.95	19.87
Township enterprise	2.08	4.35	17.81	29.41	93.46
Household loan	−0.32	9.22	31.31	13.07	89.51

Source: Investigation and Statistic Bureau, PBC.

At the end of 1987, there were more than 2100 rural credit cooperative unions across the country. They serve as a clearing center and management agency of rural credit cooperatives. They also act as a correspondent agency for each individual rural credit cooperative with the financial institution in the cities. The rural credit cooperative reform occurred alongside the rapid development of the commodity economy in the rural area and great increases in farmer's income. Total deposits and loans of all rural credit cooperatives reached the record-breaking amount of 12.29 billion yuan. The average per-capita deposit was 118 yuan. Annual data for rural credit cooperatives are given in table 3-1.

In addition to the rural credit cooperative, there are also different types of financial institutions operated by farmers in the countryside. In essence, most of them are cooperatives and are classified as 1) farmers mutual funds, 2) mutual savings funds to relieve poverty, 3) financial trust cooperative, 4) farmers mutual insurance cooperative, and 5) farmer's share funds.

1.3.4.2. City Credit Cooperatives. Most city credit cooperatives are concentrated in the big and medium-sized cities instead of in the country side, where rural credit cooperatives were founded. The development of city credit cooperatives has also been very fast. The total number has increased from 1207 at the end of 1985 to 2326 at the end of June 1988. The city credit cooperative is a collective-owner financial institution. It is operated independently and is responsible for its own profits and losses. It is not allowed to affiliate with any other institutions or government agencies. The city credit cooperatives are operated under the direct direction of PBC, unlike the rural cooperatives, which are supervised by the ABC.

All city credit cooperatives must open deposit and loan accounts with the local PBC. They must submit credit and cash plans and other accounting and financial reports to the local PBC to facilitate the supervision by PBC. They are also required to pay reserve deposits according to the prescribed ratio and to apply the same State-Fixed interest rates for deposit-taking and loan-granting as the other financial institutions. The city credit cooperative can raise equity capital only from collective and individual enterprises, as well as individual households. The minimum equity capital is 100,000 yuan.

The business scope for each city credit cooperative is as follows:

1. to take deposits and grant loans only with collective and individual enterprises in the city;

Table 3-2. Basic Statistics of City Cooperatives (End Third Quarter of 1987) (10 Thousand Yuan)

Province	Number of city cooperatives	Balance of Deposit	Balance of Loan	Profit Realized	Equity Share Collective	Equity Share Individual
Henan	259	89,975.82	60,980.24	1,853.18	1,682.91	1,325.02
Hebai	48	10,709	8,675	451	214	241
Hunan	18	6,350	5,316	57.9	120.25	118.35
Guangdong	57	8,998.39	18,915.2	211.8	894.57	488
Guangxi	55	20,609	9,596	448.57	220.36	139.3
Sichuan	108	12,521.8	13,310.2	235.8	967.71	807.04
Guizhou	16	7,637.2	6,306.3	103.4	48	237.8
Yunnan	10	5,348.7	3,463.8	178.8	48.3	7.7
Shanxi	30	15,763.27	11,749.65	390.29	235.6	138.86
Gansu	20	7,680	4,433	165	174	150
Qinghai	6	1,539.4	836	40.41	0.9	21.5
Ningxia	2	525	262	2	2	15.55
Xinjiang	12	786	887	10.89	37.5	64.1
Total	1,550	540,577.34	480,754.15	10,368.06	10,368.83	8,791.37

Source: Administration of Financial Management, PBC.

2. to take individual savings deposits; and
3. to handle those securities approved by PBC.

The rapid development of the city credit cooperative is a natural result of the emergence of numerous collective and individual enterprises in China and can be seen from the data in table 3-2.

There are also 10 leasing companies and 34 security firms that have been set up in recent years. To date, the total number of nonbank financial institutions is almost 63,000.

1.4. Insurance Company

1.4.1. The People's Insurance Company of China (PICC). PICC was formed on October 20th, 1949, with the head office in Beijing. Since then, it has branched out through the country. From 1949 to 1959, the total income premiums from policy sales reached 1.6 billion yuan, yet the total claims paid were only 0.3 billion. The surplus was used for general economic rehabilitation. Due to historical reasons, all domestic business was suspended from 1959–1979. PICC resumed writing all classes of insurance business at the end of 1979. There has been a tremendous development in all aspects ranging from income premium, types of business written to the size of the company itself, etc. Between 1980 and 1987, the company's income premium rose at an annual rate of 50%. At the end of the first quarter of 1988, PICC's accumulated income from both domestic and foreign business reached 9.1 billion yuan, the amount of the claims paid totaling 3.3 billion yuan.

Since 1980, a profound change has taken place in China's domestic insurance. The types of insurance written have extended from enterprise property insurance alone before reinstatement of business to over 130 lines. Among these are conveyances, cargo transportation, household property, breeding, plantation, industrial life, personal accident, and old age pension for employees in collectively run enterprises. The types of foreign business written are now close to 80 in number as opposed to over 20 types in the past. The new additions comprise coverages involving comparatively complicated technologies, such as off-shore oil exploration, nuclear power station, etc. PICC now covers most types of insurance in international markets. Although the world insurance markets have slowed in recent years. PICC has nevertheless increased business interflows with its counterparts in various parts of the world through writing reinsurance business after an in-depth investigation and study of the world markets.

Concurrent with the increase in its business portfolio and expansion of its servicing area, the number of employees of the company has expanded correspondingly. PICC at present maintains more than 2700 branches and subbranches in 28 provinces, autonomous regions, and municipalities (except Tibet and Taiwan) with a workforce of over 67,600. To meet the need of business development, a great number of insurance agents have been set up in various cities and towns.

1.4.2. New Insurance Companies. Since 1988, in order to break the monopoly of insurance business by PICC and to encourage competition in the insurance market, the Chinese Government has approved four insurance companies and has also permitted some commercial banks to enter the insurance market. Those newly established insurance companies are Life Insurance Company of China, Life Insurance Company of Sichuan, Pingan Insurance Company of Shenzhen, and Agriculture Insurance Company of Xinjiang Autonomous Region. Moreover, there are also insurance activities conducted by cooperatives or mutual funds.

1.5. Postal Savings

One of the byproducts of economic reforms has been a sharp increase in both household disposable income and savings. The marginal propensity to save has risen to record levels, especially in the rural areas, where per capita income has nearly tripled in the past eight years. The existing banks and nonbank financial institutions could not accommodate the savings increases from households. Upon an agreement reached between the PBC and the Ministry of Post and Telecommunication, the postal savings business was reinstituted in the spring of 1986, after a period of nearly 30 years.

The advantage of postal savings is manifold. There are post offices in each village and a number in each city. Nearly 90% of post offices could be delegated to taking deposits. This saved the considerable expense of opening branch offices of a bank. At the end of 1986, there were 2794 postal savings offices with a total balance of savings deposits of 56 billion yuan. At the end of 1987, the postal savings offices increased to 9477 with a total savings-deposit balance of 3.76 billion yuan.

1.6. Emerging of Financial Markets

The emerging of financial markets in China has aroused great interest from the financial community all over the world. To see the first financial market operating in a socialist state, missions from Wall Street, London, Paris, Frankfurt, and some eastern countries have visited China frequently during recent years. For example a delegation of the New York Stock Exchange, headed by Chairman John Phelan, came to Beijing in May 1986 to attend a joint seminar.

1.6.1. The Background of the Opening Up of Financial Markets. Before economic reform, the funds management system was based on the vertical allocation system through the big specialized banks that were established and operated in accordance with the principle of "money goes with materials." During that period, the financial market was rejected. All specialized banks have had their own funds from the time the central bank system was set up. To date, the banks' flow of funds still has not greatly broken away from the pattern of vertical transfer. Under this pattern, the horizontal flow of funds, wide-ranged mobilization, flexible finance and the efficent utilization of funds are constrained both vertically by bank segmentation and horizontally by regional segregation, thus obstructing the horizontal flow of commodities, services, and technologies. This leads to a slower economic development than would otherwise be the case.

With the deepening of economic and financial reform, the market mechanism has been gradually introduced into the national economy; markets of consumer goods, producer goods, technologies, etc. are being set up one by one and have developed in different places. Moreover, the role of banking has been gradually recognized by the public, and financial instruments are beginning to become diversified. The monetary authorities realize more clearly that it is not only necessary to improve the financing channels, but it is also imperative to open up other channels, develop multiple financial instruments and financing institutions, and set up the financial markets according to the principles of a planned commodity economy. These facilitate horizontal economies, increase the coverage and efficiency of finance, improve the central bank's macroeconomic control, and maintain stable economic development. Furthermore, it is also necessary to gradually develop financial mechanisms with various assets and channels that will integrate direct and indirect finance and satisfy different demands of the borrowers and lenders as well. It is to achieve these objectives that the monetary authority of China has permitted and fostered open financial markets. This has marked an important break with traditional socialist economic theory and practice.

1.6.2. The Current Situation of the Financial Market in China. In recent years, financial markets have been opened up in the following fields:

1.6.2.1. The Interbank Lending Market. On January 7, 1986, the State Council promulgated the *Provisional Regulations of the People's Republic of China on the Control of Banks*, which explicitly states that "funds may be loaned between specialized banks and . . . the inter-bank rates between specialized banks shall be agreed upon through negotiation between the two parties." Based on this regulation, interbank lending activities began to increase vigorously. By the end of 1987, interbank lending markets had been established across the country in most provinces. In particular, the markets centered in Wuhan, Shenyang, Shanghai, Kaifeng, and a number of other cities experienced the most rapid development.

There are three aspects of interbank lending and borrowing. The first is the interregional lending and borrowing network, which has greatly promoted lending activities among financial institutions. Statistics show that the accumulated interbank transactions exceeded 200 billion yuan in 1987. The second is to establish a interbank market. In this market, the interest rate is determined by the supply and demand of funds, and the amount and maturity of lending are negotiated by the borrowers and lenders themselves. The third is lending through an agreement reached between different financial institutions. The specialized banks and their branches and subbranches at various localities are the main participants of the interbank market, and nonbank financial institutions such as trust and investment companies, credit cooperatives in urban and rural areas, etc., also play an active part in the market.

1.6.2.2. The Commercial Bill Acceptance and Discount Market. In 1982, intercity acceptances were first being introduced on a trial basis in Shanghai, and a year later in the cities of Chongqing, Shenyang, etc. Based on these experiments, the PBC promulgated the *Provisional Regulations on the Acceptance and Discount of Bills of Exchange* in December 1984. As a result, discount and rediscount of acceptances by commercial banks has now become regular business. Nevertheless, there are imbalances in the development among regions due to different economic conditions, with a number of cities such as Shanghai and Shenyang recording the highest rate of growth in business of volume, while others are just beginning.

1.6.2.3. Securities Market. The securities market in China is also called the long-term financial market. The maturity of the securities issued in this market are over one year. At present, the kinds of securities issued in China are as follows:

Treasury Bill. The treasury bill (TB) is issued by the Ministry of Finance. *Unlike U.S.* Treasury bills, which mature within one year, Chinese TBs mature in five years, similar to U.S. Treasury notes. Since 1981, TBs have been issued every year. By the end of 1987, the total accumulated value of the TBs issued reached 36 billion yuan; half of them were purchased by institutions and the other half went to individual purchasers. The annual interest rate of the TB is 6% for institutional purchasers and 10% for individual purchasers. TBs are sold to institutions and individuals by banks that act on behalf of the Ministry of Finance.

Bonds for the Key Construction of the State. This is kind of government bond issued by the Ministry of Finance. The maturity of the bond is three years. The annual interest rate is 6% for institutional purchasers and 10.5% for individual purchasers. In 1987, China issued 5.5 billion yuan of these bonds. These bonds were introduced in 1987 to alleviate the shortage of funds for state construction and to support the construction of the state's key projects. Individuals can buy bonds according to their own wishes, but institutions must buy the bonds according to quotas assigned by the state.

Bonds for the Construction of Key Enterprises. The maturity, interest rate, and repayment methods are all determined by the issuing enterprises. In 1987, China issued 4.5 billion yuan of these bonds. They are only sold to state-owned and collective-owned enterprises and institutions, not to individuals.

Enterprise Bond (corporate bond). These are bonds issued by enterprises with legal entities. They were first issued in 1984. Since then great progress has been made in the development of this bond market. The maturity of the majority of the bonds is less than three years, mostly one year. According to the Provisional Regulation for the Administration of Enterprise Bonds issued by the State Council, enterprises must first get the approval from the PBC before they issued any bonds. The states control the total amount of enterprise bonds issued, and the interest rates for bonds should not exceed 40% of the saving deposits rate with the same maturity.

Financial Bonds. Financial bonds are issued by financial institutions. In July 1985, with the approval of the PBC, the ABC and the ICBC began to issue 820 million yuan bonds sold only to individuals. The maturity was one year and the annual interest rate was 9%. Since then, the specialized banks in China have begun to issue financial bonds with maturity of one to three years, annual interest rates ranging from 9% to 11%. In addition, in November 1986, the Shanghai Branch of the ICBC issued 100 million yuan of local financial bonds with maturity of 14 months and as annual interest rate of 9%.

Shares. At present, the majority of the stock shares issued in China are preferred shares. Most of the shares issued by enterprises have a maturity less than five years, with fixed interest rates and dividends, but the annual return rates are not allowed to exceed 15% of the face value of the share. By the end of 1986, shares issued with fixed maturity amounted to 93% of the total shares issued—that is, most of the shares issued by the enterprises are "bond typed" shares. At present, there is a strict control over the issue of shares.

China has a primary market for securities, and this market has been growing rapidly. China's secondary security market was established only in 1986. At present, it is still in its initial stage. On August 5, 1986, Shenyang, China's fourth largest city, opened the first trading market for securities. The market was organized by Shenyang's Trust and Investment Company. One month later, on September 26, 1986, Shanghai, China's largest city, opened its first trading market for shares. The market was organized by Jinan Branch of the CITCO. Since then, trading markets for securities have been set up in many cities. At present, there are more than 50 securities markets all over China.

In April 1988, China opened trading markets for TBs in seven cities. Later on, the market expanded to 54 cities in China. By the end of 1988, markets opened all over China. As mentioned above, the market for TBs is the largest in China. Among the 60 billion yuan bonds issued, TBs accounted for two thirds. It can be expected that, with the opening of the TB secondary market, the usefulness of TBs will be greatly enhanced.

1.6.2.4. Foreign Exchange Market. In 1988, a number of local governments established foreign-exchange adjustment centers to facilitate foreign exchange transactions. Eligible Chinese enterprises, foreign enterprises, joint venture enterprises, and foreign investment funds are allowed to sell and buy foreign exchange through the centers, and prices are allowed to float according to supply and demand within a preserved range. By the end of 1988, about 39 cities, mostly coastal cities, had established foreign-exchange adjustment centers. The annual volume of turnover is around US$ 6.3 billion.

All in all, the financial market in China is currently at a stage of being opened up and developed, and further steps in this direction are intended.

In light of the realities of the country as well as the need for overall economic development, the basic strategy is to open up and improve the financial market step by step in a systematic way, e.g., from a short-term market to a long-term one, from trial cities to other cities, from coastal areas to inland areas, from developed regions to less developed regions.

2. A Brief Account of the Evolution of China's Banking Structure

Since the credit reform of 1955, the Chinese banking structure has followed the Soviet model. Under this system, the PBC was a monopoly bank. In domestic banking, it acted as the "center of cash, credit and settlement," from which the supply of money originated, into which currency held in the public sector was deposited, and through which inter-public-unit payments were made.

The function of the PBC under this system was twofold. First, by overseeing the bank account of each state enterprise, it maintained a microfinancial surveillance over these firms and ensured that they would operate according to the credit plan. Secondly, the PBC had a macromonetary function aimed at quantitative control of money supply and the prevention of inflation. Actually, in performing the surveillance function, the PBC became a captive of the state enterprise and, effectively, a limitless supplier of money.

The PBC had to carry out the macromonetary control function in a passive and accommodating way. Bank loans were granted only on the basis of short-term inventory, so in reality the PBC adopted the "real bills" doctrine. Moreover, the PBC could not limit the creation of currency since currency could be withdrawn from the PBC for transactions involving the nonpublic sector, and the PBC had no control over the size of these transactions. Therefore, it could only attempt to influence the quantity of money in circulation through currency absorption. The main instrument of absorption was to increase saving deposits from the household. As a result, saving deposits occupied a much more strategic position in China than in the West.

In 1979, China entered a new stage of economic reform and development. In October 1984, the Communist Party of China at its First Plenary Session of the 12th Party Congress adopted the *Decision on Reform of Economic System*. In the Decision, the Central Committee decided on the further implementation of the policy of stimulating the domestic economy and opening it up to the outside world. In addition, the Decision accelerated economic system reform; to give farmers more freedom to cultivate and sell their crops; to give enterprises more managerial autonomy; and to set up a market system aiming to promote the development of a socialist commodity economy. Thus banks, loans, interest rates, and exchange rates became important instruments of macroeconomic control.

On September 17th, 1983, the State Council made the decision that the PBC should function solely as the Central Bank of China instead of functioning dually as both as issuing bank and a commercial bank. Thus, the PBC became an integral part of the government that exercises supervision over all financial institutions. It is a bank of the government, an issuance bank, and a bank's bank, but it also has the function of administration and management of finance on behalf of the central government.

The opening of financial markets is important for banking structure reform. Beginning in 1985, both money and capital markets emerged not only in the big cities but also in some medium-sized cities. The objectives of banking structure reform may be summarized as follows:

1. To encourage competition in the banking industry in order to increase the economic efficiency of both banks and nonbank financial institutions, in part by breaking down the oligopoly of the large specialized banks.
2. To expand the magnitude of credit. In the past, only banking credit was permitted in China. Commercial credit among enterprises, private credit, or any other form of credit was strictly prohibited. This was a serious obstacle for the development of the economy. The breakdown of the oligopoly of the big banks and the establishment of different kinds of financial institutions stimulated an increase in deposits. From 1978 to 1987, the annual growth rate of banking deposit jumped from 10% to 28%; likewise, by the end of 1987, loans were 4.9 times the amount of loans in 1978. Thus, the banking system became a crucial financial resource for the development of the national economy.
3. To facilitate the internationalization of banking. Prior to 1978, the economic policy of China was based on the closed-door approach. At the time, China had very few economic relations with the outside world. The economic and banking reform together with the open door policy, has developed international financial activities on a large scale. After it resumed its seat in the IMF and World Bank, China also joined the African Development Bank in May 1985, and in March 1986 the PBC became a regular member of the Asian Develop-

ment Bank. At the same time, other financial institutions began to interact with foreign banks and institutions. Now, BOC ranks 22nd among the 100 big banks in the world, and ICBC ranks 14th. At the same time, more than 100 foreign banks and other financial institutions have established their offices in China. This greatly promoted the financial cooperation between Chinese banks and foreign banks.

3. Current Regulation and Supervision

3.1. The Central Bank—The People's Bank of China (PBC)

The PBC was established on December 1, 1948, as both a commercial and a state bank. Under the decision made by the State Council in 1984, the PBC functioned entirely as a central bank no longer dealt with enterprises and individuals. The principal tasks of the PBC are spelled out in the Provisional Regulations of the People's Republic of China on the Control of Banks (Bank Control Regulation), promulgated January, 7, 1986 by the State Council, as follows:

1. research and develop national guidelines and policies for financial activities and arrange for their implementation after approval by the State Council;
2. research and draft financial legislation;
3. formulate basic regulations for financial business;
4. control the issue of currency, regulate circulation, and maintain currency stability;
5. control interest rates on deposit and loans, and set the rate of exchange between Renminbi and foreign currencies;
6. devise state credit plans, exercise centralized control over credit funds, and exercise uniform control over the working capital of state enterprises;
7. control foreign exchange, bullion, and the offical foreign exchange and gold reserves;
8. examine and approve the establishment, reorganization, and merger of specialized banks and other finanical agencies;
9. control, coordinate, supervise, and inspect the operations of specialized banks and other financial institutions;
10. manage the state treasury and distribute government bonds;
11. control the shares, bonds, and other securities of enterprises, and control the money market;

12. engage in relevant international financial activities on behalf of the government: and
13. control the state's insurance enterprises, in accordance with the provisions of the state laws and administrative regulations.

3.2. Planning for Banks

The principal plans for banks in China are the overall credit plan and overall cash plan, which form a part of the national economic plan. These two plans are drawn up by the PBC in conformity with expected demand and supply of money and overall balance between money flows and commodity flows. The preparation and implementation of these two plans assist the performance of the national economic plan, guide banking operations, and help the banks to play their role.

3.2.1. Overall Credit Plan. The plan covers sources and uses of funds. Sources of funds include capital and reserves of banks and nonbank financial institutions and budget appropriations for bank deposits. Uses of funds include loans, overdrafts, gold, and foreign exchange reserves. The head office of the PBC sets the annual credit targets for the provincial, municipal, and autonomous regional branch offices, which in turn work out quarterly credit plans on the basis of the annual targets and report to the head office to be put on record. The same principle of unified control is adapted by commercial banks and nonbank financial institutions. The credit quotas for enterprises are allocated according to the priorities laid down in the credit structure agreed upon between the banks and the relevent ministries of the central government. The provincial, municipal, and autonomous regional branch bank offices examine the performance of the credit plan monthly and quarterly, discover problems, and take measures to ensure the realization of the plan.

3.2.2. Overall Cash Plan. The plan covers cash receipts and payments. Cash receipts include receipts from the retail sale of commodities, services, taxes, saving deposits, remittance, and others. Cash payments are payments of wages and other payments to individuals, payments for purchases of agricultural and sideline products, administrative and business expenses and bonuses, procurement of industrial and mining products, and saving deposits cashing and remittances. The system of overall cash-plan control is basically similar to that of the overall credit plan control.

3.3. Cash Control

Cash control is a very important mechanism to provide efficient circulation of money. According to state regulations, the PBC exercises cash control over all enterprises, government agencies, army units, and schools. The specialized banks and other financial institution exercise cash control over those units keep accounts with these institutions. The scope of cash control is as follows:

1. a limit is set to cash retained by units, and the extra cash must be turned over to the bank or financial institution;
2. transactions between units must be settled through bank accounts, except for limited payment in cash that is in conformity with state provisions and approved by the bank;
3. the use of cash by units is mainly for payments to urban and rural residents, miscellaneous small payments between units, and payments by units for purchases of limited amount of products from urban and rural fairs;
4. purchases of commodities and raw materials by a unit from other places should be paid through a bank account instead of in cash, except for special cash with the approval of the bank; and
5. units with a large volume of cash transactions are required to draw up a cash receipt and expenditure plan.

3.4. Supervision of Specialized Banks and Other Financial Institutions

The head office of specialized banks, other commercial banks, and national trust and investment corporations are required to submit the following information to the head office of the PBC for examination and approval:

1. business guidelines and policies;
2. activities outside the allocated scope of business;
3. codes of regulations falling outside current regulations for financial business, or involving other special banks requiring uniform regulations;
4. formulation and amendment of articles of association;
5. establishment of branches abroad; and
6. reports on the performance of credit and cash plans, statistic reports, and operational reports.

The establishment of branches and subbranches by specialized banks and other nationwide financial institutions shall be reviewed and approved as follows:

1. head offices of financial institutions branches and subbranches are to be reviewed by PBC head office and approved by the State Council;
2. provincial branches of the applicant bank should submit the application to the head office of PBC for approval;
3. local and municipal subbranch applications are to be submitted by provincial applicant bank branches to provincial branches of the PBC for approval; and
4. applications of operational units below the country level are required to submit by district and municipal subbranches of applicant banks to local and municipal branches of the PBC for approval.

If any specialized bank branches and offices fail and are to be closed, the insolvent entity must apply to the original approving unit two months prior to closing of business. After approval, assets and liabilities shall be liquidated and discharged under supervision of the unit that made the original approval. Because all financial institutions in China are state-owned or collective-owned or backed by state-owned banks, no bank failure has yet occurred.

Individuals are forbidden to establish banks and carry on financial businesses.

3.5. Interest Rates

Before the economic reform, interest rates were so low and uniform that they had lost all impact on the mobilization and allocation of capital. There were only two different interest rates for saving deposits: one for current saving accounts and another for fixed saving accounts. Loan rates were the same for all credit to industrial and commercial enterprises, regardless of the duration of the loans, the uses to which the loan were granted, and whether the loans were overdue. Changes were introduced by the State Council in 1979. All interest rates are now prescribed by the PBC after receiving approval by the State Council, except the interbank rates on the money market, which are determined by supply and demand. As a result, interest rates for all deposits were substantially raised eight times beginning from 1979. They were also diversified according to the duration of deposits. Interest rates on bank loans were also increased and

Table 3-3. Deposit and Loan Rates of ICBC (annual rate, March 15, 1989)

Deposit Rates	%	Loan Rates	%
1. Residential Saving Deposit		1. Working Capital Loan	
Current account	2.88	Loans to industrial and commercial enterprise	11.344
One year	11.34		
Three years	13.14	Loans to procure cereals, cotton, and edible oil	9.00
Eight years	17.64		
2. Government Agency Deposit		2. Fixed-Asset Loan	
Current account	2.88	Below one year	11.34
Time deposit	Same as residential time deposits	From 1–3 years	12.78
		From 3–5 years	14.40
		From 5–10 years	19.20

Note: The interest rates mentioned in the above table are only a small part of the interest structure of the ICBC.
Source: The planning department of the PBC.

Table 3-4. Interbank Rates of Selected Money Markets, 1989

Market	Date of Transaction	Number	Amount of Transaction (10 Thousand)	Duration (day) Longest	Shortest
Kunming ABC money market	Feb. 4–15	3	910	30	10
Shenyang financial center	Feb. 4–16	21	4,700	30	20
Wuhan money market	Feb. 15	4	1,750	25	7
Hangzhou money market	Feb. 1–18	8	590	30	10
Zhengzhou money market	Feb. 1–18	10	2,630	30	20
Tianjin PBC money market	Feb. 13–18	10	2,900	30	3
Nanjing ICBC money market	Feb. 13–18	2	500	1	1
Shanghai ICBI money market	Feb. 13–18	42	79,300	8	1
Hefei ICBC money market	Jan. 1–Feb. 20	15	4,680	60	16

Source: *Financial Times*, Feb. 23, 1989, published by Financial Time Press, Beijing, PRC.

varied with the term of maturity and the purpose of the loan. Furthermore, the banks could now add a 20% to 50% surcharge on the interest for overdue loans, for loans to be used to cover working capital that was judged excessive, and for loans caused by overruns in capital construction. The local branch of specialized banks are given a degree of freedom and flexibility in charging different rates for different clients (see tables 3-3 and 3-4). The general term is that the rate of interest should be used as an economic instrument of monetary control so as to direct capital to the more efficient enterprises, and to mobilize more financial savings from the public to curb the ongoing inflation.

3.6. Monetary Policy

As the monetary authority in China, the PBC is obligated to promote monetary stability and enhance the development of the national economy. Monetary policy in China is designed to operate at two different levels. First, within the framework of expected output and price developments, the PBC set up an overall credit plan, which includes credit provided to the specialized banks and other commercial banks. The implementation of the credit plan depends on regulations defining the deposit base of the specialized banks, other commercial banks and non-bank financial institutions, deposit requirements, and rediscount rates. All government accounts are to be held at the PBC, while other deposits are to be made specialized banks, other commercial banks, and nonbank financial institutions. Specialized banks, other commercial banks, and nonbank financial institutions must in turn place 12% of their deposits with PBC. When combined with those governing government account deposit, these requirements ensure that the PBC has direct control over about 40% of the total deposit base. Specialized banks and other commercial banks can supplement their loanable funds by borrowing from the PBC at 7.2% per year. The differential is intended to discourage the specialized and other commercial banks from borrowing from the PBC.

Second, within the restrictions imposed by the PBC, the specialized banks and other commercial banks use their own devices to ensure that their credit and deposit policy is consistant with the PBC's monetary policy. To enable them to remain within their credit limits, the banks are given direction in their lending. Credit worthiness of projects is to receive greater emphasis than in the past, with bank managers given greater latitude to withhold loans to enterprises that are unable to repay the loans in time. To assist the banks managers in rationing credit, interests on bank loans have been increased rapidly. Rates on working capital loans, for example, have been increased from 5.04% in 1979, to 7.2% in 1985, to 7.92% in 1987, to 11.34% in January 1989. Furthermore, the bank manager is empowered to vary, within certain margins, the interest rates charged.

3.7. Foreign Exchange Control

The central government pursues the policy of centralized control and unified management of foreign exchange. According to the Provisional Regulations for Foreign Exchange Control of the PRC promulgated by the State Council on December 18, 1980, the principal objective of foreign exchange control is to increase national foreign-exchange income and to economize on foreign-exchange expenditure in order to expedite the economic growth and safeguard the rights and interests of the country. All foreign-exchange receipts and expenditures, all issuance and circulation of payment instruments in foreign currency, and all flows into or out of the PRC of foreign exchange, precious metals, and payment instruments in foreign currency are governed by these regulations. The administrative organ in charge of foreign-exchange control is the State General Administration of Exchange Control (SGAEC).

Originally, the BOC was the only specialized foreign-exchange bank. Beginning from 1987, all specialized banks and other commercial banks, as well as some of nonbank financial institutions (for instance, trust and investment companies, finance companies, and financial leasing companies), were approved by SGAEC to handle foreign exchange operations, foreign-exchange trust deposit, lending, investment, financial leasing, guarantee, and other business.

In 1985, the State Council also promulgated the *Regulations Governing Foreign Banks and Joint Chinese-Foreign Banks in Special Economic Zones*. These regulations were formulated with a view to expanding international economic and financial relations so as to promote the economic growth rate of the special economic zones. The PBC may grant its approval to foreign and joint Chinese–foreign banks to engage in part or all of the following business operations:

1. granting loans in local and foreign currencies and discounting bills;
2. inward remittances from foreign countries and regions, and foreign-exchange collections;
3. settlement of export transactions and outward documentary bills;
4. exchange in foreign currencies and foreign-currency bills;

5. local and foreign-currency instruments;
6. local and foreign-currency guarantees; and
7. buying and selling of securities.

4. Development of Banking

Before economic reform, the banking operations of PBC were very simple. They could be summarized as *deposit, loan, and remittance*. But economic reform expanded these powers.

4.1. Extending Short and Medium-Term Equipment Loans

This was a very innovative addition to the banking operation. This type of loan was without precedent in the history of the PBC. It was first instituted in 1979. The State Council endorsed its significance by allocating to the Bank 2 billion yuan in 1980 and another 4 billion yuan in 1981. The loans were intended to help light industries utilize their plants more fully, to replace old equipment, and to introduce technological innovations in order to expand production. Such loans were not to be used for large-scale capital constructions or for building new plants. Priority was given to industries and enterprises that could raise production quickly, and emphasis was placed on the loans that could increase the efficiency of the borrowers. The duration of these loans could be from one to five years. Funds for the repayment of principal plus interest would come from the borrowing units' profits and depreciation. All of these funds were formerly remitted to the state as budget revenue, but now they could flow to the bank instead.

The granting of short and medium-term loans represented a significant departure from traditional Chinese banking. It violated all three basic banking principles adopted from the Soviet Union in the 1950s. First was the separation of funds from the budget and from the bank. Under this principle, bank loans to enterprises were to cover only working capital of a temporary and seasonal nature. They were not to be used for equipment and fixed assets. The main purpose of the new short and medium-term loans was contrary to this principle. Second, the new loan was longer than one year. Third, the real bill doctrine was violated since this kind of loan is granted for renovation and new equipment. It is no longer backed by commodity inventory.

Table 3-5. Loans to township enterprises and Farmhouseholds (RMB 100 million yuan)

Loans to township enterprises	287.7	348.9
Loans to farm households	64.11	106.01

Source: Almanac of China's Finance and Banking, 1988, p. 64.

4.2. Loans to Urban and Rural Collectives and Individual Enterprises or Households

A second new development in banking since 1979 was the emphasis given to loans to urban and rural collective enterprises and to individual enterprises or households. The ICBC granted loans for inventory and for small-scale equipment purchases to collective-owned urban units, factory cooperatives, and individual enterprises. The ABC also granted loans of the same nature to township industrial enterprises, collective agricultural enterprises, and individual farm households (see table 3-5).

Most of these borrowers provided goods and services to local communities and nearby cities, such as machinery spare parts, garments, kitchen facilities, meats, poultries, fruits, vegetables, and repairs. Formerly, loans were rarely available to these enterprises and units. There were two reasons for this new credit policy. First, it would encourage production by small, decentralized units of the economy, specifically the development of the township industrial enterprises in the rural area, which, in turn, would provide a greater variety of consumer goods and services and a higher standard of living for the people. Second, it would alleviate both urban and rural unemployment, particularly the surplus labor force in the rural area after the introduction of new contracts for production with remuneration linked to output. This development was a reversal of past policy, in which bank loans were used as an instrument for socialization, so that loans were generally reserved for the more centralized units, such as the urban state enterprises and the rural communes.

4.3. The Introduction of Trust Deposits and Custodian Accounts

Trust deposits and custodial accounts were necessitated by the increased autonomy of state enterprises. Whereas previously all enterprise profit and depreciation allowances had to be submitted to the state budget, these enterprises were now able to keep a share of their profits to be used as worker's welfare funds or for future investment. Thus, for the first time, funds were at the disposal of these firms. These off-budget funds have increased rapidly and now total more than 200 billion yuan.

Trust deposits are really time-deposit accounts for the state enterprises; their duration could vary, and the longer the term, the higher the interest rates. The specialized banks could also serve as a custodian and invest the trustor's deposit funds in areas or enterprises specified by the trustor.

After the national conference of PBC held at Xiamen in 1980, all banks in large and medium cities began to establish trust and investment departments. By the end of June 1982, there were more than 620 trust and investment departments at the banks. Among these, 186 were affiliated with the PBC (later on transferred to ICBC), 266 affiliated with the PCBC, 20 affiliated with the ABC, and 96 affiliated with the BOC. Furthermore, many municipals and coastal port agencies also set up trust and investment companies to raise funds for development of their local infrastructures. In addition, the State Council also authorized the BOC and many national and local trust and investment companies to handle international trust business.

The Bank Control Regulations of January 7, 1986 spelled out clearly that:

> trust and investment companies may be established to handle such things as capital and asset trusts, asset custodianships, financial leasing, economic consulting, issuing of securities, and investment ... (and) trust and investment companies established by specialized banks in large and middle-sized cities shall be independent legal entities, shall carry out independent accounting, and shall be subject to the leadership of the PBC in their business operations.

In April of the same year, the PBC published *Provisional Regulations Governing Financial Trust and Investment Institutions*, in which the details of financial trust activities, such as planning control, ratio of required deposits, criteria for starting operations business scope and business management, etc. were described. These regulations subject financial trust activities to state macroeconomic control comparable to that imposed on banks.

4.4. Reform of the Measures for Settlement of Account (Mode of Payment)

The Chinese measures for financial settlement were adopted from the Soviet Union in the 1950s. They are conducive to a highly centralized planned economy. Thus, they are designed as a means to exercise state control, instead of providing banking service to the client. But since China is in a period of transformation from a centralized economy to a decentralized economy, the payments system requires modification and updating.

The old measures of settlement of account were as follows:

Settlement of account between different localities	Collection against acceptance
	Authorized collection
	Remittance
	    Letter remittance
	    Teletransfer
	    Draft of remittance
	Domestic letters of credit
	Commercial paper for discount

Settlement of account in the same city	Acceptance Check Authorized to pay Collection without acceptance Authorized collection

The major defects of the above measures of settlement of account are

1. large amounts of cash tied up by both the sellers and buyers;
2. a long time to clear payments between both parties;
3. different measures for specific types of transaction;
4. large arrears between sellers and buyers; and
5. banks forced to grant credit in the nature of advancement, which may lead to excessive credit expansion.

In view of the above defects and the drastic change in the national and financial structures, the PBC published *Report of Reform of Settlement of Account* on August 22, 1988. The Report proposed major changes in principles, the concept of credit, concrete arrangements, and the management of settlement of account. The Report instituted a new system of measures for settling accounts, with drafts, promissory notes, and checks as the most important means. The report abolished collection against acceptances, domestic letters of credit, authorized collection, collection without acceptance, and certified checks, and at the same time adopted bank draft, commercial paper, bank promissory notes, checks, and authorized collection as the instruments to carry on the settlement of account in order to simplify and at the same time of accommodate various new types of commodity transaction and economic activities.

To expedite the change of the settlement of account, the PBC and the big specialized banks were authorized to establish clearing centers in the cities equipped with electronic computers and electronic communication networks.

4.5. Resumption and Development of Bilateral Clearing with Socialist Countries

Bilateral clearing with socialist countries began in the 1950s. Initially, China had signed trade and payment agreements with the Soviet Union and a number of Eastern European socialist countries. On the basis of these agreements, a protocol of settlement and payment procedures was developed by the state banks of the countries. The volume of trade between China and Soviet Union and other socialist countries increased rapidly. In 1959, the trading volume between China and the Soviet Union had reached 1.9 billion rubles (equivalent to US$ 2 billion). About three quarters of China's total foreign trade volume was transacted with socialist countries. In the 1960s, for political and diplomatic reasons, trading volume between China and other socialist countries fell sharply. By 1969, the trading volume between China and Soviet Union had dropped to only 25 million rubles and was negligible with Eastern European countries. In total, trading volume between China and other socialist countries represented only 1% of China's total foreign trade volume. However, since 1983, the trading volume between both the Soviet Union and Eastern European countries and China has increased drastically.

The important clearing and payment arrangements for such trade are as follows:

1. A bilateral clearing account by the state bank of both countries in each other's name. For instance, the BOC will open an account in the name of the Foreign Bank of Soviet Union, and vice versa. All payments of goods and incidental expenses will be put through these two accounts.
2. Clearing currency. Most of the clearing currency is Swiss franc. However, in quite a few cases the US$ is adopted.
3. Prompt payment.
4. Swing credit. All trade and payment agreements have credit limits in Swiss francs, but the amount is different for different countries.

In the early 1950s, both parties adopted letters of credit as the means of payment. In order to accelerate the payment to the exporter, prompt payment was introduced in 1955. After the exporter dispatches the goods in accordance with the conditions for delivery and the separate sales contract, he presents the required documents to the exporter's country's bank. After the bank checks the documents and finds them in order, the bank makes payment to the exporter immediately, and at the same time debits the clearing account of the importer's bank and mails the documents, together with a debit note, to the importer's bank. When the importer's bank receives the documents and the debit note, it credits the account of the exporter's bank and collects the money from the importer.

5. Internationalization and Globalization

5.1. Overseas Chinese Financial Institution

Before the founding of the PRC, BOC already had its branches in the U.S.A., Europe, Australia, and East Asian countries. In 1979, a basic guideline for the work of BOC's overseas branches was developed: pursuant to the state open-door policy, the BOC shall develop its business activities by adopting the operation procedures generally prevailing in modern international financial institutions. Under such a principle, the overseas branches of BOC have achieved a rapid growth in business over the past nine years. In addition to its basic overseas branch network, including branches in Luxembourg, New York, Caymen, Sydney, Tokyo, Macao, Paris, and Frankfurt. Moreover, the center of the BOC group in Hong Kong, including Bank of Communication, Nanyang Commercial Bank Ltd., etc. (13 banks), was increased in a wide range. The increase of capital was brought about in the local financial circles and was most conducive to the prosperity and stability of the Hong Kong and Macao economy.

The 13 banks in the BOC group have developed different areas of expertise in investment banking, capital markets, and treasury management, in addition to the traditional trade finance and mortgage loan business. The Hong Kong government figures, which break down market share by country of beneficial ownership, show that the BOC group accounted for 19.7% of total deposits in 1987, up considerably from 15.5% in 1985.

There are also five overseas Chinese insurance companies, under

Table 3-6. Foreign Financial Institutions in China (End of 1987)

City	Bank	Insurance Company	Security Firm
Beijing	80	14	9
Qingdao	2		1
Shanghai	28		4
Guangzhou	22		
Shenzhen	7		
Xiamen	3		
Zhuhai	1		
Dailian	12		
Tianjin	5		
Wuhan	1		
Nantong	1		
TOTAL	190	14	14

Source: Almanac of China's Finance and Banking 1988, p. 126.

the direction of PICC, in Hong Kong, Macao, Singapore, London, and other major cities. The China Insurance Company Ltd. is the biggest, with branches in Hong Kong, Singapore, and Macao, followed by the Taiping Insurance Company Ltd., with two branches in Hong Kong and Singapore, the Ming An Insurance Company (H.K.) with its head office in Hong Kong, and the China Life Insurance Company Ltd. with its head office in Beijing and branches in both Hong Kong and Singapore. The smallest is the China Reinsurance Company Ltd. in Hong Kong.

5.2. Foreign Financial Institutions in China

In 1979, the Chinese government promulgated regulations to allow foreign financial institutions to set up branches and representative offices in China, to introduce more foreign capital and expertise of foreign banks and institutions. The first foreign bank opened in China was the representative office of the Export and Import Bank of Japan in December 1979. Since then, a total of some 50 banks, including the Bank of Tokyo, Sanwa Bank of Japan, Bank of America, The Chase Manhattan Bank N.A., Barclays Bank, and Banque Nationale de Paris, have opened representative offices in Beijing.

In February 1983, the PBC published regulations governing the establishment of foreign and overseas Chinese financial institutions in China.

Table 3-7. Bonds Issued by Chinese Government Agency and Financial Institutions (1980–1987)

	Tokyo	Frankfurt	Hong Kong	Singapore	London
International Trust and Investment Corp.	130B, Yen 188M, US$	150M, MK	700M, HK$ 10B, Yen		
Bank of China	155B, Yen 150M, US$	150M, MK 200M, US$		200M, US$	200M, US$
Investment Enterprise Co. Fujian	250B, Yen				
Trust and Investment Co. of Shanghai	25B, Yen				
International Trust and Investment Corp. of Guangdong	20B, Yen		50M, US$	50M, US$	
International Trust and Investment Corp. of Tianjin	10B, Yen				
Ministry of Finance		500M, MK 800M, MK 200M, US$			
TOTAL	365B, Yen 250M, US$		10B, Yen 700M, HK$ 50M, US$	250M, US$	200M, US$

Source: State Foreign Exchange Control Administration of China.

These permit foreign and overseas Chinese foreign institutions to open representative offices or branches in China's big cities and special economic zones. As a result, many major Western security companies and insurance companies entered China to look for more business. At the end of 1987, the total number of foreign financial institutions in China was 190. (These are listed in table 3-6.) The Office of Foreign Banks largely act as a liaison office between Chinese enterprises and foreign customers.

5.3. Foreign Loan Obligation

Because China is still a developing country, it must borrow convertible currency abroad. The total balance of such foreign loans at the end of 1988 was US$ 30 billion. A certain portion of loans were short-term loans from Western commercial banks. Most of the long-term loans were from international financial institutions, such as the World Bank, the IMF, and Asian Development Bank, as well as ODA from friendly foreign countries. Beginning in 1982, China began to issue bonds on foreign financial markets, mostly concentrated in Japanese yen. The composition of these loans is shown in table 3-7.

4 BANKING IN THE EUROPEAN ECONOMIC COMMUNITY: STRUCTURE, COMPETITION, AND PUBLIC POLICY

Joseph Bisignano

In most countries, banking is a heavily regulated industry. "Indeed, banking is among the most heavily regulated of economic activities."[1] And even after years of attempts in several countries to disencumber this industry from regulations that foster inefficiencies and, contrary to original intent, distort incentives for risk-taking, it remains highly regulated. Governments have played a major role in shaping the nature of bank loan markets and deposit contracts in attempts to provide countries with a particular kind of financial service industry, together with a variety of explicit and implicit support systems. This role has had the good effect of securing considerable financial stability in many industrialized economies during the postwar period. At the same time, in some cases the price of this stability has been an inefficient industry for certain types of financial services and at times has stunted the growth and efficiency of competing capital markets. In a few cases, it has also exposed governments to substantial financial risk and losses.

Member states of the European Economic Community (EEC) have recently embarked upon an ambitious program of increasing competition in financial services within the Community. Indeed, they are attempting to accomplish in a few years what the United States has yet to complete, that being the freedom of establishment of banking branches and subsidiaries in all member states, with the ability to offer a wide variety of banking and financial securities services. The integration of banking markets in the EEC is being fostered by a novel philosophical approach to cross-country financial integration, based on three general principles: *minimal harmonization of regulations, mutual recognition* of rules and regulations, and *home country control*. The first principle requires that only several fundamental banking regulations and procedures be cemented by Community legislation. The second and essential principle of mutual recognition provides that each member state basically accepts as applicable within its own boundaries the regulations (importantly with respect to permissible activities) established in other member states. This, in effect, provides free access to domestic markets for all Community members, even if certain of the specified list of activities are prohibited to domestically established financial institutions.[2] And thirdly, banks operating in other EEC member countries are to be subject to the control and supervision of their home authorities.

The objectives of the EEC's 1988 Second Banking Directive are indeed ambitious. One need only recall that full integration of financial services in the EEC to date has been hampered by significant restrictions on capital flows. And some countries, such as Italy, have up to 1989 not permitted the complete freedom to establish bank branches anywhere within their national boundaries. Hence the two principles on which the new EEC banking market is to be constructed, "to safeguard certain fundamental public goods by the passage of some minimal Community legislation" and "to entrust everything beyond this minimum to regulatory pluralism," will represent a major change in the regulatory frame of reference we use to understand the European banking industry.[3]

The aim of this essay is to provide a broad-brush background of the structure, competition, and some of the major public policy issues associated with banking in the EEC and to relate these topics to the proposed EEC single market in financial services. However ambitious the attempt to paint a picture of these three areas, any effort will likely be partial and incomplete, given the variety of changes in banking and securities markets that have taken place in Europe during the past few years, and the changes that will occur with the creation of a single market in financial services as a result of 1992 EEC initiatives. Some small treatment will also be given to nonbanking financial services. Because of the number of countries involved, we will not attempt a detailed country-by-country survey. Several countries that are members of the EEC are treated in this volume, and several comparative studies of banking structure and regulation in the EEC are available, even if not all are up to date.[4] We will try to describe some of the broad similarities and sharp differences that exist in the EEC banking industry. Although not a member of the EEC, but because of its significance in both European and international banking, Switzerland is also mentioned at times.

To help focus some of the public policy concerns with the structure of the EEC banking industry, we begin with a small amount of economic theory. This theory attempts to define the nature of the banking contract and banking services, the role of information and monitoring in banking, and some of the reasons for the establishment of public policy related to banking. Section 2 provides a broad description of the banking industry and capital markets in the EEC. Section 3 reviews some of the background leading up to the objectives and components of the EEC's Second Banking Coordination Directive. Section 4 focuses on the possible competitive implications of a single EEC banking market. Finally, section 5 reviews what we think are some of the major public policy issues that derive from an integrated single market in banking services in the EEC.

1. The Role of Banks and the Role of Public Policy in Banking

One of the basic roles of a financial system is to facilitate the intertemporal transfer of real resources via the extension of credit. The transfer of real resources is effected by the transfer of financial claims, claims to a future exchange of means of payment. The transfer of financial resources may take place directly between borrowers and lenders, as in securities markets, or through credit. The *payments system*, the accounting system for transfers of liquid wealth between parties, is typically operated by the banking system. In some countries the postal system continues to provide an efficient payments mechanism, complementing the role in this area performed by banks.

The extension of credit requires a transfer of information from borrower to lender and a monitoring of the credit quality of the borrower. The transfer of information, the *information trade*, may take place directly between borrower and lender, or between the borrower and an intermediary, who accumulates a variety of loan contracts and finances them with his own capital and borrowed resources. The borrowed resources in the case of the bank may be convertible into cash or transferred to another party on demand. The intermediary/lender in these cases acts as an information assembler and sorter, who prices the loan contract based on his ability to evaluate the information provided by the borrower. Similarly, there is an information trade between the lender (depositor) and the intermediary. The intermediary, as borrower, also needs to establish the quality of his credit. This information transfer is usually aided by the role of the government, which may require certification of the intermediary and may establish the range and limits of the intermediary's activities, as well as providing assurances as to the ability of the intermediary to satisfy claims held against it.

Because of the difficulty in gaining and evaluating credit information by lenders, and given the incentive of the borrower to shield information that could be costly to reveal, in terms of the price of the loan, there exists an asymmetry in the information available to the two parties to the loan contract.[5] Specialization in the gathering, sorting, and monitoring of information on the credit quality of the borrower may be best performed by an intermediary rather than through the capital markets, at least for some types of borrowers.[6] In those cases where the borrower has an established "borrowing reputation" and/or where public-disclosure rules lower information costs and permit credit evaluation by individual lenders, the debt contract may be formed directly between borrower and lender, sidestepping the intermediary. But in the case where the intermediary comes between the ultimate borrower and lender, one can picture the ultimate lender (depositor) as effectively delegating the credit screening, monitoring, and enforcing roles to the intermediary (bank), for which the lender pays an implicit fee. Hence, the depositor is in a sense buying a portfolio of loans and is paying the intermediary to screen and monitor the credit quality of borrowers. At the same time, the intermediary houses a diversified loan portfolio. This diversification permits the intermediary to increase its risk tolerance with respect to each loan, thereby reducing the cost of risk-bearing.[7] In those cases where the intermediary and the borrower share information over an extended period of time, information that may be closely held by the intermediary, and where the borrower and lender are each heavily dependent on each other (and where the intermediary may even have an equity interest in the borrower), both borrower and lender are sharing not only information but the combined "risk" of the two institutions. In such relationships, the asymmetries in information are reduced and therefore the threat of credit rationing as well.[8] Another form of closely held information by banks is the deposit history of the borrower who is also a depositor with the bank. The bank may judge the credit quality of the borrower by monitoring the behavior of the borrowers' deposit balances, information that is not available to others.[9] Thus the bank trades on inside information—in the good sense of the term—with the knowledge of the borrower, reducing the cost to the borrower and the risk aversion of the lender.

The problem of informational asymmetries between borrower and intermediary also exist between the intermediary and the depositor. Banks screen and monitor borrowers and enforce loan performance. However, depositors are now confronted with the difficulty of evaluating the performance of these functions but are not given access to the inside information shared between borrower and intermediary. (This problem is also faced by banks who lend in the interbank market.) The asymmetry in information between the bank and the depositor gives rise to potential real economic and financial instability, because some of the bank's assets are highly illiquid, while a large portion of its liabilities, in the form of deposits, are withdrawable on demand or, as in the case of large CDs, are of short-term maturity. These characteristics of the bank's balance sheet and the information structure make the financial institution potentially unstable. The potential intermediary instability is the result of balance-sheet illiquidity, which is dependent both on the confidence of the depositor in the asset quality of the intermediary and on the depositor's confidence in the ability of the intermediary to obtain credits from other lenders, public and private. The faith in the intermediary may be threatened by the lack of depositor knowledge of the quality of the intermediary's asset portfolio and cost and maturity structure of its liabilities, and is aggravated because the intermediary may not be able or may not desire to share such information with depositors. Furthermore, the stability of bank short-term liabilities will depend on depositors' perceptions and expectations of other depositors' behavior. Hence, there is a need for backup liquidity support, which may be provided by a lender of last resort or some mechanism to ensure the stability of deposits, such as deposit insurance. In turn, real economic activity can be threatened by severe disruption in the banking industry when contracts between depositor and intermediary and intermediary and borrower are not renewed.[10] Recognizing the strategic role of banks in influencing aggregate economic behavior, banks have historically been heavily regulated and supervised with the objectives of ensuring stability by 1) restricting or limiting banking powers; 2) protecting the public in the event of bank failure; and 3) protecting the interests of consumers in their relationships (as borrowers and lenders) with banks.[11]

The stability of the banking industry can be enhanced in one respect by reducing the threat of bank runs by government intervention in the form of deposit insurance or through the provision of less explicit assurances to depositors. (Deposit insurance provided by the government is not unique to the United States, but neither is it as ample elsewhere, nor as strategic to the assumed "stability" of the banking system. However, it is of note that the EEC Commission in 1986 recommended the introduction of deposit guarantee schemes in all member countries.) At the same time, the elimination of bank deposit runs via government deposit guarantees may create so-called moral hazard problems, in that the provision of deposit insurance may alter the asset risk preferences of banks, as banks attempt to exploit the competitive advantage of having government-backed liabilities or implicit government guarantees on the value of intermediary deposits. At the same time, depositors are likely to reduce their surveillance of the intermediary, given guarantees on the nominal value of their deposits. Hence, a government guarantee designed to ensure the stability of bank deposits may have the perverse effect of significantly altering the risk incentives of bank managers, shareholders, and depositors. The existence of this moral hazard problem is argued by some to justify such banking regulations as minimum liquid balances, minimum capital standards, and restrictions on deposit rates.[12]

A demand by banks for banking regulation and supervision may emerge in response to the negative externalities that a bank may potentially face as a consequence of the risk-taking behavior of other banks. Again, the problem arises because of informational asymmetries, in this case *between* banks, as well as between banks and depositors, where one bank has only partial knowledge of the risk characteristics of another bank's assets or of the stability of the other bank's deposits.[13] Such a demand for regulation and supervision could arise from banks active in the interbank market, where knowledge of the risk exposure of borrowing banks may be slight or difficult to obtain and where it may be difficult or impossible to achieve private agreements or accepted norms on bank risk-taking behavior.

Three aspects of banking, then, may give rise to potential instability: the liquidity of bank deposits, the illiquidity of some assets, and informational asymmetries in the loan and deposit markets. The close interrelationships between banks also raises the potential for difficulty in one bank to be transferred to another, threatening the entire banking system.[14] Guaranteeing stability in the system by means of government deposit guarantees or implicit commitments creates its own problems of moral hazard. One answer to the potential moral hazard problem is to severely regulate and supervise the activities of banks, e.g., by limiting the maturities of or rates of interest paid on deposits; prohibiting or limiting certain types of investments; restricting particular kinds of financial activities, securities brokerage, or underwriting activities, or the maturity of loan contracts; restricting branching within a country; or limiting competition by restricting the entry of both domestic and foreign banks into the domestic market. At the bottom of many such regulations appears to be the desire to guarantee financial stability by restricting competition. In this fashion stability is paid for by the consumers of banking services, that is, depositors and borrowers. These, of course, are not the only reasons for banking regulation, but they appear to underlie the justification for certain types of regulation in a number of countries.[15]

A strong argument for the need for regulation and supervision in banking is often allied with the role of banks in the payments system, with particular emphasis in recent years on the large-dollar electronic-payments system involving the clearing of both domestic and foreign payment balances.[16] This has been of particular concern in the United States, where the intraday credit arising from funds transfer and book-entry securities on large-dollar payments networks has made the U.S. Federal Reserve a large unsecured creditor.[17] In answer to this concern, it has been argued that the moral hazard problem in banking could be reduced by recognizing that not all banking and related financial activities need to be regulated and insured to the same degree. The payments system could be made safe, some argue, by having separately capitalized institutions that hold only safe assets, say government securities, and act as a mutual fund offering transactions services.[18]

We quickly notice that the issue of securing stability of the payments system by separating payments from nonpayments-related financial services opens up an important and broader topic central to banking in the EEC, namely, that of *corporate separateness* and the interrrelation between banking and commerce. First, what operations ought to be permitted under the umbrella of a bank, or, as in the case of the United States, a bank holding company? And can the activities of the bank's subsidiary, or that of the bank holding company, from the point of view of securing the safety of the banking system, be economically separated from the bank in the eyes of the public?[19] Second, is it desirable to permit commercial enterprises to own banks or for banks to have large equity interests in nonfinancial firms? The answer to these questions turns in part on how the banking authorities are able to structure regulations and banking supervision so that the government does not implicitly become the ultimate risk bearer for the banking system and also does not implicitly extend its limited security umbrella to nonbanking activities.

As the trend in banking moves towards fewer and larger institutions, both in Europe and in the United States, the moral hazard problems in banking might be expected to grow, both because of the belief that some institutions are too big to fail without endangering the entire financial system and because of the inability to prevent increasingly larger public and private banks from leveraging the implicit value of implicit or explicit government commitments to the banking industry by taking on risks that they believe are implicitly being shared by the government.[20] As the EEC moves to a banking environment characterized by greater domestic and foreign competition, larger institutions, an expanded menu of permissible activities, and generally reduced direct government intervention in the pricing and provision of financial services, banking authorities will be confronted with one simple question: To what extent will banking structures in Europe be determined by the discipline of the market and to what extent by the system of regulations and safety net provisions provided by the government?

2. EEC Financial Institutions and Markets: An Overview

2.1. The Role of Capital Markets

Although the analogy is of limited applicability, it is useful to keep in mind that the financial sectors of several EEC member countries resemble in part the industrial sector of many developing countries. One segment is a member of a competitive international market, where competition is severe, profit margins are thin, and there is considerable freedom of entry (e.g., wholesale banking, Eurobanking, Eurocapital markets, and reinsurance). A second domestic segment is heavily regulated and protected from foreign competition, profit margins are often higher than in the competitive sector, prices and/or commissions are fixed, and the industry is characterized as offering a limited product mix and at times suffering from sizable and visible inefficiencies (e.g., domestic retail banking, domestic capital markets, life and casualty insurance).[21] While the analogy may falter when pushed hard, it serves to focus our attention on the fact that the financial services industry in several European countries is basically a dual economy.

Viewed from the perspective of national flow-of-funds or sectoral balance-sheet data, most private nonfinancial sectors in the EEC obtain much of their external financing from banks. The reasons for the comparative structural weakness, until recently, of many European capital markets are many and varied. A number of factors have contributed to the relative dominance of banks over capital markets in providing finance to the company sector: 1) the organization of the banking system, with special credit institutions, sometimes government controlled and subsidized, structured to provide long-term finance to companies or to housing or special financing to the agricultural sector, or in which long-term debt issuance is performed by banks and funds reloaned to corporations; 2) inflation, which has discouraged the holding of long-term, marketable financial assets; 3) the dominant role of government financing in some capital markets, which during certain periods effectively crowded out private short- and long-term debt issuance; 4) in some cases the preferences of nonfinancial companies to seek close, long-term relations with reliable financial sources, instead of a fragmentation of debt claims on capital markets, and through which informational asymmetries might be reduced through a close client/agent relationship; and 5) simple government and corporate politics.[22] In some cases, with Germany the dominant example, the capital market is much less a separate capital market and might be thought of as having been largely collapsed into the banking system.[23]

Table 4-1 provides a snapshot of the liability structure of nonfinancial companies in six major countries, four of which are members of the EEC. Although the portion of bank financing as a percentage of the total financing of the nonfinancial sector varies from year to year, table 4-1 shows the typical prominent position of banks in most European countries vis-à-vis, say, the United States, in financing the nonfinancial company sector. Note, in particular, the significant role of German banks in providing long-term financing to businesses. The importance of the banking system as both creditors to the German nonfinancial sector and as sources of financial assets can be seen in tables 4-2a and 4-2b. At the end of 1988, for example, almost 60% of the total liabilities of the nonfinancial sector in Germany were to banks and only 16.2% were in securities issues. Some authors have characterized the modest utilization of securities in the financing of the German corporate sector as a "structural weakness," given the insignificant market for industrial bonds and the limited utilization of equity issuance.[24] As recently as 1982, the German central bank called attention to "the narrowness and low capacity of the German share market."[25]

Conscious of the long-standing compartmentalization and specialization of French financial intermediaries and the bias towards short-term financial asset holdings in France, since the late 1970s a series of governmental reports and laws have sought to increase the scope and efficiency of French capital markets. In doing so they also sought to move the French financial system away from intermediated finance towards greater

Table 4-1. Liabilities of Nonfinancial Companies and Bank Lending

Items	United States 1978	United States 1988	Japan 1978	Japan 1988	Germany 1978	Germany 1988	United Kingdom 1978	United Kingdom 1988	France 1978	France 1988	Italy 1978	Italy 1988
As a percentage of total credit market debt of company sector												
Debt of nonfinancial companies[a]												
Loans from banks-	30	27	46	67	87	88	72	88	66	61	84	65
of which: long-term	(3)	(1)	n.a.	n.a.	(56)	(58)	(0)	(0)	(44)	(42)	(33)	(22)
Other loans[b]	19	17	48	20	7	6	17	8	19	20	6	19
Securities (excluding shares)	51	56	6	13	6	6	11	4	16	19	10	16
Total	100	100	100	100	100	100	100	100	100	100	100	100
Memorandum items												
Shares on issue (market value)	103	133	32	64	47	56	168	268	26[c]	32[c]	41	116
Trade and other domestic nonmarket debt	40	28	59	40	21	29	92	68	n.a.	n.a.	0[d]	15[d]

As a percentage of total credit market claims of banks

Credit market claims of banks[e]

Loans to companies	20	21	35	54	32	28	59	48	67	59	45	52
Loans to personal sector[f]	47	52	37	26	28	29	17	46	23	24	8	10
Loans to nonresidents	6	2	—	—	9	12	—	—	—	—	—	—
Loans to public sector	—	—	8	1	16	15	24	6	—	—	6	5
Securities (excluding shares)	27	25	20	18	15	16	—	—	10	17	41	33
Total[g]	100	100	100	100	100	100	100	100	100	100	100	100

As a percentage of total credit market debt of all nonfinancial sectors[h]

Shares of total market

Companies' credit market debt	21	20	46	44	34	28	19	20	34	23	28	28
Bank credit market claims	32	27	61	55	93	87	34	23	49	37	45	32

[a] For Germany, producing enterprise sector.
[b] From insurance companies, other financial institutions, public sector and nonresidents.
[c] Nominal value.
[d] Other domestic nonmarket debt only.
[e] For the United States, commercial banking; for Japan, banks, etc. (excluding trust business); for France, banks, including nonbank financial institutions; for Italy, banks, including special credit institutions.
[f] Including loans for housing.
[g] Excluding loans to other financial institutions and, in the case of the United Kingdom, lending to nonresidents.
[h] For the United Kingdom, domestic nonfinancial sectors only.

Source: BIS estimates based on national sectoral balance-sheet data, which differ conceptually from country to country.

Table 4-2a. Financial Assets and Liabilities of Domestic Nonfinancial Sectors in Germany, End 1988[a]

Items	In Billions of Deutsche Mark	As a Percentage
Financial assets	4,071.4	100.0
Funds placed with:		
banks (except funds invested in bank bonds)	1,904.6	46.8
other financial institutions	715.7	17.6
of which: insurance companies	(595.1)	(14.6)
securities markets	712.5	17.5
of which		
bonds (including bank bonds)[b]	(482.9)	(11.9)
shares[c]	(223.2)	(5.5)
Other claims		
on domestic sectors	343.2	8.4
on the rest of the world	395.3	9.7
Liabilities[d]	3,782.6	100.0
Loans/funds from:		
banks	2,235.9	59.1
other financial institutions	321.4	8.5
of which: insurance companies	(189.8)	(5.0)
securities issues	613.7	16.2
of which:		
bonds[e]	(436.8)	(11.5)
shares[f]	(167.9)	(4.4)
Other liabilities		
to domestic sectors	318.7	8.4
to the rest of the world	292.9	7.7

[a] For methodological notes, see Deutsche Bundesbank Special Series No. 4. Discrepancies in the totals are due to rounding.
[b] At market prices: DM 482.4 billion.
[c] At market prices: DM 529.0 billion.
[d] Including shares in circulation.
[e] At market prices: DM 438.9 billion.
[f] At market prices: DM 566.3 billion.
Source: Deutsche Bundesbank Special Series No. 4.

financing in open money and capital markets. The *Monory Law* of 1978 provided a major impetus to the restructuring of the French capital markets, using the attractive carrot of tax incentives to personal shareholding. Net investment in French shares, up to a specified limit, were made deductible from taxable income. Spurred by the 1982 Dautresme

Table 4-2b. Net Sales of Bonds and Shares in Germany (in Billions of Deutsche Mark)

Year	Bonds[a]					Shares		
	Total Bonds	Bank Bonds	Industrial Bonds	Public Bonds[b]	Foreign Bonds[c]	Total Shares	Domestic Shares[d]	Foreign Equities[e]
1980	52.6	41.5	−1.3	4.9	7.3	10.5	6.9	3.6
1981	73.1	70.5	−1.0	−2.6	6.2	10.2	5.5	4.7
1982	83.7	44.8	−0.6	28.6	11.0	9.2	5.9	3.3
1983	91.3	51.7	−0.6	34.4	5.7	15.6	7.3	8.3
1984	86.8	34.6	−0.2	36.7	15.7	12.0	6.3	5.7
1985	103.5	33.0	0.3	42.7	27.5	18.5	11.0	7.5
1986	103.9	29.5	0.2	57.8	16.4	32.3	16.4	15.9
1987	113.0	28.4	−0.03	59.8	24.8	16.6	11.9	4.9
1988	89.9	−11.0	−0.1	46.2	54.8	33.5	7.5	26.0

[a] Net sales at market value plus/less change in issuers' portfolios of their own bonds.
[b] Including Federal Railways and Federal Post Office.
[c] Net purchases (+) or net sales (−) of foreign bonds by residents, transaction values.
[d] At issue prices.
[e] Net purchases (+) or net sales (−) of foreign equities by residents; transaction values.
Source: Monthly Report of the Deutsche Bundesbank, August 1989 Statistical Section, adaptation of table VI.1.

Report, the *Delors Law*, enacted in January 1983, was directed specifically at increasing business use of the French capital markets and reducing their dependency on the banking system for financing.[26] In addition to relaxing the conditions for nonvoting share issuance and revising the tax benefits available from personal investment in French shares, the Delors Law is said to have provided a legal framework that permitted the introduction of a variety of new financial techniques, such as floating-rate bonds, convertible bonds, bonds with warrants, investment certificates, and participating shares.[27] Venture capital was also encouraged through the creation of a special type of closed-end fund, *fonds communs de placement à risques*, in which under the Delors Law at least 40% of the funds had to be placed in unlisted securities. In addition, the moribund secondary equity market was replaced by the *second marché*, similar to NASDAQ in the United States, with requirements for listing established and auditing eased. Reforms also did not escape the French short-term money market following the enactment of the Delors Law. The development of a commercial paper market in the mid-1980s and the loss of the banking system's monopoly in subscribing for Treasury bills meant that banks were losing two major sources of high-grade short-term assets.[28] The increasingly competitive money and capital markets in France, stimulated by legislation and the resulting disintermediation, in turn caused banks to respond by offering investment funds, SICAVs and FCPs, with the previous deposit funds now placed in the bond market. And more recently (in 1988) the asset side of bank balance sheets was altered by the ability of banks to securitize bank loans (Fonds Commun de Créances).[29]

As a consequence of legislation aimed at increasing competition in French money and capital markets and reducing the country's dependency on bank-intermediated finance, in a relatively short time France greatly transformed its financial system.[30] The dual financial economy has been replaced by a much more integrated and competitive financial structure. Disintermediated financing by nonfinancial companies rose from 30%–35% to over 50% by 1986. Even the French Treasury now supplies securities to the market primarily via an auction system and seldom through a Treasury bond syndicate. And the improved liquidity for conventional Treasury bonds, the 1986 introduction of a government bond futures market (MATIF) and options contracts, and the more efficient settlement procedures for certain government securities all contributed to increasing the attractiveness and substitutability of French government bonds internationally.[31]

In attempting to draw a sharp contrast between recent French and German money and capital market developments, we should not be lured into the conclusion that in some sense the new system of greater nonintermediated finance in France is a more efficient and competitive framework than the dominance of the bank-intermediated financial system in Germany. There are a number of factors that determine the desirability of one financial system over another. For example, because bank monitoring may considerably reduce information problems such as those that exist with capital market financing, firms with close and long-standing bank ties may be less liquidity constrained that those that depend on capital market financing.[32] It is also sometimes argued that financial intermediation makes private saving easier and thereby increases the proportion of income saved, resulting in lower interest costs to borrowers and higher returns to savers.[33] The competitive structure of the banking industry would also influence governments' desires to stimulate the growth of money and capital markets at the expense of banks. Germany and France provide an interesting vantage point from which to initially view European banking and capital markets. Germany is often, and in part mistakenly, viewed as a financial system dominated by universal banks, with underdeveloped money and capital markets. France, on the other hand, has made major structural changes in its money and capital markets, creating considerable direct competition between intermediated and nonintermediated sources of finance. As a result, bank-intermediated finance in Germany, as a percentage of the financing of the nonfinancial company sector (seen in table 4-1), remained fairly stable between the late 1970s and late 1980s, while capital market financing has been on the rise in France.[34] These two financial systems provide a useful backdrop against which to view capital markets in other EEC countries.

Because Dutch *universal banks* provide a wide range of financial services—commercial and investment banking, equity broking, and even insurance—the Netherlands' financial system is often compared to that in Germany. Yet there are some significant institutional differences that alter the mix of intermediated and nonintermediated credit flows in the Netherlands. Much of the long-term business financing in the Netherlands is obtained from institutional investors. Long-term borrowing is also available by direct issuance of debt on the capital markets, although the availability of this source is limited to large, well-known firms.[35] The increased corporate use of capital markets in recent years is the result of the January 1986 deregulations regarding the issuance of guilder-denominated instruments. These restrictions were related to minimum maturity requirements for guilder-denominated bearer securities.[36] As in France, the aim was to increase the use of nonintermediated finance.

Two distinctive features of the Dutch capital market are the large role played by the private placement market and the heavy capital market demands made by the the central government. Institutional investors are estimated to account for as much as 60% of the domestic supply of capital market funds, which derive from the existence of a funded pension system. Many of these funds are placed in the large "private loan market," which is quantitatively larger than the domestic "public capital market." But even with the central government absorbing as much as 60% of total capital market supply in recent years and the continued growth of the large private placement market, the industrial sector has once again begun to tap the domestic equity market after years of absence from this source of financing.[37] Also, Amsterdam might be considered continental Europe's London with regard to equity trading, particularly foreign equities. After London, the Amsterdam equity market has the highest equity market capitalization as a percentage of GNP (as of December 1987) in Europe—more than twice that of Germany—with half of the listed stocks being foreign.[38]

Table 4-3. Bonds and Government Securities: Issues and Stocks in Italy (in Billions of Lire)

Items	Stock (December 1988)	Gross Issues 1987	Gross Issues 1988	Net Issues 1987	Net Issues 1988
Public sector	804,637	406,116	531,585	83,987	102,544
Treasury bills	244,835	316,111	409,411	25,171	36,275
Treasury credit certificates	346,265	55,480	27,350	35,268	−7,849
Treasury bonds	146,180	19,020	75,383	13,538	59,781
Special credit institutions	165,903	44,028	53,789	13,522	20,906
Certificates of deposit	43,818	18,929	32,000	2,510	12,940
Firms and public corporations	36,739	7,383	5,195	4,037	809
Total	1,007,279	457,527	590,569	101,546	124,259
As a percentage of GDP	93.4	46.7	54.7	10.4	11.5

Source: Banca d'Italia, Ordinary General Meeting of Shareholders, abridged report for the year 1988, p. 113.

Until recently, discussion of the Italian capital markets was largely synonymous with a discussion of Italian public finance. The dominance of the government in the Italian securities markets can be quickly grasped by considering both total bond stocks and government securities outstanding at the end of 1988 and net and gross new issues, seen in table 4-3. At the end of 1988, the public sector accounted for approximately 80% of outstanding bonds and government securities, and during 1988 represented about 82% of all net issues.

Italy provides a classic example of how inflation and government indebtedness can dry up the capital market for private enterprises. Inflation during the 1970s helped shrink what was once a reasonably developed private bond market. With inflation high and, not surprisingly, the private nonbank sector's liquidity preferences short, the banking system was the major purchaser of government securities, in turn offering the private nonbank sector variable interest-rate deposits. This condition changed during the 1980s, in part caused by the decline in inflation and a shift in private liquidity preferences, as the household sector moved heavily into direct purchases of government securities, resulting in a major disintermediation of the banking industry.[39]

As a consequence of years of high inflation and massive public-sector indebtedness, Italy is only recently beginning to organize something approaching developed money and capital markets.[40] Traditionally, medium- to longer-term financing was provided by special credit institutions, with commercial banks limited (officially) to offering credits of up to 18 months' maturity. The recent major innovation in the capital markets was not in the bond market but, unlike most other countries in the EEC, in the equity market. Although several pieces of legislation were aimed at reviving the equity market during the 1970s, the real push came in 1983 in the form of investment funds, supervised by the Banca d'Italia and CONSOB (the Companies and Stock Exchange Commission). Lower inflation, enhanced corporate profitability, and improved regulation and supervision of investment funds and portfolio management companies gave an enormous push to the equity market in Italy. By 1986, Italy was observing an unprecedented volume of new share issues.[41]

There is no real private corporate bond market in Italy, since medium- and long-term financing is obtained from Italy's so-called special credit institutions. And a commercial paper market is in its infancy. Hence discussion of money and capital market growth in Italy in recent years is largely confined to discussion of improvements in the secondary market for government securities, the growth of unit trusts, and equity financing.[42] For the private financial sector, Italy must be considered a bank-dominated center, with incipient growth in its capital markets. The growth in equity finance in Italy may receive a further push from governmental actions in 1987 designed to permit commercial banks to establish merchant banking subsidiaries, which would be able to take significant equity interests in private companies.[43] To date, merchant banking in Italy has been dominated by one institution, Mediobanca, a major shareholder in some of Italy's large corporations.

The Italian capital market can be pictured to be similar to that of Germany in having little in the way of a well-developed bond market in corporate debt, but unlike Germany in having seen significant growth and development in its equity market. However, to be fair, the innovations, competitiveness, and openness of Italian capital markets have not rivaled those seen in France since the late 1970s.

Belgium is another country whose domestic capital market is largely moribund, save for the primary market financing of the government deficit. Recent efforts to bring smaller firms to the equity market, for example, have not been successful. Long-term business financing for large firms is conducted by a government institution, the National Industrial Credit Company, while smaller firms obtain longer-term finance from the National Fund for Credit to Trade and Industry. The former institution acts as a major financial intermediary in Belgium, issuing bonds on tap to households and financial institutions. Hence the bond holdings of households and nonfinancial institutions are largely those of intermediaries, mainly government controlled. Like Italy, most of the financing of the business sector in Belgium is intermediated.[44]

In searching for the reasons for the size, growth, and efficiency of domestic capital markets in the EEC, and in general the extent of non-intermediated finance, one can see from the above examples several major contributors: 1) the structural organization of the "banking system," in the broadest use of the term; 2) government "management" of the banking sector, including government-administered financial firms; 3) the use of the banking sector as a source of government finance via direct and indirect taxation, including reserve requirements and inflation; 4) the size of the government's indebtedness vis-à-vis the availability of domestic saving; 5) the legal prohibition on the use of certain types of financial instruments and hedging techniques; 6) taxation and regulation of capital market activities, including turnover taxes, disclosure requirements, and the availability of related hedging instruments; 7) differences between countries in the taxation of interest, dividends, and capital gains; and 8) issues related to monetary control. Why, for example, has the French government in recent years sought to streamline the French government bond market and create bond futures and options markets, while we have seen the first futures contract on German government bonds originating in London? In a broad sense, the answer to such questions revolves around legal issues and the advantages or disadvantages assumed to derive from intermediated finance.

One clear advantage of intermediated finance is tax revenue. France, for example, has had higher taxes on saving than most other European countries. Moreover, banks are required to inform the government tax authorities of individual savings income. Hence there is a clear incentive for individuals in some European countries to invest in Eurobonds in Luxembourg, where there are no withholding taxes, no reporting of savings income to the tax authorities for nonresident investors, and no registration of bond holders.[45] In Denmark and the Netherlands, on the other hand, bank interest income is reported to the tax authorities. And in Switzerland, the taxation of bank interest income begins at the source. Arguably the most cited example of a European tax deterrent to investment in domestic capital markets is that of the Belgian dentist who invests in ecu bonds in Luxembourg to escape the Belgian 25% withholding tax.

Escaping the tax man is of no small relevance to the form of individual and business saving in the Europe. The experience of Germany during 1989 is an example of how sensitive European capital flows appear to be to the differential treatment of deposit and security income. In the past several years, a number of countries have eliminated so-called *coupon taxes* for nonresidents. Partly in response to the 1988 announcement that Germany was to reinstitute a withholding tax on domestic interest income, nonresident purchases of long-term financial assets in Germany "fell by no less than DM 30 billion in 1988 to just under DM 10 billion. Such a low figure as this was not even recorded during the period of pronounced weakness of the Deutsche Mark at the beginning of the 1980s."[46] At the same time, domestic German investor purchases of foreign long-term assets mushroomed, doubling between 1987 and 1988 to DM 88 billion. It was thus with some relief that the Bundesbank welcomed the elimination of withholding taxes on domestic interest income, which took effect in July 1989.[47] Soon after the announcement, long-term capital inflows began to improve.

The above discussion has had one notable omission, that of the United Kingdom. And even here the general characterization of European domestic capital markets seems to prevail. Bank financing in the United Kingdom from the early 1970s has been the dominant source of finance for industrial and commercial enterprises, with fixed-interest sterling

Table 4-4. Industrial and Commercial Companies' Borrowing and Financing in the United Kingdom (in Millions of Pounds Sterling)

				Financed by:				
					Capital Issues			
Years	Net Financing Requirement (− = Surplus)	Bank Borrowing[a]	Other Borrowing (Incl. Issue Dept. Bills)[b]	Ordinary Shares (+ Capital Issues Overseas)	Fixed Interest (Debentures and Preference Shares)	Total	Overseas Investment Inflow	Decline in Financial Assets (− = Increase)
	+	−	−				−	=
1963	798	537	130	130	211	341	62	−272
1964	1,361	752	167	168	249	417	101	−76
1965	1,248	497	237	81	345	426	110	−22
1966	1,189	187	138	137	452	589	168	107
1967	665	333	122	96	351	447	211	−448
1968	1,000	569	167	351	185	536	241	−513
1969	1,734	664	220	188	335	523	148	179
1970	1,878	1,126	354	75	193	268	367	−237

1971	1,046	734	244	199	285	484	299	−715
1972	1,375	2,987	128	395	267	662	−52	−2,350
1973	3,178	4,805	748	211	87	298	480	−3,153
1974	6,299	4,112	92	49	27	76	1,233	786
1975	1,099	547	645	947	257	1,204	1,112	−2,409
1976	2,623	2,672	438	795	56	851	1,175	−2,513
1977	499	2,471	502	792	−46	746	1,117	−4,337
1978	1,871	2,319	−91	754	−41	713	642	−1,712
1979	4,802	3,936	545	820	5	825	417	−921
1980	5,344	6,356	296	862	523	1,385	1,907	−4,600
1981	3,364	5,750	1,762	1,626	738	2,364	1,061	−7,573
1982	6,433	6,586	2,967	990	245	1,235	1,400	−5,755
1983	−1,615	1,618	−116	1,826	608	2,434	1,820	−7,371
1984	1,920	7,300	1,637	1,425	248	1,673	−2,731	−5,959
1985	7,180	7,704	1,045	4,177	816	4,993	−329	−6,233
1986	10,792	9,417	1,261	6,919	490	7,409	2,994	−10,289
1987	23,729	13,003	−1,597	17,144	534	17,678	2,909	−8,264
1988	42,513	29,614	2,880	7,665	1,207	8,872	3,813	−2,666

[a] Including Bank of England Issue Department transactions in commercial bills.
[b] − = repayment of borrowing.

Sources: Bank of England; Central Statistical Office.

finance largely unavailable from the mid-1970s to the mid-1980s.[48] Conscious of the weakness in the sterling paper market, the British government since 1982 has tried to encourage growth in this market through changes in tax law (regarding deep discount bonds), changes in regulations aimed to improve the financing of one- to five-year corporate bonds, and permission for companies to issue sterling commercial paper.[49] These efforts were strengthened by London's "Big Bang," which improved the number and capitalization of securities houses, improving distribution and secondary market trading potential. Not least of all, the British government's reduced borrowing requirements also have helped to breath life back into the sterling bond market. In addition, while bank borrowing continues to dominate the financing of U.K. industrial and commercial enterprises, as displayed in table 4-4, a notable change has been the growth in ordinary share issuance since 1985, spurred by the rise in British equity prices.

Elsewhere in the EEC, the story is that of a revival of capital market activity with a modestly reduced reliance on bank finance. Although accounting for only 10% of total new funding (bonds and shares) in 1987, Portugal's private enterprises have increased their reliance on open capital markets at the expense of the banking system.[50] As recently as 1984, Portuguese households held about 90% of their financial assets in time, savings, and emigrant's deposits. In 1989 this percentage was reduced to 42%, with about 45% of their financial assets held in Treasury bills and other securities.[51] While the aggregate shift of private and public enterprises to capital market financing in Portugal is still limited, it has nonetheless grown dramatically in the period from 1984 to 1987, amounting to 23% of new external financing in 1987 (although still only 10% for private enterprises). Although banks may dominate the provision of funds to businesses in Portugal, as they do in most other EEC member states, clearly there has been a major revival, and in some cases new birth, in capital market financing.

The above short discussion of several European capital markets provides only a partial view of a broad movement in European finance: the revival of growth in domestic capital markets. Yet many of the major elements of change have been noted. With long-term capital markets for many years dominated by government borrowers, banks and/or special credit institutions have been the major source of longer-term financing for the nonfinancial corporate sector. Only in recent years has there been anything like a revival in equity financing, aided by the rise in equity prices beginning around 1983, the growth of institutional investors, and government attempts to restructure and improve the technical efficiency of equity markets. The banking system, broadly defined, has been the primary source of finance for domestic firms and households. The domestic capital market has in many cases been the fund-raising turf of governments and, as in Germany, of banks.

2.2. The Role of Banks

The nature of banking in the EEC is almost as diverse and idiosyncratic as the languages and customs of its members. To describe the banking industry generally, we begin very broadly with David Pyle's definition of the essential characteristic of a financial intermediary: "it issues claims on itself and uses the proceeds to purchase other financial assets."[52] Add to this Santomero's three primary activities of banks: 1) asset transformation, involving asset diversification, asset (credit risk) evaluation, and the transformation of large-denomination financial assets into smaller-denomination assets; 2) the creation of a medium of exchange through their supply of demand deposits; and 3) the intermediation function involving the tranformation of deposits into loans and the arbitrage across markets offering uncertain rates of return.[53]

Recall that in defining what is a bank, Corrigan placed special emphasis on Santomero's second aspect of banking—the issuance of transactions accounts. Given the nature of this liability, which is eligible for immediate withdrawal, and the nature of its assets, most of which are not marketable and bear a risk of default, it is often argued that the activities of banks require the support of a "public safety net—deposit insurance and access to the lender of last resort—which is uniquely available to banks."[54] With this in mind, we come to a unique characteristic of *banking* vis-à-vis other financial activities: the role of the government in helping to ensure the viability of a particular kind of private market activity. In most kinds of private-market activity, the viability of the institution is determined by its capital. The risk sharing that takes place in the private firm is between equity holders and creditors. Because bondholders and equity holders do not equally share in both profits and loss, the equity holder obviously has greater preference for risk, since if the firm is profitable the proceeds are rewarded to the shareholders, while if the firm is bankrupt, the loss is shared between the two claimants, and with limited liability to equity holders.

The argument has been made by some finance theorists that the major role of the government in banking in many countries, either in providing implicit support guarantees or in providing credible but underpriced deposit insurance, has caused banks to substitute government "equity" for private equity. In some countries, such as the United States, this may explain the relatively low capital base of commercial banks and thrift institutions, compared with nondepository financial institutions. In other countries, the low capital base may be explained by direct government ownership or control of banks and the heavy regulatory and nonformal government constraints placed on banks. This argument requires one to think of government as having a large implicit equity stake in banking, even to the point that the government equity stake may reduce the incentive to increase the private capital base of banks.[55]

The above argument suggests that, unlike most other private-market activity, in banking the ubiquitous contingent lender/equity holder in case of loss is usually assumed to be the government, either through a government-sponsored deposit insurance program, direct intervention in the case of loss to reimburse depositors, or through some, possibly temporary, support via the lender-of-last-resort function. Golembe (1989), for example, identifies the two most important public policy objectives of bank regulation and supervision to be the protection of the public against bank failure and to "guard against banking power."[56]

The role of the government as a contingent creditor or implicit shareholder creates a moral hazard problem in that the presence of some form of public backing, ultimately the taxpayer, may significantly alter the risk preferences and incentives of bank managers and shareholders, who may attempt to leverage the contingent support role of the government.[57] The moral hazard problem for banks, and the conflict between equity holders and creditors, is heightened by the fact that banks are usually much less capitalized than nonfinancial corporations.[58] Hence, the contingent risk borne by the government in attempting to ensure the efficient provision of a public good is increased the greater the leveraged position of the banking system. Indeed, government-sponsored deposit insurance permits the substitution of deposit insurance for equity capital, particularly when the deposit insurance is underpriced for high-risk banks. The bank depositors' protection then becomes less the equity base of the bank and more the equity base of the government—that is, its taxing authority. The government's contingent risk is in turn managed by regulations and supervision (e.g., by monitoring the risk-taking activities of banks; restricting their ability to engage in certain kinds of activities or to offer certain kinds of liabilities; restricting their ability to attract deposits by limiting deposit rates and/or the maturities on deposits; limiting or prohibiting their equity relationship with nonfinancial enterprises; and, as seen in the recent international agreement among G-10 countries on bank

Table 4-5a. Statistical Summary of the Ownership of Top Banks in the EEC, 1987[a] (arithmetic means)

Number of Banks in Banker Top 500		Assets (in Millions of U.S. Dollars)	Pretax Profits	Pretax Profits/ Assets	Pretax Profits/ Capital	Capital/ Assets	Net Interest Income/ Assets	Employees
Private	69	37,601	207.2	0.77	16.36	4.81	3.01	15,948
		(1.15)	(1.61)	(0.89)	(0.80)	(0.48)	(0.59)	(1.36)
Public (central and local government)	67	31,133	158.9	0.61	14.30	3.70	2.14	7,261
		(1.09)	(1.43)	(1.10)	(0.66)	(0.54)	(0.60)	(1.48)
Cooperative	14	41,402	242.8	0.89	17.31	5.16	2.06	12,124
		(1.36)	(0.95)	(0.60)	(0.40)	(0.58)	(0.62)	(1.69)
Mutuals	12	10,421	77.5	0.81	14.78	6.14	3.99	4,419
		(0.50)	(0.64)	(0.46)	(0.52)	(0.39)	(0.29)	(0.56)

[a] Classification after Revell (1987). Large German savings banks are controlled by local government organizations and therefore are classified as public rather than mutual organizations. Figures in parentheses are standard deviations/means.

Source: P. Molyneux. "An Analysis of the Structure and Performance Characteristics of Top EC Banks and the Strategic Implications of 1992," *Revue de la Banque,* June 1989.

Table 4-5b. Sector Distribution of the 100 Largest EC Banks, 1987

		Total Assets	
Sectors/Number of Banks		In Billions of U.S. Dollars	In Percentages
Public	42	1,859.9	37.9
Cooperative	9	538.7	11.0
Mutual	5	75.9	1.5
Private	44	2,432.4	49.6
Total	100	4,906.9	100.0

Source: J. Revell. "Bank Preparations for 1992: Some Clues and Some Queries," *Revue de la Banque*, March 1989.

capital standards, by setting minimum acceptable standards for capital related to the assumed risk characteristics of their assets and certain banking service activities).

As the EEC moves to a unified market in financial services, the future activities of EEC banks are expected to change, and with them the public policy concerns of central banks and banking regulators and supervisors. The background and elements of this planned unification will be discussed in section 3. This section will attempt to provide a broad overview of the similarities and differences in banking institutions and markets in the EEC. The theoretical background above may help as a frame of reference in understanding some of the similarities and differences in banking and banking regulation in the Community.

A summary view of some industrial-organization aspects of banking in the EEC may be seen in tables 4-5 to 4-9. Note that, measured by the number of banks in the Banker Top 500, there are almost as many publicly owned banks in the EEC as privately owned banks (table 4-5a). Interestingly, the size, pretax profits performance, and capital/asset ratios of these two groups of banks are not widely different. The private banking sector is somewhat larger, employs twice as many individuals, while their pretax profits as a percentage of capital or assets are quite similar. However, as would be expected, the capital/asset ratios for private banks are somewhat larger than for publicly owned institutions.

Although most countries in the EEC have three to five large, well-known banks, there is only modest concentration in the two largest banking sectors, Germany and the United Kingdom, where banking regulations do not severely restrict domestic or foreign competition (table

Table 4-6. Market Concentration and Size of Banking Sectors in the EEC, 1986[a]

Countries and Number of Banks in Market		Size of Banking Sector[b] Assets (in Billions of U.S. Dollars)	Concentration as a Percentage of Total Market[c]			
			Assets		Deposits	
			5-firm	3-firm	5-firm	3-firm
Germany	4,465	1,465.0	31.2	21.2	30.5	19.1
United Kingdom	661	1,337.8	32.6	26.5	30.3	21.6
France[d]	367	1,012.6	63.0	42.3	65.2	45.5
Italy	980	529.2	55.1	35.2	68.5	41.6
Spain	349	332.3	34.7	21.9	38.8	24.3
Netherlands	81	272.3	—	71.3	—	83.9
Belgium	86	228.3	84.7	57.1	87.5	59.0
Luxembourg[e]	120	198.1	22.4	16.7	—	16.5
Denmark	216	111.9	50.9	36.7	58.6	45.3
Greece		48.4	—	—	—	49.7
Portugal	40	43.3	—	49.7	—	49.6
Ireland	43	22.1	—	71.0	—	—

[a] The market size figure for Greece is a deposits figure.
[b] Sources of information for banking sector size; OECD (1988) and various central bank publications.
[c] 3-firm and 5-firm concentration ratios calculated using data taken from the consolidated accounts published in *The Banker* "Top 500."
[d] The number of banks in France increases to around 6,000 if mutual assocations are included.
[e] Only 12 of the 120 Luxembourg banks are domestic institutions.
Source: P. Molyneux. "An Analysis of the Structure and Performance Characteristics of Top EC Banks and the Strategic Implications of 1992," *Revue de la Banque*, June 1989; data derived from OECD (1988) and various central bank publications for banking sector size. Banker (1988) is used for estimating the concentration ratios. Note that this table includes savings banks, among other institutions, in the definition of the banking sector.

4-6). (We should note one qualification. The concentration figures do not necessarily capture the concentration in the domestic banking market in some cases, since much of the business in markets such as London and Luxembourg is distinctly international and a sizable portion of the deposits interbank deposits.) Concentration would appear to be promoted by nationalization in France and branching restrictions in Italy, although in the latter case, these are currently being eased.[59] As might be expected, concentration is highest in some of the smaller countries, such

Table 4-7. EEC Banking Concentration: Assets of Five Largest Banks as a Percentage of Total Banking and Total Financial System Assets, 1987

Countries	Assets as a Percentage of Total	
	Banking System	Financial System
France	79.2	53.1
Italy	60.4	37.9
Spain	74.9	47.9
United Kingdom	35.7	33.1
Germany	62.0	28.5

as the Netherlands, Belgium, and Ireland. And although Italy, France, and the United Kingdom have population sizes that are roughly similar, Italy is notable for having fewer commercial banks.[60]

With the coming integration of financial markets in Europe, bank ownership becomes an important issue. Molyneux argues that one of the significant characteristics of continental European banking markets is the much bigger role played by publicly controlled institutions compared with the British banking market.[61] For example, in Italy there are six *public charter banks*, whose capital is held directly or indirectly by the government and whose boards of directors and senior executives are appointed by the government.[62] The largest bank in Italy, Banca Nazionale del Lavoro, is a member of this group. In France, 39 banks were nationalized in 1982. While several banks have in recent years been privatized, including one of the big three, Société Générale, a sizable portion of the banking system remains in government hands. France also has several large mutual and cooperative banks that have been under government control since before World War II, the largest of which, Crédit Agricole, is the largest bank in the EEC.[63] In terms of the number of branches, the mutual and cooperative banks in France outnumber the branches of ordinary commercial banks.

Two other characteristics of banking in the EEC are the large number of special credit institutions, some with special lending status either with respect to particular lending maturities or with activity directed at particular sectors, and the regional orientation of many banks and credit institutions. Germany, for example, has a variety of banks specializing in special types of lending activity: mortgage banks, building societies, installment credit institutions, banks targeting small and medium-sized firms, and some banks that primarily finance exporters. France too has a

Table 4-8. European "Commercial Banking" Market Saturation Data, 1986 (Year-End Data)

Countries	Population[a]	Number of Banks	Number of Branches	Population/ Branch	Number of Employees	Employees/ Branch	Assets[b]	Assets/ Branch[c]	Assets/ Employee[c]	Population/ Employee
Belgium	9.9	85	3,646	2,702	50,624	13.9	108.7	29,813	2.147	195
Denmark	5.1	83	2,131	2,403	35,565	16.7	25.0	11,732	0.703	144
France	55.4	386	9,917	5,584	229,197	23.1	282.3	28,466	1.232	242
Greece	10.0	32	1,311	7,605	36,382	27.8	10.4	7,933	0.286	274
Ireland	3.6	36	675	5,259	15,800	23.4	14.2	21,096	0.901	225
Italy	57.2	162	5,878	9,735	191,871	32.6	114.5	19,486	0.597	298
Luxembourg	0.4	127	300	1,230	11,971	39.9	56.8	189,333	4.745	31
Netherlands	14.6	83	2,500	5,859	63,000	25.2	110.7	44,280	1.757	232
Portugal	10.2	21	1,215	8,420	44,122	36.3	15.4	12,642	0.348	232
Spain	38.6	138	16,498	2,342	157,595	9.6	110.6	6,704	0.702	245
United Kingdom	56.9	578	14,300	3,979	403,000	28.2	1,008.2	70,503	2.502	141
Germany	61.1	308	6,382	9,571	191,300	30.0	283.5	44,422	1.482	319
Total	323.0	2,039	64,753	4,988	1,430,427	22.1	2,140.4	33,054	1.496	226

[a] In millions.
[b] In billions of U.S. dollars.
[c] In millions of U.S. dollars.

Source: "European Banking Integration in 1992," Salomon Brothers, June 1989; Primary source, European Banking Federation. Note that this table differs from table 4-6 in restricting the definition of the banking market to include only commercial banks.

Table 4-9. Structure and Performance Characteristics of the Top Banks in the EEC for 1987[a] (arithmetic means)

Countries and Number of Banks in The Banker Top 500		Assets (in Millions of U.S. Dollars)	Pretax Profits Mean (in Millions of U.S. Dollars)	Pretax Profits/ Assets	Pretax Profits/ Capital	Capital/ Assets	Net Interest Income/ Assets	Employees	Branch Networks
Germany	44	33,876	161.1	0.47	14.52	3.17	1.57	5,555	944
		(1.10)	(1.32)	(0.74)	(0.60)	(0.31)	(0.63)	(1.86)	(3.79)
United Kingdom	15	46,204	113.0	0.68	7.22	6.44	3.21	31,413	1,642
		(1.19)	(4.96)	(1.56)	(2.45)	(0.44)	(0.32)	(1.19)	(0.67)
France	20	59,444	299.5	0.55	15.77	3.40	2.89	19,339	1,417
		(1.14)	(1.19)	(1.09)	(0.82)	(0.53)	(0.72)	(1.17)	(1.83)
Italy	33	25,793	200.1	1.08	18.14	5.71	2.73	7,009	342
		(0.94)	(1.08)	(0.72)	(0.53)	(0.48)	(0.45)	(1.00)	(1.96)
Spain	13	22,423	254.5	1.22	22.12	5.86	4.99	11,826	1,120
		(0.72)	(1.02)	(0.46)	(0.54)	(0.40)	(0.18)	(0.79)	(0.65)
Netherlands	5	64,772	340.8	0.53	13.77	3.97	2.49	21,588	1,069
		(0.38)	(0.50)	(0.23)	(0.14)	(0.26)	(0.37)	(0.47)	(0.78)

Country									
Belgium	9	30,420 (0.66)	110.1 (0.74)	0.46 (0.50)	14.69 (0.35)	2.99 (0.46)	2.20 (0.25)	6,927 (0.81)	710 (0.64)
Luxembourg	6	10,289 (0.40)	66.3 (0.84)	0.57 (0.42)	18.69 (0.47)	3.55 (0.42)	2.46 (0.54)	3,973 (1.35)	303 (1.76)
Denmark	8	12,904 (0.43)	64.6 (0.94)	0.49 (0.63)	7.63 (0.64)	6.88 (0.21)	3.42 (0.59)	4,557 (0.31)	247 (0.27)
Greece	3	14,368 (0.95)	45.0 (0.35)	0.52 (0.63)	18.30 (0.48)	2.78 (0.39)	0.66 (0.39)	10,388 (0.60)	379 (0.35)
Portugal	4	8,612 (0.46)	53.0 (1.37)	0.51 (0.92)	15.52 (0.42)	3.20 (0.53)	2.64 (0.36)	7,495 (0.25)	136 (0.07)
Ireland	2	14,881 (0.06)	208.0 (0.04)	1.48 (0.09)	24.2 (0.09)	6.13 (0.05)	4.51 (0.06)	9,221 (0.07)	239 (0.07)

[a] Figures estimated by author. Data taken from *The Banker* "Top 500" of which 162 banks were EEC-based banks. Figures in parentheses are standard deviations/means.

Source: P. Molyneux. "An Analysis of the Structure and Performance Characteristics of Top EC Banks and the Strategic Implications of 1992," *Revue de la Banque*, June 1989.

variety of speciality banks, such as the Crédit Foncier de France in the mortgage financing arena and Crédit National specializing in industrial and commercial lending. In some cases, banks that originally had somewhat restricted lending targets, such as the Istituto Mobiliare Italiano in Italy, specializing in industrial lending, have expanded over time and offer a very wide variety of financial services. Indeed, the term *savings bank* as opposed to *commercial bank* can be very misleading. In Italy, for example, the *casse di risparmio*, savings banks, can perform many of the functions performed by *banks*, which in the American context means commercial banks. It is hence risky to conclude from viewing the number of so-called special credit institutions in these countries that the financial system is fragmented or compartmentalized.

A good example of the regional orientation of banking in Europe is the 12 German Girozentralen (Landesbanken), semipublic wholesale banks owned jointly by state governments and regional saving banks. While acting as the state banks for the 12 federal states and as clearing houses for the regional saving banks, they offer most forms of typical commercial banking services. The largest of them, Westdeutsche Landesbank, is about the fourth largest bank in Germany. Similarly, the five regional Zentralbanken operate as clearing associations for credit cooperatives and together with their central institution, the Deutsche Genossenschaftsbank, are essentially universal banks and compete with the major German commercial banks. Both Landesbanks and the regional Zentralbanks have recently been discussed as potential areas of merger activity in German banking.[64]

Another organizational characteristic in several EEC countries is the close ownership and management participation by banks of nonfinancial firms. The country often pointed to in this regard is Germany, where banks are the dominant direct source of finance for nonfinancial enterprises, also underwriting marketable securities and even distributing them to bank customers. Cable reports that at the beginning of the 1980s, German banks held almost 10% of the seats on the boards of the largest 100 German enterprises.[65] The banks also own large blocks of shares in German nonfinancial firms and effectively control even more through the use of proxy voting for their customers.[66] Recently, it also has been estimated that the ten largest banks in Germany have majority control in 27 of the 32 largest industrial firms.[67] Concerned with the concentration of economic influence, the German parliament is considering the desirability of limiting banks' ownership and control of German industry.

The close joint owner/creditor relationship of banks to nonfinancial firms has been argued to reduce potential information asymmetries between debtor and creditors and thus reduce lending costs and potential credit rationing. It may also reduce placement costs for marketable securities. At the same time, however, it raises the important question of potential conflicts of interests for universal banks such as those in Germany and the Netherlands. This was a major concern of the Gessler Report, which considered the strengths and weaknesses of the German universal banking system.[68] Spain and France are two other cases where bank ownership of equity in nonfinancial corporations is sizable. Although banks in several other countries in the EEC are permitted to hold equity in nonfinancial corporations, in many cases there are significant limitations on participations.

An important banking industrial organization question in the EEC concerns the ownership of banks by nonfinancial firms. In most countries of the EEC, nonfinancial firms are not permitted to own banks, although some participation is permitted. The issue of bank ownership by nonfinancial enterprises is most heated in Italy. There is no legislation in Italy that prohibits industrial firms from purchasing banks. The issue became a live one in 1986 when Bank of America put up for sale its Italian bank subsidiary and two major industrial firms expressed interest. The Banca d'Italia has strongly opposed ownership of banks by industrial groups, although minority shareholding has been permitted. In the end the subsidiary, Banca d'America e d'Italia, was purchased by Deutsche Bank.[69]

One of the goals of European financial market integration is to take advantage of the economies of scale in banking that have not yet been exploited. In some countries where a large number of small banks exist, such as in Italy, some economies of scale may be available. Yet even though banking concentration seems particularly high in only a few countries (France, Belgium, the Netherlands, Spain), as a group, banking concentration appears substantial. Salomon Brothers estimates that of the 2039 banks in Europe at the end of 1986, 25 banks (the largest five in France, Italy, Spain, the United Kingdom, and Germany) captured approximately 70% of the total assets.[70] It should also be noted that outside the United Kingdom, only four banks in the EEC have wholly owned retail banking operations outside their home country. Hence one can conclude for retail banking in the EEC that any major inroads by foreign competitors have yet to be seen. In Germany, which appears to have relatively low banking concentration ratios in spite of the assumed dominance of the big three banks, the large regional saving banks offer substantial competitive impediments to profitable foreign entry into the retail banking market. The somewhat oligopolistic structure of retail

Table 4-10. Gross and Net Margins in Banks, 1982

	Percentage of Average Total Assets	
Countries and Banks	Gross Earnings Margin	Net Earnings Margin
Belgium		
Large banks	3.36	0.78
Commercial banks	3.01	0.77
Savings banks	2.70	1.06
Germany		
Large banks	4.35	1.23
Commercial banks	3.30	1.07
Giro banks	0.86	0.38
Savings banks	3.79	1.59
France		
Large banks	2.94	0.93
Commercial banks	2.98	1.01
Italy		
Large banks	2.92	0.86
Commercial banks	3.23	1.36
Savings banks	4.52	1.98
Netherlands (1981)		
Commercial banks	2.91	1.00
Savings banks	2.75	0.79
United Kingdom		
Large banks	4.72	1.44
Trustee savings banks	5.83	1.75
Building societies	1.78	0.50

Source: OECD Costs and Margins in Banking, Statistical Supplement, 1985.

banking in the EEC is expected by some investigators to remain for some time, even after the removal of remaining capital flow barriers, the greater freedom of banking establishment, and the improved competitive pricing of banking services.[71]

Before considering the general structure of services offered by banking systems in the EEC, we briefly consider banking profitability.[72] Data on bank profits in Europe are both dated and difficult to use in making cross-country comparisons. Nonetheless, what data are available (seen in tables 4-10, 4-11a, and 4-11b) suggest that Italy, the United Kingdom, and Spain have had the most profitable banking sectors, measured with respect to GDP and loans outstanding (Table 4-11a). Gross earnings margins (Table 4-10) for large banks appear to be particularly high in the

Table 4-11a. Profit Before Tax of Banks, 1982

Countries	In Millions of ecu	GDP in Percentages	Loans Outstanding in Percentages
Belgium	389	0.45	0.32
Germany	5,024	0.84	0.63
Spain	2,482	1.24	1.4
France	2,317	0.42	0.35
Italy	3,658	1.03	1.8
Netherlands	365[a]	0.32	0.35
United Kingdom	4,032	0.95	0.68

[a] 1981.
Source: "The Cost of Non-Europe" in *Financial Services*, Vol. 9, Price Waterhouse, Commission of the European Community, table 3.28, 1988.

United Kingdom and Germany. Countries where there appears to be high concentration in banking, such as Belgium and the Netherlands, have not necessarily experienced the highest profitability.

Using more recent data, table 4-11b shows the high net interest income as a percentage of assets in Spanish banking. These high intermediation margins are said to result from the modest sophistication of Spanish savers.[73] The high margins are evident in both commercial and saving banks, but particularly in the latter, which are heavily involved in retail banking. However, table 4-11b also suggests that pretax profits as a percentage of equity in Spanish banking are lower than in the other countries shown, reflecting high personnel and operating costs. The large intermediation margins in Spanish banking are one reason some consider Spain an attractive market for foreign banks.

2.3. Banking Services in EEC Member States and Switzerland

Among EEC countries and Switzerland, five countries are typically characterized as having universal banking systems, offering a host of banking and security services. These countries are France, Germany, Italy, the Netherlands, and Switzerland.[74] The usual characterization, however, may be somewhat misleading. Recent liberalization in the United Kingdom has resulted in a wide variety of security services offered

Table 4-11b. Comparative Measures of Bank Profitability (as a Percentage of Total Assets in 1986)

	Commercial Banks						Saving Banks			
Item	Germany	France	Italy[a]	Spain	United States	Japan	Germany	Italy	Spain	United States[b]
Net interest income	2.46	2.72	3.02	3.73	3.34	1.27	3.18	2.78	4.68	2.13
Net noninterest income	1.09	0.46	1.31	0.87	1.42	0.31	0.35	0.92	0.66	0.94
Pretax profits	0.79	0.38	0.50	0.81	0.80	0.52	0.94	0.92	0.91	1.14
Pretax profits/equity	16.9	14.9	17.2	14.4	13.0	22.7	25.1	26.1	16.9	20.3

[a] Data for Italian commercial banks are for 1985.
[b] Data for U.S. saving banks are for 1985.
Source: Boletin Economico, March 1988, Banco de España, "Analisis Comparativo de la Rentabilidad del Sistema Bancario Español". See also Lygum, Perée, and Steinherr (1989) for discussion of Spanish bank profitability.

by British banks. Spanish banks are also clearly universal banks.[75] On the other hand, universality in principle does not necessarily imply universality in practice. For example, in Germany, the textbook example of a universal banking system, securities underwriting activity is largely dominated by the major three banks. Germany's commercial banking system is indeed more heterogeneous than homogeneous because of the significant role played by the large regional saving banks and special credit institutions, such as mortgage banks, installment credit institutions, and the postal giro and saving bank system.

In comparison to the United States, where banking has two major but increasingly blurred services-separation lines—one geographic, continuing to restrict free branching between states, and another functional, separating commercial from investment banking—banks in the EEC are free to engage in the provision of most financial services. The one exception in most countries is insurance, and even here the barriers are being reduced, in particular in Germany. Yet in some cases universal banks are restricted, at least nominally, with respect to the maturity of credits offered. In Italy, for example, bank commercial loans are usually not expected to be of maturity longer than 18 months, although overdraft facilities effectively provide longer-term financing, and recently commercial banks have been permitted to provide some medium-term financing. In addition, in some instances commercial banks are primarily short-term borrowers and are restricted from issuing long-term bonds. Because Germany is often used as the classic example of a universal bank, able to both borrow and lend both in the short and long term, it is common to attribute the same characteristics to other EEC banking systems with so-called universal banking attributes. The analogy is of only limited use. And universality in German banking also has its limits. The German Bundesbank has at times argued against the development of particular financial instruments, markets, and techniques that might impair their monetary control.[76] Thus, *universal banking* should not be confused or equated with *unrestricted banking*. Nor should it be forgotten that, as in Germany and the Netherlands, some universal commercial banking markets face strong competition from large and aggressive saving banks and special credit institutions, and even nondepository institutions such as pension funds.

In Switzerland, another heralded universal banking center, there is considerable specialization in particular kinds of banking business, such as portfolio management, foreign exchange, and gold operations.[77] And because of the existence of a stamp duty on securities transactions, the Swiss banks have very little activity in the issuance and trading of

Eurobonds, other than those denominated in Swiss francs, over which they have a monopoly on issuance, due to the success of the Swiss National Bank in restricting the issuance of Swiss franc-denominated bonds to within Swiss borders.

In the U.S. context, *nonbanking financial services* as described in most member states of the EEC are often provided directly under the aegis of the bank itself rather than through a separate subsidiary, with the exception of insurance. And whereas in the United States nonbanking financial services are often legally organized, together with banking services, under the corporate umbrella of a holding company, the holding-company legal structure in the EEC is commonly used to affiliate banking institutions with nonfinancial enterprises, such as in Belgium and France. In the United Kingdom, for example, only one of the large London clearing banks is organized under a holding-company structure. To add confusion to the matter, one should also note that when it is suggested that a particular financial service can be provided by the bank, the service is sometimes available from a subsidiary of the bank, even though the bank itself may be legally capable of providing the service. These issues suggest that describing the services provided by "banks" in the EEC depends on the legal structure of the financial system and banking custom. In some cases, a country may not have a truly universal banking system, but a commercial bank may still provide a service, such as insurance or merchant banking, through a closely associated affiliate or subsidiary. In short, a financial service may not be provided in-house both because it is not permitted and in other cases because it is not desired.

The United Kingdom has moved closer to the model of a continental universal bank as a result of the 1986 change in legislation that eliminated the functional separation of securities agents (brokers) and market-makers (jobbers) and the opening up of membership to the stock exchange. The deregulation of the London capital market saw both foreign and domestic banks rush into the securities market, with major investments in security market-making firms.[78] The large British banks were then capable of offering traditional domestic lending/deposit-taking services, international banking services, securities services to corporate and individual clients, merchant banking, and even (unlike some of their continental colleagues) life insurance, since several of the major clearing banks own life insurance firms.[79] The 1986 "Big Bang" in London has been rather costly for some firms entering the securities market as market-makers. The rush for position in London's gilt market by both domestic and foreign banks and security houses resulted in significant excess supply, with several British and American firms subsequently leaving the market.[80]

It is also nearsighted to focus primarily on commercial banks when considering the structure of the U.K. financial services industry. Indeed, the industry more nearly resembles a financial services bouillabaisse. In recent years, the market has seen an insurance firm purchase a stockbroker, a clearing bank purchase a large real estate agency, a unit trust firm issue credit cards, a large life insurance company sell unit trusts and mortgages, building societies sell insurance, unsecured personal loans, and credit cards, and a merchant bank sell mortgages and life insurance.[81] And in an arrangement with savings banks from ten other European countries, some U.K. saving institutions are planning to offer mutual funds denominated in European currency units. Britain provides a ready illustration of how difficult it has become to continue to define and regulate financial institutions along institutional rather than functional lines.

The push to expand financial product lines has also been evident in Germany, where banks have entered one arena previously thought somewhat sacrosanct: life insurance. In the competition for *Allfinanz*, the provision of the gamut of financial services under the name of the same institution, two of Germany's three largest banks have taken on insurance services, challenging some of Germany's large independent insurers.[82] The German insurance market is the largest in the EEC, estimated to account for about 33% of all premium income.[83] It is also thought to be very profitable. In the desire to take advantage of any remaining economies of scale or scope, some of the larger universal banks also are buying into Germany's specialized finance institutions, such as the Bausparkasse, which are building societies. At the same time, there have been merger proposals between several regional cooperative banks.

While there are few financial service areas in which German banks as a group are not highly competitive, there have been some areas where the German financial system, partly because of legal barriers and custom, and partly because of a conservative regulatory framework, lost ground to foreign competitors. In response, two recent developments have increased the efficiency of securities trading in Germany. One is the organization of Germany's several stock exchanges, and another is the provision of financial hedging instruments. In January 1989 a legislative bill revised the stock market law permitting the establishment of an options and futures exchange. This new activity was partly a reaction to the trading of German government bond futures begun in September 1988 on the London International Financial Futures Exchange (LIFFE).

The efficiency of equity trading in Germany also has been enhanced by the technical coordination and cooperation between the eight regional stock exchanges. One of the remaining impediments to equity trading in Germany remains the equity turnover tax, which has encouraged the trading of German shares on foreign bourses.[84] While these improvements in the provision of financial services have not originated with the banking industry, they have made banks more competitive as Europe moves closer to an integrated financial market.

The services provided by Italy's banks and nonbank financial institutions have also expanded in recent years, particularly in the nonbank financial services area. Portfolio management, leasing, factoring, merchant banking, and mutual-fund-type investments have all grown rapidly since the mid-1980s, many of these services being offered by subsidiaries of banks.[85] More efficient bank branching in Italy has resulted from the elimination of restrictions on the transfer of branches. The next step anticipated is a liberalization of rules concerning the opening of new branches, with the authorities concerned about the risks of overbranching and the threat to bank profitability. One notable weakness in the private financial market in Italy is life insurance, which has actually declined in terms of its share of total premiums.[86] The weakness in the provision of private life insurance contracts is attributed to the large state pension system, a source of considerable concern given demographic trends in Italy.[87]

The services available from French banks in recent years have mirrored changes in other banking centers. While considered to have a universal bank structure, French banks sometimes have been characterized as suffering from excessive compartmentalization as well as excessive public control. However, the competitive efforts seen in French capital markets have also been noticeable in French banking. Some of these efforts are seen in the variety of bank services that combine securities and loan characteristics, such as commercial paper backed by a bank credit line, participation shares, and subordinated bonds.[88] And as mentioned earlier, banks have been very active in the marketing of investment funds, SICAVs, and FCPs.

French banking also will likely be involved in the future opening up to cross-border competition of the large European insurance industry. The EEC Competition Commission in 1989 recommended an initiative that would permit the cross-border marketing of group life insurance and private retirement funds throughout the Community.[89] French banking became involved in the insurance competition fray when a prominent French bank launched a hostile takeover attempt of both a major insurance company and a large financial holding company.[90] The structure of the banking services industry in the EEC will be shaped in part by the links that banks forge with the insurance industry, which will in turn require a reshaping of regulation and supervision. The issues of corporate separateness in banking and the need to insulate the banking part of a financial conglomerate from its nonbanking affiliates may be a serious issue in Europe as competition for financial services increases as a result of the EEC's 1992 program of financial integration.

3. 1992 Banking Integration in the European Community: Objectives, Structure, and Obstacles

Economic integration in the EEC, which comes under the sign of 1992, can be thought of as basically completing the objectives of the original EEC Treaty. This integration may be broadly defined as the freedom of economic movement (capital, goods, workers), freedom of economic establishment, and freedom of provision of services within the borders of the EEC. This section will consider some of the parameters of the 1992 program as it applies to financial services and to banking in particular.

The objectives of the 1992 initiative for the financial services industry are a paraphrase of the objectives just noted—freedom to establish anywhere in the Community, freedom to provide throughout the Community financial services that are permitted to be offered in the home country, and the freedom of capital movements. Because capital usually flows to that area where its after-tax return is highest, the existence of some substantial differentials in taxation in the Community will also test the ability of the member states to fully liberalize capital flows, with France and Italy the countries usually identified as having the greatest concern.[91]

The integration of the financial services industry in the EEC has been spurred by five official European Commission documents: 1) the 1977 First Banking Coordination Directive; 2) the 1985 Commission White Paper, "Completing the Internal Market"; 3) the 1987 document "The Creation of an European Financial Area"; 4) the 1987 "Single European Act," legislation that supplemented the EEC Treaty and aimed to create by 31st December 1992 "an area without frontiers in which the free movements of goods, persons, services and capital is ensured" (article 8A); and 5) the Commission's draft 1988 "Second Banking Coordination Directive," which in revised form was officially adopted in December 1989. The development of Commission thinking and the program to complete the internal market, of which financial service is only a part, is a broad subject beyond the area of this chapter.[92] What we wish to provide below is a description of the general structure of the internal market program and some of the difficulties it may face when confronted with existing banking structure in the Community.

Between the First (1977) and Second (1988) Banking Coordination Directives, the EEC Commission went from a broad declaration of the right to establish credit institutions in the Community, with supervision based on home control central to a small set of harmonization objectives. During the period between the two directives, an important shift in thinking took place regarding the most efficient manner of attaining economic integration and harmonization rules for the Community. This revision was apparent in the 1985 White Paper. The plan was to achieve the harmonization of standards across the Community not by attempting to secure complete uniformity of rules but through the minimal harmonization of a small set of basic laws and regulations.[93]

The transition from the First Banking Directive in 1977 to the Second in 1988 was not one in which a particular thread can be said to have been followed. The 1977 directive set up a framework on which further agreements on banking harmonizations could be constructed. In 1983 a directive was agreed to that set out the principle of supervision on a consolidated basis. In 1986 the Commission also issued two nonlegally-binding recommendations; one on the monitoring and control of large exposures of credit institutions, and another regarding deposit guarantees, encouraging member states in which they were absent to introduce them by 1990.[94]

This series of directives was still far from complete in securing an integrated EEC banking market. Capital flow restrictions were still in effect in a few countries; authorization by the host-country supervisory authorities had to be secured to operate in another member state; host-country regulations and supervision constrained the activities of the guest institution; and in many countries, branches of foreign banks had to be backed by so-called *endowment capital*, rather than by the capital of the parent institution.[95]

The Second Banking Coordination Directive spelled out the objectives and procedures for integration earlier defined in the 1985 White Paper. The White Paper's reference to the provision of financial services gave prominent mention to the "Cassis de Dijon" judgment in arguing for the "free circulation of financial products." The Commission considered that it should be possible to facilitate the exchange of such "financial products" at a Community level, using minimal coordination of rules (especially on such matters as authorization, financial supervision and reorganization, winding up, etc.) as the basis for mutual recognition by member states on what each does to safeguard the interests of the public. Such harmonization, particularly as regards the supervision of ongoing activities, should be guided by the principle of "home country control."[96]

The objectives of the Second Banking Coordination Directive are clearly spelled out in the explanatory memorandum accompanying the articles of the draft Directive:

Main objectives of the Proposal
1. The proposal for a Second Banking Coordination Directive is the centrepiece of Commission proposals for the banking sector in the context of the completion of the Internal Market by 1992. Along with the liberalisation of capital movements and other accompanying Community instruments in the Banking sector (on own funds, large exposures, harmonised solvency ratio, deposit guarantee system), it is intended to:
   — remove the remaining barriers to freedom of establishment in the banking sector;
   — provide for full freedom of services.
2. The approach in the Directive is firmly based on the White Paper concepts of *harmonisation of essentials*, *mutual recognition* and *home country control*. The aim is that there should be a *single banking license* valid for both establishment and freedom of service no later than the end of 1992.[97] (Emphasis ours).

Table 4-12 details the banking services covered in the Second Banking Directive, services that in principle are free to be traded across borders of EEC member states and to which the principle of mutual recognition is to apply. The single banking license for EEC banks and the list of permissible banking activities effectively "has been drawn up on a liberal universal banking model."[98] As stated in the Second Banking Directive, the most far-reaching group of activities concern banks' activities in securities, including: "trading for own account or account of customers in all forms of security (short and long-term); participation in share issues and the provision of services related to them; portfolio management and advice."

The principle of mutual recognition of laws, regulations, and administrative practices with regard to the provision of financial services cannot of course be implemented without some basic common guarantees of financial stability, this being embedded in the "harmonization of essential standards." The Second Banking Coordination Directive states that "home country control" of banks operating in other EEC member states is *contingent* on 1) the harmonization of minimum capital for authoriza-

Table 4-12. Second Banking Coordination Directive Commission of the European Communities: List of Activities Subject to Mutual Recognition

1. Acceptance of deposits and other repayable funds from the public
2. Lending[a]
3. Financial leasing
4. Money-transmission services
5. Issuing and administering means of payment (e.g., credit cards, travelers checks, and bankers' drafts)
6. Guarantees and commitments
7. Trading for own account or for account of customers in:
    (a) Money market instruments (checks, bills, CDs, etc.)
    (b) Foreign exchange
    (c) Financial futures and options
    (d) Exchange and interest-rate instruments
    (e) Transferable securities
8. Participation in share issues and the provision of services related to such issues
9. Advice to undertakings on capital structure, industrial strategy, and related questions, and advice and services relating to mergers and the purchase of undertakings
10. Money brokering
11. Portfolio management and advice
12. Safekeeping and administration of securities
13. Credit reference services
14. Safe custody services

[a] Including, inter alia, consumer credit; mortgage lending; factoring, with or without recourse; and financing of commercial transactions (including forfeiting).

Source: Second Council Directive on the Coordination of Laws, Regulations and Administrative Provisions Relating to the Taking-up and Pursuit of the Business of Credit Institutions and Amending Directive 77/780/EEC, Annex, December 1989.

tion and continuing business; 2) supervisory control of major shareholders and of banks' participation in the nonbank sector; 3) sound accounting and control mechanisms; and, in addition, 4) aid in ensuring solvency and the protection of depositors, legislation on own funds, and a harmonized solvency ratio.[99]

Previous to the single market program (the "Completing the Internal Market" White Paper), the EEC had adopted *full harmonization* as the principle of economic integration; simply put, everyone in the Community was to play by the same well-defined and agreed-upon rules. However, the presumption under which the internal market will operate is along the lines of the Cassis de Dijon case—namely, financial activities permitted in a member state are permitted in every other member state if the activity is defined as permissible and does not pose a threat to the public interest in the host market.

The sweeping nature of the Second Banking Directive (which authorizes a single banking license in which a bank authorized to operate in its home market is immediately eligible to operate in any member state subject to the rules of its home country) quickly raises the question of whether regulatory authorities will allow local banks to operate on the same footing as foreign institutions operating in the domestic market. Some EEC countries, for example, permit the payment of interest on demand deposits, and others do not; variable rate mortgages are common in some national markets, but not in others. The Second Banking Directive leaves little doubt that there will be few levers to pull to prohibit foreign banks from offering services that are not available from domestic institutions.

> Where the competent authorities of a host Member State ascertain that an institution having a branch or providing services within its territory is not complying with the legal provisions adopted in that State pursuant to the provisions of this Directive involving powers of the host Member State competent authorities, those authorities shall require the institution concerned to put an end to that irregular situation.[100]

The regulatory framework set by the Second Banking Directive is also characterized by the absence of any European banking supervisory authority. The authorities of the licensing country are the ultimate supervisors and regulators of their institutions, wherever they may be operating in the Community. Hence competition can be expected to take place on two levels: competition in the provision of specific financial services and competition in regulations.[101] Over time what will emerge from this federal system of banking licensing, regulation, and supervision will largely depend on how member states respond to competition that may place their banks at a competitive disadvantage within their home markets. The novelty of the EEC's new banking regulatory framework is that the level of regulation will be strongly market-determined, and, some argue, "more responsive to market conditions than one designed ex ante by a supernational body, and then revised subject to long and variable lags."[102] The implicit assumption in such a system is that competition among regulators will not degenerate into a "competition in laxity," which might potentially weaken the overall stability of the European banking system, with the end product of a lowest-common-denominator regulatory structure.[103] Hence, it is not possible to describe a fixed banking regulatory structure in the EEC, since by design the regulatory structure is expected to evolve toward a competitive equilibrium. A component of this structure will include some regulations and agreements that are organized and mutually agreed upon by banking regulators and supervisors of the member states, such as the recent agreement on minimum bank capital standards.

Although the 1977 First Banking Coordination Directive reduced the number of barriers to the establishment of banks in the EEC (for example, by 1989 the ability to refuse a banking license on grounds of economic need was prohibited), a number of barriers existed both with respect to the establishment and to the provision of banking services. Licensing requirements, endowment capital for a branch in another member state, exchange controls, and restrictions on services were still in effect in several countries in the Community.[104] To provide an overview of some of the existing barriers, we present below some of the findings of the study conducted for the Commission by Price Waterhouse.[105]

One of the major obstacles to the integration of financial markets in the EEC has been the continuing use of exchange controls, in particular in France, Italy, and Spain. While Italy liberalized capital flows to varying degrees in recent years, the complete freedom of capital movements was only recently permitted. France recently had restrictions on the opening of foreign bank accounts and some constraints on loans to nonresidents. But in a bold move, on January 1, 1990, France removed its remaining exchange controls, six months in advance of the original European Community schedule.[106] Spain is anticipated to retain exchange controls for some time.[107] Nonetheless, in 1988 there was some significant liberalization of cross-border transactions in unit trusts, unlisted securities, and national securities listed on foreign bourses in several countries of the EEC.

The EEC/Price Waterhouse 1988 study of regulatory barriers to trade and establishment in banking considered the banking practices in eight countries (Germany, the United Kingdom, Italy, Belgium, the Netherlands, France, Luxembourg, and Spain). Specifically, the study focused on requirements for establishing a banking operation, regulations restricting foreign acquisitions or participations in a bank, and restrictions on the type and range of permitted financial activities and services. An interesting conclusion of this study was the finding that within the EEC there was little "overt discrimination" against nondomestic banks. However, this does not mean that entry was easy or that barriers to trade in financial services were absent.[108] Barriers to trade in banking were thought to exist more in the practice than in the letter of the regulatory provisions.

Differences in banking regulations that might restrict trade, however, are not difficult to identify. The requirement that foreign branches maintain a minimum endowment capital is common to all countries with the exception of the United Kingdom. Minimum endowment-capital requirements were identified as a major restriction on banks within the EEC operating outside their home country. Some countries also impose minimum solvency ratios (gearing ratios), which create distortions both between banks in different countries and between banks and other financial entities that do not have the same solvency requirements. In some countries of the Community, *comfort letters* (a sort of support guarantee from the parent bank or supervisor) are required, with the requirement of such letters being of some importance in Italy. Restrictions on foreign acquisitions or participation in domestic banks exist in Italy, France, and Spain, and prior supervisory-authority authorization is required throughout the Community. For example, France requires that the foreign purchase of more than 20% of a bank's capital has the approval of the Ministry of Finance and the Banque de France. With respect to the provision of banking services, Spain and Italy both have rules that limit the services that can be provided by a foreign bank. For example, in Spain a foreign bank is limited to three branches, and in Italy there are individual lending limits for branches of foreign banks.[109] And in several countries it has been common practice that domestic bond offerings are lead-managed by a domestic institution.

The development of the issue of EEC banking reciprocity vis-à-vis non-EEC institutions has been of keen concern to banks outside the Community. Yet banking reciprocity agreements in Europe are nothing new. Even before the 1985 White Paper, several member states in the Community had banking reciprocity restrictions. The 1984 OECD study of obstacles to international trade in banking services found that the principle of reciprocity was contained in national banking legislation in several countries (e.g., Canada, Italy, Spain, Switzerland), and in several others (e.g., France, Denmark, Ireland),[110] reciprocity was administratively important even when not embodied in legislation. In Germany, a reciprocity guideline applied to non-EEC banks in relation to the lead management of foreign DM bond issues. A similar reciprocity guideline is in place in the United Kingdom (with a U.K. institution as coleader). In addition, the United Kingdom's 1986 Financial Services Act gives broad powers to the Treasury to use against EEC or non-EEC countries that do not extend reciprocity privileges. The Netherlands is another EEC country with reciprocity guidelines regarding the lead management of domestic currency-denominated bond issues. In short, reciprocity has for some time been a common principle for certain kinds of EEC banking and securities activities.

The final draft of the Second Banking Coordination Directive, adopted in December 1989, contained an article regarding relations with third countries that differed considerably from the original proposed directive. The February 1988 draft directive suggested that the Commission would examine whether credit institutions in the Community "enjoy reciprocal treatment" in third countries, in particular with regard to the establishment of subsidiaries and the acquisition of participations in credit institutions. This reciprocity language raised considerable concern in a number of countries for a variety of reasons. One reason was the continued separation of commercial and investment banking in some countries, such as the United States and Japan. In the end, the finally-agreed-upon provision with respect to relations with third countries took the form of a reciprocal national treatment principle; non-EEC banks operating in the EEC will be only required to establish that Community banks have the equivalent treatment as non-EEC banks in the latter's respective home markets.[111] At the same time, however, the EEC's Banking Federation, a European banking trade organization, identified a number of countries said to restrict the activities of foreign banks, presumably identifying them for further EEC scrutiny.[112] The country most prominently mentioned is Japan.

An area where the issue of reciprocity may have an important influence on EEC finance, and directly on banking activity, is corporate takeovers. The EEC is still in the process of establishing a common set of rules on takeover bids. Reciprocal treatment on takeovers vis-à-vis non-EEC countries is said to be favored by the EEC's Economic and Social Committee.[113]

Taxation and capital standards also have differentiated the banking environment in the EEC. EEC member states face a variety of difficult forms and rates of taxation, as well as various types of tax-free saving vehicles. In France, for example, there are a variety of saving deposits, some of which are exempt from taxation. (For example, passbook accounts such as *livrets A* with the Caisses d'Epargne and *livrets bleus* with Crédit Mutuel are tax free, while nonnegotiable bank saving certificates are taxed at a rate of 45%.) Taxes differ widely on interest income, dividend income, and capital gains, depending on the residency of the

Table 4-13. Withholding Taxes in the European Community (as a Percentage of Interest and Dividend Income)

Countries	On Interest Paid To		On Dividends Paid To	
	Residents	Nonresidents	Residents	Nonresidents
Belgium	25	25	25	25
Denmark	0[a]	0	30	30
France	—[b]	0–51	0	25
Germany	0[c]	0[c]	25	25
Ireland	0–35	0–35	0	0
Italy	12.5–30	12.5–30	10	32
Luxembourg	0	0	15	15
Netherlands	0[a]	0	25	25
United Kingdom	25	25	0	0
Greece	—[d]	49	42–53	42–53
Portugal	30	30	12	12
Spain	20	20	20	20

[a] Banks report interest income to the tax authorities.

[b] Recipients can choose to pay 27% or 47%, depending on the savings instrument, or to lump interest income with other incomes. Banks report interest income to the tax authorities.

[c] Banks do not report interest income to the tax authorities.

[d] Corporations pay 25%: individuals pay 8% plus an amount liked to graduated rates applicable to income taxes.

Note: Rates indicated are subject to restrictions and exemptions.

Source: Arthur Andersen, Morgan Guarantee, World Financial Markets, September 9, 1988.

recipient, and on security trading. The reporting by banks to the tax authorities of interest income also differs among EEC member states. Bank secrecy laws, in addition, vary considerably across countries. Table 4-13 lists the range of withholding taxes on interest and dividend income received by EEC residents and nonresidents. Differences in capital gains taxation are in some cases quite substantial and of considerable concern to countries like France, which, because of its high capital-gains taxes, might induce large capital outflows now that capital flows are completely liberalized.[114]

The massive long-term capital outflow experience of Germany in 1988–1989 was in part attributable to the reimposition of a 10% withholding tax on interest income. Similar problems, but on a much smaller

Table 4-14. Reserve Requirements in EEC Countries, Mid-1988

Countries	As a Percentage of Demand Deposits in Banks
Belgium	0.0
Denmark	0.0
France	5.0
Germany	6.6–12.1
Greece[a]	7.5
Ireland	10.0
Italy[a]	25.0[b]
Luxembourg	0.0
Netherlands	—[c]
Portugal	15.0
Spain[a]	18.5
United Kingdom	0.5

[a] Required reserves are remunerated to some degree.

[b] Applied against the increase in deposits since May 1984; the effective level of required reserves is close to 20%.

[c] A small, variable, and remunerated reserve requirement was introduced in May 1988.

Source: Morgan Guaranty Trust (1988); Levich (1989).

scale, occurred in the Netherlands in 1987 with the announcement of bank reporting of deposit interest to the tax authorities. These instances of a capital flight of sorts suggest that both short- and long-term capital flows are indeed quite sensitive to tax differentials.[115] France has been most insistent on the need to harmonize tax treatment in the Community and has expressed concern over what the absence of tax harmonization might do to French saving flows once the Single Market in finance is put in place. Tax- and income-reporting harmonization will be a difficult issue to handle on the road to financial integration in the EEC, given the requirement that any agreement on a common tax policy for the EEC will need unanimous agreement among members.[116] On other internal market harmonization issues, the Single European Act substituted a unanimous voting requirement in the European Council with qualified majority voting.[117]

Although not a part of the planned harmonization agenda, since it relates to issues of monetary control, another important tax is that of reserve requirements on bank deposits. Table 4-14 shows the wide range of reserve requirements in the Community, ranging from zero in

Belgium, Denmark, and Luxembourg to 25% in Italy. Reserve requirements can be considered a tax on financial intermediation. As such, they are an element of the differential tax structure in the Community and provide a competitive advantage to those countries in which they are particularly low.

Bank capital standards is one area where significant harmonization has recently been achieved among Community members, following the 1987 *International Convergence of Capital Measurement and Capital Standards*, an agreement reached by the Basle Committee on Banking Supervision (comprising representatives of the central banks and supervisory authorities of the Group of Ten, Switzerland, and Luxembourg). The subject of "appropriate" or "desirable" capital standards is thorny both theoretically and practically. The assumption often made by bankers is that bank capital is more expensive than noncapital liabilities, although academics argue that there is no strong theoretical or empirical support for this proposition.[118] In fact, banks are usually much more highly leveraged than nonbank financial institutions and nonfinancial corporations.

Without detailing the differences in approaches to the bank capital-adequacy issue, two general frameworks have been employed in the past by most countries in both defining capital and measuring the capital base.[119] One approach relates capital to total assets, without distinguishing between different types of assets and their associated credit or interest-rate risks (the so-called *gearing ratio*). A second approach relates capital to some risk–asset measure, derived from an accounting of the risk perceived to be inherent in different categories of bank assets and off-balance-sheet financial services (the so-called *weighted risk–asset ratio*). The Basle Committee's agreement on bank capital is in the second tradition, in which levels of capital for internationally active banks are related to the credit risk of both on-balance-sheet assets and off-balance-sheet bank activities.[120] The bank capital agreement employs a weighted risk ratio where different categories of assets and off-balance-sheet activities are weighted according to assumed levels of riskiness. The agreement also defines two types of capital: core capital (composed of equity capital and published reserves from posttax retained earnings) and supplementary capital (consisting of various other categories of reserves and provisions). The target standard ratio of capital to weighted risk assets is established at 8%, of which core capital is to be at least 4%. Internationally active banks in the participating countries to the agreement are expected to achieve this common minimum standard by the end of 1992.

The EEC Commission has pursued an initiative similar to the Basle bank capital adequacy agreement. (The Directive on Own Funds and the Solvency Ratio Directive have not yet been finalized.) The proposed Solvency Directive also suggests a minimum risk-weighted capital ratio of 8%. The definition of capital under the proposed directive is similar to that in the Basle agreement. However, some differences in capital definitions exist for a number of countries. For example, under the German Capital Principle I, only equity capital and published reserves count as "liable funds." Hence, the proposed EEC bank capital initiative has met with some concern from the Bundesbank and the German Supervisory Office.[121] Nonetheless, the proposed EEC own funds and capital ratio initiatives are interpreted as being in general agreement with the Basle Supervisors' Committee agreement; the EEC initiative is expected to be applicable to all banks within the EEC, and not only those defined as international banks.[122]

The Second Banking Coordination Directive's aim was clearly to eliminate the myriad of explicit administrative restrictions on banking establishment and the provision of services that exist in the EEC. This was most efficiently effected, as we have noted, by the principles of mutual recognition and home-country control of banks operating outside their home market. But this plan could only be put in place if all Community members agreed to a "harmonization of essential supervisory standards," such as the capital adequacy standards just mentioned. The harmonization program was designed to cover supervisory control of major shareholders and of banks' participations in the nonbank sector; accounting and control mechanisms; minimum capital for authorization and continuing business; own funds; and a harmonized solvency ratio. As of end-1992, a host country will not be able to require a bank already established elsewhere in the Community to be authorized in order to operate on host ground. And no longer will any member states be able to require the branch of a bank established in another member country to have its own endowment capital. The EEC has effectively searched for a common banking establishment, services, and a regulatory common denominator in order to increase the efficiency of the banking sector in Europe. The impact no doubt will be to negate Pecchioli's earlier appraisal of permissible banking activities in the OECD, to the effect that "there is no common approach within the OECD area to regulatory provisions affecting the range of services that can be offered by banking institutions."[123] Two questions that remain are the likely competitive impact of these changes and the public policy problems they might create.

4. Competitive Implications of a Single EEC Banking Market

The topic of this section is the prospective competitive environment in banking in the EEC. This includes the potential effect of a single EEC banking market on prices, efficiency, and banking mergers and acquisitions activity. Before addressing these issues, it is worth noting that some of the competition in the provision of financial services may come from outside the banking industry, specifically from the nonintermediated finance area. From the period (approximately) 1960–1970 to 1970–1980 the banking system in Europe grew (as measured by total assets of deposit money banks) at a greater rate than secondary bond markets (as measured by the growth of outstanding issues on secondary markets). However, from 1980–1985 the growth of secondary bond markets outpaced the growth of the European banking industry.[124] And in some countries, such as Germany, the relative importance of commercial banks (measured as a percentage of assets of all financial institutions) vis-à-vis other financial institutions declined, while that of insurance companies and other deposit institutions rose.[125]

Three factors have helped to change the competitive environment in European banking: 1) the significant decline since 1980 in the number of countries in the EEC having interest-rate controls/regulations or interest-rate cartel agreements; 2) the development and improvements in short-term money, bond, and equity markets; and 3) the deregulation of fees and commissions on financial services. At the end of 1980, many countries in the EEC plus Switzerland had either controlled or regulated interest rates or interest-rate cartel agreements, the exceptions being Germany, Italy, and the Netherlands.[126] At the end of 1987, Belgium, France, Greece, Portugal, and Switzerland continued to have some controls or cartellike agreements regarding interest rates. In some cases, interest-rate regulations encouraged the growth of previously underdeveloped financial markets. An example of the recent use of interest-rate controls to channel funds to an underdeveloped securities market is the French case, where the use of regulations on short-term deposit rates combined with market-determined long-term rates resulted in a desired shift in household savings to the long-term capital market.

Table 4-15, adapted from Bröker (1989), provides a partial list of the introduction of negotiable money market instruments in several EEC countries since the 1960s. Competitive short-term open financial markets have made it more difficult for deposit and/or lending-rate regulations or cartels to continue. This competitive pressure should become even

Table 4-15. Introduction of Negotiable Money Market Instruments in Selected EEC Countries

Countries	Period of Introduction			
	Before 1960	1960–1970	1971–1980	1981–1987
Denmark			TB (1976)[a]	
France				CD, CP (1985), TB (1986)
Greece			CD (1975)	TB (1985)
Italy			CD (1979)	
Netherlands				CD, CP (1986)
Portugal				TB (1985), CD (1987)
Spain		CD (1960)		TB (1981), CP (1982)
United Kingdom	TB	$CD (1966) $CD (1970)		$CP (1986)

[a] Reintroduction after 20 years.
Note: TB: Treasury bills; CD Certificates of Deposit; CP: Commercial Paper.
Source: Adapted from G. Bröker, Competition in Banking, OECD (1989), table 3.2,

stronger as the Community moves to a single banking market. In addition, the well-known 1986 deregulation of the London Stock Exchange and move to negotiated commissions and reductions in the securities commission rate in France, Germany, the Netherlands, and Switzerland have increased the competitive structure of secondary markets in bonds and equities.[127] As a result, banks in Europe are now facing much more efficient and competitive securities markets than they were at the beginning of the 1980s. Greater competition in European banking is being induced by the increasing growth and efficiency of its money, bond, and equity markets. And the increased market determination of interest rates, financial service fees, and commissions is making it more difficult for bank interest rates and banking markets to be regulated and cartelized.

The competitive gains expected as a result of the 1992 EEC Single Market in financial services are based on data developed by Salomon Brothers (1989) and on a study conducted by Price Waterhouse for the European Commission.[128] (The latter study covered the prices for 16 financial products or services: seven banking services, five insurance services, and four brokering or security services.) Table 4-16 displays data on price differentials in several banking services provided by European banks. A wide differential in bank service charges is apparent. Table 4-17 shows estimates of the possible declines in aggregate financial services prices resulting from the EEC internal market program. And table 4-18

Table 4-16. Price Differentials in European Banking Products, 1986

Products	Belgium	France	Italy	Luxembourg	Netherlands	Spain	United Kingdom	Germany	Average
Commercial loans[a]	1.80	1.75	2.05	2.00	2.70	2.25	2.75	2.00	2.16
Consumer loans[a]	2.40	8.00	n.a.	2.80	5.20	5.40	8.60	9.20	5.90
Credit cards[a]	18.80	7.40	19.80	9.20	15.00	13.20	12.20	16.80	14.10
Mortgages[a]	1.92	2.61	1.40	n.a.	1.37	3.20	1.16	2.30	2.00
Foreign-exchange drafts[b]	0.14	0.21	0.17	0.18	0.07	0.40	0.16	0.18	0.19
Travelers check negotiation[b]	7.30	7.50	6.60	5.00	7.20	7.00	5.00	5.00	6.30
Current accounts[c]	$0	$11	$266	$9	$0	$2	$124	$130	$68
Letters of credit[d]	1.15	0.88	1.03	1.20	1.10	1.50	1.02	0.85	1.09

[a] Margin in percentage points over money market rates.
[b] Percentage of nominal value.
[c] Annual cost of average account.
[d] Percentage of nominal value for three-month letter of credit.
Source: Salomon Brothers, "European Banking Integration in 1992," June 1989, figure 14.

Table 4-17. Possible Impacts on the Prices of Financial Products through Completion of the EEC Internal Market (As a Percentage)

Countries	Theoretical, Potential Price Reductions	Indicative Reductions	
		Range	Centre of Range
Spain	34	16–26	21
Italy	29	9–19	14
France	24	7–17	12
Belgium	23	6–16	11
Germany	25	5–15	10
Luxembourg	17	3–13	8
United Kingdom	13	2–12	7
Netherlands	9	0–9	4
Average for the eight countries	21	5–15	10

Source: "The Economics of 1992," European Economy, 35 (March 1988), 90.

gives a detailed breakdown of the estimated changes in prices of banking, securities, and insurance services expected to result from the internal market. The gains are considerable: in aggregate terms, a reduction of 10% in the cost of financial services in the EEC, amounting to approximately ecu 21 billion or 0.7% of GDP. The largest declines in financial services prices are expected in Spain, which some target as a prime candidate for entry based on assumed relative banking profits. This may be one of the reasons why the Bank of Spain has encouraged the merging of Spanish banks. The smallest price declines are for Luxembourg, the United Kingdom, and the Netherlands, with Belgium, France, Germany, and Italy occupying the middle group. In banking, the greatest competitive pressures are in the retail market and for small-to-medium size firms in the corporate banking market, with the wholesale banking market assumed to be already very competitive.[129]

There is a good deal of debate as to where the competitive pressures will geographically emerge, as well as the extent to which there exist potential gains to be had from economies of scale and scope in European banking. Judging by the estimated size of spreads in banking (prime or base lending rates less estimated bank borrowing rates) and existing levels of banking concentration, Gilibert and Steinherr (1989) identify Denmark, France, Germany, the Netherlands, and the United Kingdom as likely to have increased competition pressure from foreign banks.[130] (Spreads between lending and deposit rates are estimated to be around 5% in France, Germany, and the United Kingdom.) They argue that

Table 4-18. Estimate of Potential Falls in Financial Product Prices as a Result of Completing the EEC Internal Market

Items	Belgium	Denmark	Spain	France	Italy	Luxembourg	Netherlands	United Kingdom
1. Percentage differences in prices of financial products[a] compared with the average of the four lowest observations[b]								
Banking								
Consumer credit	−41	136	39	105	—[d]	−26	31	121
Credit cards	79	60	26	−30	89	−12	43	16
Mortgages	31	57	118	78	−4	—[d]	−6	−20
Letters of credit	22	−10	59	−7	9	27	17	8
Foreign exchange	6	31	196	56	23	33	−46	16
Travelers checks	35	−7	30	39	22	−7	33	−7
Commercial loans	−5	6	19	−7	9	6	43	46
Insurance								
Life	78	5	37	33	83	66	−9	−30
Home	−16	3	−4	39	81	57	17	90
Motor	30	15	100	9	148	77	−7	17
Commercial fire, theft	−9	43	24	153	245	−15	−1	27
Public liability	13	47	60	117	77	9	−16	−7
Securities								
Private equity	36	7	65	−13	−3	7	114	123
Private gilts	14	90	217	21	−63	27	161	36
Institutional equity	26	69	153	−5	47	68	26	−47
Institutional gilts	284	−4	60	57	92	−36	21	—[d]

Table 4-18. (Continued)

Items	Belgium	Denmark	Spain	France	Italy	Luxembourg	Netherlands	United Kingdom
2. Theoretical, potential price reductions[b]								
Banking	15	33	34	25	18	16	10	18
Insurance	31	10	32	24	51	37	1	4
Securities	52	11	44	23	33	9	18	12
Total	23	25	34	24	29	17	9	13
3. Indicates price reductions[c] All financial services								
Range	6–16	5–15	16–26	7–17	9–19	3–13	0–9	2–12
Center of range	11	10	21	12	14	8	4	7

[a] See table 5.1.3 for definitions of the financial products.
[b] The figures in part 1 of the table show the extent to which financial product prices, in each country, are above a low reference level. Each of these price differences implies a theoretical potential price fall from existing price levels to the low reference level. Part 2 sets down the weighted averages of the theoretical potential price falls for each subsector.
[c] Indicates that price falls are based upon a scaling down of the theoretical potential price reductions, taking into account roughly the extent to which perfectly competitive and integrated conditions will not be attained, plus other information for each financial services subsector, such as gross margins and administrative costs as a proportion of total costs.
[d] Observations for consumer credit in Italy and mortgages in Luxembourg were not obtained, and have been represented in the calculations of the larger aggregates. The data for institutional gilt transactions in the U.K. were not available on a comparable basis, and so the figures for institutional equity transactions were used in the calculations.

Source: Price Waterhouse; "The Economics of 1992," *European Economy* 35 (March 1988), 91.

Spain and Belgium have large banking networks with low to moderate profit levels, and thus are less attractive to foreign banks. On the other hand, Molyneux (1989) suggests that acquisitions by foreign banks are likely in the United Kingdom, Germany, Italy, and Spain, with France an unlikely candidate, since those banks that appear as desirable acquisition targets are already controlled by large financial institutions. Some security houses argue that in fact the list of eligible private European bank takeover targets is a short one.[131] The large public ownership of banks in some countries, combined with a possible reluctance to see extensive foreign ownership, particularly of major institutions, and the limited number of available banks for sale suggest that 1992 will not likely lead to a flurry of bank takeovers.

The issue of acquisition or merger activity among large banks is obviously a source of political concern. Some argue that it is unlikely that there will be a merger or acquisition joining two large or core banks from different member states, since governments are likely to intervene to prevent such a transaction. However, in the future the ability of governments in the EEC to block a large bank merger or acquisition will depend on the development of Community company law. If this future legislation permits incorporation as an EEC corporate entity, the ability of any government to block a merger or acquisition could be seriously limited.[132] The current efforts of the European Commission to rule on large mergers could greatly alter the future financial structure of Europe.[133]

Two factors that influence the attractiveness of European banks as takeover or merger candidates are profitability and *Q-ratios*, the latter defined as the ratio of the market (or replacement) value of the firm to its book value. The United Kingdom is often identified as having the most profitable banking sector, even though it is also the market identified as the most competitive, with over 500 foreign banks competing with domestic institutions.[134] (It is well known that for EEC banks there is often little relationship between profit performance and the degree of competition or banking concentration.) The Danish and German banking sector rank second and third, respectively, in terms of net earnings.[135] Although Spain has been identified by some as an area of likely increased foreign competition, profits in Spanish banking are not particularly high and are heavily dependent on the large differential between borrowing and lending rates, which is expected to decline after 1992.[136]

Aliber (1984) has identified Q-ratios in banking as an indicator of anticipated profitability and/or the cost of capital. Firm expansion is expected when the Q-ratio exceeds unity and contraction when less than

Table 4-19. Selected Q-Ratios in Banking

Countries	Market Price/Book Value (Average 1974–1982)	Market Price/Book Value (1978)
France	0.89	0.94
Switzerland	1.65	1.61
Germany	1.34	1.43
United Kingdom	0.59	0.68
Japan	1.92	1.62
United States	0.9	0.87
Spain	1.62	1.10

Source: Reported in Ballarin, Gual, and Ricart (1988) and Caminal, Gual, and Vives (1989). These figures incorporate earlier works by Aliber and Dermine.

unity. The high Q-ratios calculated by Aliber for Japanese banks for the early 1980s appear in retrospect to have been a good lending indicator of that country's success in international banking during the second half of the 1980s. No complete study of Q-ratios in EEC banking is available. Table 4-19 provides banking Q-ratios for seven countries, derived from several independent studies. Although the data are not current, they suggest that Spain may indeed be an acquisition prospect in an expanded European banking market. However, in terms of purchase value, the United Kingdom would appear to offer attractive possibilities, since its Q-ratio of less than unity suggests that the market price of the banking sector is less than its book value.

It appears unlikely that the opening up of the European banking market will lead to large acquisition activity, for some of the reasons already mentioned and for the most persuasive argument, namely, that the number of available candidates is simply not that great. Rather, banking experts anticipate that a more likely outcome will be cross-border cooperative efforts, in which banks in different geographical markets attempt to take advantage of each other's comparative strengths and distribution networks. An example referred to in the past was the exchange of 10% participations by the Belgian Société Générale de Banque and Amro Bank in the Netherlands. However, as an indication of the difficulty of such efforts, the joint participation agreement was later reversed. Another recent example is the 5% exchange between Banco Santander of Spain and the Royal Bank of Scotland in 1988.[137]

The potential for change in the competitive climate in European banking begs the usual question of the available gains from banking size. Will Europe in a dozen or more years find itself with fewer independent banks and increased concentration in banking? In some countries, such as Italy and Spain, where regional banking markets have been previously protected (e.g., restrictions on branching in Italy depending on bank size), fewer banks are likely to result. However, some countries may find that increases in bank size may be limited by the thinness of their existing capital bases, which could come under additional pressures as the Basle Supervisors' bank capital standards are put into place. But lacking such constraints, will increased efficiency/profitability gains come from an increase in the average size of banks?

Most of the research on economies of scale in banking is with reference to the U.S., and the general conclusion of this work is that there are few economies of scale beyond banks of a very modest size.[138] A recent study comparing Swiss and German banks, London consortium banks, and New York State commercial banks also found little relationship between profitability and bank size.[139] Many analysts have accepted this literature as applicable to European banking and have suggested that we should not expect increased efficiencies from size resulting from the EEC's single market in financial services.[140] Central bankers and the European Commission, on the other hand, have argued the reverse, that increased size means increased efficiency.[141] On the other hand, some argue that is is not size per se that yields increased efficiency in banking but the fact that there is jointness or interdependence in the production of financial services, commonly called *economies of scope*, and these efficiency gains are substantial for the universal bank.[142] At the same time it is argued that economies of scope in banking are difficult to prove empirically.

If we admit that there are some limited economies of scale in banking but possibly significant economies of scope, one can use two complementary arguments proposed by Aliber to suggest that the number of banks in the EEC may likely decline and the average size increase; firstly, that in general the number of banks in a country will be greater the more extensive is the scope of regulation, and, secondly, the number of banks will be larger the larger is the number of separate regional banking markets.[143] Since the EEC banking regulatory harmonization efforts are likely to create a more competitive market environment in banking, along the lines suggested by Giddy (1985), Kane (1987), and Padoa-Schioppa (1988), it is likely that fewer rather than more banking regulations will exist in Europe in the long run. And given the certain decline in regional banking markets, with or without national borders around them, we should anticipate fewer separate banking institutions in Europe and a larger average-size bank. All the same, based in part on the Bank of England's survey of the U.K. financial services industry and the expected impact of the single European market, it is most probable that European retail financial markets will continue to remain fragmented for some time, given both the difficulty of implementing a Community-wide network in retail financial services and the scarcity of large-scale retail networks available for purchase in the markets described as "attractive".[144]

5. Public Policy and the Single Market in Banking Services

An evaluation of the public policy (regulatory and prudential supervisory) aspects of the EEC's efforts to integrate the banking industry is bound to be partial and incomplete for three reasons. Firstly, several of the aspects of protective regulation in EEC banking have yet to be finalized. The original Second Banking Coordination Directive proposal, for example, refers to two earlier Commission recommendations regarding large exposure and deposit guarantee schemes that were anticipated to be transformed into Commission directives. This work has yet to be completed. Secondly, differences in regulatory systems in the Community over time will be reduced as competition between regulatory systems leads to some sort of competitive equilibrium.[145] And thirdly, the regulatory structure, both in individual countries and at the European Commission level, will adapt to the competition in banking markets that follows the 1992 program. For example, European banking may be more oligopolistic after a period of adjustment to the new regulatory and freedom-of-entry environment. The fallout from London's deregulation of the securities industry and the major overhaul of its financial regulatory structure (the Financial Services Act), followed by revisions in the overhaul, suggest that regulatory and competitive market structures are jointly and endogenously determined. The degree of competition in European banking markets and the regulatory response will in turn be determined by the contestability of these markets—that is, the sensitivity of financial prices and the response of existing firms to potential competition. In the first instance, competition is likely to be severest in those areas of banking where sunk costs are lowest and new entrants can best trade on a name established in other European banking markets.[146]

An initial public policy concern with the single-market program in banking might best be gained from considering the Bank of England's survey "The Single European Market":

> A number of firms felt that the combination of expanding financial services activity and intensified competition could increase the level of risk in the financial markets. Increased risk could arise from several sources. In particular, the survey suggested a tendency among some corporate consumers, as well as suppliers, of financial services to feel they ought to be "in on 1992" (as happened in the United Kingdom with "Big Bang"). This could lead to corporate reorganizations (expansion, diversification, new investment) based less on a realistic assessment of opportunities and threats than on concern "not to miss the boat", or for reasons of "public profile", or simply out of fear. Some non-EEC (notably US and Japanese) institutions also appeared to feel pressure to "do something" about "1992". These risks could be exacerbated by the advent of relatively inexperienced (or unscrupulous) firms in newly deregulated sectors. It was thought quite possible that some of these negative effects of increased competition could appear before the potential benefits begin to be felt.[147]

This practical concern with the advent of new competitive conditions in a single European financial market reflects the expectation that the state of nature in banking is likely to change, but with only limited understanding of the form and magnitude of the potential changes. From a financial regulatory/supervisory point of view, the issue that should be given considerable attention is the possibility of a rise in the moral hazard problem in the new competitive banking environment. Here a formal definition is useful.

> Moral hazard may be defined as actions of economic agents in maximizing their own utility to the detriment of others, in situations where they do not bear the full consequences or, equivalently, do not enjoy the full benefits of their actions due to uncertainty and incomplete or restricted contracts which prevent the assignment of full damages (benefits) to the agent responsible. It is a special form of incompleteness of contracts which creates the conflict between the agent's utility and that of others. Such incompleteness may arise due to several reasons: the coexistence of unequal information and risk aversion or joint production, costs and legal barriers to contracting and costs of contract enforcement.[148]

The potential for an unexpected rise in competitive risk (a change in the state of nature) in retail banking (an industry, as mentioned at the start of this chapter, that historically has been heavily regulated) suggests that a major public policy concèrn ought to be public policy itself—that is, the reaction of public policy to structural changes in European banking markets. The experience of the crisis in the U.S. thrift industry is one example—and one will do—of how public policy grossly underestimated the potential risks from deregulation, which carried with it a large moral hazard problem.[149] The risk that governments and monetary and regulatory authorities could unwittingly increase the moral hazard problem as the banking industry in Europe becomes more concentrated is reflected in the concern raised by Tobin with regard to the issue of failures of financial institutions.

> Given the proclivity of the monetary and financial regulators for averting failures of large depositories, proposals to restructure the financial system should guard against changes that make rescues even more compelling.... The system of depositories (the United States) is drifting toward oligopoly of giant nationwide banks and bank holding companies, and to conglomerates engaged in a host of financial and non-financial businesses. An unfortunate byproduct of this drift would be that the government would be so fearful of the consequences of a failure of these giants that their survival would be guaranteed—whatever the nature of their difficulties, whether they presented any threat to the payments system or not, indeed whether they were connected to financial or non-financial activities.[150]

As they move into a new competitive environment, the one significant advantage European banking markets have in comparison to prederegulated U.S. banking markets is the existing structure of banking regulation. European banking regulations, using the terminology of Revell, are heavily biased towards "prudential regulations" rather than "structural regulations," where the former involves controls of balance-sheet items like liquidity and solvency, and the latter relates to permissible activities, establishment and banking rules, and controls in interest rates and financial service prices.[151] Some of the problems the United States encountered in deregulating its financial system resulted from the earlier dominance of structural regulations. However, a major disadvantage European banking markets have vis-à-vis American markets is the continued role of the government sector in banking.

Given Europe's history of heavy direct government involvement in banking, how governments (regulators, treasuries, monetary authorities) distance themselves from their banking institutions in an attempt to require greater private absorption of risk and less implicit or explicit government guarantees, yet at the same time ensure financial stability through appropriate supervisory practices and regulatory requirements, should have some impact on the success of the single market in European banking services. Encouraging the banking sector to bear the risk on

Table 4-20. International Comparison of Deposit Insurance Systems

Countries	Coverage (Domestic Currency)
EEC countries	
Belgium	B. fr. 500,000
France	Fr. fr. 400,000
Germany	30% of equity
Netherlands	Fl. 35,000
Spain	Pts. 1,500,000
United Kingdom	75% of deposits up to £20,000
Denmark	D. kr. 250,000
Italy	Lit. 3,000,000,000
Portugal[a]	Limited to one bank
Greece[b]	None
Ireland[c]	IR£ 15,000
Luxembourg[b]	None
Other countries	
United States	$100,000
Japan	Yen 10,000,000
Canada	Can.$60,000

[a] Only deposits with the state-owned Caixa Feral de Depositos, which accounts for around one quarter of the banking system, are formally insured, directly by the government, for historical reasons. The creation of a deposit insurance system is currently in preparation, in compliance with an EC recommendation.

[b] None as of 1987; see Pecchioli (1987), annex XII. Note that all countries in the EEC currently without deposit guarantee schemes are in the process of planning their implementation in response to an EEC Commission recommendation.

[c] cf. *Financial Times*, "Financial Regulation Report." September 1989, regarding the Central Bank Act 1989 in Ireland.

ventures for which they expect to be the beneficiaries is of considerable importance if the industry is likely to become more concentrated, if greater foreign activity is expected in domestic markets, and if banks are to become involved in a wider variety of financial activities. We can identify (at least) three areas of potential moral hazard problems in European banking, not necessarily a result of but certainly contingent on a more highly competitive and interrelated European banking market: government-administered deposit insurance programmes; commercial enterprise ownership or control of banks, and assumed implicit guarantees of support by the central bank or the government (i.e., treasury), partly as a result of increased firm size and concentration in banking.

As the U.S. experience with its thrift industry has shown, any restructuring of the financial systems that carries the possibility of increasing the risks taken by the banking system should at the same time include a serious reevaluation of the efficiency of the deposit insurance system: efficiency in the sense of ensuring that deposit insurance is not used as an implicit leverage for the risk-taking of the institution's new activities.[152]

> The existence of a federal safety net for depository institutions—consisting of federal deposit insurance, the discount window, and guarantees of the payments mechanism—will inevitably lead some owners and managers of firms that benefit from the safety net to increase their willingness to expose their depositories to excessive risk. The problems raised by such actions are endemic to all insurance programmes, public and private.[153]

The U.S. experience with deposit insurance both for commercial banks and savings institutions suggests that there are two components of such insurance: firstly, the explicit contractual obligation, and secondly, the implicit guarantee of deposits above the contractual maximum.[154] The implicit deposit guarantee arises in those cases where the activities of banks, particularly large banks with new or large exposure activities, have the potential to increase the risk faced by all major bank players. This so-called *systemic risk* potential may arise, for example, in the case of LDC debt, leveraged buy-out activities, or payments settlement risk. The likelihood of a major financial restructuring increasing any implicit or explicit assurances by the authorities, as in the U.S. thrift industry case, should provide an incentive for financial authorities to consider the importance of market discipline in inducing banks to monitor, control, and limit their risk exposure.

The moral hazard problem cannot be contained by explicit regulation alone.[155] Regulation must be reinforced by some market mechanism that creates an incentive for banks to limit their risk exposure and not to attempt to profit from explicit or assumed government guarantees. In addition, the moral hazard problem created by deposit insurance requires the institution of careful bank examination and supervision procedures. For example, the U.S. experience with bank failures in the early part of the century revealed that the difference in failure rates between national banks and state-chartered banks, with the latter having a significantly higher failure rate, can in good part be explained by the superior supervision and examination of national banks.[156]

At the present time, moral hazard in European banking created by deposit insurance is not a big issue, since explicit deposit insurance is not of general public concern. (Some even argue that it is completely ignored by the public.)[157] Compared with U.S. deposit insurance, deposit insurance coverage in banks of the EEC is relatively modest and does not have advertising value, as in the United States.[158] Nonetheless, a number of countries are reexamining the adequacy of their deposit insurance systems. Greater cross-border competition in retail banking could ignite increased public concern with the adequacy of deposit insurance coverage offered by a nondomestic institution, with deposit insurance becoming a means of attracting retail deposits in foreign markets. Hence the demand for government-sponsored deposit insurance programs could rise both from the public and from the banks. It is possible that new entrants into foreign retail banking markets without extensive branch networks will need to compete both with "name" and higher deposit rates to attract funds, and with greater deposit guarantees to ensure their stability, thereby providing the ingredients for an incipient moral hazard problem.[159]

One can argue that many European banking markets already have considerable deposit insurance coverage, although most of this insurance is implicit, since 1) explicit bank failures are rarely permitted to occur, and 2) in some countries many of the large banks are directly or indirectly controlled by the government. Intervention by the finance or monetary authorities to arrange the merger of a weak or failing institution with a healthy one should be considered a form of deposit insurance. Indeed, such implicit deposit insurance may pose more of a potential moral hazard problem to the authorities than explicit insurance, because the insurance is basically free to the insured institution. In the United States, big banks in effect have 100% deposit insurance due to the too-big-to-fail doctrine, as recently argued by the Chairman of the Federal Deposit Insurance Corporation.[160] Deposit insurance for smaller institutions is argued by some to be necessary for competitive reasons. The test of European implicit deposit insurance may arise when inefficient institutions meet with aggressive foreign entry.

A second potential moral hazard problem in European banking is related to the issue of bank ownership or control by nonfinancial enterprises. Here the danger is the apparent risk of conflict of interest and the risk that the public umbrella of security provided to the banking institution will be implicitly extended to related commercial enterprises. This issue is of some importance in countries where the banking industry is in the process of restructuring and anticipating greater domestic and foreign competition and, in particular, where it is in need of capital reinforcement. The subject of the control of banks by industrial and other nonfinancial groups is particularly important in Italy. Presently, there is a limit of 20% ownership of a bank by an industrial firm. It is argued that Italian banks are in need of high capital requirements to aid in their expansion and to facilitate the announced privatization of some public-sector banks.[161] Such capital infusions, it is argued, are more likely to be available from foreign financial institutions and from the Italian industrial sector. Greater influence in Italian banking of domestic nonfinancial groups is also recommended in order to increase the efficiency of the banking sector, given the previous restructuring and internationalization of some parts of Italian industry.

Countering this argument is that of the governor of the Banca d'Italia, who argues that separation of banking and commerce is necessary to prevent conflicts of interest and "is also intended to avoid undue extension of the powers and sphere of action of the central bank."[162] The threat to stability is that of contagion: that the problems in the industrial firm with controlling interest in a bank could easily spread to the bank. The danger, as suggested by Ciampi, is that intervention by the central bank as lender of last resort would be indirectly supporting the nonbanking component of the conglomerate.[163] Such an implicit and incipient extension of the powers of the central bank to aid a commercial enterprise could provide a serious increase in the moral hazard problem already existing in banking. Italy is not alone in confronting the need for capital in its banking sector and the question of the desirability of the separation of banking from commerce. France also faces the requirement of additional bank capital, a difficulty compounded by the large government stake in the banking industry. Any future privatization of government-controlled banks may raise the question of how to best handle the moral hazard problem and banking/commercial enterprise linkages. In addition, a potential moral hazard problem may exist in some countries where banks are permitted to take substantial equity interests in industrial concerns, with Germany being the dominant European example in this regard.[164] On the other hand, several countries in the EEC, such as Belgium and Denmark, allow only limited share ownership of nonfinancial firms by banks, in part as a result of the bank problems caused by failing industrial firms during the 1930s.

While Community-wide agreements to limit bank ownership of equities may appear desirable from the point of view of limiting potential contagion coming from the nonfinancial enterprise, it may at the same time diminish some of the gains from close debtor/creditor relationships, which permit greater information sharing and superior monitoring on the part of the bank. It also begs the question of how commercial bank ownership or joint operations in nonbanking financial activities, such as insurance or corporate securities sales and underwriting, limits contagion problems, which bank/industrial-firm interrelationships somehow cannot avoid. The important issue may be not whether banking and nonbanking financial services activities can be efficiently and safely provided under the same corporate umbrella, while banking/commercial interrelationships provide insurmountable risks, but whether the corporate legal structure can be arranged so that there is legal and publicly perceived corporate separateness between banking, nonbanking financial, and commercial activities. Whether such corporate separateness can be achieved and potential moral hazard problems limited depends in good part on the quality of the supervisory and regulatory authorities in assuring separateness and on actual market experience with such institutions. The German banking example seems to indicate that in some countries financial conglomerates with strong equity ties to industry have existed without creating undue moral hazard difficulties. On the other hand, in other countries moral hazard problems in banking do not appear to have been severely reduced by limiting equity participations by banks in industrial firms or the reverse.

Lastly, one might conjecture that the opening up of a single market for financial services in Europe may have caused an overestimation of the gains to be had from increased financial integration and/or an underestimation of the risks involved. The reluctance of managers to recognize that, in the words of Guttentag and Herring, "shock probabilities" have increased after they have made major commitments to new markets and activities could aggravate the moral hazard problem faced by European central banks and regulatory/supervisory authorities.[165] This could be a serious problem where banks are weakly capitalized and/or where historically governments have played a major role in managing, directly or indirectly, banking activities and in providing capital or backup support in times of financial difficulty. A sort of "disaster myopia" is used to describe the slow reaction of banks to debt-servicing problems that arose before the debt crisis in 1982.[166] A similar problem, but of the regulatory myopia sort, existed with the growing crisis in the U.S. savings bank industry in the 1980s. Here moral hazard problems were introduced by an increase in non-risk-based deposit insurance, a regulator/supervisor that had divided responsibilities between promoting an industry and ensuring its soundness, and political involvement in regulatory decision making. Competitive risk myopia in European banking could also arise with the growth of a European banking oligopoly, in which case a moral hazard threat may emerge from the establishment of a few very large European financial conglomerates.[167] These potential dangers exist to some degree in several of the countries of the EEC. They point to the need for a strong cooperative banking supervisory review and greater public disclosure, as banks enter a new European financial marketplace. In a broad context, these dangers may also point to the need to limit the implicit or backup role of government in private financial market risk-taking. Greater freedom in banking to establish and compete, both geographically and functionally, will require that the private market more efficiently allocate both risk and reward.

Acknowledgments

The views expressed in this chapter are those of the author and not necessarily those of the Bank for International Settlements. A number of individuals have been of assistance in the preparation of this article, both in terms of advice and the provision of data and technical assistance. I wish to thank Robert Aliber, Palle Andersen, Henri Bernard, Claudio Borio, Didier Bruneel, Creon Butler, Phil Davis, Jean Dermine, Charles Freeland, Peter Hayward, Michael Hutchison, George Kaufmann, John Kneeshaw, Christopher Kwiecinski, Joël Metais, José Ramalho, Gerald Randecker, Paolo Marullo Reedtz, Ana Maria Sanchez Trujillo, and Paul Van den Bergh. And my thanks to Rosemary Munday for typing several drafts of the manuscript.

Notes

1. "Obstacles to International Trade in Banking Services," *Financial Market Trends*, March 1984, OECD, p. 1.
2. The papers by Padoa-Schioppa (1988) and Zavvos (1988) provide general introductions to the aims and strategies of the EEC's planned integration of the financial sector.
3. Padoa-Schioppa (1988), p. 51.
4. See, for example, Hendrie (1988), Dale (1984), and, with reference to the United Kingdom, Hall (1989).
5. Leland and Pyle (1977) provide one of the early analyses of financial intermediation and information asymmetries.
6. A formal model showing the dominance of financial intermediation over direct lending (nonintermediated finance), based on the cost of monitoring and the size of investment projects, is presented in Williamson (1986).
7. Diamond (1984) argues that the aggregate cost of monitoring may be high when there are many lenders. There may also be a "free-rider problem" when one lender fails to monitor, attempting to exploit the monitoring of others. The outcome is for some lenders (banks) to monitor and to essentially sell this service to other lenders (depositors). Similarly, one bank may initiate a large loan and then "downstream" parts of the loan to other banks,

who participate in part on the basis of the credit review of the loan-originating bank. Contract enforcement may also be more efficient when there are fewer lenders. This service is similarly sold by the intermediary to the depositor.

8. Close institutional relationships between commercial banks and industrial corporations are argued by some to result from the reduction in informational asymmetries, with Germany often being cited as an example. See, for example, Cable (1985).

9. This argument is made by Black (1975) and revived by Fama (1985).

10. Diamond and Dybvig (1983) provide an analysis of bank deposit contracts and show that government provision of deposit insurance may be superior to contracts that prevent bank runs.

11. See Golembe (1989), for example, on the broad long-term trends in U.S. banking regulation. He argues that in the United States, banking is increasingly becoming somewhat of a public utility industry, with regulation increasingly becoming more important than supervision.

12. See Freeman (1988). Postlewaite and Vives (1987) provide a model in which there is a positive probability of a bank run even when the competitive equilibrium is unique.

13. The endogenous demand for banking supervision is described in Marquardt (1987).

14. Some have argued that the basis for banking regulation and supervision is not to guarantee the stability of deposits of any individual bank but to prevent individual failures from leading to other failures that would undermine the entire industry. See Baltensperger and Dermine (1987). This would then raise the potential problem of "too big to fail," in which institutional size would itself create a moral hazard problem for the banking authorities. A too-big-to-fail banking environment may act in effect as 100% deposit insurance for large banks. Deposit insurance for smaller banks may in turn be required to ensure their competitiveness with larger institutions.

15. As argued by Baltensperger and Dermine (1987) it is difficult to separate the motivations for banking regulation. Monetary and credit control also would be an important motive for banking regulation. For example, the reluctance of the Bundesbank to have short-term financial assets compete with traditional bank deposits appears to have been motivated by concern with the stability of the demand for money in Germany.

16. See Corrigan (1986).

17. The potential problems faced by the U.S. central bank related to payments systems have recently been studied by the Federal Reserve's task force on controlling payments system risk; see Lindsey (1988).

18. This position is taken by Pierce (1986), in opposition to that taken by Corrigan (1982). The importance of the payments system in Corrigan's view of the financial world is quickly revealed in his definition of a bank and the public policy implications of this definition: "The definition is deceptively simple: a bank is any institution that is eligible to issue transaction accounts. If an institution meets this definition, it would (1) be eligible for government deposit insurance; (2) have direct access to the discount window; (3) be subject to reserve requirements; and (4) have direct access to Federal Reserve payment services, particularly the wire transfer system" (p. 2). The conditions required to insulate banks from problems occurring in their nonbank affiliates is considered in Chase (1988).

19. On the issue of the corporate separateness doctrine, Corrigan (1986) quotes Walter Wriston, the former chairman of Citibank: "For example, it is inconceivable that any major bank would walk away from any subsidiary of its holding company. If your name is on the door, all of your capital funds are going to be behind it in the real world. Lawyers can say you have separation, but the marketplace is persuasive, and it would not see it that way" (p. 27).

20. Even someone as cautious and thoughtful as Tobin has recently argued that " . . . I see no convincing macro-economic reason for the US government to guarantee that a large depository will not be allowed to fail." See Tobin (1987), p. 169. Similarly, Corrigan (1986) states: "To put it directly, the freedoms contemplated by the current market environment must include the freedom to fail. And, by extension, the financial system must be a system in which discipline operates through prior restraints, . . ., and not by falling into situations in which restraint and discipline are achieved only as a by-product of instability and failure" (p. 50). Kaufman (1989) examines some of the real and imagined dangers resulting from the failure of large depository institutions. A former chairman of the FDIC has also argued that failure to close some large U.S. thrift institutions promptly not only did not prevent failure but ultimately resulted in much larger losses than would have resulted if failure had been permitted to take place earlier. See Isaac (1989). The "crisis" in the U.S. federal deposit insurance system is examined in Kane (1985).

21. This useful analogy is taken from Abraham (1989).

22. Borio (1989) finds that countries with a highly leveraged company sector are often those in which the banking sector is the dominant supplier of funds; in some cases, these countries have significant direct or indirect equity interests in the nonfinancial business sector.

23. Friedmann and Herrmann (1987) provide a broad overview of the German capital market and the dominant role played by the banking system. The structure and determinants of bank intermediation in Italy are considered in Monti and Porta (1981).

24. See Friedmann and Herrmann (1987), p. 74.

25. "Report of the Deutsche Bundesbank for the Year 1981," p. 22.

26. See Metais (1985).

27. Metais (1985), p. 101.

28. See Bruneel (1987). The two "waves" of financial disintermediation in France during the 1980s arising from the introduction of new marketable financial assets and the creation of mutual fund institutions are described in Bruneel (1989).

29. See "La Titrisation des Créances Bancaires", Les notes bleues, Actualité, No. 408, 31 octobre 1988. Securitization was in good part aimed at giving banks greater flexibility with respect to their mortgage portfolios.

30. See Lebegue (1985) and Frank (1988). De Boissieu (1989) estimates that, as late as 1981, approximately 80% of the financing of the French economy was intermediated.

31. See Evans and Alcamo (1988). The reforms of French capital markets also greatly altered the sources of government financing. Between 1978 and 1983 approximately 70% of general government borrowing took place through financial institutions. During 1984-1985 only 47% of general government financing was intermediated. See Bruneel (1987).

32. In an investigation of Japanese business investment, Hoshi, Kashyap, and Scharfstein (1989) found that firms with close bank ties had investments that were much less sensitive to liquidity than firms that resorted to capital market financing. Bank monitoring was argued to be costly for firms, but the advantage was to reduce information problems and liquidity constraints.

33. See Kaufman (1981), pp. 65-76.

34. The Deutsche Bundesbank (1989) argues that the recent improvement in corporate liquidity in Germany and the use of "sophisticated financial management techniques" has reduced the close relationship between the major German corporations and the "principal bankers."

35. See Hendrie (1988), p. 260.

36. See Hogeweg and Van Straaten (1987).

37. See Hogeweg and Van Straaten (1987), pp. 129–130.
38. See Hawawini and Jacquillat (1989), table 1.
39. See Caranza, Panetta, and Pepe (1987).
40. See Hendrie (1988).
41. See Banca d'Italia, *Economic Bulletin*, October 1986, p. 36.
42. See Dini (September 1988). Patarnello (1989) describes recent changes in the Italian secondary government bond market.
43. See "Italians Sweep Aside 50-year Curb on New Merchant Banks", *Financial Times*, February 9, 1987.
44. With regard to recent developments in the Belgian capital market, see Abraham (1989) and Baudewyns and Maes (1987).
45. See McDougall (1989) on the importance of taxation in European financial integration. The 1987 Single European Act has been propelled in part by the use of majority voting in the EEC Council of Ministers. On the issue of taxation, however, veto power of any one member still prevails.
46. "Report of the Deutsche Bundesbank for the Year 1988," p. 47.
47. See "Monthly Report of the Deutsche Bundesbank," June 1989, p. 14.
48. See Threadgold (1987).
49. Government efforts to revive the sterling bond market are reviewed in Plenderleith (1989). Plenderleith's characterization of London's capital market might well be appropriate for other European capital centers: "We have become accustomed in London to a structure in which the bond market means essentially the government bond market—the gilt-edged market . . . but alongside it there is developing a corporate bond market, a sovereign bond market and an array of markets in derivates—futures, options, warrants, swaps and other techniques for capital market financing" (p. 387).
50. See Lygum, Ottolenghi, and Steinherr (1988).
51. Lygum, Ottolenghi, and Steinherr (1966), table 6.
52. Pyle (1971), p. 737.
53. See Santomero (1984).
54. Corrigan (1982), p. 2.
55. These arguments are presented in Kane (1985).
56. Golembe (1989), p. 181.
57. The classic case in recent years has been the massive failure of the U.S. saving institutions. See Brumbaugh, Carron, and Litan (1989). William Isaac, former chairman of the U.S. Federal Deposit Insurance Corporation, in hindsight argues that the bailing out (payment in full) of all depositors in the cases of the Bank of the Commonwealth, Detroit (1972), the U.S. National Bank of San Diego (1973), and Franklin National Bank (1974), were "serious policy mistakes." See Isaac (1989), p. 3.
58. This point is also mentioned by Robert Hall in commenting on the paper by Brumbaugh et al. (1989). The lower capitalization of banks has for some time been argued to result from government provision of flat-rate deposit insurance. Peltzman (1970) is one of the earliest to argue this point. See also Benston et al. (1986), chapter 7.
59. Molyneux (1989). Most data on sectoral ownership of banking institutions are somewhat dated. Revell (1988) estimates that as of 1983, the central government's share of the banking industry, measured as a percentage of total banking assets, was about 61% in France, 40% in Italy, and 22% in Belgium.
60. Note that the figures for Italy in table 4-6 are for commercial banks. Lane (1988) reports that there are in fact 1109 separate "banks" in Italy.
61. Molyneux (1989), p. 362.

62. See Hendrie (1988) and "The Cost of Non-Europe in Financial Services", EEC (1988), p. 323 for details. Five of the ten largest banks in Italy are public charter banks.

63. See Revell (1989) and "The Top 500," *The Banker*, July 1988.

64. See the *Euromoney* supplement, "Towards a Single Market," September 1988, with regard to potential changes in the German banking market.

65. Cable (1985), p. 119.

66. Germany and Japan both have a long history of simultaneously holding large debt and equity claims on nonfinancial corporations. See Borio (1989) and *59th Annual Report*, Bank for International Settlements, June 1989, pp. 85–86.

67. See "German Banks Facing Curbs", *International Herald Tribune*, November 8, 1989, and "The Deutsche Bank Juggernaut will Keep On Rolling", *Euromoney*, January 1990, regarding the concentration of banking power in Germany.

68. See Krummel (1980).

69. See "Ciampi Tries to Set Bank Takeover Rules," *Financial Times*, November 29, 1986, and Pepe (1986).

70. See Salomon Brothers, "European Banking Integration in 1992," and Hanley et al. (1989), p. 10.

71. Hanley et al. (1989), p. 38.

72. A recent study of the determinants of bank profitability is Bourke (1988).

73. See Lygum, Perée, and Steinherr (1989).

74. Cumming and Sweet (1987–1988) provide a concise analysis of financial structure in the G-10 countries.

75. The six large commercial banks in Spain account for about 50% of total commercial bank assets. There is now little legal distinction between commercial and saving banks in Spain, as a result of recent legislation, and saving banks are competitive in many of the same areas as commercial banks. However, saving banks are more retail institutions with little foreign activity. See Lygum, Perée, and Steinherr (1989) for a recent review of the Spanish financial system.

76. See Boreham (1985), part II.

77. See Christensen (1986) for a review of Swiss financial markets and Plott (1989) on recent attempts of the Swiss Cartel Commission to increase competition in Swiss banking. Switzerland's stamp duty and withholding tax have effectively aided its competitor to the north, Luxembourg. See also Laurie (1988).

78. The immediate cause of the change in British capital market legislation was the potential for prosecution of the stock exchange under antitrust law. The longer-term reason for the "Big Bang" was the elimination of exchange controls in 1979 and the opening up of the London market to foreign competition after the deregulation of the New York capital market in 1975. See the *Annual Report*, Bank for International Settlements, June 1987, pp. 81–82.

79. See Hendrie (1988), p. 345.

80. See "The gilt Markets' Vanishing Act," *The Economist*, September 17, 1988 and "And Profits Desert the City, Too," *The Economist*, June 4, 1988. Among those leaving the primary gilt market were Lloyds Bank, Chemical Bank, and Citicorp.

81. See "Big Bang in Britain's High Street," *The Economist*, October 15, 1988.

82. The two banks are Deutsche Bank and Commerzbank. See "Commerzbank Seizes Allfinanz Initiative," *Financial Times*, August 8, 1989 and "Europe's Insurers Draw a Bead on 1992," *The Economist*, October 28, 1989.

83. "The Cost of Non-Europe," in *Financial Services*, Vol. 9, p. 394.

84. See "Sweeping Away Frankfurt's Old-Fashioned Habits," *The Economist*, January 28, 1989.

85. Much of the factual material here is taken from Ciampi (1989).
86. "The Cost of Non-Europe," in *Financial Services*, Volume 9, p. 111.
87. Not necessarily an impediment to improve services in banking, but also not a guarantee, is the large portion of the Italian financial industry directly or indirectly administered by the public sector, representing 65% of total deposits. Ciampi (1989), p. 27.
88. See Lebegue (1985). An analysis of competition in the French banking industry is available in the study by the Association Française des Banques, "La Concurrence Bancaire en France et en Europe," 1987.
89. See "Brittan Seeks Open Market in Finance, Pension Funds," *Wall Street Journal*, September 1, 1989.
90. See "Storming France's Insurance Barricades," *The Economist*, August 26, 1989.
91. The absence of successful tax harmonization in the EEC has been of recent concern to the Banca d'Italia, which has argued that the lack of tax harmonization will possibly mean higher interest rates in Italy. Moreover, should Italy be required to alter its taxation of capital gains and earnings on bank deposits to match those of lower taxation countries, the result would likely mean an increase in the government's budget deficit.
92. Key (1989), Gilibert and Steinherr (1989), and Morgan Guarantee's World Financial Markets (September 1988) provided overviews of the internal market program as it applies to finance.
93. Paragraphs 77-79 on the Commission's 1985 White Paper adopted the principle of mutual recognition. In cases where harmonization of regulations and standards is not considered essential from either a health/safety or an industrial point of view, immediate and full recognition of different quality standards, food composition rules, etc., must be the rule (p. 22). The origin of this point of view appears to have been the important European Court of Justice's decision in the Cassis de Dijon case, which stated that a member state could only create an import barrier to secure the satisfaction of routine basic requirements. See Key (April 1989) for details.
94. See Zavvos (1988) and the 1988 Annual Report of the Banking Federation of the European Community for a review of EEC banking and financial market legislation.
95. See Dermine (1989).
96. "Completing the Internal Market" (COM (85) 310 Final), pp. 27-28.
97. "Proposal for a Second Council Directive on the Coordination of Laws, Regulations and Administrative Provision Relating to the Taking Up and Pursuit of the Business of Credit Institutions," Commission of the European Community, (COM (87) 715 Final), February 16, 1988, p. 1. of Explanatory Memorandum.
98. "Completing the Internal Market" (COM (85) 310 Final), Explanatory Memorandum, p. 2.
99. "Completing the Internal Market" (COM (85) 310 Final), Explanatory Memorandum, p. 3. The proposed EEC banking solvency directive was one of the difficult hurdles for all Community members to jump. Germany, for example, had sought better treatment of mortgage finance than that contained in the original draft directive.
100. "Second Council Directive...", December 15, 1989 (Second Banking Directive), article 21, para. 2.
101. The expectation of competition in banking regulations is suggested by Micossi (1988) and Padoa-Schioppa (1988), among others.
102. Levich (1989), p. 27.
103. Both Giddy (1985) and Kane (1987) view this competition in banking regulation in a sort of *contestable markets* framework, in which the demand for the services of regulators is a derived demand, stemming from the demand for the financial service by the public. The system that emerges, as argued by Giddy, will depend on whether regulators compete

in order to draw business to their respective local markets or collude to establish some mutually agreed-upon level of regulatory services.

104. A concise view of the background to the Second Banking Coordination Directive and the important role of two European Court of Justice decisions with regard to establishment requirements and the freedom of services is given in Fitchew (1987).

105. See "The Cost of Non-Europe" in *Financial Services*, Volume 9, Commission of the European Communities, Section 4, "Barriers to Integration in Financial Markets", pp. 102–135.

106. See "France Prepares Early End to All Exchange Controls," *Financial Times*, December 12, 1989.

107. With wide interest-rate differentials inducing currency appreciation, in February 1989 Spain introduced temporary measures to restrain capital inflows. Foreign borrowing with maturities of less than three years was prohibited, and 30% of foreign currency and convertible peseta borrowing were required to be deposited with the central bank.

108. And, as argued by Dasgupta and Stiglitz (1988), small barriers to entry can be sufficient to create substantial monopoly and oligopoly power. Oligopoly power may also result from large sunk costs in an industry.

109. The restriction on branches of foreign banks in Spain does not apply to foreign banks established in Spain before 1978, when the restriction was imposed. Some foreign banks have quite extensive branch systems in Spain.

110. See "International Trade in Services: Banking," OECD, 1984, pp. 13–15. The EEC's 1977 First Banking Coordination Directive also contained a reciprocity principle that was to be applied to banks with head offices outside the EEC.

111. Article 9 of the final version of the Second Banking Directive reads, "[W]henever it appears to the Commission... that Community credit institutions in a third country do not receive national treatment offering the same competitive opportunities as are available to domestic credit institutions and that the conditions of effective market access are not fulfilled, the Commission may initiate negotiations in order to remedy the situation" (para. 4). Also, see "1992 Update," *The Banker*, August 1989.

112. "EEC Bankers Identify Possible Targets for Reciprocal Action," *Financial Times*, August 17, 1989. An extensive discussion of the reciprocity issue is found in Key (1989), pp. 59–75.

113. "Brussels Fights for Accord on Takeover Bids," *Financial Times*, October 2, 1989.

114. The French concern over differential taxation in the EEC is echoed in Lebegue's comments in McDougall (1988). The Lebegue report for the Conseil National du Crédit (1988) suggested that without fiscal harmonization in the Community, France faces the risk of a disruption of both intermediated and nonintermediated finance. See Lebegue (1988) and Achard (1987). Pietrafesa et al. (1989) present a comprehensive study of the taxation of financial income in the EEC.

115. The issue of differential taxation is not limited by any means to these issues alone. In the United Kingdom, for instance, there is concern with differences in the tax treatment of unit trust umbrella funds based in the United Kingdom and those in Luxembourg. Another important issue is the potential effect of differential taxation on takeovers. See the Bank of England's "The Single European Market: Survey of the U.K. Financial Services Industry" (1989).

116. Article 17 of the Single European Act states that the European Council acting unanimously "shall adopt provisions for the harmonisation of legislation concerning turnover taxes, excise duties and other forms of indirect taxation to the extent that such harmonisation is necessary to ensure the establishment and the functioning of the internal market."

117. Luxembourg is argued by some to be one of the most resistant to fiscal changes, in particular with respect to a universal withholding tax, changes in banks secrecy laws, harmonization of indirect taxes, and the placement of a value-added tax on gold transactions. See Laurie (1988). Levich (1989) argues that without a change in bank secrecy laws and the imposition of a withholding tax on interest income, Luxembourg, with the best treatment of capital gains in the Community, looks to gain from a European single market in financial services.

118. Schaefer (1987) makes this point.

119. This summary of capital adequacy frameworks is taken from the Committee on Banking Regulations and Supervisory Practices, Report No. 5, Basle (1986).

120. See "International Convergence of Capital Measurements and Capital Standards", Basle (1988).

121. These concerns were raised by Johann Wilhelm Gaddum, a member of the Directorate of the Deutsche Bundesbank, in a speech in Bonn on July 18, 1988 to the German Saving Bank Academy.

122. The Second Banking Coordination Directive also contained a provision on qualified participations in an institution that is defined as neither *credit* nor *financial* (a limit of 15% of own funds and 60% on total participations) (article 12). In addition, in 1986 the EEC Commission issued a recommendation on the monitoring and control of large exposures of credit institutions, suggesting that "credit institutions may not incur an exposure to a client or group of clients when its percentage value exceeds 40% of own funds." Note that this was a recommendation, not official legislation. See *Official Journal of the European Communities*, February 4, 1987.

123. Pecchioli (1987), p. 57.

124. See Bröker (1989), annex II, tables 3-3 and 4-4.

125. Bröker (1989), annex II, table 3-2.

126. Bröker (1989), table 3-1, pp. 50–70 provides an excellent review of the factors that have contributed to increased price competition in banking in the OECD area.

127. The Swiss Cartel Commission, with the support of the Swiss National Bank, has increasingly brought pressure on Swiss bank cartel agreements, such as on brokerage, commissions, and the loyalty pledge of the major banks' underwriting syndicate.

128. The results of the Price Waterhouse survey and estimates of the expected price reductions in financial services are summarized in "The Economics of 1992," *European Economy*, March 1988.

129. See Gilibert and Steinherr (1989) on the issue of shifts in competitive pressure in the EEC, as a consequence of the single market program.

130. See Gilibert and Steinherr (1989), tables 2 and 3.

131. See the Salomon Brother study by Hanley et al. (1989). This study concludes that there are quite simply few European banks for sale. Of those available, this study identifies U.K. banks as likely takeover targets.

132. These points are mentioned by Revell (1988). Crabbe (1989) provides some speculative discussion on which banks in the Community are likely merger or takeover targets. In France, for example, he could identify only one possible takeover target, particularly given the government's hand in the banking system. Molyneux (1989) conjectures that foreign bank acquisitions are unlikely to involve large institutions. A list of recent mergers and acquisitions in European banking is contained in Hanley et al. (1989), figure 16.

133. Currently mergers in the EEC are subject to both national laws and the antitrust rules of the EEC. However, a potential merger that is denied by the Commission cannot be permitted by a member state. See Rose (1989) on EEC antitrust activity and authority.

134. Comparative profits performance in banking is usually based on the OECD study, "Bank Profitability" (1987). The 1989 study by Banque Indosuez (1989) (see references) provides a good review of bank earnings, profitability, and operating expenses.

135. See the Banque Indosuez (1989) study, p. 22.

136. The high intermediation margins in Spanish banking are examined in Caminal, Gual, and Vives (1989). The interest-rate spread is said to be 6.1% in Spain, compared with an average of 4.1% for the EEC. The authors note that Spanish banking is characterized by high labor costs and the highest operating costs in the EEC, suggesting inefficiencies due to the highly regulated and protected nature of the industry. Gross earnings in banking are the highest in the Community (1984–1986), but net pretax profits have been below average. However, the Spanish banking sector has recently improved its cost performance considerably. See Hanley et al. (1989), p. 67. The merger of Banco de Bilbao and Banco de Vizcaya in October 1988 is cited as an example of the recent increased competitiveness and profitability in Spanish banking.

137. German banks have also established joint relationships with Spanish banks. Hanley et al. (1989) provides considerable detail on recent merger and acquisition activity in European banking.

138. See, for example, Gilligan, Smirlock, and Marshall (1984), and Benston, Hanweck, and Humphreys (1982).

139. Schuster (1984).

140. An example is Gilibert and Steinherr (1989).

141. See Dini (1989), p. 9.

142. Revell (1987) makes this argument, suggesting that the "scope of the business conducted by a particular bank determines its optimum size" and the optimum size of the domestic market. This would appear to imply that with an improved European market for banking services, there could indeed be an increase in the size of some of the large universal banks.

143. Aliber (1989).

144. See the Bank of England's "The Single European Market: Survey of the U.K. Financial Services Industry," pp. 2 and 15. The markets thought attractive in this survey were France, Italy, and Spain.

145. Padoa-Schioppa (1987) has emphasized this competitive aspect of "regulatory pluralism" in Community banking legislation.

146. On the issue of sunk costs and imperfect and impacted information in determining entry into existing markets, see Martin (1989). In contestable markets, potential competition results in the absence of any economic rents being earned from those already in a market: so-called *incumbency rents*. Moreover, the sequence of entry into a market should not be a significant determinant of differential profits or market share. Hence, potential competition (the threat of market entry) is as good as actual competition in preventing the rise of monopoly power. However, in contestable markets, price is driven to equal average cost and not marginal cost. Contestable markets, in their pure form, assume that market entry is free and exit costless. Such hypothesized markets are used as a benchmark to study industrial organization and are often thought of as markets subject to hit-and-run entry. See Baumol (1982) and Gilbert (1989) for nontechnical reviews of the theory.

147. "The Single European Market", Bank of England, May 1989, p. 18.

148. Taken from *The New Palgrave: A Dictionary of Economics*, Vol. 3, J. Eatwell et al., editors. See also Arnott and Stiglitz, pp. 383–384. M.J.B. Hall (1989), for example, argues that in the United Kingdom "it is far from certain that the issue of JMB (Johnson Matthey Bankers) has not created a dangerous moral hazard for the banking industry" (p. 140).

149. The recent U.S. saving and loan experience has not gone unnoticed in Italy; the need for greater supervisory vigilance to accompany the increase in European banking competition is emphasized by Ciampi in Bancaria (1989).

150. Tobin (1987), p. 170. On the same issue, see Corrigan (1986).

151. See Revell (1981).

152. Kuprianov and Mengle (1989) provide an interesting review of the motivation and limitations of deposit insurance and alternatives to deposit insurance. Barth and Bradley (1989) review the history of deregulation and government deposit insurance in the U.S. thrift industry and emphasize the need for a rule in the event that the insurance fund is hit with catastrophic losses. See also Pennacchi (1987) on the underpricing of deposit insurance. White (1989) provides a historical review of factors that contributed to the financial crisis in the U.S. thrift industry.

153. Congressional testimony of Governor Manuel J. Johnson (1989), p. 9.

154. See James (1989) for an analysis of how LDC lending by U.S. banks created "implicit deposit insurance," given that the likelihood of simultaneous LDC defaults represented a systemic risk.

155. This point is emphasised in the paper by Kuprianov and Mengle (1989). Baer and Brewer (1986) analyze the role of market discipline on large U.S. banks introduced by the use of large uninsured CDs. The risk premium on uninsured large CDs is one method by which the market signals to banks its evaluation of bank risk exposure and acts to cause banks to better monitor that exposure.

156. See Benston et al. (1986).

157. See Baltensperger and Dermine (1987, 1989). Guttentag and Herring (1988) and Mussa (1986) discuss how measures aimed at assuring "safety and soundness" to depository institutions may indeed protect depositors but only at the cost of exposing taxpayers.

158. Baltensperger and Dermine (1989) state that the advertising of deposit insurance is even prohibited in Germany. Kuester and O'Brien (1989) show that the value of U.S. deposit insurance to bank shareholders can be quite significant. Using data on 234 bank holding companies, they found that the value of deposit insurance averaged between 0.5 and 2 cents per dollar of bank liabilities.

159. The issue of deposit insurance and bank failures is of recent concern in France. See "La Faillite, Nous Voilà!", *Le Monde Affaires*, April 8, 1989. Deposit insurance at fixed premiums may also create "perverse risk incentives" for bank managers and shareholders when they are confronted with increased competition and the availability of a greater schedule of financial services. Deregulation thus creates the need for greater supervision and greater capital, reducing the incentives for the leveraging of governmental guarantees. See Merrick and Saunders (1985) on the risk incentives created by fixed premium deposit insurance.

160. L. William Seidman, Chairman of the FDIC, clearly identified the too-big-to-fail doctrine for big banks with 100% deposit insurance. See "Seidman Warns Against Insurance Cut," *American Banker*, October 18, 1989.

161. See Monti (1988).

162. Ciampi (1988). See also Pepe (1989).

163. Ciampi (1988). Kane (1989) also warns of the "unintended subsidies to banks" derived from implicit government financial guarantees.

164. Otto Graf Lambsdorff has suggested with regard to large German banks that " ... in the combination of providing equity, providing credit, the seats on the supervisory board, the exercise of proxy votes in shareholder meetings, that in all this an accumulation of economic power has been constituted and is being further constituted that carries in it the

possibilities of abuse." See "The Deutsche Bank Juggernaut will Keep Rolling On," *Euromoney*, January 1990.
165. See Guttentag and Herring (1986).
166. See Guttentag and Herring (1986).
167. See the discussion in Fouquet (1989) on the future of European banking.

References

Abraham, J.-P. "The Process of Change in Belgian Banking," Research Papers in Banking and Finance, No. 88/6, Institute of European Finance, University College of North Wales, Bangor, 1988.

Abraham, J.-P. "The Process of Change in Belgian Capital Markets: Recent Developments and European Perspectives," Research Papers in Banking and Finance, No. 89/3, Institute of European Finance, University College of North Wales, Bangor, 1989.

Achard, P. "Le Marché Unique de 1992: Perspectives pour les Banques, les Assurances et le Système Financier Français," Rapport au Ministre d'Etat, December 1987.

Aliber, R.Z. "Regulation, Protection, and the Structure of the International Banking Industry", mimeo, Graduate School of Business, University of Chicago, 1989.

Aliber, R.Z. "International Banking: A Survey," *Journal of Money, Credit and Banking* (November 1984), pp. 661–678.

Arnott, R.J. and J.E. Stiglitz. "The Basic Analytics of Moral Hazard," *Scandinavian Journal of Economics* (1988), pp. 383–413.

Association Française des Banques. "La Concurrence Bancaire en France et en Europe", October 19, 1987.

Baer, H. and E. Brewer. "Uninsured Deposits as a Source of Market Discipline: Some New Evidence," *Economic Perspectives*, Federal Reserve Bank of Chicago, September/October 1986, pp. 23–31.

Baltensperger, E. and J. Dermine. "European Banking, Prudential and Regulatory Issues," mimeo, paper prepared for presentation at the INSEAD Conference on European Banking after 1992, Fontainebleau, France, January 1989.

Baltensperger, E. and J. Dermine. "The Role of Public Policy in Ensuring Financial Stability: A Cross-Country, Comparative Perspective," in Richard Portes and Alexander K. Swoboda, (eds.), *Threats to International Financial Stability*. Cambridge: Cambridge University Press, 1987.

Banco de España. "Analisis Comparativo de la Rentabilidad del Sistema Bancario Español," *Boletin Economico* (March 1988), pp. 11–20.

Bank of England. "The Single European Market: Survey of the UK Financial Services Industry," May 1989.

Banking Federation of the European Community. *Annual Report*, 1988.

Banque Indosuez. Impact de la Creation du Marché Financier Intégré Européen

sur le Secteur des Banques et des Assurances, Service des Etudes Economiques et Financières, mimeo, September 1988.
Ballarin, E., J. Gual, and J.E. Ricart, "Rentabilidad y Competividad en el Sector Bancario Español. Un Estudio Sobre la Distribucion de Servicios Financieros en España," mimeo, IESE, Documento de Trabajo, No. 25, 1988.
Barth, J.R. and M.G. Bradley. "Thrift Deregulation and Federal Deposit Insurance," *Journal of Financial Services Research* (September 1989), pp. 231–259.
Baudewyns, J. and G. Maes. "Organisation and Regulation of the Capital Market in Belgium," in *Changes in the Organisation and Regulation of Capital Markets*. Basle: Bank for International Settlements, March 1987.
Baumol, W.J. "Contestable Markets: An Uprising in the Theory of Industrial Structure," *American Economic Review* (March 1982), pp. 1–15.
Benston, G.J., G.A. Hanweck, and D.B. Humphreys. "Scale Economies in Banking: A Restructuring and Reassessment Part I," *Journal of Money, Credit and Banking* (November 1982), pp. 435–456.
Benston, G.J., R.A. Eisenbeis, P.M. Horvitz, E.J. Kane, and G.G. Kaufman. *Perspectives on Safe and Sound Banking* (a study commissioned by the American Bankers Association). Cambridge, MA: The MIT Press, 1986.
Benston, G.J., R.D. Brumbaugh Jr., J.M. Guttentag, R.J. Herring, G.G. Kaufman, R.E. Litan, and K.E. Scott. "Blueprint for Restructuring America's Financial Institutions: Report of a Task Force," The Brookings Institute, Washington, D.C., 1989.
Black, Fischer. "Bank Funds Management in an Efficient Market," *Journal of Financial Economics* (1975), pp. 323–339.
Boreham, G.F. "European Banking Developments—Lessons for Canada," *Canadian Banker* (February 1985), Part I, pp. 19–24; (April 1985) Part II, pp. 18–22.
Borio, C.E.V. "Leverage and Financing of Non-financial Companies: An International Perspective," Bank for International Settlements, BIS Economic Papers No. 27, Basle, May 1990.
Bourke, P. "International Comparisons of Bank Profitability," Research Monographs in Banking and Finance, No. 7, Institute of European Finance, University College of North Wales, Bangor, 1988.
Bröker, G. "Competition in Banking, Trends in Banking Structure and Regulation in OECD Countries," Organisation for Economic Co-operation and Development, Paris, 1984.
Brown, B. International Banking Centres. Euromoney Publications, 1982.
Brumbaugh, R.D. Jr., A.S. Carron, and R.E. Litan. "Cleaning Up the Depository Institution Mess," *Brookings Papers on Economic Activity*, No. 1, 1989, pp. 243–295.
Bruneel, D., "Recent Developments in the French Financial System and their Economic Policy Consequences," in *Changes in the Organisation and Regulation of Capital Markets*. Basle: Bank for International Settlements, March 1987.

Bruneel, D., "Recent Evolution of Financial Structures and Monetary Policy in France," in Donald R. Hodgman and Geoffrey E. Wood (eds.), *Macroeconomic policy and economic interdependence*, MacMillan, 1989.

Bruni, F., "Banking and Financial Reregulation towards 1992: The Italian Case," paper presented at the Conference on European Banking after 1992, INSEAD, Fontainebleau, February 9–10, 1989.

Bulletin of the European Communities, Supplement 2/86, "Single European Act."

Cable, J. "Capital Market Information and Industrial Performance: The Role of West German Banks," *The Economic Journal*, (March 1985), pp. 118–132.

Caminal, R., J. Gual, and X. Vives, "Bank Runs as an Equilibrium Phenomenon," *Journal of Political Economy* (June 1987), pp. 485–491.

Caminal, R., R. Gual, and J. Gual. "Competition in Spanish Banking", mimeo, January 1989.

Caranza, F., F. Panetta, and R. Pepe, "Recent Changes in the Organisation and Regulation of the Capital Market in Italy," in *Changes in the Organisation and Regulation of Capital Markets*. Basle: Bank for International Settlements, March 1987.

Castello-Branco, M.J. and J. Pelkmans (eds.). "The internal market for financial services," European Institute of Public Administration, Proceedings of the colloquium organized by the European Institute of Public Administration, February 24–25, 1987.

Cecchini, P. (with the collaboration of M. Catinat and A. Jacquemin). *1992 le Défi: Nouvelles Données Économiques de l'Europe sans Frontières* (the Cecchini Report), Flammarion, 1988.

Chase, S.B. "Insulating Banks from Risks Run by Non-Bank Affiliates," in *The Financial Services Industry in the Year 2000: Risk and Efficiency*, Proceedings of a Conference on Bank Structure and Competition, May 11–13, 1988, Federal Reserve Bank of Chicago.

Christensen, B.V. "Switzerland's Role as an International Financial Center," Occasional Paper No. 45, Washington, DC: International Monetary Fund, July 1986.

Ciampi, C.A. "Separation Prevents Conflicts of Interest," *Financial Times*, December 1, 1988, Section IV, III*.

Ciampi, C.A. "The Governor's Concluding Remarks," Ordinary General Meeting of Shareholders, Banca d'Italia, Rome, May 31, 1989.

Ciampi, C.A. "Address by the Governor of the Bank of Italy at the Annual Meeting of the Italian Bankers Association Held in Rome", June 27, 1989.

Ciampi, C.A. "Le Scelte di Fondo nell'Evoluzione del Sistema", *Bancaria* (July/August 1989), pp. 100–103.

Commission of the European Communities. "Completing the Internal Market," White Paper from the Commission to the European Council, Brussels, June 14, 1985.

Commission of the European Communities. "Creation of an European Financial Area," Brussels, November 4, 1987.

Commission of the European Communities. "The Cost of Non-'Europe' in Financial Services," *Research on the "Cost of non-Europe," Basic Findings*, Vol. 9, Price Waterhouse.

Commission of the European Communities. "The Economics of 1992; An Assement of the Potential Economic Effects of Completing the Internal Market of the Euopean Community," *European Economy* 35 (March 1988).

Commission of the European Communities. "Creation of a European Financial Area," *European Economy* 36 (May 1988).

Commission of the European Communities. "Proposal for a Second Council Directive on the Co-ordination of Laws, Regulations and Administrative Provisions Relating to the Taking-up Pursuit of the Business of Credit Institutions," Brussels, February 16, 1988 (so-called proposed Second Banking Directive).

Commission of the European Communities. Second Council Directive of 15th December 1989 on the Co-ordination of Laws, Regulations and Administrative Provisions Relating to the Taking-up and Pursuit of the Business of Credit Institutions and Amending Directive 77/780/EEC, Brussels.

Committee on Banking Regulations and Supervisory Practices (The Cooke Committee). "Report on International Developments in Banking Supervision," Report No. 5, Bank for International Settlements, Basle, September 1986.

Committee on Banking Regulations and Supervisory Practices. "International Convergence of Capital Measurement and Capital Standards," Basle, July 1988.

Conti, V. "Margini, Costi e Prospettive Strategiche per le Agiende di Credito: Alcuni Confronti Internazionali," Collana Ricerche No. R89-2, Banca Commerciale Italiana, Milano, February 1989.

Corrigan, G.E. "Financial Market Structure: A Longer View," Seventy-Second Annual Report, for the year ended December 31st, 1986, Federal Reserve Bank of New York.

Corrigan, G.E. "Are Banks Special?" Annual Report 1982, Federal Reserve Bank of Minneapolis.

Crabbe, M. "Which Banks in Europe can be Bought?" *Euromoney* (August 1989), pp. 59-64.

Croham, D. "Reciprocity and the Unification of the European Banking Market," Group of Thirty, Occasional Papers No. 27, New York, 1989.

Cumming, C.M. and L.M. Sweet. "Financial Structure of the G-10 Countries: How Does the United States Compare?" Quarterly Review, Federal Reserve Bank of New York, Vol. 12, No. 4, Winter 1987-1988, pp. 14-25.

Dale, R. *The Regulation of International Banking*, Cambridge: Woodhead-Faulkner, 1984.

Dasgupta, P. and J.E. Stiglitz. "Potential Competition, Actual Competition and Economic Welfare," *European Economic Review* (1988), pp. 569-577.

de Boissieu, C. "The French Banking Sector in the Light of European Financial Integration," paper prepared for the INSEAD Conference on European Banking after 1992, February 1989.

de Larosière, J. "The Requirements of the Monetary Authorities with Regard to the New Risks, and How These Requirements are Changing in Preparation for the Single Internal European Market Due at the End of 1992," speech to the Asset-Liability Manager Seminar organized by *Banque*, May 18, 1988.

De Felice, G., D. Masciandaro, and A. Porta. "Evoluzione del Sistema Bancario nella Struttura Finanziaria e Problemi di Regolamentazione: un'Analisi Comparata," in Francesco Cesarini, Michele Grillo, Mario Monti, and Marco Onado (eds.), *Banca e Mercato, Riflessioni su Evoluzione e Prospettive dell'industria Bancaria in Italia*, Societa Editrice Il Mulino, 1988.

Dermine, D. "Home Country Control and Mutual Recognition", paper presented at the SUERF (Société Universitaire Européene de Recherches Financières) Colloquium, October 12th–14, 1989, Nice.

Deutsche Bundesbank. "Longer-Term Trends in the Banking Sector and Market Position of the Individual Categories of Banks," Monthly Report of the Deutsche Bundesbank, April 1989, pp. 13–22.

Deutsche Bundesbank. "The Longer-Term Trend of Inflows of Funds to Banks," Monthly Report of the Deutsche Bundesbank, October 1985, pp. 25–36.

Diamond, D.W. "Financial Intermediation and Delegated Monitoring," *Review of Economic Studies* (1984), pp. 393–414.

Diamond, D.W. and P.H. Dybvig. "Bank Runs, Deposit Insurance, and Liquidity," *Journal of Political Economy* (June 1983), pp. 401–419.

Dini, L. "The Italian Financial System in the Perspective of 1992," address to the Italian Chamber of Commerce for Great Britain, Conference on Target 1992, London, September 23, 1988.

Dini, L. "Liberalisation of Financial Services in the European Community: the Case of Italy," address at the International Centre for Monetary and Banking Studies, Geneva, March 14, 1989.

Eatwell, J., M. Milgate, and P. Newman (eds.). *The New Palgrave: A Dictionary of Economics*. London: Macmillan, 1987.

Escande, J.-P. "L'harmonisation Monétaire et Financière au Sein de la C.E.E.," *Journal Officiel de la République Française* (novembre 1987).

Euromoney. "Towards a Single Market, 1992," a supplement to *Euromoney* and *Corporate Finance*, September 1988.

European Bond Commission. *The European Bond Markets*. Chicago: Probus Publishing Company, 1989.

Evans, E. and B. Alcamo. "US and French Treasure Yields: How Close a Link?" International Bond Market Analysis, Salomon Brothers, May 10, 1988.

Fama, E. "Banking in a Theory of Finance," *Journal of Monetary Economics* (January 1980), pp. 39–57.

Fama, E. "What's Different about Banks?" *Journal of Monetary Economics* (January 1985), pp. 29–39.

Fitchew, G. "Towards a Completed Internal Market in Financial Services: The White Paper and Beyond", in M.J. Castello-Branco and J. Pelkmans (eds.), *The Internal Market for Financial Services*, European Institute of Public Administration, 1987.

Fouquet, C. 'L'Avenir des Services Financiers," *Eurepargne*, (October 1989), pp. 29–36.
Frank, D. "Reach for the Sky," (French bond market), *The Banker* (March 1988), pp. 19–20.
Freeman, S., "Banking as the Provision of Liquidity," *The Journal of Business*, (January 1988), pp. 45–64.
Friedmann, W. and H. Herrmann. "Recent Changes in Capital Markets in Germany," in *Changes in the Organisation and Regulation of Capital Markets*. Basle: Bank for International Settlements, March 1987.
"German Banks Found Short of Capital Rule," *American Banker*, August 16, 1989, p. 2.
Gertler, M. "Financial Structure and Aggregate Economic Activity: An Overview," working paper No. 2559, National Bureau of Economic Research, April 1988.
Giddy, I.H. "Domestic Regulation versus International Competition in Banking," *Kredit und Kapital* (1985 supplement), Heft 8, "Internationales Bankgeschäft.", pp. 195–209.
Gilbert, R.J. "The Role of Potential Competition in Industrial Organisation," *Journal of Economic Perspectives* (Summer 1989), pp. 107–127.
Gilibert, P.L. and A. Steinherr. "The Impact of Financial Market Integration on the European Banking Industry," European Investment Bank, EIB Papers, No. 8, March 1989.
Gilligan, T., M. Smirlock, and W. Marshall. "Scale and Scope Economies in the Multi-Product Banking Firm," *Journal of Monetary Economics* (May 1984), pp. 393–405.
Golembe, C.H. "Long-Term Trends in Bank Regulation, *Journal of Financial Services Research* (September 1989), pp. 171–183.
Golembe, C.H. and J.J. Mingo. "Can Supervision and Regulation Ensure Financial Stability?", in "The Search for Financial Stability: The Past Fifty Years, a conference sponsored by the Federal Reserve Bank of San Francisco, June 23–25, 1985.
Grilli, Vittorio. "Europe 1992: Issues and Prospects for the Financial Markets," *Economic Policy* (October 1989), pp. 387–421.
Guttentag, J.M. and R.J. Herring. "Disaster Myopia in International Banking," *Essays in International Finance*, No. 164, Princeton University, September 1986.
Guttentag, J.M. and R.J. Herring. "Prudential Supervision to Manage Systemic Vulnerability," mimeo, International Banking Center, The Wharton School, May 1988.
Hall, Maximilian J.B. *Handbook of Banking Regulation and Supervision*. London: Woodhead-Faulkner, 1989.
Hanley, T.H., J.D. Leonard, D.B. Glossman, D.I. Oddis, S.I. Davis, W. Vincent, S. Lewis, R. Napier, and T. Kitagawa. "European Banking Integration in 1992," Salomon Brothers, June 1989.
Hawawini, G. and B. Jacquillat. "European Capital Markets: The Road to 1992

and Beyond," February 1989, paper prepared for presentation at the INSEAD Conference on European Banking after 1992, Fontainebleau, France.

Hendrie, A. (ed.). *Banking in the EEC, 1988: Structure and Sources of Finance*. London: Financial Times Business Information.

Hogeweg, G.P.J. and A.J. Van Straaten. "Recent Changes in the Organisation and Regulation of the (Netherlands) Capital Market: Causes and Expected Consequences," in *Changes in the Organisation and Regulation of Capital Markets*. Basle: Bank for International Settlements, March 1987.

Hoshi, T., A. Kashyap, and D. Scharfstein. "Bank Monitoring and Investment: Evidence from the Changing Structure of Japanese Corporate Banking Relations," Finance and Economics Discussion Series, No. 86, Division of Monetary Affairs, Federal Reserve Board, Washington, DC, August 1989.

International Monetary Fund. "International Capital Markets: Developments and Prospects," April 1989.

Isaac, W.M. "Deposit Insurance Reform: Banking's Top Priority," The Golembe Reports, CHG Consulting Inc., June 12, 1989.

James, C. "Empirical Evidence on Implicit Government Guarantees of Bank Foreign Loan Exposure," Carnegie-Rochester Conference Series on Public Policy, Vol. 30, spring 1989.

Johnson, M.H. Testimony before the Sub-committee on Financial Institutions, Supervision, Regulation and Insurance of the Committee on Banking, Finance and Urban Affairs, U.S. House of Representatives, 19th September 1989.

Kane, E.J. *The Gathering Crisis in Federal Deposit Insurance*. Cambridge, MA: MIT Press, 1985.

Kane, E.J. "Competitive Financial Reregulation: An International Perspective," in R. Portes and A.K. Swoboda (eds.), *Threats to International Financial Stability*. Cambridge: Cambridge University Press, 1987.

Kane, E.J. "Financial Regulation in a Shrinking World," paper prepared for the Conference on Globaliszation of Financial Markets, Federal Reserve Bank of Chicago, November, 2–3, 1989.

Kaufman, G.G. *Money, the Financial System, and the Economy*, 3rd edition. Houghton Mifflin Company, 1981.

Kaufman, G.G. "Bank Runs: Causes, Benefits and Costs," *The Cato Journal* (Winter 1988), pp. 559–587.

Kaufman, G.G. "Are Some Banks too Large to Fail? Myth and Reality," mimeo Loloya University of Chicago, September 1989.

Kemp, L.J. *A Guide to World Money and Capital Markets*. London: McGraw-Hill, 1981.

Key, S.J. "Financial Integration in the European Community," International Finance Discussion Papers, No. 349, April 1989, Board of Governors of the Federal Reserve System.

Key, S.J. "Mutual Recognition: Integration of the Financial Sector in the European Community," *Federal Reserve Bulletin*, September 1989, pp. 591–609.

Krummel, H.J. "German Universal Banking Scrutinised: Some Remarks Concerning the Gessler Report," *Journal of Banking and Finance* (March 1980), pp. 33–55.

Kuester, K.A. and J.M. O'Brien. "Bank Equity Values, Bank Risk and the Implied Market Value of Banks' Assets, Liabilities and Deposit Insurance," Finance and Economics Discussion Series. No. 98, Federal Reserve Board, Washington, DC, November 1989.

Kuprianov, A. and D.L. Mengle. "The Future of Deposit Insurance: An Analysis of the Alternatives," Economic Review, Federal Reserve Bank of Richmond, May/June 1989, pp. 3–15.

Lane, D. "Italy Focus: Outlook: Rainy with Sunny Spells," *The Banker* (August 1988), pp. 41–46.

Lascelles, D. "EC Bankers Identify Possible Targets for Reciprocal Action," *Financial Times*, August 17, 1989.

Laurie, S. "The Switzerland of the Future?" *The Banker* (November 1988), pp. 42, 45–46, 49.

Lawrence, C. "Banking Costs, Generalised Functional Forms, and Estimation of Economies of Scale and Scope," *Journal of Money, Credit and Banking* (August 1989).

Lebegue, D. "Modernising the French Capital Market," *The Banker* (December 1985).

Lebegue, D. "La Fiscalité de l'Épargne dans le Cadre du Marché Interieur Europeen," rapport du groupe de travail du Conseil National du Crédit, June 1988. (Summary in Les Notes Bleues, fiche de lecture, No. 402, September 25, 1988).

Leland, H.E. and D.H. Pyle. "Information Asymmetries, Financial Structure and Financial Intermediation," *Journal of Finance* (May 1977), pp. 371–387.

Levich, R.M. "The Euro-Markets after 1992," NBER Working Paper No. 3003, June 1989.

Lindsey, D.E. "Controlling Risk in the Payments System", Report of the Task Force on Controlling Payments System Risk to the Payments System Policy Committee of the Federal Reserve System, Board of Governors of the Federal Reserve System, August 1988.

Lygum, B., D. Ottolenghi, and A. Steinherr. "The Portuguese Financial System," European Investment Bank, EIB Papers No. 7, December 1988.

Lygum, B., E. Perée, and A. Steinherr. "The Spanish Financial System," EIB Papers, No. 12, European Investment Bank, December 1989.

Marquardt, J.C. "Financial Market Supervision: Some Conceptual Issues," BIS Working Paper No. 19, Bank for International Settlements, Basle, May 1987.

Marsh, D. "French Banking and Finance: Winds of Change," *The Banker* (April 1985), pp. 91–95.

Martin, S. "Sunk Costs, Financial Markets, and Contestability," *European Economic Review* (July 1989), pp. 1089–1113.

McDougall, R. "Papering over the Euro-cracks," *The Banker* (November 1988), pp. 22–26.

Merrick, J.J. Jr. and A., Saunders. "Bank Regulation and Monetary Policy," *Journal of Money, Credit and Banking* (November 1985), pp. 691–717 part 2.

Metais, J. "Equity Finance in France after the Monory and Delors reforms," *The Banker* (April 1985), pp. 97–105.

Metais, J. "International Strategies of French banks", in Christian de Boissieu (ed.), *Banking in France*, London: Routledge, 1990, pp. 136–187.

Micossi, S. "The Single European Market: Finance," Banca Nazionale del Lavoro Quarterly Review, June 1988, pp. 217–235.

Molyneux, P. "An Analysis of the Structure and Performance Characteristics of Top EC Banks and the Strategic Implications for 1992," *Revue de la Banque* (June 1989), pp. 359–366.

Monti, M. "Banks' Capital Needs will be High if Restructuring is to Go Ahead," *Financial Times*, December 1, 1988, Section IV, III*.

Monti, M. and A. Porta. "Bank Intermediation under Flexible Deposit Rates and Controlled Credit Allocation: The Italian Experience," in A. Verheirstraeten (ed.), *Competition and Regulation in Financial Markets*. London: Macmillan Press, 1981.

Morgan, J.P. "Financial Markets in Europe: Toward 1992," *World Financial Markets*, (September 1988), pp. 1–24.

Mussa, M. "Safety and Soundness as an Objective of Regulation of Depository Institutions: Comment on Karaken," *Journal of Business*, (January 1986), pp. 97–117.

Organisation for Economic Co-operation and Development. "Obstacles to International Trade in Banking Services," *Financial Market Trends* (March 1984) No. 27, pp. 1–16.

Organisation for Economic Co-operation and Development. *International Trade in Services: Banking*. Paris, 1984.

Padoa-Schioppa, T. "Towards a European Banking Regulatory Framework," Economic Bulletin, Banca d'Italia, February 1988, pp. 49–53.

Patarnello, A. "Recent Trends on the Secondary Market for Government Bonds in Italy," *Revue de la Banque*, (September 1989), pp. 431–432.

Pecchioli, R.M. "Prudential Supervision in Banking," Organisation for Economic Co-operation and Development, 1987.

Peltzman, S. "Capital Investment in Commercial Banking and its Relationship to Portfolio Regulation," *Journal of Political Economy* (January/February 1970), pp. 1–26.

Pennacchi, G.C. "A Re-examination of the Over- (or Under-) pricing of Deposit Insurance," *Journal of Money, Credit and Banking* (August 1987), pp. 340–360.

Pepe, R. "Riflessioni e Confronti in Tema di Separatezza tra Banca e Industria", Temi di Discussione, No. 76, Banca d'Italia, Servizio Studi, October 1986.

Peyrelevade, J. "Europe Financière et Monétaire," Commissariat Général du

Plan, La France, l'Europe. Xeme Plan 1989–92, Paris, June 1989.
Pierce, J.L. "Financial Reform in the United States and the Financial System of the Future," in Y. Suzuki and H. Yomo (eds.), *Financial Innovation and Monetary Policy: Asia and the West*. Tokyo: University of Tokyo Press, 1986.
Pietrafesa, N. et al. "La Tassazione delle Rendite Finanziare nella CEE alla Luce Della Liberalizzazione Valutaria," Temi di Discussione del Servizio Studi, No. 114, Banca d'Italia, February 1989.
Plenderleith, I. "The Development of the Sterling Bond Market", Quarterly Bulletin, Bank of England, August 1989, pp. 383–387.
Plott, D. "Swiss Bank Battle Heats Up as Panel Insists on its Plan," *Wall Street Journal*, August 30, 1989, p. 9.
Postlewaite, A. and X. Vives. "Bank Runs as an Equilibrium Phenomenon," *Journal of Political Economy*, June 1987, pp. 485–491.
Pyle, D.H. "On the Theory of Financial Intermediation," *Journal of Finance* (June 1971), pp. 737–747.
Renard, F. "La Faillite, Nous Voilà!", *Le Monde, Supplement*, April 8, 1989, pp. 8–9.
Revell, J. "The Complementary Nature of Competition and Regulation in the Financial Sector," in A. Verheirstraeten (ed.), *Competition and Regulation in Financial Markets*. London: The Macmillan Press, 1981.
Revell, J. "Mergers and the Role of Large Banks," Research Monographs in Banking and Finance, No. 2, Institute of European Finance, University College of North Wales, Bangor, 1987.
Revell, J. "Comparative Concentration of Banks," *Revue de la Banque* (April-May 1988), pp. 33–38.
Revell, J. "Bank Preparations for 1992: Some Clues and Some Queries," *Revue de la Banque* (March 1989), pp. 185–194.
Rose, M. "EC Merger Control in the Doldrums," *Mergers and Acquisitions International* (September 1989), pp. XXV–XXIX.
Santomero, A.M. "Modelling the Banking Firm: A Survey," *Journal of Money, Credit and Banking*, 16(4) (November 1984, part 2), pp. 576–602.
Santomero, A.M. "European Banking in post-1992: Lessons from the United States," paper prepared for the Conference European Banking after 1992, INSEAD, Fountainebleau, France.
Schaefer, S.M. "The Design of Bank Regulation and Supervision: Some Lessons from the Theory of Finance," in R. Portes and A.K. Swoboda (eds.), *Threats to International Financial Stability*. Cambridge: Cambridge University Press, 1987.
Schuster, L. "Profitability and Market Share of Banks," *Journal of Bank Research* (Spring 1984), pp. 56–61.
Threadgold, A. "Organisation and Regulation of the Domestic UK Capital Market: Causes and Expected Consequences of Recent Changes," in *Changes in the Organisation and Regulation of Capital Markets*. Basle: Bank for International Settlements, March 1987.

Tobin, J. "The Case for Preserving Regulatory Distinctions," in *Restructuring the Financial System*, a symposium sponsored by the Federal Reserve Bank of Kansas City, August 20–22, 1987.

White, A.P. "The Evolution of the Thrift Industry Crisis," Finance and Economics Discussion Series, No. 101, Federal Reserve Board, Washington, D.C., January 1989.

Williamson, S.D. "Costly Monitoring, Financial Intermediation and Equilibrium Credit Rationing," *Journal of Monetary Economics* (September 1986), pp. 159–179.

Wolfson, M.H. "The Causes of Financial Instability," Finance and Economics Discussion Series, No. 78, Federal Reserve Board, Washington, D.C., June 1989.

Zavvos, G.S. "The Strategy of the EEC for the Banking Sector," *The Irish Banking Review* (Spring 1988), pp. 53–64.

Zavvos, G.S. "The EEC Banking Policy for 1992," *Revue de la Banque* (March/April 1988), pp. 7–20.

5 THE FRENCH FINANCIAL SYSTEM

L. Beduc F. Ducruezet and P. Papadacci

1. The Structure of Financial Institutions and Markets

The 1984 Banking Act (see section 2) not only redefined the notion of banking operations substantially, but also entirely overhauled the classification of credit institutions into different categories (see appendix 2). These institutional decisions, and a trend towards growing uniformity in the activity of institutions under pressure of competition, have made the traditional distinctions between commercial banks, investment banks, and medium- and long-term lending banks obsolete.

1.1. Banks

Henceforward, the term '*bank*' refers to institutions that may conduct all types of operations; they are consequently pivotal in the financial community. These banks, be they members of the French Bankers' Association (AFB) or mutual or cooperative banks, account for almost half of the net assets of the entire French banking system. They hold 55% of all deposits (excluding short-term securities such as certificates of deposit) of nonfinancial agents, make 54% of loans to customers, and hold 45% of credit institution portfolios.

1.1.1. The AFB Banks. This category of universal banks, all of which must belong to be the AFB and which numbered 408 on December 31, 1988, includes institutions of widely differing size. Its membership includes three major national institutions (Banque Nationale de Paris, Crédit Lyonnais, and Société Générale) and five other banks whose total assets exceed 100 billion francs (Banque Française du Commerce Extérieur, Banque Paribas, Crédit Commercial de France, Banque Indosuez, and Compagnie Bancaire). These eight institutions account for 55% of the total assets of AFB banks. They are followed by 59 banks with total assets of between 10 and 100 billion francs, and 194 with total assets of between 1 and 10 billion francs. The three national banks aside, AFB banks are customarily divided into Paris-based banks (131), provincial banks (63 banks), capital markets banks (20), banks that operate primarily in the French overseas departments or territories (18), foreign banks (162), and banks whose registered offices are in the Principality of Monaco (11). In addition to their aggressiveness in the domestic market (through financial innovations, new types of lending, etc.), the AFB banks have expanded their operations abroad substantially (opening branches and agencies, intervening in world markets, etc.).

The AFB banks hold 29% of nonfinancial agents' deposits and make 34% of loans to customers and hold 35% of credit-institution portfolios.

1.1.2. The Mutual or Cooperative Banks. A second category of institution in the French banking system consists of mutual or cooperative banks. Their field of operations is narrower than that of the AFB banks. These mutual or cooperative networks are affiliated with the "social" or non-profit-making economy, which has grown under the wing of the State. Within the framework of this relationship, these institutions enjoy certain privileges, such as making State-subsidized loans, but they are allowed to deal only with a limited category of customer (farmers, craftsmen, etc.) who are members of these institutions and own (often token) shares in their capital.

These banks hold 26% of nonfinancial agents' deposits, make 20% of loans, and hold approximately 10% of all types of securities. The major institutions are the Crédit Agricole, the Banques Populaires, and the Crédit Mutuel. These institutions are losing their distinctive character as the State phases out the subsidies on certain types of loan. They operate in an increasingly competitive sector. Consequently, they are gradually coming to function like universal banks and are even starting to do business with nonresident customers.

1.2. Savings Institutions

1.2.1. Savings Banks and Provident Funds. These are divided into two separate networks. The Caisse Nationale d'Epargne is not a credit institution, but is part of the network run by the Post Office. The Caisses d'Epargne et de Prévoyance are credit institutions within the meaning of the Banking Act and are subject to a central organ, the Centre National des Caisses d'Epargne et de Prévoyance (CENCEP). The savings banks enjoy a privilege in the form of the savings passbook called the livret A, which bears tax-exempt interest (currently 4.5% per annum). Conversely, they are entitled to lend to individuals only. Only in the last few years have the Caisses d'Epargne et de Prévoyance been allowed to manage checkable sight deposits, and they are now allowed to make loans to small and medium-sized firms.

1.2.2. The Caisse des Dépôts et Consignations (CDC). The CDC is a legally and financially autonomous publicly owned institution. It performs tasks entrusted to it by the State, and its management is controlled by Parliament via a supervisory commission.

Most of the funds deposited in the livret A passbooks are centralized by the CDC, which uses them mainly to finance low-cost housing. The CDC also centralizes all or part of the special-regime savings deposits, i.e., the savings banks' ordinary taxable savings passbooks (livret B), housing savings accounts and schemes, "popular" savings passbooks, and industrial development accounts; the latter three vehicles are tax exempt. The CDC takes direct deposits from a clientele made up of public institutions, public subsidized housing organizations, property finance companies, and retirement and sickness insurance institutions (social security organizations, pension funds, mutual companies), as well as from notaries public and other government-appointed officials. Monies placed on consignment represent only a tiny portion of the CDC's resources.

In all, the Caisses d'Epargne et de Prévoyance account for 22% of customer deposits with credit institutions. The CDC, Caisses d'Epargne et de Prévoyance, and the Caisse Nationale d'Epargne combined manage 33% of money assets of resident nonfinancial agents, make 17% of loans, and holds 40% of all types of securities.

1.3. Specialized Credit Institutions

1.3.1. Finance Companies. These are credit institutions with a limited field of operations, that are not authorized to receive funds from the public at less than two years' initial term except on a subsidiary basis. However, these institutions are now entitled to issue bills (comparable to certificates of deposit) with a minimum maturity of 10 days. But the finance companies obtain half of their resources by means of refinancing with the banks, to which they are very frequently linked by ownership.

Some of these institutions operate within a preestablished regulatory framework, i.e., mutual guarantee cooperative companies, saving–lending institutions, property finance companies, overseas finance companies, telecommunications finance companies, property companies for commerce and industry, energy-conservation investment finance companies, and regional finance companies.

The other finance companies are authorized individually on the basis of one of the following criteria regarding their aims:

- to provide a particular type of finance (credit, leasing, rental operations with an option to purchase) for a diversified clientele and for various purposes;
- to provide finance to a single category of customers (individuals, businesses, local authorities) in all forms and for all purposes;
- to finance a particular type of item (producer goods, property, cash shortages, consumer goods) for a diversified clientele and by all possible procedures;
- to finance the acquisition of goods or services supplied by an industrial or commercial corporation to all possible types of clientele and by all means of financing; or
- to perform factoring operations or issue and manage means of payment.

Finance companies differ greatly in size: at the end of 1988, the smallest had total assets of less than 10 million francs, and the largest had total assets in excess of 70 billion francs. Finance companies combined account for 13% of lending.

1.3.2. Securities Houses and Brokerage Firms. Under Section 99 of the Banking Act, the principal activity of securities houses is the management of securities portfolios, receiving customers' preassigned deposits, or the investment of such securities as del credere agents. After a period of decline until 1980, this category of institution has grown strongly, especially since 1985, and has undergone far-reaching changes. Formerly often controlled by individuals, securities houses are now usually subsidiaries of major banking groups and engage in new types of operation such as intervention in the negotiable debt securities markets or the MATIF (Marché à Terme International de France), and the issue of short and medium-term paper.

Brokerage firms, which have replaced the former *agents de change* or stockbrokers, enjoy a monopoly in quoting and trading in securities. Certain brokerage firms have also opted for the status of securities houses as authorized by the Act.

1.3.3. Specialized Financial Institutions. This category embraces a small number of credit institutions that have been entrusted by the State with a permanent public-interest task. There were 32 such institutions at the end of 1988, including 21 regional development companies. Specialized financial institutions operate in a variety of fields on behalf of all kinds of economic agents, i.e.,

- property finance, notably for individuals (Crédit Foncier de France, Comptoirs des Entrepreneurs, Caisse de Garantie du Logement Social);
- producer-goods finance, for industrial and commercial firms (Crédit National, Crédit d'Equipement des Petites et Moyennes Entreprises, regional development companies);
- local government finance (Crédit Local de France);
- finance for operations with foreign countries (Caisse Centrale de Coopération Economique); and
- capital markets operations (Matif S.A., Société des Bourses Françaises).

Specialized financial institutions account for 16% of total lending, 9/10ths of it long-term. They obtain their resources primarily from bond issues in France and on the international markets, and from refinancing on the interbank market.

Like the mutual banks, specialized financial institutions are under pressure to adapt to changes in their environment as public involvement decreases. To stem the loss of market shares, certain specialized financial institutions are now diversifying. In some cases they have formed or acquired subsidiaries in order to circumvent their rigid original status.

1.4. Insurance Companies

Insurance companies are subject to supervision by the Insurance Department (Ministry of Economy and Finance) and are governed by regulations specific to their industry. In France, insurance companies form a separate institutional sector, distinct from financial institutions. Life insurance and capital accumulation absorb a third of their premium income, and general insurance the remainder.

At the end of 1987, there were 557 direct insurance companies subject to the French Insurance Code and established in the form of public limited companies (Sociétés Anonymes) pertaining to the public and private sector or mutual companies. Of these, 441 wrote general insurance business and 116 wrote life insurance and capital accumulation business. In addition, 20 companies[1] were engaged exclusively in reinsurance.

Alongside a large number of medium-sized companies, there are several groups of international scale that dominate the national market by their relative size: 10 companies account for 52% of general insurance business and 20 groups account for 86% of the life insurance market. Leading French insurance groups include nationalized companies such as Union des Assurances de Paris, Assurances Générales de France, Groupe des Assurances Nationales, and private-sector companies such as Axa-Midi, Victoire, etc.

Despite the preponderance of compulsory levies (taxation and social security contributions) in the funding of pension schemes and the welfare system, the insurance industry plays a growing role in the management of savings. Authorized by section 11 of the Banking Act to conduct all types of banking operations, the insurance companies have profited from fast-growing demand for life insurance and capital accumulation products[2] since the beginning of the 1980s to develop a diversified range of financial products, generally combined with favorable tax treatment. These compete with or supplement the savings products offered by the banks. Particularly worth mentioning are capital accumulation certificates (securities maturing in 7–30 years), which life insurance companies alone are entitled to issue and market. The total amount outstanding for this category of certificates (73 billion francs at the end of 1987) is rising very fast.

Because they manage huge mass of capital generated by the mutualization of risks proper, the insurance industry is an active institutional investor in the capital market. However, the companies are subject to regulatory restrictions[3] as to the structure of their investments. Insurance companies' securities portfolios represent more than 3/4 of total investment outstanding, i.e., 550 billion francs out of a total of 717 billion

THE FRENCH FINANCIAL SYSTEM 251

francs at the end of 1987 (see appendix 3). Moreover, the insurance sector accounts for 19.2% of total French stock market capitalization for bonds and 15.2% for equities.

1.5. E. Financial Markets

Following reforms introduced since 1985, the *short-term* money market has been subdivided into two compartments: the interbank market and the money market.

1.5.1. The Interbank Market. This market, to which credit institutions alone have access, is where refinancing operations take place between those institutions holding surplus cash and those in need of liquidity. The Banque de France occasionally intervenes in this market to fine-tune the system by supplying or withdrawing liquidity for short periods (24 or 48 hours) (see section 3.4.2).

In all cases, operations entered into on the interbank market are recorded in the books of the Banque de France, which makes this the market for central bank money.

The interest rates formed on this short-term money market are signposted by those at which the Banque de France conducts its official operations (see section 3.4.1).

1.5.2. The Money Market. The money market is open to all economic agents, financial and nonfinancial alike, via the authorized holding of all negotiable short-dated securities with maturities ranging from 10 days to 7 years. These securities are issued by the banks (certificates of deposit), by the other credit institutions (financial institutions' and finance companies' bills), by companies (commercial paper), and by the central government (Treasury bills). These securities are not listed on the stock market but are traded over the counter on regulated markets. They have replaced a proportion of time deposits by allowing holders to obtain liquidity more readily simply by selling them; in addition, with the exception of Treasury bills, they are often issued at the investor's request for a duration to suit his needs.

The *long-term* money market is also subdivided into two compartments: the securities market and the mortgage market.

1.5.3. The Securities Market. In France, the securities (or capital) market has grown strongly for almost a decade now due to several convergent favorable factors. To begin with, there has been heavy demand for capital to finance the government budget deficit (the central government being the leading issuer of bonds), and to strengthen credit institutions' capital and other permanent resources. Second, positive and regularly rising real interest rates have stimulated demand for bonds, while increasing profits in most companies in recent years have made it easier to place new equity issues. Lastly, tax incentives have encouraged individuals to build up securities portfolios. These incentives operate both at the time of purchase of securities (on condition that they are held over a certain period of time) and on receipt of revenues (tax-exempt amount or withholding tax), or when capital gains are realized (tax-exempt amount) at the time of disposal.

The capital market too has seen many innovations, particularly in the bond market, with floating rate and reviewable rate issues, issues in which bonds belonging to a single core issue are issued in several *tranches* (*obligations assimilables du Trésor*—fungible Treasury bonds), the possibility of hedging interest-rate risks by means of futures trading on the MATIF, and subordinated and participating loan stocks (hybrid securities, midway between equities and bonds).

1.5.4. The Mortgage Market. Under the supervision of and organized by the Crédit Foncier de France, the mortgage market was created in 1966. Its purpose was to lengthen the duration and lower the cost of property finance by allowing lenders to trade their mortgage claims on certain conditions. The scale of refinancing on this market has diminished since 1970 and is now marginal.

Credit insititutions may now sell claims, notably ones representing home loans, under a technique known as *securitization*, recently introduced in France. However, preliminary work on building portfolios of homogeneous claims of sufficient quality to attract investors is liable to delay launch of the first *fonds commun de créances* (mutual funds that securitize debts receivable).

Generally speaking, it is important to note the growing role of indirect holdings of securities (money market instruments and marketable securities) by nonfinancial agents via *undertakings for collective investment in transferable securities* (UCITS) (or *organismes de placement collectif en valeurs mobilières* (OPCVM)). These organizations currently play a crucial role in developing and leading the money and capital (bond especially) markets. The UCITS outweigh the traditional institutional investors (insurance companies and pension funds) and are responsible for the sharp growth in repurchase operations, which offer yields close to market rates while preserving a high level of liquidity.

1.5.5. Modernization of the Financial Markets. Modernization was designed partly to attract investors by offering a range of instruments covering all maturities from the very short term to the long term and by ensuring satisfactory liquidity via a busy secondary market, and partly to facilitate the transmission of short-term interest-rate changes into long-term rates.

While the first objective has amply been achieved, the second still faces obstacles, one of whose consequences notably has been a reversal of the yield curve reflecting long-term interest-rate expectations, conflicting with the rates set for short-term capital within the framework of monetary policy.

1.6. Internationalization

French credit institutions have been actively involved in the worldwide internationalization of banking, which has expanded rapidly over the past two decades. The banks developed a dense network of overseas establishments. Foreign banks have steadily increased their presence in France during the same period.

1.6.1. French Credit Institutions' Establishments Abroad

1.6.1.1. The Leading French Banks Have Built Up a Dense International Network. French credit institutions now operate the world's third largest network of foreign establishments, behind Japan and the United States.[4] At the end of 1987, 47 credit institutions under French control were represented abroad in the form of 287 branches, 307 subsidiaries, 246 affiliates, and 249 representative offices. Their combined investments totalled 28 billion francs (see appendices 4 and 5).

Banks account for the overwhelming percentage of the international network, with 97% of total capital invested abroad by French credit institutions at the end of 1987. Moreover, the concentration is particularly sharp among banks per se: on December 31, 1987, out of 238 banks under French control, only 34 were engaged in business abroad via branches, subsidiaries, or affiliates, and banks belonging to the seven leading banking groups[5] (i.e., 26 institutions) accounted for virtually all of the investment concerned.

Lastly, although geographically diversified, the French foreign banking network remains concentrated

- in two areas, namely Europe and North America, which account for almost two thirds of capital invested; and
- on a small number of countries: the United States and Switzerland account for a quarter of investment, and the five main host countries for almost half of the capital invested abroad.

1.6.1.2. Credit Institutions Expanded their International Network Remarkably Between 1970 and 1983, but Have Marked Time Since Then. The foreign network of French institutions is the outcome of several periods of expansion, and some of their establishments abroad date back many years. The network underwent a thorough transformation between the early 1970s and the middle of the 1980s.

Responding to changes in the international economic environment (e.g., strong growth in the Euromarkets and gradual integration of financial markets) and in national regulations (quantitative credit controls, move towards universal banking), the major institutions strengthened their overseas presence and redeployed their network geographically. They have sought to position themselves favorably in the major traditional and new financial centers and to improve their earnings. Consequently, investment abroad by banks under French control was multiplied by 8.4 between 1974 and 1984, growing from 2.3 billion francs to 19.4 billion francs, in current francs.

This trend went hand in hand with a significant strengthening of French banks' presence in North America and Asia, at the expense of geographic areas in which they had been present for much longer, such as Europe and Africa (see appendix 6).

Earnings from operations initiated by the foreign network have deteriorated noticeably since 1983, owing to shrinking margins and rising international sovereign risks. Consequently, there has been a distinct slowdown in the pace of expansion abroad.

With the prime aim of improving earnings and bringing their own funds into line with new international risk–asset ratios, the leading French banks have recently attempted

- to rationalize their networks, reviewing the density of their branch network and shifting the distribution between different forms of investment in favor of subsidiaries (see appendix 7); and
- to target their activities more precisely by geographical zone and host country.

1.6.2. The Presence of Foreign Financial Institutions in the French Banking System

1.6.2.1. A Steadily Growing Banking Population. Paris has always welcomed foreign institutions. Only in the 1960s, however, did the number of foreign banks in France begin to grow steadily. Between 1960 and 1970, the number of foreign banks grew from 33 to 58, then to 122 in 1980 and 168 in 1988 (see appendix 8).

At the end of December 1988, foreign-controlled banks accounted for 41% of the population of AFB banks, and their share of overall AFB banking activity[6] amounted to 20% (see appendix 9).

Ranking of foreign banks by geographic origin reveals

- the importance of European Community-based banks (37% of the total population), including 27 of the top 50 institutions in the Community;[7] and
- the large number of banks based in the United States (29) in the overall foreign banking population (168), given the number of countries represented in France (38).

1.6.2.2. The Accelerating Internationalization of the Financial System Since 1985. In the recent period, the easing of regulatory restrictions (abolition of quantitative credit controls, gradual liberalization of exchange controls), the modernization of financial structures (stock market reform, creation of the MATIF and the MONEP[8]), and improvement in market procedures (introduction of continuous quotation, appointment of primary dealers in Government securities) have all helped to promote Paris as a financial center. These far-reaching changes have in turn attracted new categories of foreign investors.

Over the past three or four years, foreigners have stepped up their presence in the French financial system, as witnessed by

- the arrival in France of some of the world's largest commercial banks and securities houses (American investment banks, U.K. merchant banks, Japanese securities houses);
- the growth in the number of foreign-owned securities houses (24 units were authorized between 1985 and 1988).

Overall, the number of foreign-controlled credit institutions rose by 33% between 1985 and 1988 to 256 (168 banks, 55 finance companies, and 33 securities houses), and 7 out of the 45 Paris brokerage firms opened their capital to foreign financial institutions in 1988.

This internationalization of the French financial system is expected to continue in the coming years. Many European credit institutions will in all likelihood be tempted to bolster their presence in each of the member countries as the single European market draws near.

2. A Brief History of the French Banking System

The French banking system is currently governed by the January 24, 1984 Act (Law No. 84–46) regarding the activities and supervision of credit institutions, commonly referred to as the *Banking Act*. This Act not only renovated but also standardized the law as applied to institutions engaging in credit activities. The chief phases of the evolutionary process from which the present banking system has grown are outlined below.

Until 1880, the Banque de France, founded in 1800, played a major role in financing the economy in addition to its currency-issuing privilege, originally received for Paris and progressively extended to the whole of France.

The major credit institutions were founded between 1850 and 1864 to perform the principal banking operations (deposit-taking and lending), whereas previously the banks concentrated primarily on placing public-sector loans and on foreign-exchange operations.

The organization of the banking system evolved pragmatically. It was notably after two spectacular bankruptcies that the prudential principles distinguishing deposit-taking business from investment banking were established. Subsequently, medium- and long-term lending banks emerged to provide finance for productive investment.

The first statute organizing the banking industry was the June 1941 Act, which in fact concerned only general-purpose banks and confirmed their method of operating on a professional and corporate basis. The mutual or cooperative banks and the specialized institutions entrusted with a public interest task remained outside the scope of this Act. The system thus created consisted of

- a Standing Committee of Banks (Comité permanent de banques) consisting of six bankers and a government representative. It regulated the workings of the banking system and banking operations and took measures concerning individual institutions;
- a Banking Control Commission (Commission de contrôle des banques) to enforce the banking regulations vis-à-vis the institutions; and

- two industry association—one for banks, the other for financial institutions—with compulsory membership for all. These associations acted as transmission belts between their members and the authorities.

A second act, passed in December 1945, nationalized the largest institutions to enable the authorities to influence the distribution of lending more directly within the framework of a planning process intended to revive the postwar economy. This Act replaced the Standing Committee of Banks by the National Credit Council, which worked closely with the Banque de France from the outset.

This system, which left the special status institutions (mutual or cooperative banks) still outside the direct purview of the monetary authorities, remained in operation for almost 40 years.

The January 1984 Act (the Banking Act) thoroughly overhauled the framework in which the banking business operates, extending the system as a whole to all legal entities, now referred to as *credit institutions*, whose regular business is to carry out banking operations.

Banking operations comprise the receipt of funds from the public (i.e., in the form of deposits, with the right to make use of them for own account but subject to an obligation to repay them), credit operations, and making available to customers or managing means of payment.

Credit operations refer to all actions by which a person, against valuable consideration, places or promises to place funds at the disposal of another person, or assumes a contingency/commitment in favor of the latter in the form of an endorsement, surety, or guarantee. Leasing, and more generally all rental operations with a purchase option, are treated as credit operations.

Lastly, all instruments that, regardless of the medium or technical process used, enable any person to transfer funds are considered means of payment.

Moreover, credit institutions may also carry out operations connected with their business, such as

- foreign exchange operations;
- gold, precious metals, and coin transactions;
- the placing, subscription, purchase, management, custody, and sale of securities and any financial product;
- advice and assistance in assets management, financial management, financial engineering, business creation and development, and acquisition of interests in companies; and
- rental of movable and real estate assets for institutions authorized to engage in leasing operations.

Credit institutions are not entitled to engage in activities other than those enumerated above on a regular basis. Such operations may, under certain circumstances, be permitted if they remain of minor importance in relation to the institution's normal business as a whole; they must not distort competition on the market concerned.

Credit institutions are authorized by the Comité des Etablissements de Crédit (Credit Institutions Committee) to operate in one of the six following categories: banks, mutual and cooperative banks, savings banks and provident funds, municipal credit banks, finance companies, and specialized financial institutions (see section 1.1).

The Credit Institutions Committee may withdraw authorization either at the institution's request, or automatically if the institution ceases to comply with the conditions to which authorization is subject. Authorization may also be withdrawn as a disciplinary sanction by the Commission Bancaire (see below).

The Banking Act instituted five bodies, two of which express opinions on credit and monetary policy (see below), the other three being responsible for supervision of the banking system (see section 3). Each of these bodies presents an annual report. Together, they represent a very thorough overview of the French banking and financial system.

The Conseil National du Crédit (National Credit Council) is consulted on the main thrusts of monetary and credit policy, and it monitors the workings of the banking and financial system. It expresses opinions and may carry out such studies as it sees fit.

The Consultative Committee, also known as the *users' committee*, scrutinizes matters pertaining to relations between credit institutions and their customers, and it proposes such measures as it sees fit in this field, notably in the form of opinions or general recommendations.

3. Regulation and Supervision

3.1. Supervisory Authorities

Despite the decompartmentalization of banking and capital markets activities, supervision of financial institutions and of markets remains fragmented between a profusion of supervisory authorities.

The very broad definition of "banking operations" adopted by the January 24, 1984 Banking Act nevertheless allows a considerable diversity of institutions with credit-institution status to be brought within the ambit of the same supervisory authorities. Moreover, the recent setting up of a body permitting consultation between the banking supervisory authorities and the market authorities represents a first step along the road to harmonization of supervisory procedures.

3.1.1. Supervision of Credit Institutions. Under section 1 of the January 3, 1973 Act, the Banque de France is responsible for overseeing the smooth functioning of the banking system. In that capacity, it is involved in the regulation and supervision of credit institutions via three bodies instituted by the Banking Act. These bodies are staffed by Banque de France personnel on secondment. They are as follows.

3.1.1.1. The Comité de la Réglementation bancaire (Bank Regulations Committee). This committee consists of six members including the Minister of Economy and Finance (Chairman) and the Governor of the Banque de France (Vice-Chairman). The Committee is entrusted with the task of "laying down general regulations applicable to credit institutions." Under section 33 of the Banking Act, it has powers to define the rules relating to capital requirements and the conditions on which equity participations may be taken in or by these institutions, conditions governing the opening of branches, conditions governing banking operations, management standards, accounting rules, instruments of credit policy, etc.

3.1.1.2. The Comité des établissements de crédit (Credit Institutions Committee). This six-member body is chaired by the Governor of the Banque de France. The Committee acts as registrar of credit institutions, making decisions pertaining to individual institutions (granting authorizations and exemptions) as provided for in the laws and regulations applying to credit institutions, with the exception of those that come within the purview of the Commission Bancaire.

3.1.1.3. The Commission Bancaire (Banking Commission). The Commission Bancaire consists of the Governor of the Banque de France (Chairman), the Director of the Treasury (directeur du Trésor), a member of the Conseil d'Etat, a judge of the Cour de Cassation (French Supreme Court) and two members appointed for their competence in the field. The Commission Bancaire wields authority over credit institutions and securities houses subject to the terms of the Banking Act. There were 2123 such institutions at the end of December 1988.

Under section 37 of the January 24, 1984 Act, the Commission Bancaire is responsible for enforcing compliance with banking regulations by credit institutions. It scrutinizes their operations and monitors their financial soundness. For this purpose, members of the staff of the Banque de France[9] conduct data analyses and on-the-spot inspection visits, which may be extended to the subsidiaries of a credit institution and to the legal entities controlling it either directly or indirectly, as well as to the other subsidiaries of those entities (section 41).

The Commission Bancaire is also invested with disciplinary powers. In case of breach of the rules of sound professional conduct, it is empowered to issue a warning or an injunction to the managers of the institution concerned. It may also inflict disciplinary and/or financial sanctions after establishing a violation of a legislative or regulatory provision, or failure to defer to an injunction. In such cases, it has the powers of an administrative court.

3.1.2. Supervision of Markets and Market Operators. The institutional structure of the capital markets was reorganized by the December 31, 1987 Act for the futures markets, the January 22, 1988 Act for the securities markets, and the August 2, 1989 Act regarding the security and transparency of capital markets. The terms of these statutes place the regulation of the markets within the competence of new regulatory bodies and strengthen the powers of the ordinary law supervisory body, the Commission des Opérations de Bourse (French Securities and Exchange Commission).

3.1.2.1. The New Stock Market Bodies. The Conseil des Bourses de Valeurs (Securities Exchange Board) is a professional body consisting of 12 members, of which 10 are elected by the brokerage firms, entrusted with regulatory and disciplinary powers.

As the higher authority responsible for organizing the market, the Board lays down general stock market regulations (standing market rules, rules regarding the listing and delisting of securities, laying down conditions for the creation and management of guarantee funds for the brokerage firms), and decides on the listing and delisting and, where appropriate, suspension of trading in securities.

With regard to the brokerage firms, it is empowered to lay down both general and individual regulatory decisions. For example, it lays down the conditions of authorization, withdrawal of authorization, and suspension of brokerage firms and spells out the prudential rules (risk asset ratio, risk distribution ratio, and liquidity ratio) applicable to them. Section 4 of the January 22, 1988 Act empowers it to authorize new brokerage firms (as of January 1, 1992). It also has the power to discipline the said firms and their employees, being entitled to sanction all breaches of statutes and regulations or failure to observe professional obligation.

The Société des Bourses Françaises (French Bourse Corporation) has the status of a specialized financial institution and is the executive body of the Conseil des Bourses de Valeurs.

The SBF is responsible for the everyday running of the market, recording and publishing deals concluded by the brokerage firms, and overseeing enforcement of the regulations laid down by the Conseil des Bourses de Valeurs. For this purpose, it has an audit unit whose task is to prevent and investigate breaches of statutes and regulations and failure to observe professional obligations on the part of brokerage firms and their personnel.

3.1.2.2. Bodies Governing the Futures Market. The Conseil du Marché à Terme (Futures Exchange Board), is a 17-member body representing credit institutions, brokerage firms, insurance companies and industrial and commercial companies. It is invested with regulatory and disciplinary powers.

The Conseil is responsible for issuing market regulations. It decides whether to list or to delist futures contracts accepted for trading on the market,[10] and makes all decisions necessary to ensure the proper functioning of the latter (e.g., laying down settlement and delivery procedures, framing the rules of supervision applicable to market operators, etc.).

Since the unification, in July 1988, of the financial instruments and commodities futures markets, the Conseil du Marché à Terme is authorized to approve the specific regulatory measures adopted by both the financial futures and commodities market committees.

In addition, it has the power to sanction operators who contravene the laws and regulations governing the market or fail to fulfill their professional obligations.

MATIF S.A. is the clearing house of the French International Futures Market, recording daily trading and guaranteeing their performance. It has the status of a credit institution (a specialized financial institution).

OMF—Organisation de marchés en France, SA—is a finance company that, in addition to organizing the OMF stock index futures market, ensures the daily clearing of operators' positions.

3.1.2.3. The Role of the Central Bank. As the monetary authority, the Banque de France closely monitors developments on the short-term money markets. The scope of its powers is spelled out in the December 14, 1985

Act on securities and broadened by recent legislation (the December 31, 1987 and January 22, 1988 Acts; see supra).

According to the terms of the December 14, 1985 Act, the Comité de la Réglementation Bancaire issues all regulations regarding the organization of markets in negotiable debt securities (certificates of deposit, bills issued by financial institutions and finance companies, commercial paper) and approves the characteristics with which issues of such securities must comply. The Banque de France takes all appropriate measures to enforce compliance with regulations, and also supervises interbank market brokers.[11]

According to the terms of the December 31, 1987 and January 22, 1988 Acts, the Banque de France expresses an opinion regarding the general regulations established by the Conseil des Bourses de Valeurs and the general regulations established by the Conseil du Marché à Terme.

It is also consulted on the listing or delisting of contracts accepted for trading on the futures market where these concern a market subject to its supervision.

3.1.2.4. The Commission des Opérations de Bourse (COB) (French Securities and Exchange Commission). This Commission is an administrative body. Although it is not a legal entity, it has its own budget.[12] The Commission des Opérations de Bourse is run by a collegiate management (a chairman appointed by the Council of Ministers, and eight members). Its task is to protect savings invested in securities, and particularly to check the quality and periodicity of the information released by listed companies and to ensure the proper functioning of the markets.

Supervision of issuers. The COB defines the content of the information to be disclosed by the issuer and delivers a certificate of authorization for each operation involving public offering complying with regulatory requirements. It may veto the listing of new securities. By virtue of its responsibility for ensuring that transactions take place regularly and fairly, the Commission des Opérations de Bourse is empowered to substitute for a defaulting issuer to disclose the latter's position to the public together with the comments of the supervisory authority. It also has the power to apply to the presiding judge of the Court of First Instance of Paris for a writ ordering the issuer to suspend operations.

Market supervision. The scope and powers of the COB have been extended by the January 22, 1988 Act on the securities markets and the August 2, 1989 Act on the security and transparency of capital markets.

As the supervisory authority of the capital and futures markets, the COB also supervises the Undertakings for Collective Investment in Transferable Securities and securities portfolio managers. These must be authorized by the COB and their operations are regulated by it (through the issuance of general recommendations and rules of professional conduct). By virtue of its responsibility for safeguarding the integrity of the market, it verifies that no one has manipulated the prices, divulged misleading information or used privileged information to his advantage: all these violations are subject to criminal sanction. For this purpose, it has powers of investigation against operators on the market, against major shareholders of listed companies, the consolidated subsidiaries of the said companies, and against any person thought capable of providing information useful to the pursuit of its task.

The COB is entitled to take financial sanctions against persons committing practices contrary to its regulations and may request the presiding judge of the Court of First Instance of Paris to order the immediate cessation of malpractice liable to injure the rights of investors.

3.1.2.5. The Commission Bancaire (Banking Commission). As the credit institutions' supervisory authority, the Commission Bancaire is responsible for overseeing market operators where these have the status of a credit institution or securities house. In virtue of its right to follow-up, the scope of its supervision may be extended to the subsidiaries of such institutions.

3.1.3. Coordination of the Work of Supervisory Authorities. Pursuant to section 21 of the January 22, 1988 Act, the Conseil des Bourses de Valeurs, the Conseil du Marché à Terme, the Commission des Opérations des Bourse and the Commission Bancaire are entitled to disclose among themselves such information as may be required in the performance of their respective tasks.

The coordination of relations between the monetary authorities and the supervisory authorities of the capital market was institutionalized in April 1988 by the setting up of the capital markets Liaison Committee. Under the chairmanship of the Director of the Treasury, this committee's membership includes the Governor of the Banque de France, the Chairman of MATIF S.A., and the Presidents of the Conseil des Bourses de Valeur and the Commission des Opérations de Bourse. It is responsible notably for organizing coordination and the release of information available on each of the market's compartments.

3.2. Main Aspects of Banking Regulations

3.2.1. Rules Governing the Right to Operate as a Credit Institution. Credit institutions are bound by the rules governing their taking-up and of the business and by the rules pertaining to their financial structure and to the extension of their activity outside the banking industry.

3.2.1.1. The Taking-Up and Pursuit of the Business of Credit Institutions. The right to operate as a credit institution is subject to authorization by the Comité des Etablissements de Crédit. Before granting such authorization, this body verifies that the company applying for authorization meets the conditions enumerated in sections 15, 16, and 17 of the Banking Act, i.e.,

- appropriateness of the company's legal form to the activities of a credit institution;
- compliance with the minimum capital requirement;
- the presence of at least two people to determine the effective direction of the institution's business policy;
- the integrity and the experience of its managers; and
- the presentation of a program of activities.

These criteria of authorization merely transpose into French law the terms of the First European Directive of December 12, 1977.

3.2.1.2. The Geographic Distribution of Branch Networks. The freedom to open, transfer convert or sell branches was restored on January 1, 1987 (Regulation No. 86-22 of the Comité de la Réglementation Bancaire) for most credit institutions, with the exception of those that collect tax-exempt savings (Crédit Mutuel and the savings banks), or which enjoy a monopoly over the distribution of subsidized loans (specialized financial institutions).

3.2.1.3. Minimum Capital Requirement. Credit institutions must have paid-up capital or, where applicable, a capital endowment whose minimum amount varies according to 1) the legal category of the institution, and 2) its total assets.

The minimum capital requirement is

- for *banks, mutual banks, and savings banks*, 15 million francs, or 30 million francs when total assets exceed 1.2 billion francs at the end of two consecutive accounting years;
- for the *municipal credit banks*, 5, 10 or 30 million francs, depending on whether total assets are below 600 million, between 600 million and 1.2 billion francs, or above 1.2 billion francs;

- for *finance companies* (excluding mutual guarantee companies and credit card issuers, subject to specific provisions), 7.5 million francs;
- for *security houses*, 5 or 10 million francs, depending on their type of activity; and
- for *specialized financial institutions*, 15 million francs, or 30 million francs where total assets exceed 300 million francs.

3.2.1.4. Equity Participation in Nonbanking Companies. Under regulation No. 85-16 of the Comité de la Réglementation Bancaire, credit institutions that own direct or indirect equirty participation[13] in nonbanking companies must remain within the following three ceilings at all times:

- no equity participation may exceed 5% of the institution's net capital resources;
- total equity participation must not exceed 50% of net capital resources;
- total equity participation giving exclusive controlling power and those in companies whose articles of association or legal form imply unlimited liability on the part of partners must not exceed 15% of net capital resources.

3.2.2. Regulations Regarding Bank Terms

3.2.2.1. Regulations Regarding Interest Payable on Credit Accounts. The payment of interest on sight deposits has been prohibited since June 1967. However, the futures markets' clearing houses were recently authorized (June 1989) to pay interest on the margin accounts placed with them as surety or cover for operations, regardless of the despositor's professional status.

The payment of interest on passbook accounts (whether or not subject to tax) is regulated, as is the payment of interest on time accounts and notes of less than three months' maturity and of an amount of less than 500,000 francs (Regulation No. 86-13 of the Comité de la Réglementation Bancaire of May 16, 1986).

3.2.2.2. Lending Rates. Credit institutions have been free to set their lending rates since April 1966. They must not, under any circumstance, exceed the ceiling rate resulting from computation according to the terms of the December 28, 1966 Act on usury.

Credit institutions are, moreover, obliged to inform their customers of the terms applied by them. In practice, direct billing[14] of banking services to private customers is relatively uncommon.

3.3. Solidarity Mechanisms

The protection of funds received from the public in France depends on a contractural deposit insurance system and a legal solidarity and guarantee scheme.

3.3.1. The Contractual Deposit Insurance System. The solidarity mechanism binding the banks was agreed in 1980 and implemented by the Association Française des Banques.

In the event of bank failure, the Association Française des Banques launches an appeal for contributions by its members. These contributions are calculated in proportion to deposits taken and are intended to compensate the institution's French franc account-holding customers. There is a ceiling on reimbursements of 400,000 francs per depositor.

3.3.2. The Legal Solidarity and Guarantee Scheme

3.3.2.1. Section 52 of the Banking Act. Under para. 2, Section 52 of the Banking Act, the Governor of the Banque de France may make arrangements with all credit institutions with a view to taking the measures required to protect the interests of depositors and third parties, to ensure the smooth functioning of the banking system, and to uphold the reputation of Paris as a financial center.

Under the legal solidarity scheme, the decision to resort to para. 2, Section 52 in case of failure of a credit institution on the one hand, and the choice of the appropriate mechanism on the other hand, are entirely at the discretion of the Governor.

3.3.2.2. Section 6 of the January 22, 1988 Act on Securities Markets. Because the brokerage firms are responsible vis-à-vis those placing orders for the delivery of securities and settlement of transactions, section 6 of the January 22, 1988 Act is designed to strengthen the security of the market by establishing a guarantee fund to cover the commitments of brokerage firms to their customers in case of failure on the part of one of them. The fund is managed by the Société des Bourses Françaises and stands at 1 billion francs.

3.4. The Central Bank, lender of last Resort

Since the abolition of the rediscounting of new export credits[15] and the removal on January 1, 1987 of quantitative credit controls, interest-rate management has become the prime instrument of monetary policy.

As lender of last resort, the Banque de France provides refinancing to the banking system, concentrating its intervention on the interbank market,[16] where the bulk of central bank money is now provided with temporary securities transactions offered under an auction procedure.

3.4.1. Official Intervention Techniques of the Banque de France

3.4.1.1. Calls for Tender. This is the main instrument used by the Banque de France to periodically supply Central Bank money to credit institutions (purchase of Treasury bills or private paper under repurchase agreements). Calls for tender are made at the discretion of the Central Bank, which sets the rate of intervention and the quantity of money that it intends to supply to credit institutions, according to the "Dutch auction" method.

3.4.1.2. Five- to Ten-Day Repurchase Agreements. Unlike the previous procedure, this is initiated by the credit institutions themselves; they may resort to this procedure daily and set the amount of their refinancing. It carries a rate 0.5% to 0.75% above that of the calls for tender and therefore is used only when the day-to-day money market rate is persistently above this ceiling.

3.4.2. Market Procedures.

In addition to the official techniques, the Banque de France can monitor bank liquidity by supplying or withdrawing liquidity on the interbank market, or by intervening in the market for negotiable debt securities, in the framework of its open market operations.

3.4.2.1. Supply and Withdrawal of Liquidity on the Interbank Market. These operations, taking the form of 24- or 48-hour repurchase agreements or reverse repurchase agreements, are concluded at prevailing market terms.

3.4.2.2. Open-Market Operations. As part of its open-market policy, the Banque de France intervenes in the money market (which is opened to all categories of economic agents) by buying or selling negotiable

Treasury bills. These outright purchases and sales currently represent only a marginal proportion of the Central Bank's intervention.

3.5. Management Standards

Under section 51 of the Banking Act, credit institutions are obliged to conform to management standards designed to safeguard their liquidity and solvency and a sound financial structure.

3.5.1. Supervision of Liquidity. Since the introduction of new regulations in February 1988, supervision of the risk of illiquidity operates at two levels:

- *A one-month ratio*, known as the liquidity ratio, which must remain above 100% at all times. The ratio is calculated for all currencies combined in all geographical zones in which credit institutions and securities houses operate. It is defined as the ratio between all or part of the current liquid assets realizable within one month on the one hand, and all or part of current liabilities and potential commitments maturing within a maximum of one month on the other.
- *Three ratios* representative of the foreseeable liquidity position at three months, six months, and nine months are, moreover, calculated at the end of each quarter for purposes of *observation*. These are not subject to any regulatory standard.

3.5.2. Supervision of Maturity Transformation. Credit institutions and securities houses are obliged to comply with a *ratio of own funds and permanent resources* designed to limit the risk of maturity transformation. This ratio was instituted in 1987 to replace the ratio of nonrediscountable medium and long-term operations and the gearing ratio, formerly applicable to banks and finance companies respectively.

The existing regulations oblige institutions subject to them to maintain a minimum ratio between 1) their own funds, provisions, and resources at more than five years, and 2) their long-term applications. After a transitional period,[17] all institutions are expected to show a ratio of 60% at least.

3.5.3. Supervision of Solvency. Introduced in 1979 for registered banks, financial institutions, and certain special-status networks, the regulations regarding solvency were extended in 1984 and 1985 to all credit institutions. They consist in the setting of a threshold (risk asset ratio) and ceilings (risk distribution ratio).

The risk asset ratio. The minimum ratio between net capital resources and total risks incurred by institutions in all geographical zones of activity is set at 5%.

The risk distribution ratio. To limit the concentration of exposure, credit institutions must at all times show that:

- their total exposure to a single customer or to a single group of customers having financial links between them does not exceed 40% of their net capital resources; and
- all exposure individually greater than 15% of net capital resources does not exceed eight times the latter.

In keeping with the European Directive of June 13, 1983 concerning the supervision of credit institutions on a consolidated basis, consolidation is mandatory for the calculation of risk asset and risk distribution ratios.

3.5.4. Monitoring Foreign Exchange Positions. Since September 1, 1989, credit institutions and securities houses engaged in foreign exchange operations[18] are obliged at all times to comply with

- a maximum ratio of 15% between their long or short position in each foreign currency and their net capital resources;
- a maximum ratio of 40% between their short positions in all foreign currencies and their net capital resources.

These ratios may be calculated on a consolidated basis.

4. Broad Trends in Banking Prudential Supervision

Banking has undergone far-reaching changes in recent years, mainly as a result of market globalization, deregulation, and greater competition.

Competition has come in part from nonbanks (insurance companies, companies belonging to the retail sector, etc.), which have begun to offer financial products, and partly from the financial markets, which have played an unprecedented role in attracting savings and granting credits.

Disintermediation and spreading competition have simultaneously generated a wave of financial innovations and a shift in the emphasis of banking activities towards market activities. The emergence and development of new risks (interest-rate risks, foreign-exchange risks, position risks, etc.) have obliged the banking authorities to improve their prudential and accounting regulations and develop their consultation with the market authorities.

4.1. Redeployment of Banking Activities

After suffering steadily shrinking margins on international operations since 1983, credit institutions have had to contend with a narrower interest-rate spread on their traditional intermediation business. This is because large corporations are now entitled to raise funds on the short-dated securities markets, and because lending terms are coming closer to those available for disintermediated financing. There has notably been a decline in lending indexed to the bank base rate in favor of loans indexed to market rates. However, banks' operating income is all the more affected by this development, since the absence of any charge for the management of means of payment and the provision of services free of charge were, until recently, offset by the size of their intermediation margin. In addition, their extremely extensive branch network represents a high structural cost.

To maintain or even boost earnings on their operations, credit institutions have first sought to stem the decline of their traditional business, refocusing their lending on households[19] and, further, sought out alternative sources of profit by developing their previously marginal service activities (financial engineering, stockmarket listing, asset management, marketing collective investment products to customers, etc.). Also, they became actively involved in arbitrage operations between the different financial markets[20] – either by operating directly or by setting up or taking over specialized institutions (capital markets banks, securities houses, brokerage firms, etc.).

In terms of income statement structure, the diversification of banking operations has reduced intermediation contribution to net banking income—from 82.4% in 1983 to 72.5% in 1987 for AFB banks—and has correlatively increased that of "securities" and "other operations," which represented 21.3% of the total in 1987, against 12.3% in 1983.

To cope with rising market risks, the supervisory authorities have moved to adapt the prudential and accounting regulations.

4.2. Improving Prudential and Accounting Regulations

The principles applied by the banking supervisory authorities have sought first to protect credit institutions against the risks of illiquidity associated with the development of operations on markets not subject to the authority of a central bank, and second (for financial futures instruments) to lay down accounting procedures that are both specific and that reflect financial realitices. Lastly, they have been designed to encourage credit institutions operating in the markets to establish adequate management and control instruments (notably for interest-rate risk control purposes).

The regulations adopted in France in the course of the recent period have laid down specific accounting rules for

- operations on financial futures instruments (notably distinguishing between hedging and speculative operations); and
- transaction portfolios.

With regard to systems of internal control, Regulation No. 88-04 of February 22, 1988 of the Comité de la Réglementation Bancaire, required credit institutions that customarily operate in the financial futures markets to set up a permanent mechanism for measuring operations, calculating their outcome, supervision and management of risks incurred, and control over internal procedures. Further, they are required to submit a quarterly report on results and positions taken to the Commission Bancaire.

Application of this regulation is simultaneously helping to improve management and supervision of market risks incurred by credit institutions and to enhance the security of the financial community.

Also with this in view, the market authorities at the same time laid down professional rules of ethics and prudential standards applicable to nonbank operators (risk asset and risk distribution ratios and minimum capital requirements for brokerage firms, for example). In addition, they have introduced mechanisms designed to keep the markets liquid (reform of the regulations governing the status of equity market makers, which came into force in July 1989).

Lastly, following the October 1987 stock market crash, the need arose to improve consultation between bank supervisors and market supervisors with a view to harmonizing the rules applicable to operators, regardless of their legal status (see section 3.1).

5. The Structural Implications of Globalization for French Financial Institutions

After having seen fairly extensive changes in their environment as a result of deregulation, globalization of financial activities, and the emergence of new financing techniques, French financial institutions can expect to undergo substantial restructuring in the near future, under pressure of intensifying European competition (free movement of capital as of July 1, 1990, Europewide integration of financial services in 1993), together with the application of international prudential rules (Cooke ratio or European capital adequacy ratio), and changes in customers' investment behavior (with the expected development of life insurance and retirement plans, a more demanding attitude towards banking services, etc.).

The consequences of globalization on banking activities, risk management and, lastly, external growth and concentration in the financial sector are examined below.[21]

5.1. The Framework of A Global Environment for Banks

5.1.1. The Globalization of Financing. The globalization of banking activities is affecting channels for the provision of finance, as well as products and institutions. The globalization of financing may be viewed as a twofold phenomenon of liberalization and internationalization of financing conditions.

The first aspect refers to a body of reforms that have sought to stimulate competition between credit institutions and enhance the role of the market in setting prices. These reforms attracted particular attention in France, where the financial system was relatively more regulated and compartmentalized than in most other OECD countries. They notably concerned a removal of quantitative controls on credit (1986), the opening of the money market to nonfinancial agents (with the introduction of commercial paper and certificates of deposit), despecialization—in a legal sense at least—of banks (the 1984 Banking Act abolished all distinctions between commercial and investment banks), the trend towards greater uniformity in lending procedures, with the decline in loans at preferential rates and inroads into certain monopolies enjoyed by the mutualist sector, etc.

Parallel to this, the growth of the capital market (notably as a result of disinflation in the 1980s and falling nominal interest rates) had the de facto effect of boosting the share of market financing in total financing to the economy (this process of disintermediation has gone into reverse to some extent since 1987).

Banking operations have become increasingly worldwide as national financial systems have been deregulated. International bank loans outstanding rose by 101% from $1785 billion in 1983 to $3591 billion in 1988.[22] Eurobond issues were multiplied by two between 1984 and 1988 (from $81.7 billion to $177.2 billion).[23] The growing interconnection of financial markets as a result of deregulation of national stockmarkets,[24] together with progress in videotext or data links, has at the same time sharply boosted international trading in the secondary markets.

A second feature of this financial globalization has been the greater fluidity of financial products. On the one hand, the introduction of new negotiable assets (certificates of deposit, commercial paper, etc.) has created a sort of continuum between deposits in the strict sense of the term and conventional securities.

On the other, the creation of floating rate bonds and the dissemination of new financial instruments for managing interest rate or foreign exchange risks have resulted in two contrasting developments. On the one hand, several previously separate features (index-linked bonds, futures instruments, options, interest-rate agreements including a risk "premium," convertible bonds combining equity and bond features, etc.) have been incorporated into a single instrument. On the other hand, the components of financial contracts have been unbundled or dissociated (e.g., currency or interest-rate swaps).

In addition to the decompartmentalization of markets and categories of financial products, distinctions between different financial institutions (notably between banks and insurance companies) have tended to become blurred. Banks have increasingly intervened in the capital markets either via "market intermediation"[25] or through active management of their assets and liabilities. More recently, banking and insurance activities have drawn closer together. Indirectly, by using certain financial instruments (such as options, caps, or floating rate bonds), the banks (and not only the banks) may on occasion find themselves selling certain types of insurance (against market risks, for example) not provided by conventional insurance companies. Also the banks, whether through subsidiaries or jointly with insurance companies, are selling an increasing number of insurance products (they accounted for 30% of the domestic life insurance market in 1988).

5.1.2. International Rules. The globalization of markets and banking activities has gone hand in hand with the establishment of international rules to hasten the process or control certain of the risks entailed in it.

The first category includes different measures pertaining to European financial integration, e.g., the freedom to market UCITS units from October 1989; the removal of controls on capital movements from July 1990; and above all the creation of a single market in financial services in 1993, in compliance with the second European directive. The latter provides for the establishment of a single authorization procedure for banks, based on the principle of mutual recognition by member states. Practically speaking, this will allow institutions authorized to engage in banking operations in their home country to conduct the same operations throughout the Community, including in States whose legislation does not allow their own institutions to engage in such activities.

Regarding the rules of prudential supervision, the application of the *Cooke ratio* (a body of standards laid down by the representatives of the Group of Ten in July 1988) for banks operating internationally requires that these banks comply with a capital adequacy ratio equal to 8% of weighted risk assets, before the end of 1992. Meanwhile, the European Community is working on the preparation of a solvency ratio applicable to all European banks, which should be very close to the BIS ratio.

5.2. The Structural Consequences of Globalization for French Banks

5.2.1. Banking Activities. The principal growth items in the banks' operating statements in recent years were securities-related activities, financial engineering, or asset management on the banks' own behalf. On the other hand, intermediation activities declined proportionally.

According to a Commission Bancaire study,[26] between 1981 and 1987, trends in net banking income by sector were as follows (in constant francs):

Securities department	+189%
Miscellaneous activities[27]	+149%
Management of means of payment	+28 %
Bank intermediation	+10 %

In structural terms, however, intermediation was still preponderant in 1987, representing 72.5% of total net income (11% less than in 1981). Miscellaneous activities increased their share to 16% (+8%), while that of "securities" departments increased 3% to 5.3%. Lastly, "management of means of payment" remained unchanged at 6.2%.

5.2.2. Trends in Banking Risks. The following major changes occurred in the financial structure of banks in the 1980s:

- growing market risks[28] due to expanding capital markets and volatile exchange rates and interest rates. Banks have increasingly resorted to new financial instruments such as swaps, futures contracts, etc. in order to manage these risks;
- rising counter-party risks due mainly to the scale of lending to the less-developed countries, but also arising out of the use of these new financial instruments. The first response to credit risks was to increase provisions.[29] Subsequent efforts gave rise to a process of reregulation, as illustrated notably by the introduction of the Cooke ratio. It is worth noting on this point that French banks will find it harder than other countries' banks to comply with the capital adequacy standard:[30] at the beginning of 1987, their weighted capital/assets ratio averaged 7.52% (and it was generally less than that for the three largest banks). Weighting aside, the capital/assets ratio for France (1987, banks in the *Banker* "Top 500") was 3.17. It was 6.19 for British banks, 5.14 for American banks, and 4.87 for Italian banks.

The banks may envisage several possible consequences of enforcement of the Cooke ratio:[31]

- an increase, ceteris paribus, in the cost of bank lending or swaps;
- a reduction in the proportion of interbank activities (which are very large in French banks);
- slower growth in lending or possible conversion of loans into negotiable bills (securitization);
- a potential increase in risky lending (given the 100% weighting for all lending to the nonbanking private sector); and
- similarly, a potential buildup of operations requiring little capital (financial engineering, M&A).

Regarding risks, while the Cooke ratio as currently in place should effectively lower the risk of lending, this would not be the case for the overall risk (switching from activities entailing a credit risk to those entailing, for example, an interest-rate risk, etc.)

5.2.3. Growing Concentration in the French Financial System

5.2.3.1. Opening Up the French Banking System. The globalization of financial activities has led to a sharp rise in French banks' establishments abroad and in those of foreign banks in France (see section). To illustrate, total investment increased from 9.1 billion francs in 1980 to 27.2 billion in 1987 (more in the form of subsidiaries than of direct investment).

Conversely, the number of foreign banks has tended to rise as a proportion of total AFB banks. Foreign banks accounted for 34.3% of the population of AFB banks in 1987 and 42.5% in 1988 (E.C. banks alone: 15.7%).

The salient features of the foreign banks' presence in France appear to be[32]

- their operations are still relatively moderate in scale (12% of lending and 10% of customer deposits in 1988). Foreign banks accounted for 19.4% of total resident banks' assets, representing a much smaller market share than for the production of goods and services; and
- foreign banks (an in particular non-European banks) specialize in capital markets operations (26.7% in 1988) due to their small branch networks (4.7% of the French bank branch network).

5.2.3.2. The Trend Towards Concentration of French Banks and Insurance Companies in Preparation for the 1992 European Market. In 1986, France had one of the most concentrated banking systems in Europe, according to the OECD.[33] The percentage of assets held by the country's five leading banks relative to the assets of all banks was 63% for France, 55.1% for Italy, 34.7% for Spain, 32.6% for the United Kingdom, and 31.2% for Germany. In view of the impending single market of 1992, it looks as if concentration in the European banking industry is going to occur more through mergers and acquisitions than through internal growth.[34]

There are several reasons why the leading banks prefer to enter alliances with other French or European banking groups:

- access to a Europewide banking network is becoming indispensable for major banks in the present commercial environment, in which:
  - services to customers are acquiring increasing importance,[35] and
  - in many cases, competition is expected to shift from products to distribution (as financial products become increasingly uniform);
- the sheer size of groups is a factor in competition between banks (notably in the case of defensive alliances);
- the need to keep pace with extensive concentration now taking place in industry; and
- the Fact that, while banks too may seek gains in terms of economics

of scale, success on this score is by no means a forgone conclusion; D.B. Humphrey, for example,[36] finds that cost dispersion for banks of comparable size is more significant than differences in costs between banks of different sizes.

Insofar as one may conjecture, the salient trends in integration of the European banking system are likely to be

- in the short term, the small number of major European banks available for acquisition or merger. This is particularly true of the French banking system, which appears to be highly concentrated;
- on the other hand, a considerable number of small banks are likely to be absorbed; here, France (after Spain and Italy) would appear to be a prominent target; and
- a proliferation of purely defensive "alliances," for example in the form of cross-shareholdings.

Lastly, one particular aspect of this concentration process could take the form of closer links between banking and insurance, known in French as *bancassurance*. This is becoming necessary under pressure of more intense competition, and facilitated by the de facto convergence of the two sectors' activities.

For the insurance companies, closer links with the banks[37] provide an opportunity of gaining access to a branch network that would allow them to withstand European competition. The banks, meanwhile, are interested in insurance as a center of productivity (life insurance and retirement savings plans are growing fast,[38] whereas banking margins on lending have tended to shrink in recent years) and as a financial resource (the insurance companies have benefited more than the banks from disinflation). More specifically, certain equity participation by insurance companies in banks may have its origin in the banks' need to increase their own funds.

6. Some Aspects of the Competitiveness of French Banks and Insurance Companies

European financial integration is expected to have two consequences: improved allocation of savings resources on the one hand, and sharper competition in the financial sector on the other.

Below is a brief survey of the chief strengths and weaknesses of French banks and insurance companies in this new competitive environment.

6.1. The Banks

6.1.1. Strengths and Weaknesses. In macroeconomic terms, French banks' main strengths in the face of competition from foreign institutions are

- the presence of some of the largest banks in the OECD, which have already acquired international stature;
- the relatively concentrated structure of the sector; and
- the large number of UCITS (50% of European UCITS in 1988).

Regarding customer relations, French banks' characteristics include:

- an extensive branch network (more extensive than in the United Kingdom, the Netherlands, or Italy, for example);
- an unequalled bank card system (a single network); and
- acknowledged know-how in the fields of investment and new means of payment systems (home banking is available to one customer in 27 against one in 40 in the United Kingdom and one in 350 in the Netherlands).

As for bank personnel, while employees' average qualifications appear to be relatively low (due to massive recruitment in the 1970s), the proportion of executive-grade personnel is rising steadily (the percentage of middle management and executive grade personnel rose approximately 4 points between 1984 and 1988, while that of clerical workers fell 8.5%). Today, French banks employ twice as many executive-grade personnel as European banks as a whole.[39]

Among their weaknesses, French banks still appear to have high administrative costs, accounting for 59% of net banking income in 1988, against 56% for German and British banks, and 46% for Luxembourg.

Second, French banks pay relatively high taxes. Corporation tax, and above all specific taxes, are higher than average for Europe. In 1987, for example, aggregate specific taxes came to 8 billion francs out of a total net income of 12.6 billion francs.[40]

Another handicap facing French banks could be the structure of their activity. Commissions still represent only a small proportion of total bank revenues: 15% of net banking income (OECD-1986), against 31% for the German banks, 38% for the British banks, and 36% for the Italian ones. Generally speaking, French banks appear to suffer from a certain lack of competitiveness in operations such as foreign exchange, public-sector bonds, mortgage lending, etc.

6.1.2. Shifting the Emphasis of Banking Activity after 1992. Conditions surrounding the activity of French banks over the coming years are expected to depend

- chiefly, in the medium run, on the effects of European financial integration;
- on trends in household savings and investment behavior: expected shift towards life insurance and retirement savings plans, more demanding attitudes to banking services and interest payments on investments; and
- on the growth of the capital markets, which is expected to be less lively in the traditional markets than in derivative ones.

Against this background, competition in the banking industry is likely to occur at two levels:

- for the big universal banks: greater competition for customers. The focus of competition would shift from head office to the branches in that case; and
- growing competition in what might be termed *delocalizable* activities: financial engineering, arbitrage operations between markets, and management of large institutional portfolios (mutual funds, capital accumulation funds). These high-margin activities are already being conducted on an international scale, and after 1992 ought rather to represent a culmination rather than the start of financial integration.

6.2. The Insurance Companies

This appears to be a dynamic sector overall; life insurance and retirement savings plans are growing fast, and the "customer base for insurance" is still in its phase of extensive exploitation. In the face of their European competitors, however, the French insurance companies' weaknesses are obvious:

- they are far less powerful than their British, German, or Dutch competitors. This situation is partly due to the existence of a more highly developed compulsory pension scheme in France. The ratio of life insurance premiums to GDP per capita is 1600 francs, against 2600 francs in W. Germany, 3142 francs in the United Kingdom, and more than 6000 francs in Japan;[41]
- the insurance companies are insufficiently represented in certain sectors: brokerage notably, and reinsurance;
- they are heavily penalized in terms of taxation: fiscal and parafiscal levies amount to 35% for health insurance and 5.15% for life insurance. The respective figures are 10% and 4.4% in W. Germany, 17% and 2% in Italy, and 0% in the United Kingdom and Spain.

Consequently, the competitiveness of the French insurance companies will very likely depend on possible reforms in taxation and the effects of restructuring and concentration now in progress, not forgetting the decisive importance of the value of the currency in a sector dependent on long-term savings.

Notes

1. Reinsurance companies are not subject to control by the Insurance Department.
2. Premium income in the life insurance and capital accumulation sector has grown at an average annual rate of 22.5% since 1980.
3. Under article R 332.2 of the Insurance Code, insurance companies are obliged to invest a minimum of 34% of their portfolios in bonds.
4. Ranked by distribution of banking systems' international holdings at the end of 1988. Source: Bank for International Settlements.
5. Banque Nationale de Paris, Société Générale, Crédit Lyonnais, Paribas, Indosuez, Crédit Industriel et Commercial, and Crédit Commercial de France.
6. Measured according to total mainland France assets.
7. Ranked by total assets by *The Banker*, July 1988.
8. Marché des Options Négociables de Paris (Paris traded-options market).
9. The General Secretariat of the Commission Bancaire is a General Department of the Banque de France.
10. The following markets come within the purview of the Conseil: the Marché à Terme International de France (MATIF-French international financial futures market) and the OMF market, on which futures and options contracts are traded. The Marché des Options Négociables de Paris (MONEP), on the other hand, is supervised by the Conseil des Bourses de Valeurs.
11. Interbank market brokers (section 69 of the Banking Act) are individuals or companies engaged exclusively in acting as intermediaries between agents on these markets. They require authorization by the Comité des établissements de crédit.

12. The budget of the COB is funded by a fee charged to all listed companies and to Undertakings for Collective Investment in Transferable Securities.

13. An equity participation in this context is defined as any interest in excess of 10% in a company's capital.

14. At the end of 1987, income from commissions represented approximately 20% of AFB banks' net operating income.

15. Medium-term export credits (EC excluded) relating to contracts signed between 1981 and 1986 alone may still be rediscounted at special rates with the Central Bank.

16. A compartment of the money market reserved for credit institutions and securities houses.

17. Due to end on December 31, 1991.

18. Institutions whose foreign exchange operations represent less than 10% of their total operations are exempted from application of this regulation.

19. Between 1985 and 1988, lending to households as a percentage of total lending by financial agents increased from 26.7% to 29.2%, while short-term revolving lending and overdrafts as a percentage of total lending to households rose from 9.5% to 15%. Source: Banque de France—Monetary Analysis and Statistics Department.

20. The outstanding amount of credit institutions' securities portfolios increased by 36% between 1985 and 1988, while off-balance-sheet operations on financial futures instruments were multiplied by 3.8 in 1988 alone.

21. Problems relating more specifically to sharpening competition in banking and insurance (under the stimulus of the 1993 European market) will be dealt with in section 6.

22. For reporting banks in the BIS zone.

23. Which may be attributable to the expanding Euroyen market, the abandonment of the "lead manager rule," and the massive utilization of swaps: 20%–30% of Eurobond issues have been linked to swaps since 1986.

24. In France notably: the replacement of stockbrokers by Brokerage Firms in 1988 and the forthcoming abolition—on January 1, 1992—of the latters' stock market monopoly, and the lifting of deduction of tax at source on interest paid to nonresidents.

25. "Distributive" techniques in the sense of Gurley and Shaw, implying not the creation of debt securities by credit institutions, but a "brokerage"-type activity.

26. Report of the Commission Bancaire 1988. The study covers a representative sample of 55% of net banking income of all AFB and mutual banks.

27. Including financial engineering and management of banks' securities and property portfolios on their own account.

28. Corresponding to interest-rate and foreign-exchange risks, which may be defined as the risk of a decline in the value of a financial instrument due to variations in interest or exchange rates.

29. The ratio of provisions for "doubtful debts" was estimated (on a sample of the 35 largest banks) at 46.6% in 1987, compared with 39% in 1986. Report of the Commission Bancaire 1988.

30. Unless their extensive provisions for risks are included under supplementary capital.

31. See notably L. Nowicki (1989).

32. See Report of the Commission Bancaire 1988.

33. See Molyneux (1989).

34. According to 80% of respondents in a survey by Arthur Andersen Consultants, "European Capital Market, Strategic Forecast."

35. This emerges in an EFMA survey (1988). According to this survey, 72% of "financial institutions" think that individual customers will be the most profitable customer segment

over the next ten years, particularly for mortgage lending and savings or retirement products.
36. "Cost Dispersion and the Measurement of Economies in Banking," Federal Reserve Bank of Richmond Economic Review—May, June 1987.
37. See D. Kessler (1987).
38. Life insurance premium income rose 35.3% in 1988. Overall insurance premium income grew by 17.5% in 1988.
39. CERC-Les Structures de Salaire dans la CEE-4th quarter 1988.
40. The tax on loans outstanding was abolished in 1989, however.
41. See M. Albert (1989).

References

Albert, M. "Compétitivité Fiscale et Monétaire de l'Assurance Française," *Revue Haute finance* (Spring 1989).
Bruneel D. "The Regulatory Framework of the French Financial Market", Banking seminar at Dubai, November 15, 1988.
Butsch, J.L. "Les Banques Françaises Face à l'Instabilité Financière," *Revue d'économie politique* (September–October 1988).
Commission Bancaire. Annual Reports 1985 and 1988.
Commission Bancaire (General Secretariat). "Implantation à l'Étranger des Établissements de Crédit à Fin 1987/October 1988."
Conseil National du Crédit: Annual reports 1986 and 1987.
Coupaye, P. "Les Banques Françaises en 1989," *Cahiers du crédit mutuel* (September 1989).
Dufloux, C. and M. Karlin. "La Réglementation Prudentielle des Banques," *Revue Banque* 489–492 (December 1988–March 1989).
Fédération Française des Sociétiés d'Assurance. 1987 Report.
Giry-Deloison, P. and P. Masson. "Les Rouages de la Globalisation," *Revue Banque* (July–August 1988).
Index. *Revue économique de la Banque Indosuez* "Impact de la création du marché intégré sur le secteur des banques et des assurances"/1st quarter 1989.
Kessler, D. "Banques et Assurances: Cohabitation, Partage ou Fusion," *Revue d'Économie Financière* (March 1987).
Molyneux, P. "An Analysis of the Structure and Performance Characteristics of Top EC Banks and the Strategic Implications for 1992." *Revue de la Banque de Bruxelles* (June 1989).
Nowicki, L. "L'impact du Ratio Cooke sur l'Activité Bancaire Internationale," *SEDEIS* (July 1989).
OECD. "Competition in Banking"/Etude publiée et 1989.
Patat, J.P. "Les Autorités Monétaires Face à l'Instabilité et aux Nouveaux Risques du Système Financier,"—*Revue d'Économie Politique* (September–October 1988).
Pécha, J. "Les Rôle des Banques Centrales sur les Marchés de Titres," Banque de France Direction des Etudes et des Statistiques Monétaires, May 1988.

Prate, A. "Perspecitve de l'Europe Financière et Monétaire," *Revue Banque* (October 1988).
Revell, J. "Bank Preparations for 1992: Some Clues and Some Queries," *Revue de la Banque de Bruxelles* (March 1989).

Appendix 1. Financial Institutions and the Treasury Classification in national accounts (base year = 1980) and monetary statistics at 1st February 1989 (DOM-TOM excluded)

	Credit Institutions and Similar Entities-S41 (M3 and its counterparts)							
Banque de France and FSC S411	Banks S412	Savings Banks S4131	Caisse des dépôts et consignations S4132	Finance Companies and Similar Entities S4141	Specialized Financial Institutions (I.F.S.) and Similar Entities S4142	Miscellaneous Financial Institutions S4143	Undertakings for Collective Investment in Transferable Securities (UCITS) (6) S42	Government S611
—Banque de France (*) —Exchange stabilisation Fund (3) (*)	—Banks member of the Association Française des banques (AFB French bankers' association) BFCE (Banque Française du Commerce Extérieur -French bank for Foreign Trade) excluded	—Savings banks and provident funds • Savings banks and provident funds • Regional financing Institutions (SOREFI Stés régionales de financement)	—Caisse des dépôts et consignations • Caisse de garantie pour le logement social IFS (*) (CGLS ex-CPHLM)	—Finance Companies (sociétés financières SF) (SCM & SOREFI excluded) • Finance companies subject to special provisions —Real estate companies for commerce and industry (Sociétés immobilières pour le commerce et l'industrie SICOMI) —SOFERGIE —Sociétés de	—Specialized financial institutions IFS • Caisse Centrale de Coopération Economique (CCCE) • Comptoir des Entrepreneurs • Crédit d'Equipment des PME (CEPME) • Crédit Foncier de France • Crédit Local de France • Crédit National • MATIF—SA—Paris Futures Clearing House	—Mutual loan funds* —Mutual guarantee insurance companies (Stés de Caution Mutuelle) (SF) (3) —Groupements professionels de répartition d'emprunts collectifs au profit d'agents non bancaires (3) (*) —Caisse Nationale de l'Industrie (CNI) (3) (*) —Caisse Nationale (3) des Banques (CNB) (*)	—Short-term closed unit trusts (Stés d'investissement à capital fixe*) —Short-term open-ended unit trusts (Stés d'investissement à capital variable SICAVs)*	—Treasury* Post-Office* (Postal Giro System current accounts)

THE FRENCH FINANCIAL SYSTEM

- Banque française du com. extérieur
- Mutual banks
- Banques populaires
- • Crédit agricole (Caisse Nal. du Crédit Agricole included)
- Mutual Credit bank (1)
- Crédit mutuel agricole rural
- Crédit maritime
- Banques du Crédit coopératif -Co-operative credit banks (2)
- Sociétés coopératives de banque -bank co-operative companies (9)
- Municipal credit banks

(SF) S.A.
- • «Emprunts caises d'épargne Ecureuil» (*)
- National savings banks (Post Office) (*)

- Financement des Télécom
- Saving-lending institutions (Stés de crédit différé)
- Public entities financing council houses (Stés de Crédit immobilier HLM) (3)
- Mortgage refinancing institution (Caisse de refinancement hypothécaire)
- • Stés financières habilitées à titre individuel (SFHTI)
- Stés de crédit-bail immobilier - real estate leasing Cies (5)
- Stés de location avec option d'achat (5)
- Stés de gestion de moyens de paiements (5)
- Autres Stés financières (4) (5) (8) (Other finance

(CCIFP) (7)
- • Stés de Développement Régional (SDR) including SOFIMAC, SOFIPARIL ET SOCREDOM
- • Société française pour l'assurance du capital risque des PME (SOPARIS) (3)
- • Société des Bourses Françaises (SBF) (French Bourse corporation)
- Entities similar to specialized financial institutions
- • Caisse nationale des Autoroutes
- • Caisse nationale des Télécommunications
- • Caisse nationale de l'Energie

- Caisse de consolidation et de mobilisation des crédits à moyen terme (CACOM) (3) (*)
- Autoroutes de France (3)*
- Comités Interprofessionels du Logement (CIL) (3) (*)

- Short-term mutual funds (Fonds communs de placement FCP)*

Banque de France and FSC S411	Credit Institutions and Similar Entities-S41 (M3 and its counterparts)							Undertakings for Collective Investment in Transferable Securities (UCITS) (6) S42	Government S611
	Banks S412	Savings Banks S4131	Caisse des dépôts et consignations S4132	Finance Companies and Similar Entities S4141	Specialized Financial Institutions (I.F.S.) and Similar Entities S4142		Miscellaneous Financial Institutions S4143		
	• Groupement de banques pour l'émission d'emprunts obligataires (GBPE) (*) (bank partnerships for bond issues)			companies) —Maisons de titres (A 99) (Securities houses A 99) —Instituts régionaux de Participation (IRP) (3) (*) —Brokerage firms (3) (10)* (sociétés de bourses)					

(1) Includes the federative Mutual Credit Bank and Mutual Credit of Brittany—Bank co-operative companies—and the Mutual credit bank of Lorraine (members of the French Bankers' Association, Association française des Banques AFB).
(2) Banque française du crédit coopératif (bank co-opérative company) and Caisse centrale de crédit coopératif.
(3) Currently not included in monetary statistics.
(4) See breakdown published in the Report of the Banking Commission (1987) (Commission Bancaire).
(5) The whole of these entitles composes the CENCEP group (apart from "other finance companies of the group").
(6) Which are "transparent" in monetary statistics.
(7) The Central clearing house (commodity market) is classified as bank (member of the French Bankers' Association AFB), by the Banking Act.
(8) Including SOFININDEX which took over UFINEX in August 1986.
(9) Includes only the Central bank for co-operative and mutual banks, Banque centrale des coopératives et des mutuelles (BCCM) and the Banque fédérale mutualiste, put together with members of the AFB at present.
(10) Brokerage firms are subject to the Banking Act only if they opt for the "article 99" of the Banking Act of 24th January 1984.
(*) Not included in the Banking Act.—Credit institutions or not.

Source: Money in 1988, Banque de France.

Institutions Financières et Trésor Public Nomenclature commune à la comptabilité nationale (base 1980) et aux statistiques monétaires—au 1-2-1989 (DOM-TOM exclus)

	Etablissements de Crédit et Assimilés—S41 (M3 et ses contreparties)						Organismes De Placement Collectif en Valeurs Mobilières (OPCVM) (6) S42	
Banque de France et FSC S411	Banques S412	Caisses d'Epargne S4131	Caisse des dépôts et consig- nations S4132	Sociétés Financières et Assimilées S4141	Institutions Financières Spécialisées et Assimilées S4142	Institutions Financières Diverses S4143		Etat S611
—Banque de France (*) —Fonds de stabilis- ation des changes (3) (*)	—Banques «AFB» non compris BFCE —Banque française du commerce extérieur —Banques mutualistes	—Caisses d'épargne et de prévoy- ance • Caisses d'épargne et de prévoy- ance	—Caisse des dépôts • Caisse de garantie pour le logement social IFS (*) (CGLS ex- CPHLM)	—Stés financières SF (hors SCM & SOREFI) • Stés financières soumises à des dispositions particulières: —Stés immobilières pour le commerce et l'industrie (SICOMI)	—Institutions financières spécialisées (IFS) • Caisse centrale de coopération économique (CCCE) • Comptoir des Entrepreneurs • Crédit d'équipement des PME (CEPME)	—Fonds communs de créances (*) —Sociétés de caution mutuelle SF (SCM) (3) • Groupements professionels de répartition collectifs au profit d'agents non bancaires (3) (*)	—Stés d'investis- sement à capital fixe (*) —Stés d'investis- sement à capital variable (SICAV) (*)	—Trésor public (*) —PTT Comptes courants postaux (*)

Institutions Financières et Trésor Public Nomenclature commune à la comptabilité nationale (base 1980) et aux statistiques monétaires—au 1-2-1989 (DOM-TOM exclus)

	Etablissements de Crédit et Assimilés—S41 (M3 et ses contreparties)						
Banque de France et FSC S411	Banques S412	Caisses d'Epargne S4131	Caisse des dépôts et consignations S4132	Sociétiés Financières et Assimilées S4141	Institutions Financières Spécialisées et Assimilées S4142	Institutions Financières Diverses S4143	Organismes De Placement Collectif en Valeurs Mobilières (OPCVM) (6) S42	Etat S611
	• Banques populaires • Crédit agricole (y.c. CNCA) • Crédit mutuel (1) • Crédit mutuel agricole rural • Crédit maritime • Banques du Crédit coopératif (2) • Sociétés coopératives de banque (9) — Crédit municipaux	• Stés régionales de financement SOREFI (SF) • S.A. «Emprunts caisses d'épargne Ecureuil» (*) — Caisse nationale d'épargne (PTT) (*)		—SOFERGIE —Stés de Financement des Télécom —Stés de crédit différé —Stés de crédit immobilier (HLM) (3) —Caisse de refinancement hypothécaire • Stés financières habilitées à titre individuel (SFHTI); —Stés de crédit-bail immobilier (5) —Stés de location avec option d'achat (5)	• Crédit Foncier de France • Crédit Local de France • Crédit National MATIF—SA—(CCIFP) (7) • Stés de Développement Régional (SDR) y compris SOFIMAC, SOFIPARIL et SOCREDOM • Sté française pour l'assurance du capital risque des PME (SOFARIS) (3)	• Caisse Nationale de l'Industrie (CNI) (3) (*) • Caisse Nationale des Banques (CNB) (3) (*) • Caisse de consolidation et de mobilisation des crédits à moyen terme (CACOM) (3) (*) • Autoroutes de France (3) (*) • Comités Interprofessionnels du Logement (CIL) (3) (*)	—Fonds communs de placement (FCP) (*)	

- Groupement de banques pour l'émission d'emprunts obligataires (GBPE) (*)

— Stés de gestion de moyens de paiement (5)
— Autres Stés financières (5) (4)
— Maisons de titres (A 99)
— Instituts régionaux de Participation (IRP) (3) (*)
— Stés de Bourse (10) (*)

- Sté des Bourses Françaises (SBF) (3)
— Institutions assimilées aux IFS
- Caisse Nationale des Autoroutes (CNA) (*)
- Caisse Nationale des Télécommunications (CNT) (*)
- Caisse Nationale de l'Energie (*)

---

(1) Inclut la Banque fédérative du crédit mutuel et la Banque coopérative et mutualiste de Bretagne—sociétés coopératives de banque—et la Banque du crédit mutuel lorrain (banque 《AFB》).
(2) Banque française du crédit coopératif (société coopérative de banque) et Caisse centrale de crédit coopératif.
(3) Non recensé actuellement dans les statistiques monétaires.
(4) Voir la ventilation publiée dans le rapport (1987) de la Commission bancaire.
(5) L'ensemble de ces unités constitue le groupe CENCEP (hors 《autres sociétés financières du groupe》).
(6) Rendus 《transparents》 dans les statistiques monétaires.
(7) La Banque centrale de compensation (bourse du commerce) est classée, par la loi bancaire, banque 《AFB》.
(8) Y compris SOFININDEX qui a absorbé UFINEX en août 1986.
(9) Inclut seulement la Banque centrale des coopératives et des mutuelles (BCCM) et la Banque fédérale mutualiste, regroupées avec les banques 《AFB》 pour le moment.
(10) Les sociétés de bourse ne sont soumises à la loi bancaire que si elles optent pour le régime de l'article 99 de la loi du 24-01-1984.
(*) Hors loi bancaire—Etablissement de crédit ou non.

Appendix 2. Breakdown by Category of Credit Institutions subject to The January 24, 1984 Banking Act (Mainland France and Overseas Departments and Territories and the Principality of Monaco)

Financial Institution	Dec. 31, 1984	Dec. 31, 1988
Banks	358	408
Mutual and cooperatives banks	195	178
Savings banks and provident funds	468	301
Municipal credit banks	21	21
Finance companies	882	1059
Specialized financial institutions	28	32
Securities houses (institutions subject to Section 99 of the Banking Act)	65	124
Total	2017	2123

Appendix 3. Distribution of Investments on December 31, 1987

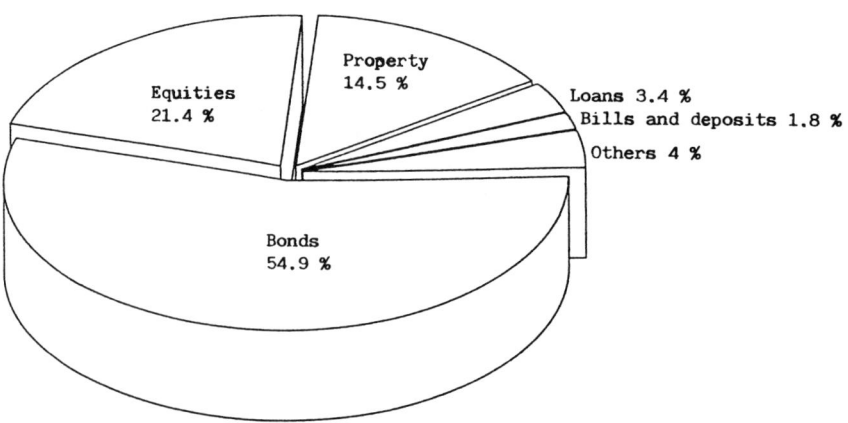

Equities 21.4 %
Property 14.5 %
Loans 3.4 %
Bills and deposits 1.8 %
Others 4 %
Bonds 54.9 %

Appendix 4. Number of French-controlled Credit Institutions Established[a] Abroad at the End of 1987 (Breakdown by Category)

AFB banks	35
Mutual banks	2
Finance companies	8
Section 99 institutions (e.g., securities houses)	1
Specialized financial institutions	1
Total	47

[a] In the form of branches, subsidiaries, interests acquired in local financial institutions, or representative offices.

Appendix 5. Foreign Establishments of French-Controlled Credit Institutions at the End of 1987

	Number of Credit Institutions with Establishments Abroad	Number of Establishments
In the form of branches	19	287[a]
In the form of subsidiaries	32	307
In the form of interests in local financial institutions	36	246
In the form of representative offices	17	249

[a] Number of branches.

Appendix 6. Geographical Analysis of Foreign Investment by French Banks

Percentage	1974	1981	1984
Europe	56.3	53.1	47.9
North America and Caribbean	10.5	17.2	18.1
Latin America	9.5	9.5	7.8
Asia	6.4	7.9	14.6
Africa	10.6	6.8	5.1
Middle East	4.5	3.3	3.9
Oceania	2.2	2.2	2.6
Total	100.0	100.0	100.0

Source: General Secretariat of the Commission Bancaire.

Appendix 7. Trends in Foreign Assets of French-Controlled Banks (Breakdown by Form of Investment)

Francs million	1978	1980	1984	1987
Investments in branches	2,965	4,144	9,173	10,491
% of investments	40.6	45.2	50.0	38.5
Subsidiaries	1,726	2,697	6,612	12,713
% of investements	27.2	29.4	34.1	46.6
Affiliates	1,665	2,322	3,081	4,062
% of investments	26.2	25.4	15.9	14.9
Total investment abroad	6,356	9,163	19,406	27,266

Source: General Secretariat of the Commission Bancaire.

Appendix 8. Foreign Establishments[a] in the French Banking System

	1960	1970	1973	1980	1984	1988
Number of banks (at end of year)	33	58	76	122	146	168

[a] In the form of branches and subsidiaries.

Appendix 9. Trends in Market Share of Foreign Banks in Overall Activities of AFB Banks

	1960	1970	1973	1980	1984	1988
As a % of total mainland France assets	7.2	12.3	14.1	15.4	19.0	19.4

Source: General Secretariat of the Commission Bancaire.

6 THE STRUCTURE OF THE ITALIAN FINANCIAL SYSTEM

G.P. Szegö and V.S. Szegö

The Italian financial system is regulated by the same laws as at the beginning of the century: a basic law on financial markets of 1913 and the banking law of 1936. During the period 1913–1936 the Italian financial system was controlled by a precise framework based upon two cornerstones: the universal bank and the confinement of all securities transactions in one of the official exchanges. Under this system, banks were allowed to make loans with arbitrary maturities and to own shares in other companies. No prudential controls were imposed. The system collapsed during the crisis of the early 1930s, when the severely undercapitalized Italian banks were overexposed in shares of industrial companies and indulged in buy-backs of their own shares. The unavoidable subsequent crisis was caused by insufficient capitalization and not by the universal banking structure.

By preventing commercial banks from granting long-term loans, the banking law of 1936, imposed a forced compliance of the golden rule of maturity matching between deposit and loans and introduced a series of administrative controls and many discretionary powers to the controlling agencies: the CICR (Comitato Interministeriale per il Credito ed il Risparmio) and the Ispettorato per la Difesa del Risparmio e l'Esercizio del Credito. After World War II and the return of the country to democratic government, the functions of the Ispettorato were transferred to the Bank of Italy, while the CICR remained as a purely political body.

The actual system, in spite of some structural shortcomings, has worked remarkably well due to the outstanding capability of the governors of the Bank of Italy, who were able to weather many storms under different regimes and circumstances.

The major obstacle to a modernization of the financial intermediation system can be attributed to the very high (and increasing) government deficit that started in the 1970s. The service of this deficit, which takes place through very frequent issues of government notes and bonds, is greatly distorting the financial flows in the country.

This situation inflates interest rates, depresses the stock market, and places a heavy burden on the production system. The current system, like most of the Italian legal system, places a heavy emphasis on administrative controls rather than on objective rules. The recent introduction of risk-adjusted capital-adequacy controls may signal a change of trend, increase stability, and abolish or decrease the possibility of political intervention on the credit sector.

Despite the strict legal separation between banks (which must both collect deposits *and* distribute short-term credit), special credit institutions (which are involved in longer maturity operations), and the other financial intermediaries (i.e., everybody who "solicits public savings"), the distiction in practice between the different intermediaries, which are controlled by different bodies, is becoming more and more blurred. Also, in view of the forthcoming European financial integration, some new laws regulating in particular the relationships between banks and nonbank industries, between banks and insurance companies, and between commercial and investment banks are being discussed.[1]

1. The Banking System

Since 1936, the Italian Banking System has been divided into two sectors: commercial banks, engaged in short-term credit, and special credit institutions, specializing in medium- and long-term operations. This distinction, however, does not imply rigid separation between short-term and long-term financial activity. First, Italian deposit banks may own shares of special credit institutions and thereby indirectly finance long-term credit activity, and some banks may operate in the medium-long term through special subsidiaries. Secondly, commercial banks may, within a limit

Table 6-1. Deposits and Loans (% Growth Ratios)

	1984	1985	1986	1987	1988	1989 (1 quart.)
Deposits	11.6	10.1	8.9	6.8	7.3	8.0
Loans	17.1	15.6	9.6	8.7	18.0	17.3
Securities of which:	7.4	6.3	6.7	0.6	−6.5	−0.4
Government securities	11.3	9.7	6.9	−1.4	−5.2	—

Source: Bank of Italy.

depending upon the amount of deposits and within 30% of their global resources, issue long-term credit. Lastly, the distinction between long- and short-term credit exists more in form than in substance. In practice, loan maturities may be extended to very long periods, mainly through overdraft facilities that are virtually evergreen.

For all categories of commercial banks, the principal source of funds are customers' deposits. The competition among banks for the acquisition of deposits has been very fierce, especially in times of liquidity shortages. The growth of deposits has been one of the objectives common to all Italian banks, sometimes at the expense of sound financial management and profitability.

However, in the most recent years, the rate of growth of deposits has slowed down (see table 6-1). Italian banks offer the range of services generally provided by their counterparts in Europe and the U.S., like lines of credit, whether unsecured or guaranteed by security transactions. The charges to customers vary from bank to bank. Italian banks normally grant their customers line-of-credit and overdraft facilities through current accounts and a variety of services such as the handling of payments and encashment.

The Italian commercial banks may be divided into seven groups according to their legal status, which roughly coincides with the form of ownership. The distinctions also affect earning distribution and the role of the government authorities in management decisions.

The seven categories of banks are

1. Public law institutions (Istituti di Credito di Diritto Pubblico)
2. National interest banks (Banche d'Interesse Nazionale)
3. Ordinary banks (Banche di Credito Ordinario)
4. Cooperative banks (Banche Popolari)

5. Savings and pledge banks (Casse di Risparimio e Monti di Credito su Pegno)
6. Rural banks (Casse Rurali ed Artigiane)
7. Branches of foreign banks

1.1. Public Law Institutions (Istituti di Credito di Diritto Pubblico)

According to the Banking Law of 1936, Banco di Napoli, Banco di Sicilia, Banco di Sardegna, Banca Nazionale del Lavoro, Istituto Bancario S. Paolo di Torino, and Monte dei Paschi di Siena are public law institutions. They are public banks owned by the Treasury and therefore their internal rules are governed by public law. Their Board of Directors is appointed by the government. Among these banks are some of the oldest existing banks, as well as some of the reincorporated central banks of the nations, which merged to form Italy in the second part of the nineteenth century.

1.2. National Interest Banks (Banche d'Interesse Nazionale)

Credito Italiano, Banca Commerciale Italiana, and Banco di Roma are national interest banks. From the legal point of view, these three banks are corporations, but the majority of their capital is owned by the (Institute of Industrial Conversion) (IRI), a government institution that took them over, saving them from bankruptcy, in 1931. As we see from tables 6-2 and 6-3 the largest Italian banks fall into these first two groups.

Table 6-2a. Banks and Authorized Branches (End 1988)

	No. of Banks	*No. of Branches*
Public law	6	2,209
National interest	3	1,273
Ordinary banks	110	3,492
Cooperative banks	127	2,800
Savings banks	85	4,187
Rural banks	726	1,419
Branches of foreign banks	38	62
Central institutes	5	5
TOTAL	1,100	15,447

Source: Banca d'Italia.

Table 6-2b. First 876 Banks: Total Resources

	No. of Banks	Resources[a] (Million Dollars)	% total
Public law	6	229,198	27.48%
National interest	3	128,301	15.38%
Ordinary banks	105	144,148	17.28%
Cooperative banks	124	104,757	12.56%
Savings banks	81	172,400	20.67%
Rural banks	523	24,824	2.98%
Branches of foreign banks	31	15,037	1.80%
Central institutes	3	15,460	1.85%
TOTAL	876	834,125	100

[a] Resources: Capital and Reserves + Deposits and Interbank funds.
Source: Il Mondo 10/31/1988.

1.3. Ordinary Banks (Istituti di Credito Ordinario)

Ordinary banks are created in the form of corporations and are subject to the rules governing private corporations and to the banking law. Most of them are private banks. Some of them are of considerable size; for instance, the largest ordinary bank, the Banca Nazionale dell'Agricoltura (BNA), is the tenth largest bank in Italy (see table 6-3). In 1989, two commercial banks—Nuovo Banco Ambrosiano and Banca Cattolica del Veneto—merged to form a new bank, Banco Ambrosiano-Veneto, which will have a deposit volume probably slightly larger than BNA.

1.4. Cooperative Banks (Banche Popolari)

A distinctive feature of cooperative banks, which have the legal form of corporations, is the fragmentation of their capital. The charter of the smaller banks (banks with capital less than L.500 million) does not allow any member to own shares in a total par value of more than L.7.5 million. Of the annual profits, 20% must be set aside for the statutory reserve (compared with the 5% normally envisaged for other types of banks). These banks are predominantly local, but some, such as Banca Popolare di Novara, Banca Popolare di Milano, and Banca Popolare di Bergamo, have extended their area of operations and have reached considerable dimension (see table 6-3).

Table 6-3. Largest Italian Banks: Accounting Data (End 1987) (in millions of dollars)

Bank	Resources in Italy[a]	Rank in Italy[a]	Total Assets	Rank in the EEC[b]	Rank in the World[c]	Deposits	Capital Funds	Loans	Net Profit	Net Interest Income	Cash Flow
Banca Nazionale del Lavoro	83,132	1	96,072	15	35	77,713	5,419	33,570	122	1,828	674
Banca Commerciale Italiana	50,520	2	62,534	31	67	47,115	3,404	20,671	247	1,271	530
Banco di Napoli	44,364	3	59,343	32	70	48,287	1,876	23,881	52	1,232	278
Istituto Bancario S. Paolo di Torino	47,098	4	73,477	26	55	43,332	3,766	25,672	420	1,328	650
Credito Italiano	45,235	5	50,448	39	82	42,643	2,592	15,075	115	1,025	319
Cassa di Risparmio delle Provincie Lombarde	44,355	6	53,891	37	77	40,227	4,128	21,140	176	1,409	736
Banco di Roma	44,268	7	56,361	34	72	42,262	2,006	16,547	0	696	128
Monte dei Paschi di Siena	39,082	8	67,183	27	60	35,994	3,086	12,670	175	1,048	620
Banco di Sicilia	24,833	9	31,140	57	115	23,486	1,346	14,885	22	826	262
Banca Nazionale dell'Agricolture	17,710	10	22,361	81	163	16,899	811	7,924	47	508	201
Banco di S. Spirito	16,743	11	19,793	88	182	15,863	880	4,712	39	405	188
Banca Popolare di Novara	16,381	12	19,108	93	189	14,995	1,387	5,415	121	582	217
Cassa di Risparmio di Torino	14,315	13	17,311	102	207	13,239	1,076	4,755	148	485	261
Banca Popolare di Milano	13,720	14	19,845	87	181	12,665	1,055	4,841	68	426	185
Cassa di Risparmio di Roma	13,707	15	20,327	85	176	12,371	1,337	5,483	70	570	356

[a] Italy's largest bank is the Banca Nazionale del Lavoro ($96,072 million in assets).
[b] Europe's largest bank is the Credit Agricole ($214,382 million in assets).
[c] The World's largest bank is the Dai-Ichi Kangyo Bank ($270,782 million in assets).

1.5. Savings and Pledge Banks (Casse di Risparmio a Monti di Credito su Pegno)

Savings banks and pledge banks are established in the form of foundations or corporations and must be authorized by a Decree of the Minister of the Treasury as corporate entities. Pledge banks, which over the years have attracted a large volume of deposits and have become predominantly credit institutions, are subject to the regulations applying to savings banks. Therefore, nowadays, the distinction between savings banks and pledge banks stands only for historical reasons. Savings banks, which are non-profit-making organizations, no longer confine their activities to the acceptance of savings deposits, but also offer their customers current account facilities and engage in all the operations that commercial banks are authorized to perform: for instance, they are empowered to grant loans and overdrafts secured by tangible property. Of the profit, 70% is allocated to reserve until it reaches 10% of the deposits; thereafter a minimum 50% of the profit is allocated to reserve and the balance to charity.

Some savings banks have reached considerable dimensions, such as the Cassa di Risparmio delle Provincie Lombarde and the Cassa di Risparmio di Torino (see table 6-3). Pledge Banks, on the other hand, are on the average very small. The largest of them is the Banca del Monte di Bologna e Ravenna, which falls in 74th place in the rank of Italian banks according to size. Its total resources amounted to L. 2,530,087 in 1988.

1.6. Rural Banks (Casse Rurali ed Artigiane)

A very large number of the 1100 banks forming the Italian banking system are rural banks. In 1915, there were 2594 rural banks, now there are 726 (see table 6-2). These banks, which have the legal status of cooperatives, perform most of the normal banking operations; however, they operate almost only at local level, and most of their lending is to their members of the cooperative.

1.7. Branches of Foreign Banks

Until late 1960s there were very few foreign banks operating in Italy, but since the early 1970s there has been a steady increase in the number of representative offices, and subsequently full branches, especially of

American banks. At the end of 1988, there were 38 foreign banks in Italy (see table 6-2).

Until 1986, Bank of America had the longest established presence, through its controlling interest in the Banca d'America e d'Italia (BAI), founded in 1917 and one of Italy's largest private banks. BAI's ownership has recently been transferred to Deutsche Bank, which became the foreign bank with largest—though indirect—branch network in Italy. In 1985 Citibank decided to increase its presence in Italy and bought from Banco di Roma a majority stake in Banca Centro Sud, a commercial bank mainly operating in the center and south of Italy. Foreign banks engage predominantly in wholesale banking. Their lira funds consist mainly of interbank deposits and, to a smaller extent, of large deposits by major industrial companies and by public institutions. Their lendings are also principally to large companies, as well as to Italian branches of foreign firms.

2. Banking Associations

The Associazione Bancaria Italiana (ABI) is the association of all banks. Membership includes the commercial banks and special credit insitutions, finance, and leasing companies. The association represents the banking sector in dealing with Parliament, government, and monetary authorities. ABI promotes agreements among banks for standardization of the terms and conditions of banking services, the development of standard contractual schemes, automation, and information gathering. The association provides advice to members on legal, fiscal, and administrative matters and, together with the Bank of Italy, has developed a deposit insurance scheme, which has been recently introduced. In addition to ABI, there exist associations for each category of banks like the Cooperative Banks Association (Associazione Tecnica Banche Popolari), the Association of Regional Special Credit Institutions (Associazione Mediocrediti Regionali), and the Savings Banks Association (Associazione Casse di Risparmio Italiane, ACRI). With objectives similar to those of the ABI, the ACRI also promoted the creation of a *savings banks advance fund* with the aim of assisting member banks at times of liquidity difficulty by providing minimum-rate and long-maturity loans.

There are a number of banking institutions whose purpose is to promote the development of banks belonging to the various categories and to provide them some centralized banking services. In addition, each functions as a "central bank" for a particular category. Among these are the

Italian Savings Bank Credit Instituion (ICCRI), the Central Banks and Bankers Institution (Istituto Banche e Banchieri, ISTBANC) and the Rural Savings Banks Credit Institution (ICCREA). These institutions provide for the distribution of financial resources within the respective category of member banks, accepting funds from those with excess liquidity and lending to those short of liquidity, collecting funds abroad and redistributing them within the system. They also issue bank drafts and effect investment in securities.

Other interbank organizations have been set up to deal in specialized fields. They include Montetitoli S.p.A., similar to Cedel or Euroclear, which acts on a fiduciary basis as a central depository and administrator for securities; Centrale Bilanci S.r.L, which collects and analyzes financial statements of all significant Italian companies, redistributing them to the member banks; and Societa' Interbancaria per l'Automazione (SIA), which acts as a centralized EDP service company mainly for Bancomat system of cash dispensers.

3. Special Credit Institutions

As already mentioned, medium- and long-term credit is only granted by special credit institutions or special credit sections of the large commercial banks. However, there is a strong two-way relationship between commercial banks and long-term special credit institutions.

Within the field of special credit, a distinction is made between *credito mobiliare*, i.e., industrial credit (for industry, public utilities, mining, film industry, shipbuilding, export-credit), and *credito immobiliare*, i.e., real estate credit, and credit for agriculture and fisheries. Some special credit institutions operate throughout the country, while others operate only regionally or in a particular market sector.

The loans granted vary in terms both from institution to institution and based on the use of the loan. Most loans are guaranteed by tangible collaterals (mortgages on real property, machinery, deposit of securities). Most credit institutions also manage various state funds to finance certain activities or to promote activities in certain areas of the country. Other special credit institutions also engage in merchant banking.

In addition to their capital, reserves, bonds, and other kinds of borrowing facilities, the special credit institutions receive part of their funds from the government, and can also borrow from the Euromarket from the European Investment Bank and from other EEC organizations.

Because these institutions cannot directly raise funds in the form of deposits, their link with commercial banks is extremely important. Commercial banks may participate in the capital of the Special Credit Institutions and provide them with financial resources. Until the early 1980s, this process took place through the purchase of the bonds issued by the special credit institutions. More recently, the special credit institutions stopped issuing bonds and the banks started lending directly to the special credit institutions in which they participate. Special credit institutions also issue medium-term maturity certificates of deposits, but the use of this borrowing instrument is not frequent.

Istituto Mobiliare Italiano (IMI), which was founded in 1931, is the most important special credit institution. Until the end of World War II, this was the only Italian financial institution for medium- and long-term financing. IMI is a public-law institution whose capital is held 50% by the Cassa Depositi e Prestiti (a public financial institutions owned by the Treasury Department) and the remainder by savings banks, credit institutions, and insurance and financial companies. IMI provides loans with term up to 20 years, is authorized to take up share holdings, and manages various state funds. Apart from the industrial credit to large-size firms, which still represents its core business, IMI is engaged through subsidiaries in a broad range of financial and capital market services such as leasing, factoring management and mutual funds, securities, retail distribution, investment and commercial banking, portfolio management for individual, banks, corporations and insurance companies, venture and growth capital, and business consultancy.

Mediobanca is a listed corporation founded in 1949 by the National Interest Banks. Most of Mediobanca's funds are provided by savings deposits collected though the three National Interest Banks. Until 1988, Mediobanca's shares were held by the three National Interest Banks and therefore indirectly by IRI; during 1988, while retaining control of the institution, the three banks have partly sold their shares to the public.

Mediobanca holds significant equity interest in a number of major Italian listed companies, such as Assicuranzioni Generali, FIAT, Snia BPD, Cantiere Burgo, Pirelli, Olivetti. It is active in investment banking, and is the credit institution most engaged in the underwriting of large securities issues floated by government and corporations. Substantially its activity is that of a merchant bank.

Crediop (Consorzio di Credito per le Opere Pubbliche) is a public-law institution and its capital is subscribed by substantially the same bodies that hold IMI's capital. Crediop was engaged principally in the financing of the Treasury and the public utilities, but since 1981, when it took over

Istituto di Credito per le Imprese di Pubblica Utilita', it has extended its operations to the industrial and export credit sector.

Efibanca (Ente Finanziario Interbancario) is a corporation whose capital is subscribed by Banca Nazionale del Lavoro, Banca Popolare di Novara, private banks, and insurance companies.

Interbanca (Banca per i Finanziamenti a Medio e Lungo Termine) is a Special Credit Institution that has the legal status of a corporation. Its capital is subscribed by Banca Nazionale dell'Agricoltura, Banca d'America e d'Italia, and other private banks.

Centrobanca (Banca Centrale per il Credito Popolare) was created in 1944 by cooperative banks. It is involved with medium-long-term industrial and agricultural credit. It is strongly linked to cooperative banks that provide funds and clients.

Since 1950, in addition to these financial institutions, which are mostly engaged with medium-long-term credit to large firms, various Mediocrediti Regionali (Regional Special Credit Institutions) have been founded. These institutions provide medium-long-term credit to the smaller firms within the region in which they operate and are directly linked to a central institution: the **Mediocredito Centrale**. This special credit institution provides financing mainly through the discounting of guaranteed bills. Besides financing Mediocrediti Regionali, Mediocredito Centrale has its own financial activity, especially in the area of export-credit.

4. Capital Markets

Possibly due to the rather recent formation of the Italian state in the 1860s, the stock market has never played a major role in the financial intermediation process. Even in the most industrially advanced region of the country, Lombardy, the Milan Stock Exchange never had any activity of a size or an economic weight comparable in any way to that of the Paris Bourse or the Amsterdam and London Stock Exchanges.

It was not until 1808, during Napoleonic times, that the first formal exchange was created in Italy, with the establishment of a stock exchange in Milan, the financial capital of Italy. Since then, nine other exchanges have been created: Rome, Turin, Genoa, Bologna, Florence, Naples, Palermo, Trieste, and Venice. The Milan Exchange is by far the largest, now accounting for about 90% of total stock trading value and 80% of bond trading.

The CONSOB (Commissione Nazionale per la Societa' e la Borsa) is the official authority designed to control capital markets and exchanges. Its main goal is to ensure that investors are provided with adequate information regarding listed companies and their operations on capital markets. The CONSOB regulates and controls the stock exchanges, all listed public corporations, and all registered auditing companies, which must certify the annual balance sheets and income statements of the listed companies. The CONSOB has the power to give authorization to listing, to force companies to give adequate information, to set up the rules regarding the contracts traded on the stock exchanges and, in case of some exceptional event, to suspend a stock from listing. (For a more detailed description of the activity of the CONSOB, see section 7). The financing of industry, with the exception of some atypical periods, has mostly taken place through the banking system, through leasing and factoring, and through government subsidies. The corporations, originally family owned, use the stock market in order to raise "risk capital," but are very careful not to lost the control of the company. This situation is still true nowadays: the stock market is fragmented into a limited set of related companies and sectors, and the majority of stock trading and changes of ownership of companies takes place outside the market.

In recent years, banks have handled 70%–80% of total stock trading and 90%–95% of bond trading. The reason for this is the much easier access for most operators to bank windows than to stockbroker firms, which do not have any sales network and are only used by the most affluent and sophisticated investors. In Italy, unlike many other countries, commercial banks cannot be members of the Stock Exchange and must use stockbrokers, who are members of the exchange, and other authorized intermediaries in order to execute the trades received by their customers. The national extension of banks' network and the large number of branches open in all cities however, give, Italian banks a definite advantage in security trading on behalf of their clients.

Since the vast majority of orders are channeled through the banks, they are able to meet orders by internal settlements between customers with matching operations without entering the Stock Exchange Clearing House. Banks thus use the stock exchange only for a small residual quota. This fact is one of the major causes for the contraction in trading volumes at the official exchanges, a contraction that severely threatens the efficiency of the stock exchange function in the price formation mechanism. In order to avoid this problem, many proposals that aim at a concentration of trading in the Exchange, as required by the increasingly ignored law of 1913, are currently being debated. All these proposals leave the banks with just the role of collecting the orders. Two important steps in this direction have been taken with the establishment of joint-ventures between banks and stockbrokers, and the creation of the Montetitoli S.p.A. (Law 19/6/1986 n.289). This is a corporation that accepts all kinds of securities for safekeeping and takes care of the trading, relevant bookkeeping and settlements. Changes in property only involve an electronic transfer from an account to another. This innovation greatly simplifies the circulation of securities both in terms of time and cost.

In addition to special credit institutions, a large number of companies engaged in financial intermediation and merchant banking (Societa' d'Intermediazione Mobiliare (SIM)) have been formed in recent years. Since SIMs do not collect deposits, they are not engaged in banking activity as defined by the Banking Law, which states that a firm can be considered a bank if and only if it is involved both in deposit taking and in credit granting this, they are not subject to the laws governing banks and special credit institutions and are not subject to the control exercised on banks by the Bank of Italy. The activity of the SIM must be authorized by CONSOB.

Recently, the government approved a draft of a law regarding the financial intermediation activity with the aim of increasing the transparency of the operations and the stability and efficiency of the market. In addition, the Governor of the Bank of Italy pointed out the necessity of introducing new controls, especially regarding capital adequacy of the SIM.

In conclusion, the current belief is that the SIM should be controlled by the CONSOB and by the Bank of Italy. While the CONSOB will take up the role of controlling the SIM from a market point of view, and therefore will promote market transparency, the Bank of Italy will set reserve requirements and control capital adequacy (see Note 1).

In the main markets there are 325 listed stocks. In addition to the main organized stock exchanges, in Italy there exists two other markets: a second market called *Mercato Ristretto* and an over-the-counter (OTC) or Third Market. The Mercato Ristretto was legally recognized in 1977 (Law 23/2/1977 n.49) after more than 20 years of autonomous unregulated activity. This market lists companies that do not have the prerequisites to be listed in the main exchange. These requirements relate not only to capital structure and profitability, but also to ownership diffusion and freedom of circulation of shares. The Mercato Ristretto lists many companies with bylaws that have some limitations on shares ownership and rights, such as

- acceptance clauses (*clausole di gradimento*)
- per-head voting power and
- limitation in the number of shares per owner.

The acceptance clause gives to the board of directors the veto power to the admission of any new stockholder. The voting right per-head close is present in the bylaws of all cooperatives banks.

While the main stock exchanges are essentially forward markets, the Mercato Ristretto allows only spot transactions with cash settlement. In the original plan, the two main functions of this market were the financing for medium and small companies and the testing of companies before entering the main market. Therefore, the legislator's aim in allowing only spot operations was to forbid the speculative activity that was rumored to be connected with forward contracts

While on the main market transactions always take place daily, until September 1987 the Mercato Ristretto had only a weekly session. After this date, daily tradings were introduced also in the Mercato Ristretto, with the aim of improving its capitalization, turnover, and efficiency.

After an initial period of success, the Mercato Ristretto experienced a sharp contraction in trading activity. The capitalization reached a peak in 1981 and then declined together with the turnover. This trend mirrors in part the events of the main market, but also implies that the Mercato Ristretto does not attract the Italian investors because of the very low diversification and a certain rigidity of the trading rules.

Currently, of about 40 stocks quoted in the Mercato Ristretto of the Milan Stock Exchange, more than half belong to banks and in particular to cooperative banks.

The market for all the transactions settled outside the two official markets is called Third Market. This market has neither official recognition or control, nor a physical location or standardized contracts. It is an OTC market, organized by stockbrokers and banks in which shares of companies that have no intention of being listed in one of the official markets are traded. Also, shares of companies waiting for official listing are negotiated in this market. This occurs because the rule for admission to the Stock Exchange requires that, prior to listing, the ownership of a company be widely distributed.

In February 1988, a secondary market for government securities was established. Before this date, most of the secondary transactions of government papers took place in the OTC interbank market, leaving the main market, in which official prices were formed, with a residual 0.10%–0.50% of the total turnover. The aim of the new market was to concentrate all transactions in one public market, thus ensuring transparency in price formation and improving the liquidity of government securities. This secondary market for government securities is a telematic market via the Reuter system in which the main 20 Italian financial intermediaries act as primary dealers. This market is still in development stage and, while it is still too early to make a complete performance evaluation, it has been characterized by an increasing turnover. More time is necessary to give a former evaluation.

4.1. Conditions for Admission to the Exchange

There are three different ways to be admitted to one of the official Italian Stock Exchanges:

1. *Admission by right.* This is granted to the following securities: government bonds, bonds with a public guarantee, local government bonds, bonds issued by some international organizations (such as European Investment Bank and International Bank for Reconstruction and Development) and saving shares.
2. *Compulsory listing.* If a company has all the required characteristics, the CONSOB can force its quotation to give to the investors all the guarantees connected with public monitoring. The CONSOB so far has very rarely used this power, although in a recent statement it has recognized the right of all interested parties to initiate the process of forced listing, even against an explicit position of the board of directors.
3. *Admission by Request.*

In 1984, the CONSOB passed a regulation unifying the conditions for admission to official listing in the Stock Exchange for shares as well as for bonds. For both types of securities, the company must satisfy the following four conditions:

1. the net value of the company must be at least, L.50 billion (= $40 million) for companies in the financial sector (banks and insurance companies), and at least L.10 billion (= $8 million) for the other sectors;
2. at least the last annual balance sheet must be certified by an accounting firm approved by the CONSOB and admitted in a special register;
3. all the last three annual income statements must show a profit; and
4. ownership of the company must be highly distributed: this implies that at least 25% of the capital has a widespread ownership.

The CONSOB has the power—typical of a discretionary legal framework—to admit to listing securities of companies that do not satisfy the above requirements.

In addition the following conditions must be met:

1. In the case of shares, no limitation on their marketability, like acceptance closes, should be imposed.
2. In the case of bonds, the conditions are the following:
   - the issue must have the minimum value of L.10 billion (= $8 million);
   - at least 25% of the issue must be characterized by a widespread ownership.

There are different ways to reach a sufficiently distributed ownership of the securities prior to listing. The distribution can be reached through an OPV (Offerta Pubblica di Vendita = Official Public Offering) of already-existing shares owned by the controlling interest of the company asking for admission to listing, or via a OPS (Offerta Pubblica di Sottoscrizione = Official Public Offering of New Shares) in the event of an increase of company's capital prior to listing.

The company that is applying for admission to listing must prove the degree of distribution of its shares by providing the Exchange with a table showing the geographical distribution of the shareholders' residence listed according to the number of shares owned.

The Law of September 15th, 1987 introduced some changes in the requirements for listing in the Mercato Ristretto by reducing the needed capital distribution from 20% to 10% of the shares outstanding. It is also sufficient that the company has one year of life and has shown profits even without having paid dividends. The company must be resident in Italy and have a net capital of at least L.1 billion ($0.8 million).

No conditions exist for admission to the unofficial OTC or Third Market.

4.2. Securities and Contracts

The vast majority of the companies that list their shares in the stock market have the status of S.p.A. (Societa' per Azioni = public corporation).

Also listed are shares of Societa' in Accomandita per Azioni (S.A.A.). The characteristics of this type of corporation is a distinction among shareholders between *soci accomandanti* and *soci accomandatari*. The latter are shareholders whose liability, like that of ordinary shareholders, is limited to the capital conferred, and the former bear an unlimited liability for debts of the corporation. Only *soci accomandatari* or their delegates can sit in the Board of Directors and control the company independently by the percentage of capital they own. There has been a recent rise in the number of such corporations as takeover-proof.

By Italian law, there exist three different types of shares: common shares, preferred shares, and saving shares.

Common shares have voting rights at all meetings of common stockholders, and all such shares are in nominative form. Voting is on the base of one vote per share. Shares must have a stated par value (*valore nominale*). In the event of the liquidation of a company, common stockholders are entitled to the assets remaining after payment to all debtholders and all other types of stockholders.

The holders of preferred stock usually do not have voting rights in regular stockholder meetings. In the case of some companies they do have voting rights in special meetings (*assemblea straordinaria*).

Preferred stocks enjoy a preferential dividend treatment, usually based on par value and not on profits and preference on the company's assets in case of liquidation. Preferred shares are nominal and subject to the same fiscal regulation as ordinary shares.

Some preferred shares are convertible in ordinary shares at certain exercise periods. In this case, their price behavior is much more closely related to that of ordinary stock.

Saving shares were instituted in 1974 and can be issued only by listed companies. These shares must provide a return of at least 55% on par value. In the case in which a dividend is paid to ordinary shares, a spread of at least 2% must be granted to saving shares. Holders of saving shares do not have any voting rights. The total amount of preferred and savings shares cannot exceed 50% of the company total issued capital.

The highly leveraged position of many companies is witnessed by the existence of bonds of different nature and in particular convertibles and warrants. These bonds must be considered an innovation for the Italian financial markets, since they became common only during the bull market of 1984–1986, though they were introduced in 1974. The issue of corporate bonds has been recently severely curtailed by the overwhelming government papers.

Convertibles bonds played an important role in the process of financial restructuring, which has characterized Italian corporations during the 1980s. The very favorable conditions of the stock market in 1984–1986

Table 6-4. Authorizations to the Issuing of Convertibles or Warrants (in Billion Liras)

Issuers	1982	1983	1984	1985	1986	1987	1988
Special Credit Institutions	862	156	367	887	2801	710	1039
Convertibles	762	56	—	787	2518	710	939
Warrants	100	100	367	100	283	—	100
Public Institutions	100	—	360	560	996	100	—
Convertibles	—	—	10	60	800	—	—
Warrants	100	—	350	500	196	100	—
Joint Stock Companies	456	598	272	786	1942	875	728
Convertibles	—	298	272	786	1572	775	691
Warrants	456	300	—	—	370	100	37
Total	1418	754	999	2233	5739	1685	1767
Convertibles	1218	354	282	1633	4890	1485	1630
Warrants	200	400	717	600	849	200	137

Source: Banca d'Italia.

allowed the issuing companies to attach a high price to the conversion option, with a substantial discount on debt cost. The same market trend favored bonds with warrants, but this new instrument has still to reach its full potential.

In most cases the warrant is autonomously traded. Nontradable warrants have been often used to support bond issues in substitution of convertibles. Recently, they have also been connected with stock issues, especially for an initial public offering, to win investors' reluctance. (See table 6-4 for a description of the development of warrants and convertibles on the Italian market.)

In addition to these securities, Italy has a number of stock option contracts and the so-called *riporti di borsa*.

Before entering into the details of these contracts, it is important to describe the structure of the settlement system in the Italian stock markets. Spot settlements (technically the payment takes three days) only apply to fixed-income securities and to shares traded in the Mercato Ristretto. All the other operations are forward contracts. In this market, settlements take place once a month. At the beginning of each year, CONSOB establishes an Exchange Calendar (Calendario Borsistico), including the monthly settlement dates. All contracts stipulated in the month are settled in the same date.

In the pure forward contract (*contratto a termine fermo*), the parties agree to trade securities at a specified time and price. When the contract is drawn up and until the settlement day, the parties are not required to take possession of the securities sold and to pay for the purchase. Because of the strong speculative opportunity offered by this contract, in order to reduce the speculation on a particular security, the CONSOB has sometimes imposed spot cash settlements and, more recently, the advance deposit of a margin or, in the case of sales, of the securities.

Another contract is the *contratto di riporto*. In this contract, as in a repurchase agreement, one of the parties transfers the property of securities to the other party at a certain price with the agreement that at a specified future date, he will receive the securities back, paying a previously established amount.

Riportato is the first party, who, selling spot to buy forward, wants to obtain short-term financing without losing the property of the securities. The second party, called *riportatore*, buys spot and sells forward to obtain a temporary use of the securities paying a certain amount. The *riportatore* can use the securities as he likes, and if they have voting rights he can also exercise them. Typically, these contracts are used to postpone to the next settlement day the obligations assumed with a previous contract that is scheduled to expire.

The price of the contract can be calculated as the difference between the spot price at which the securities are sold and the forward price at which they are bought back. When the prices are equal, the contract is stipulated at par; if the spot price is lower than the forward, we have the *riporto in senso stretto* which is basically a short-term loan; finally, if the spot price is higher than the forward price, we have a *deporto*, which is technically a loan of securities.

The operation, which is very simple in its essential structure, is somewhat more complicated in the Italian market, since the market works discontinuously on a set of predetermined settlement days.

Italian option contracts are called *contratti a premio*. The most used contract is the *contratto dont* (call option), which gives the right to buy securities at a stated price. The price of the contract is expressed as a margin on the spot price of the security in the stipulation day.

The *stellage* contract gives the holder the option to buy or sell a certain number of securities. This contract then always ends with a transaction, either of purchase or sale.

Less common are the put contract, which gives the right to sell securities at a stated price or lose the premium, the strip contract, which gives the option to buy a certain number of securities or to sell twice that quantity, and the strap contract, which gives the choice between buying a stated number of securities or selling half of them. All these options

Table 6-5. Milan Stock Exchange: Forward Contracts, Options, and *Riporti* (Parvalue of Exchanged Contracts in Billion Liras)

	1984	*1985*	*1986*	*1987*	*1988*
Forward contracts	7,143	26,317	66,661	41,967	41,269
Options	—	5,208	10,602	11,020	11,385
Riporti	5,647	6,882	12,981	14,359	11,600

Source: Comitato Direttivo degli Agenti di Cambio—Milan CONSOB.

must be exercised at a certain day (*risposta ai premi*) fixed by the Exchange Calendar.

Table 6-5 gives a description of the development of pure forward contracts, options, and *riporti* on the Milan Stock Exchange. The market of government securities has already been mentioned; its rapid development reflects the large volume of Treasury papers issued in order to finance the budget deficit (table 6-6).

There is a wide variety of government securities bearing different terms and maturities. Ordinary Treasury bills (*Buoni Ordinari del Tesoro* (BOT), which have maturities up to one year, are the most important source of funds for the government: such short-term securities finance more than 30% of the total deficit. Investors bid through stockbrokers or banks at fortnightly auctions of BOTs.

Other sources of funds for the Treasury are Certificati di Credito del Tesoro (CCTs) and Buoni del Tesoro Pluriennali (BTPs). These securities have maturity from 4 to 10 years; CCTs bear a floating-rate interest adjusted semiannually to the BOT yield plus a spread, while BTPs are straight bonds. In addition, there are two types of securities denominated in Ecu: Buoni del Tesoro in Ecu (BTEs) and Certificati del Tesoro di Ecu (CTEs). They bear different maturities. The majority of Treasury papers are held by the households: the share in the hands of the Bank of Italy and of the banking sector has been steadily declining (table 6-7).

4.3. New Issues

Between 1984 and 1987, in connection with the bull market and the establishment of mutual funds, a considerable number of new companies were admitted to the stock market (see table 6-8). Indeed, in spite of the rather complicated procedure required, 40 new companies were listed in

Table 6-6. Italian Public-Sector Deficit: Sources of Financing.

Period	Medium-Long-Term Securities	of Which B.I.	BOT BTE	of Which B.I.	C/A Post Offices Resources	of Which C/A	Treasury C/A	Foreign Loans	Other	Total Deficit	Creation of Monetary Base
86	87,073	7,905	9,697	1,402	4,525	11,267	718	856	−3,259	110,159	10,994
87	56,090	1,311	27,482	−4,515	9,274	12,925	781	6,067	2,420	114,258	9,240
88	60,792	4,215	41,982	−5,274	4,331	10,763	−2,505	4,227	3,130	125,405	2,677
88.II	13,150	−141	13,025	1,177	−1,626	218	−1,058	284	−597	24,454	−454
88.III	11,686	2,028	22,005	−1,172	3,521	1,101	−205	2,447	2,091	42,851	3,423
88.IV	24,490	3,503	484	838	−3,406	6,836	−1,299	698	2,047	31,149	−766
89.I	4,356	−1821	21,266	2,224	−1,018	2,027	−48	2,847	1,257	30,735	−309
89.II	16,661	6,408	747	−3,726	−8,826	1,334	448	1,538	2,156	13,610	−7,716
89.III	16,284	−3,438	8,131	−2,568	6,539	1,548	498	3,627	3,610	39,739	−20
88 GEN-NOV	58,594	1,315	42,025	−5,558	8,477	4,184	−1,796	3,865	1,509	118,654	5,677
89 GEN-NOV	52,887	6,627	38,541	−4,722	2,329	5,571	1,010	8,582	6,947	114,857	3,883
86	79.04%	7.18%	8.80%	1.27%	4.11%	10.23%	0.65%	0.78%	−2.96%	100.00%	9.98%
87	49.09%	1.15%	24.05%	−3.95%	8.12%	11.31%	0.68%	5.31%	2.12%	100.00%	8.09%
88	48.62%	3.36%	33.48%	−4.21%	3.45%	8.58%	−2.00%	3.37%	2.50%	100.00%	2.13%
88.II	53.77%	−0.58%	53.26%	4.81%	−6.65%	0.89%	−4.33%	1.16%	−2.44%	100.00%	−1.86%
88.III	27.27%	4.73%	51.35%	−2.74%	8.22%	2.57%	−0.48%	5.71%	4.88%	100.00%	7.99%
88.IV	78.62%	11.25%	1.55%	2.69%	−10.93%	21.95%	−4.17%	2.24%	6.57%	100.00%	−2.46%
89.I	14.17%	−5.92%	69.19%	7.24%	−3.31%	6.60%	−0.16%	9.26%	4.09%	100.00%	−1.01%
89.II	122.42%	47.08%	5.49%	−27.38%	−64.85%	9.80%	3.29%	11.30%	15.84%	100.00%	−56.69%
89.III	40.98%	−8.65%	20.46%	−6.46%	16.45%	3.90%	1.25%	9.13%	9.08%	100.00%	−0.05%
88 GEN-NOV	49.38%	1.11%	35.42%	−4.68%	7.14%	3.53%	−1.51%	3.26%	1.27%	100.00%	4.78%
89 GEN-NOV	46.05%	5.77%	33.56%	−4.11%	2.03%	4.85%	0.88%	7.47%	6.05%	100.00%	3.38%

Source: Analysis F.A., Milan.

Table 6-7. Total Issues of Stock: Breakdown by Ownership (Data in Billion Lira)

	BOT	CCT	BTP	Other Govern. Stocks	Total Govern. Stocks	Bonds ICS	Bonds of State and Pub. Companies	Shares
Bank of Italy								
1988 gen—ago	−4,131.2	−3,004.0	−602.3	−1,214.3	−8,951.8	33.1	−1.0	24.4
1989 gen—ago	−2,208.3	1,861.3	3,061.1	−757.6	1,956.5	−5.4	3.6	52.1
Banks								
1988 gen—ago	−4,431.8	−9,647.2	1,589.9	−3,548.0	−16,037.1	−5,074.7	−1,795.9	327.2
1989 gen—ago	−6,219.0	−18,200.0	n.d.	n.d.	−24,419.0	−9,900.0	n.d.	n.d.
Other Investors								
1988 gen—ago	36,246.8	14,217.7	24,604.5	5,882.9	80,951.9	10,162.2	2,443.6	4,229.2
1989 gen—ago	32,977.7	27,480.0	12,294.9	3,720.8	76,473.4	13,112.7	−337.6	3,597.3
Cassa Depositi e Presiti								
1988 gen—ago	—	—	—	−58.3	−58.3	371.0	−0.7	—
1989 gen—ago	—	—	—	−22.0	−22.0	51.6	−1.4	—
Total net issues								
1988 gen—set	34,979	−2,715	36,480	2,191.0	70,935	6,392	779	5,757
1989 gen—set	28,648	14,074	20,221	4,577.0	67,520	3,702	−732	5,174

Source: Analysis F.A., Milan.

Table 6-8. Milan Stock Exchange: Main Indicators (1980–1988)

Year	Number of Listed Companies	Number of Listed Shares	Capitalization (bn L.)	Trading Volume Yearly (Total)	Trading Volume Daily (Average)
1980	134	174	23,543	7,343	29
1981	132	178	28,749	12,334	49
1982	138	190	27,299	3,770	15
1983	139	201	34,698	5,880	23
1984	143	213	49,793	7,143	28
1985	147	214	98,195	26,315	104
1986	184	284	190,914	66,571	265
1987	205	316	140,723	41,566	164
1988 (8.7)	210	321	147,542	20,882	158

Source: Sole 24 ore.

1986, and between 1983 and 1986 there were a total of 62 new listings. This trend has now completely stopped.

A recent study of the Bank of Italy points out that in 1985, the first year of exceptional growth, the earnings/price ratio was 5%, very close to the real interest rate in the financial market, which means that the stock market upsurge was based on correct expectations about companies earnings.

5. Mutual Funds

Most of the trading volume in the Italian capital markets is generated by mutual funds, which are a recent addition to the Italian financial markets. They were first introduced in 1983 (Law 23/3/1983 n.77) and started their activity in 1984. Mutual funds are managed by corporations that are allowed to invest the funds provided by the subscribers in stocks, bonds, and money market instruments. These funds are granted a very attractive tax status that, together with the bull market of 1984–1986, favored a massive investment by households. The establishment of mutual funds had an important impact on the market structure, attracting into the Stock Exchange household savings that were traditionally channelled into bank deposits.

Mutual funds are legally distinct from their management companies and are regulated by the Bank of Italy. In particular, the management of mutual funds must obey the following rules:

- never sell short;
- never make a forward purchase behind the next settlement day;
- neither lend nor borrow, with the exception of borrowing from a bank giving securities as a guaranty, but only up to 5% of the capitalization of the fund; and
- the fund cannot invest in shares of the company that manages the fund, nor in other funds. The fund can, however, invest in shares of companies that control its management company, but for no more than 2% of the outstanding shares and without exercising voting rights.

The fund must follow strict guidelines that are aimed to force risk diversification and to protect the investors:

- the fund can own shares of unlisted companies, provided that the annual balance sheet of the issuing companies is certified; however, the percentage invested in such securities cannot exceed 10% of the fund; and
- the fund cannot own more than 5% of the outstanding shares of any listed company or 10% of any unlisted one.

The success of mutual funds among households can be evaluated by their increasing number: at the end of their first year of activity, 1984, there were 10 funds, with total assets of L.1.164 billion ($0.9 million); at the end of 1986, the number of funds had increased to 60, with total assets of L.65,000 billion ($52 million). Even after the market peak of May 1986 and the break of October 1987, their number has kept growing, reaching 89 as of July 1988. The downturn in the Italian stock market that started at the beginning of 1987 has initiated a severe crisis in the mutual funds: their capitalization has been declining since then.

6. History of the Italian Banking System

Since the 1880s, the development of the industrial sector and the growing need of financial resources have helped banking and financial activity to flourish. However, the strong link between bank and industry and the growth of speculative activities, especially in the field of real estate, caused an excessive risk concentration.

The first crisis in modern times came at the beginning of the 1890s and involved at first the industrial sector and then the banking industry. To meet the growing need for liquidity on the part of the banking system, central banks (there were six banks empowered with the right of issuing currency, i.e., the central banks of the original independent states that merged to form Italy) issued additional notes. However, this caused a rapid inflation. In 1893, Banca Romana, the former Church State bank, was found to have permitted an illegal circulation of banknotes that exceeded by 60 million liras its legal limit; the bank was liquidated and its assets absorbed by three of the other issuing banks, namely, Banca Nazionale Toscana, Banca Toscana, and Banca Nazionale, which then combined to create the Bank of Italy. Between 1893 and 1894, other large banks has to be liquidated: Societa' Generale di Credito Mobiliare, Banca Generale, Banca Tiberina, Banco di Sconto e Sete, Banca di Milano, and Istituto di Credito Meridionale.

In 1894, with the support of German and Swiss capital, the Banca Commerciale Italiana was founded. This event was the result of the growing financial and political relationship between Germany and Italy that began in the early 1890s as a result of the increasing need of the newly founded Italian State to finance its deficit and of the political difficulties with France, the former major source of capital. The largest German financial institutions contributed to the creation of this new bank. Their effort was not only financial; their longer experience in banking, and especially in managing a universal bank engaged in activities both in the short and in the long term, made it possible for Banca Commerciale Italiana and for Credito Italiano, founded the year after, to survive until the crises that involved the whole Italian banking system after the World War I.

The 1907 crises, which impacted the banking business worldwide, caused only minor difficulites in Italy. This was partly due to the new tendency of the Central Bank to regulate the banking business and to control the circulation of money.

The investments, which during World War I were mostly channeled to the very lucrative and stable heavy industry, suddenly became very risky ofter the war, since these industries had to face problems connected with industrial postwar conversion. Many banks violated the principle of risk diversification and were involved in the forthcoming crises. They ended up with worthless credits or retained parts of the shares of their own debtors. The liquidation of the large Banca Italiana di Sconto in 1921 was so dramatic that it effectively marked the end of the universal bank and the beginning of a new banking structure founded on the separation of short-term and medium-long-term lending.

In the following years, the first attempts to control the banking business were made, and in 1926 a decree on savings protection was passed. The underlying philosophy of this law was that banks' financial distresses and liquidations are dangerous for the whole economy and that depositors should be protected by means of an adequate control of the banking activity.

This decree, however, could not prevent the 1929 economic crisis from affecting the banking system. In 1931, Banca Commerciale Italiana, Credito Italiano, and Banco di Roma all asked for the help of the authorities: they owned debts of insolvent industrial corporations and shares of the same. Even worse, buy-back operations that were performed in order to substain the value of their own stock had drastically reduced their capital.[2]

The need to clarify the relationship between bank and industry was felt strongly. In 1931, IMI was constituted to absorb the industrial shares retained by banks, and in 1933 IRI (Istituto per la Ricostruzione Industriale = Institute for Industrial Reconversion) took over the three troubled banks.

The underlying principle of the 1936 banking reform was that "the acceptance of deposits and the provision of credit are public-interest functions." All operations involving the stability of the banking system therefore had to be authorized. At that time, the bank-controlling authority was the Ispettorato per la Difesa del Risparmio e l'Esercizio del Credito. The law, which is still in full force today, established a number of rules and defines the authorities designated to control the banking activity and to implement the monetary policy. However, it contained many discretionary aspects, allowing ample space for more direct intervention by Mussolini's regime. The structure of the state was completely altered: Italy was then under a dictatorship, and the state was directly managing many of the most important corporations in Italy.

The law was based on the incorrect assumption that bank failures were caused by maturity mismatch and not by insufficient capitalization. As a result, it put a straightjacket on the Italian banking system.

With the return of democracy after World War II, the power of the Ispettorato per la Difesa del Risparmio e l'Esercizio del Credito was transferred to the Bank of Italy. In the 1950s, the banking system was involved in the problem of reconstruction of the war-damaged industries and infrastructures and in managing the funds connected with the Marshall Plan.

THE STRUCTURE OF THE ITALIAN FINANCIAL SYSTEM   319

The history of the banking system since the 1960s is characterized mostly by rules and regulations imposed by the authorities that reduced more and more the margin of freedom of banks to operate.

In 1962, for the first time since the end of World War II, the Italian commercial balance showed a deficit of 1.252 billion dollars. To finance this deficit, the Treasury issued debt instruments and placed them within the banking system. This was the beginning of a period of strong dependence of the Treasury on the banking system, caused by the necessity to find placement for the larger and larger amounts of papers that had to be issued. The Bank of Italy was bound to purchase all debt papers issued by the Treasury and not sold to the public.

This formal relationship lasted till 1982 and ended with the so-called divorce between the Bank of Italy and the Treasury; thereafter bank holdings of government securities declined (see table 6-9). After 1982 the

Table 6-9. BOTS and Government Securities by Type of Ownership

	1980	1984	1988
BOTS			
Households	43.3	64.9	79.2
Credit institutions	50.5	29.3	9.7
Others	6.2	6.8	11.1
GOVERNMENT SECURITIES			
Households	34.4	44.7	55.0
Credit institutions	63.5	46.3	27.6
Others	2.1	9.0	17.4
TOTAL			
Households	39.6	53.3	63.0
Credit institutions	63.5	46.3	21.7
Others	4.5	7.6	15.3

Households: Ratio of BOTS and Government Securities on Total Financial Activities

1980	1984	1988
13.4	26.3	32.1

Banks: Assets Composition

	1984	1988
Loans	53.5	62.4
Securities of which:	46.5	37.6
BOTS and Government	30	25.4

banking system had no formal obligation towards the Treasury to subscribe the public debt.

From 1973 to 1988, the Bank of Italy adapted direct measures to restrict credit and at the same time to achieve its target of placing Treasury debt instruments and facilitating the financing of special credit institutions. In 1973 a *portfolio constraint* was introduced. This measure compelled banks to invest part of their resources in bonds issued by special credit institutions. According to the 1973 directive, banks had to invest 6% of the total amount of deposits existing at end 1972 in certain fixed-income securities. This percentage was increased to 12% in 1974. This limitation to free bank-asset management was in force until 1978, when it was reduced to 6.5% of the incremental resources. In 1975, another restriction was placed on the form of compulsory reserve. Before that time, the compulsory reserve that each bank was obliged to hold at the Bank of Italy consisted of cash, Treasury papers, and bonds issued by the special credit institutions; however, the ruling of 1975 stated that the amount to be allocated to the compulsory reserve (15% of monthly increases in deposits) should be only in cash.

Besides this portfolio constraint, the Bank of Italy also used another direct tool to restrict credit: the *ceiling on lending growth*, which was in force almost continuously from 1973 to 1982 and was renewed for short periods in 1986 and 1987. This ceiling consisted in the establishment of a maximum rate of expansion of bank lending. It had the effect of directly controlling the volume of banking activity and of substantially reducing the independence of each bank.

The banking system, in compliance with the goals of the 1936 Banking Law, increasingly became an instrument at the disposal of the authorities and the main tool for actuating the government monetary policy. All operations such as bank mergers and acquisitions or the opening of a new branch needed authorization from the Bank of Italy, and the Bank of Italy had the power to set up the closure of a branch for reasons of economic efficiency or geographical location. It is therefore obvious that in this kind of environment the Italian banking system was completely unprepared for the process of "Europeization" that was beginning to take place in the late 1970s. In gradual steps during the 1980s, the government and the Bank of Italy have eliminated part of the heavy constraints and promoted efficiency and competition. The most important issues are transformation of state-owned banks into public corporations; their partial privatization and increase in size through mergers and acquisitions; and the formation of multifunctional financial intermediation groups involved in short-term and long-term banking activities as well as merchant banking, leasing, and factoring—i.e., promoting the concept of universal banking at a group level (see Note 1).

7. Major Regulatory Agencies

The basic provisions governing the credit sector are contrained in the Banking Law of 1936. This legislation vests the responsibilities for guidance and control of the credit system essentially in the CICR (Interministerial Committee for Credit and Savings) and the Bank of Italy. The former is a political body composed of the Ministers of Treasury, National Budget, Public Works, Agriculture, Industry, Foreign Trade, and State Holding, while the latter is a technical institution. The Governor of the Bank of Italy attends the meetings of CICR.

The CICR is vested with decision-making powers regarding all matters concerning savings and credit, as well as with guidance of surveillance of the banks. The CICR collaborates with the Bank of Italy in formulating its decisions and in implementing them. The law regulating the main Italian autonomous regions (Sicily, Trentino-Alto-Adige) vests local authorities with some powers concerning the establishment of banks operating exclusively within such regions.

The Bank of Italy is a public-law institution with a capital of L.300 million subscribed to by savings banks, public-law institutions, national interest banks, and social security and insurance institutions. Affiliated to the central bank is the Italian Foreign Exchange Office (UIC), responsible for ensuring compliance with foreign-exchange regulations on the basis of instructions issued by the Ministry of Foreign Trade, and for managing the official currency reserves.

In addition to controlling the credit system and performing its central banking functions, the Bank of Italy also issues banknotes and is responsible for management of the Treasury's liquidity position.

In the area of control of the credit system, the basic legislation invests the Bank of Italy with very wide powers, including that of issuing directives regarding minimum share capital or endowment funds of the banks; ceilings on bank lending and deposit rates and on service charges; distribution of credit among the various investment categories; establishment of the ratio between capital and reserve funds and investment in real estate and shares; ceilings on the volume of lending abroad; authorization for the establishment of the percentage of profits to be allocated to reserves; authorization for participation in syndicates for the placement of securities not issued or guaranteed by the government; and authorization to open a new bank or a new branch or to merge or acquire another bank. A further function of the Bank of Italy is to ensure the adequate diversification of banking system risks. The Bank of Italy has the right to inspect all banks and to put them under a specially appointed management in case of wrongdoings or financial difficulties. In order to avoid risk resulting from the concentration of loans to the same borrower, a centralized information service, known as the risks registry (Centrale Rischi), was established in March 1964. In this way the Bank of Italy is informed on the global debt position of an individual customer within the entire banking system. Banks have access to information concerning their own customers.

All shares, bonds, and debentures issued by banks or companies must be authorized by the Bank of Italy.

In 1974 the National Commission for Corporation and Exchange (CONSOB) was instituted. The function of the Commission is to maintain surveillance over capital markets and to ensure that listed companies provide the market with adequate information. For listed companies, the Commission has the authority to force them to produce consolidated accounts, to give public information regarding matters of interest, and to inspect them.

In addition, all balance sheets of listed companies must be delivered to the Commission before and after their approval by the stockholders. Any stockholder whose holdings exceed a certain percentage of the capital of a listed company must declare this to the Commission.

As for the duties towards the Stock Exchange, the Commission is entrusted with powers regarding the determination of the Exchange Calendar, the prerequisites for admission to the Exchange, the types of admitted contracts, the formation of prices, and intermediation rates.

The President of the Commission must keep the Minister of Treasury informed of any event of particular importance; the Minister may then inform the Parliament. On March 31st of each year, the Commission must provide the Minister of Treasury with a report regarding the measures taken and the planned activity.

The same law of 1974 gives a precise definition of the concept of *public savings solicitation*, which includes any public announcement and offering of securities, even through the mail or any other communication means. In all these cases, permission of the CONSOB must be secured.

The Stock Broker Council (Comitato Direttivo degli Agenti di Cambio) is a technical body elected in each exchange by the local stockbrokers. Its main function is to supervise the market in its daily operations to guarantee a smooth development of the transactions. The

CONSOB delegates to this council some of its control powers on the day-to-day operations.

The Comitato Direttivo manages the mutual fund of the stockbrokers (required by law) and uses it to settle insolvencies. Before intervening with this guarantee fund, the Comitato can favor a friendly settlement of the insolvency. The Comitato Direttivo sets up the Stock Exchange official listing, collects the daily price of stocks and bonds and the value of the exchange rates, and appoints a Commissario di Borsa (Exchange Commissioner), in whom are vested responsibilities regarding the Exchange administration. The Commissioner has the power to suspend transactions of a security if its daily price variation exceeds 20% for stocks and 10% for bonds.

8. Rules and Regulations of the Banking System

8.1. Entry Restrictions

The Banking Law requires banks to obtain the authorization of the Bank of Italy both to open a new bank or a new branch. Up until 1985, the Bank of Italy had the power to deny the authorization for reasons like economic efficiency, competition, and geographic location. In 1985, a law was passed in compliance with the EEC Directive 780/77. As a result, the Bank of Italy cannot deny authorization when the prescribed prerequisites on capital adequacy and the trustworthiness of the owners are met. The same rules apply to the opening of new branches and to foreign banks.

8.2. Interest Rates and Charges

In Italy, the role of the Central Bank and of the Treasury in determining interest rates is perhaps more important than in other countries. The Treasury's heavy deficit exerts considerable pressure on the money and financial markets. These markets provide the principal source of financing of government debt. Further, considerable influence is exerted by the monetary authorities through the determination of compulsory bank reserve requirements and the interest paid on the reserves, which is now fixed at 5.5%. When compared with the much higher yields charged by banks on their loans to customers, this rate results in an appreciable loss of earnings for the banks. Banks must recoup this loss of earnings by changing their loan customers higher rates.

Until the early 1980s, both deposit and lending rates were decided by the banks under the supervision of ABI. This practice has been discontinued with the aim of making the banking system more competitive.

Italian banks pay interest on checking accounts. The banks charge to their clients the costs for each check purchased and a fee for each operation. In addition, banks profit from the time float between the instant in which a check is deposited and the time in which the amount is at disposal of the client. A similar practice of "back-value dating" applies when the account is debited a few days before the actual date of the transaction. Recently, ABI, together with the Bank of Italy, promoted the disclosure of banking rates and charges: banks were encouraged to publicize their general contract conditions.

8.3. Economic Concentration

Even though in the last years official policy has been in favor of an increased market concentration, the Italian banking system is still one of the least concentrated markets in the industralized world (see table 6-10).

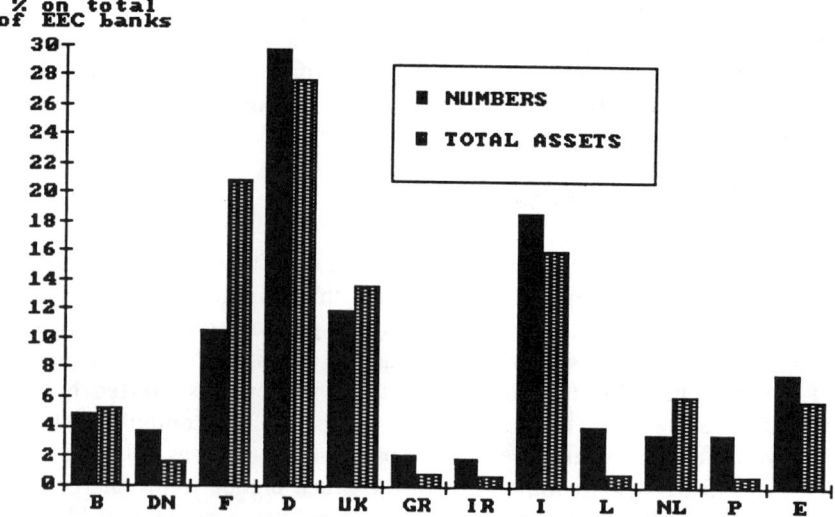

Figure 6-1. The 159 Largest European Banks: Situation Per Country. *Source*: ABI Annual Report 1988.

Table 6-10. Banking Concentration Ratios: 1983[a]

	Banks			All Banking Institutions		
Country	3	5	10	3	5	10
UNCONSOLIDATED[b]						
Germany	43	60.7	69.4	16.6	24	38.2
Italy	28	40.8	61.3	17.5	25.5	40.4
Spain	28.3	42.6	57.9	17.6	26.3	35.7
France	48.5	57.4	—	33.1	47.3	60.9
Belgium	51.6	75	97.5	35.8	52.1	67.7
Ireland	48	—	—	40	—	—
Switzerland	70.6	74.7	79.8	44.8	51.5	59.3
Sweden	76.4	88.8	97.4	52	60.4	67.5
CONSOLIDATED[c]						
Germany	44.5	60.3	68.8	15	22	35
Great Britain	24.4	34	38.8	21.3	29.7	37.1
Spain	38.4	59.7	77.9	23.8	37.2	58.2
Italy	—	—	45.4	—	—	41.3
France	51.8	68.7	—	35.1	53.6	70.5
The Netherlands	69.3	83.9	89	58.7	72.9	81.5

[a] Calculated as the concentration of total banking assets within the first 3, 5, 10 largest institutions.

[b] Except that in the case of France and Spain, for which total assets of foreign branches are included, total assets are calculated only on the basis of internal branches.

[c] Except that in the case of Italy, for which only banking shares have been consolidated, for the other countries accounts have been consolidated on the basis of all shares.

Source: Revell, Jack, "Uno studio comparato della concentrazione bancaria," Banca Impresa e Societa, N.3, Dec. 1987.

Figure 6-1 shows that the number of Italian banks that fall in the group of the 159 largest European banks is considerable. However, the largest of these, the Banca Nazionale del Lavoro, is only the 15th largest (see also table 6-3).

Changes in concentration depend on the restrictive measures adapted by the authorities in terms of geographical expansion, mergers, and acquisitions. It is also affected by the fact that most (60%, taking into account the deposit level) of the Italian commercial banking system is either owned or controlled by the state. The largest nonstate bank, the Banco Ambrosiano-Veneto, which was formed very recently from the merger of two banks, is only the tenth bank in the country. The Italian banking system is segmentated into a large number of mostly medium-

and small-sized banks that operate only at a local level. In view of 1992, when Italian banks will have to face the competition of other EEC banks, the need to increase the average size of banks is strongly felt.

8.4. Capital Adequacy

Since 1987, in compliance with the agreement between the countries reporting to the Bank of International Settlements, banks are bound to maintain two minimum capital ratios. The first ratio is a risk ratio: total assets multiplied by risk coefficients cannot exceed 12.5 times capital, or in other words the capital should be at least equal to 8% of total risky assets. The second ratio required is a capital-dimension ratio: total assets cannot exceed 22.5 times capital, which equals to a capital-to-assets ratio of 4.4%. Table 6-11 shows the capital adequacy of the Italian banking system. One fifth of Italian banks do not meet this capital ratio currently, compared with one fourth of all European banks.

8.5. Role of the Central Bank as Lender of Last Resort

In the context of its central bank functions, the Bank of Italy provides to the banks rediscount services (on promissory notes, Treasury bills, coupons of securities issued or guaranteed by the government, and pledge notes) and advances on securities. Ordinary advances, for a term of four months but renewable at maturity, can be granted on current accounts and on all securities issued or guaranteed by the government. A commit-

Table 6-11. Banks: Capital Adequacy

	December 1987		December 1988	
	Risk Coef.	*Size Coef.*	*Risk Coef.*	*Size Coef.*
Largest, large, and medium-size banks	9.80	5.87	8.80	5.86
Small- and smallest-size banks	16.10	8.23	15.18	8.39
Cooperative banks	18.11	9.51	15.60	8.90
Savings banks	13.11	6.65	13.28	7.90
Rural banks	22.65	9.67	22.02	9.94
Branches of foreign banks	—	4.55	—	4.32
Total of the system	12.80	9.67	11.82	6.98

Source: Banca d'Italia.

ment fee is charged on the amount available for drawings. Fixed-term advances must be utilized and repaid at maturity (up to 22 days). Some penalties are charged by the Bank of Italy on those financing operations transacted with the same bank within a short period of time: this additional charge increases with the frequency of such operations.

8.6. Insolvency Regulation

In the case of insolvency, banks are not subject to the normal liquidation processes, which apply to other companies. Because banking is a matter of public interest, the Bank of Italy has a major role in the liquidation of a bank. In such cases, with some rare exceptions, the Bank of Italy imposes a period of controlled management *amministrazione straordinaria*. The management of the bank is taken over by a special commission chosen by the Bank of Italy. After this period, which may last for one year at the most, the bank is either liquidated or acquired by another bank or returns to normal activity. In 1974, a law was passed according to which the Bank of Italy could grant advances substantially free from interest charges to banks that had assumed liabilities of liquidated banks and therefore bore losses. In this way, the burden of the loss was made substantially public. This system proved itself to be effective until 1984. In 1984 the bankruptcy of the Banco Ambrosiano caused a large loss of about L.2000 billion. This showed that, in the case of large banks, the application of the 1974 Law could present some inconveniences. In this way, the loss was made substantially public. In 1987, the Interbank Fund for Depositors' Protection (Fondo Interbancario per la Tutela dei Depositanti) was constituted with the approval of both the Bank of Italy and government. Compared with the previous system, the fund is characterized by four main features: 1) the fund bears the legal form of a syndicate of banks; 2) to take part in the Fund, banks must keep certain levels of risk concentration, profitability, and solvency; 3) the premiums are charged to the member banks according to the amount of deposits; and 4) the guarantee is not complete: interbank deposits are excluded, and deposits of more than L.200 million ($143 thousand) are not guaranteed in full.

9. Major Current Problems

As mentioned, the Italian banking system is going through a period of intense change. The old concepts of banking as a public service has been replaced by the more actual idea that banks have the goal to produce profits. The authorities have gradually reduced reliance on heavy-handed direct constraints on banking operations and have shown more concern for competition and efficiency.

On the international side, the process of deregulation within the EEC and the integration of European capital markets has brought to the surface both the problem of competition with foreign banks and of regulation of new areas of activity. Any regulation must be in compliance with the EEC directives. In 1992, Italian Banks will have to face the competition of the other EEC banks, most of which are larger in size and with greater experience in many fields. They will have to face in particular the universal banking system that has become the standard model in the EC countries.

The authorities have recently suggested the form of a multifunctional banking group as a means to allow banks into medium-long-term financing and collateral financial activities. The structure of the group has yet to be defined; broadly it consists of a group at the head of which there could be either a bank or a financial institution controlling all other members. Italian banks will therefore be able to engage, although indirectly, in all those activities performed by universal banks. This solution will enable banks to take advantage of the synergies deriving from the integration of the various components of the group. However, the formation of a multifunctional banking group may give rise to many problems concerning its structure, in particular regarding possible conflicts of interest within the group itself.

In 1981, the CICR issued a regulation that allows the banks to acquire shares in other firms without any authorization of the Bank of Italy. However, the regulation imposes some limits on the acquisitions commensurate with the capital of the acquiring bank.

The regulation explicitly lists the types of eligible shares as

- shares of other banks
- shares of companies enganged activities collateral to banking
- shares of "investment banks" fully owned by banks
- shares of auditing compaines

The regulation specifies percentage limits of the acquirable shares in each of the previous cases commisurated at times on the capital of the bank, at times on the capital of the acquiree. The acquisition of shares in foreign companies is subject to authorization and is limited to shares of either banking institutions or of companies directly engaged in activities connected to banking.

In 1987, another regulation added to shares of merchant banks to the list of retainable shares, thereby permitting banks to operate on capital markets and to participate in syndicates for the issue of securities. In order to avoid conflicts with the still-existing prohibition to retain shares of industrial companies, specific limits are imposed on the activity of such merchant banks.

Two problems must still be solved. There is a need to clarify the relationships between banking and commerce and between banking and insurance. The law specifies limits on the number of banking shares that may be acquired by industrial companies. Anybody acquiring more than 10% of a bank and every further 2% must obtain an authorization from the Bank of Italy. Industrial companies cannot own more than 20% of a bank. The authorities seem favorable to waive this limit, since it is likely that the interrelation between bank and industry could provide synergies, expecially in periods in which industries earn high profits. On the other hand, the relationship could create a conflict of interest between shareholders and debtors. It is felt, however, that this problem could be solved with adequate controls.

As for the relationship between bank and insurance, the 1981 Regulation of the CICR does not allow banks to own any shares of insurance companies. Some banks were able to overcome the prohibition by buying the shares through their special sections of medium-long-term credit, for which the limit was not in force. The abolition of this limit would permit the realization of further economies and competition with banks of other European countries in which such prohibition do not hold. Many projects are now being debated in Parliament: the rules concerning the new Societa' d' Intermediazione Finanziaria (Financial Intermediaries), the transformation in public corporations of (some) of the state banks, and the problem of the cross-ownership between banks and industry (see Note 1).

10. Conclusions

The Italian banking and financial system is going through a period of rapid changes and internationalization. The current system will be poorly able to compete with those of the other European countries after 1992. The post-1992 regulatory priniciples of EC have the aim of forcing integration. As known, the EC system is based on two principles:

- mutual recognition of national regulatory frameworks; and
- home-country control.

The relationships between country regulations will become very similar to those between states in the U.S.A., but the differences between regulations will be much wider. The different structure of the financial system in the various countries and the different range of activities allowed to banks does not allow us to fully anticipate the consequences of 1992. It is, however, clear that banks from countries that allow a comparative larger range of activities will have some advantages with respect to the domestic banks of stricter host countries.

As quite correctly pointed out in a recent OECD report (Bröcher, 1989),

> ... a bank, which is member of a stock exchange in its home country, would have access to stock exchange membership of all other EC countries including those with stock exchange monopolies. Thus banks from countries with high-grade universal banking systems would obtain "better than national treatment" in any host country with a low-grade universal banking system.

One very interesting development that we are now witnessing in Europe is the strong increase in cross-country bank mergers and acquisition activities. The aim is that of creating European multinational banking groups with the aim of using for each financial service the bank of the group regulated by the country for which this service is subject to the most benign legislation. For example, Italian banks have been buying French banks with the aim of selling French-law mutual funds, which are much less constrained that the Italian funds.

In the European Community, the "common position" approved in July 1989 on the list of specific activities that will be considered as banking activities, and therefore controlled by the home-country regulatory agencies, coincides with the list of activities performed by German banks, with the sole absence of insurance brokerage. A financial service company, involved in one of the financial servies considered as a banking activity by the Community, in order to be granted the freedom of operating in an unrestricted way in all EC countries, must be fully owned by a bank. We do not think that Italy can afford not to follow the other European countries into a more liberal definition of banking activities.

A clear move towards universal banking will be advisable. We hope that the current political debate will give birth to a more efficient and deregulated system. The last relevant point that should be underlined is the emphasis given by the Governor of the Bank of Italy, Mr. C.A. Ciampi, on the efficiency of the banking system (Banca d'Italia, 1988a). He pointed out the responsibility of each bank in "evaluating the opportunities and the areas of profits" in terms of geographical expanison. For the first time, the Bank of Italy has hinted at the fact that allowing the banking system to operate more autonomously may not be in conflict with the issue of stability of the banking system, which for a long time was the major goal pursued by the Italian authorities.

The Italian parliament is in the last stage of a debate on three different laws directly pertaining the financial system. These laws will control the percentage of a bank capital, which each nonbank entity can own (15%), the relationships between banks, capital markets, stockbrokers, and other financial intermediaries, and the creation of universal banking conglomerates (see Note 1).

Acknowledgments

The authors wish to thank, without implicating, Prof. Tancredi Bianchi for his useful comments about the Italian banking system. The financial support of CNR, Comitato per le Scienze Economiche, Sociologiche e Statistiche is gratefully acknowledged.

Notes

1. During 1990 and 1991 four new laws on financial intermediation were passed by the Italian Parliament, in particular on bank ownership and on the SIM.
2. Now buy-back operations are possible only within certain limits. The Law n.30 in 1986 determined that such operations must have the shareholders' approval, and that the period, the number of shares, the minimum and maximum acquisition prices should be stated. Moreover, the maximum amount of acquirable shares is strictly defined by the amount of retained earnings and disposable reserves resulting from the last balance sheet.

References

Banca d'Italia. *Italian Credit Structures Efficiency, Competition and Controls.* London: Euromoney Publications, 1984.
Banca d'Italia. Annual Report 1988a.
Banca d'Italia. "White Paper on the Payments System in Italy," 1988b.
Brōcher, G. *Competition in Banking.* Paris: OECD, September, 1989.
Pecchioli, R.M. *The Internationalization in Banking. Policy Issues.* Paris: OCDE, 1983.

7 THE EVOLUTION OF JAPANESE BANKING AND FINANCE

Thomas F. Cargill and Shoichi Royama

1. Introduction

The emergence of a modern financial framework in Japan is a relatively recent event compared to the financial history of other industrialized countries. Banks offering intermediation services were established shortly after the Meiji Restoration in 1868 when Japan adopted a national policy of industrialization in order to achieve economic parity with the West. The banking system's role was to mobilize the country's financial resources to support industrialization and economic growth.

The banking and financial systems were one and the same in the early years of Japanese finance. Despite the evolution of nonbank financial institutions and direct markets, especially in the last two decades, bank finance continues to dominate the flow of funds in Japan.

The banking and financial systems have evolved through major transitional stages during a little more than one century of history: 1) undisciplined expansion of bank notes in the 1870s that initiated the establishment of a central bank—the Bank of Japan (BOJ)—to control the currency component of the money supply and to increase government supervision over financial institutions; 2) financial collapse in the mid-

1920s associated with events surrounding a devastating earthquake in 1923; 3) structural changes marked by the concentration of intermediation services into a smaller number of financial institutions initiated in the late 1920s that continued to the end of World War II; 4) mobilization of financial resources to support war preparation and the war itself during the 1930s and first half of the 1940s, respectively; 5) reorganization of the financial system during the U.S. occupation in the second half of the 1940s; 6) the provisim of financial support for the reindustrialization and reestablishment of Japan as a major force in the world economy during the High Growth Period (HGP) from the mid-1950s through the early 1970s; 7) initiation of financial liberalization in the mid-1970s that has continued to the present; and most recently, 8) a dramatic increase in Japan's financial importance to the world economy resulting from unprecedented current account surpluses in the 1980s in the context of increasing financial integration and rapid growth of global money and capital markets.

Japan's emergence as a financial superpower has been clearly reflected by the shift in the relative financial roles of Japan and the United States. The United States has become a net debtor nation while Japan has assumed the role as the world's largest creditor nation. At the end of 1987, the U.S. net external liability stood at $368.2 billion dollars. In contrast, Japan had a net external asset position of $240.7 billion dollars while West Germany's net external asset position of $83.3 billion dollars placed that country in a distant second place.

Japan's emergence in recent years as a major financial force in the world economy is fully reflected by the domestic and international growth of banks. Japanese banks have become the largest in the world. In 1988, ten largest banks in the world were Japanese; Dai Ichi Kangyo is the largest bank in the world, with assets totaling $380 billion at the end of September 1988. Japanese banks have expanded internationally in ways significantly different than in the 1970s. Prior to 1980, the majority of international activities on the part of Japanese banks were associated with trade financing; however, since 1980 Japanese international banking activities have broadened significantly to direct competition with domestic banks for both retail and wholesale business in the United States, the United Kingdom, and other countries as well as assuming an increasing role in the Eurocurrency markets (Ostrom, 1988; Zimmerman, 1988). In short, Japan has become a financial superpower in banking and finance.

This chapter describes the evolution of Japanese banking and related financial institutions and offers some insights into the structure of banking

THE EVOLUTION OF JAPANESE BANKING AND FINANCE   335

and finance in Japan and how the financial structure has changed in recent years. This objective is carried out in the next seven sections. In section 2, we provide an overview of Japan's flow of funds from the mid-1950s through the mid-1980s. Sections 3 and 4 discuss specific financial institutions and the regulatory institutions in Japan, respectively. Section 5 presents a brief history of banking through the 1980s. Section 6 discusses several issues related to the so-called "unique" characteristics of Japanese banking during the HGP and whether the particular method of transferring funds in Japan during the HGP precludes neoclassical analysis. Section 7 discusses the transition of Japanese finance and banking that started in the mid-1970s. Section 8 discusses several issues raised by the transition of finance and banking and recent proposals as of mid-1989 designed to restructure Japanese banks in the light of the new economic and technological environment. Section 9 ends the chapter with a short concluding statement.

2. Japan's Flow of Funds

The financial system of any country is represented by the institutional framework that channels funds from surplus to deficit sectors. Table 7-1 presents the sectoral financial balances of the major nonfinancial sections of the Japanese economy over the period from 1954 through 1985. During the post-World War II period through 1975, the household sector was the primary surplus sector and the corporate sector the primary deficit sector. The central-government sector was generally a small surplus sector over this period and, combined with other public-sector deficits, the overall public sector was a deficit sector approximately equal to one third the size of the corporate sector. This pattern of flow of funds changed dramatically after 1975. The central government and hence the overall public-sector deficit increased by 100% and the corporate-sector deficit decreased by 50%. The shift of the government sector as the largest deficit sector has had profound effects on the Japanese financial system and has been a primary force of financial liberalization.

There are several classification schemes that can be used to characterize the transfer of funds from surplus to deficit sectors, and the approach here is based on the following taxonomy: 1) negotiated versus open-market transactions; 2) indirect versus direct financial markets; 3) bank versus nonbank financial intermediation; and 4) private versus public or government-sponsored financial markets and institutions.

Table 7-1. Surplus or Deficit Position of Major Nonfinancial Sectors as % of GNP

Fiscal Year	Personal	Corporate	Central GVT.	Public Sector Other	Total	Rest of World
1954	6.5	−3.9	0.1	−2.1	−2.0	−0.5
1955	7.6	−4.4	−0.6	−1.6	−2.2	−0.9
1956	7.0	−7.0	1.2	−1.3	−0.1	0.1
1957	7.1	−9.8	1.9	−1.2	0.7	2.0
1958	6.3	−4.5	0.8	−1.2	−0.4	−1.4
1959	9.5	−7.7	0.2	−1.0	−0.9	−1.0
1960	8.9	−9.0	1.5	−1.0	0.5	−0.3
1961	8.8	−11.5	2.4	−1.6	0.8	1.8
1962	9.0	−8.0	1.5	−2.6	−1.1	0.1
1963	7.7	−7.5	1.1	−2.5	−1.4	1.1
1964	9.3	−7.6	0.3	−2.6	−2.3	0.6
1965	7.9	−4.5	0	−3.2	−3.2	−1.1
1966	9.1	−4.8	−0.8	−3.3	−4.1	−1.2
1967	9.4	−7.3	−0.7	−2.4	−3.1	0.2
1968	9.1	−6.7	0	−2.8	−2.8	−0.7
1969	8.7	−6.9	0.6	−2.2	−2.8	−1.3
1970	8.2	−7.2	1.3	−2.3	−1	−1
1971	9.6	−6.3	0.9	−2.8	−1.9	−2.5
1972	11.5	−7.9	0.6	−3.3	−2.7	−2.2
1973	8.8	−7.6	1.1	−3.9	−2.8	0
1974	10.3	−8.5	0.7	−4.4	−3.7	1
1975	10.5	−4.1	−2.7	−4.6	−7.3	0.1
1976	11.4	−3.9	−3.5	−4.1	−7.6	−0.6
1977	11.2	−2.6	−4	−3.3	−7.3	−1.5
1978	11.1	−1	−5.4	−3.7	−9.1	−1.7
1979	9.2	−3.1	−4.5	−3.5	−8	0.9
1980	8.3	−3.5	−3.2	−3.6	−6.8	1
1981	11.2	−3.1	−3.8	−3.6	−7.4	−0.5
1982	10.8	−3.2	−3.9	−3.0	−6.9	−0.7
1983	10.4	−1.8	−3.9	−2.9	−6.8	−1.8
1984	9.3	−0.7	−3.3	−2.5	−5.8	−2.8
1985	9.5	−1.7	−2.1	−2.0	−4.2	−3.6
Average						
1954−1985	9.2	−5.5	−0.8	−2.7	−3.6	−0.6
1954−1974	8.6	−7.1	0.7	−2.4	−1.7	−0.3
1975−1985	10.3	−2.6	−3.7	−3.3	−7.0	−1.0

Note: Corporate sector includes both nonfinancial and financial corporations.
Source: Bank of Japan, Flow of Funds Accounts, each year.

2.1. Negotiated versus Open Market Transactions

Negotiated debt transactions are customer relationship oriented, multidimensional in terms of the services provided, long-term, and frequently implicit rather than explicit. In negotiated transactions, the actual transfer of funds and the price at which funds are exchanged represent only two specific aspects of the relationship between borrower and lender. In contrast, open-market transactions are essentially defined by price and quantity, limited in terms of the services provided as part of the borrower-lender relationship, short-term, and frequently explicit rather than implicit.

The distinction between negotiated and open-market transactions can be motivated by considering a basic function of the financial system—the supply of liquidity in an imperfect information environment. Individuals sell assets in the financial system to acquire liquidity in two ways: by selling assets to financial intermediaries or by selling assets in open markets.

In the case of intermediation, the borrower negotiates the terms of the transaction (e.g., price, collateral) with a particular buyer. The more imperfect the information retrieval system and the more individual-specific the characteristics of the financial asset, the greater the tendency for this form of obtaining liquidity to become the basis for establishing a long-term relationship between the lender and the asset supplier. Hence, bilateral or negotiated forms of providing liquidity provide a foundation for customer-relationship-based financial transactions, and the greater the costs of obtaining information, the more likely it is that the customer relationship will evolve into a long-term relationship that covers services other than the provision of liquidity.

Liquidity can also be obtained in an open market where the borrower sells assets in a market composed of a large number of participants. While this method requires a mediator, i.e., a broker or exchange agent, the potential sellers and buyers of assets are many. In this setting there is little interest in knowing nor any need to know, specifics about the two parties to the transaction. Rather, the participants' concern is entirely with the price, quantity of funds, and asset quality. Open markets require some commonly agreed method for judging asset quality and some method of obtaining information in a cost-effective manner. The distinction between negotiated and open-market transactions is straightforward in concept and similar to the distinction made by Williamson (1975) between markets and hierarchies; however, it is not easily amenable to measurement. Cargill and Royama (1988, chapter 2) and Royama (1986) offer a

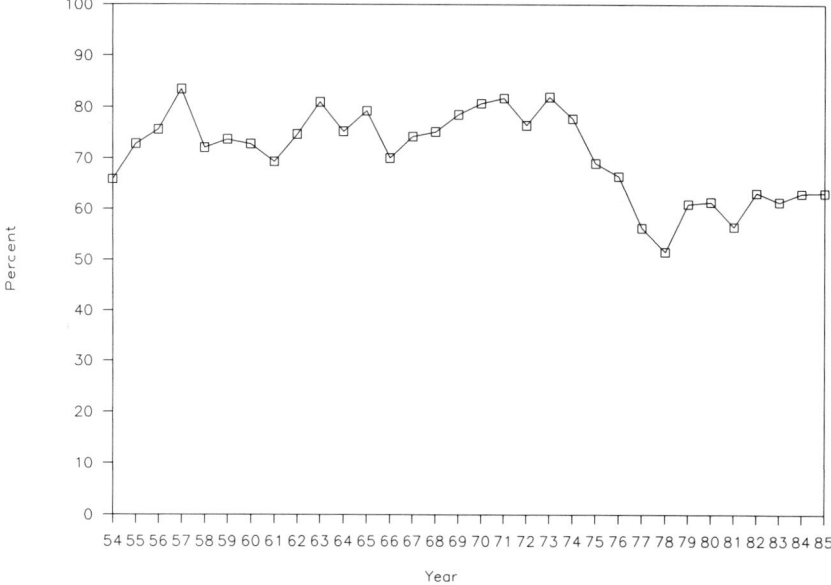

Figure 7-1. Percentage of Funds Obtained by Nonfinancial Borrowers Classified as Negotiated Transactions, 1954–1985. *Source*: Flow of Funds, Bank of Japan.

decomposition of the Japanese flow of funds over the period from 1954 to 1985 in terms of the four-part taxonomy: indirect-negotiated, indirect-open market, direct-negotiated, and direct-open market.

Figure 7-1 suggests that negotiated transactions have played a major role in Japan, and although they have declined in importance since 1975, they continue to dominate Japanese finance.

2.2. Indirect versus Direct Finance

The financial system can also be characterized in terms of indirect and direct finance as originally suggested by Gurley and Shaw (1960). Indirect or intermediation financial markets have played a large role in the flow of funds in Japan; in fact, indirect finance represented the only viable funding channel for most of the postwar period. Figure 7-2 illustrates the indirect finance ratio over the period from 1954 through 1985.

The indirect finance ratio has been steadily declining since 1975, and many observers regard this as strong evidence that the structure of the

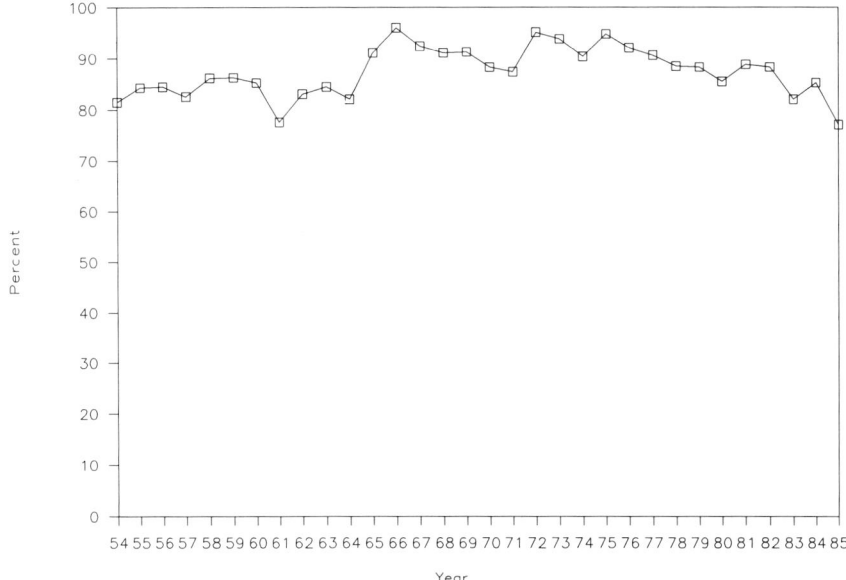

Figure 7-2. Percentage of Funds Obtained by Nonfinancial Borrowers Through Indirect Financial Channels, 1954–1985. *Source*: Flow of Funds, Bank of Japan.

Japanese financial system is changing and that the emergence of direct finance is a necessary outcome of the liberalization process. Nevertheless, it would be hasty to conclude that the past dominance of indirect financing is weakening in Japan; for example, the indirect finance ratio previously demonstrated a downward trend between 1966 and 1971, when it fell from 96.0% to 87.4%. While it is reasonable to argue that the recent decline in the indirect finance ratio is consistent with expanded money and capital markets, one should exercise caution in predicting the continued decline of indirect finance in Japan given the importance of customer relationships that permeate almost all aspects of economic life in Japan.

2.3. Banks versus Nonbank Financial Institutions

The banking system in Japan consists of several classes of institutions offering deposit and loan services to be discussed in more detail in the following section. Flow-of-funds data in figure 7-3 suggest that Japanese

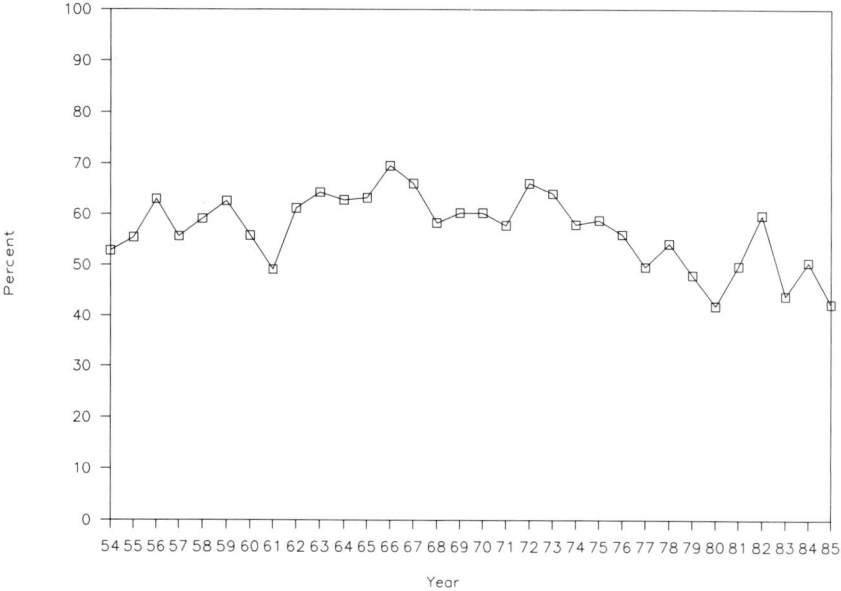

Figure 7-3. Percentage of Funds Obtained by Nonfinancial Borrowers Through the Banking System, 1954–1985. *Source*: Flow of Funds, Bank of Japan.

banks dominate intermediation finance; however, there has been a noticeable decline in bank market share since 1975.

2.4. Public versus Market Financial Intermediation

Figure 7-4 illustrates the percentage of funds supplied to nonfinancial borrowers by public or government financial institutions in Japan from 1954 through 1985. Public financial intermediation in Japan has played and continues to play a major role in the financial system. Much of the public financial intermediation has been directed toward the country's infrastructure in terms of allocating funds while the private institutions have supplied funds to the business sector; thus, there has been little competition between public and private institutions in terms of supplying funds. In terms of obtaining funds, however, public and private institutions have become more competitive, and intense debate has arisen in Japan as to the role of public financial intermediation in a more liberalized environment.

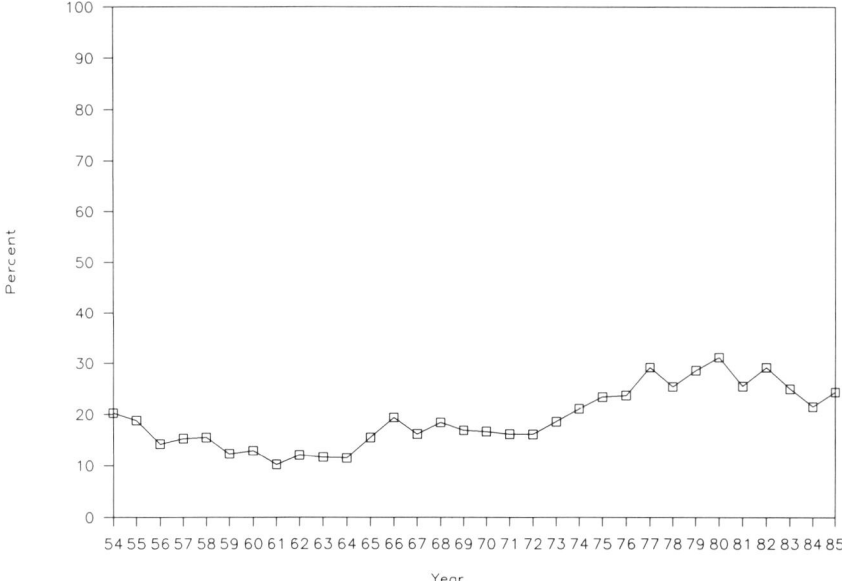

Figure 7-4. Percentage of Funds Obtained by Nonfinancial Borrowers Through Public Financial Institutions, 1954–1985. *Source*: Flow of Funds, Bank of Japan.

3. Institutions for Intermediation Finance

Table 7-2 and 7-3 present information on the types and sizes of Japanese financial institutions.[1] The structure of intermediation finance has remained essentially constant over the past two decades; however, financial liberalization has begun to blur the portfolio distinctions between the various institutions.

Japan possesses a variety of financial institutions that provide intermediation finance classified into three categories in the flow-of-funds tables: banks, other private financial institutions, and public financial institutions.

The banking system is composed of five different types of banks: city banks (including one specialized foreign exchange bank), regional or local banks, long-term credit banks, trust banks, and foreign banks.

There are 13 city banks, one of which is a specialized foreign exchange bank,[2] located in the major population centers of Japan such as Tokyo and Osaka in addition to having branches located throughout the country

Table 7-2. Private Financial Institutions in Japan (100 Million Yen)

Institution	Size in Terms of Deposits, Bank Debentures, Trusts, and Others Issued								Share (%) 1955	Share (%) 1987	Size in Assets[a] 1987	Share (%) 1987	# of Inst. 1987	# of Branches 1987	Annual rate of growth in size (%)						
	End of 1955	End of 1960	End of 1965	End of 1970	End of 1975	End of 1980	1985	1987							55–60	60–65	65–70	70–75	75–80	80–85	85–87
City banks[b]	25,560	59,445	131,902	252,022	553,236	898,233	391,618	1,758,797	40.33	22.45	2,509,891	25.05	13	3,437	18.4	17.3	13.8	17.0	10.2	9.2	12.4
Regional banks	11,794	29,752	71,902	147,363	345,182	609,886	955,046	1,144,735	18.61	14.61	1,294,066	12.92	64	7,164	20.3	19.3	15.4	18.6	12.1	9.4	9.5
Long-term credit banks	3,438	10,528	26,739	57,617	141,366	223,810	362,117	434,293	5.42	5.54	561,277	5.60	3	83	25.1	20.5	16.6	19.7	9.6	10.1	9.5
Trust banks (banking account)	1,087	3,374	8,930	19,338	41,758	58,736	96,203	115,837	1.72	1.48	390,553	3.90	7	401	25.4	21.5	16.7	16.6	7.1	10.4	9.7
Trust banks (trust account)[c]	3,514	17,360	36,078	75,586	202,938	366,368	542,652	721,236	5.54	9.21	1,440,098	14.38	7	—	37.6	15.8	15.9	21.8	12.5	8.2	15.3
Sogo banks[d]	4,254	11,458	32,862	64,158	161,490	273,113	386,453	457,376	6.71	5.84	514,794	5.14	68	4,417	21.9	23.5	14.3	20.3	11.1	7.2	8.8
Sinkin banks	3,041	9,890	31,748	78,857	197,006	343,003	504,820	599,017	4.80	7.65	697,533	6.96	455	7,551	26.6	26.3	20.0	20.1	11.7	8.0	8.9
Credit cooperatives	458	2,044	8,086	20,421	51,370	87,609	128,612	152,037	0.72	1.94	162,689	1.62	439	2,899	34.9	31.7	20.4	20.3	11.3	8.0	8.7
Labor credit associations	136	431	1,226	3,685	13,487	29,678	49,522	56,520	0.21	0.72	60,765	0.61	47	635	25.9	23.3	24.6	29.6	17.1	10.8	6.8
Shoko-chukin bank	565	1,702	1,391	12,032	34,740	56,713	91,638	103,203	0.89	1.32	110,514	1.10	1	98	24.7	-4.0	54.0	23.6	10.3	10.1	6.1
Agricultural cooperatives	4,161	9,627	29,717	72,997	184,243	320,821	476,360	531,769	6.56	6.79	472,229	4.71	4,092	16,364	18.3	25.3	19.7	20.3	11.7	8.2	5.7
Life insurance companies	1,888	7,435	22,219	58,139	127,942	259,689	529,451	776,116	2.98	9.91	792,584	7.91	24	—	31.5	24.5	21.2	17.1	15.2	15.3	21.1
Non-life insurance companies	858	1,895	4,090	11,906	32,756	61,574	106,283	158,128	1.35	2.02	175,242	1.75	23	—	17.2	16.6	23.8	22.4	13.5	11.5	22.0
Foreign banks	—	—	—	—	—	15,058	24,656	15,254	—	0.19	134,250	1.34	81	115	—	—	—	—	19.7	10.4	-21.3
Others[e]	2,625	6,482	230	66,785	165,263	350,843	656,703	810,230	4.14	10.34	701,359	7.00	—	—	19.8	-48.7	210.9	19.9	16.2	13.4	11.1
Total	63,379	171,423	407,120	940,906	2,252,777	3,955,114	302,134	7,834,548	100.00	100.00	10,017,844	100.00	—	—	22.0	18.9	18.2	19.1	11.9	9.8	11.5

[a] Total assets for columns from City banks to Shinkin banks, and sum of cash, deposits, loans, and securities for columns from Credit cooperatives to Others.
[b] The Bank of Tokyo, the only foreign-exchange bank, is included.
[c] Total of trust accounts of trust banks and those of a city bank (Daiwa Bank) and two regional banks in Okinawa.
[d] Almost all Sogo banks converted to ordinary banks in February 1989.
[e] Others include The Zenshinren bank, National Federation of Credit Cooperatives, National Federations of Labor Credit Associations, Mutual Federations of Agricultural Cooperatives, Fishery cooperatives, Credit Federations of Fishery Cooperatives, Securities finance companies.

Table 7-3. Government Financial Institutions in Japan, Fiscal Year-End 1987

Institution	Branches	Assets	Percent
The Japan Development Bank	2	¥82,019	9.1%
The Export-Import	1	43,041	5.9
The Shoko Chukin Bank	98	115,674	12.9
The People's Finance Corporation	151	56,127	6.3
The Housing Loan Corporation	2	304,125	33.9
The Agricultural, Forestry and Fisheries Finance Corporation	21	54,921	6.1
The Small Business Finance Corporation	8	52,089	5.8
The Hokkaido and Tohoku Development Corporation	3	8,491	0.9
The Japan Finance Corporation for Municipal Enterprises		118,234	13.2
The Okinawa Development Finance		8,691	1.0
Corporation Fund for Overseas Economic Cooperation		44,573	5.0
Total	336	897,985	100.0

Source: Bank of Japan, Economic Statistics Monthly.

and the world. City banks are generally the largest banks and primarily service the corporate or large business sector. City banks obtain funds from the corporate and personal sector in the form of demand and time deposits with maturities of no more than two years. As of 1981, time deposits can automatically be extended for one year, thus increasing to three years the maximum maturity. During the 1980s, city banks significantly directed loan activity toward households and small businesses, although large corporate borrowers continue to be the major borrower.

The regional or local banks are more numerous than the city banks and have a portfolio structure similar to city banks; however, they are generally smaller and located in areas outside of the major population centers. Their portfolio activities are confined to a regional area, and they service a wide range of small- to medium-sized business enterprises. Since liberalization began, regional banks have increased their lending to larger businesses, which previously relied almost entirely on city bank credit. Prior to 1989, there were 64 regional banks; however, almost all *Sogo* or mutual banks converted to regional bank status, so there are now about 130 regional banks.

Branches of both city and regional banks are restricted by the Ministry of Finance (MOF); however, the MOF uses its administrative control over branches to encourage expansion of smaller rather than larger banks.

There are three long-term credit banks (the Industrial Bank of Japan, the Long-Term Credit Bank of Japan, and the Nippon Credit Bank). They provide loans up to ten years to business enterprises and obtain funds by issuing bank debentures of one and five years in maturity. While long-term credit banks are permitted to hold deposits of client enterprises and governmental entities, they are prohibited from accepting individual deposits as a general source of funds.

There are seven trust banks that make long-term loans to business enterprises and obtain funds from managing trust accounts.

In addition to domestic banks, there are 81 foreign banks operating in Japan as of 1987, which are now permitted to offer most of the same services as domestic banks. Foreign banks play a minor role in Japanese finance, however. Even as recently as year-end 1987, foreign bank assets represented 2.8% of all bank assets in Japan. The phrase *all banks* frequently encountered in Japanese financial statistics is defined to include city banks, regional banks, long-term credit banks, and trust banks. Even though foreign financial institutions now have greater access to Japan's domestic financial system than in the past, Japanese consumers of financial services prefer domestic to foreign banking institutions, other things held constant.

There are a variety of other private financial institutions that provide banking-type services to specific sectors of the economy or offer non-deposit financial assets to the public, such as life insurance policies. There are almost 1000 financial institutions organized to finance small business enterprises that are not serviced by either city or regional banks. These include the *Sogo* or mutual banks, credit associations, credit cooperatives, and others that deal primarily with smaller manufacturing and commercial enterprises. There are a large number of institutions that service the financial needs of agriculture, forestry, and fishery activities. In addition to institutions that provide banking services to small manufacturing enterprises and specialized sectors, there are over 40 insurance companies, over 200 securities companies, and several housing finance institutions.

To augment the private financial institutions and to support politically favored sectors of the economy, there exist a number of governmental financial institutions such as the Japan Development Bank, the Export-Import Bank, and other public financial institutions. These institutions do not issue transaction or other types of deposits; rather, they are fund allocators. They obtain funds through the Fiscal and Loan Program of the MOF that in turn is funded by the postal savings and social insurance system. In this regard, the postal savings system (PSS) represents the largest financial institution in the world in terms of deposits and accounts for most of the flow of funds through public financial institutions. The PSS held deposits at end-1988 of $940 billion dollars (¥124.5 = $1.00) and held about 30% of deposits of the general public. The funds available to the PSS make it several times larger than the Federal Reserve of the United States. It has also become a controversial issue in Japan, since the MOF has provided the PSS with regulatory advantages in terms of deposit ceilings, and, until the recent tax reforms of 1986 that essentially ended the *maruyu* system, PSS deposits had considerable tax advantages.[3]

4. Regulatory Institutions

Japanese regulatory institutions are a product of the historical and political evolution of the country.[4] Japan has traditionally lacked an emphasis on decentralized decision making, democratic-type institutions, and openness to political or economic markets. In addition, Japan is geographically a small country without separate regional political and economic institutions. Japan does not have the same degree of legalistic perspective common to many Western countries. Individual responsibilities and conflicts are defined and settled more by administrative guidance by a central authority, rather than by explicit law and interpretations of the law through the court system. Thus, Japanese financial regulation 1) is centralized in a small number of entities; 2) lacks a regional or dualistic perspective; and 3) establishes and enforces the regulatory parameters via an administrative and informal process.

Specifically, the MOF is the primary regulatory authority over the financial system, followed by the Bank of Japan (BOJ) as a distant second and the Ministry of Posts and Telecommunications (MPT) as an even more distant third. The MOF combines the functions of the U.S. Treasury, Office of Management and Budget, Internal Revenue Service, Securities and Exchange Commission, Commodities Futures Trading Commission, Office of the Comptroller of the Currency, activities of the Justice Department and Federal Trade Commission related to the financial system, state banking and insurance regulators, supervisory functions of the Federal Reserve, Federal Deposit Insurance Corporation, Federal Savings and Loan Insurance Corporation, Federal Home Loan Bank Board, National Credit Union Administration, and state credit union regulatory agencies. The MOF derives power from the Banking Law, Securities and Exchange Law, Insurance Business Act, Trade and Foreign

Exchange Control Law, and other legislation. The MOF's influence over the domestic and international financial system is thus substantial and pervasive. There exists no counterpart to the MOF in the United States.

The extent of the MOF's power is reflected by article 26 of the Banking Law:

> When the Minister of Finance deems it necessary in the light of a bank's business situation or financial position, he may direct that it be enjoined from conducting business in whole or in part, transfer its property to the competent authorities, or take any other necessary measures.

The same power is granted the MOF for almost every other sector of the financial system.

The MOF is composed of seven Bureaus. The Finance Bureau and the Budget Bureau are responsible for the government's fiscal program, while financial regulation is administered by the Banking Bureau, Securities Bureau, and International Finance Bureau. Through these bureaus the MOF sets interest-rate ceilings on deposits (except postal savings deposits), examines financial institutions, supervises the deposit insurance system, defines permissible and nonpermissible portfolio activities of financial institutions and markets with regard to both domestic and international financial transactions, licenses and supervises banks and other depository institutions and other financial institutions, licenses securities companies, supervises a number of public financial institutions such as the Japan Development Bank, and develops overall financial policy.

The MOF sets and ensures maintenance of the regulatory parameters by a process referred to as *administrative guidance*, which enhances its power of control far beyond that suggested by the formal legal parameters. Administrative guidance involves interpretations of existing laws and regulations conveyed to the concerned parties in a verbal form, but sometimes in a written form. Noncompliance by market participants is unlikely because they cannot "shop" for a more favorable set of regulations as they sometimes can in the United States, and they fully recognize that they will require MOF permission and support for continued operation. Because the majority of financial regulation in Japan is defined and enforced by administrative guidance, the liberalization of the financial system during the past decade has largely been an administratively directed process (Cargill and Royama, 1988).

The MOF, however, does not have complete regulatory control. There are five areas of financial regulation for which the MOF either involves other entities or other entities assume a dominant role without explicit influence from the MOF:

1. The BOJ is consulted on almost all of the major regulatory decisions of the MOF.
2. The BOJ plays a formal role in setting deposit-rate ceilings at private financial institutions (Suzuki, 1987, p. 148), and these in turn are influenced by the particular direction of monetary policy being pursued at the time.
3. The BOJ has primary jurisdiction over the interbank market.
4. The "window guidance" or loan expansion limits for private financial institutions is largely under the control of the BOJ, especially since the early 1970s. Despite its deemphasis since 1980, window guidance remains a viable monetary policy instrument should the BOJ resort to tight monetary policy. It was effectively used in 1979 with regard to city bank loans; however, BOJ policy has generally been expansionary since 1980.
5. Deposit rates on postal savings accounts are regulated by the MPT rather than the MOF or the BOJ. In addition, the MPT has been rather open about providing the PSS with a regulatory advantage by setting the rates usually above those paid by private financial institutions. While the PSS lost a major tax advantage as a result of the 1986 tax reform that ended the exclusion of interest income on small deposits from taxes, it received authority at the same time to diversify its asset portfolio into open-market assets subject to a limit determined yearly by the MOF. Previously, the PSS transferred all of the funds to the Trust Fund Bureau of the MOF.

In addition, the MOF does not present itself as a unified regulatory authority. Each bureau of the MOF is provided with a high degree of independence in its respective area of responsibility, and intense conflicts between different bureaus have occurred in the past (Horne, 1985).

In summary, while the MOF does not have exclusive control over the regulatory parameters, it is the primary financial regulatory authority of the Japanese financial system. While the existence of separate bureaus in the MOF generates a multiplicity of sorts in Japan, Japanese financial regulation is far more unified than in the United States. There exists a strong tradition in the MOF to work out differences of opinion between the bureaus in order to present a unified regulatory approach. In addition, financial regulation is defined and enforced via a process of administrative guidance in contrast to the situation in the United States where financial regulation is codified and enforced via law and court rulings.

5. A Brief History of Japanese Banking

This section offers a brief review of the more important periods in the evolution of the Japanese banking system from the second half of the nineteenth century to the early 1970s. The following section will focus on the period since the early 1970s to the present.

5.1. Early Period

The Meiji Government was formed in 1868 to modernize and establish Japan as a major industrial country replacing the feudal regime maintained by the Tokugawa Shogunate. As part of the modernization effort, Japan established a national banking system in 1872 based on the system established in the United States by the National Currency Act of 1863 (revised as the National Bank Act of 1864). Approximately 150 national banks were given the right to issue national bank notes as well as to accept deposits and to make short-term business loans. In the late 1870s, national bank notes expanded rapidly in response to government expenditures to repress an uprising in Kyushu. Rapid inflation and bank failures threatened the newly organized government. The MOF in 1881 began a reorganization effort to establish a central bank with the sole right of issuing bank notes and withdrawing inconvertible national bank notes from circulation in order to bring inflation under control and restore public confidence in the nation's money supply.

The BOJ was established in 1882. Since national banks could no longer issue currency, they reverted to "ordinary bank" status, accepting deposits and specializing in short-term business financing. Private commercial banking was officially legalized by the 1890 Bank Law. The BOJ and the MOF provided regulatory oversight, and the government established other private, quasigovernmental, and governmental institutions to meet needs not being satisfied by commercial banks. In 1874 the PSS was established, followed by quasi-government institutions such as the Yokohama Specie Bank (1880) and the Industrial Bank of Japan (1902).

Despite the monopolization of currency issuance by the BOJ, Japanese banks expanded rapidly, as did other related financial institutions. In 1913, there were 1,457 ordinary banks, 52 specializing in financing limited types of activities, banks, and 684 small savings banks in operation (Schiffer, 1962, p. 20). In addition, there were several quasigovernment institutions as well as the PSS.

During the second half of the nineteenth century through the 1920s,

Japanese banking developed in an environment of limited government regulation compared to the present; however, self-regulation and cartelization of the market did exist with tacit government approval. Teranishi (1990) has recently argued that the pre-World War II period of Japanese finance relied on a "process of free competition." While the view that Japanese prewar financial and banking system was one of free competition is debatable, the prewar system differed from the postwar period in two respects: explicit government regulation characterized the postwar period, and the postwar period was probably less competitive than the prewar period. There has never been a period in Japanese banking similar to the "free banking" experience of the United States that occurred during the period from 1837 through the late 1850s.

5.2. Financial Panic in the 1920s

An important change in the nature of government regulation and the structure of banking occurred during the late 1920s when the banking system collapsed. The origin of the financial collapse partly arose from the economic effects of a major earthquake (measuring 7.9) striking Tokyo on September 1, 1923. The earthquake caused widespread destruction in the Kanto Plain and other parts of eastern Japan and left 133,000 dead. To reduce the adverse impact on the economy, commercial bills drawn or payable to commercial banks in the areas hit by the earthquake were rediscounted by the BOJ with the understanding that the government would cover any losses. Known as earthquake bills, their aggregate total was estimated at 2.1 billion yen as of March 1927. Of these, the BOJ had rediscounted bills of 430 million yen. The rediscount period had been extended twice and had only 200 days remaining in March 1927, when the Budget Committee of the Lower House (House of Representatives of the Diet) began debating a bill to extend measures for compensating earthquake-bill losses.

Opposition parties vigorously argued that the rediscounting of earthquake bills favored banks and businesses with strong political ties. The debate was intense; for example, Minister of Finance Naoharu Kataoka's appearance before the Lower House was interrupted by severe heckling many times as he argued that rescuing financially troubled banks was of the utmost urgency. To stress the need for action, he stated that the Tokyo Watanabe Bank, a medium-sized commercial bank, had ceased operations at noon that day. While the Watanabe Bank had already been experiencing cash-flow problems prior to the debate, it was still in operation at the time of Kataoka's remarks. Kataoka's remarks, however, generated deposit withdrawals that forced the bank's closure. The failure of the Watanabe Bank triggered a run on many smaller banks that possessed insufficient funds to cover depositors' withdrawals. This in turn caused a general bank panic and numerous bank failures.

The bank panic of 1927 had a profound effect on attitudes about the safety of a less than completely regulated banking system that had permitted the formation of a large number of institutions. As a result, a Bank Law was enacted in March 1928 that greatly expanded government regulation and supervision over banking and encouraged an amalgamation and consolidation of Japanese banking that continued until the end of World War II. At that time, only 61 banks remained in operation along with several hundred small specialized financial institutions. In addition, concern for the stability of the financial system was reflected by strict segmentation of financial markets, a characteristic of Japanese finance that continues despite almost 15 years of financial liberalization. The extended regulatory control of the financial system limited the role of competition, and the consolidation of banking into fewer institutions made it easier for self-regulation and the cartellike structure of financial institutions to further restrain competitive forces.

5.3. Consolidation of Banking and War Mobilization in the 1930s

Developments in banking during the 1930s were characterized by a continuation of the concentration of banking activities into a small number of more closely supervised institutions and mobilization of the country's financial resources to support the military buildup.

The consolidation of banking into a smaller number of institutions started after the 1927 panic accelerated in the early 1930s. The share of ordinary bank deposits held by Japan's five largest banks at the end of 1922 (Mitsui, Mitubishi, Sumitomo, Yasuda, and Daiichi) amounted to 19%. The five-bank concentration percentage increased to 24% by year-end 1926, 31% by year-end 1927, and 41% by year-end 1932. The 1928 Bank Act forced smaller banks that could not meet their financial obligations to merge. As a result, commercial banks numbering 1,420 at the end of 1925 shrunk by two thirds to 466 by the end of 1935. The government also embarked on a program to improve industrial efficiency by streamlining industry. Many industrial cartels, mergers, and trusts of different entities came to dominate Japan's economy. The ultimate effect of these efforts was the creation of the *zaibatsu*, which means *business* (*zai*) and *groups* (*batsu*)—a type of holding company made up of manufacturing, trading, and financial entities under the control of wealthy families. Mitsui, Mitsubishi, Sumitomo, and Yasuda were the largest of the ten or so *zaibatsus*.

The government dramatically extended its influence over the economy with the passage of three economic control acts in the late 1930s. The Provisional Fund Control Act of 1937 required government approval to establish a company, increase capitalization, merge with another, change business goals, issue new stock, or to expand, renovate, or newly invest in plant and equipment. Government approval was also required to borrow from a financial institution or sell equities or bonds. In addition, autonomous controlling entities were established for each category of financial institution. Guidelines for granting government approval were established by categorizing industries according to their role in meeting military demand, their contribution to Japan's international balance of payments, and their productive capacity.

The National Mobilization Act of 1938 forced further consolidation of the banking system as part of an extensive governmental effort to mobilize the country's real and financial resources for war. The number of banks declined from 186 in 1931 to 61 by the end of the war.

In 1942, the Bank of Japan Act became law and further extended the influence of the government over the financial system. Prior to 1942, the BOJ had been regulated by a series of bylaws. The first article of the law stated that the BOJ would act to encourage the appropriate development of the Japanese economy. The central bank was to carry out its activities with reference to the policies of the government and would henceforth, be fully dependent on the government.

5.4. Post-World War II Developments Through the Early 1970s

Rebuilding the devastated nation, shifting industrial capacity for peacetime production, and establishing an industrial and financial framework that would support Japan's long-term goal of parity with the West were high priorities of the government after World War II. In addition, the U.S. Occupation played a role in influencing the restructuring of the economy and the financial system. In terms of restructuring the postwar financial and banking system, however, an important caveat needs to be emphasized. The structure of the financial system that emerged by the end of the U.S. Occupation was not a new creation; rather, it reflected characteristics and developments that were firmly in place both before and during the war. It is best to view the post-World War II financial system as the outcome of an evolutionary process rather than a discrete change from prewar Japan (Hamada and Horiuchi, 1987).

The U.S. Occupation played some role in shaping the postwar Japanese financial system; however, U.S. influence on balance did not significantly influence financial patterns that had already been firmly established.

The objectives of the U.S. Occupation can be summed up as the *democratization* of Japanese political institutions, society, and the economy. With regard to Japanese finance, the U.S. dissolved the *zaibatsu*, redefined the relationship between the BOJ and the government, and applied Glass–Steagall—type restrictions to bank activities in the securities market.

In December 1947, the Elimination of Excessive Concentration of Economic Power Law was passed to dissolve the *zaibatsu*. A total of 165 million shares of large companies valued at 7.57 million yen were to be sold to the public by 1951. These shares were sold through the Holding Company Liquidation Committee to the general public. Banks that held shares in *zaibatsu* companies were also required to sell their shares. The 1947 measure was originally intended to dissolve several large banks; however, the need for large banks led to a decision to exempt banking and trust institutions from the application of the 1947 law. Since interest rates were administratively set by the banks along with MOF participation, the 1947 Temporary Interest Rate Adjustment Law was introduced to exempt interest—rate determination from the Anti-Monopoly Law enacted April 1947.

The Public Finance Law of March 1947 prohibited the BOJ from direct acceptance of newly issued government bonds and prohibited government borrowing from the BOJ.

As part of the dissolution of the *zaibatsu*, the stock exchanges were reorganized to encourage broad distribution of equities. A 1948 revision of the 1947 Securities and Exchange Law known as Article 65 separated banking and securities activities. This provision was based on the Glass–Steagall restrictions imposed in the United States by the 1933 Banking Act.

There is little doubt that the U.S. Occupation had some impact on the Japanese financial system; however, one can easily exaggerate its importance. In general, U.S. Occupation policies consistent with well-established patterns of Japanese finance persisted after the end of the occupation, while those inconsistent with Japanese finance were modified over time.

For example, while the *zaibatsu* structure of trade and finance was dissolved, it was replaced by the main bank system—an organizational structure that has a number of characteristics in common with the *zaibatsu*. These were groups of businesses controlled by wealthy families. The largest and most powerful of the approximately ten groupings were Mitsui, Mitsubishi, Sumitomo, and Yasuda.

The period from the mid-1950s after the end of the U.S. Occupation just prior to the first oil-price shock in 1973 is referred to as the *high growth period* (HGP). During this period, real GNP grew at annual rates of around 10%. The banking and financial system continued their evolutionary development during the HGP in ways that were not markedly different than manifested in the prewar periods.

Specifically, the following characteristics came to define Japanese banking and finance: 1) specialization; 2) dominance of intermediation finance and, within intermediation finance, dominance of bank finance and negotiated as opposed to open-market transactions, 3) extensive regulatory constraints defined and enforced via administrative guidance and self-regulation; 4) focus on industrialization, export-led economic growth, international isolation, and high household saving; and 5) emphasis on collateralization as a way to limit bank risk at the micro level and limit inflation at the macro level. Let us briefly discuss each of these characteristics.

5.4.1. Specialization. The establishment of specialist institutions in different fields was thought to promote the utilization of their particular expertise. The further specialization of the financial system after the war and binding limits on entry of new financial institutions were a continuation of prewar trends. The city and regional banks were responsible for servicing the short-term needs of business, while the long-term capital requirements of business were addressed by establishing long-term credit banks and trust banks. A specialized institution was established to service foreign exchange transactions following the prewar Yokohoma Specie Bank. In addition to these specialist institutions that were privately owned and operated, government financial institutions, such as the Japan Development Bank and the Export-Import Bank of Japan, the Small Business Finance Corporation, and the Agriculture, Forestry, and Fisheries Finance Corporation were founded to supplement private-sector financing needs. The smaller financial institutions were reorganized into mutual banks (Sogo bank), credit associations (Shinkin bank), and others in order to provide capital to small and medium-size business while financial institutions specific to agriculture and forestry were established.

The principle of financial specialization was further implemented with the separation of commercial from investment banking by the Securities and Exchange Law of 1948 (particularly article 65) modeled after the 1933 Glass–Steagall Act in the United States. The separation of domestic from international finance was enforced by the 1949 Foreign Exchange Control Law.

5.4.2. Dominance of Indirect-Negotiated Financial Transactions and Customer Relationships: The Main Bank System. The emergence of the banking system as the center of postwar Japan was a continuation of prewar developments; however, banks assumed even more importance than they had during the prewar periods. The increased role of banks and the growing importance of customer relationships were the result of five considerations:

1. Banks were the only established institutional entity that could mobilize and allocate the extremely short supply of capital in postwar Japan. In addition, banks were the only institutions that had access to subsidized credit through the discount window of the BOJ. In contrast to the Federal Reserve, the BOJ encouraged banks to rely on discount window funds as a normal source of funding.
2. Negotiated transactions were better suited to the imperfect information environment in postwar Japan. Japan had never developed a financial disclosure framework, and long-term customer relationships were well suited to processing information in a capital-short environment.
3. While points 1 and 2 were sufficient to assure a prominent place for banks, the absence of government debt further assured that direct money and capital markets were unlikely to develop as an alternative funding source for business.
4. International financial isolation and restrictions over capital flows denied businesses offshore funding sources of any type.
5. The equity market was not a satisfactory source of funds.

The role of bank finance and, more importantly, the role of negotiated or customer relationships in postwar Japan cannot be underestimated. The particular form of the relationship in postwar Japan is known as the *main bank system*—a unique industrial structure that has little counterpart in the United States.

The main bank system is an evolutionary form of the prewar *zaibatsu*. The *zaibatsu* groups were officially disbanded during the Occupation, since they were viewed as perpetuating an uneven distribution of income, as anticompetitive, and as playing a role in Japan's militarism that eventually led to World War II. Even before the official end of the Occupation, however, the *zaibatsu* structure reemerged in a looser form in which the city banks were elevated to leadership status for six major groups: Mitsui, Mitsubishi, Sumitomo, Fuji (successor to Yasuda), Dai-chi Kangyo (1971 combination of Dai-chi and Kangyo), and Sanwa. The leadership role of the large banks was a natural outcome of the capital shortage and the fact that large banks had direct access to BOJ credit.

The company groups that emerged after the end of World War II are referred to as *keiretsu* or *affiliations of firms* and differ in four ways from the earlier *zaibatsu* groups. First, the large city banks play the leadership role in the most important *keiretsu* groupings, whereas in the *zaibatsu* groupings financial institutions played a subordinate position. Second, reciprocal shareholding among member firms including the city banks and other financial institutions in the group replaced ownership by families in the earlier *zaibatsu* groupings. Third, the *keiretsu* members are more loosely connected than previously, though the interconnections between members are still highly valued and constitute an important part of the industrial and financial structure of Japan. Fourth, the *keiretsu* groupings are much more varied than the *zaibatsu* groups. Major groupings employ a city bank in the leadership role; however, other groupings employ other financial institutions in the leadership role, and some groupings even exclude financial institutions.

5.4.3. Regulatory Constraints. The postwar Japanese financial system was highly regulated, with open-market-type forces severely constrained. Virtually all interest rates were subject to ceilings; financial institutions were segmented in terms of maturity, sources of funds, and asset diversification; entry was restricted in almost every financial market to both new Japanese institutions and to foreign financial institutions; and capital flows were subject to binding regulation. While there is little doubt that the postwar Japanese financial system was one of the most regulated, administratively controlled, and inflexible of the industrial nations, there is an important caveat.

The extensive regulatory environment and the absence of market-sensitive interest rates did not imply the absence of competition;[5] however, competition was nonprice oriented rather than price oriented. There existed intense competition among banks to establish customer relationships with new and dynamic businesses as well as to enhance relationships previously established. At the same time, this type of competition limited the efficiency of the market, since consumers of financial services were presented with limited choices, entry to financial markets was restricted, and key elements of the negotiated transactions between banks and their customers were not subject to market forces.

The regulatory framework of postwar Japan did witness a fundamental change in the form of regulation. In the prewar periods, the MOF played a much smaller role in defining the regulatory parameters; rather, the MOF permitted various forms of self-regulation by the market in the form of restrictions on portfolio activities, interest rates, and entry. These restrictions had tacit permission and encouragement from the government. For example, interest-rate restrictions were almost all established and enforced by the banks, since there was no legal framework for setting interest-rate ceilings with the exception of a usury law passed in 1877. Interest rates on both deposits and loans were established by agreement and self-regulation of the banks themselves. In 1901 the Osaka Bankers Association agreed to a common deposit-rate structure for their member institutions, which was followed in 1902 by the Tokyo Bankers Association. In 1918 the Tokyo Bill Exchange required all members to participate in the common deposit-rate structure. Loan rates were similarly agreed upon. These voluntary arrangements were also made with respect to other portfolio activities, and operated without fundamental change and had tacit government approval until the end of the war.

After the war, the government through the MOF assumed a more aggressive approach to defining and enforcing the regulatory parameters. The Temporary Adjustment of Rates of Interest Law enacted December 1947, for example, shifted responsibility for interest-rate regulation from the market to the government. Since 1947, the MOF has taken the lead in setting deposit-rate ceilings as well as other regulatory parameters; however, self-regulation remains an important part of Japanese financial regulation. A variety of self-imposed constraints on portfolio activities continue to persist in Japan, especially over bond undewriting activities, that continue to have tacit MOF approval.

5.4.4. Objectives of Financial Regulation. The financial system had always been concerned with industrialization and export-led economic growth, and much of the regulation that had evolved through the end of the war directed the financial system to support Japan's industrial objectives. This focus continued in the postwar period. Aside from the usual objectives of financial regulation to limit risk and provide a framework for controlling the money supply, financial regulation in Japan explicitly concerned itself with the following: 1) industrialization, 2) economic parity with the West, 3) export-led economic growth, 4) international isolation, and 5) high household saving.

Again, it should be kept in mind that both formal regulation by the MOF and self-regulation by the market combined to support these objectives. As a result of this overriding concern with industrialization and export-led economic growth, consumer and mortgage credit constituted a small portion of the flow of funds compared to other industrialized economies.

5.4.5. Collateralization. The issuance of earthquake bills without regard to collateralization and the subsequent banking problems in the late 1920s strongly reinforced the attitude by both the regulatory authorities and the banks of the need to limit bank risk. As a result, the principle of collateralization has played a major role in the flow of funds. Every bank loan requires some form of explicit colleralization, and this requirement until recently had even been extended to domestic bond placements.

This concern with collateralization is reminiscent of the real-bills doctrine that required every bank loan to be supported by goods in process of production. And like the real-bill doctrine, the collateralization principle in Japan had both a micro and a macro implication. At the micro level, collateralization was supposed to limit system risk by reducing individual bank credit risk; at the macro level, collateralization was supposed to make it more likely that the money supply would match the needs of trade and reduce the possibility of inflation.

Japan has experienced a number of inflationary periods with severe economic consequences, and as a result places a higher concern on controlling inflation than is found in many other industrialized economies. This is clearly reflected by some of the reforms enacted in the early postwar years. The Public Finance Law of 1947 and establishment of the Policy Board of the BOJ in 1949 were designed to limit the potential for inflation. The former banned the issuance of government bonds and the latter ensured the "democratic" administration of monetary policy by including representatives from the BOJ, MOF, and financial institutions on the Policy Board of the BOJ. The potential for inflation was further reduced when the *Dodge line* was adopted in 1949 on the recommendation of the Detroit banker Joseph Dodge. The Dodge line committed the government to a balanced budget. While small amounts of government debt were issued after 1965, the Dodge line restraints held firm until central government deficits after 1975 required the issuance of large amounts of government debt.

6. "Uniqueness" of Japanese Banking and Finance Prior to the Initiation of Financial Liberalization

The economic and technological environment changed radically in the mid-1970s, which in turn initiated a transition in Japanese finance and banking that continues to the present. The transition has fundamentally changed the role of banking; however, before focusing on the most recent evolution of banking and finance in Japan, we need to clarify some views that were widely held until a few years ago about Japanese finance.

First, was Japan's financial system during the HGP unique in terms of the dominance of indirect finance, business "overborrowing," bank "overloan," and uneven endowment of funds among financial institutions? The view that these characteristics[6] made Japan's financial system unique has been widely held in Japan and later argued in English by Suzuki (1980). Second, did the absence of flexible prices and open markets render the HGP structure of banking and finance incapable of neoclassical analysis? Does one need to adopt an "eclectic" approach, as suggested by Wallich and Wallich (1976)? The inability to use neoclassical profit maximization analysis to understand Japanese finance was widely held in Japan, and Wallich and Wallich's contribution influenced many English readers.

Both of these views are part of the general view that Japanese finance is unique and unlike any of the financial structures found among the industrialized nations. While these views are no longer widely held, it will be useful to briefly discuss each one, since they have played an important role in attempts to study Japanese finance.

6.1. Four "Unique" Characteristics of Japanese Finance

It is not clear whether the four phenomena—dominance of indirect finance, business overborrowing, bank overloan, any uneven endowment of funds among banks—are themselves unique, a reflection of unique characteristics of the activities of corporations and financial institutions, a reflection of the specific regulatory parameters imposed on the financial system, or some combination of influences. In addition, it is not obvious that the four phenomena are only to be found in Japan. U.S. money center banks, for example, have been net borrowers of federal funds since the mid-1960s, while regional financial institutions have allocated their uncommitted risk capital in the federal funds market.

Suzuki (1980) has offered the most well-known interpretation of the dominance of these forces. Suzuki argues that the four financial phenomena are intimately linked to an economy whose growth is fueled by capital spending and exports and that such phenomena are a natural outcome when interest rates are held artificially low and when the free, cross-border flow of capital is restricted. If correct, this view suggests that the uniqueness of Japan's financial structure is the result of regulatory parameters that, in the case of restrictions on capital flows, cannot be regarded as unique to Japan.

Despite the plausibility of the above argument and the wide acceptance that Japan achieved much of its economic success by artificially keeping interest rates low, there is reason to doubt that a policy of artificially low interest rates was a characteristic of the Japanese financial system during the HGP.

What is actually meant by a policy of maintaining artificially low interest rates? This question is less clear than as it first appears. Neither is it apparent in what manner artificially low interest rates are related to the high economic growth. A policy of holding interest rates artifically low is widely understood as 1) using noneconomic measures to keep interest rates at a level below market equilibrium and 2) employing noneconomic methods to allocate funds (i.e., credit rationing) to deal with the excess demand for funds arising under such circumstances. What is the relationship between either policy and high economic growth, and how would each policy promote economic expansion?

Macroeconomic reasoning suggests that the combined use of easy monetary and balanced fiscal policies could maintain effective demand at a level equal to productive capacity and to incline the structure of effective demand towards investment, thereby furthering capital formation. In the postwar economic climate of Japan, however, policies based on this reasoning would almost certainly generate inflationary monetary growth. Therefore, a policy of maintaining artificially low interest rates or rates set below market levels via interest-rate regulations and administrative guidance over financial institutions was adopted to keep interest rates lower (thereby stimulating investment) and to control the money supply (liquidity) at the same time (Tachi, 1963).

Not all observers agree with this scenario. Some argue that since artificially low interest rates are held at a level below the point of market equilibrium, the amount of savings, and consequently the amount of investment, will fall below their potential under free market conditions over the long term (Kosai and Ogino, 1980). This is particularly true when savings are elastic relative to interest rates over the long run. In short, the savings rate would decline with artificially lowered interest rates. Therefore, as long as the marginal capital coefficient operates independently of the existence of a policy of maintaining artificially low interest rates, the pace of economic growth will be slower when such a policy is employed than under free market conditions. In other words, a policy of maintaining artificially low interest rates actually limited the potential growth of the Japanese economy.

It is not even clear that interest rates were maintained below market levels, since effective interest rates were higher than reported rates. Compensating balance requirements were high during the HGP, so effective loan rates may not have been maintained at an artificially low level. The so-called unique characteristics of Japanese finance—dominance of indirect finance, overborrowing of business corporations, overloan of banks, and the uneven endowment of funds availability among city and regional banks—are not necessarily unique characteristics of the Japanese financial system. To the extent that they reflect regulatory constraints, the uniqueness of the Japanese financial system is thereby reduced, since many of the same type of constraints were present in other countries. While much attention has been devoted to maintaining low interest rates as a unique characteristic of Japanese finance, it is not clear how this contributed to economic growth.

Whether the Japanese financial system, particularly during the HGP, was unique or not cannot be easily answered by focusing on structural issues such as artificially low interest rates or restrictions on capital flows. Rather, two approaches are inseparable in considering the distinctiveness of the Japanese finance: structural issues and issues concerning the behavior of market participants. Stated another way, the second issue focuses on whether the portfolio choices of Japanese financial institutions, corporations, and households could be viewed as being particularly distinctive in Japan. We now turn to a consideration of this issue with regard to the main bank system.

6.2. Inappropriateness of the Neoclassical Analysis to Japanese Finance

It is now widely accepted that Japanese portfolio behavior during the HGP can be understood as rational behavior subject to explicit and implicit constraints. The apparent inflexibility of interest rates in the HGP and the lack of open markets does not imply an absence of profit-maximizing behavior or the need to adopt an eclectic approach to understanding Japanese finance during this period.

Risk assessment in Japan has traditionally relied on the type of information about borrowers that emerges from long-term customer relationships between financial institutions and demanders of financial services. In such an environment, inflexible interest rates and the lack of open markets are consistent with rational economic behavior whose objective is to distribute risk and provide liquidity in an imperfect information and capital shortage setting (Elston, 1981; Horiuchi, 1989; Horiuchi, Packer, and Fukuda, 1988; Nakatani, 1984; Osano and Tsutsui, 1985; Sheard, 1984).

The financial system reflects this particular approach to finance in two important respects. The flow of funds is dominated first by transactions based on negotiated or customer relationships rather than open-market transactions, and second by the role of the main bank system in postwar finance.

There are major economic reasons for the existence of *keiretsu* groupings. They reduce the overall level of risk through mutual support of financial, service, and product interdependence. They allow each member access to a wide variety of financial and nonfinancial services because of the diverse membership. Low-risk members can borrow from banks and simultaneously act as intermediaries to the higher-risk members by providing trade credit. In fact, trade credit in Japan as a percent of total financial assets has been over three times as large as in the United States in the twentieth century (Goldsmith, 1985, p. 155). The city banks in the company groups also provide a substitute for an extensive and reliable financial disclosure framework that did not exist during the HGP.

The *keiretsu* groups are designed to achieve long-term and stable economic performance for its members, reflecting an important element of Japanese culture. Research suggests that the major objective of the members of the group is not high profits per se, but stable profitable performance over the long run based on a set of explicit and implicit mutual insurance contracts between members (Nakatani, 1984). This inturn enhances the strength of the group over time.

7. Japanese Finance in Transition: Mid-1970s to Present

The most recent changes in finance and banking in Japan can best be understood by considering three aspects of the process: 1) the catalysts that initiated the process, 2) the market and regulatory responses to the catalysts, and 3) the form of the process.

7.1. Catalysts for Financial Liberalization

During the HGP period, the financial system effectively transferred the large surpluses of the household to the corporate sector. Monetary policy through most of the period was constrained by maintenance of the exchange rate of 360 yen per dollar. However, in the late 1960s monetary policy shifted to a more continuous expansionary mode to accommodate government desires to maintain high growth into the 1970s and to offset the effects of the "Nixon shocks." The expansionary monetary policy, however, resulted in high inflation that reached over 20% in 1973, at which time the BOJ initiated a tight monetary policy.

The effects of the tight monetary policy, coincided with the first oil-price shock. The economy thus experienced a severe disinflationary process that eventually brought the inflation rate down to about 7% in 1975. The long-run real performance of the economy, however, was fundamentally altered by the oil-price shock.

The natural growth path of real GNP shifted downward after 1973, which in turn shifted the established flow of funds patterns. The corporate sector deficit declined by almost 50% while the central government deficit increased by almost 100% by 1975 (table 7-1). The household surplus remained largely unchanged. The shift in the flow of funds set into motion a number of forces that initiated the transition of Japan's financial system to a more flexible, open, and competitive system than had existed during the HGP.

Funding the deficits presented the MOF with a difficult problem in the context of a financial system without open money and capital markets (Cargill and Royama, 1988; Feldman, 1986). Previously, government debt had been placed in the market by selling the debt to a captured syndicate of financial institutions and securities companies at above market prices. The MOF restricted the development of a secondary market by prohibiting financial institutions from reselling the debt. The financial institutions were willing to absorb the debt, since they anticipated that it would be purchased at prices generating a positive capital gain within one year by the BOJ. The securities companies were willing to absorb the debt, since they could use the government bonds as the basis for the unofficial *gensaki* market. Most importantly, the amount of debt prior to 1975 was small, since the central government budget was essentially balanced.

The situation drastically changed after 1975, when the debt placements become increasingly larger each year and market participants resisted MOF's efforts to place the debt at abovemarket prices. This situation established a quid pro quo relationship between the financial system and the MOF in which market participants required financial liberalization as the price for absorbing the government debt.

Banks became advocates for liberalization because they had lost market share in the total flow of funds. The decline in the corporate sector deficit reduced the dependence of the corporate sector on bank credit. Thus, banks saw financial liberalization as a way to reestablish and to expand market share in the total flow of funds.

Securities companies become advocates for liberalization because the development of open money and capital markets and internationalization of finance would offer new opportunities to expand their role in the financial system.

The corporate sector became an advocate for liberalization because it experienced an increase in liquidity after 1973 as a result of a slower rate of investment. In addition, it became less dependent on the banking system and found that it no longer needed the large compensating balances typically required by banks during the 1960s and early 1970s (Takeda, 1985). Thus, the corporate sector saw liberalization as a way to enhance profits and diversify its activities into financial asset management.

The household sector became an advocate for liberalization because its willingness to hold a limited set of financial assets at regulated interest rates was no longer being compensated by high rates of real income growth. In addition, the aging of the population placed more emphasis on establishing a wider range of financial assets for retirement in the absence of an extensive government-supported retirement system. However, the household sector was not in the same political position as the banks, securities companies, or the corporations to influence the liberalization process. Thus, despite the household sector's advocacy of financial liberalization, its influence was minor compared to the other sectors.

The catalysts for financial reform in Japan thus emerged from the real sector in the sense that the oil-price shock fundamentally altered the growth potential of the economy, with corresponding shifts in the flow of funds patterns. Inflation and high rates of interest played a relatively minor role compared to their importance in the United States.

Two other catalysts added momentum to the financial reform process, but in less direct ways. First, the abandonment of the fixed exchange rate after 1973 placed increasing pressure on Japan to liberalize domestic finance. Japan's role in international trade and the flexible exchange-rate system were incompatible with a rigidly regulated domestic financial structure and the absence of open money and capital markets. The requirements of a flexible exchange-rate system would have eventually required financial liberalization (Suzuki, 1986), though liberalization would not have occurred as rapidly in the absence of the decline in income and the corresponding shift in the flow of funds. Second, in the early 1980s, U.S. pressure on Japan to "internationalize" the yen, increase foreign financial institution access, and increase the pace of domestic liberalization also provide a catalyst for further reforms (Frankel, 1984).

7.2. Market and Regulatory Response to the Catalysts

In contrast to the situation in the United States, regulatory rather than market innovations have dominated the reform process in Japan. Regulatory reform has also been concerned with a much broader range of issues, institutions, and markets than in the United States. Cargill and Royama (1988, appendix) provide a detailed chronology of regulatory changes that have been made from 1975 to 1987[7] and are categorized according to specific aspects of the financial and monetary structure they directly impact: money market, interbank market, capital market, new services and financial assets, interest-rate liberalization, internationalization, and monetary policy. Together, regulatory changes directed toward these areas have transformed the Japanese financial system from a rigid and inflexible structure to one that now is more flexible and competitive than previously.

The money market has expanded during the past decade and now includes *gensaki*, large CDs, Euroyen deposits, yen-denominated bankers acceptances, commercial paper, and six-month Treasury bills. Money market interest rates are market determined, and money markets have wide market participation.

The interbank market has been a focus of separate regulatory reform. The BOJ in 1978 ended the quotation system, which limited interbank rate movements, and has permitted increasing access to the market. Debate continues as to whether the BOJ continues to exercise administrative guidance over the market; however, interbank rates are more flexible than previously, and the BOJ regards the market as liberalized.

The capital market has expanded significantly as a result of the growth of government debt. Both the new and secondary issue markets have expanded. The corporate bond market, however, has not expanded nearly as much: collateralization requirements limit the flexibility of corporate bond issues; cartellike agreements among banks and securities companies impose a variety of restrictions on bond issues that limit their flexibility as a funding source;[8] large corporations continue to value

Table 7-4. Percentage of Japanese Company Fund Raising in Foreign Capital Markets, 1977–1986

Year	Percent
1977	17.1%
1978	18.0
1979	24.9
1980	26.4
1981	28.1
1982	36.3
1983	45.5
1984	47.3
1985	50.7
1986	45.7

Source: Figures provided by Horiuchi (1989, p. 32).

customer relationships with city banks; and corporations can now borrow in foreign markets, which they have resorted to increasingly (table 7-4). The equity market, despite being the largest in the world in terms of capitalization, is still not regarded as a flexible source of funds given extensive interfirm holdings of equity among firms in the main bank system structure (Nakatani, 1984).

A variety of new financial services and assets have been introduced during the past decade. Most of the money market instruments have been introduced since 1979. Financial institutions have been permitted to issue combination-type deposits, resident foreign-currency deposits, and money market certificates whose interest rate is tied to the CD rate. Investment companies have been authorized to issue investment funds of various types.

The internationalization of domestic finance became official policy in 1980 when the Foreign Exchange and Foreign Trade Control Law was amended to incorporate the principle of liberalized capital flows. As a result, a large number of restrictions on the inflow and outflow of capital have been relaxed since 1980, and there now exists a close interface between domestic money market and international interest rates. Foreign institutions have been give greater access, and foreign securities companies have been admitted to the Tokyo Stock Exchange. In December 1986, the Tokyo International Banking Facility opened; however, further changes in tax and regulatory conditions will be needed to render this offshore facility attractive to foreign capital (Rosenbluth, 1989); for example, securities activities are generally prohibited in the offshore market. While the yen does not yet play a role in international finance consistent with Japan's role in international trade, there is little doubt that the yen will become a more widely used international reserve and investment asset, Japan having now become a major world financial center.

Interest-rate liberalization has occurred in selected areas of the financial system. Interest rates are essentially unregulated on money market instruments, the new-issue market for medium- and long-term government bonds, the secondary bond market, the six-month Treasury bill, foreign-currency deposits, money market mutual funds, and large-denomination time deposits. In addition, loan interest-rate restrictions have been relaxed. At the same time, deposit-rate ceilings still affect about 70% as of 1989 of the total bank deposits; however, the ceilings have been adjusted more frequently. Regulatory authorities have accepted the principle of first liberalizing interest rates on large deposits, with small deposit liberalization to be considered in the future.

Monetary control-related issues such as reserve requirements have not been a major issue in the reform process of Japan, as they have been in the United States. At the same time, the BOJ has been required to adjust its operating procedures in response to the changing financial environment as part of its strategy to maintain low and stable inflation. In 1978 the BOJ began announcing money supply projections for each quarter about one or two weeks before the quarter. These are not annual monetary aggregate targets as employed by the Federal Reserve, but are projections or forecasts of future money supply growth to highlight the BOJ's concern about the money supply and price stability. In 1979 the BOJ added CDs to the official money supply measures. The BOJ has gradually shifted emphasis from credit allocation controls such as "window guidance" to instruments more in tune with a liberalized financial environment. In particular, the BOJ has made efforts to develop open-market operations as a major policy instrument to better take advantage of the growing links between interest rates and expenditures created by financial liberalization.

7.3. Process of Financial Liberalization

There are three distinct characteristics of the financial reform process in Japan that have been extensively discussed elsewhere (Cargill and

Royama, 1988): 1) the process has been administratively directed and incremental; 2) the process has been smooth and lacking the types of disruptions in the financial system common in the United States during the 1970s and early 1980s; 3) the process has been characterized by regulatory rather than market innovations and lacks the intense regulatory-market conflicts common in the United States.

8. Financial Liberalization and Negotiated-Based Intermediation Finance

The transition of Japanese finance can best be thought of as a process of securitization[9] in the sense that a shift is occurring from bilateral, negotiated, or customer-based ways of obtaining liquidity to methods that rely on the exchange of assets for liquidity in open, less regulated, and wide-participation markets. This is the basic nature of the financial transition in Japan that had its origin in the growth of central government debt after 1975 and the associated growth of the primary and secondary government securities market.

The securitization process in the sense of the term as used in Japan has been manifested by several major developments since the mid-1970s: 1) development of markets for CDs, bankers' acceptances, commercial paper with unregulated interest rates; 2) willingness of the regulatory authorities to adjust regulated interest rates on deposits in line with market interest rates as well as to remove ceilings on selected deposits; 3) relaxation of restrictions on the inflow and outflow of capital, which has brought about a close interface between domestic and international interest rates; 4) initial steps toward establishment of a short-term government securities market; and 5) changes in monetary policy that now emphasize open-market operations based on the interest rate-expenditure channel compared to pre-1975 monetary policy techniques (Fukui, 1986; Suzuki, 1986).

The effects of the securitization process can be seen in four areas: 1) decline in the indirect finance ratio since 1975; 2) decline in the market share of the banking system, 3) decline in the role of negotiated transactions in the flow of funds; and 4) decline in the role of the main bank system.

It may be too early to predict further declines in the indirect finance ratio and, in any event, the securitization process does not necessarily mean the demise of financial institutions—only a change in their nature of the relationship to borrowers.

In contrast, there is no doubt that securitization implies the decline of negotiated transactions, which in fact has taken place, as illustrated in figure 7-1. Related to the overall decline in negotiated transactions, securitization has also reduced the role of banks in the flow of funds (figure 7-3) and weakened the main bank system. Horiuchi, Packer, and Fukuda (forthcoming) and Horiuchi (1989) found that the percentage of funds obtained from the main bank by a major corporation (defined as a company listed in the first section of the Tokyo Stock Exchange) has exhibited a general downward trend since 1962.

The securitization process has had fundamental effects on the structure and banking and finance; however, the transition has been fairly steady and gradual since 1975. We should not expect to see dramatic changes in Japanese finance at any one time. The incremental approach has been effective in Japan because the successful price-stabilization policies of the BOJ has maintained a small gap between regulated and unregulated interest rates (Cargill and Hutchison, 1988).

9. Implications of Financial Liberalization and Securitization in Japan

The securitization of finance in Japan has raised a number of issues regarding banks and other financial institutions. Three of the more important issues are 1) conflicts between specialization of financial activities and securitization; 2) increased risks for individual financial institutions and, hence, implications of the securitization process for system risk; and 3) influence of global financial markets on Japanese banks and other financial institutions.

9.1. Specialization and Securitization

Discussions are presently underway by the MOF to deal with conflicts between the traditional institutional specialization of finance in Japan and the developing securitization process, which by its nature requires ease of substitution between different financial channels. The Financial System Research Council (1987) has considered a number of possibilities and recently (May 1989) identified five possible policies that could be taken in the near future to restructure the Japanese financial system, all of which would be designed to reduce the degree of specialization.

The possible options are as follows: 1) to permit mutual entry of existing financial firms (banks, securities houses, trust banks, long-term credit banks, and so on) in each other's market area; 2) to permit entry to other industries in the form of subsidiary entities; 3) to establish new financial institutions with wide-ranging portfolio powers subject to specific, but very loose restriction; 4) to permit bank holding-company organizations; and 5) to permit universal banking.

The five options were considered in light of the following generally accepted principals: 1) enhanced competitiveness in the financial service industry is a necessary condition for increasing the availability of assets and services to the economy; 2) the financial structure must be internationally compatible with other financial structures, especially those of major industrial powers; 3) the financial structure must reduce the potential for unfair trade practices; and 4) the financial system must be able to manage individual institution risk in such a manner as not to increase system risk.

In terms of these considerations, options 1, 4, and 5 were dropped from the list of the feasible future trajectories for Japan's financial system. Options 1 and 5 were considered too radical of a change in Japan's financial structure, and option 4 was eliminated because Japanese law does not permit holding-company structures. The Financial System Research Council released its report May 1989 (in Japanese only at the time of this writing) to be followed by extensive discussions on how to implement the recommendations. The Council then will make recommendations to the MOF as to the structural changes required in the 1990s.

9.2. System Risk

In the past, Japanese financial institutions have operated with limited portfolio flexibility and therefore have had limited opportunities to assume risk. As the transition toward securitization and open markets continues, however, individual institutions are faced with new portfolio choices that involve more risk that is less susceptible to assessment than previously: interest-rate risk, credit risk, liquidity risk, and exchange-rate risk. Pettway, Tapley, and Yamada (1988), for example, found evidence that bank risk measured by bank stock price variation has increased in the past decade. Credit risk, in particular, has become a more serious problem as a result of lending in international markets and the decline in the importance of the main bank system. The close relationship between banks and their borrowers and the main bank's role as spokesperson for the business provided an efficient forum for assessing and monitoring credit risk. As this system declines in importance, publicly available financial disclosure frameworks become more important.

While regulatory authorities have recognized the need to monitor and regulate financial institution risk more than previously, little has been accomplished beyond the discussion stage. In this respect, there has been a considerable amount of debate between the BOJ and the MOF over deposit insurance. Not entirely unexpectedly, the debate concerns regulatory turf as much as it does substantive issues regarding government deposit guarantees.

The deposit insurance system was established in 1971 and modeled after the U.S. system, with some notable exceptions: membership is compulsory for almost all private financial institutions that offer banking services; private financial institutions have management representation on the Deposit Insurance Corporation (DIC); and the DIC is capitalized in equal parts by the government, the BOJ, and private financial institutions. The MOF dominates the DIC. Even though the Vice-Governor of the BOJ is appointed the Governor of the DIC, other officers and management appointments must be approved by the MOF. And while the DIC is permitted to borrow from the BOJ, such borrowing is subject to approval by the MOF.

Government deposit guarantees have not received the amount of attention they have in the United States, for three reasons. First, there have been very few failures of financial institutions in Japan during the postwar period. A few Sogo banks have encountered viability problems; however, the MOF and the BOJ moved quickly to merge them with stronger institutions as well as to provide direct management of their operations. No losses were experienced by depositors, however. Second, the small number of banks in Japan make it relatively easier for regulatory authorities to monitor risk and reduce the probability of being surprised. Third, Japanese regulatory authorities are far more willing to intervene in the operations of any financial institution they perceive as experiencing problems compared to regulators in the United States. In particular, the BOJ under pressure form the MOF in 1965 bailed out Yamaichi Securities company through the discount window.

9.3. Globalization of Finance

Increased internationalization has been a major feature of Japan's financial system during the past decade. Some of the indices of internationalization include the following:

1. Currently, foreign-exchange transactions in Tokyo exceed those in the United States, and Japan has assumed second place behind London in terms of foreign-exchange transactions.
2. Despite the unattractive tax and regulatory constraints, the Tokyo offshore market has grown rapidly since its establishment. As of year-end 1986, the Tokyo offshore market held assets of $94 billion dollars, equal to about one third those of the New York's International Banking Facility. By year-end 1987, however, the two markets were about equal in size, and by year-end 1988, the Tokyo market exceeded the New York market; however, much of this volume represents fund movements between banks (Rosenbluth, 1989, p. 89).
3. Japanese banks and other financial institutions are far more dependent on international activities than previously. This is especially the case for the city banks and other large financial institutions. For example, all banks (city banks, long-term credit banks, and trust banks) received 42.4% of their revenue from international activities in 1987, and the largest of these institutions had an even higher dependence on international activities.
4. Japanese financial institutions have expanded activities to a number of overseas markets. International banking business in the past was confined to supporting Japanese trade in manufactured products; however, these institutions now engage in a wide variety of activities in overseas markets. At the same time, the Japanese financial system has become more open to foreign entities. After 1985, the number of foreign institutions operating in Japan increased greatly, as did the number of Japanese institutions operating abroad.

The globalization of finance has reinforced the securitization process in two ways:

1. Globalization has brought increasing pressure to establish an open short-term government securities market that would provide a low-risk short-term financial asset in which to hold yen. The MOF in 1987 began to issue six-month Treasury bills as a step toward a short-term securities market. However, there is considerable debate about the speed with which such a market will be established in Japan. The MOF has shown considerable resistance to a short-term market because at present, the BOJ purchases almost all short-term government debt at subsidized prices.
2. Globalization has forced the regulatory authorities to place banks and other institutions conducting international transactions on a more comparable basis with institutions in other countries. In July 1987,

the Bank for International Settlements established uniform capital ratios that all major banks in the G-10 countries and Luxembourg must achieve by the end of 1992.

10. Concluding Comments

The Japanese financial system has relied extensively on negotiated financial transactions with implicit pricing, and less on open-market transactions with explicit pricing, than has been the case in the United States. In the mid-1970s, however, new economic and technological forces generated pressure on the Japanese financial system to increase the role of open-market-based financial transactions. As a result, the financial system is now more open and more competitive in terms of price competition than previously.

The transition of finance has reduced the role of the banking system in the flow of funds in two ways. First, banks now provide a somewhat smaller percentage of funds to the nonfinancial sectors of the economy than previously. Second, there is evidence that the main bank system is less important than it was even a decade ago.

Whether commercial banks can maintain or enhance their market share remains uncertain. Regulatory authorities are currently in the process of deciding fundamental structural questions about the future financial structure. If the past regulatory attitude is any indication, the banking system will be allowed considerable flexibility in securities markets that will at least permit them to maintain current market-share levels.

In any event, there is little doubt that even if banks remain a dominant force in Japanese finance, the role of negotiated transactions will continue to decline. In this respect, Japanese finance is converging to the type of open-market environment of the United States. Nevertheless, Japan's financial transition is a slow process and despite all of the rhetoric toward competition, the financial structure is likely to evolve into something much less competitive than in the United States.

Acknowledgments

Professor Royama is a member of the Securities Exchange Council at the Ministry of Finance and chair of the Ad Hoc Committee on Research of the Fundamental Issues in the Securities Market. The authors express appreciation to George Benston and George Kaufman for comments on an earlier draft of this chapter; however, they are responsible for any remaining errors.

Notes

1. This section draws from Cargill and Royama (1988, pp. 21–32).
2. The Bank of Tokyo is specifically authorized by the Foreign Exchange Control Law as of 1954 to be principally engaged in foreign-exchange transactions and international finance; however, the Bank of Tokyo is now generally regarded as a city bank, and the majority of banks are permitted to conduct foreign-exchange transactions.
3. Feldman (1986), Hayashi (1985), and Suzuki (1987) provide greater detail on Japan's PSS.
4. This section is taken from Cargill (1989).
5. Cargill (1988) and Sakakibara and Feldman (1983) provide detail on these points.
6. While the indirect finance ratio concept is familiar, the other tems with respect to Japan are less familiar. Overborrowing refers to the exceedingly small amounts of equity capital and an excess of borrowed funds in the capital structure of borrowers, primarily corporations. Overloan refers to the dependence of financial institutions, particularly the major banks, on borrowing from the BOJ. Stated another way, Japanese financial institutions were exceedingly illiquid because deposit growth could not match credit demand. The uneven endowments of funds availability refers to the situation where the large financial institutions (e.g., the city banks) were perpetually short of funds and had to borrow from other financial institutions in the interbank market to make up the difference. These concepts are discussed in greater detail by Suzuki (1980).
7. A summary of more recent liberalization efforts is provided by Choy (1988).
8. Horiuchi (1989) provides a concise discussion of market-imposed constraints on domestic bond issuance.
9. The term *securitization* is used somewhat differently than in the United States. Securitization in Japan refers to a major restructuring of financial flows rather than merely the extension of bank activities into the securities markets.

References

Cargill, Thomas F. *Central Bank Independence and Regulatory Responsibilities: the Bank of Japan and the Federal Reserve*. Saloman center for the Study of Financial Institutions and Markets, New York University, 1989.

Cargill, Thomas F. "Competition and the Transition of Finance in Japan and the United States," *Journal of Comparative Economics* 12 (September 1988), 380–400.

Cargill, Thomas F. and Michael M. Hutchison. "The Bank of Japan's Response to Macroeconomic and Financial Change," in Hang-Sheng Cheng (ed.), *Monetary Policy in Pacific Basin Countires*. Norwell, MA: Kluwer Academic Publishers, 1988.

Cargill, Thomas F. and Shoichi Royama. *The Transition of Finance in Japan and the United States: A Comparative Perspective*. Stanford, CA: Hoover Institution Press, 1988.

Choy, Jon. "Financial Liberalization in Japan: Update and Impact—Two Part Report 6A and 6B," Japan Economic Institute, Washington, DC, 1988.

Elston, C.D. "The Financing of Japanese Industry," Bank of England, *Quarterly Bulletin* (December 1981), 510–518.

Feldman, Robert Alan. *Japanese Financial Markets: Deficits, Dilemmas, and Deregulation*. Cambridge, MA: The MIT Press, 1986.

Feldman, Robert Alan. "The Future of Japanese Banking," presented at the Japan Economic Seminar, Brookings Institution, Washington, DC, November 18, 1988.

Financial System Research Council. *Report on Specialized Financial Institution System in Japan*, December 1987. Translated into English by Federal of Bankers Associations of Japan, Tokyo.

Frankel, Jeffrey, A. *The Yen/Dollar Agreement: Liberalizing Japanese Capital Markets*. Washington, DC: Institute for International Economics, 1984.

Fukui, Toshihiko. "Recent Developments of the Short-Term Money Market in Japan and Changes in Monetary Control Technics and Procedures by the Bank of Japan," Special Paper No. 130, Research and Statistics Department, Bank of Japan, Tokyo, 1986.

Goldsmith, Raymond W. *National Balance Sheets*. Chicago: University of Chicago Press, 1985.

Gurley, John G and Edward S. Shaw. *Money in a Theory of Finance*. Washington, DC: Brookings Institution, 1960.

Hamada, Koichi and Akiyoshi Horiuchi. "The Political Economy of the Financial Market," in Kozo Yamamura and Yasukichi Yasuba (eds.), *The Political Economy of Japan, Vol. I, The Domestic Transformation*. Stanford, CA: Stanford University Press, 1987.

Hayashi, Toshihiko. "The Postal Savings System in Japan: A Roadblock to Interest Deregulation?" Working Paper E-85-10, Hoover Institution, Stanford University, 1985.

Horiuchi, Akiyoshi. "Informational Properties of the Japanese Financial System," *Japan and the World Economy* 1 (1989),

Horiuchi, Akiyoshi, F. Packer, and S. Fukuda. "What Role has the 'Main Bank' Played in Japan?" *Journal of Japanese and International Economics* 2 (1988), 159–180.

Horne, James. *Japan's Financial Markets*. Sydney, Australia: Allen & Unwin, 1985.

Kosai, Yutaka and Yoshitaro Ogino. *The Contemporary Japanese Economy*. London: Macmillan, 1980.

Nakatani, Iwao. "The Economic Role of Financial Corporate Grouping," in Masahiko Aoki (ed.), *The Economic Analysis of the Japanese Firm*. Amsterdam: Elsevier Science Publishers, 1984.

Osano, H. and Y. Tsutsui. "Implicit Contract in the Japanese Bank Loan Market," *Journal of Financial and Quantitative Analysis* 20 (1985), 221–229.

Ostrom, Douglas. "Japanese Banks in the United States," Japan Economic Institute, January 22, 1988.

Pettway, Richard H., T. Craig Tapley, and Takeshi Yamada. "The Impacts of Financial Deregulation Upon Trading Efficiency and the Levels of Risk and Return of Japanese Banks," *Financial Review* 23 (August 1988), 243–268.

Rosenbluth, Frances McCall. *Financial Politics in Contemporary Japan*. Ithaca, NY: Cornell University Press, 1989.

Royama, Shoichi. *Financial Liberalization*. Tokyo: Tokyo University Press, 1986. [In Japanese].

Sakakibara, Eisuke and Robert Alan Feldman. "The Japanese Financial System in Comparative Perspective," *Journal of Comparative Economics* 7 (March 1983), 1–24.

Sheard, Paul. "Financial Corporate Grouping, Cross-Subsidization in the Private Sector and the Industrial Adjustment Process in Japan, Parts 1 and 2," Discussion Paper Series, Osaka University, August 1985.

Suzuki, Yoshio. *Money and Banking in Contemporary Japan*. New Haven, CT: Yale University Press, 1980.

Suzuki, Yoshio. *Money, Finance, and Macroeconomic Performance in Japan*. New Haven, CT: Yale University Press, 1986.

Suzuki, Yoshio (ed.). *The Japanese Financial System*. Oxford: Clarendon Press, 1987.

Suzuki, Yoshio. "Japanese Monetary Policy under the Floating Exchange Rate Regime," working paper, Bank of Japan, 1988.

Takeda, Masahiko. "A Theory of Loan Determination in Japan," *Monetary and Economic Studies*, Bank of Japan, Institute for Monetary and Economic Studies, 3 (May 1985), 71–114.

Tachi, Ryuichiro. "Zaisei kin'yu seisaku" ["Monetary and Fiscal Policies"], in *Sengo nihon no keizai seicho* [*Postwar Japanese Economic Growth*]. Tokyo: Iwanami Shoten, 1963.

Teranishi, Juro. "Financial System and the Industrialization of Japan: 1900–1970," paper presented at the Money Markets and Monetary Policy in the Pacific Basin Conference sponsored by the Federal Reserve Bank of San Francisco, July 26–27, 1990.

Wallich, Henry C. and Mable I. Wallich. "Banking and Finance," in Hugh Patrick and Henry Rosovsky (ed.), *Asia's New Giant*. Washington, DC: The Brookings Institution, 1976.

Williamson, O.E. *Markets and Hierarchies: Analysis and Antitrust Implications*. New York: Free Press, 1975.

Zimmerman, Gary C. "The Growing Presence of Japanese Banks," *Weekly Letter*, Federal Reserve Bank of San Francisco, October 28, 1988.

Appendix: Chronology of Major Changes in the Japanese Financial and Monetary Environment, 1975–1990

This chronology is based on information provided by the Economic Planning Agency, Institute of Monetary and Economic Studies of the BOJ, the MOF, the Japan Securities Research Institute, the OECD, and the U.S. Treasury Working Group. A version covering the 1975–1986 period was represented in Cargill and Royama (1988). The current version was updated with information provided by the Institute of Monetary and Economic Studies. A great debt is owed to the staff of the Institute's Division II and in particular to Mr. Katagi, Mr. Kotani, and Mr. Kubo for help in preparing the material.

IMPACT KEY:
1 = Money market
2 = Interbank market
3 = Capital market
4 = New financial asset or service
5 = Internationalization of finance
6 = Interest-rate liberalization
7 = Tactics of BOJ policy

Date	Type	Impact
1972		
August	• Sogo account authorized (combined demand and saving deposit account).	4
1975		
August	• Ad hoc provision accepted to permit year-by-year acceptance of the Budget Law, which prohibits deficit financing.	3
November	• Joint operations of cash dispensers begun among city and regional banks in large cities.	4
1976		
March	• Circular notice issued by MOF concerning gensaki transactions that officially recognized a market that had emerged in the late 1940s by securities companies. Gensaki transactions represent the resale or repurchase of government bonds at a fixed price for a fixed time period, usually three months.	1
1977		
January	• Discount five-year maturity bonds issued. Previously only ten-year maturity bonds issued.	3
April	• Government-bond-purchasing syndicate members authorized to sell deficit-covering government bonds held more than one year.	3, 6

THE EVOLUTION OF JAPANESE BANKING AND FINANCE

Date	Type	Impact
June	Deficit-covering bonds are issued to cover current-account central government deficits. • Bank permitted more freedom to manage yen conversion with respect to their cash position.	5
October	• Syndicate members authorized to sell construction government bonds held more than one year. Construction bonds are issued to finance public works projects.	3, 6
1978		
January	• MOF initiated the sale of government bonds held by the Trust Fund Bureau on a bidding basis.	3, 6
February	• Publication of over-the-counter quotations of government bonds by the Securities Dealers Association of Japan.	3, 6
June	• Medium-term (three year) government bonds issued on a bidding basis.	3, 6
	• Operations by the BOJ purchase government bonds from syndicate members executed on a bidding basis.	3, 6, 7
	• Increased flexibility in quotation of the call rate and permission to resell bills at a free rate from a date one month after purchase.	1, 2, 4, 6, 7
July	• BOJ commenced announcing money forecasts on a quarterly basis.	7
August	• Securities Dealers Association of Japan commenced publishing bid and asked quotations of representative issues of government bonds.	3, 6
October	• Quota relaxed on sales of securities in the gensaki market by city banks (5 billion to 20 billion yen).	1, 6
October–November	• Call instrument with seven-day term at a free rate established, bill instrument with a one-month term at a free rate established, and rates on over three-months bills liberalized.	1, 2, 4, 6, 7
1979		
February	• Nonresidents' ban on acquisition of yen-denominated bonds abolished; the marginal reserve requirements on nonresidents' free yen deposits also abolished except for gensaki transactions.	5
March	• Sears, Roebuck the first foreign firm to issue unsecured yen-denominated bonds in Japan.	3, 5

Date	Type	Impact
April	• Quotation system for the interbank call rate abolished; a call instrument with 2–6 day term established.	1, 2, 6, 7
	• Quota further relaxed on security sales in the gensaki market by city banks (20 billion to 50 billion yen).	1, 6
May	• Negotiable CDs introduced with unregulated interest rates and issues limited to 10 percent of banks' net worth, minimum of 500 million yen and 3–6 month maturity.	1, 4, 6
	• Restrictions on nonresidents' gensaki transactions removed; nonresidents permitted to purchase yen-denominated CDs.	1, 5
	• Medium-term (two-year) government bonds issued on a bidding basis.	3, 4, 6
June	• Restrictions on short-term impact loans made by foreign banks removed; impact loans are unrestricted borrowing in a foreign currency by residents.	4, 6
	• Short-term impact loans by Japanese foreign-exchange banks authorized.	4, 6
	• BOJ adopted a "quick" system for purchasing outstanding government bonds: timely and flexible buying operations in small lots.	3, 6, 7
October	• Quotation system for over two-month interbank bill rate abolished.	1, 2, 6, 7
1980		
January	• Medium-term government-bond fund authorized for securities companies. This is an open-type investment fund in small denomination (100,000 yen), possessing limited transaction features and in which more than half of the funds are invested in medium-term government bonds. Interest rate is not officially regulated; however, MOF influences rate via "moral suasion."	3, 4, 6
	• Ceiling on bank CD issue raised to 25 percent of net worth, to take effect January–March 1980.	1, 4, 6
March	• Interest rates on free yen deposits held by nonresident official institutions liberalized.	5, 6
	• Medium- and long-term impact loans by Japanese foreign-exchange banks authorized.	4, 5
	• Ceilings on foreign banks' issurance of yen-denominated CDs increased to 20 percent of yen-denominated assets by second-quarter 1981.	1, 4, 5, 6

Date	Type	Impact
	• Joint operation of cash dispensers begun by six city banks (SICS).	4
April	• Joint operation of cash dispensers begun by the remaining seven city banks (TOCS).	4
	• Quota relaxed on sales of securities in the gensaki market by city banks.	1, 6
	• Ceiling on bank CD issue raised from 25 to 50 percent of net worth, to take effect April–June 1981.	1, 4, 6
May	• Limitations on the sale of outstanding government bonds by syndicate members reduced from one year to seven–nine months after issue date.	3, 6
June	• Medium-term (four-year) government bonds issued on a bidding basis.	3, 4, 6
October	• Joint operations cash dispensers begun by 63 regional banks (ACS).	4
	• Joint operation of cash dispensers begun by 71 sogo banks (SCS).	4
November	• Joint operation of cash dispensers begun by 158 shinkin banks (SNCS); all shinkin banks now participate.	4
	• Financial institutions with surplus funds, such as regional banks and trust banks, permitted to borrow on the call market while investing funds in the bill market.	2
	• Four major securities companies (Nomura, Yamaichi, Daiwa, and Nikko) permitted to borrow in the call market subject to a 20 billion yen ceiling each.	2
December	• Amendments made to the Foreign Exchange and Foreign Trade Control Law: Permission no longer required for impact loans; import usance facilities by usance bill for one year or less liberalized; and shift made from the nonresident free yen account system (yen account convertible into foreign currencies held by nonresidents) to a nonresident yen account.	5
	• Major foreign-exchange banks exempted from the requirements to report on the issue of foreign-currency securities, such as overseas CDs, and on the acquisition of foreign-currency securities (over one year).	5

Date	Type	Impact
	• Banks authorized to undertake limited participation in overseas syndicated yen-denominated loans.	5
	• Resident foreign-currency deposits in foreign-exchange banks liberalized (3 million yen ceiling per deposit removed).	5, 6
	• Ceiling raised on foreign-exchange banks' conversion of foreign currency into yen.	5
1981		
April	• City banks authorized to lend in the call-loan market.	2, 6
	• Restrictions on city bank gensaki purchases removed.	1, 6
	• Limitations on the sale of government bonds by syndicate members (financial institutions) relaxed from 7–9 months to 100 days after issue date.	3, 6
May	• Amendments made to the Bank Law designed to define the functions of both domestic and foreign banks, to take effect April 1982.	5
	• BOJ commenced selling holdings of short-term government securities on the open secondary market.	1, 6, 7
June	• New type of maturity-designated bank time deposit (Kijitsu-shitei-teiki) introduced in which depositor can withdraw funds at any time after one year so long as depositor designates maturity; interest calculated on a compound basis.	4
	• New type of loan trust fund ("Big") account introduced for trust banks for two maturities (two and five years); interest calculated on a compound basis.	4
July	• Subsidiaries of Japanese banks permitted to lend Euroyen up to one year to finance trade with Japan.	5, 6
September	• Government issued six-year nonmarketable bonds.	3, 4
October	• Accumulation type of government-bond fund account authorized for securities companies; this is a closed-type investment fund of long-term government bonds.	4

Date	Type	Impact
December	• New type of bank debenture ("Wide") authorized for long-term credit banks; interest calculated on a compound basis for five years.	4
	• Borrowing on the call market authorized for eight medium-sized securities companies (up to 5 billion yen per company) and call-borrowing ceiling for the four large companies raised from 20 billion to 30 billion yen.	2, 6
1982		
January	• Two additional medium-sized securities companies permitted to borrow in the call market.	2, 6
February	• New type of property-accumulation designed bank time deposit authorized; the deposit is applicable to the special tax-exempt plan called "worker's property accumulation plan."	4
April	• Call-money brokers permitted to deal in the TB market.	1, 2
	• Tokyo Stock Exchange removed restrictions imposed on membership of foreign securities companies.	3, 5
	• Yen/dollar swap limits raised for foreign banks.	5, 6
May	• Japanese banks permitted to lend long-term yen abroad to borrower of their choice.	5
	• Domestic sales authorized of foreign-denominated commercial papers and CDs previously issued abroad according to MOF guidance.	1, 5, 6
July	• Government-bond fund with profits retained until maturity ("Jumbo") established by securities companies.	4
October	• Property-accumulation pension instruments established by private financial institutions and the PSS that are applicable to the special tax-exempt plan called "worker's property accumulation plan."	4
November	• Open type of government-bond funds (Rikin funds) established by securities companies. The funds are designed only for interest accruing on government bonds that is automatically invested every interest-payment date; after 30 days investor can withdraw funds at any time.	4

Date	Type	Impact
1983		
January	• Regulations on yen-denominated foreign bonds relaxed (e.g., approval period reduced to 3–6 months).	3, 4, 5
	• Eligibility standards for issuing unsecured convertible bonds relaxed.	3, 4
February	• Quota for the issuance of yen-denominated CDs by foreign banks increased to 30 percent of yen-denominated assets.	1, 4, 5, 6
	• Ceiling on bank CD issues to be raised step by step from 50 to 75 percent of bank net worth, the last stage effective January–March 1984.	1, 4, 6
April	• Joint operation of cash dispensers begun by the seven trust banks (SOCS).	4
	• Banks permitted to offer over-the-counter sales services for newly issued long-term government bonds.	3, 4
	• Limitations on yen/foreign-currency swaps relaxed by authorized foreign-exchange banks.	5
May	• Postal insurance system permitted to invest in foreign bonds.	5
June	• Restrictions lifted on the ban on short-term Euroyen loans to nonresidents; however, Euroyen lending plans are subject to reporting requirements.	5
	• Securities companies permitted to make loans on the security of government bonds.	3, 4
August	• Government-bond time deposits established by banks.	3, 4
September	• Government-bond trust accounts established by trust banks.	3, 4
	• New type of combined account ("High Pack") established by securities companies with limited transactions features.	4
October	• Banks permitted to offer over-the-counter sales of newly issued medium-term government bonds.	3, 4
	• Government-bond discount bank debenture account established by long-term credit banks. This is an instrument composed of medium-term government bonds and discount bank debentures in which the interest on government	3, 4

Date	Type	Impact
December	bonds is automatically reinvested in the discount bank debenture. • Issuance of yen-denominated CDs relaxed further by foreign banks (to 50 percent of yen-denominated assets).	1, 4, 5, 6
1984		
January	• Two city bank cash dispenser systems (SICS and SOCS) integrated into one service network (BANKS).	4
	• Minimum denomination of bank CDs lowered from 500 million to 300 million yen.	1, 4, 6
	• Sales of U.S. housing mortgage bonds (GNMA bonds) begun.	3, 4, 5
March	• Tokyo Stock Exchange relaxed restrictions on the listing of foreign companies.	3, 5
April	• Participation of foreign-securities companies in government-bond underwriting syndicate authorized.	3, 5
	• Real-demand rule regarding forward foreign-exchange contracts abolished. This rule restricted trade in forward yen only as counterpart of actual trade transactions.	5
	• Shinkin bank and securities company offered new financial instrument composed of a medium-term government-bond fund and ordinary deposit.	3, 4
	• Domestic sales of foreign-denominated CDs and commercial paper authorized for banks and securities companies.	1, 4, 5, 6
	• Ceiling on bank CD issues raised from 75 to 100 percent of bank net worth, effective April 1985.	1, 4, 6
	• Guidelines on the issue of Euroyen bonds by residents relaxed so that the number of domestic companies authorized to issue Euroyen bonds is enlarged.	4, 5
	• Overseas yen lending by authorized foreign-exchange banks liberalized.	4, 5
	• Restrictions relaxed further on issuance of yen-denominated foreign bonds.	4, 5
May	• Permission granted to government to issue foreign-currency-denominated national bonds (Nakasone bonds) abroad.	4, 5

Date	Type	Impact
June	• Public-bond dealing by financial institutions initiated.	3, 4
	• Restrictions on the conversion of foreign currencies into yen (the Yen-Ten restrictions) for financial institutions removed.	5
	• Restrictions on short-term Euroyen lending to residents removed.	5
	• Financial institutions commenced dealing on their own account outstanding government bonds on the secondary market.	3, 4, 6
July	• Eligibility standards for offering yen-denominated foreign bonds relaxed.	3, 4, 5
October	• Three foreign banks permitted to commence selling and buying on their own account outstanding government bonds on the secondary market.	3, 4, 5, 6
November	• Six foreign banks permitted to make over-the-counter sales of newly issued government bonds.	3, 4, 5
December	• Non-Japanese residents authorized to issue Euroyen bonds.	4, 5
	• Removal of withholding tax imposed on the interest earnings of nonresidents on Euroyen bonds issued by Japanese residents.	5
	• Euroyen CD issues by Japanese banks (through their overseas branches and subsidiaries) by Japanese securities companies (through their overseas banking subsidiaries), and by foreign banks permitted.	4, 5
	• Foreign banks authorized to establish trust banks in Japan.	4, 5
1985		
February	• Exchange dealers permitted to handle domestic interbank direct deals and international transactions of Broker's Broker.	5
March	• Initiation of Money Market Certificates (MMCs) that are not subject to deposit-ceiling regulations (minimum denomination of 50 million yen and 1–6 month maturity). Rate tied to the CD rate; however, MMCs are not negotiable.	4, 6
	• Permission granted to engage in simultaneous buying and selling transactions by city banks in the bill market. Previously, the buy-sell transactions were separated by at least one day.	2, 6

THE EVOLUTION OF JAPANESE BANKING AND FINANCE

Date	Type	Impact
	• Banks authorized to issue overseas convertible corporate bonds.	3, 5
	• Banks authorized to establish financial investment consulting companies.	1, 3, 4
April	• CDs further liberalized: denomination reduced from 300 million to 100 million yen, maturity reduced from three months to one month, and ceiling on issuance rate raised from 75 to 100 percent of the bank's net worth.	1, 4, 6
	• Transactions fee reduced for large-denominated stock sales on consignment.	3
	• Foreign-currency-denominated CPs and CDs further liberalized (denomination reduced and ratings terms more flexible).	1, 4, 5, 6
	• Medium- and long-term Euroyen loans to nonresidents liberalized.	4, 5
	• Euroyen convertible bonds issued by residents initiated.	3, 4, 5
	• Withholding tax abolished on nonresidents' interest income on investment in Euroyen bonds issued by residents.	5
	• Nonresidents' Euroyen bond issuance relaxed.	3, 4, 5
	• Bond-rating agencies established.	3, 4
May	• Securities companies resumed buying bills (they had been prohibited from buying bills in early 1970s).	2, 6
June	• A yen-denominated bankers' acceptance market established.	1, 5, 6
	• A bill market instrument with 5–6 month maturity to achieve greater maturity dispersion established.	2, 4, 6
	• Financial institutions permitted to sell government bonds (issued on the operating account) after 60 days from the previous 100-day interval.	3, 6
	• Securities companies authorized to make loans secured by public bonds within certain limits.	3, 4
	• Bank dealers' participation in Broker's Broker transactions authorized.	1, 3, 4
	• Introduced dual-currency bond.	5
	• Nine foreign banks licensed as trust banks.	5
	• Legal preparations made for the establishment of a futures bond market.	3, 4, 6

Date	Type	Impact
July	• Call-market transactions authorized without collateral.	2, 4, 6
	• Qualification standards relaxed for resident issues of Euroyen convertible bonds.	3, 4, 5
August	• Securities companies authorized to issue large-lot bond investment trust accounts (FFFs), which consist of a position in a portfolio of national bonds and debentures (bank or corporate) with five-year maturities; interest rate subject to MOF administrative guidance.	3, 4, 6
	• Transactions conditions in call market relaxed.	2, 6
	• Fifteen-year domestic straight-bond market initiated.	3, 4
	• Domestic issuance of foreign-currency-denominated bonds resumed.	3, 4, 5
	• World Bank issued dollar-denominated bonds (Shogun bonds) in Tokyo market.	3, 4, 5
September	• Banks and securities companies authorized to offer joint-participation loans in which the securities companies hold the collateral.	3, 4
October	• Ceiling on CD issuance enlarged from 100 to 150 percent of the bank's net worth.	1, 4, 6
	• Interest rates liberalized on large-denominated time deposits (more than 1 billion yen) with two-year and less maturities.	4, 6
	• A futures government-bond market established in Tokyo Stock Exchange.	4, 5, 6
	• Variety of bonds fully redeemable at the redemption date increased.	3
	• Broker's Broker charge on Tokyo Stock Exchange transactions reduced.	3
	• Foreign banks authorized to participate in trust banking activites.	4, 5
	• Qualification standards relaxed for residents' issuance of Euroyen straight bonds.	4, 5
November	• Ceiling on borrowing in the call market by securities companies increased.	2, 6
Decmber	• Securities companies authorized to issue a new Money Trust Fund (HIT) account with essentially a one-year maturity. Interest rate subject to administrative guidance of MOF.	4, 6
	• Permission granted to issue bonds with negotiable warrants.	3, 4

THE EVOLUTION OF JAPANESE BANKING AND FINANCE 387

Date	Type	Impact
1986		
January	• Initiation of TB gensaki operations between the BOJ and money market dealers, TB obligations have two-month maturities and are almost entirely absorbed by the BOJ.	1, 4, 6, 7
February	• Issurance of short-term (six-month) government bonds.	1, 4, 6, 7
	• Foreign securities company membership on Tokyo Stock Exchange relaxed; three U.S. companies become members.	3, 5
March	• Securities companies authorized to issue long-term government-bond fund; interest rate is under administrative MOF guidance.	3, 4, 6
	• BOJ initiated open-market operations in CDs.	7
April	• Ceiling on issuance of CDs enlarged from 150 to 200 percent of bank's net worth, and upper maturity limit raised from six months to one year.	1, 4, 6
	• Upper maturity limit of MMC raised from six months to one year.	4, 6
	• Minimum large-denominated time deposit reduced from 1 billion to 500 million yen.	4, 6
	• Selling government bonds relaxed further by financial institutions from 60 to 40 days (operating account bonds) and from 100 to 40 days (investment account bonds).	3, 6
	• Settlement procedure for government-bond transactions changed to increase bond market flexibility.	3
	• Securities companies authorized to engage in broking of yen-denominated bankers' acceptance market.	1, 4, 6
	• Authorized maturity for Euroyen CDs extended from six months to one year.	1, 4, 5, 6
	• Admitted foreign banks to issue Euroyen bonds provided that they will not bring back to Japan the proceeds from their Euroyen bond issues.	5
	• Several measures passed, designed to increase flexibility of nonresident Euroyen bond market.	5
May	• Deposit-insurance system revised to increase maximum insurance level from 3 million to 10 million yen.	4
	• Progressive reserve requirements introduced.	7

Date	Type	Impact
	• Various required financial ratios for financial intermediaries revised.	—
September	• Minimum denomination of MMCs reduced from 50 million to 30 million yen.	4, 6
	• Minimum large-denominated time deposit reduced from 50 million to 30 million yen.	4, 6
	• Ceiling on issuance of CDs increased from 200 to 250 percent of bank's net worth.	1, 4, 6
December	• Offshore banking facility established in Tokyo.	4, 5, 6

Note

The addendum to this appendix appears on page 591 of this book.

8 BANK STRUCTURE IN SWITZERLAND

Urs W. Birchler and Georg Rich

1. Description of Current Structure of Financial Institutions and Markets

In Switzerland, most financial institutions are organized as universal banks. As in most other Continental European countries, banking legislation does not distinguish between commercial and investment banks. In principle, any institution authorized to operate as a bank may offer the entire gamut of banking services, including underwriting, securities trading, and portfolio management. The only exception is insurance, which needs a different license. In practice, only the largest banks may be characterized as truly universal banks; most of the smaller institutions are more or less specialized. In official statistics, Swiss financial institutions are classified into eight major groups: the four big banks, cantonal banks, regional and savings banks, Raiffeisenkassen, private banks, foreign banks, miscellaneous other banks, and finance companies. The 20 largest Swiss banks are listed in table 8-1.

The first group, which comprises three very large banks and one smaller institution, conduct a wide range of banking activities. They play an important, if not dominant, role in the domestic market. In addition,

Table 8-1. The 20 Largest Swiss Banks (Billions of Dollars, End of 1989)

Rank	Name of Bank	Type	Total Assets	Fiduciary Accounts	Total Assets and Fiduciary Accounts
1.	Union Bank of Switzerland	B	112.3	27.0	139.3
2.	Swiss Bank Corporation	B	103.6	17.2	120.8
3.	Credit Suisse	B	75.0	19.9	94.9
4.	Cantonal Bank of Zurich	C	25.2	0.4	25.6
5.	Swiss Volksbank	B	24.6	1.0	25.6
6.	Swiss Association of Raiffeisenkassen[a]	RA	19.8	—	19.8
7.	Bank Leu	O[b]	9.5	1.1	10.6
8.	Cantonal Bank of Berne	C	8.2	0.1	8.3
9.	Cantonal Bank of St. Gall	C	7.5	0.1	7.6
10.	Cantonal Bank of Lucerne	C	7.3	0.3	7.6
11.	Banque Cantonale Vaudoise	C	7.3	1.1	8.4
12.	Banca della Svizzera Italiana	O	5.8	3.7	9.5

13.	Cantonal Bank of Thurgau	C	5.7	0.1	5.8
14.	Crédit Foncier Vaudois	C	5.6	0.0	5.6
15.	TDB American Express Bank	F	5.3	5.5	10.8
16.	Neue Aargauer Bank	R	4.9	0.1	5.0
17.	Basellandschaftliche Kantonal-bank	C	4.7	0.0	4.7
18.	Hypothekarkasse des Kantons Bern	C	4.7	0.0	4.7
19.	Graubündner Kantonalbank	C	4.5	0.1	4.6
20.	Banque Paribas (Suisse) SA	F	4.4	1.5	5.9

[a] All cooperatives, excluding the central bank.
[b] This institution was statistically treated as a big bank until 1989.

B: Big bank
C: Cantonal bank
R: Regional bank
RA: Raiffeisenkassen (loan associations)
O: Other Swiss-owned bank
F: Foreign-owned bank

Source: Swiss National Bank, *Das Schweizerische Bankwesen*. Swiss-franc values were converted to U.S. dollars at the average exchange rate for December.

they are engaged in a thriving international business, the significance of which has risen rapidly since the end of World War II (table 8-2). They not only constitute the key actors in the domestic money and foreign-exchange markets, but are also prominently involved in underwriting, securities trading, and portfolio management.

In contrast to the four big banks, the cantonal and regional banks are active mostly in the domestic market. Although they are universal banks too, they tend to emphasize mortgage lending. Similarly, the Raiffeisenkassen, for the most part, act as mortgage lenders. The private banks stress portfolio management, while the foreign banks are specialized in foreign-exchange trading, trade finance, underwriting, securities trading, and portfolio management. The finance companies, as a rule, do not accept deposits from the public but are involved in various kinds of capital market and lending activities.

Considering the prevalence of universal banks in Switzerland, we shall structure our discussion as follows: In section 1.1, we discuss the activities of the four big banks and the private banks. In this context, it should be kept in mind that most of these institutions act both as commercial and investment banks. Section 1.2 covers the cantonal and regional banks, as well as the Raiffeisenkassen. The finance companies are examined in section 1.3, while section 1.6 is devoted to the foreign business of Swiss-controlled banks, as well as the Swiss business of foreign-controlled banks. Section 1.4 describes insurance, pension funds, etc. The money and capital market activities of Swiss financial institutions are described in section 1.5, rather than under the headings for the individual groups of financial institutions.

1.1. Commercial Banks

1.1.1. The Four Big Banks. This group comprises the three most important Swiss financial institutions, that is, the Union Bank of Switzerland, the Swiss Bank Corporation, and Credit Suisse. The other institution (Swiss Volksbank) is considerably smaller than the Big Three, resembling a large cantonal bank in terms of size. Until 1989 the big banks included a fifth, still smaller institution (Bank Leu, which became part of the Credit Suisse holding structure).

In contrast to most of the smaller institutions, the five big banks are thoroughly universal banks. They pursue all lines of banking business, including trade in gold and other precious metals, as well as the Swiss speciality of accepting fiduciary funds.

Since the end of World War II, the big banks have served as the

Table 8-2. Composition of Assets and Liabilities of Swiss Banks (Billions of Dollars, End of Year)

Year	Total Assets or Liabilities	Assets		Liabilities		Net Foreign Assets	Net Foreign Fiduciary Assets[a]
		Domestic	Foreign	Domestic	Foreign		
1950	6.7	6.1	0.6	6.1	0.6	−0.0	n.a.
1955	9.0	8.2	0.8	8.0	1.0	−0.2	n.a.
1960	13.7	11.9	1.8	11.9	1.8	−0.0	n.a.
1965	23.7	19.4	4.3	19.3	4.4	−0.1	n.a.
1970	48.7	32.3	16.4	34.6	14.1	2.3	n.a.
1975	122.3	79.7	42.6	89.0	33.3	9.3	2.7
1980	274.9	172.3	102.6	195.1	79.7	22.8	9.1
1985	370.4	223.4	147.0	256.7	113.6	33.4	17.3
1989	660.2	416.8	243.4	463.3	196.9	46.6	44.0

[a] Until 1973, included in net foreign assets.

Source: Swiss National Bank, *Das Schweizerische Bankwesen*. See table 8-1 for the conversion of Swiss-franc to dollar values.

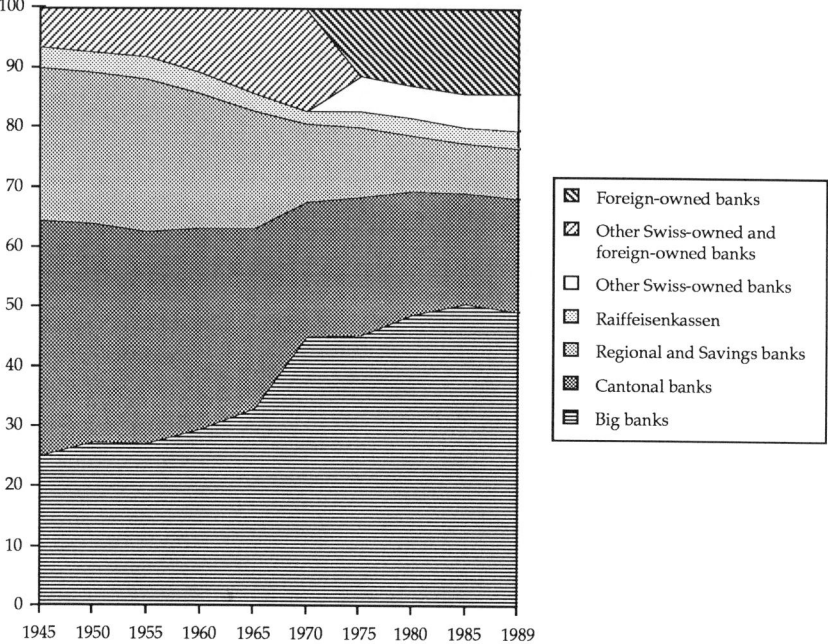

Figure 8-1. Market Shares in Total Assets of the Banking System 1945–1989 (Percent).

principal driving force behind the growth of the Swiss financial system. From 1950 to 1989, their share of the Swiss banks' total assets (including finance companies) rose from 28% to 49% (figure 8-1 and table 8-3). In the domestic market, the big banks expanded their business by opening branches throughout Switzerland and by taking over smaller institutions. The expansionist drive of the big banks largely accounts for the fact that in per capita terms, the number of bank branches is higher in Switzerland than in any other country. The marked expansion of the big banks' domestic business, however, was not the main source of their rapid growth. It was dwarfed by the explosive development of their foreign activities, which was particularly pronounced in the late 1960s (table 8-2).

The big banks—at least the Big Three—are represented on all the major financial markets of the world. Their international strength derives mainly from their active role as portfolio managers, underwriters, and participants in the interbank deposit market. In particular, they dominate the underwriting market for securities denominated in Swiss francs.

Table 8-3. Market Shares in Total Assets of the Banking System 1945–1989 (Percent)

Year	Big Banks[a]	Cantonal Banks	Regional and Savings Banks	Raiffeisenkassen	Other Swiss-Owned	Foreign-Owned	Total
1945	25.1	39.5	25.6	3.3	6.5		100
1950	27.6	36.5	25.1	3.4	7.4		100
1955	27.2	35.6	25.5	3.6	8.1		100
1960	29.7	33.6	22.6	3.4	10.7		100
1965	33.1	30.2	19.5	3.1	14.1		100
1970	45.0	22.7	13.0	2.3	17.0		100
1975	45.5	23.1	11.6	2.7	5.8	11.3	100
1980	48.9	20.7	9.4	2.7	5.4	12.9	100
1985	50.7	18.5	8.3	2.7	5.7	14.1	100
1989	49.2	18.8	8.5	3.0	6.1	14.2	100

[a] Including Bank Leu.
Source: Swiss National Bank, *Das Schweizerische Bankwesen*.

Although the size of the Big Three is impressive by Swiss standards, they do not rank among the very largest financial institutions of the world. They prefer to strengthen their profitability and capitalization, rather than to maximize their asset growth.

Another reason for the big banks' strength is in their solid domestic deposit base. Deposits from nonbank customers, including medium-term bonds (the so-called *Kassenobligationen* or *bons de caisse*), account for over one-half of their aggregate liabilities (table 8-4). Their fiduciary accounts are another important source of funds. Banks normally place these funds in the interbank market in their own name but at risk of the depositor. Frequently, they channel these funds to their own foreign branches, which in turn redeposit them with other banks. Thanks to their fiduciary accounts, the big banks are able to play a major role on the interbank deposit market.

Loans are the most significant item on the asset side of the big banks' balance sheets. About half of their aggregate loans consist of mortgages. In Switzerland, mortgages typically take the form of floating-rate loans. In recent years, fixed-rate mortgages have become increasingly important. Currently, they account for about one third of aggregate mortgage loans. Loans to foreigners, notably export credits, also figure prominently among their assets. As a by-product of their loan business, they offer such traditional off-balance-sheet services as credit lines, documentary credit, and guarantees.

Forward exchange commitments are another important off-balance-sheet item of the big banks. These commitments not only serve as a means of covering open on-balance-sheet positions in foreign exchange, but also reflect the big banks' dominant role in the Swiss foreign-exchange market. Roughly one third of the big banks' gross earnings arise from their foreign-exchange and precious-metals trade. Another third derives from various types of fees (brokerage and underwriting fees, fees on loans and fiduciary accounts), while the remainder is attributable to financial intermediation.

1.1.2. Private Banks. The private banks are the oldest Swiss financial institutions. Out of the 22 private banks still existing today, 17 institutions are over 100 years old. Seven institutions date back to the eighteenth century. The private banks are unincorporated firms whose owners are personally and fully liable for all the debts of their firms. For this reason, the private banks need not comply with all the provisions of the Swiss Bank Act, which governs the activities of Swiss banks. In particular, they

Table 8-4. Stylized Balance Sheet of Main Banking Groups (All Banks and Finance Companies) (Billions of Dollars or Percent, End of 1989)

	Big Banks[a]	Cantonal Banks	Regional and Savings Banks	Foreign Banks	Total[b]
Assets					
Cash, interbank assets, money market paper	101.5 (27.9)	16.9 (12.1)	3.7 (6.2)	39.9 (49.3)	182.0 (26.0)
Securities	20.6 (5.7)	9.1 (6.5)	4.3 (7.3)	9.1 (11.3)	47.5 (6.8)
Customer loans	113.8 (31.3)	21.7 (15.6)	9.7 (16.3)	23.6 (29.2)	185.4 (26.5)
Mortgages	94.8 (26.1)	81.9 (58.7)	37.8 (63.8)	2.3 (2.8)	227.5 (32.5)
Loans to the public sector	7.3 (2.0)	5.1 (3.7)	1.7 (2.8)	1.4 (1.7)	15.9 (2.3)
Other assets	25.7 (7.1)	4.8 (3.4)	2.1 (3.5)	4.6 (5.7)	40.7 (5.8)
Total assets	363.6 (100)	139.5 (100)	59.3 (100)	81.0 (100)	698.9 (100)
Liabilities					
Interbank liabilities	87.0 (23.9)	8.5 (6.1)	3.9 (6.5)	43.0 (53.2)	151.1 (21.6)
Demand deposits	30.7 (8.4)	8.3 (5.9)	4.6 (7.8)	7.2 (8.9)	59.7 (8.5)
Time deposits	110.7 (30.4)	24.8 (17.8)	6.0 (10.2)	13.9 (17.2)	168.6 (24.1)
Savings deposits	45.3 (12.5)	43.0 (30.8)	19.8 (33.4)	0.9 (1.2)	117.2 (16.8)
Medium and long-term bonds	41.9 (11.5)	41.1 (29.5)	19.7 (33.2)	2.6 (3.2)	112.3 (16.1)
Other liabilities	25.8 (7.1)	8.0 (5.7)	2.5 (4.2)	5.7 (7.1)	46.0 (6.6)
Capital	22.3 (6.1)	5.8 (4.2)	2.9 (4.8)	7.5 (9.3)	44.1 (6.3)
Total liabilities	363.6 (100)	139.5 (100)	59.3 (100)	81.0 (100)	698.9 (100)

[a] Including Bank Leu.
[b] 355 banks.
Source: Swiss National Bank, *Das Schweizerische Bankwesen.* See table 8-1 for the conversion of Swiss-franc to dollar values.

do not have to meet capital requirements and publish financial statements unless they publicly declare their willingness to accept deposits.

The private banks specialize in portfolio management and the related business of securities trading. They participate both in the underwriting market and secondary securities trading. The lion's share of the private banks' gross earnings arises from portfolio management, secondary securities trading, and underwriting. Less important sources of earnings are foreign-exchange and precious-metals trading, as well as capital gains on securities.

The number of private banks—73 in 1950—has shrunk drastically in recent years. Many institutions have been converted to joint-stock companies. Portfolios are managed to an increasing extent by joint-stock banks or by private portfolio managers without the status of a bank.

1.2. Thrift, Savings, and Other Depository Institutions

1.2.1. Cantonal Banks. In principle, the Swiss Bank Act does not distinguish among various types of banks. The Act deviates from this principle only in four cases: the cantonal banks, the private banks, the foreign-owned banks, and the finance companies. The Act mentions these institutions explicitly because some of its provisions do not apply to them. According to articles 3 and 4 of the Act, the cantonal banks are defined as banks established on the basis of cantonal legislation (Switzerland operates a three-tier system of government, with the cantons placed between the Confederation and the municipalities). Although Switzerland is divided into 26 cantons, there are 28 cantonal banks. Two cantons (Vaud and Geneva) operate two cantonal banks each.

Most cantonal banks possess the following characteristics:

- They are state-owned banks, since their capital is in the hands of the cantons. In recent years, a few cantonal banks have started to issue nonvoting shares to the general public.
- Their activities are monitored and their deposits are guaranteed by the respective canton.
- They do not pay income or corporate profits taxes, but are required to hand over their profits to the canton.
- Their ability to conduct foreign business is restricted by cantonal legislation. In 1985, the cantonal banks established a joint venture, called the Swiss Cantobank, in which most of them participate. Through that institution, organized as an ordinary commercial bank,

BANK STRUCTURE IN SWITZERLAND 399

rather than as a cantonal bank, they attempt to gain direct access to foreign markets.

Despite these common attributes, the various cantonal banks differ substantially in terms of size and business activities. Measured by total assets, 10 cantonal banks rank among the top 20 Swiss institutions (table 8-1), but many are very small. While the largest cantonal banks pursue lines of business similar to the big banks (except that they are barely involved in foreign markets), the smallest institutions resemble savings banks. Although mortgage loans account for roughly 60% of the cantonal banks' assets (table 8-4), that percentage varies from one third to nine tenths for the individual institutions. To finance their mortgage loans, the cantonal banks rely heavily on savings deposits and medium-term bonds. The share of the cantonal banks in aggregate bank assets shrank from 37% in 1950 to 19% in 1989 (figure 8-1 and table 8-3). The main beneficiaries of this development were the big banks. Three factors explain the erosion in the cantonal banks' competitiveness:

- When the cantonal banks were established in the nineteenth century, they were not only expected to generate profits but also to achieve social objectives, such as furthering the growth of the cantonal economies, as well as promoting home ownership and thrift. These obligations conflict with their desire to compete with the privately owned banks on an equal footing.
- Political interference by cantonal governments tends to dampen the entrepreneurial spirit of the cantonal banks.
- Since the domestic business of Swiss banks has grown less rapidly than their international operations, the cantonal banks have been unable to participate much in the most lucrative lines of activity.

1.2.2. Regional and Savings Banks. Besides the cantonal banks, Switzerland features 210 regional and savings banks. Their characteristics and business activities are similar to those of the cantonal banks. They play an important role as mortgage lenders. Mortgages account for about 60% of their total assets (table 8-4). They finance their mortgage loans mainly by accepting savings and other deposits from the general public.

As in the case of the cantonal banks, the size of the regional banks varies enormously, with assets of the individual institutions ranging from $5 billion to less than $4 million. Moreover, their market share has declined in the same way and for similar reasons as that of the cantonal banks. In 1950, they still accounted for 25% of the Swiss banks' total assets, as compared with a market share of 9% at the end of 1989 (figure 8-1 and table 8-3).

Since most regional banks are small, they strive to cooperate in an increasing number of areas. In particular, they have established their own clearing system for interbank payments.

1.2.3. Raiffeisenkassen. The Raiffeisenkassen are tiny banks located mainly in rural areas and run largely by part-time staff. They are organized as cooperatives with their own legal identity. The members of these cooperatives are jointly liable for any losses incurred by depositors. Furthermore, the Raiffeisenkassen only lend to their members against collateral.

Although the Raiffeisenkasen account for merely 3% of the Swiss banks' aggregate assets, they have successfully fended off the larger banks and have managed to preserve their traditional market share. Their strength resides in their low production costs and their concentration on a small number of banking activities, notably mortgage lending. The individual cooperatives may avail themselves of various services provided by a common institution, called the central bank of the Raiffeisenkassen. It manages the liquidity of the individual cooperatives and advises them on legal and accounting matters. Though small in comparison to the other banks, the Raiffeisenkassen would rank sixth on the list of the largest Swiss banks (table 8-1) if they constituted a single institution.

1.3. Investment and Merchant Banks

As we mentioned at the outset, the universal bank constitutes the prevalent type of financial institution in Switzerland. The only Swiss institutions resembling Anglosaxon-type investment banks belong to the colorful group of finance companies. In Switzerland, there are close to 2000 finance companies pursuing a wide array of financial activities. A minority of about 140 companies are regarded as banklike institutions (or near banks) and, therefore, come within the realm of the Swiss Bank Act. To qualify as banklike, a finance company's assets must be similar to those of a bank, that is, they must include loans, securities, or participations. Banklike finance companies in turn are classified into two categories. Finance companies falling into the first category are regarded as banks. They must comply with all the provisions of the Swiss Bank Act and are supervised in the same fashion as banks. Banklike finance companies belonging to the second category must comply only with one portion of the Bank Act, notably a reporting requirement (see section 3.2).

To qualify as a banklike finance company belonging to the first category, an institution must satisfy at least one of three requirements:

- It publicly declares its willingness to accept deposits from the nonbank public
- It refinances loans by borrowing funds on the interbank market
- It is active in the underwriting business

The banklike finance companies represent one of the most dynamic segments of the Swiss financial system. In the past 20 years, their number has tripled, mainly as a result of the influx of foreign-controlled institutions. These account for almost 80% of the total.

The attractiveness of the Swiss-franc underwriting business (see section 1.5) and regulations of the Swiss National Bank (SNB), Switzerland's central bank, largely explain the rapid growth of banklike finance companies. The SNB must authorize capital exports taking the form of either credit or primary issues of securities (maturing in more than one year). According to the SNB's regulations, only banks and banklike finance companies located in Switzerland are eligible for authorizations. For this reason, many finance companies, notably foreign-owned institutions, have striven to achieve banklike status.

Foreigners intent on establishing a banking operation in Switzerland frequently opt for a banklike finance company rather than a full-fledged bank. Several factors explain that preference for finance companies. Homecountry legislation may preclude parent companies that do not themselves possess the status of a bank from establishing a banking subsidiary in Switzerland. Furthermore, if a foreigner merely wishes to engage in a small range of banking activities, a finance company may be more suitable than a bank. Another reason lies in the fact that until the end of 1989, institutions specializing as underwriters were considered to belong to the second category of banklike finance companies. Foreigners interested in underwriting often preferred to open a banklike finance company because Swiss reciprocity rules for the admission of foreign banks (see section 3.2) did not apply to secondcategory institutions.

1.4. D. Insurance, Pension Funds, etc.

The Swiss insurance sector comprises both public and private suppliers. The federal government provides compulsory old-age, disability, un-

Table 8-5. Pension Funds: Structure of Assets (Percent, End of 1987)[a]

Real estate	17
Mortgage loans	8
Loans to employers[b]	17
Mutual funds (real estate and shares)	7
Shares	7
Fixed-interest securities	30
Liquid assets	10
Other	4
Total	100

[a] Latest data available.
[b] Important in the case of public-sector funds.
Source: Federal Office of Statistics.

employment, and employment-related accident insurance. The federal old-age and disability insurance schemes are supplemented by 15,000 pension funds operated by the individual employers. Various public and private institutions offer health and accident insurance, while life and casualty insurance is largely the responsibility of the private sector.

In 1988, total assets of private insurance companies and the federal government insurance schemes, excluding pension funds, amounted to roughly $79 billion and $10 billion, respectively. Private insurance companies held more than 50% of their assets in the form of fixed-interest securities and loans. About a third of the total was invested in real estate and mortgages, while shares accounted for only 5%.

At the end of 1987, Swiss pensions funds managed $125 billion worth of assets (equivalent to 18% of total assets of Swiss banks and finance companies). Since 1985, membership in a pension fund has been compulsory for virtually all employees in Switzerland. However, most employees were already insured voluntarily before membership became compulsory. The composition of the pension funds' assets is shown in table 8-5.

Insurance companies and pension funds are both customers and competitors of the banks. They avail themselves of portfolio-management and securities-trading services provided by the banks. In particular, they tend to acquire a major portion of bonds issued in the Swiss capital market. To an increasing extent, the pension funds also purchase shares. Large pension funds have begun to write options on their holdings of shares in an effort to limit the variability of the return on their investments.

In other areas, the institutional investors compete with the banks. Both the insurance companies and the banks offer voluntary retirement savings plans supplementing the pension funds and the federal old-age insurance scheme. Institutional investors and banks also compete on the mortgage market. However, from 1978 to 1989, the share of outstanding mortgage loans granted by insurance companies and pension funds fell from 13% to 10%, while the banks increased their share from 82% to 88%.

1.5. Financial Markets

1.5.1. Money Market. Unlike the banking system, the money market is not highly developed in Switzerland. Three factors account for the rudimentary state of the Swiss money market. First, the high degree of concentration in the Swiss banking system and the prevalence of branch banking imply that liquidity needs are frequently satisfied by fund transfers within institutions, rather than between institutions. Furthermore, as indicated above, smaller institutions like the regional banks and the Raiffeisenkassen operate clearing systems that reduce the necessity of resorting to the money market. In the case of the cantonal banks, the Cantonal Bank of Zurich, the largest institution in that group, has taken on the role of a clearing house for most of the smaller establishments. Consequently, the regular participants in the Swiss money market number less than 50, including the SNB and a few institutional investors, with the SNB and the Big Three calling the tune.

A second reason for the underdeveloped state of the Swiss money market resides in the fiscal and debt-management policies of the federal and local governments. On the whole, the various levels of government have successfully achieved budgetary balance, after incurring substantial deficits in the 1970s and early 1980s. Thus, they no longer appear as net borrowers on the domestic money and capital markets. Furthermore, to absorb short-term fluctuations in their cash flow, they have traditionally preferred to build up buffer stocks of short-term assets, notably time deposits with domestic banks, rather than to issue short-term debt.

Third, the Swiss tax system has impeded or prevented the evolution of markets in short-term paper claims. It features a turnover tax (stamp tax) on transactions in both the primary and secondary markets for paper claims. Due to the high level of the stamp tax rates (0.15% of the face value, each time paper issued by domestic debtors is sold; 0.3% in the case of paper issued by foreign debtors), the cost of issuing short-term paper claims is prohibitive.

The principal money market instruments are Swiss-franc interbank deposits and foreign-exchange swaps. Both instruments are not subject to stamp tax. Foreign-exchange swaps normally take the form of U.S.-dollar interbank deposits that are covered in the forward exchange market. At present, the swap market is probably the most active and efficient segment of the Swiss money market. It owes much of its importance to the activities of the SNB. Since the beginning of the 1980s, foreign exchange swaps have served as the principal instrument of Swiss monetary policy.

Short-term paper claims, by contrast, are virtually unknown in Switzerland. In particular, there are no markets for certificates of deposit and commercial paper issued by domestic borrowers. The only short-term paper claims used to any significant extent are special commercial bills, issued to finance inventories of essential raw materials that Swiss companies must hold in order to enable them to cope with wars and other national emergencies. Until recently, the SNB and the banks, under an arrangement with the federal government, were prepared to discount or rediscount special commercial bills at preferential rates to lower the cost of carrying these obligatory inventories.

A technique occasionally used to avoid the stamp tax is to issue book claims that do not assume the form of paper. The federal government regularly issues such claims, with terms to maturity of up to six months, but the amounts outstanding are small. Recently, the World Bank and private borrowers have begun to experiment with book claims too. Interestingly, the federal government played a pioneering role in developing this instrument because the stamp tax hindered its own debt management.

1.5.2. Capital Market. In contrast to the money market, the Swiss capital market is one of the most active and efficient in the world. Thanks to a high domestic savings rate, Switzerland began to export capital as early as in the sixteenth century. The need to place funds abroad provided a strong impetus to the early development of a vigorous capital market. Other sources of strength are the absence of significant restrictions on international capital flows, a low domestic inflation rate that renders the Swiss franc one of the most widely used currencies in the international underwriting markets, as well as the important role of the major Swiss banks as international portfolio managers. Owing to the size of their portfolios, the major banks possess remarkable placing power, enhancing their competitiveness in the underwriting markets.

Table 8-6. Capital Exports (Subject to Authorization): Breakdown by Foreign Countries or Regions

Country or Region	Billions of Dollars		Percent	
	1988	1989	1988	1989
EC	12.3	5.8	35.4	22.5
EFTA	3.7	1.2	10.6	4.8
Other Western Europe	0.1	0.2	0.3	0.6
Eastern Europe	1.0	2.0	2.9	7.7
Japan	10.6	12.7	30.5	49.5
United States and Canada	3.9	1.8	11.2	6.9
Australia, New Zealand	0.9	0.2	2.5	0.6
Caribbean	1.0	1.1	2.8	4.3
Other Countries	1.3	0.8	3.9	3.2
Total	34.8	25.6	100.0	100.0
of which: development organizations[a]	1.1	1.2	3.2	4.6

[a] Included in the country of domicile.
Source: Swiss National Bank, *Monatsbericht*.
Swiss-franc values were converted to U.S. dollars at the average exchange rate for the respective year.

In 1989, Swiss residents issued in the domestic capital market $8.7 billion worth of bonds, as well as $3.1 billion worth of equity. The bulk of bonds was sold publicly; only a small part consisted of private placements. The most important debtors were banks and other financial institutions. They accounted for more than half of the value of new bond issues. The share of the three levels of government, by contrast, only amounted to 13%.

Issues of debt and equity by foreigners, which reached $19.3 billion in 1989, far exceeded sales by domestic residents. The relatively high volume of foreign issues testifies to the importance of the Swiss capital market as an international source of funds. The single most important borrowing country was Japan, accounting for roughly 30% and 50% of total issues in 1988 and 1989, respectively (table 8-6). Japanese-controlled banks and finance companies were actively engaged in underwriting Japanese debt and equity. Straights made up two thirds of bonded debt issued by foreigners in 1985–1988, but less than one third in 1989 (table 8-7). The rest consisted of convertible bonds and debt embedded with options or warrants. Equity-related instruments have become increasingly

Table 8-7. Capital Exports (Subject to Authorization): Breakdown According to Instruments, 1985–1989 (Billions of Dollars)

Year	Bonds[a]			Loans	Total
	Straights	Convertibles	With Options		
1985	10.8	2.6	1.7	4.0	19.1
1986	17.1	2.4	4.2	4.4	28.1
1987	16.1	4.6	3.5	7.6	31.7
1988	17.9	7.7	1.8	7.5	34.9
1989	5.7	10.8	2.6	6.5	25.6

[a] Including equity.
Source: Swiss National, Bank, *Monatsbericht*.
See table 8-6 for the conversation of Swiss-franc to dollar values.

important in the Swiss capital market during the past decade. Their popularity dropped sharply after the stock market crash of 1987, but recovered again in 1989.

As we mentioned in section 1.3, primary issues of securities by foreigners with terms to maturity of over a year must be authorized by the SNB. In practice, the SNB no longer restricts capital exports but automatically approves foreign issues in the domestic market. At this moment, only one other restriction remains in effect. To keep the Swiss-franc underwriting business in Switzerland, the SNB only allows financial institutions located in Switzerland to act as lead managers and to participate in syndicates issuing either Swiss-franc securities or dualcurrency securities with a link to the Swiss franc. With the help of foreign central banks, the SNB has been able to suppress primary issues of Swiss-franc securities in foreign capital markets. These efforts do not mirror protectionistic instincts on the part of the SNB, but are designed to shield the domestic underwriters from the ill effects of the stamp tax.

The stamp tax has hurt the Swiss capital market in two other respects. On the one hand, Switzerland does not possess significant primary markets for foreign-currency securities because such issues would be subject to the stamp tax. Inasmuch as Swiss-controlled banks participate in underwriting foreign-currency securities, they conduct this business at their foreign subsidiaries, notably those in London, in order to avoid the stamp tax. On the other hand, secondary trading of Swiss-franc securities has moved abroad, but little is known about the extent of this exodus.

The structure of the Swiss underwriting market has changed considerably in recent years. Until the end of the 1970s, its principal feature was the prevalence of tightly knit cartel arrangements. The membership of the various syndicates was fixed, with the market dominated by the big banks. The syndicates tended to fix prices and restrict entry of new firms. Moreover, they divided up the market among themselves according to rigid rules. Swiss capital export controls served to sustain these cartel arrangements and to petrify the domestic underwriting market. The relaxation of capital export controls in the 1980s, coupled with the globalization of capital markets and the entry of new foreign-controlled financial institutions, enhanced the competitiveness of the Swiss underwriting market. New syndicates emerged that were keen on innovation, while the rigid structures of existing syndicates were loosened. Since 1984, 20%–30% of primary issues have been underwritten by syndicates formed on an ad hoc basis. The enhanced competitive spirit also affected pricing in the underwriting market. Although Swiss commissions (up to 3%) are high by international standards, the costs to debtors are frequently lower because competition forces the syndicates to grant concessions through the pricing of the issue. The lead managers, therefore, often have to accept terms at which they will have difficulties placing their issues. As a rule, Swiss syndicates purchase the entire issue from the debtor at the agreed price and sell it to the investors at their own risk. The stamp tax due on primary issues is double the standard rates because the authorities assume that underwriting entails two taxable transactions, that is, a sale of securities by the debtor to the syndicate, followed by a sale by the syndicate to the investors.

1.5.3. Stock Exchanges. The bulk of secondary trading of securities, including bonds, takes place at the three Swiss stock exchanges of Zurich, Basle, and Geneva. In May 1988, Swiss banks established the world's first fully electronic options and futures exchange, called SOFFEX (Swiss Options and Financial Futures Exchange), where puts and calls on the 11 most important stocks listed on the Swiss stock exchange are traded. SOFFEX also features options on an index of stock prices, that is, the Swiss Market Index. Recently, index and interest rate futures have been listed.

Responsibility for supervising Swiss securities markets is vested in the cantons, rather than the federal government. The three major stock exchanges are semiprivate institutions, governed by cantonal laws, while the four small ones are purely private organizations. Like the small stock exchanges, SOFFEX is not supervised by any cantonal authorities, but rests on self-regulation by its members.

Swiss stock exchanges are divided into two compartments, called the main and adjunct stock exchange. Officially listed securities are traded on the main stock exchange. The adjunct stock exchange (or premarket dealing) features either existing securities that do not fulfill the requirements for being listed on the main compartment or newly issued securities expected to be listed there shortly. Trading pits are set up for the various categories of securities, at which traders shout their bids and offers (*à la criée* system). Most stocks and bonds are traded sequentially. At each pit, only a single listing is traded at any moment, with a few minutes allotted to each listing. Sequential trading, of course, is not suitable for listings on which investors would like to write options and futures contracts. For this reason, the 11 stocks covered by SOFFEX (and 26 other securities) are now traded continuously. After closing hours of the stock exchanges, the banks continue to trade securities on a lively over-the-counter market. Official market-makers do not exist in Switzerland, but underwriters of newly issued securities occasionally undertake to support the market prices of their issues. At SOFFEX some banks set bid and ask prices on one or several contracts.

1.6. Internationalization

As we saw in the preceding sections, Swiss banks maintain close links to the rest of the world. At the end of 1989, 118 foreign-controlled banks, as well as 17 branches of foreign banks and 110 foreign-controlled finance companies, were active in Switzerland. They employed a total of 19,000 persons. Conversely, domestic banks operated 91 foreign branches. In addition, they maintained about an equal number of subsidiaries abroad, as well as over 100 representative offices.

While in the domestic market the banks deal largely with nonbank customers, roughly half of the Swiss banks claims on and liabilities to foreign residents represent interbank funds, with the bulk held in short-term form. Since the beginning of the 1970s, foreign claims have exceeded liabilities by increasing amounts, reflecting Switzerland's role as a net exporter of capital. Roughly two thirds of foreign claims and four fifths of foreign liabilities of Swiss banks (including branches abroad) are denominated in foreign currencies, particularly in U.S. dollars.

Table 8-8 provides a breakdown of the Swiss bank's foreign claims and liabilities vis-à-vis individual countries or regions of the world. At the end

BANK STRUCTURE IN SWITZERLAND 409

Table 8-8. Swiss Banks' Assets and Liabilities vis-à-vis Foreign Countries or Regions (Billions of Dollars, End of 1989)

	Balance Sheet Items			Fiduciary Accounts			Total[a]
	Assets	Liabs.	Net Position	Assets	Liabs.	Net Position	Net Position
U.S.	40.7	19.5	21.2	1.9	4.2	-2.2	19.0
Japan	19.3	4.6	14.7	0.8	0.3	0.4	15.1
EC	97.8	79.5	18.3	145.4	46.8	98.7	117.0
• U.K.	42.8	25.9	16.9	44.7	8.9	35.8	52.8
• W. Germany	10.8	11.5	-0.3	4.8	5.1	-0.3	-0.6
• France	12.1	9.8	1.6	14.3	8.2	6.1	8.4
• Italy	9.1	9.3	-0.2	1.5	10.3	-8.8	-8.9
• other EC	23.0	23.4	-0.4	80.1	14.3	65.7	65.3
EFTA	10.4	3.6	6.8	2.7	1.3	1.4	8.2
Other industrial countries[b]	7.8	5.5	2.3	5.3	5.4	-0.1	2.2
Eastern Europe	5.1	1.7	3.4	0.1	0.1	0.0	3.5
Caribbean	10.6	16.7	-6.0	6.6	21.0	-14.4	-20.4
Latin America	6.1	8.3	-2.2	1.1	10.8	-9.7	-11.9
Middle East	4.0	10.6	-6.6	0.7	24.5	-23.8	-30.4
Asia, Pacific Islands[c]	8.2	9.8	-1.7	0.7	6.0	-5.2	-6.9
Africa[d]	2.2	3.3	-1.0	0.6	6.9	-6.4	-7.4
Unallocated[e]	2.4	8.5	-6.1	0.0	0.2	-0.2	-6.3
Total	214.5	171.5	43.0	166.0	127.4	38.6	81.6

[a] 137 international banks.
[b] Canada, Australia, New Zealand, South Africa, Turkey plus West-European nonmembers of EC or EFTA
[c] Except Japan.
[d] Except South Africa.
[e] Mainly claims and liabilities in precious metals.
Source: Swiss National Bank, *Das Schweizerische Bankwesen*. See table 8-1 for the conversion of Swiss-franc to dollar values.

of 1989, Swiss banks, including their foreign branches, were net creditors vis-à-vis the highly industrialized countries. By contrast, they maintained a net debtor position vis-à-vis the Middle East, the Caribbean, and Latin America. These patterns are even more pronounced if the Swiss banks' fiduciary deposits are taken into account.

The most internationalized segments of Swiss banking involve such off-balance-sheet activities as foreign-exchange dealing, portfolio management, and underwriting. According to statistics collected by the Bank for International Settlements in 1989, the Swiss foreign-exchange market was the fourth largest in the world. Unfortunately, no reliable data exist on the size and attributes of portfolios managed by Swiss banks. As regards underwriting, we showed above that the bulk of primary issues in the Swiss capital market (71% in 1988 and 62% in 1989) originated with foreign debtors. A large fraction of foreign securities underwritten by Swiss banks are ultimately purchased by foreigners, as indicated by the fact that aggregate primary issues in 1988 and 1989 were three to four times larger than the surplus of the Swiss balance of payments on current account. Thus, Swiss banks not only serve as instruments for exporting capital, but also play an important role as intermediaries between foreign borrowers and foreign lenders.

2. A Brief History of the Development of the Current Banking Structure[1]

Swiss banking is not an old industry. As late as in the eighteenth century, very few banks existed in Switzerland. Although the industrial revolution hit Switzerland at a relatively early stage, demand for credit remained low for a long time. Until the middle of the nineteenth century, the Swiss economy was dominated by small firms that relied extensively on retained profits as a source of finance. Moreover, there was no need for capital imports. On the contrary, Switzerland had tended to export capital since the sixteenth century. For these reasons, the first banks that sprung up in the second half of the eighteenth century were established mainly for the purpose of placing domestic funds abroad.

The fiscal behavior of Swiss governments was another factor keeping domestic credit demand low. The governments of Zurich and Berne, in particular, tended to run budget surpluses. The absence of major wars from the sixteenth century onwards contributed to the healthy state of public finances. This contrasts sharply with the experience of other European countries, where the need to finance governments deficits provided a strong impetus to the establishment of banks. The international posture of early Swiss bankers gave rise to a paradoxical situation. At the end of the eighteenth century, Swiss bankers, notably private bankers from Geneva, already played an important role on the major foreign financial markets, while the domestic banking system was still in an embryonic state.

After the end of the Napoleonic wars, the growth of the Swiss banking system slowly began to take off. Much of its early development occurred in the period 1840–1880. At first, this period witnessed a rapid proliferation of savings banks that were established partly for philanthropic reasons. Through 1880, over 200 savings banks were set up in Switzerland. Railway construction and the emergence of big industrial companies served as another driving force behind the early development of the Swiss banking system. The traditional mode of ploughing back retained profits proved inadequate for financing these projects. New sources of finance were required. To this end, the first joint-stock banks, the forerunners of the present big banks, were established. The joint-stock banks not only played a key role in financing the industrial revolution, but they were also instrumental in the formation of the first Swiss insurance companies and stock exchanges.

The middle of the nineteenth century also saw the creation of the first mortgage or regional banks. To this day, mortgage lending has remained one of the most important activities of Swiss banks. In addition, most cantons decided to set up cantonal banks. These institutions, which also stressed mortgage lending, were either newly established or resulted from takeovers of existing privately owned banks.

The cantonal banks, together with a few privately owned banks, also undertook to issue notes. In 1848, Switzerland became a unified country with a central government. Under the new political regime, Switzerland introduced a uniform monetary standard, modeled after the bimetallic system of France, that replaced the existing multiplicity of currencies. Gold and silver coins served as legal tender. Furthermore, banks were authorized to issue notes, convertible into gold or silver coins at fixed exchange rates. Upon establishment of the Swiss National Bank at the beginning of 1907, there were 36 banks of issue in Switzerland. Since 1907, the note issue privilege has been vested exclusively in the SNB.

Around 1880, the explosive growth of the Swiss banking system began to slow down. The rate at which new banks were established not only declined markedly, but the frequency of bank failures also rose. The Swiss banking system passed through a prolonged period of structural change and gradually assumed its present form. The most significant structural change was the evolution of the universal bank as a means of diversifying risk. The degree of concentration of the Swiss banking industry also increased. After a peak in 1880, the number of banks began to shrink, a process that continued intermittently until the 1930s. The trend toward greater concentration was accompanied by a rapid spread of branch banking, especially after the turn of the century. Another structural change was a strong increase in the internationalization of banking. Toward the end of the nineteenth century, foreign banks started to penetrate Switzerland, while the domestic institutions undertook to expand their foreign business. Switzerland once again turned into a capital exporter, after having temporarily borrowed funds abroad in order to finance new industries and railways. At the eve of World War I, the size of Swiss net foreign assets in per capita terms was probably unmatched by any other country.

After a brief period of prosperity in the 1920s, Swiss banks were thrown into a serious turmoil by the Great Depression. They incurred huge losses as a result of the slump in economic activity, the collapse of the gold standard, and the imposition of exchange controls in Germany. Among the eight major banks operating at that time, three institutions failed or were rescued by the authorities. A total of about 40 other banks failed, equalling over 10% of existing institutions. The financial crisis prompted the authorities to tighten up bank supervision. In 1934, the Swiss Bank Act was passed. It transferred to the federal government the responsibility for supervising banks. After the devaluation of the Swiss franc in 1936, the Swiss economy, including the banking system, slowly recovered again.

Since Switzerland was able to stay out of World War II, it was spared the economic devastation of its neighboring countries. Swiss banking activity continued to expand, albeit at a modest pace. Owing to the high domestic savings rate and the efficient domestic capital market, the Swiss government managed to finance its huge war-time budget deficits by issuing long-term securities to the public, rather than by money creation. During World War I, by contrast, money creation had served as an important source of government finance.

The recovery of the European economies after World War II, as well as the liberalization of trade, triggered a renewed surge in Swiss banking activities. The number of banks that had reached a low in the Great Depression began to rise again. It has increased steadily since, except for a temporary decline during the recession of 1974–1975. The number of bank branches has grown even more rapidly. Total assets of Swiss banks and finance companies climbed from $6.7 billion at the end of 1950 to

$660.2 billion at the end of 1989 (table 8-2). Valued in Swiss francs, they rose by an average of 9.8% per year over that period. The banks' asset growth clearly exceeded the growth in nominal GNP, averaging 7.0% per year from 1950 to 1989. In the second half of the 1960s, in particular, the Swiss banks took a "great leap forward" that reflected a renewed surge in their foreign business, as well as a marked increase in domestic economic activity. Data on the assets and liabilities of Swiss Banks and finance companies, broken down by banking groups, are presented in table 8-4.

3. Current regulation and supervision of banking

3.1. Major Regulatory Agencies

In Switzerland, bank supervision is entrusted to the *Federal Banking Commission* (FBC). The FBC is an independent authority. It is attached to the Ministry of Finance for administrative purposes, but receives no instructions from the government. It comprises seven to nine commissioners appointed by the federal government. Among the commissioners, only the president of the FBC holds a full-time appointment; all the others perform their duties part-time. The commissioners are in turn assisted by a secretariat made up of full-time staff members.

The FBC enforces the Swiss Bank Act, as well as two ordinances based on this Act. Swiss banking legislation closely circumscribes the supervisory powers of the FBC. Inasmuch as it leaves room for discretion, the FBC may pass supplementary regulations in the form of circular letters to the banks. The FBC is also responsible for licensing new banks and for deciding whether finance companies or other nonbanks conducting banking business should be brought within the realm of the Swiss Bank Act.

The FBC relies on an indirect approach of supervising banks. It rarely examines banks on the spot. Instead, it delegates that task to the external auditors of the banks. The banks are legally obliged to have their books examined by auditing firms, requiring a permit from the FBC to carry out their duties. The banks' auditors must report annually to the FBC. In particular, they must check whether their clients have complied with Swiss banking regulations and must report violations to the FBC. If they neglect to perform their duties properly, they are liable to criminal prosecution.

The *Swiss National Bank*, by contrast, has no authority over prudential supervision. However, as a lender of last resort to the domestic banks, the SNB shares with the FBC the responsibility for maintaining the stability of the Swiss financial system.

In addition to the FBC and the SNB, the *Swiss Bankers' Association* may be regarded as an institution fullfilling supervisory functions. The SBA is an organization representing 450 member banks. It not only acts as a lobby of the banks, but has also concluded a variety of conventions among its members. These conventions serve two fundamentally different purposes. On the one hand, they establish codes of conduct supplementing Swiss banking legislation. On the other hand, they constitute cartel arrangements restricting competition among banks.

3.2. Types of Regulations

As was pointed out above, Swiss banking legislation is applicable to banks and any other institutions pursuing banking activities. Anyone intending to open a bank in Switzerland must apply for a *license* from the FBC. The license is granted if the applicant meets certain minimum conditions with regard to organization and management of the prospective bank. Should an already existing bank fail to satisfy these conditions, the FBC may revoke its license.

Various provisions impinge upon the structure of the banks' balance sheets. The banks must comply with risk-weighted *minimum capital requirements* against their assets, as well as their off-balance-sheet positions. The capital requirements are applicable to the banks' domestic and foreign operations, including their foreign subsidiaries. At the end of 1989, required capital averaged approximately 8% of bank assets. In addition, banks are subject to *liquidity requirements*, stipulating minimum holdings of both cash reserves and total short-term assets. They are also obliged to report to the FBC *loans to and deposits from individual customers* exceeding certain percentages of total capital and short-term liabilities, respectively.

Besides its emphasis on adequate capital and liquidity of domestic financial institutions, Swiss banking legislation contains few other provisions guaranteeing the *safety of bank deposits*. In the event of bank runs, individual institutions may ask the federal government to lift temporarily their obligation to pay out cash on demand. Moreover, owners of savings deposits hold a limited first claim on the assets of an insolvent bank. In contrast to many other countries, Switzerland does not have a deposit insurance scheme. In lieu of deposit insurance, the Swiss Bankers' Association has concluded a convention among its members. The participating banks are prepared jointly to guarantee the savings deposits at insolvent institutions. This convention is little known among the Swiss public and has never been used. As indicated above, the deposits at the cantonal banks are partly guaranteed by the respective cantonal governments.

Swiss banking legislation also contains various provisions on the *admission of foreign banks*. As pointed out in section 2, foreign banks have been active in Switzerland for a long time. They conduct their business through subsidiaries, branches, agencies, and representative offices. To establish a bank in Switzerland, foreigners must not only comply with all the requirements existing for Swiss nationals but also with a few additional provisions aimed specifically at applicants from abroad. These additional requirements are insignificant, save for the obligation that the country whose banks seek admission to Switzerland must accord reciprocal treatment to Swiss banks. The FBC has attempted to enforce this reciprocity rule liberally. In particular, it does not insist on mirror-image reciprocity. Thus, it does not demand that Swiss banks in other countries be able to engage in exactly the same range of activities as foreign banks in Switzerland. In the case of the United States, the FBC only admits banks from states that accord reciprocal treatment to Swiss banks.

Foreign-controlled subsidiaries, branches and agencies may engage in the same activities as domestically controlled banks. Foreign-controlled subsidiaries must comply with all the provisions of Swiss banking legislation, including capital requirements. Foreign-controlled branches and agencies are governed by a separate ordinance based on the Swiss Bank Act. They need not comply with Swiss capital requirements but instead must hold 10% of their assets in Switzerland. In line with the Basle Concordat, they must also demonstrate that they are adequately supervised by their parent-country authorities.

3.3. Role of the Central Bank

As with other central banks, the Swiss National Bank is obliged to act as a lender of last resort to the banking system. It has traditionally interpreted its lender-of-last-resort role restrictively. As a rule, the SNB is only prepared to provide liquidity assistance in exceptional circumstances. It is willing to intervene in the event of major liquidity problems that may threaten the stability of the domestic financial system. In the SNB's view, liquidity problems arising from the interbank payments system do not call for central-bank action, at least not in normal circumstances. The banks should maintain sufficiently high cash reserves in order to be able to absorb normal fluctuations in their payments flows. Should the SNB be compelled to intervene, it prefers to provide liquidity assistance to the market as a whole, rather than to individual banks. Its reluctance to deal with individual banks derives from two observations. First, if caught in a liquidity squeeze, a solvent bank should always be able to get the required funds on the money market, provided the aggregate supply of liquidity is adequate. Second, owing to the rapid development of financial activities outside the banking system, liquidity problems may erupt increasingly in the nonbank sectors of the economy. Therefore, the SNB should not direct its liquidity assistance exclusively at the banks.

4. Major Current Operating and Regulatory Problems

4.1. Banks

4.1.1. Strengthening the Solvency of Banks. Although the Swiss approach to bank supervision has worked well, a few gaps in the domestic supervisory system remain. In line with similar efforts in other countries, Swiss supervisory authorities currently focus their attention on consolidation and capital adequacy.

Until recently, Swiss banking legislation only applied to institutions located in Switzerland, as well as to the foreign branches of domestic banks. Switzerland was among the first countries to modify this approach and to shift to a consolidated system of bank supervision, that is, to extend supervision to the foreign subsidiaries of domestic banks. A consolidated approach is followed in three regulatory areas: licensing of banks, calculation of required capital, and control of exposure vis-à-vis individual borrowers or depositors. An unresolved issue is how required capital should be determined in the case of bank holding companies, since these are not mentioned explicitly in the Swiss Bank Act.

Swiss banks are well capitalized as compared with financial institutions in other countries. For this reason, they are able to satisfy without difficulty the minimum capital requirements recently set by the Basle Committee on Banking supervision, even if their substantial hidden reserves are disregarded. To date, Switzerland has not fully switched to the Basle framework on capital adequacy because Swiss requirements already cover some types of risk (especially price risk) on which the Basle Committee has not yet passed any recommendations. A partial adaptation to the Basle framework occurred on January 1, 1990. Swiss capital requirements were extended to most of the banks off-balance-sheet positions. But Swiss authorities took pains not to tighten capital requirements. Therefore, they took advantage of the less stringent Basle rules by relaxing these requirements in two other areas. They adopted the Basle Committee's treatment of foreign assets, as well as its formula for subsuming subordinated bonds in required capital.

4.1.2. Competitive efficiency. In Switzerland, supervision of the financial sector focuses on the banks, even though banking business is increasingly conducted by near-bank competitors, notably finance companies. This development not only widens the gaps in the Swiss supervisory system, but also distorts competition between the tightly supervised banks and the less regulated near banks. For this reason, on January 1, 1990 Swiss authorities extended the legal definition of a bank. Finance companies involved in underwriting or important lending activities are now also regarded as banks and, therefore, must comply fully with Swiss banking legislation. In particular, if treated as banks, foreign finance companies must satisfy Swiss reciprocity rules (see section 3.2). While finance companies now compete with banks on an equal footing, it is possible that the intensity of competition will decline as a result of extending the reciprocity rules to the finance companies. To mitigate this problem, existing finance companies will be exempted from the reciprocity rules by a grandfathering clause.

Competition among Swiss banks has traditionally been restricted by cartel agreements at the national and local levels. Owing to stiff international competition, the significance of these agreements is declining. In addition, the Swiss Cartel Commission has demanded that various restrictive agreements be lifted. As a consequence, the banks have abandoned some of their restrictive practices (e.g., an agreement fixing rates on small time deposits). However, they insist on retaining all the other agreements contested by the Commission (mainly agreements fixing portfolio management fees and commissions on securities traded in the secondary market, as well as an agreement establishing rules about membership in underwriting syndicates). This matter is currently examined by the federal minister of the economy, who is empowered to dissolve restrictive agreements contested by the Commission. To date, the Commission has not investigated local restrictive agreements fixing interest rates on various types of bank loans, including mortgages. These agreements have already been weakened or abandoned as a result of increased competition in financial markets.

4.1.3. Warding Off Funds from Criminal Sources.

Swiss banks are often accused of serving as a safe haven for funds gained from unsavory activities. Swiss banking secrecy, it is widely believed, helps to conceal these funds from law enforcement agencies. Although these accusations are justified to some extent, we should nevertheless emphasize that many critics of Swiss banks misunderstand the nature of Swiss banking secrecy. Banking secrecy by itself is not a uniquely Swiss institution. In most countries, banks are not allowed to disclose information on individual customers. The distinguishing feature of Swiss banking secrecy resides in the fact that the criminal authoritices must prosecute ex officio bank officials suspected of breaching secrecy. This does not imply that secrecy is absolute. The banks must disclose to Swiss authorities information on customers involved in criminal activities. Swiss authorities are also prepared to assist foreign governments in investigations of criminal activities by customers of Swiss banks. However, they provide legal assistance only if the offense concerned is subject to criminal prosecution under Swiss law. In practice, this condition attached to legal assistance tends to raise four problems:

1. Swiss authorities are unable to provide legal assistance on cases involving international transfers of foreign exchange and capital that are illegal in other countries. In Switzerland, there are virtually no restrictions on imports and exports of foreign exchange or capital. Even so, according to an agreement concluded between the FBC and the Swiss Bankers' Association (see below), the banks are not to help customers who wish to transfer funds to Switzerland illegally.
2. As far as tax offenses are concerned, Swiss legislation draws a distinction between tax evasion (providing false information on tax returns) and tax fraud (forging documents and engaging in similar criminal activities in connection with filing tax returns). Tax fraud is a criminal offense in Switzerland, but not tax evasion. Therefore, Swiss authorities only provide legal assistance in cases involving tax fraud.
3. Insider trading has been a criminal offense in Switzerland since the beginning of 1989. Therefore, Swiss authorities now provide legal assistance on insider trading cases.
4. Only since August 1990, money laundering has been a criminal offense in Switzerland. Simultaneously, banks and other professional asset managers have been legally obliged to verify the identity of their customers. Further measures to curb money laundering are presently under discussion.

Contrary to a popular misconception, anonymous bank accounts do not exist in Switzerland. In particular, the famous numbered accounts are not, as is widely believed, anonymous accounts. The banks use numbered accounts merely to ensure that only a handful of officials know the names of their customers. As a matter of fact, the banks are required to verify to the best of their abilities the true identity of their account holders. The same requirement applies to holders of fiduciary accounts and safe deposit boxes. If customers place funds with the banks through such middlemen as lawyers or nonbank portfolio managers, the latter must disclose the identity of the true owners of these funds. Furthermore, banks are not to assist their customers in capital flight and attempts to deceive foreign authorities. These requirements are laid down in the agreement mentioned above that was concluded between the FBC and the Swiss Bankers' Association in 1987. It replaced an earlier agreement concluded in 1982 between the SNB and the banks and in July 1990 was supplemented by the mentioned article on money laundering in the penal code.

4.2. Capital Markets

The operating and regulatory problems of Swiss stock exchanges are also debated extensively. The Swiss stock exchanges are frequently criticized for following a parochial approach to trading that is at odds with the current trend toward globalization of capital markets. While this criticism is partly justified, the strengths of Swiss stock exchanges should not be overlooked. In the following, we shall briefly describe the main strengths and weaknesses of Swiss stock exchanges.

The principal strength of Swiss stock exchanges lies in an efficient settlement system. To facilitate settlements, the stock exchanges are supported by a number of institutions operated by the banks. The Swiss Securities Clearing Corporation (SEGA) is responsible for settling domestically issued securities, while the Swiss Corporation for International Securities (Intersettle), established in June 1989, settles transactions in foreign securities. SOFFEX also involves a highly efficient settlement system.

Critics of the Swiss stock exchanges tend to stress several shortcomings. First, the transparency of securities trading leaves something to be desired. Banks need not execute buying and selling orders by their customers at a stock exchange. Instead, the normal procedure involves two steps. In a first step, banks net internally buying and selling orders for the individual listings. If buying orders fail to match selling orders, the banks subsequently purchase or sell the balance at a stock exchange. Thus, only a fraction of customer orders actually passes through a stock exchange. Although banks are legally required to offer or charge market prices to their customers, it is not always easy to determine the market price applicable to internally netted securities, notably in the case of listings traded sequentially. Furthermore, the stock exchanges until very recently were loath to publish statistics on the volume of securities traded. Due to the paucity of data, it was virtually impossible to appraise the liquidity of Swiss securities markets.

In response to this criticism, the stock exchanges have undertaken to improve the flow of statistical information. In 1989, reported turnover on the seven Swiss stock exchanges and on the over-the-counter market totaled $979 billion. From 1950 to 1989, its annual growth calculated in Swiss francs averaged 13%, with a particularly pronounced expansion setting in after 1980. Furthermore, in 1989, daily turnover of the 11 SOFFEX stocks averaged $125 million or 0.37% of the market value of outstanding shares. That percentage roughly matches the levels recorded for similar stocks at major foreign stock exchanges. The average daily volume of SOFFEX reached 24,600 contracts in 1989. Index options accounted for almost half of the total. The Swiss stock exchanges list a number of privately written options that successfully compete with SOFFEX.

A second shortcoming resides in the procedures employed for listing securities on the Swiss stock exchanges. The responsibility for listing securities issued by Swiss residents rests with the individual stock exchanges, which do not apply uniform criteria in this regard. Until very recently, securities issued by foreign residents could be listed only upon approval by the Swiss Admissions Board, a semiprivate body. The Federal Department of Finance was entitled to send an observer to the deliberations of the Board. At present, the future of the Board is uncertain because the SNB, which signed the agreement establishing the Board but did not participate in its deliberations, has withdrawn from this body. The SNB opposes the discriminatory treatment of foreign securities, as well as the Board's insistence on rating the creditworthiness of foreign borrowers wishing to have their securities listed on the Swiss stock exchanges. According to the SNB, uniform criteria should be applied to domestic and foreign securities. Furthermore, the Board, the SNB maintains, should tighten up the reporting requirements for Swiss and foreign borrowers whose securities are listed on domestic stock exchanges, in lieu of rating their creditworthiness.

A third shortcoming arises from the restrictions Swiss corporations may impose on the voting rights attached to their shares. In Switzerland, corporations may issue registered, bearer, and nonvoting shares. In the case of registered shares, existing shareholders may confer upon the board of directors the authority to curtail or lift the voting rights of new buyers of shares. This device is frequently employed to prevent foreign control of domestic corporations, to forestall unfriendly takeovers, or to keep out groups of investors that might challenge existing management. As a result, bearer and nonvoting shares normally command a premium over registered shares. Besides possible detrimental effects on the efficiency of domestic corporations, the fetters on voting rights tend to diminish the attractiveness of Swiss shares and to impair the liquidity of domestic securities markets. Under the revised Swiss corporate law, which will come into force in 1992, the transfer of voting rights can only be denied on grands of statutory per capita limitations.

In this context, some critics argue that the bulk of the restrictions on voting rights should be replaced by new regulations on takeovers of listed corporations. For this reason, the Association of Swiss Stock Exchanges adopted a takeover code. It stipulates that offers to take over partially or fully a listed company must be disclosed to the public. The offer must identify the prospective buyer of the company's shares and list his existing participation. Moreover, the offer must remain valid for at least one month and must show the price at which the buyer is willing to acquire the shares. The takeover code also stipulates that all existing shareholders be treated equally.

Since the takeover code is a private contract between the stock exchanges, it cannot be easily enforced. However, the members of the stock exchanges have agreed not to participate in takeover attempts violating the code. The code is unlikely to resolve all the problems posed by takeovers of listed companies. Many critics believe that the code is biased against prospective buyers of listed companies and, therefore, will not do much to eliminate the inefficiencies caused by Swiss restrictions on voting rights.

A fourth shortcoming concerns the supervision of Swiss secondary markets for securities. As we pointed out above, in principle, the cantons are responsible for supervising securities trading. This implies that both the market participants and the stock exchanges are supervised in a fragmented and heterogeneous manner. Inasmuch as banks engage in securities trading, the federal authorities, through the FBC, supervise the market participants. While the members of the stock exchanges normally consist of banks, numerous near banks and nonbanks are also involved in securities trading. At present, only the Canton of Zurich supervises the activities of these nearbanks and nonbanks. Although the need for a uniform system of supervising Swiss securities markets is widely accepted, public opinion is divided as to the means by which this objective should be achieved.

5. Globalization

5.1. Domestic Bank Structure

Swiss financial markets have traditionally been open to foreigners. Therefore, as we pointed out above, foreign-controlled banks and finance companies play an important role in Switzerland. Foreign banks and finance companies, along with the big Swiss-controlled banks, are active in such areas as underwriting securities issued by foreigners, managing foreign portfolios, and dealing in swaps, futures and options. Thus, increased globalization bears mostly upon the foreign business of banks.

Foreign-controlled financial institutions, by contrast, have not penetrated the market segments that are typically dominated by domestically controlled banks (table 8-4). In particular, they are little involved in the mortgage and savings deposit business, even though no significant legal barriers to entry exist to these markets. Until recently, mortgage lending by foreign-controlled banks was hampered by the severe Swiss restrictions on foreign ownership of domestic real estate. However, foreign-controlled banks are now allowed to keep for two years real estate they acquire from insolvent mortgage debtors. Nevertheless, foreign-controlled banks stay away from the mortgage and savings deposit business. They are not sufficiently well known among the Swiss public and do not possess enough branches to compete effectively with the domestic banks in these areas.

Although banks specializing in the traditional domestic financial activities are sheltered to a large extent from foreign competition, they face the challenge of having to perform successfully in markets with little prospect of rapid growth. As we saw earlier, the foreign business of Swiss banks has expanded much more strongly than their domestic business. Some of the domestically oriented banks, therefore, seek refuge in increased cooperation or mergers with other institutions.

5.2. Participation of Domestic Banks in Other Countries

Swiss banks—which have long been active abroad—are benefiting from the efforts of many countries to remove controls on international capital flows and barriers to entry in domestic financial markets. Liberalization of financial markets in Japan and the EC, in particular, has prompted Swiss banks to strengthen their presence in these parts of the world. An additional inducement for setting up foreign branches or subsidiaries arises from the fact that, mainly for the tax reasons mentioned earlier, important market segments have developed abroad. There are no significant primary and secondary markets for foreign-currency securities in Switzerland (Eurobonds and Euronotes). Moreover, even the Swiss-franc money and secondary securities markets have partly moved abroad, notably the markets for currency and interest-rate swaps, as well as for backup facilities denominated in Swiss francs. Therefore, banks cannot participate in all aspects of the Swiss-franc business unless they are present in the important foreign financial centers. Although the big banks are increasingly becoming international, they attempt to preserve their Swiss character by following defensive strategies, such as limiting foreign ownership of their shares, and offensive strategies, such as setting up multinational bank holding companies or cooperating with foreign financial institutions. The domestically oriented banks, by contrast, find it too risky and costly to establish branches or subsidiaries in other countries.

5.3. European Integration

Although not a member, Switzerland already maintains close economic links to the European Communities. In 1989, the EC countries absorbed 57% of aggregate Swiss commodity exports and furnished 71% of imports. Since commodity imports from the EC far exceed exports, Switzerland is an important market for Community producers. Swiss and Community financial markets are also closely integrated. At the end of 1989, the share of the EC in the Swiss banks' aggregate foreign assets and liabilities (including fiduciary funds) amounted to 63.9% and 42.3%, respectively (table 8-8). Thus, Swiss banks are substantial net creditors vis-à-vis the EC. The high degree of financial integration with the EC is attributable to the fact that Switzerland never restricted significantly international capital flows.

Liberalization of capital flows and deregulation of financial markets within the EC is likely to affect Swiss banks in positive and negative ways. On the one hand, these developments will open up new opportunities for Swiss banks in the EC. On the other hand, the traditional competitive edge of Swiss banks will be blunted, since liberalization and deregulation will strengthen the financial markets of the EC. On the whole, we expect Swiss banks to benefit, rather than to suffer, from European integration.

Nonmembers of the EC have expressed some concern about the Community's intention to liberalize internal trade in financial services. EC banks and securities dealers (as well as non-life-insurance companies) will be able to open branches freely throughout the Community. Subsidiaries of banks and securities dealers from non-EC countries will be granted the same privileges as their EC counterparts. To obtain a license for operating subsidiaries in the EC, non-EC banks and securities dealers will have to meet uniform Community requirements. In particular, the EC will insist on a still vaguely defined reciprocity rule. That rule should not hurt Swiss financial institutions. As pointed out above, Switzerland itself applies a reciprocity requirement that most of the EC countries presently meet. Conversely, Swiss banks maintain branches or subsidiaries in most EC countries.

In all likelihood, the EC will enforce its reciprocity rule in a fashion similar to Switzerland. It will probably employ that rule for opening up the financial markets of highly protectionist nonmembers, rather than for shielding its domestic markets from non-EC competition. We expect the new EC reciprocity rules to be more beneficial to Swiss-controlled banks than the existing national regimes. If a Swiss-controlled subsidiary is admitted to one EC country, it will automatically be allowed to do business elsewhere in the EC. Only for EC branches of non-EC banks will the existing national regimes remain in force. Furthermore, the EC seems to envisage settling conflicts with nonmembers over reciprocity by negotiation, rather than retaliation. For these reasons, it is highly unlikely that in the future Swiss authorities will refuse to admit banks from any member country of the EC.

As European integration progresses, Switzerland will probably be compelled to adapt various domestic rules and regulations to those of the EC. In the areas of banking and finance, the need for adaptation will comprise

- modifying or removing the Swiss stamp tax;
- modifying Swiss restrictions on the transfer of ownership of shares issued by domestic corporations; and
- reconciling the Swiss takeover code with that of the EC.

Many of these difficulties cannot be resolved unless jurisdiction over Swiss securities markets is passed from the cantons to the federal government.

An interesting approach to furthering integration of Swiss and Community financial markets was adopted in the case of the insurance industry. In 1989, Switzerland concluded with the EC an agreement eliminating barriers to entry in the nonlife sector of the insurance industry. Swiss non-life-insurance companies, which have been active in the various EC countries for a long time, are now able to operate in the EC on the same terms as their Community counterparts. In return, Switzerland is committed to accord reciprocal treatment to Community non-life-insurance companies. Switzerland is not obliged automatically to comply with Community laws on insurance. In case of conflicts, the agreement features a mechanism for reconciling differences between Swiss and Community legislation. This agreement—the first of its kind—could serve as a model for cooperation between the EC and nonmembers in other areas. Even so, the EC is no longer inclined to negotiate with Western European nonmembers on a country-by-country basis. Instead, the EC prefers to deal with the European Free Trade Association as a whole, of which Switzerland is a member.

6. The Future of the Swiss Banking System in a Global Environment

The globalization of financial markets will expose domestic banks to stiffening competition from within Switzerland and from abroad. Although Swiss banks are well prepared for competing in global markets, they clearly realize that many of their traditional comparative advantages are fading or becoming less important:

- Most Continental European countries are liberalizing international capital flows and deregulating their financial markets. Therefore, Swiss banks are facing more and more competition from institutions in other Continental European countries whose financial markets are becoming increasingly attractive to foreign investors.
- Swiss banks tended to benefit from the relatively low inflation rates in Switzerland and from the strength of the Swiss franc on the foreign-exchange market. This comparative advantage has also been eroded to some extent as member countries of the EC have successfully lowered their domestic inflation rates.
- As the importance of institutional investors increases, the traditional strengths of Swiss banks—confidentiality and ability to tailor their services to the needs of individual customers—will lose some of

their appeal. However, Swiss banks are adapting quickly to the new environment by improving their investment advice, rectifying the shortcomings of Swiss stock exchanges, and by promoting their off-balance-sheet business.
- Although Switzerland remains a country with relatively low taxes, it has ceased to be a tax haven. The stamp tax, in particular, seriously impairs the international competitiveness of Swiss banks.
- Swiss banking secrecy has lost some of its glitter. Swiss authorities are more willing than in the past to provide legal assistance to foreign governments and to lift banking secrecy if customers of Swiss banks are charged with criminal activities.

Even though the adjustment to globalized markets raises various difficulties, Switzerland still offers an environment conducive to banking. Political neutrality and stability, a strong tradition of free enterprise and free financial markets, and an independent central bank sustain the prosperity of the domestic banking system. The competitiveness of Swiss banks is enhanced by their long-lasting international experience and their high capitalization. Furthermore, since the major institutions are universal banks with a multitude of branches, they are able to diversify their business. Diversification in turn reduces their vulnerability to difficulties in individual regions, industries, and areas of finance. Swiss banks are also well prepared for globalization in a technical sense. They may rely on a skilled labor force working in an highly computerized economy. In the past, Swiss banks, and industrial firms for that matter, were forced repeatedly to adapt to a changing domestic and international environment. We expect Swiss banks to meet decisively and successfully the challenges of globalization.

Acknowledgments

We are greatly indebted to Daniel Zuberbühler, Daniel Beck, and Peter Klauser for their very helpful comments on this chapter.

Note

1. This chapter is partly based on Ritzmann (1973).

References

Christensen, Benedicte V. *Switzerland's Role as an International Finance Center*, Occasional Papers, No. 45. Washington, DC: International Monetary Fund, 1986.

Corti, Mario A. "Switzerland: Banking, Money, and Bond Markets", in George Giddy (ed.), *International Finance Handbook*, Section 4.6, Vol. 1. New York: John Wiley & Sons, 1983, pp. 1–50.

Federal Banking Commission. *Jahresberichte (Rapports de gestion)*, 1987 and 1988.

OECD. *Switzerland, OECD Economic Surveys*. Paris: OECD, 1986/87.

Ritzmann, Franz. *Die Schweizer Banken. Geschichte—Theorie—Statistik*. Berne and Stuttgart: Paul Haupt, 1973.

Swiss National Bank. *Das schweizerische Bankwesen*. Zurich, 1988 and 1989.

Swiss National Bank. *Monatsbericht*. Zurich, April and May, 1990.

Union Bank of Switzerland. *Swiss Federal Banking Law, Federal Law relating to Banks and Savings Banks, Including Implementing Ordinance*. Zurich, 1990.

9 COMPETITION, DIVERSIFICATION, AND STRUCTURAL CHANGE IN THE BRITISH FINANCIAL SYSTEM

David T. Llewellyn

The British financial system has a dual structure with two parallel financial systems since it is both the national system of the United Kingdom, but also one of the world's major international financial centers and hosts the largest component of the Eurocurrency and bond markets. In 1989, of the 551 banking institutions authorized in the U.K., 256 were foreign and 68 were U.K.-incorporated subsidiaries of overseas institutions. Authorized banking institutions from 64 countries had offices in the U.K. Of the £1000 billion of assets of banks in the U.K., 59% are denominated in foreign currency, and the foreign-currency assets of foreign banks in the U.K. represent 83% of the total, with the largest single component being that of Japanese banks. Thus, in terms of volume of assets, the foreign-currency business of banks in the U.K. is considerably larger than sterling domestic business.

Analyzing the structure of U.K. banking, when the industry is in the midst of an uncompleted phase of major structural change and financial innovation as great as any experienced this century, immediately presents major methodological problems. The business of banking is changing in two fundamental ways: 1) banks have increasingly become multiproduct firms, encompassing a range of services far wider than the traditional role of asset-liability transformation, and in particular fee income and off-balance-sheet business have increased; and 2) the traditional structured or specialist basis of the British financial system has given way (under the pressures of competition, technology, and deregulation) to a more conglomerate structure that has eroded the traditional distinctions between the major areas of finance.

The theme of this chapter is that the British financial system is in the midst of a period of major structural change as all types of financial institutions are diversifying their range of business under the impact of greatly intensified competitive pressures, international pressures, major changes in the structure and style of regulation, technology, and changes in the market environment. In the process, traditional distinctions between specialist financial institutions are being eroded, nonbank financial institutions are conducting traditional "banking business," banks are conducting "nonbanking" financial business, and nonfinancial companies (e.g., retail stores) are also entering into the business of financial services.

The structure of the chapter is as follows. Section 1 reviews the nature and form of structural change and financial innovation in the British financial system. Section 2 considers the role and impact of the most powerful pressure—competition—producing structural change and what might be predicted for a financial system subject to more intensive internal and international competitive pressures. Section 3 considers two potential problem areas related to recent trends (profitability and the viability of financial conglomerates), and Section 4 discusses the issues in the context of international competitive pressures that might be expected as a result of the "1992 arrangements" in the EC.

1. Structural Change

1.1. Central Structural Issue

At the risk of oversimplification, financial services can be broadly divided into six categories: commercial banking, investment/merchant banking, insurance, fund management, housing finance, and securities trading. The central strategic issue of any financial system is that of *separation* versus *integration*, though in practice it is almost invariably a question of the balance between the two polar cases. In the former, different categories of finance are conducted by specialist institutions with clear demarcation lines between different types of activity and institution.

With an integrated or conglomerate system, all (or a wide variety) of functions are performed by single institutions with little to delineate the different functions of different institutions.

Since regulatory arrangements in this dimension are different in different countries, this creates potential competitive distortions for those institutions that conduct business in several countries, in that under host-country regulatory regimes they are legally able to conduct business in foreign countries from which they may be debarred in their own. Conversely, under home-country regulatory regimes, foreign institutions may be able to conduct business in a country from which domestic institutions are debarred. The globalization of banking and financial markets, and the increasing integration of markets domestically and internationally, create pressures on regulation that is not competitively neutral as between institutions within a national system and between countries. Thus, regulation (legal or informal) that enforces limits on the range of business (e.g., between investment and commercial banking) is likely to be undermined via global competitive pressures. Eisenbeis (1989) suggests that regulation that constrains one set of institutions creates opportunities for nondomestic institutions to secure competitive advantages, induces domestic residents to use foreign institutions and markets, and drives domestic institutions overseas.

In those countries where regulation, or restrictive practices, has traditionally enforced separation, these impositions tended to be liberalized over the 1980s. This has been the result of several interacting and simultaneous pressures: global competitive pressures; the evolving diversification strategies of financial institutions seeking competitive advantages through the offer (sometimes on a global basis) of a full range of financial services and the alleged synergies associated with economies of scope; the intensification of competitive pressures in institutions' traditional markets and business areas; and the requirements of competitive neutrality in regulation as, through financial innovation, distinctions are eroded between different types of financial intermediation mechanisms (e.g., banks and capital markets) and instruments. In the U.K., the prevailing political orthodoxy of the 1980s was that diversification should not be impeded because it implies financial services being supplied under more competitive conditions with a presumed benefit (in terms of efficiency, choice, and price) to the consumer.

Many countries are moving further along the structural spectrum towards the conglomerate end. It is a process that, once begun, is difficult to halt, since the process itself creates competitive distortions to the extent that allowable diversification between potentially competing sets of hitherto differentiated institutions is not symmetrical and equal in both directions. A major factor in the early 1980s behind the demand by U.K. building societies for an extension of their powers was the move by the banks into the mortgage market. Similarly, banks in many countries (including those where regulation impedes it) have sought to diversify into the securities industry both to regain business lost through securitization but also because, as a result of financial innovation, the distinctions between banking and capital market facilities have become less powerful.

The main arguments in favor of allowing banks to diversify relate to the potential risk-reducing qualities of a diversified business; the ability to increase and widen the source of profits with potential systemic advantages; the benefits to be derived from increasing competition in the provision of financial services, and to generate alleged benefits of economies of scale but most especially of scope.

On the other hand, there are several reasons why separation might be desired. It can be viewed as one way of dealing with potential conflicts of interest that can arise in institutions conducting a wide range of business. It also makes regulation easier in that if the objective is to regulate *functions*, there is a clearly defined set of *institutions* performing each function. It also means that to a large extent regulation can be "subcontracted" to the functional sectors themselves: such self-regulation through "clubs" has been a distinctive feature of regulation in the U.K., and it has many advantages (Llewellyn, 1986). The regulatory authorities might also take the view that risks are reduced through limiting the range of business activities, and that systemic risk is lowered by, for instance, reducing the danger of contamination of one part of the business (e.g., banking) by risks in other parts (e.g., insurance). Diversification also widens the range of activities against which the lender-of-last-resort function and deposit insurance is provided.

Depending upon the type and correlation of risks involved, diversification can have the effect of improving the risk-return tradeoff (Boyd and Graham, 1986) but in the process induce institutions to incur more rather than less risk. Diversification may improve upon the set of risk-return opportunities available to a financial institution, as indicated in figure 9-1. If, prior to diversification, the institution chose point X, the new opportunities available to it involve a choice of several possibilities compared with the previous set of options: 1) more risk with a higher return than before, (A); 2) a higher return for the same risk (B); 3) a higher return and lower risk (C); 4) lower risk and the same return (D); and 5) a lower return with a lower risk (E). There is no necessary presumption that institutions will choose a less risky portfolio, and some analysis argues that institutions will do so only if shareholders of the

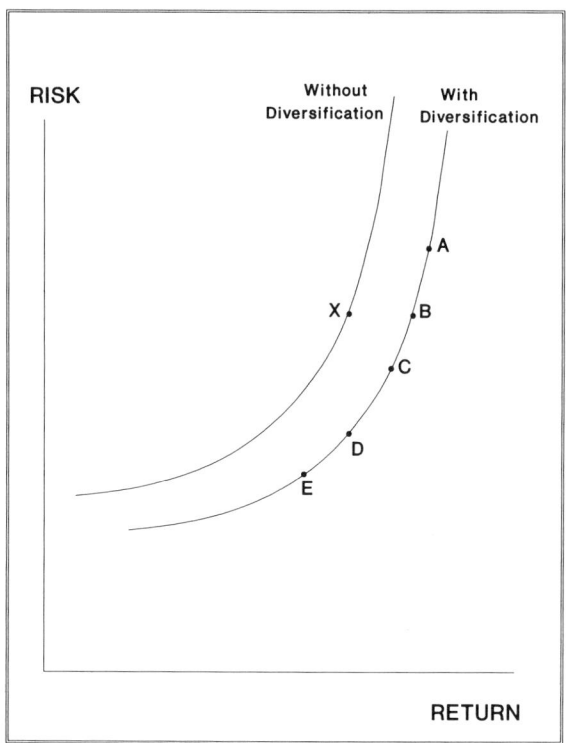

Figure 9-1. Risk-return Tradeoff.

institution are risk averse and unable to diversify their asset portfolios directly in the securities market. Thus it is theoretically possible that allowing diversification will have the effect of increasing risk, and the evidence from U.S. studies is ambiguous. Gilbart (1988) finds there is no a priori reason for supposing that diversification reduces overall risk, since it depends upon a complex of factors including the expected profitability of the new area, its inherent riskiness, the correlation with existing parts of the business, the relative size of the different business areas, and the extent of any synergies implied with alleged economies of scope. However, Clark (1988) in a survey of economies of scale and scope suggests that in general large diversified deposit institutions have not enjoyed a cost advantage over smaller, more specialized institutions. Boyd and Graham (1986) find no evidence either way with respect to risk enhancement or reduction. Overall, U.S. studies point to no unambiguous conclusions about the effect of diversification on risk, efficiency, and profitability. There seems to be little evidence of significant economies of scale.

Separation may also be favored as a means of minimizing any alleged possibility of a concentration of power in the financial system, which in turn has two dimensions: issues related to competitiveness, and the increased systemic cost if conglomerates fail. Diversification may have the effect of reducing risk in the sense of reducing the *probability* of failure. On the other hand, it may raise the systemic *cost* of failure, because a wider range of financial activities is involved. If diversification reduces risk (probability of failure), there is a tradeoff in allowing diversification between lower risk and higher systemic cost, which may mean that a regulator would choose not to allow diversification even though risk would be reduced, or to allow diversification but providing the components were separately capitalized.

1.2. Diversification: Strategic Options

This central issue relating to the structure of the financial system has five key dimensions:

1. the extent of allowable diversification by financial institutions;
2. the distinction between whether a bank or other financial institution provides an *own-service* from its own resources (implying that the risk is on the balance sheet and that capital has been allocated for it) or whether it acts solely as a *marketing agent* for another company, such as, for instance, when a bank or building society acts as an agent for an insurance company;
3. the separation between financial and nonfinancial companies;
4. the distinction between diversification and ownership; and
5. the extent to which diversification requires separate management and capitalization.

The first issue relates to the extent to which financial institutions are able to offer a wide range of financial services. When *separation* is the norm, as historically it has been in the U.K., the separation relates to differences between types of financial institution, between banking and the capital market, and between finance and industrial and commercial companies. Such separation may be imposed by regulation or be chosen for business reasons, though in some cases it may reflect restrictive practices and self-imposed anticompetitive arrangements.

Diversification is an ambiguous concept, most especially when considering risk characteristics. A financial institution (say, with an existing specialized and narrow range of business) wishing to diversify by offering a wider range of services has three basic strategic options: 1) it can develop what can be termed *own diversification*, where new business (e.g., potential insurance liabilities for a bank) is developed internally and placed on the balance sheet as the institution provides the service itself with its own resources; 2) it can purchase an existing supplier of the service (e.g., a bank buys an insurance company); or 3) it can enter into an agency arrangement whereby it sells the product of an existing independent supplier of the service: *agency diversification*.

There is a major difference between the first two options and the third. In the former case, the risk of the new business is borne by the diversifying institution, the balance sheet is constrained, and equity capital must be allocated to the new business to cover the new balance-sheet exposure risk. Comparing options 1 and 2, in principle the firm is indifferent when the cost of purchasing an existing company equals the start-up cost of providing the new service from within the firm. On the other hand, there is a risk premium to be taken into account through developing the diversified business internally (it could prove not to be successful or more difficult to develop) whereas the purchase route immediately absorbs an ongoing and presumably successful business. It also means that the acquiring institution buys the reputation and skills of the other firm and immediately gains the scale of the firm rather than building up scale through organic growth. Thus option 2 is an attractive option for a diversifying institution, and in general is the method used when banks diversified into securities trading.

In terms of risk analysis, the crucial distinction is between *own* and *agency* diversification. In the former case, the relevant criteria relate to how the new business affects the risk characteristics of the new combined balance sheet and exposure (e.g., covariance of risks, etc.). In practice, a major form of diversification is where an institution provides a wide range of services by acting as a sales agent for other institutions that absorb the balance sheet and capital risks. Obvious recent examples are where building societies have arrangements with life assurance companies and sell the latter's products. The fees earned raise the rate of return on assets and equity, and such returns may not be highly correlated with existing returns.

The *agency* form of diversification has become a significant feature of the British financial system and, as argued in section 4, may become a feature of EEC transnational business arrangements is the financial sector. A parallel could be drawn with other industries. The majority of goods are not bought directly from the manufacturer but from a store selling a wide range of goods produced by different manufacturers. The rationale is simple; the optimum scale and structure of production is different from the optimum scale and structure of distribution with the result that the producer (for a fee) subcontracts the sales process.

Traditionally, services are different, since by their nature they are delivered directly by the producer. There is no inherent reason why this must be the case. There are many advantages to such *agency* diversification: institutions may link complementary expertise; the different institutions may offer mutually advantageous economy of access by utilizing each other's delivery systems; they share each other's reputation advantages; they avoid many of the management problems of a diversified business; learning costs are avoided, as are the substantial start-up costs involved with *own diversification*; and fee income is generated without encumbering the balance sheet. At the systemic level, the *agency* route enables firms to diversify without raising the number of suppliers.

An intermediate route, between *own* and *agency* diversification, is where joint-venture companies are formed between different types of financial institutions, with each contributing its own expertise. A recent example in the U.K. is with the National Provincial Building Society, which has established a life assurance company as a joint venture with a major insurance company (General Accident).

The third dimension relates to the extent to which a formal separation is made between financial and nonfinancial companies, and the extent to which the latter are able to offer financial services. This amounts to the issue of whether, for business or regulatory reasons, finance should be regarded as an exclusively specialist activity. In most countries, there is a traditional distinction between finance and nonfinance companies, although this is breaking down. In the U.S., for instance, Sears Roebuck is one of the largest suppliers of financial services, and in the U.K. Marks and Spencer has a banking license and supplies a range of financial services, including credit. Allowing nonfinance companies to own banks could offer the advantages of diversification and widen the sources of capital for banks, although, as noted by Corrigan (1987), this is questionable unless the underlying profitability of banking is sound. But the difficulties are substantial: 1) the potential conflicts of interest are serious; 2) the commercial company might be motivated by a desire to gain access to a cheap source of finance, such as insured deposits (Roberts, 1987); 3) it potentially widens the area of the lender-of-last-resort function; 4) the question arises as to whether it is appropriate for unregulated and unsupervised commercial companies to own banks; and 5) the bank within the holding company could be used to supply cheap loans to other parts of the group, since any diminution of profits and/or rise in risk is unlikely (except in the extreme case) to raise the cost of funds to the bank. Again the issue arises as to whether the risk to the shareholder of the holding company is more efficiently diversified directly in the capital market by holding equity in a diverse range of companies or via a holding of equity in a conglomerate. Only if there are clear identifiable synergies is the latter a more efficient diversification strategy.

The issue of *separation* versus *integration* relates both to the range of allowable business and to the extent of interlocking ownership structures both within the finance sector (e.g., whether a bank can own an insurance company) and between financial institutions and nonfinance companies. These are distinct and separate issues in that, for instance, while Marks and Spencer has a banking license and sells financial services, it is open to considerable doubt at this stage whether the Bank of England would allow it to purchase an existing clearing bank or an insurance company (Leigh Pemberton, 1987).

A fifth issue, in the event that diversification into major new and different areas is allowed, relates to the extent to which the different functional areas can be managed and capitalized in an integrated manner, or whether integration by ownership is allowed while the management and/or capitalization must be kept separate. The latter is one way of handling the potential conflicts of interest involved in conglomeration and avoiding the risks of contamination, although by the same token it denies the economies of scale in the use of capital (Barge, 1985) and may impede marketing and delivery strategies.

The major remaining form of separation in the U.K. is that between insurance underwriting and banking. Loehnis (1987) notes that, while there has been no legal inhibition, the regulatory authorities have discouraged banks from entering into insurance (most especial general insurance) business due largely to fear of conflicts of interest between depositors and policyholders, and the risk of contamination. The Governor of the Bank of England (*Banking World*, August 1987) has said:

> We would not find it so difficult if the size between them were disproportionate in the sense that an insurance company that knows its business could probably safely carry a much smaller bank with its different sorts of risks, and vice versa. If you had two very large insitutions I think the problem of two totally different operations which are basically highly geared could lead to the dif-

ficulty of measuring capital and liquidity. This could set a problem not only for the group management and the group board, but also for the supervisors. We would perhaps be more reluctant about the acquisition if the two parts were of more equal size. There may well be a difference too, in assessing risks, capital, liquidity, gearing and so on, between life insurance and general insurance. I cite that as a simple illustration of the problem of the expertise required to make the right judgements.

The issue is discussed further in Bank of England (1984). Opinion seems to be shifting in favor of a more accommodating stance with respect to links between banking and insurance. There are now a number of U.K. insurance companies with interests in small deposit taking companies, and some large commercial banks own small insurance subsidiaries. The Trustee Savings Bank has recently purchased an insurance company, and a major mutual building society (Britannia) plans to purchase a mutual life assurance institution. Loehnis (1987) has stated, "What we want to avoid is insurance companies and banks of similar size forming links, but that would not necessarily preclude the building up of one within the other by organic growth, and in a few specific cases permission has been given for a significant minority stake in one to be held by the other." However, it is open to question whether in the U.K. this would extend to an ownership link or merger between a major insurance company and a major bank.

1.3. Structural Change and Financial Innovation

A central feature of the British financial system over the 1980s was an unprecedented combination (both historically and internationally) of structural change and financial innovation (Bank of England, 1983). Structural change is about how the basic functions of a financial system are performed by markets and institutions, the business structure of component institutions and markets, and changes in the market and institutional mechanisms through which financial intermediation and other services are provided.

Financial innovation has two central features: the creation of new financial instruments, techniques, and markets, and the unbundling of the separate characteristics and risks of individual instruments and their reassembling in different combinations (Llewellyn, 1988a). In the process, four central features of financial innovation emerge: it increases the range, number, and variety of financial instruments; it combines characteristics of instruments in a more varied way and widens the combination of characteristics, thereby reducing the number and size of discontinuities in the spectrum of financial instruments (a process of "spectrum filling"); it has the effect of eroding some of the differences between different forms of intermediation as, for example, where Floating Rate Notes and Note Issuance Facilities link banks and capital markets; and it has the effect of integrating financial markets, since many instruments straddle several simultaneously. Eisenbeis (1987) also suggests that some financial innovations create instruments that perform functions similar to those traditionally provided by financial intermediaries that may have the effect of lowering the demand for the services of intermediaries.

There has been a close parallel in the U.K. between structural change in the financial system and the process of financial innovation in two respects: they both imply an erosion of traditional distinctions and boundaries (a distinction between *institutional* and *instrument* integration), and both have been induced by the same pressures of competition, technology, changes in regulation, international competitive pressures, and changes in the market environment. Structural change in the financial system has involved the erosion of traditional demarcations between different subsectors of the system: *institutional integration*. Similarly, financial innovation has the effect of eroding distinctions between financial instruments and intermediation mechanisms: *instrument integration*. Over the 1980s, structural change and financial innovation were twin components of the same process: the development of a more integrated, less specialist financial system. In the process there has been a steady erosion of traditional distinctions in several dimensions: between the business of different types of institutions, between instruments, between wholesale and retail sectors, (for instance, money market interest rates are now available on retail deposits, and corporate banking products such as CAPS and COLLARS have become available in the retail mortgage market), between capital market and banking facilities, and also between functions as, for instance, where NIFs offered by banks represent a form of insurance. In the process, the British financial system has shifted perceptibly from its historical differentiated form to a more conglomerate structure.

1.4. Historic Characteristics and Structure

For most of this century, the structure of the British financial system was remarkably stable; historically it has been a highly structured system based on specialist and differentiated financial institutions and markets with clear functional demarcations between them (Revell, 1973). The City of London historically has organized itself on a highly specialist basis. In particular, and in common with many other financial systems (most notably the U.S., Canada, Japan, and Australia) but in contrast to many in Europe, there has been a clear functional distinction between the major business areas of commercial banking, investment banking, housing finance, insurance, fund management, and securities trading. However, this structured system, in contrast to the experience in other structured systems, has not been predominantly a product of official and legal regulatory limits on the range of business activities (except in the case of building societies) but more a function of restrictive practices, anticompetitive mechanisms, and self-imposed constraints. On the other hand (and for reasons already outlined), the regulatory authorities have been sympathetic to this structured approach.

1.5. Current Trends

The major structural changes that have dominated the more recent evolution of the British financial system (most especially since 1980) relate to competition, the process of diversification, the undermining of the historic structured system, the form and extent of regulation, the increasing internationalization of finance, and the acceleration in the pace of financial innovation. At the same time the business of "banking" has changed: a shift from wholesale to retail banking (discussed below), the provision of a wide range of financial services, and the development of off-balance-sheet business (Lewis, 1988). The traditional monopoly of banks in the money transmission service has also been challenged, most notably by building societies.

Overwhelming all other forces has been the role of competition as the competitive environment has intensified within and between subsectors of the system. In the process, the specialist basis of financial institutions has been powerfully eroded as diversification has produced a trend towards financial conglomerates. This has been a comparatively easy process in the U.K., since historic demarcations have been largely self-imposed rather than forced by legislation. At the same time regulation has become more formalized and explicit, and competitive pressures have undermined most of the traditional features of self-imposed regulation based upon restrictive practices.

The dominant change, and one that has been both created by competitive pressures and in itself reinforcing them, is the proccess of diversification and the erosion of the historic structured basis of the financial system. The process of diversification has involved existing institutions widening the range of products and services, and institutions purchasing firms in other sectors. The 1980s witnessed mergers and purchases between banks, securities traders and brokers of various kinds, insurance companies, investment managers and advisers, and estate agents. Banks, building societies, and insurance companies now offer a full range of financial services both via their branch network and agency arrangements. This has been occurring across the full range of financial institutions and markets. The clearing banks have bought securities trading firms and merchant banks, and they also own unit trusts (thus merging four areas of finance that have traditionally been kept separate). One bank has also bought an insurance company. At the same time, the process of diversification into a limited range of financial services includes nonfinance companies such as the BAT company and Marks and Spencer (which holds a banking license). Marks and Spencer, a nationwide retail store, launched its own unit trust in October 1988, which it sells through a directly owned subsidiary. Several national retail stores (with access to a large number of personal customers) offer credit card services and personal loans. Thus conglomeration has come to straddle financial and nonfinancial companies.

Building societies are similarly diversifying. From being a set of highly specialized institutions, whose business was exclusively to collect retail savings deposits to finance mortgage loans, they are emerging as diversified retail banks encompassing consumer lending, insurance under-writing, stock exchange brokerage services, portfolio management, and money-transmission services that have hitherto been the monopoly of a small number of clearing banks.

1.6. Shift to Retail Banking

One of the ways in which banking changed during the 1980s was in the switch at the margin in the balance between wholesale and retail (personal sector) banking, and from international to domestic business. Three major factors account for this. Firstly, the financial position of the corporate sector improved over the period, and the rising rate of return on capital and overall profitability reduced the corporate sector's dependency on external finance in general and bank finance in particular, which reversed the trend of the 1970s (Llewellyn, 1985). Secondly, and for similar reasons, banks had greater recourse to the capital (debt and equity) market for a higher proportion of their external financing needs. At the same time, there was a major stock-adjustment by the personal sector, with a substantial and simultaneous rise in the proportion of both financial assets and liabilities relative to income (Llewellyn, 1989).

However, a further dominant factor was the effect of competitive pressures, which, towards the end of the 1970s and into the 1980s, were considerably greater in wholesale and international markets and lending to the corporate sector than in retail and personal sector markets. This was visible in terms of the finer margins on on-balance-sheet loans to the corporate sector, and the profitability of some wholesale business had become very low. There are several reasons for this: 1) the corporate sector has traditionally had access to a larger number of banks than has the personal sector; 2) for corporate business, the capital market is a potential competitor to banks, and the securitization process indicates that shifts can be made when conditions are conducive; and 3) it is also the case that the capital market has been particularly innovative over the 1980s. The corporate sector also has international banking and capital market options that further intensify competitive pressures on U.K. banks' corporate sector business.

The impact of this apparent strategic shift is indicated in table 9-1, which shows that banks are now recycling deposits from the personal sector into loans to that sector, and are recouping as business deposits a large proportion of their loans to business. In contrast in the early 1980s, banks were in effect in the business of transforming personal-sector deposits into loans to the corporate sector. Hence, it would appear that increasing competition in the banks' "traditional" wholesale, corporate, and international markets has induced them to diversify their business towards the personal sector, which was perceived to be relatively more profitable. The rationale of the strategic shift can also be seen in the comparison between the relative profitability of the banks' domestic and international business: 1) domestic profits as a proportion of assets are around three times as great as profits on international business; 2) there was a rise in the basic profitability of domestic business, which is not the case for international business; and 3) the recent provisioning problems have been associated exclusively with international assets. The major growth areas for the banks have been personal mortgage lending and both lending and deposits to "other financial institutions" (OFI). As a proportion of assets, lending to the personal and OFI sectors increased from 18% to 32% and from 15% to 24%, respectively, over the period

Table 9-1. U.K. Monetary Sector: Position Against Sectors (£ Billion)

	1980			1983			1987		
	Liabilities	Assets	Net	Liabilities	Assets	Net	Liabilities	Assets	Net
Public sector	1.6	17.3	15.7	3.2	18.4	15.2	7.7	16.0	8.3
Other financial institutions	7.3	8.5	1.2	15.1	15.4	0.3	48.0	48.0	—
Industrial and commercial companies	13.6	29.4	15.8	21.8	35.6	13.8	46.5	67.2	20.7
Persons	27.7	9.6	−18.1	40.8	29.6	−11.2	56.6	64.6	8.8
Small businesses	8.9	7.4	−1.5	12.7	14.4	1.7	15.1	22.4	7.3

1980 to 1987. Over the same period, lending to industrial and commercial companies and unincorporated businesses fell from 53% to 33% and from 14% to 11% of total lending, respectively.

1.7. Securities Industry

The most far-reaching structural change centers on the securities industry following the "Big Bang" in 1986 (Goodhart, 1987; Hall, 1987). This represents an instructive case study of the pressures inducing structural change. Historically, this sector has been highly regulated through practices enforced by the London Stock Exchange (LSE). Since 1908, stock exchange practice was based upon a strict *single capacity* rule, which meant that member firms were either brokers or jobbers (market-makers) in securities (equities and government and corporate bonds but not Eurobonds) but could not be both. Prior to the "Big Bang," the stock exchange consisted of 4852 individual members in 209 member firms (predominantly partnerships). Most of these firms (192) were brokers acting as agents for investors (arranging deals on their behalf with the jobbers for a minimum commission). Traditionally, member firms had to be partnerships. But changes to this rule in 1969 allowed member firms to become limited companies and to take outside shareholders, though a limit of 10% was placed on shareholdings in a member firm by any single nonmember. This was raised to 29.9% in 1982, but the fact that member firms could not be wholly owned by a single nonmember meant that firms could not be part of wider groupings.

Thus, the historic distinction and separation between banking and securities trading (enforced by law in some countries) was in the U.K. financial system the product of self-imposed arrangements. No change in the law was required to end this major feature of the British financial system.

The rule book of the LSE was never applied to the very much larger Eurobond market in London where trading arrangements have always been different in four major respects: banks were not excluded as traders and market-makers, there was no single-capacity operation, no fixed minimum commission charges were enforced, and trading has always been screen-based rather than on the floor of an exchange. In fact it was the set of rules and restrictive practices enforced by the LSE that induced the Eurobond market to develop outside the ambit of the stock exchange. In 1986 the LSE and International Securities Regulatory Organization (the self-regulatory organization set up by the Eurobond market) were merged to form a unified securities market known as the International Stock Exchange and regulated in common by The Securities Association.

As a result of the "Big Bang" and deregulation in the stock exchange and the securities industry, British and foreign banks have become major elements in the securities industry as part of integrated financial groups comprising commercial banking, merchant banking, securities broking, and market-making, together with fund management components. In October 1986, fixed commissions for securities trading in the London market were ended following the agreement between the government and the Stock Exchange. In March of the same year, Stock Exchange rules were changed to allow 100% outside ownership of stock broking and jobbing firms. The resulting massive capital injection by a wide range of British and foreign banks has changed the U.K. market in two major respects: the hitherto separate and specialist roles of market-maker and broker (enforced by internal regulation since 1908) have been abandoned, and all the major securities firms have become parts of integrated financial institutions. In terms of U.S. experience, this is tantamount to May Day in 1975 and the abolition of Glass–Stegall occurring simultaneously (Jacomb, 1985).

This represents a substantial package that has been a major, if not central, ingredient of structural change in the British financial system evident during the 1980s. The catalyst was the decision of the government to refer the rule book of the LSE to the RTPC. But the old system would have changed without this, due to global competitive pressures. The restrictive practices were causing the LSE to lose market share even of domestic trading of domestic securities. Stock exchange firms were undercapitalized, which made it difficult to compete with the more highly capitalized firms in the U.S. After the abolition of exchange controls, the international portfolio diversification of major institutions was conducted predominantly by foreign intermediaries, and this clearly exposed the weaknesses of the British market (Leohnis, 1987). The abolition of exchange control in 1979, coupled with developments in information and trading technology and the growing power of large institutional traders who could take advantage of these factors to bypass the LSE, meant that uncompetitive practices could not be sustained. Perhaps the most indicative symptom of an unsustainable system was the development of the Eurobond market outside the traditional market and set of restrictive practices. This represents a major example of the power of global competitive pressures, and the impact of technology, having a decisive influence on the structure of a financial system.

2. Analysis of Competition and Its Effects

A central theme has been that the dominant pressure inducing structural change in the financial system has been competition and the greatly intensified competitive environment that has prevailed in the 1980s. The financial system of the 1980s has been an industry subject to increased competitive pressures both within and between subsectors. In order to focus the discussion, it is instructive to consider what would normally be predicted in an industry that is subject to more competition. This is summarized in table 9-2; the experience of the recent evolution of the financial system indicates that the model applies as much to the finance industry as to any other.

The analysis of competition in finance has a particular bearing with respect to 1992 and the EEC (see section 4) because the completion of the "internal market" is unambiguously about competition. The framework outlined in this section is one that is directly relevant to a consideration of the likely impact in some EC countries of the 1992 arrangements.

2.1. Efficiency

The first proposition, though perhaps the most important, is difficult to test in practice. Nevertheless, all sectors are under pressure to improve efficiency and control costs. Certain indications, however, suggest that

Table 9-2. Impact of Competition

1. The most efficient firms would become yet more efficient, and the average efficiency of the industry would rise.
2. The pricing of the product would tend to eliminate any excess demand that might previously have existed.
3. Internal cross-subsidies, and pricing structures not based on cost or risk considerations, would tend to disappear.
4. The industry would likely experience more mergers as the less efficient firms found the competitive environment too demanding.
5. There would be considerable pressure towards the elimination of any cartel that might exist over the fixing of the industry's prices.
6. Restrictive practices would be competed away through circumvention.
7. Overall profitability is likely to decline.
8. The overall risk characteristics of the industry are likely to increase.
9. Firms seek to diversify.
10. Exits.

the basic efficiency of the system has increased. In wholesale banking, domestic and international competition has eroded lending margins, and the abolition in 1983 of the building society cartel (where the margin used to be set at a level sufficient to maintain the less efficient societies in business) has increased pressure on less efficient building societies. Across the board, clearing banks are also under increased pressure to control operating costs.

One particular aspect of efficiency associated with competitive pressures has developed in the mortgage market with the emergence of securitized mortgages and partnership arrangements. In both cases, overall efficiency is raised because some institutions concentrate on that part of the lending process in which they have a comparative advantage. Both mechanisms are based upon there being three functions in a loan: an *initiating procedure, administration* of the loan, and the *holding of the asset*. Traditionally all three functions have been performed by the same lending institution, which seeks a borrower and makes the loan, administers the loan contract, and holds the loan as an asset on the balance sheet. There is no reason, however, why the functions should not be split if different institutions have different comparative advantages and efficiency in different functions. A building society or a retail bank may have a comparative advantage in the first two functions and hence would be efficient at initiating and adminstering mortgages. On the other hand, because of funding or capital constraints, it may be less efficient than some other institution (such as a wholesale bank with no retail branches) at holding the asset. In this case, overall efficiency is increased if each institution exploits its comparative advantage: the first institution initiates and administers the loan, while the second holds the mortgage as an asset. This particular innovation raises efficiency through a process of decomposing the lending process and exploiting the different comparative advantages.

A similar analysis applies to some new financial instruments (such as swaps) where each borrower funds in his most efficient way (even though that is not his preferred way) and subsequently makes a swap with another borrower who has the opposite comparative advantage and preferences.

2.2. Elimination of Excess Demand

The second proposition in table 9-2 is that competition has the effect of eliminating any excess demand (queues) that might exist, which implies that the price is set below the market clearing level. The building society cartel was operated in this way, with queues for mortgages being the norm prior to 1983. An excess demand implies that some consumers would be prepared to pay a higher rate of interest than that being charged. This was sustainable for two reasons, both associated with an uncompetitive mortgage market: 1) the building societies were part of a cohesive, cooperative industry and until 1983 operated a collective cartel, and 2) they were not subject to external competition, since banks entered the mortgage market in a significant way only in 1981. If competition develops (either internally or from outside), competitors bid away the excess demand by raising the rate of interest to the market-clearing level. Thus the effect of competition in this case is to raise the mortgage rate, eliminate excess demand, and increase the supply of loans. In practice, excess demand has been eliminated in the mortgage market since the entry of banks in the early 1980s.

2.3. Cross-Subsidies

All multiproduct firms have the problem of identifying and allocating costs to each business area (including capital costs). Proposition 3 in table 9-2 relates to pricing policies. When competitive conditions vary between different business areas of an institution there is scope for *cross-subsidizing*. This implies a pricing policy that does not fully reflect differences in cost and risk, and frequently means that prices are set high in one market (where competition is less) and low in another such that the former effectively cross-subsidizes the latter. This need not imply offering one service at a loss, but may mean that fixed costs are not allocated to it. As competition intensifies, such cross-subsidies are normally competed away. In effect, new entrants target on the subsidizing component of competitors' business, which undermines the latter's ability to price the subsidized component at a low level.

Two examples of how competition has eroded cross-subsidies are in the mortgage market and securities trading. Traditionally, and when not subject to external competition, building societies charged higher rates of interest on large mortgages compared with smaller mortgages, even though they were in practice less risky and cheaper to administer. This implied a perverse pricing strategy with low risk and large mortgages cross-subsidizing higher risk and more costly mortgages. This would not be sustained in a highly competitive market, since new entrants would secure a high-risk-adjusted rate of return by competing away the large mortgages (by slightly under-cutting building societies) and leaving building societies with the less profitable business. This is how the banks behaved when they entered the mortgage market in the early 1980s. This had the effect of forcing building societies to reverse their pricing policies, and it is now more common for large mortgages to be offered at a lower rate of interest.

A second example is in the pricing of securities trading. As a result of the stock exchange fixing minimum dealing charges, large institutional traders were not able to bargain over commission charges, which implied that they did not secure the benefits of their large volumes. This had the effect of a cross-subsidy to personal customers whose charges were lower than would otherwise have been the case had charges for institutional traders been lower than the minimum allowed. One of the predictable features of the "Big Bang," as was also the case following similar changes on the New York Stock Exchange in 1975, is that charges for large trades have been reduced, and there is some evidence that those for small trades have risen.

The position becomes more complex when a particular product performs several services simultaneously, and when it is difficult to unbundle the components. In this case it is difficult to identify and price separately the subsidizing and subsidized components. An example is "free banking" on current accounts that are both deposits and a part of the money transmission service offered by banks. Generally, banks do not charge for the use of current accounts (while they remain in credit), but similarly do not pay interest on credit balances. This implies a cross-subsidy from those who hold large average balances (effectively an interest-free loan to the bank) to those who make many transactions and hence impose costs on the bank that are not recouped from the customer. This implicit cross-subsidy would be eliminated if the market rate of interest were paid on all outstanding balances while the economic cost was charged for all services. This would induce customers to maintain higher average balances and at the same time seek to reduce their costs by, for instance, greater use of credit cards so as to minimize the number of transactions.

Leaving aside the question of tax efficiency (i.e., interest received is taxed while the subsidy received by no charges is not) the problem arises because consumers are using both services of a current account, and everyone is a subsidizer and a recipient of a subsidy. The position is therefore not as clear-cut as when the subsidizing and receipt of the subsidy involve different customers who can be targeted by competitors. However, although it is more difficult in practice to identify the subsidizing and subsidized customers, the pricing arrangements makes it potentially attractive for competitors to bid for transactions balances. With the change in regulation in the 1986 Building Societies Act, several building societies have done this. Banks have also begun to pay interest on current accounts with large average or minimum balances, though without simultaneously levying charges.

In a competitive market, with building societies now able to compete for money transmission business, it is doubtful that the clearing banks will be able to permanently avoid the logic of paying interest on credit balances and charging economic prices for all services, most especially since the latter can be avoided by increased use of credit cards, which also lower the costs to banks. The building societies that offer current account facilities all pay interest on outstanding credit balances, and this has undoubtedly been a spur to the banks to do likewise.

2.4. Mergers

Proposition 4 of table 9-2 has been a feature of the building society sector, with the number of societies declining from 273 in 1980 to 138 by the end of 1987. There will likely be substantial pressures for a further concentration in the industry. To the extent that scale is a factor in market success (e.g., in computer facilities and the ability to offer a wider range of services), this will be reinforced in the medium term. Regulation will also be a pressure on smaller societies in that they do not have the same range of powers (either on asset or liability diversification) as the larger societies.

It is likely, therefore, that the number of societies will continue to decline and the industry will become yet further concentrated. In practice, future concentration will more likely involve a merging of medium-sized societies. In effect, the 20% of business undertaken outside the ten largest societies will be undertaken by considerably fewer societies. The number of institutions will be reduced in three ways. The traditional route has been through mergers, and this will continue. But since the 1986 Building Societies Act, all societies now have the option of converting from mutual to PLC status, and this can be done either as an independent institution or with a view to being absorbed by an existing institution such as a bank or insurance company. Some medium-sized institutions will appear attractive to other institutions as a route to selling retail financial services to the personal sector. This conversion and absorption route could imply more competitive pressures for the larger societies in that it gives greater access to the personal sector to a wider range of competitor institutions.

2.5. Cartels and Restrictive Practices

Competitive pressures make it difficult to sustain a non-market-clearing pricing structure. Similarly, if a cartel fixes prices at a level that creates excessive profits, competition may develop from outside the cartel. It was competitive pressure from the New York Stock Exchange (where large U.K. investors could transact at lower dealing charges) that was the major factor undermining the minimum commission charges enforced by the London Stock Exchange. For a cartel to be effective, the industry must be cohesive and not subject to external competition. This was true of the building society and the stock exchange price-fixing arrangements until the early 1980s. In the case of the former, the cartel was abandoned in 1983 after the entry of banks into the mortgage market. Competition from New York, after technology developments made it feasible for U.K. investors to trade in New York, was the dominant factor undermining the price-fixing arrangements on the London stock exchange.

The argument above is a particular example of the more general proposition that competition undermines all forms of restrictive practices through circumvention. If it is technically possible to do so, customers seek to avoid the restrictions by dealing outside the cohesive group maintaining them.

2.6. Erosion of Profitability

A normal expectation is that competition has the effect of eroding profitability, most especially as new firms enter the industry. This has clearly been the case in international banking, wholesale banking generally, and in securities trading in the U.K. since the "Big Bang." It is not, however, invariably the case, and the outcome depends upon how the industry operated before the entry of competition and specifically upon whether it was previously seeking to maximize profits. An instructive case study is provided by building societies where profitability (absolutely and in terms of the rate of return on assets and capital) rose during the 1980s, notwithstanding the more competitive climate. This is associated in part with the operation of the cartel prior to 1983, which had the effect of maintaining the mortgage rate below the market clearing level. With the abolition of the cartel, profits rose since the same margin was earned on an increased volume of mortgages. Thus profits can be increased due to the stock-adjustment effect of moving to a market-clearing, profit-maximizing position.

2.7. Risk

A major issue in finance is the extent to which (if at all) deregulation (externally imposed or internally generated) induces excessive competition and excess capacity with the potential for increased instability in the financial system. Competition may have the effect of increasing risk in two ways: 1) by increasing the variability of profits, and 2) by inducing lending criteria to be relaxed. This latter seems to have been the case in international lending during the 1970s, and the evidence indicates that the risks on building-society mortgage lending increased in the early stages following the entry of banks. This was associated, in part, by lending bigger multiples of borrowers' income and a higher proportion (sometimes 100%) of the value of the property. It is likely that risks rose to the extent that, by previously maintaining excess demand, building societies rationed out less creditworthy borrowers. An alternative is via the effect on interest rates, in that a more competitive environment might be expected to raise both the volatility of interest rates (competing institutions engage in active liability-management) and their absolute level to the extent that in the noncompetitive (cartelized) regime, interest rates would be set below the market clearing level. Using the model of Klein (1971) and Monti (1972), and in the context of deregulation of deposit rates, Baltensperger and Dermine (1987) suggest that a more competitive market environment will not induce banks to take more risks, since in the model used the lending side is independent of the deposit side. However, they make no reference to any previous regime of credit rationing or to the standard Stiglitz and Weis conclusion.

2.8. Diversification

Competition developing in a firm's existing market is likely to induce diversification. This has been true across the board in the financial system, as has been described. For instance, a major competitive influence on building societies has been a strategic decision adopted by their banking competitors over the 1980s to target the personal sector for retail deposits, lending to this sector, and the provision of financial services generally.

2.9. Exits

In the final analysis, and failing other strategies, the ultimate effect of competition is to induce exits from the industry as the industry becomes overcrowded, and the more efficient force the exit of the less efficient. In practice this has not been a common reaction in the financial system. However, one example has been in the securities industry. One of the features of the "Big Bang" was a substantial rise in the number of market-makers both in the gilts and equity markets. New entrants were anticipating a sharp rise in turnover following the abolition of minimum commissions; this had previously been the effect in New York following similar reforms in 1975. In practice, the required increase in turnover to enable the much larger number of market-makers to remain profitable was not a realistic proposition. In the event, and especially after the stock-market collapse in October 1987, the volume of transactions actually declined sharply. This subsequently induced several equity and gilts market-makers to withdraw within the first two years of the new market structure. At the same time several firms have announced that they will no longer service personal accounts below a certain figure.

3. Problem Issues

3.1. Excess Capacity and Profitability

Partly as a result of banks' strategic shift towards retail banking and financial services during the 1980s, competitive pressures have intensified in retail banking, and this is likely to be intensified further as a result of the 1992 EEC arrangements to be discussed in the next section. The possibility arises that the provision of retail financial services is becoming an overcrowded industry. A wide range of institutions (clearing banks, insurance companies, foreign banks, building societies, and even non-financial firms) have targeted the personal sector simultaneously. There are many reasons why financial institutions or firms generally seek to diversify: to maintain profitability in the context of more competition in traditional markets, to reduce risk by less concentration, to reap economies of scope, to reduce excess capacity, because of a presumed high profitability of existing suppliers or because competitors have higher costs, to compete away cross-subsidies, etc. The profitability of diversification, however, depends in part upon what is happening to the demand for the product. If demand is rising strongly, it can make profitable an area that, for a particular institution, might not have been profitable before. The demand can be met by a new institution without taking business from others. If, on the other hand, demand is static, the net result is that all have a smaller volume of business, and it is almost certain that profitability is lowered.

Given the extent and magnitude of the shift towards selling financial services to the personal sector, it is difficult to avoid the conclusion that strategies are being built on optimistic assumptions about the size and profitability of the market. Competition (domestic and international) eroded the profitability of parts of wholesale banking in the 1970s as more firms (often foreign banks) entered the market. The same is likely to happen in the retail sector in the 1990s.

It is normally (though by no means invariably) to be expected that increased competition leads to a decline in profitability. It is, therefore, something of a paradox that in the case of both the clearing banks and building societies, basic profitability increased over the 1980s at a time when the competitive environment intensified considerably. Profitability is measured not in terms of absolute profits but in terms of the rates of return on assets (ROA) and equity (reserves for building societies, i.e., ROE). In the case of banks, the low figure for 1987 reflects a distortion due to the exceptional provisions for bad debt made in that year. The sample includes the four largest banks and four large building societies. Table 9-3 shows that for building societies there has been a sharp trend rise in the ROA since 1982 from 0.80% to 1.25%. For banks, the ROA rose sharply after 1984. The ROE measures show a trend rise for building societies after 1982 (from 24% to 31%) and for banks there was a very sharp rise from 17% in 1983 to 26% in 1986.

When considering the reasons for the apparent paradox, and drawing implications for the future, a distinction is made between *cyclical, stock-adjustment*, and *permanent* factors. To the extent that the explanation for the rise in profitability relates to either of the first two, the rise is likely to be temporary. *Stock-adjustment* factors occur when there is a once-and-for-all single and finite shift to a new position that is neither subsequently reversed nor continuous at the same rate. This change may be substantial while the stock adjustment is being made, but is nevertheless finite in nature.

In general, bank profitability (i.e., as measured by ROE and ROA) can rise for five reasons:

1. An endowment effect raises overall profitability.
2. The nature of business is changing in a way that generates profits without increasing assets. Off-balance-sheet earnings raise the measured ROA and ROE, even though the true profitability of the asset base might be declining.
3. Margins are raised on all business, perhaps because of bouyant demand or strategic decisions to raise profitability.
4. The asset mix changes, with a switch from low to high margin assets.

THE BRITISH FINANCIAL SYSTEM

Table 9-3. Banks and Building-Society Rates of Return

Rate of Return	1980	1981	1982	1983	1984	1985	1986	1987
1. Rate of return on assets								
• Banks	1.37	1.24	0.85	0.83	0.81	1.09	1.21	0.10
• Building societies	0.70	0.89	0.80	1.00	0.85	1.14	1.20	1.25
2. Rate of return on equity								
• Banks	23.3	23.0	17.2	16.9	19.1	25.5	26.1	2.2
• Building societies	22.4	27.7	24.0	28.4	25.8	30.5	30.8	31.0
3. Rate of return on capital								
• Banks	13.3	13.1	11.8	11.3	11.3	12.5	13.1	1.3
4. Equity/assets ratio								
• Banks	5.9	5.4	5.0	4.9	4.2	4.3	4.6	5.0
5. Capital/assets ratio								
• Banks	7.6	7.2	7.2	7.3	7.2	8.7	9.2	8.6

In this case (as happened in 1986 and 1987 for both domestic and international business), margins in both can decline while overall the ROA is increased.
5. There is a fall in the cost of bank liabilities relative to other market interest rates.

The endowment effect (given that banks do not pay interest on all deposits) is cyclical in nature and is associated with the movement in interest rates. There was something of this effect operating at times during the 1980s, though the impact has been steadily declining and will decline further, since competition has the effect of eroding the proportion of accounts upon which no interest is paid.

A major factor in profitability trends has been a change in the nature of the banking business. Banks are not exclusively asset-liability transformers (absorbing deposits with one set of characteristics and creating assets with a different set). Increasingly they earn income off the balance sheet through the provision of various services. This necessarily increases the measured rate of return on assets. Over the 1980s, the proportion of the banks' total income generated through off-balance-sheet activity rose from 11% in 1980 to 17% in 1987. Thus the measured ROA and ROE can be maintained because the nature of the business is changing. Banks have also benefited from the cyclical effect of an exceptionally strong and sustained demand for mortgages and consumer credit.

Perhaps the most important contribution came from a strategic shift (stock-adjustment) that banks made from wholesale to retail banking activity during the 1980s. Competitive pressures during the 1970s substantially eroded the profitability of wholesale banking (domestic and international) which, combined with the strong growth in the demand for retail loans, induced a major strategic shift by banks towards the retail sector. Such business is considerably more profitable, and hence such a shift will necessarily raise measured profitability. This represents a competitive response of diversification in order to maintain overall profitability.

Analyzing profitability trends is a complex process. Nevertheless, abstracting from the detail, the rise in bank profitability (in terms of the rate of return on assets and equity) over the 1980s was dominated by four factors:

1. A change in the nature of banking business with the growth of fee income and other off-balance-sheet business.
2. The cyclical effect associated with the unprecedented rise in the demand for credit, most especially from the personal sector.

3. A stock-adjustment effect of a shift, at the margin, from wholesale to retail banking.
4. The rise in the ROE associated in part with a substantial rise in loan capital issued by banks following a change in capital regulations in the early 1980s by the Bank of England. This had the effect of allowing a multiple rise in bank assets on the basis of a fixed volume of equity; hence, the ROE would rise. Since there is a regulatory limit on the extent to which loan stock can be counted as capital, the shift towards loan capital was a stock adjustment rather than a continuing flow, and hence is not a means of continuing to raise the ROE.

Thus to a significant extent, the predicted long-run effect of increased competition on profits has been concealed by two stock adjustments and a strong cyclical effect.

To some extent, two potential problems for banks (a capital constraint and the impact of competition on profitability) were concealed during the 1980s. The former was because of the facility to raise capital via subordinated debt. Over the period 1980–1987, the six major clearing banks raised a total of £7.3 billion in such capital due to an accommodating change in the Bank of England's regulation with respect to capital (Llewellyn, 1988b). The stock adjustment to the regulatory limit having been made, capital must now be raised predominantly through equity; retained earnings (which implies profits) and new issues. The problem with this is that, given current price–earnings ratios (which for the bank sector overall currently stand at 5.6 against 12.9 for all shares in the FT 500 Index), the average cost of new capital will rise sharply.

The decade of the 1980s may therefore come to be viewed as a transitional phase. During the 1970s, competitive pressures in wholesale banking eroded profitability. The 1980s could prove to be transitional in the sense of the various stock adjustments and the cyclical effect, in which case the 1990s could be a period when competitive pressures begin to seriously erode overall bank profitability. It is difficult to avoid the conclusion that the 1990s will be a more difficult period for bank profitability, most especially if the retail financial services sector is becoming overcrowded. There are several grounds for a less optimistic view of future profitability than might be suggested by recent trends:

- the underlying effect of competition;
- the ending of the beneficial stock-adjustments;

- the lesser ability to engage in cross-subsidizing, most especially with respect to current accounts;
- the further erosion of the banks traditional "endowment effect" as the average cost of retail funds rises;
- the ending of the boom in consumer lending;
- a reduction in the underlying profitability of credit cards;
- a rise in the average cost of capital in the context of banks having reached the regulatory limit (as a proportion of the capital base) with respect to loan-stock capital.

The banks will respond, and this is likely to include a further attempt to expand off-balance-sheet income, which will change yet further the nature of banking business.

3.2. Financial Conglomerates

The second problem area identified relates to the trend towards diversification and the emergence of financial conglomerates, the wisdom of which might be questioned on grounds of efficiency. There is no certainty that financial institutions have the necessary managements skills to handle a very diversified business where the technicalities can be complex. There may also be doubt in some cases about whether, for instance, the different ethos and cultures of clearing banks, merchant banking, and broking can be mixed; the "deal-orientated" culture of securities trading does not easily fit within the ethos of a clearing bank (Gardener, 1988). Evidence indicates that alleged "synergy" is difficult to identify and achieve when totally different cultures and practices are brought together. This appears to be most evident in the case of the American banks who bought/created U.K. securities trading firms.

Those who are skeptical of the financial conglomerate strategy believe that conflicts of interest cannot be avoided, that the costs of policing all the complex boundaries (Chinese Walls and complicance officers) in an attempt to avoid them are high, and that the risk remains of losing clients when breaches are published. These costs may outweight the alleged benefits of synergy and economies of scope even when they can be identified. In some cases, size has proven to be a problem with unwieldly structures, internal tensions, and information and control problems.

This in turn raises the question of the extent to which the different facets of a conglomerate are managed independently, and of the type of control systems within the administrative structure. The dilemma is that, if the different areas are integrated so as to secure the advantage of the consumer of a "department store," then questions arise about whether such a diverse but integrated business can be effectively managed. On the other hand, if (perhaps because of a regulatory requirement) different elements of the conglomerate are established as semi-autonomous companies, the question arises as to whether there is any advantage to the user of financial services and whether the firm secures the alleged synergies. Loehnis (1987) considers the distinct possibility that in the U.K. regulatory context, costs of supervisory compliance might come to outweigh the potential gains in synergy within a financial conglomerate.

Within the financial sector where conglomerates are emerging, a warning that diversification may not always be successful is provided by the "lifeboat" organized by the Bank of England in 1974. Here the biggest institutions that had to be rescued were former successful specialist HP finance houses, such as UDT, Bowmaker, and Mercantile Credit, which had recently diversified into lending to property developers. The wide-ranging diversification of business by the big U.K. banks has not always been conspicuously successful. Another example of such diversification by commercial banks is to be found in their move into medium-term sovereign lending. Some of the problems encountered may be attributable to many of the banks being new to this type of business. In general, the traditional wisdom and expertise of bankers engaged in international lending is located in the merchant banks, not the clearing banks.

There are also implications for the role of the central bank as a lender of last resort in that, while a functional approach to regulation may be adopted, it is companies and not functions that become insolvent. With a diversified company, the central bank cannot readily discriminate between those activities that need to be supported in the national interest and those that can be allowed to fail, most especially, for instance, if depositors interpret the failure of a subsidiary with dedicated capital as a sign of weakness of the banking group. It is not clear that requiring dedicated capital to bank subsidiaries effectively protects the bank either from contagion or from a responsibility to support its subsidiaries.

4. The 1992 Dimension

The analysis of integration between markets in financial assets has been well developed. Analogously, in terms of the provision of more general financial intermediation services, arbitrage would tend to eliminate national differences in the supply price of financial intermediation, which can vary between countries for three general reasons: 1) differences in efficiency; 2) different regulatory "taxes"; and 3) differences in the competitive environment enabling a higher level of monopoly profits or inefficiency in one system compared with another. In principle, a high price in one national system would be competed away either through the entry of foreign firms or by the users of financial services using foreign mechanisms (Llewellyn, 1988c). The same effect could be achieved via a "contestable markets" mechanism (Baumol, 1982). In practice, though it varies considerably between countries and for different users, this process can be impeded by exchange control, together with information and transactions costs.

4.1. The 1992 Dimension

None of the factors that have induced the globalization of finance (competitive pressures, financial innovation, technology, deregulation, abolition of exchange control, etc.) have a specifically European dimension (Llewellyn, 1988c). At the same time, there has been little globalization of retail banking. Whilst this has been true to date, the position could change in the 1990s. Potentially the arrangements envisaged for the post-1992 EEC represent a major change in the market environment for all financial institutions and suppliers of financial services.

There are considerable differences in the price, range, and quality of financial services available in different EC countries. There are three main factors accounting for this: 1) differences in basic efficiency in different financial services; 2) different types of constraining regulation imposed in different countries; and 3) differences in the basic internal competitive environment, which sustains a higher level of cost and/or profits in some systems compared with others.

Future progress towards the completion of the "internal market" in finance has been made possible through a new approach that led to the Second Banking Directive being issued in January 1988. Instead of requiring a high degree of prior harmonization, four new principles have been established, and it is these that make 1992 significant:

- A set of commonly agreed upon basic regulatory requirements (e.g., with respect to capital requirements);
- The *home* country of an institution will be responsible for regulation and supervision;
- There is to be a mutual recognition by all Member governments of

each others' regulatory arrangements. However, *host* authorities will remain responsible for the regulation and supervision of subsidiaries and the branches of non-EC countries' institutions; and
- There is to be greater freedom of entry.

The Second Banking Directive will add a specifically European dimension to competition in financial services. This is a major change, for it establishes the principle of freedom of establishment and the provision of cross-border services within the Community. The overriding principle is that if an institution is authorized in one member country it is deemed to be similarly authorized in *all* other Member states; an institution wishing to provide services in another Member state will not need separate authorization, whether the provision of services is to be via location in other countries or via cross-frontier trade.

Under the Second Banking Directive, a list of activities defines *banking business* for which a single license would apply throughout the EEC. This list adopts the *universal banking* principle, which includes securities-related and advisory services in addition to commercial banking services. The principle of the single license implies that, providing the home country of a bank permits the banks to engage in one of the specified banking activities, then those banks may engage in that activity in all other EEC countries, even if the activity is prohibited to domestic banks of the host country. It is likely, therefore, that competitive pressures will force a high degree of regulatory convergence, implying that the universal banking model will become the norm throughout the EEC. This would imply major changes in some EEC countries.

In combination, these points represent a substantial package and will make a significant contribution to the development of the common market in financial services. Above all, it implies (in some EC countries more than others) a major intensification in competitive pressures. It is well established that in some countries the financial system has many restrictive practices, cartels, other anticompetitive mechanisms, high costs, excess capacity, and inefficient mechanisms. All of these can in principle be competed away.

Clearly, the greatest impact will be felt in those countries where internal regulation is most constraining, where internal competitive pressures are weakest (perhaps because of cartels or restrictive practices), and where entry barriers have been most formidable. For instance, the impact within the British financial system may not be substantial: competitive conditions are already demanding, there is no exchange control, all major EC banks already have a presence in London, there are no restrictions on the range of business, and branches are not required to have dedicated capital. In other words, there have been no regulatory limits preventing EC institutions from developing business within the U.K.; in general entry into the U.K. will be no easier after 1992 than it is now. On the other hand, British institutions will gain through greater access to other EC markets.

4.2. Retail Banking

When considering the implications of 1992, it is necessary to distinguish between wholesale and retail banking because the competitive conditions in these sectors vary both within and between countries. In wholesale banking, business tends to be large scale and institutions may have comparatively few but large customers. The key is that delivery can be made without the necessity of a network of branches. Retail banking, on the other hand, involves a large number of small accounts and access has usually been via a branch network. The cost considerations are therefore fundamentally different. In some (though by no means all) EC countries, further competition in wholesale banking will be limited because in this sector competition has already become *global* rather than specifically *European*. However there are still some EC countries with only a limited range of financial instruments and facilities even for large corporate customers, and where regulation limits the entry of foreign institutions. Even in these countries, however, large firms usually have access to foreign and international markets, and so they already have access to a wide range of facilities not available within their own country. Nevertheless, in some EC countries where entry and access barriers have been formidable, there will be scope for foreign competition in wholesale banking business as a result of the Second Banking Directive.

The central issue for competing banks is access to potential customers and the creation of effective delivery systems for financial services. Whatever the type of business being considered, for provision to be effective an institution needs access to potential customers; this is likely to be secured differently for retail as opposed to wholesale banking services, and different banks will develop different approaches. Access can be secured in five basic ways: 1) by building a location, i.e., establishing a European network of branches; 2) by mergers, where two institutions of different nationality merge so that a single institution has universal access in both countries; 3) through the purchase of a company in another country that has ready access to customers; 4) through developing business links with institutions in other countries so that the partner gives access to its customer base and acts in some cases as an agent; or 5) via trade, though there has to be effective communication between the customer in one country and the supplier of a banking service in another.

Some banks and other financial institutions will seek a pan-EC strategy via transnational mergers. There are several examples to date, including that of UAP (the largest French insurance group) and Sun Life Assurance (U.K.) planning to exchange shareholdings and cooperate on future international development. Prior to that, UAP had acquired a major stake in the largest Belgian insurance group. In some countries (perhaps Spain and Italy) there will be powerful competitive pressures on small banks to merge or join larger groups. In 1987 Deutschebank acquired Bank of America's 100-branch network in Italy, and Credit Lyonnais of France acquired Nederlander Crediet Bank (a Dutch subsidiary of Chase Manhattan Bank), which absorbed 127 branches and a 7% market share. Other examples include the acquisition by Banco Santander of Spain of a substantial equity stake in Instituto Bancario Italiano and the participation of Midland Bank in Euromobiliare.

The logistical and cultural merging of different nationalities of banks can prove to be a formidable and hazardous undertaking. This is one reason why pan-EC strategies may stop short of full merger or acquisition and take the form of joint ventures and various forms of cooperative arrangements. The "link" method is potentially powerful and is likely to emerge as a major business route because it enables different institutions to exploit their different comparative advantages. This has recently been used in the U.K. mortgage market and has enabled foreign institutions without an internal branch network to access retail customers.

In practice, and given the expense of developing a new branch network, this is likely to be a major implication of the Second Banking Directive and its effect upon the future evolution of European financial institutions. Such links, and joint ventures designed to exploit different comparative advantages, will become increasingly common between institutions in different countries. Foreign institutions will be holding assets that have been originated and administered by domestic institutions. This will prove to be a major way of foreign institutions gaining access to personal customers without the necessity of a branch network. It represents a method of gaining access to customers without incurring substantial costs through a branch network.

On the other hand, the impact should not be exaggerated, since there is a strategic dilemma in the choice between creating a new branch network in a foreign country *versus* an acquisitions strategy. Although in general retail banking is more profitable than wholesale banking in virtually all systems (partly because competition in the latter is already global in nature), it can be difficult and expensive to gain access. The strategic problem arises because retail financial services are economic only at a certain minimum volume; thus retail banks rely upon a large number of small accounts, whereas some wholesale banking can be profitable with a small number of large accounts, and this has implications for how risks are handled. If foreign banks set up *branch* networks, they will seek to recoup the high costs of entry by not undercutting indigenous institutions, but they in turn are likely to lower prices in the face of increased competitive pressures. At the same time, this strategy is likely to create an excess number of branches. New entrants must also face a lack of local expertise and an innate reservation of retail customers to dealing with unfamiliar foreign institutions. An alternative strategy is simply for foreign banks to acquire domestic banks and run them as before. But in this case there may be little of the alleged synergy of larger-scale operation to be gained. There will also be a reluctance of the regulatory authorities to allow their large banks to move into foreign ownership lest they lose supervisory and monetary policy control over them.

4.3. Competition

Overall, the major implications of the 1992 ambitions will be to further intensify the competitive environment in which (most especially retail) financial services are provided. This cannot fail to have major strategic implications for the suppliers of financial services, perhaps most especially with respect to business linkages between different nationalities of financial institutions. This could represent a further significant element in the structural change of the financial system.

The 1992 arrangements unambiguously represent a more competitive market in financial services, both wholesale and retail. This will place substantial pressure on EC financial institutions to change. Small institutions, without a multinational presence, may not have the economies of scale or geographic penetration to provide the range of services required to remain competitive. They may be squeezed out of important multinational markets, as happened in the U.S. with small regional banks and thrifts. It is likely, therefore, that there will be a major restructuring of EEC banking.

The internationalization of finance, and the generally more intensive competitive environment this creates, brings with it major implications for the regulation and supervision of financial institutions. The original strategy for the development of a common market was via changes in regulation. It was based upon a high degree of prior harmonization so that competition between institutions of different Member states would be effective and fair. The rationale of harmonization is that no institution would gain a competitive advantage in the common market because they were regulated more lightly. In this way regulation was to precede competition. The current strategy (i.e., based upon the mutual recognition of the regulatory arrangements of other Member states) will likely mean that in practice, competitive pressures will force a high degree of regulatory convergence so as to avoid unintended competitive advantages and disadvantages for institutions of different countries. This implies that there are likely to be significant changes in regulation in some EC countries following the competitive effects of the Second Banking Directive. Indeed, the Directive recognizes the need for a degree of coordination in regulatory and supervisory arrangements. The major implication of the directive is that governments will no longer be able to impose their own regulations on institutions of other countries providing they are authorized in a Member state.

To be effective, the nature and form of regulation must reflect the competitive environment, and this now has a powerful international dimension. Financial institutions are increasingly competing in a global rather than purely national financial system and, to do so effectively, they often need to offer services similar to all potential competitors. If they are able to offer a particular service in one country, there are inevitable pressures to seek to generalize this. Secondly, if a regulator that restricts a particular activity in its own country requires that this is also maintained when institutions are operating in other countries (where no local regulation imposes the same requirements), then these institutions are placed at a competitive disadvantage in developing a global competitive strategy. On the other hand, if diversification is allowed in third markets, the anomaly emerges that an institution is able to undertake business in a foreign center that it cannot legally undertake in its own country. This creates pressures for change: the institutions increase their pressure for domestic regulatory reform.

4.4. The U.K. Position

On the face of it, although by no means immune from the competitive pressures implicit in the 1992 arrangements, the British financial system and London as an international financial center are well placed both to meet the opportunities created and to address the internal competitive challenges. This is not to say that some smaller banks, and some building societies, will not be the target of acquisition strategies of foreign banks viewing such acquisitions as an obvious entry mechanism for the development of retail financial services. Although building societies are mutual, they have the facility to convert to company status with a view to being immediately absorbed by another institution.

The British financial system is well placed, since it is Europe's strongest financial services sector and already competes effectively in international markets. The provision of a wide range of financial services is very competitive compared with some other EEC members. It starts from a competitive position of strength. Secondly, the British financial system is already the most open in the EEC in that the entry requirements for banks are the least restrictive. Thus it should be no easier for foreign banks to enter after 1992 than before, and those institutions with domestic or international ambitions in the U.K. are probably already in place. Thirdly, it has the advantage of "critical mass" as an established international financial center and, to the extent that non-EEC institutions perceive new business opportunities in the EEC as a whole via location in one of its centers, London has an initial advantage. To the extent that competition develops in retail financial services, the cost considerations noted earlier need to be weighed. However, there are banks and building societies with a good retail base that could be the target for acquisition and/or merger.

While the "internal" financial system may not be powerfully affected, the role of London as an international financial center could be adversely affected, though again the impact is likely to be small. In the first place, though not related specifically to 1992, there is an issue with respect to regulation that has become more restrictive. Secondly, the abolition of the requirement of dedicated capital for bank branches in EC countries removes one of the competitive advantages of London as a foreign location for community banks; the U.K. is alone among EC countries in not requiring branches of foreign banks to have dedicated capital. Thirdly, it must be assumed that efficiency in other financial centers will increase as a result of potential competitive threats and that governments will encourage this. This may mean that, to the extent that banks in some member countries undertake activities overseas because of internal controls, restrictions, and inefficiencies in their home base, London could lose business due to repatriation of activities. One example, parallel with the previous experience of the U.K., is that the ending of fixed minimum commission charges on the Paris stock exchange could lead to a repatriation of business in French equities conducted in London to the market in France. It is also clear that other centers (Paris and Frankfurt) have ambitions to compete with London as an international financial center, and the efficiency improvements due to competitive pressures may remove some of the advantages currently enjoyed by London. Competitive pressures are also likely to induce a process of regulatory convergence, thus reducing competitive advantages created by different regulatory regimes.

References

Baltensperger, E. and J. Dermine. "Banking Deregulation in Europe," *Economic Policy*, 4, 63–109 (1987).
Bank of England. "Competition, Innovation and Regulation in British Banking," *Quarterly Bulletin* 23, 363–376. (September 1983).
Bank of England. "Insurance in a changing Financial Services Industry," *Quarterly Bulletin* 24, 195–199. (June 1984).
Barge, J. "Goodhart's Law Strikes Again," *The Banker* (July 1985), pp. 27–31.
Baumol, W.K. "Contestable Markets: An Uprising in the Theory of Industry Structure," *American Economic Review* 72, 1–15.
Boyd, J.H. and S.L. Graham. "Risk, Regulation and Bank Holding Company Expansion into Non-banking," Federal Reserve Bank of Minneapolis, *Quarterly Review* (Spring 1986), pp. 2–17.
Clark, J.A. "Economies of Scale and Scope at Depository Financial Institutions: Review of the Literature," Federal Reserve Bank of Kansas City, *Economic Review* (September 1988), pp. 16–33.
Corrigan, E.G. Commentary in *Restructuring the Financial System*. Kansas City: Federal Reserve Bank, 1987.
Eisenbeis, R.A. "Can Regulatory Reform Prevent: the Impending Disaster in Financial Markets?," in *Restructuring the Financial System*. Kansas City: Federal Reserve Bank, 1987.
Eisenbeis, R.A. "The Impact of Securitisation and Internationalisation on Market Imperfections," in E.P.M. Gardener (ed.), *The Future of Financial Systems & Services*. London: Macmillan, 1989.
Gardener, E.P.M. "A Strategic Perspective on Banking Financial Conglomerates in London After the Crash," mimeo, Bangor University, 1988.
Gilbart, R.A. "A Comparison of Proposals to Restructure the US Financial System," Federal Reserve Bank of St. Louis, *Review* 70, 58–75 (July 1988).
Goodhart, C.A.E. "Structural Changes in the British Capital Markets," in D. Currie et al. (eds.), *The Operation and Regulation of Financial Markets*. London: Macmillan, 1987.

Hall, M.J.B. *The City Revolution: Causes & Consequences*. London: Macmillan, 1989.
Jacomb, M. 'Will the City of London Survive the Revolution," *Journal of Royal Society of Arts* (October 1985), pp. 15–30.
Klein, M.A. "A Theory of the Banking Firm," *Journal of Money, Credit and Banking*, 3, 205–218 (1971).
Leigh-Pemberton, R. "Ownership and Control of UK Banks," Bank of England, *Quarterly Bulletin* 27, 525–526 (November 1987).
Lewis, A. "Off Balance Sheet Activity," in J.S.G. Wilson (ed.), *Managing Bank Assets and Liabilities*. London: Euromoney Publications, 1988.
Llewellyn, D.T. *The Evolution of the British Financial System*. London: Chartered Institute of Bankers, 1985.
Llewellyn, D.T. *Regulation and Supervision of Financial Institutions*. London: Chartered Institute of Bankers, 1986.
Llewellyn, D.T. "Analisis basico de la innovacion financiera," *Papeles de Economia Espanola* 21 (1988a), pp. 24–38.
Llewellyn, D.T. "Capital Adequacy," in J.S.G. Wilson (ed.), *Managing Banks Assets and Liabilities*. London: Euromoney Publications, 1988b.
Llewellyn, D.T. "Financial Intermediation and Systems: Global Integration," in D. Fair, and C. Boissieu (eds.), *International Monetary and Financial Integration: The European Dimension*. Hague: Kluwer, 1988c.
Llewellyn, D.T. "Structural Change in the British Financial System," in D.T. Llewellyn, (ed.), *Reflections on Money*. London: Macmillan, 1989.
Loehnis, A. "Financial Restructuring: The British Experience," in *Restructuring the Financial System*, Kansas City: Federal Reserve Bank, 1987.
Revell, J.R.S. *The British Financial System*. London: Macmillan, 1973.
Roberts, S.M. Commentary, in *Restructuring the Financial System*. Kansas City: Federal Reserve Bank, 1987.

10 THE UNITED STATES FINANCIAL SYSTEM

Herbert L. Baer and Larry R. Mote

1. Introduction

The U.S. financial system is easily the largest in the world—although that position stands to be challenged by a unified European financial market—and, in many respects, the most advanced. It also has the greatest diversity of institutions, the widest variety of instruments, and the most highly developed derivative markets. In many areas of finance, it leads in innovation. It is also one of the most idiosyncratic financial systems in the world, characterized by an oddly parochial set of laws and regulations that both impair competition and shield inefficiency. Because of these anomalies, which are apparent to even the most casual student of financial systems, the U.S. system is not one that other countries with less fully developed economies and financial systems would be well advised to emulate, at least not in every detail. However, much can be learned from a careful examination of both the strengths and weaknesses of the U.S. system.

This chapter provides basic information on the structure, composition, and general mode of operation of the U.S. financial system. However, it focuses most heavily on financial supervision and regulation, because these are the primary avenues through which public policy affects the efficiency and stability of the system. It seeks to identify those practices and approaches that may objectively be deemed to be superior to others, as judged by the nearly universally accepted criteria of safety, or the absence of severe financial disturbances that spill over to the real sector of the economy; operational efficiency, or the ability to execute financial transactions quickly and with a minimum expenditure of real resources; and allocational efficiency, or the channeling of real resources to those uses that provide the greatest social benefit as reflected in relative rates of return.

2. Basic Characteristics of the U.S. Financial System

The U.S. financial system possesses three characteristics that differentiate it from the financial systems of other countries. These are its extreme degree of fragmentation, as reflected in the enormous number of individual institutions; its unparalleled degree of diversity; and the relative importance of direct finance, i.e., the raising of funds by the issue of open-market instruments such as stocks, bonds, and commercial paper.

2.1. Fragmentation

The extreme fragmentation of the U.S. financial system is most evident in the structure of the banking industry, which consists of nearly 13,000 independently chartered commercial banks of greatly varying size and diversification. However, fragmentation is also apparent in the wide range of different types of financial institutions specializing in one or a few financial services and in the division of regulatory authority between the federal government and the 50 states and, at least at the federal level, between separate agencies for each of the major categories of institutions.

This fragmentation is due partly to historical accident, partly to a strong commitment to states' rights within the federal system, and partly to effective lobbying by small banks seeking protection from the competition of large institutions. At present, branching by both state-chartered banks and (under the policy of deference to state law embodied in the McFadden Act of 1927 as revised by the Banking Act of 1933) federally chartered banks is governed by the laws of the individual states. Until recently, many of these laws either prohibited or severely restricted branch banking.

In recent decades, fragmentation has been slowly eroded by the elimination of restrictions on branch banking within states, the spread of regional interstate banking compacts among the states permitting holding-company acquisitions across state boundaries (Frieder, 1986), the drive by banks and other institutions to broaden their permissible activities, and the growing recognition that regulation by function, rather than by charter, becomes a virtual necessity as institutions with different charters increasingly compete with one another (Angermueller, 1987). Nonetheless, fragmentation remains a distinguishing feature of the U.S. banking system and one that has made it difficult to achieve agreement with foreign countries regarding the regulatory treatment of foreign institutions within each country.

2.2. Diversity

The second identifying characteristic of the U.S. financial system—which, however, does not clearly distinguish it from the financial systems of several other industrialized countries—is its great diversity, as reflected in the large number of different types of institutions and the enormous differences in their degree of specialization. Thus, there are at least 20 fairly well-defined and distinct types of financial institutions in the United States and considerable heterogeneity within each of these basic types. At the same time, there is considerable overlap in their functions. For example, savings and loan associations, mutual savings banks, and mortgage banking companies are all active on the asset side in originating and servicing residential mortgages, although the first two of these generally hold the mortgages in their portfolios while mortgage banks sell most all of theirs to institutional investors. Similarly, consumer finance companies, credit unions, and industrial banks specialize in originating and holding relatively small installment loans to individuals, while differing considerably in their sources of funds. Sales finance companies specialize in supplying credit to retailers, which in turn finance purchases by their customers. Factors are highly specialized firms that purchase the accounts receivable of retailers, usually on a nonrecourse basis. While most consumer lending institutions are independent of commercial and industrial firms, a few of them, known as captive finance companies, are owned by major automobile or appliance manufacturers and, at least initially, specialized in financing purchases of their parent firms' products. But other, more diversified financial institutions, particularly commercial banks, are heavily engaged in both residential mortgage and consumer installment lending.

2.3. Relative Importance of Direct Finance

The third identifying characteristic of the U.S. financial system is the unusually high proportion of credit extended through the sale of securities. Like the financial systems of many other countries, that of the United States is characterized by a mixture of intermediation finance, involving lending to ultimate borrowers by financial intermediaries that then sell their own "indirect securities" in the form of deposits and other obligations to the public, and direct finance, in which the public extends credit directly to the ultimate borrower through the purchase of primary securities in the open market. It is sometimes argued that the relative importance of the securities markets in the U.S. financial system is evidence of its advanced state of development. Partly because of the breadth and resiliency of these markets, the United States, virtually alone in the world, is able to conduct its domestic monetary policy almost exclusively through open-market purchases and sales of government securities.

In contrast, intermediation finance accounts for a much higher proportion of total credit in most other countries, including such highly developed ones as West Germany and Japan. In recent decades, little more than 10% of the external funds raised by nonfinancial corporations in these two countries has been obtained by the sale of securities, as opposed to nearly 50% in the United States. Like virtually all other countries, they find it necessary or desirable to conduct monetary policy primarily through changes in the interest rate at which the central bank stands ready to lend to commercial banks.

That being the case, it might be viewed by some as retrogression that, throughout most of the twentieth century, the share of intermediation finance increased in the United States. An alternative interpretation is suggested by the fact that, while intermediation has increased both absolutely and relatively, securities markets have continued to expand. This indicates that the increased importance of intermediation finance reflects a broadening of participation in the financial markets to include a larger proportion of the population, particularly lower-income groups that lack the means and sophistication to enter the securities markets. This interpretation is supported by data from the Federal Reserve's Survey of Changes in Family Finances, which show that the proportion of the population holding indirect securities has greatly increased over the past several decades, and by the fact that, even as the securities markets have continued to grow, individuals have increasingly chosen to participate in them through such institutional investors as mutual funds and pension funds.

Several recent intercountry comparisons suggest that there are some important tradeoffs between having highly efficient securities markets and having a well-developed system of intermediation finance. More importantly, the choice between the two may not be as clear-cut as was once believed (Goodman, Cumming, and Kumekawa, 1984; Langohr and Santomero, 1984). Finally, financial institutions are increasingly, albeit to varying degrees, involved in both traditional intermediation markets such as bank lending to business and the purchase and sale of financial instruments in the organized capital markets.

3. Most Important Types of Financial Institutions

In order to highlight the varying degrees of participation by U.S. financial institutions in the two basic types of finance, the descriptions of the most important types of financial institutions in this section are arranged roughly according to where the institutions stand on the spectrum from intermediation finance to direct finance. The traditional depository institutions are listed first, followed by more specialized lending institutions. Then come such institutional investors as insurance companies, pension funds, and mutual funds that may be viewed as marginal financial intermediaries, in that they carry out most of their operations on the asset side of the balance sheet in the securities markets. Investment banks, brokers, and dealers, whose operations are largely in the securities markets, are listed last.

3.1. Commercial Banks

3.1.1. Current Position. Commercial banks have been the dominant type of financial institution in the United States throughout its history. Although the degree of their dominance has declined significantly since the latter part of the nineteenth century, commercial banks are still by far the most important type of financial institution in terms of their total assets, accounting for roughly 30% of the total. A comparison of banks' share of the total assets of financial institutions for various years between 1950 and 1989 is shown in table 10-1.

U.S. banks were derived from the British model and originally engaged primarily in short-term lending to commercial enterprises. However, in responding to the demands of the marketplace, U.S. banks found ways to extend longer-term loans to business for the purchase of plant and

Table 10-1A. Total Financial Assets (Billions $)

	1950	1960	1970	1980	1988	1989
Commercial banks	147.7	224.2	489.7	1,226.1	2,383.5	2,548.1
Savings and loans	16.9	71.5	170.9	613.7	1,359.9	1,268.1
Mutual savings banks	22.4	41.0	79.3	171.5	280.0	283.3
Credit unions	1.0	6.3	18.0	69.0	196.2	203.4
Life insurance companies	62.6	115.8	200.9	464.2	1,113.3	1,219.7
Other insurance companies	11.7	26.2	49.9	174.3	434.4	472.0
Finance companies	9.3	27.6	64.1	202.4	489.3	525.3
Security broker/dealers	4.0	6.7	16.2	45.9	140.5	255.0
Total	275.6	519.3	1,089.0	3,007.1	6,397.1	6,774.9

Table 10-1B. Share of Total Financial Assets (Percent)

	1950	1960	1970	1980	1988	1989
Commercial bank	53.6	43.2	45.0	42.1	37.3	37.6
Savings and loans	6.1	13.8	15.7	20.4	21.3	18.7
Mutual savings banks	8.1	7.9	7.3	5.7	4.4	4.2
Credit unions	0.4	1.2	1.7	2.3	3.1	3.0
Life insurance companies	22.7	22.3	18.4	15.4	17.4	18.0
Other insurance companies	4.2	5.0	4.6	5.8	6.8	7.0
Finance companies	3.4	5.3	5.9	6.7	7.6	7.8
Security broker/dealers	1.5	1.3	1.5	1.5	2.2	3.8
Total	100.0	100.0	100.0	100.0	100.0	100.0

equipment. Over the years they have gradually broadened their assets and liabilities to the point that they may be considered the most diversified type of financial institution in the country. Although commercial and industrial loans remain their largest single category of loans, they are heavily represented in consumer loans, residential real estate loans, agricultural loans, and loans to other financial institutions, as shown in table 10-2.

3.1.2. Business Lending. As their name suggests, commercial banks have long been important suppliers of credit to commercial enterprises. Indeed, under the Real Bills Doctrine promulgated by Adam Smith (1776) and endorsed by a long line of respected economists and bankers, banks should lend exclusively to commercial firms only on a short-term

Table 10-2. Loans of Domestic Commercial Banks: Consolidated Report of Condition, December 31, 1988

Loan Type	Million $	Percent
Commercial and industrial	497,156	29.3
Consumer	361,993	21.3
Residential real estate	318,902	18.8
Other real estate	333,530	19.6
Agricultural production	29,824	1.8
Depository institutions	34,222	2.0
Other	121,926	7.2
Total	1,697,553	100.0

basis and only for purposes involving the production or distribution of real goods. Such loans should also be "self-liquidating," in the sense that they could be repaid with the proceeds from the sale of the goods being financed. If banks would observe these limitations, it was argued, they would always be in a position to pay off their depositors. Additionally, the total volume of money and credit would adjust automatically to the "needs of trade," as reflected in the demand for business credit. This doctrine, often referred to in the United States as the "commercial loan theory of banking," received lip service from several generations of bankers and was built into the Federal Reserve Act in the form of a requirement that only commercial paper meeting its criteria could serve as collateral for loans from the Federal Reserve's discount window. Although Professor Lloyd Mints provided what was widely viewed as the definitive refutation of the doctrine (Mints, 1945), it continues to have its adherents to this day.

Since the turn of the century, commercial banks have lost market share in commercial lending to a variety of other types of financial institutions. It is estimated that their share of total business financing has fallen from about 60% in 1900 to roughly 20% in 1989. Life insurance companies have made major inroads in long-term lending, particularly commercial mortgage lending; commercial finance companies have grown rapidly as suppliers of fully secured credit to small and medium-sized businesses; and trade credit has become a major source of short-term credit to many small businesses. Thus, banks today supply a relatively small and declining proportion of all external funds raised by nonfinancial corporations (Hoskins and Weston, 1970). Be that as it may, commercial and industrial loans remain the largest single asset category on banks' balance sheets, though they have declined from about 70% of the total in 1910 to about 30% at the end of 1989. Most importantly, commercial banks remain one of the few sources of short-term, unsecured credit to business and are clearly the primary source of such credit to small businesses.

At the present time, commercial banks are undergoing a new challenge to their preeminence in commercial lending resulting from technological advances in information processing and transmission that have called into question banks' longstanding informational advantage derived from their customer relationships. Even where banks have been able to maintain their advantage in originating loans, the greater volatility of interest rates in recent years, in conjunction with the increased regulatory burden of capital and reserve requirements resulting from the higher level of interest rates, has made it increasingly uneconomic for banks to fund and hold such assets (Rose, 1982; Baer and Pavel, 1988). Accordingly, they are becoming much more originators and sellers of loans and much less long-term investors. In seeking ways to enhance the appeal of these assets to investors, banks have been driven to develop further the techniques of securitization pioneered by the Federal National Mortgage Association, the Government National Mortgage Association, and the Federal Home Loan Mortgage Corporation to foster the growth of a secondary market for home mortgages. These techniques have included, in addition to the bundling of heterogeneous collections of loans into single, less risky securities offering either fixed coupons or the payment of principal and interest on a pass-through basis as it is received, various guarantees or credit enhancements to overcome investors' resistance to taking on unfamiliar risks (Pavel, 1989).

3.1.3. Real Estate Lending. Loans secured by real estate are among the most illiquid of assets and have long been considered dangerous for institutions with predominantly short-term liabilities. Indeed, a number of state-chartered banks in New England failed in the early 1800s as a consequence of ignoring this principle and investing heavily in loans secured by farmland. Faced with unexpectedly large deposit withdrawals, they came to grief because of the illiquidity of these loans. Hence, it is not surprising that U.S. commercial banks largely avoided such lending in the latter part of the nineteenth century. Not only did most of the states eventually enact laws restricting such lending, but the National Banking Act of 1864 prohibited national banks from making real estate loans. This prohibition was not eliminated until 1900, when it was replaced by a restriction limiting the real estate loans of national banks to the lesser of their capital and surplus or 50% of their time and savings deposits.

Commercial banks greatly expanded their real estate lending in the 1930s when mortgages insured by the Federal Housing Authority first became available. However, in recent decades they have been active primarily in the market for conventional mortgages, which, however, tend to be to the most creditworthy borrowers. As of the end of 1988, mortgage loans secured by residential real estate, primarily one-to-four family dwellings, constituted 19% of aggregate commercial bank loans. Since 1987, the dollar amount of residential mortgage loans originated by commercial banks has exceeded that of savings and loan associations.

3.1.4. Consumer Installment Lending. It was not until the 1920s that commercial banks made any serious effort to enter the consumer lending business. Conventional banking doctrine held that lending for purposes of consumption, rather than production, was poor banking practice at best. Thus, as in the case of residential mortgage lending, commercial banks demonstrated an eagerness to enter the field only after others had demonstrated its safety and feasibility. They were moved to do so by a decline in the profitability of their traditional commercial lending business attributable to the sharply increased use of internally generated funds by business in the 1920s. Among the immediate consequences of this development were the repayment by large corporations of a large proportion of their external debt and a sharp reduction in their short-term borrowing from banks. In time, of course, the banks became formidable competitors in the consumer lending market and today are the largest single source of such credit. As of year-end 1988, the average bank held 21% of its loan portfolio in consumer loans, and banks in the aggregate held some 45% of outstanding consumer installment debt.

3.1.5. Liability Structure. On the liability side, U.S. banks have moved from near total reliance on demand deposits in the early 1950s to a situation at the end of 1989 in which demand deposits and other checkable deposits accounted for only 21% of their total liabilities. This change in composition has largely reflected the impact of the prohibition of interest on demand deposits during an extended period of rising interest rates and the growing importance at the largest banks of nondeposit liabilities such as federal funds borrowing, subordinated debt, etc. Data on U.S. banks' liabilities for several years between 1950 and 1989 are provided by table 10-3.

3.1.6. Off-Balance-Sheet Activities. Traditionally, the intermediation activities of most banks were reflected in their balance-sheet assets and liabilities. However, reduced information costs, greater emphasis on trading activities, impaired capital, and attempts to avoid regulatory taxes

Table 10-3A. Total Commercial Bank Liabilities (Billions $)

	1950	*1960*	*1970*	*1980*	*1988*	*1989*
Checkable deposits	95.7	123.7	182.5	328.2	551.3	548.9
Small time and savings	36.6	71.9	179.9	473.6	1,069.4	1,167.6
Large time deposits	0.0	1.1	52.6	243.8	361.9	379.6
Federal funds and RPs	(0.1)	(0.3)	4.7	114.8	217.6	265.6
Corporate bonds	0.0	0.0	2.1	6.3	17.2	18.6
Other	5.0	9.7	45.8	91.0	224.2	227.6
Total	137.2	206.1	467.6	1,257.7	2,441.6	2,607.7

Table 10-3B. Share of Total Commercial Bank Liabilities (Percent)

	1950	1960	1970	1980	1988	1989
Checkable deposits	69.8	60.0	39.0	26.1	22.6	21.0
Small time and savings	26.7	34.9	38.5	37.7	43.8	44.8
Large time deposits	0.0	0.5	11.2	19.4	14.8	14.5
Federal funds and RPs	(0.1)	(0.1)	1.0	9.1	8.9	10.2
Corporate bonds	0.0	0.0	0.4	0.5	0.7	0.7
Other	3.6	4.7	9.8	7.2	9.2	8.7
Total	100.0	100.0	100.0	100.0	100.0	100.0

on low-risk activities arising from reserve requirements, deposit insurance premiums, and minimum equity capital requirements have combined to shift banks away from traditional lending and deposit-taking activities. For those U.S. commercial banks reporting such activities, the nominal value of off-balance-sheet activities exceeds total on-balance-sheet assets (see table 10-4).

Some off-balance-sheet activities are driven primarily by banks' growing role as brokers and market makers in the market for foreign exchange and interest-rate risk-management products. On a dollar basis,

Table 10-4. Commitments and Contingencies, Off-Balance-Sheet Items (Foreign and Domestic): Consolidated Report of Condition, December 31, 1988

Item	Million $	Percent
Foreign exchange	1,684,057.1	51.7
Lease financing	642,841.8	19.7
Futures	408,646.2	12.5
Stand-by LOC	168,914.8	5.2
Options	96,690.0	3.0
Loans sold w/o recourse	72,000.0	2.2
Commercial LOC	29,826.2	0.9
When-issued securities	13,413.9	0.4
Securities borrowed/lent	10,695.8	0.3
Acceptances	4,299.5	0.1
Other	128,158.7	3.9
	3,259,554.0	100.0
Notional value of interest-rate swaps	928,661.0	
Total assets of banks with off-balance-sheet items	2,672,986.2	

Source: All items from call report except loans sold.

foreign-exchange trading is the leading off-balance-sheet activity. At year-end 1988, the contingent liabilities arising from interbank trading of foreign exchange were $1.6 trillion, compared with total assets at U.S. banks of $2.6 trillion. Because foreign-exchange trades are not currently subject to netting or variation margin and are not settled through delivery vs. payment, banks bear risk that their trading partner will fail. With trading growing at 30% annually, some banks are seeking to reduce these steadily escalating risks by creating a clearing house to net foreign currency transactions (Baer and Evanoff, 1990).

Interest-rate swaps, another important off-balance-sheet activity, were first introduced in 1981. At year-end 1988, the notional value of interest-rate swaps at U.S. banks was nearly $1 trillion. If attempts to form a foreign exchange clearing house are successful, it is likely that a similar approach will be taken with swaps. The boom in interest-rate swaps has led banks to increase their activity in futures markets. Futures are frequently used to hedge temporary imbalances in the swap book. More generally, banks use futures markets to rapidly alter their interest-rate risk profiles. The value of open futures positions at U.S. banks is about $400 billion.

Other off-balance-sheet activities primarily serve as substitutes for on-balance-sheet activity. Standby letters of credit, used to guarantee contract performance, are comparable in risk to commercial loans. At year-end 1988, U.S. commercial banks had $168 billion of standby letters of credit outstanding, up from $37 billion in 1980. Attempts to avoid regulatory taxes appear to have played an important role in the rapid growth of standby letters of credit during the 1980s (Baer and Pavel, 1988). However, making them subject to the new risk-based capital requirements has reduced their attractiveness.

Selling commercial loans without recourse is another important off-balance-sheet activity. Unlike other off-balance-sheet activities, loans sold without recourse generate no legal risk for the selling bank. However, banks may choose to repurchase loans whose quality has deteriorated in order to preserve their reputations as trustworthy trading partners. As of mid-year 1989, U.S. commercial banks had $72 billion of commercial loans sold outstanding, up from an estimated $25 billion in 1985. Loan sales have been driven in part by the need to diversify loan portfolios in the face of a boom in large merger-related lending, in part by the desire of some banks to conserve relatively scarce capital, and in part by a desire to avoid regulatory taxes.

3.1.7. Other Services. Banks are also engaged in a number of non-credit, fee-for-service activities, such as investment advising, foreign-exchange trading, and underwriting and dealing in U.S. government securities and general obligations of states and municipalities. Moreover, through separately incorporated subsidiaries, their parent holding companies may engage in securities brokerage, equipment leasing, mortgage banking, underwriting credit life insurance, and, to a limited degree, underwriting and dealing in corporate debt securities, as well as a number of other activities that the Federal Reserve Board has approved for bank holding companies. Banks continue to seek to expand the extent of their involvement in securities and insurance activities. These are areas that are currently the subject of great controversy and are discussed further in the section on major problems.

3.1.8. Outlook for U.S. Banks. Although commercial banks have lost their dominant position in lending to the largest corporations, they retain much of their advantage as unsecured lenders to small and medium-sized businesses. Moreover, they have long been the leading suppliers of consumer credit and recently overtook the savings and loans associations as the leading source of new residential mortgage loans. In conjunction with their growing off-balance-sheet activities and their expansion, through nonbank subsidiaries of their holding companies, into new activities, these facts suggest that banks are likely to remain the most important financial institutions in the United States for some time to come (Kaufman, Mote, and Rosenblum, 1983).

3.2. Thrift and Other Depository Institutions

3.2.1. Thrift Institutions. Like U.S. commercial banks, U.S. mutual savings banks and savings and loan associations were descended from similar institutions in England and Scotland. In both cases, they were first established to provide a service that the commercial banks had failed to offer. The first mutual savings bank in the United States was the Philadelphia Savings Fund Society, which was established in 1819 (Krooss and Blyn, 1971). However, within the year it was joined by the Bank for Savings in New York and the Provident Institution for Savings in Boston. Mutual savings banks were established exclusively to encourage thrift among the working class, a task that the business-oriented commercial banks had generally disdained. Because federal charters were not available for savings banks until 1982, they have been confined to the Eastern Seaboard and those few states in other areas of the country that permit their establishment. The relatively slow growth of population and economic activity in these areas has led to a drastic reduction in savings banks' share of total assets of financial institutions.

The first building and loan association was established in Birmingham, England in 1781 to extend loans to factory workers for the purchase of their own homes. Similarly, the first building and loan association in the United States, the Oxford Provident of Frankford, Pennsylvania, was established in 1831 to enable workers in the textile and tanning mills to purchase homes. As was noted above, this was a service that traditional banking theory held to be inappropriate for commercial banks. However, in a rapidly growing country like the United States at that time, there was a heavy demand for residential loans. Thus, a ready-made market existed for any institution capable of supplying it. Savings banks and savings and loan associations were essentially the only institutional suppliers of such credit for many years until national banks were permitted to make real estate loans in 1900.

Despite their name, mutual savings banks have always stood in a debtor–creditor relationship to their depositors. However, building and loan associations (now generally called savings and loan associations) were long characterized by their mutual form of organization under which their members, or savers, were the legal owners of the association. Their claims on the association were considered shares, rather than deposits, and they were paid dividends on their shares rather than interest. More recently, the mutual form has become something of a fiction, since savings and loans generally require prospective members to sign a proxy delegating their voting rights to existing management. One of the major developments in the thrift industry in the last decade has been the conversion of a large number of savings and loans to stock ownership. While resulting in increased accountability to shareholders, this movement has raised serious questions of equity in the distribution of the institutions' accumulated surplus.

Although the most rapid growth of U.S. thrift institutions dates from the passage of the Federal Home Loan Act as part of the New Deal legislation of the early 1930s, so do their most pressing problems of today. By giving government sanction to the long-term, fixed-rate, fully amortized home mortgage; by allowing thrift institutions holding large proportions of their assets in residential mortgages to deduct from their income for federal income tax purposes extremely generous loan loss provisions; and by providing long-term credit at subsidized rates to thrift institutions through the Federal Home Loan Banks, federal legislation made home ownership more attractive and feasible for a broader segment of the population than ever before in history. But it also sowed the seeds of today's problems by encouraging the specialization in long-term assets financed by short-term deposits that has made the thrift industry so vulnerable to interest-rate risk.

This vulnerability was dramatically revealed during the first "Credit Crunch" in 1966, when interest rates rose sharply under the pressure of accelerating inflation and government borrowing to finance the military buildup for the Vietnam War. As deposit rates rose, many thrift institutions experienced earnings squeezes. A prophetic paper by Federal Reserve Governor Andrew Brimmer urged measures to reduce the vulnerability of savings and loans associations to interest-rate risk (Brimmer, 1968). The measures taken at the time—ample provision of credit by the Federal Home Loan Banks and the extension to savings and loan associations of below-markct ceilings on interest rates on deposits— enabled thrift institutions to weather the immediate crisis. However, these measures further encouraged thrifts' excessive reliance on long-term, fixed-rate mortgages and contributed to disintermediation and the development of such unregulated outlets for savings as money market mutual funds that characterized later periods of credit stringency in 1969 and the mid- and late 1970s (Carron, 1982).

Despite recommendations by the Commission on Money and Credit (1961), the President's Committee on Financial Institutions (1963), and the President's Commission on Financial Structure and Regulation (1971) that deposit rate ceilings be liberalized, that asset powers of thrift institutions be enlarged to lessen their reliance on mortgage lending, and that adjustable rate mortgages be introduced to reduce thrifts' exposure to interest-rate risk, none of these was carried out before 1979. In that year federally chartered savings and loans were permitted to make variable rate mortgages. Add to this excessively restrictive environment the perverse incentives associated with flat-premium deposit insurance, and the thrift industry was a disaster waiting to happen. In the spring of 1980, interest rates rose to levels not seen since 1929, followed shortly by the most severe recession of the post-World War II era in 1982. This rendered two thirds of the industry insolvent. At the end of 1981, the net worth of the industry was estimated to be a negative $100 billion (Kane, 1985). Hoping to help the industry diversify and "earn its way" back to health, Congress enacted laws in 1980 and 1982 phasing out interest rate ceilings and authorizing thrifts to undertake new activities including real estate development and equity risk investments. The ensuing crisis in the thrift industry and the legislative and regulatory responses to it are discussed in the section on major problems.

3.2.2. Credit Unions and Industrial Banks. In recent decades, credit unions have been the most rapidly growing depository institutions in the United States, albeit from an extremely small base. Originally established as mutual organizations designed to offer reasonably priced personal loans and savings facilities to members belonging to a particular affinity group, such as a business firm, trade union, or governmental unit, they retain their mutual form but have generally escaped their original membership restrictions. Indeed, a few of them have grown to be among the largest financial institutions in their respective states. For example, as of the end of 1986, the Mid-States Corporate Credit Union of Oak Brook, with $1.3 billion in assets, was the 13th largest depository institution headquartered in Illinois.

Aided by special tax treatment and often receiving subsidized in terms of office space, equipment, and personnel from the affinity group with which they are associated, credit unions are often criticized by their principal competitors as having unfair competitive advantages. The commercial banking industry, in particular, has lobbied long and hard to have credit unions' special treatment under the federal income tax laws repealed, but so far with little success. Like savings and loan associations, credit unions command a large constituency of members and considerable sympathy from legislators because of their perceived role as suppliers of credit to small borrowers.

Whereas credit unions are chartered by both the federal government and the individual states and are to be found throughout the country, industrial banks (or Morris Plan Associations, as they are called in Pennsylvania and a few other eastern states) exist only in a few regions of the country. They are important only in Colorado, where they account for a major share of the retail lending business. Specializing in making small loans to consumers, industrial banks obtain their funds by issuing time deposits and by borrowing from commercial banks.

3.3. Finance Companies and Other Specialized Lenders

3.3.1. Consumer and Sales Finance Companies. Near the end of the nineteenth century, a large and increasingly prosperous middle class bent on improving its standard of living created a potentially enormous demand for consumer credit. At the time, the only sources of such credit were pawnbrokers and what today would be known as "juice" loan operators—essentially underworld purveyors of credit at exorbitant rates. The Russell Sage Foundation laid the basis for a thorough reform of consumer credit in the United States by drafting a model Uniform Small Loan Law early in this century. Several states, beginning with New York in 1905, enacted legislation based on the model law that licensed so-called *small loan companies* to make small, fully amortized personal loans at relatively high but controlled rates. By the time of the First World War, such companies had been established in virtually all of the states and dominated the market for consumer installment credit.

As increasing numbers of consumers earned incomes sufficient to enable them to afford the purchase of automobiles and major appliances, their demand for short-term credit to finance such purchases expanded rapidly. To satisfy this demand, a new type of financial institution, the sales finance company, arose in the early 1900s. Established in some cases by existing consumer finance companies, these institutions entered into agreements with retailers to finance purchases of their products by consumers meeting basic credit standards. They also financed retailers' inventories through what are widely known as *floor plan* loans, fully secured by specific units of the product. Some of these companies, such as General Motors Acceptance Corporation and Westinghouse Credit Corporation, were established by manufacturers to facilitate sales of their products at the retail level and are often referred to as *captive* finance companies even though financing of their parents' products is now a small part of their total business. However, as manufacturers, particularly automobile companies, have made increasing use of sales incentive programs based on favorable financing terms, the proportion of these manufacturers' sales financed by their captive finance companies has risen sharply over the past few years.

Finance companies raise the funds that they lend through varying combinations of equity financing, borrowing from commercial banks, and the issuance of bonds and commercial paper—often with the backing of a formal line of credit at a commercial bank. The commercial paper issued by the largest and most creditworthy finance companies is generally recognized to be of higher quality than that of most industrial companies and is separately designated as *finance company paper*. There has not been a default by a major finance company since the 1930s, and despite the difficulties recently experienced by banks and thrift institutions, most finance companies remain well capitalized and soundly managed.

3.3.2. Commercial Finance Companies and Factors. Although commercial banks remain the preeminent source of short-term loans to business, their credit standards and emphasis on unsecured lending traditionally prevented them from serving a large class of legitimate but highly risky businesses. Many of these firms obtain the bulk of their financing from suppliers in the form of trade credit. However, these firms have requirements for working capital and for the financing of plant and equipment expenditures that trade credit is ill-equipped to supply. This gap in the spectrum of credit services available to business led, in the first decade of this century, to the establishment of a largely unregulated and highly specialized type of lending institution called commercial or business finance companies. These companies specialize in lending to small and middle-market firms that, because of their small size, lack of credit history, or simply the newness or inherently risky character of their business, have not qualified for bank financing. They protect themselves from default risk by lending almost exclusively on a fully secured basis. Thus, a vital ingredient of their administration of loans is frequent on-site inspections of borrowing firms' physical assets.

Among the most highly specialized and least understood types of financial institutions in the United States are so-called *factors*, which provide financing exclusively through the purchase of accounts receivable, either on a recourse or nonrecourse basis. They are similar to commercial finance companies inasmuch as they typically lend on a fully secured basis. However, factoring, particularly when done on a nonrecourse basis, requires careful and expert analysis of a firm's customer credit risk and, given the incompleteness of the data usually available on which to base such an analysis, a willingness by the factor to incur a fair amount of residual risk. Because of its inherent riskiness, this type of financing tends to be relatively expensive and is used only by firms unable to qualify for a better alternative.

3.3.3. Mortgage Banks. Based on their assets alone, it is questionable whether mortgage banking companies deserve more than a footnote in a brief overview of U.S. financial institutions. At the end of 1989, their total assets amounted to only $100 billion, or 2% of the total for all financial institutions. However, the role played by mortgage banks in the mortgage market is much greater than their assets would suggest. More importantly, their activities provide a prototype for the major transformation in the activities of banks and thrift institutions that has occurred over the past decade and is still in progress.

Mortgage banks originate mortgage loans and then sell almost all of them to institutional investors such as life insurance companies and pension funds, while retaining, in most cases, the responsibility, and attendant fees, for servicing them. In 1989 mortgage banks originated mortgages in the amount of $500 billion, or 25% of all new mortgages.

Although the buying and selling activities of the Government National Mortgage Association (Ginnie Mae), the Federal National Mortgage Association (Fannie Mae), and the Federal Home Loan Mortgage Corporation (Freddie Mac) have done much to expand the size and increase the liquidity of the secondary mortgage market, the market itself is anything but new, and mortgage banks have been a major participant since the 1930s.

This experience is extremely important because of the lessons it holds for banks and thrift institutions, which over the past decade have increasingly become originators of loans that they then sell, either in their original form or bundled and securitized, to institutional investors or the general public. This is one way that depository institutions have found to shift credit or interest-rate risks that they are unwilling to bear onto others who are. It has also been a way to avoid regulatory costs, such as reserve and capital requirements, that are assessed on the basis of assets or liabilities on the balance sheet (Baer and Pavel, 1988). Outright sales of loans without recourse will continue to provide an escape from these costs, but loan sales and credit enhancement activities that involve the creation of contingent liabilities are subject to capital requirements under the international risk-based capital standards scheduled to be fully implemented in 1992.

3.4. Insurance Companies

Dating from the 1750s, insurance companies are not only the oldest type of financial intermediary in the United States, but also (if the assets of life and casualty insurance companies are considered together) are second in importance only to commercial banks. Because of the contingent nature of their obligations, insurance companies are often viewed as being fundamentally different from other financial intermediaries. However, even when they confine themselves to selling pure insurance with no element of saving (as, for example, in the case of "term" life insurance), insurance companies continuously receive premium payments that must be invested to cover expected losses and expenses in a competitive insurance market. However, the intermediation function of insurance companies has been prominent since the advent in the 1840s of "whole" life insurance, which combines term insurance with an element of saving. Indeed, that combination proved so popular that its introduction marked the beginning of a spectacular period of growth that saw life insurance—which, though dating from the establishment of the Corporation for

Relief of Poor and Distressed Widows and Children of Presbyterian Ministers in 1760, had always lagged fire and marine insurance in terms of growth and profitability—eventually account for nearly three quarters of the total assets of the insurance industry.

The investment policies of life and casualty insurance companies differ systematically, reflecting the different types of risks they insure. Because life insurance companies insure against highly predictable events leading to payouts at determinate dates several decades in the future, they invest to lock in returns over a long investment horizon. Thus, their portfolios are dominated by corporate bonds and mortgages, supplemented by relatively small amounts of U.S. government securities. As life insurance companies have sold more variable annuities in recent years, they have expanded their holdings of corporate equities.

In contrast, casualty insurance companies insure against relatively short-term, highly volatile events. Consequently, they invest primarily in shorter-term assets, including U.S. government securities. However, because all of their income is taxable, almost 50% of their assets are held in general obligations of state and local governments to take advantage of their exemption from the federal income tax. Casualty companies hold only about 30% of their assets in corporate bonds and stocks and virtually none in mortgages.

Insurance is one of the few financial industries to be regulated almost exclusively at the state level. Life insurance, in particular, is subject to extensive prudential regulation designed to assure that death benefits are paid as promised. In recent years, the insurance commissioners of some states, notably Pennsylvania, have become more concerned with consumer issues and have become more aggressive in challenging premium increases, companies' abandonment of unprofitable lines of insurance, etc.

3.5. Pension Funds

After credit unions, private and public pension funds have experienced the most rapid asset growth of any broad category of intermediaries since 1950. Designed to assure workers and their families an income after retirement, they are largely a development of the twentieth century. But while private pension funds were adopted by many companies under the pressure of collective bargaining by unions, public pension funds were an outgrowth of President Franklin D. Roosevelt's New Deal of the early 1930s and the changed view of the role of government that it reflected.

By far the largest pension plan in the United States is the federal government's Old Age, Survivors, and Disability Insurance, often referred to simply as Social Security. With over 200 million members, of which some 50 million are currently receiving benefits, OASDI is designed to provide a floor to individuals' retirement incomes.

On a "pay-as-you-go" basis until recently, OASDI had accumulated reserves of only $189.5 billion as of the end of 1987, raising concerns that eventually a much smaller proportion of the population that was employed would have to support the benefits paid to a growing proportion of retirees. Among the changes suggested to contain the rise in benefit payments have been less complete indexing for inflation, later retirement ages, and the taxation of benefits to those with substantial additional sources of income. However, there is enormous public opposition to such tampering with Social Security benefits. Nonetheless, under a financing plan developed by the President's National Commission on Social Security Reform in 1983, current contribution rates have been increased, and the OASDI program is projected to be in close actuarial balance, on average, over the period 1984–2060.

The fastest-growing segment of the pension market has been the funds operated by state and local governments for their employees. Between 1950 and 1983, their assets grew from $5.3 billion to $316 billion and now cover some 15 million employees. More than a third of their assets are invested in corporate and foreign bonds, with slightly less than a third in corporate stock and a slightly smaller amount in government securities, and the remainder divided among mortgages, state and local securities, and other assets. Both because they tend to invest more conservatively than private pension funds and because state and local governments have not increased their contributions in step with the growth of promised benefits, many of these funds are underfunded. Thus, many jurisdictions have committed themselves to substantial tax increases at some future date.

With nearly a trillion dollars in assets as of year-end 1987, noninsured private pension funds account for more than half of all pension fund assets and cover over 50 million employees. In an effort to keep employer contributions low, they invest much more aggressively than state and local government pension funds. Over half of their assets is invested in corporate stocks, about a fourth in U.S. government securities, and only about a sixth in corporate and foreign bonds. Cash, mortgages, and other assets make up the remainder. Another $500 billion of pension fund assets is in insured plans managed by life insurance companies.

It became widely known in the 1970s that pension funds owned a large and growing share of total corporate equities outstanding. This led a number of scholars and members of Congress to express concern that pension funds were in a position to control much of U.S. industry through their shareholdings (Soldofsky, 1971). Congressional hearings were held to ascertain the extent and distribution of pension funds' holdings of corporate stock and to solicit proposals for policies to mitigate their effects. However, relatively few cases were found where one or a few pension funds held controlling interests in corporations.

Because of a number of cases in which employees lost pension benefits as a result of fraud or mismanagement, Congress enacted the Employee Retirement Income Security Act (ERISA) in 1974 to establish reporting and vesting requirements and to define fiduciary responsibilities for the trustees of private pension funds. In 1985, the Pension Benefit Guaranty Corporation was established within the Department of Labor to insure private pension plans. A growing concern in recent years has been that, in some corporate takeovers, the acquiring company has stripped the target company's pension plan of funds that, though not legally required to fund contractual benefits, were economically necessary to assure that such benefits could be paid in the event of a substantial change in interest rates or other factors affecting investment performance.

3.6. Mutual Funds

Conventional mutual funds, or open-end investment companies as they are sometimes called, purchase stocks or bonds or some combination thereof, depending on the purpose and investment philosophy of the fund, using funds raised by the sale of their own shares. These shares are issued and redeemed at the initiative of the fund's investors. Because the price of the fund's shares varies with the value of its portfolio of securities, many do not consider mutual funds to be true financial intermediaries. Although they are able to offer investors diversification, denomination intermediation, and delegated monitoring—three of the traditional functions of financial intermediaries—in exchange for an annual management fee set as a fixed percentage of assets, they do not offer a capital cushion to limit customer risk exposure. In some sense, therefore, they stand at the boundary between direct and indirect finance.

During the 1980s, horseholds came to rely much more heavily on mutual funds as a vehicle for investing in stocks and bonds, at the same time that they reduced the share of their assets held in corporate securities. In 1970, only 6% of household corporate securities holdings were in the form of mutual fund shares. By 1988, mutual funds accounted for 18% of households' securities holdings. As of the end of 1988, 2286 mutual funds held $537.9 billion in assets, roughly half those of life insurance companies or private pension funds and roughly equal to those of state and local government pension funds or finance companies. After growing rapidly in the 1960s and 1970s, when they increased their share of total assets of financial intermediaries from 1% to 4%, they have since tended to grow at a rate close to the average for all intermediaries.

Money market mutual funds, similar in structure to traditional mutual funds in that they raise funds by selling shares to the public, were established for entirely different reasons and invest in an entirely different range of assets. Founded in the early 1970s as a means of offering small savers competitive rates of return in the face of legal ceilings on the interest rates banks and thrift institutions could pay on deposits, money market funds invest almost exclusively in very high quality, short-term securities like large bank certificates of deposit, Treasury bills, commercial paper, and other similar securities. Though their obligations are legally shares rather than deposits, most funds stand ready to redeem them at par to keep them competitive with deposits. Free of interest-rate ceilings and reserve requirements, money market funds grew extremely rapidly after their introduction, reaching over $200 billion in assets by 1982. Their growth has slowed considerably since the deregulation of interest rates paid by depository institutions was largely completed in the early 1980s. As of the end of 1988, they had 54.7 million shareholder accounts, and their total assets were $272.3 billion.

3.7. Investment Banks, Brokers, and Dealers

Most U.S. investment banks combine, in varying proportions, the activities of underwriting new issues of securities, serving as retail or institutional brokers with respect to most securities, and serving as a dealer or market maker with respect to a smaller number of securities. In addition, they trade and invest for their own account and engage in a number of other activities, such as arranging mergers and acquisitions, lending on margin to customers, managing mutual funds, and providing investment advice.

In 1988, investment banks underwrote a total of $408.8 billion in bonds and $57.8 billion of stocks. New issues are purchased from the issuer at the public offering price less the agreed-upon spread. Spreads on long-term, high-quality corporate bonds have usually been slightly less than

1% of the public offering price, while those on issues of common stock have been somewhat higher.

Both corporate debt and corporate equity underwriting are highly concentrated, with no more than two dozen firms accounting for the lion's share of the underwritings and the top eight firms accounting for 80% or more of the total. It is believed that this concentration reflects the importance of reputation in obtaining underwriting clients. This high level of concentration suggests the possibility of monopoly profits in the industry, and depending on the years chosen, annual returns on equity in investment banking do indeed appear to exceed those in most other industries, averaging more than 20% for the largest investment banking firms in the years immediately preceding the 1987 crash. However, they also tend to be considerably more volatile, and it is difficult to judge the industry's competitiveness based on profit behavior alone. Some additional evidence is provided by the fact that commercial banks are so eager to get into the industry and by the zeal with which the Securities Industry Association has fought that attempted entry.

For most investment banking firms, brokerage commissions and gains from trading activities account for a much larger share of total revenues than underwriting. However, since industry agreements to fix commissions were outlawed in 1975, brokerage has become considerably more competitive, and the share of total revenue from commissions fell from over half to about 25% of the total in 1987—even though the number of shares traded on the New York Stock Exchange increased ninefold between 1975 and 1988. Revenues from trading and investment rose from 8% of the total in 1973 to 22% in 1988, and revenues from underwriting remained unchanged at about 9%. Another area experiencing big increases has been providing advice in mergers and acquisitions, although data on that activity alone are not available.

Although the National Association of Securities Dealers lists about 3000 members, the size distribution of securities firms, like that of commercial banks, is highly skewed. Most are very small, locally oriented, highly specialized firms. At the other extreme are a relatively few nationally known firms with capital of several hundred million to a few billion dollars, offices numbering in the hundreds, and employees numbering in the thousands. By far the largest is Merrill Lynch, which has nearly twice the capital and number of employees as its closest competitor.

In recent years, the investment banking industry has undergone drastic shrinkages in profits, offices, and employees, with the number of employees at securities and commodities brokers and dealers falling from 516,000 to 509,000 between 1987 and 1988 and net income of the securities industry falling from $8.3 billion in 1986 to $3.1 billion in 1987. There have been numerous announcements in recent years of investment banks withdrawing from areas considered unlikely to generate satisfactory profits in the near future, in particular retail brokerage and municipal bond trading, as well as mergers of established firms designed to achieve cost savings.

4. Securities, Futures, and Options Markets

As noted earlier, the size, depth, and sophistication of its markets for securities and other open-market instruments have long been recognized as among the greatest strengths of the U.S. financial system. In contrast to its commercial banking system, U.S. securities markets have often set the pace for the rest of the world. Following the Great Depression, the United States led the world in the development of laws requiring corporations selling securities to the public to disclose adequate information on their financial condition. The United States is also home to the world's principal futures and options exchanges. Beginning in 1974, these exchanges pioneered the trading of futures and options on financial instruments. Finally, the U.S. also set the pace in deregulating trading commissions when it outlawed joint setting of commissions in 1975.

The deregulation of commissions on securities trades in combination with public disclosure and the growing importance of institutional investors such as insurance companies and pension funds has led to a dramatic increase in trading activity in U.S. financial markets. Between 1970 and 1988, the number of shares sold annually on organized exchanges grew from 4.5 billion shares to 52.5 billion shares. Over the same period, average daily transactions of dealers in U.S. government securities rose from $18 billion to $100 billion. Even more dramatic growth was experienced by the nation's futures and options exchanges. Between 1980 and 1988, the number of contracts traded on the nation's futures and options exchanges grew from 12.4 million to 437 million, with the bulk of the growth occurring in contracts on financial instruments. Much of the success of financial futures, particularly stock index futures, has occurred at the expense of existing cash markets like the New York Stock Exchange. This has helped fuel attempts to reduce the attractiveness of futures markets through more stringent regulation.

Regulation of financial trading is divided among a number of entities. The Securities and Exchange Commission (SEC) regulates the trading of securities and options on securities, while the Federal Reserve regulates margin levels on loans financing securities positions. The Commodities Futures Trading Commission regulates the nation's futures markets. The market for U.S. government securities is regulated by the Treasury and the Federal Reserve. In contrast to banking, self-regulatory organizations play an important role in many markets for financial instruments.

The 1980s witnessed a major change in the nature of trading on U.S. markets for securities and other financial instruments. Traditionally, most trading activity was channeled through organized exchanges. However, trading in U.S. government securities, foreign exchange, mortgage-backed securities, and over-the-counter swaps and options all ballooned during the 1980s. Trading in these markets is conducted on a bilateral basis rather than through organized exchanges. As the volume of trading in these markets grew, the absence of centralized netting and delivery arrangements became increasingly troublesome to participants. The result has been proposals for the creation of clearinghouses for interdealer markets. The first of these, the Government Securities Clearing Corporation, was created in 1986 and began multilateral netting of government securities transactions in July 1989 (Parkinson, 1990). As more of these clearinghouses come into existence, the distinctions between interdealer markets and organized exchanges will begin to blur.

Another major development in U.S. securities markets has been the growing importance of private placement as an alternative to public issuance of securities. Privately placed securities can legally be sold only to institutional investors exceeding a certain size. Privately placed securities must also be held for two years before they can be sold. In 1988, 25% of new equity and 37% of new corporate bonds were issued through private placement. In 1980, only 20% of corporate bonds had been issued through private placement issues. The increasing share of private placements reflects the growing importance of well-informed institutional investors and the rapid expansion in the number and size of hostile takeovers and leveraged buyouts. Both of these factors have raised the perceived costs of disclosure requirements. Recognizing the growing importance of private placements, the Securities and Exchange Commission has adopted rules that will permit the trading of privately placed securities among eligible investors two years after their issue date. Several exchanges are already competing to serve this new market by providing an electronic trading system for these securities.

In the United States, in contrast to other countries, the stock market crash of October 1987 and the "minicrash" of October 1989 have provoked much analysis of federal regulation of financial markets (Presidential Task Force on Market Mechanisms, 1988). Some have argued that the sharp slides in the stock market that occurred in the second half of the 1980s were the result of excessive speculation facilitated by low margins on stock index contracts. Others have argued that the declines would not have been as sharp if trading halts on the various exchanges had been coordinated and if more sophisticated clearance and settlement systems had been in place. Some place the blame on a specialist system that is ill-equipped to deal with the heavy volume of trading that has come to characterize the stock market. Still others argue that a consolidation of the SEC and the CFTC is necessary to ensure consistent regulation. There is little evidence to support any of these propositions (Miller, 1988). Moreover, with the exception of arguments about the need for improvements in the clearing system, it is often debatable whether supporters of a particular policy are being motivated by a desire to improve the efficiency of the U.S. financial system or by the possibility of using government regulation to gain or maintain a competitive advantage.

5. Brief History of U.S. Banking, 1782–1980

The casual observer's first impression of the U.S. banking system is very often one of perplexity. Despite its high state of development, the system seems unnecessarily cumbersome and complex. Institutions clearly competing with one another are subject to different and largely independent regulatory bodies. Most institutions are subject to regulation by more than one regulatory agency, and there is often disagreement and jurisdictional conflict between these agencies (Hackley, 1966). The distribution of authority between state and federal agencies appears to be arbitrary. Finally, the natural desire by agencies to enlarge their constituencies has at times led to "competition in laxity" in terms of the stringency of regulation, a competition that has variously been touted as one of the major srengths or condemned as the primary weakness of depository institution regulation in the United States. There have been numerous calls over the past several decades for fundamental changes in both the structure and substance of financial regulation. In order to avoid throwing out the good with the bad in the existing system, it is essential to understand its rationale, however valid or mistaken that might be. But it is impossible to understand the U.S. banking system without reference to its origins and to several major events that shaped current public policy toward banking—in particular, the defeat of the Second Bank of the United States, the Free Banking Era, the Civil War, the Panic of 1907, and the banking collapse of the early 1930s.

5.1. Origins of U.S. Banking

During the colonial era there was essentially no domestic banking system in what is now the United States. According to Benjamin Klebaner, "The American colonies had no banks for clearing business transactions, and the underdeveloped state of short-term credit arrangements hampered commerce" (Klebaner, 1974). Distrusting the colonists' ability to conduct a business calling for both intelligence and prudence, the British forbade them to establish banks.

Once independence was achieved, financial matters were at the forefront of controversies faced by the new Congress and President. Although suspicion of all banks was widespread and continued so through the mid-1800s—a number of states banned banking in the 1830s—sentiment in the major cities clearly favored their establishment. The first domestically chartered bank in the United States was the Bank of North America, chartered by the Continental Congress in Philadelphia in 1782 at the initiative of Robert Morris. Shortly thereafter, banks were established in many other states as well, and, by 1800, some 29 were in operation, including the First Bank of the United States.

It is well known that Alexander Hamilton championed the establishment of a national bank to exercise some discipline over the practices of the growing number of state banks, particularly their tendency to overissue bank notes. In 1791, the federal government granted a 20-year charter to the First Bank of the United States. Headquartered in Philadelphia, with branches in five other major cities, the Bank provided banking services to the federal government, served as its fiscal agent, and engaged in a general commercial banking business. Most importantly, it performed the rudimentary central banking function of limiting the note issues of state banks by accumulating their notes and then presenting them for immediate redemption in specie. This latter activity angered many state bankers and their political allies and, in conjunction with the public's deep-seated hostility to centralized control of money and credit dating from the establishment of the Bank of England in 1694 (Shull, 1983) and the highly unpopular ownership by foreigners of a large part of the First Bank's stock, proved fatal to attempts to extend the Bank's charter when it expired in 1811.

5.2. The Second Bank of the United States

The demise of the First Bank of the United States was followed by renewed overissues of bank notes by the state banks. These resulted, in

1814, in the first general suspension of redemption of bank notes into specie in U.S. banking history and led to sharply increased variation in the discounts at which bank notes were exchanged. The objections of the U.S. Treasury to this state of affairs led to the chartering of the Second Bank of the United States in 1816. By this time the number of banks in the United States had risen to 246. Located, like the First Bank, in Philadelphia, the Second Bank engaged in essentially identical activities. However, it had more capital, a larger number of branches, and was wholly domestically owned. Initially plagued by poor management and by the State of Maryland's attempt to tax its Baltimore office, the Bank was strengthened by the 1819 Supreme Court decision in *McCulloch v. Maryland* protecting it from prohibitive taxation by the states. Under the management of Nicholas Biddle, the Bank enjoyed a decade of prosperity and provided an effective discipline over note issue by the state banks. However, "Biddle's Bank" incurred the enmity of President Andrew Jackson, who vetoed its attempted rechartering by Congress in 1832, eventuating in its conversion to a Pennsylvania charter when its federal charter expired in 1836. Thereafter, there was essentially no federal presence in commercial banking until 1863.

5.3. The Free Banking Era, 1837–1863

American thinking about the appropriate role of government in banking has been heavily influenced by the conventional wisdom regarding the so-called Free Banking Era. However, recent historical scholarship has called into question many of the prevailing views regarding the actual events during that era and, more importantly, their interpretation. Thus, it is essential that we sketch the broad outlines of both the conventional wisdom and the revisionist views that have gained currency over the past several decades.

The period 1837–1863 takes its name from the "free banking" laws enacted by a number of states beginning with Michigan in 1837 and followed by New York and Georgia in 1838 and, more than a decade later, by 16 other states. Prior to the enactment of these laws, a bank charter could be obtained only through an act of the state legislature. As one might expect, such a requirement was conducive to bribery and favoritism and had the effect of greatly limiting entry into banking. In order to eliminate the arbitrariness and corruption that attended the chartering process, most of the states enacted laws subjecting banking to the general incorporation laws governing the chartering of other types of business. These laws permitted anyone to obtain a bank charter who met certain standardized requirements regarding capital, number of directors, and other provisions designed to protect the public. In addition, most of the free banking laws contained limitations on the number of offices at which a bank might conduct business—a provision aimed at "wildcat banking," or the practice of issuing notes at one office but only redeeming them at another, generally inaccessible office—and restrictions on the amount of bank notes that might be issued, generally in the form of a requirement that the note issue be tied to the value of state bonds held by the bank.

This massive liberalization of entry into banking produced an explosion of new banks and note issues, followed shortly by large numbers of bank failures. One of the more disastrous experiences was in Michigan, where some 40 new banks were chartered in 1837, the year that its Free Banking Law was enacted. Within two years, 36 of those banks had failed, resulting in losses to noteholders estimated at $4 million, or about 45% of Michigan's annual income in 1840 (Rolnick and Weber, 1982). The problems associated with the absence of a uniform national currency, already serious when there were only a few dozen banks issuing their own bank notes, were greatly multiplied when the number of banks neared 5000 just before the Civil War. Decisions by businesses regarding the exchange rate at which they should accept payment in the bank notes of particular banks necessitated the use of bank note reporters, large directories containing pictures and ratings of all known bank note issues. Necessarily, the published information lagged actual changes in banks' conditions, and this problem was exacerbated by counterfeit issues and issues of nonexistent banks that rivaled in number the legitimate issues. Charles Calomiris (1991) has shown that the discounts at which particular issues traded varied systematically with the cost of obtaining information on the issue, as reflected by the distance from the issuing bank.

Although the above-mentioned problems constituted important inefficiencies in the monetary system, the most serious criticisms of the banking system concerned its susceptibility to liquidity panics and suspensions of payment in gold. Throughout the nineteenth century, at roughly 10 to 20-year intervals, there were liquidity panics characterized by large withdrawals of specie from banks, sharp increases in the number of bank failures, and, in several cases, general suspensions of payment in gold. For the most part, these panics were triggered by local economic disturbances that led to defaults on loans that threatened the solvency of one or more banks and induced depositors to withdraw specie from the banks. In a fractional reserve banking system, absent an outside source of specie reserves, this inevitably caused a number of banks to fail. The resulting suspensions of payment, often initiated by the banks acting collectively and validated by the state legislature after the fact, further disrupted commerce and often resulted in recessions.

Be that as it may, many recent scholarly works have concluded that the problems of free banking have been exaggerated and that, on balance, the system worked reasonably well. One of the earliest writers to challenge the conventional view was Paul B. Trescott, who wrote in 1963:

> On the whole, the banking system mirrored the society as a whole—diverse, disorderly, growing rapidly but at an uneven pace of fits, jerks, and starts—enterprising and progressive, but not overly scrupulous. Bank credit had played a big role in financing the westward movement of population, cultivation, and transportation. It underwrote much of the high level of international commerce and shipping, and it contributed significantly to the capital needs of up-and-coming industrial development (Trescott, 1963, p. 38).

5.4. The National Banking System

By the early 1860s, complaints regarding the lack of a uniform currency, as well as the instability of the banking system and its perceived impact on money and the trade cycle, had been rife for several decades. The necessary impetus for enactment of reform legislation was provided by the outbreak of the Civil War, in particular the difficulties the Union was experiencing in financing the war effort. Thus, a key element of the legislation enacted in 1863 as the National Currency Act and reenacted with minor revisions the following year as the National Banking Act (since renamed the National Bank Act) was a requirement that the newly authorized national banks could issue National Bank Notes in an amount not to exceed 90% of the market value of their holdings of U.S. government securities. It was anticipated that this provision would create a strong demand for such securities, thereby greatly facilitating the Treasury's task of financing the war.

Other key features of the National Bank Act were the establishment of the Comptroller of the Currency, an agency within the Treasury Department, to charter, regulate, and supervise national banks; the imposition of reserve requirements ranging from 10% to 25%, depending on location, against the deposits of national banks; and a requirement that national banks contribute gold or silver with a value equal to 5% of their outstanding National Bank Notes to a Specie Redemption Fund held by the Comptroller of the Currency. The act also prohibited national banks from making loans secured by real estate and empowered the

Comptroller to regulate the types of investment securities that national banks might hold. Finally, it required national banks to submit periodic reports to the Comptroller and to undergo, at their own expense, periodic examinations by National Bank examiners.

The National Banking Act's establishment of a bond-secured national currency is reminiscent of the similar provision in the free banking laws of the states. Indeed, as Ross Robertson pointed out in his history of the Comptroller's office, the National Banking Act was patterned after the free banking laws in many respects, and some of its language was actually borrowed verbatim from the New York Free Banking Law (Robertson, 1968). Although there had been no discussion of limiting branching in the legislative history of the act and although the act explicitly stated that state banks converting to national charters might keep their existing branches, early Comptrollers read the reference to the "place" where the national banking association would carry on its business in the singular as prohibiting the establishment of additional branches. This interpretation was not successfully challenged until the early 1920s. Thus, according to Professor Robertson, the fragmented structure of the U.S. banking system was the inadvertent result of a literal reading of borrowed language carelessly incorporated into the National Banking Act.

Because of the greater restrictiveness of the federal law, only about 400, or fewer than a third, of the 1466 state banks had converted to national charters by the end of 1864. In order to force state banks to convert, Congress imposed a 10% per annum tax on state bank notes in the spring of 1865. This measure met with instant success, resulting in an increase in the number of national banks from 467 in 1864 to 1,640 in 1868 and a reduction in the number of state banks from 1,089 to 247. However, the number of state banks began to grow again in 1869, when they discovered that they could conduct a banking business without issuing their own bank notes by offering their customers checking accounts. By the turn of the century, state banks again outnumbered national banks by a large margin, an advantage they have retained to the present, although some 70% of total bank deposits are held by national banks.

Given its purposes, the National Banking Act can be said to have produced mixed results. It clearly enlarged the market for U.S. government securities, albeit somewhat belatedly, facilitating the financing of the war effort. It provided the country, for the first time, with a safe, uniform currency; no holder of National Bank Notes ever suffered losses. On the other hand, the act did not succeed in its purpose of supplanting the state banking systems. Most importantly, although it brought uniform standards to the regulation and supervision of national banks, it failed to eliminate the periodic liquidity panics, bank failures, and losses to depositors that had disrupted the financial system in earlier years.

5.5. The Panic of 1907 and the Federal Reserve Act

A liquidity panic occurred in 1907 that, though having little lasting economic effect, did much to change the face of U.S. banking regulation. Centered in New York City, the panic caused serious difficulties for several large New York banks and a suspension of payment in gold. Congress responded by enacting the Aldrich–Vreeland Act of 1908, which authorized the use of clearinghouse certificates to settle interbank accounts during future panics and established a National Monetary Commission to study the monetary and financial systems of the United States and other countries and offer recommendations for reform.

The commission released its final report in 1910. Among its recommendations were that the United States should establish a central bank to serve as a source of reserves during liquidity panics, that banks should be given greater power to establish branches, and that banks should be able to borrow from the central bank on collateral consisting of high-quality commercial bills.

These recommendations proved to be extremely controversial, and Congress spent the next few years quarrelling over which, if any, of them should be adopted. There was particularly heated disagreement between those who viewed a central bank as necessary and desirable and those who were opposed to any form of centralized control of money and credit. During the extended legislative debate, the proposals were altered to such a degree that some authors have claimed that the legislation ultimately enacted owed little to the commission's recommendations (Warburg, 1930). Be that as it may, in December 1913, the Congress passed the Federal Reserve Act and President Woodrow Wilson signed it into law.

Virtually every provision of the act was a compromise, the product of political give and take. It established, for the first time in U.S. history, a formal central banking system. Paradoxically, however, that system was highly decentralized, consisting of a five-man Federal Reserve Board in Washington, whose members were appointed by the President with the advice and consent of the Senate, and as many as 12 autonomous regional Federal Reserve Banks owned and largely controlled by the privately owned commercial banks that chose to join the system. As this implies, membership in the Federal Reserve System was voluntary, a necessary concession to those who viewed the establishment of any kind of central bank as the path to tyranny. The act imposed reserve requirements on member banks that were similar in structure and magnitude to those imposed on national banks by the National Banking Act. However, these requirements, unlike those of the 1864 act, could not be satisfied by holding deposits at other commercial banks, but only by holding legal currency or deposits at a bank's regional Federal Reserve Bank. The act thereby avoided the National Banking Act's pyramiding of reserves under which country banks held their reserves in the form of deposits with Reserve City banks, which in turn held their reserves as deposits with Central Reserve City banks, a system that was often held to exacerbate panics. The Real Bills Doctrine was embodied in the Federal Reserve Act in the form of a requirement that member banks could borrow from the Federal Reserve Banks' discount windows only on collateral consisting of "eligible paper"—essentially commercial paper meeting the criteria of the doctrine.

Most observers judged the Federal Reserve System a success during its first decade and a half of operation. Although some criticized it for permitting a deep, if short-lived, recession in 1921, it is important to remember that the System was not originally established to conduct countercyclical monetary policy. That was an activity that evolved gradually during the 1920s as System officials discovered the powerful effects of their purchases and sales of government securities on financial markets and the economy generally. The 1920s were a generally prosperous decade, marked by great progress in industry and finance, rapid economic growth, and a relatively stable price level. The Federal Reserve essentially eliminated seasonal fluctuations in interest rates, which had long been blamed for precipitating liquidity panics—a view that, to be sure, is far from universally accepted.

However, this prosperity did not extend to the agricultural sector and rural America. The enormous expansion in agricultural output during World War I led to serious overcapacity and depression in peacetime. In combination with the increased use of the automobile, which eliminated the economic function of many small towns, defaults on loans attributable to the distress in agriculture contributed to the failure of an average of 500 banks a year during the 1920s. Because these were primarily small banks in rural towns that had become redundant economically and because their failures did not produce any serious spillover effects onto other banks or financial markets, they did not provide any grounds for faulting either Federal Reserve monetary policy or banking regulation.

However, toward the end of the decade, the Federal Reserve encountered a dilemma that provided a stiff test of its capabilities. Although commodity prices were generally level or declining after 1927, stock prices exploded. The Federal Reserve was faced with a choice between dampening speculation through a rise in interest rates, thereby risking a recession, and ignoring the speculation to maintain the level of spending in the economy. It belatedly chose the former, a defensible policy under the circumstances, but one that was ultimately overdone. Unfortunately, the System's ability to cope with the spreading evidence of depression was undermined at a crucial juncture in 1929 by the death of its greatest intellect, Benjamin Strong, President of the New York Federal Reserve Bank (Chandler, 1958). The result was a paralysis that allowed the nation to slide into the longest, and one of the deepest, depressions in American history.

5.6. The Great Depression and the Banking Act of 1933

There remains considerable disagreement among scholars regarding the importance of monetary policy in precipitating the depression, and no attempt will be made here to resolve that question (see Temin, 1976). However, one thing on which most scholars agree is that, once the depression was underway, the failure of the Federal Reserve to provide sufficient reserves to the banking system to offset the massive withdrawals of currency by the public exacerbated the banking crisis, eventually resulting in the failure of 9,000 banks between 1930 and 1933, and permitted a sharp decline in the money stock that deepened and greatly prolonged the depression (see Friedman and Schwartz, 1963; Wheelock, 1989).

At the time, however, the prevailing view was that the banking collapse was the inevitable result of the banks' imprudent behavior in the 1920s. Among the activities of banks most severely criticized at the time were their entry into consumer and real estate lending, their granting of term loans to business, and their sharply increased participation in investment banking activities. Finally, it was alleged that they had engaged in overaggressive competition for deposits, which in turn caused them to "reach for yield" by lowering their credit standards. Given this diagnosis, it is not surprising that the Banking Act of 1933, enacted by Congress during the fabled first 100 days of the Roosevelt administration, was designed to prevent a recurrence of the banking collapse by imposing severe restrictions on entry into banking, the types of assets banks might acquire, and the entry of banks into activities considered excessively risky.

Among other things, the Banking Act of 1933, as revised by the

Banking Act of 1935, reorganized the Federal Reserve System, concentrating more authority in the Federal Reserve Board in Washington and formally authorizing the Federal Open Market Committee; prohibited the payment of interest on demand deposits and limited the interest rates payable on time deposits; tightened restrictions on the chartering of new national banks; restricted national bank holdings of corporate debt securities to "investment grade" securities; imposed margin requirements on loans secured by, and for the purchase of, corporate stocks; gave national banks the same intrastate branching powers as state banks in the same state; separated full-service commercial and investment banking; and introduced federal deposit insurance. The act also gave the Federal Reserve Board the power, for the first time, to vary reserve requirements within a range of 7% to 21%. The Board promptly misused this power in 1937, sharply raising reserve requirements to eliminate what it perceived as the inflationary potential inherent in banks' enormous holdings of excess reserves. However, because banks were holding these reserves as protection against a feared resumption of the bank runs of the early 1930s, they responded to the increase in required reserves by curtailing their lending, thereby aborting the recovery of early 1937 (Morrison, 1966). Indeed, Milton Friedman and Anna Schwartz have charged that the Banking Act of 1933 gave the Federal Reserve new powers as a reward for misusing the powers that it already had (Friedman and Schwartz, 1963). Be that as it may, the Banking Act of 1933 shaped U.S. banking regulation for the next half-century.

5.7. Banking Recovery and the Deregulation Movement

Although the new legislation adopted at the trough of the Great Depression was clearly very restrictive, it initially had little effect. Demoralized by bank runs and by the persistence of the depression, banks were in no hurry to enter new, risky activities. Even absent the Banking Act of 1933, many banks probably would have exited the investment banking business. Interest rates on time and savings deposits fell well below the ceilings established under the act. Not until the late 1950s did the restrictions imposed by the Banking Acts of 1933 and 1935 become seriously binding. At that time, bankers began to push seriously for their relaxation. They were aided in this effort by the fact that stability prevailed in the industry, with unusually stable interest rates and an annual number of bank failures rarely exceeding ten.

5.7.1. Research on Banking Panics. The process of deregulation was also abetted by the results of research that called into question the traditional interpretations of the banking collapse of the 1930s and earlier panics and crises and pointed out the costs of anticompetitive regulations. Several studies examined the credit standards of lenders in the 1920s and found that there had been no discernible deterioration in the ex ante quality of loans in the latter years of the decade, as had been charged earlier. Studies of bank failures in the early 1930s failed to find any evidence that they were associated with unduly high rates of interest on deposits (Cox, 1966; Linke, 1966). Even more surprisingly, other studies have shown that the widespread belief that the investment banking activities of commercial banks had led to large numbers of bank failures is entirely unfounded (White, 1983; Flannery, 1984).

More recently, other aspects of the conventional wisdom concerning the free banking era have been subjected to critical scrutiny. For example, Arthur Rolnick and Warren Weber have questioned two assertions about the era: that wildcat banking was widespread and that it was largely responsible for the bank failures that occurred. What they found, instead, was that wildcat banking had been much less pervasive than is commonly supposed and that the primary cause of bank failures during the era was declines in the prices of state bonds held by banks (Rolnick and Weber, 1982). Similarly, studies of unregulated banking in other countries suggested that competitive banking is not necessarily unstable (White, 1984).

Because of the therapeutic effects of failure and exit in other sectors of the economy, scholars and regulators have sought ways to reconcile the occurrence of individual bank failures with the stability of the *banking system*. Especially encouraging in this endeavor was research suggesting that bank failures are not necessarily more disruptive in their effects than the failure of firms in other important industries (Alhadeff, 1962). Other research focused on ways to limit spillover effects in the form of runs from the failure of individual banks (Tussing, 1968). Careful analysis of the evidence from panics and crises in the eighteenth and nineteenth centuries led several scholars to conclude that the so-called contagion effects of bank failures depend heavily on the policy followed by the central bank (Gilbert and Wood, 1988; Gorton, 1988). More recently, it has been shown that contagion was neither as common nor as serious as has been commonly supposed (Kaufman, 1986). Finally, evidence from the ongoing crisis in the thrift industry suggests that a refusal to let market discipline operate and to close insolvent institutions promptly can cause a difficult situation to escalate into a major disaster (Kaufman, 1990; Barth, 1990).

5.7.2. Research on Competition and Regulation. Also lending support to the deregulation movement has been the enormous amount of research on financial structure and regulation done at universities and the bank regulatory agencies over the past three decades. Originally focused on topics of use to the bank regulatory agencies in administering the Bank Holding Company and Bank Merger Acts, this research also examined the effects of geographic restrictions, interest-rate ceilings, and other financial regulations.

Among the findings concerning the nature of competition in financial services were the following: Markets for consumer loans and deposits and small business loans tend to be relatively localized (Chandler, 1938; Alhadeff, 1954; Hodgman, 1961; Kaufman, 1966; Edwards, 1964; Kaufman, Mote, and Rosenblum, 1982); concentration in local markets adversely affects the price and quality of service received by customers (Kaufman, 1966; Edwards, 1964; Heggestad and Mingo, 1976; Murphy and Weiss, 1969; Beighley and McCall, 1975; Rhoades, 1977); competition between different types of institutions only rarely modifies conclusions regarding the effects of bank mergers (Rhoades, 1979); and economies of scale in the production of most banking services are modest beyond relatively small levels of output, corresponding to banks with total assets of no more than $25 to $200 million (Greenbaum, 1967a; Bell and Murphy, 1968; Benston, Berger, Hanweck, and Humphrey, 1982; Benston, Hanweck, and Humphrey, 1983).

Research findings relevant to policy toward geographic expansion and enlarged powers for depository institutions include the following: multioffice banking organizations, whether multibank holding companies or branch banks, tend to have higher loan-to-asset ratios than unit banks, suggesting that they are able to reduce their risks through geographical diversification (Lawrence, 1967; Horvitz and Shull, 1964; Galbraith, 1963); branch banking leads to a greater number of banking facilities, particularly in metropolitan areas, providing customers with more convenient access to banking services (Shull and Horvitz, 1964; Woods, 1970; Savage and Humphrey, 1979; Evanoff, 1988); and entry, either by branching or by the establishment or new banks, is an extremely important determinant of competitive performance in banking (Motter and Carson, 1962; Fraser and Rose, 1972). The evidence on economies of scope—i.e., efficiencies resulting from producing banking and other financial services such as insurance or underwriting and dealing in securities together rather than separately—is generally scarce and inconclusive (Gilligan, Smirlock, and Marshall, 1981; Goldberg, Hanweck, Keenan, and Young, 1988).

Finally, research on the effects of interest-rate regulation suggests that limitations on the interest rates payable on deposits have highly undesirable long-run effects in terms of inequities to depositors, costs of avoidance, and ultimately the emergence of nonregulated competitors like money market mutual funds (Kane, 1970). Similarly, usury ceilings, which limit the interest rates charged on loans, have the longer-term effect of reducing supply and rationing less creditworthy borrowers out of the market (Vandenbrink, 1982).

5.7.3. Conclusions. Together, the findings of recent studies of the causes and effects of bank runs and crises in the nineteenth century, the causes of the banking collapse of the 1930s, and the impacts of structure and regulation on banking performance provide a solid intellectual foundation for recent actions to deregulate the financial system. In many areas, research remains well ahead of events. For example, the payment of interest on demand deposits is still prohibited, though the adverse effects of this restriction have been largely vitiated by the advent of NOW accounts and overnight repurchase agreements, and the Glass–Steagall and McFadden Acts remain nominally intact, though heavily eroded by regulatory interpretations (Kaufman and Mote, 1990; Wriston, 1986). On the other hand, several issues remain in doubt, most prominently the optimal way in which to restructure depository institutions so as to enable them to broaden their activities without subjecting the financial safety net to ever greater risks.

6. Current Regulation of Depository Institutions

The content and jurisdictional structure of financial regulation in the United States are closely intertwined. Because of the large number of depository institutions and the many regulators, regulation has generally taken the form of formal laws and regulations as opposed to informal understandings, as has long been the practice in England and other countries with more concentrated banking systems. Similarly, the division of authority between state and federal regulatory agencies has at times made regulatory competition a factor in determining restrictions on activities, capital, and branching and has helped to prevent their content from becoming overly repressive.

Technological change, increased volatility of interest rates, and declines in the profitability of traditional banking activities have profoundly changed both the structure and the content of U.S. financial regulation over the past three decades. This section provides a brief overview of the structure and content of U.S. regulation of depository institutions as of early 1990, including as much description of recent developments as seems necessary for an understanding of current issues.

6.1. Regulatory Structure

Regulation of depository institutions in the United States is itself both a result of and a component of the forces that have produced the extreme fragmentation and diversity of U.S. financial institutions. It is, therefore, not surprising that the U.S. regulatory structure also embodies those characteristics. Regulation is fragmented in at least four different ways: by type of charter; by source of charter (federal or state); by geography; and, to some degree, by function.

Historically, type of charter has played a major and perhaps inordinate role in determining the identity of an institution's regulator and the nature and stringency of the regulation to which it is subject. Thus, even though commercial banks, savings and loan associations, mutual savings banks, and credit unions have many areas of overlap in the services that they provide, they are regulated by wholly separate entities. The primary regulator of a federally chartered bank (a national bank) is the Office of the Comptroller of the Currency, an agency within the U.S. Treasury. The primary regulator of a federally chartered savings and loan association or federal savings bank is the Office of Thrift Supervision, formerly a part of the independent Federal Home Loan Bank Board, now defunct, and now also a part of the Treasury. The primary regulator of a federally chartered credit union is the Credit Union National Administration, an independent regulatory agency. In contrast, the primary regulator of a state-chartered institution is an agency of the state that chartered it (institutions within the District of Columbia are subject to federal regulation).

However, the fact that an institution's charter determines its primary regulator does not imply that it is regulated exclusively by that agency. For example, state-chartered banks that qualify for, and choose to have, federal deposit insurance are also subject to examination and certain types of regulation by the Federal Deposit Insurance Corporation (FDIC). Insured state-chartered banks that choose to become members of the Federal Reserve System are also subject to examination and regulation by that body. Since national banks are required to be members of the Federal Reserve System and since all Federal Reserve members must be insured, national banks are subject to regulation by all three federal bank regulatory agencies.

Fortunately, in the interests of minimizing regulatory overlap, the three federal banking agencies agreed in 1938 to a division of their responsibilities under which the Comptroller of the Currency examines only national banks, the Federal Reserve System examines only state-chartered banks that choose to be members of the System, and the FDIC examines only federally insured state-chartered banks that are not members of the Federal Reserve System. In 1979, to help standardize the examination procedures of the federal bank and thrift supervisory agencies, Congress established the Federal Financial Institutions Examination Council. In contrast to examinations, where the division of authority is entirely voluntary, the Bank Merger Act of 1960 formally divided authority to approve mergers among the three federal agencies, depending on the status of the bank resulting from the merger.

Finally, there is some division of regulatory authority based on function, rather than type of charter. For example, all issues of debt and equity securities by financial institutions that meet statutory size and maturity criteria are subject to regulation by the Securities and Exchange Commission (SEC). Price-fixing agreements, mergers that may result in a reduction in competition, and other possible violations of the U.S. antitrust laws are subject to enforcement actions by the Antitrust Division of the Department of Justice. Subsidiaries of bank holding companies that provide credit life insurance or other insurance services are regulated by the insurance commissioners in the states where they are licensed. However, there is considerable support for expanding the principle of functional regulation, in particular to subject banks' securities underwriting, brokerage, and dealing activities to SEC regulation (Angermueller, 1987).

Beginning with the Commission on Reorganization of the Federal Government (Hoover Commission) in the early 1950s, there have been numerous proposals to consolidate some of the regulatory and supervisory functions of the three federal bank regulatory agencies. Often, these suggestions have been motivated by a desire to eliminate duplication and improve efficiency. As noted above, however, much duplication and waste of resources were eliminated by the interagency agreement on examinations.

On the other hand, there have been frequent clashes between the agencies over the interpretation of statutory provisions that they jointly administer, particularly in the area of bank mergers in the 1960s and

1970s (Hall and Phillips, 1964), bank securities powers in the late 1960s (Hackley, 1966), and more recently in the area of bank capital requirements. These clashes, which at times have led to forum shopping and have threatened to undermine the regulatory process itself, have also motivated some proposals for reorganization.

The most recent recommendations for reorganizing the regulatory agencies to achieve wide notice were those of the Vice President's Task Force on Regulation of Financial Services, chaired by then-Vice President George Bush, which advocated in earlier drafts of its final report a drastic reduction in the regulatory powers of the Federal Reserve, the replacement of the Comptroller of the Currency by a new national bank regulatory agency, and the transfer of responsibility for federal regulation of state banks from the Federal Deposit Insurance Corporation to a new state bank regulatory agency. However, the only major changes in the organization of the regulatory agencies in recent years were the result of the Financial Institutions Reform, Recovery and Enforcement Act of 1989. They included the abolition of the Federal Home Loan Bank Board; the relocation of its Office of Thrift Supervision into the Department of the Treasury; the transfer of its responsibilities for overseeing the Federal Home Loan Banks to a new agency, the Federal Housing Finance Board; and the transfer of administrative responsibility for the Federal Savings and Loan Insurance Corporation's insurance fund (renamed the Savings Association Insurance Fund or SAIF) to the FDIC. Still pending is a controversial proposal to merge SAIF with the Bank Insurance Fund (BIF).

6.2. Prudential Supervision and Regulation

Important though the division of authority between the states and the federal government and between the various agencies is, the crucial questions regarding regulation concern its substance. This section and the following four will consider in turn the major types of banking regulation: prudential supervision and regulation; limitations on interest rates paid and charged; restrictions on the scope of activities; geographic restrictions; and antitrust regulation.

6.2.1. Supervision versus Regulation. It has become customary in the United States to distinguish supervision from regulation, although the dividing line between the two is rather fuzzy. In general, regulation consists of the promulgation of formal, written rules to govern bank behavior, such as prohibitions on holding certain types of assests, maximum rates of interest payable, etc. Supervision, on the other hand, consists of monitoring an institution's behavior and the exertion of informal pressure, often through the examination process, to modify that behavior in a way deemed conducive to the institution's long-term safety. Supervision involves a greater degree of subjectivity and less definite sanctions than regulation. But, clearly, it shares many of the same goals and, at the margin, the two are substitutable for one another.

6.2.2. Portfolio Restrictions. Prudential supervision and regulation have typically focused on banks' portfolios. As noted earlier, national banks were long prohibited from making real estate loans and are still subject to limits on such loans based on their capital and/or time and savings deposits. They may not, in general, have total loans outstanding to a single borrower in excess of 15% (formerly 10%) of their total capital and are highly restricted as to the loans they may make to officers, directors, and employees. They may own U.S. government or municipal general obligation bonds in any amount, but may purchase corporate bonds only from a list of "investment grade" securities maintained by the Comptroller of the Currency. They may not own corporate equities, with a few exceptions such as securities acquired through customer defaults on loans. Margin requirements limit the amount they are permitted to lend on the security of common stocks. Finally, since enactment of the International Lending and Supervision Act of 1983, banks and bank holding companies have been subject to mandatory capital requirements. Because of the great emphasis placed by regulators on the concept of "capital adequacy," it is discussed separately below.

In addition to the above-mentioned formal regulations mandated by statute, there are a number of less formal restrictions enforced through the examination process. These include limits on concentrations in particular industries in the loan portfolio, requirements for documentation of loans, and requirements that loans to relatives, etc., be made on an arms-length basis. Generally speaking, these restrictions are of a more subjective nature, and their enforcement comes under the rubric of supervision as opposed to regulation.

6.2.3. Capital Adequacy. Capital adequacy, variously defined, has long been a key focus of the bank supervisory process. Indeed, a constant complaint of supervisors over the past half-century or more has been that the most commonly used capital ratios—capital/deposits, capital/assets, and capital/risk assets—have all declined more or less continuously.

Indeed, if one considers only the capital/assets ratio, the downward trend has been evident at least since the early nineteenth century. At that time, a ratio of 70% was not uncommon (Lindow, 1963). By 1870 the ratio of primary capital to assets at all commercial banks in the United States was down to 35% (Kaufman, 1986). Thereafter, the ratio declined to 30% by 1890, 20% in 1910, and 12% in 1920. By the end of World War II, the ratio bottomed out at about 6% before rising to around 8% in the 1950s.

Despite regulators' frequently expressed concern that the level of capital in the banking system was too low, they were unable or unwilling to enforce a higher level. In part, this was because, except in the case of newly chartered banks, there was no statutory capital requirement. In principle, the FDIC and the Federal Reserve could have enforced higher levels of capital by terminating banks' deposit insurance or membership in the Federal Reserve System. However, they were reluctant to take such drastic actions, particularly the Federal Reserve, which was already experiencing heavy attrition in its membership. Initially, they rationalized the problem away by arguing that the capital/risk assets ratio was a more appropriate measure of capital adequacy than the traditional capital/ assets or capital/deposits ratios. By the mid-1950s the Federal Reserve had developed the Form for Analyzing Bank Capital, or ABC Form, which provided a formula for calculating a bank's minimum adequate level of capital based on the riskiness of its assets and the volatility of its liabilities, as determined from the experience of the 1930s (Robinson and Pettway, 1967). But capital continued to decline during the 1960s even relative to this standard.

Scholars turned their attention to the bank capital adequacy problem in the late 1960s, examining, in particular, the relationship between various measures of capital and the likelihood of failure. By and large, such studies found that levels of capital were poor predictors of failure (Cotter, 1966; Meyer and Pifer, 1970; Apilado and Gies, 1972; Dince and Fortson, 1972). Moreover, by the early 1970s lagging profits had displaced low capital ratios as the major concern of the banking industry and its regulators (Van Horn, 1972). Either ignoring or dismissing as invalid the primary rationale for regulating banking, which is based on the external costs associated with bank failures, several scholars concluded that the optimal capital ratio was that yielded by the free market (Pringle, 1967; Robinson and Pettway, 1967).

The Comptroller of the Currency was the first of the federal regulatory agencies to deemphasize the traditional capital ratios, citing their "arbitrary" nature and the fact that they ignore a number of important factors, including "the quality of management; liquidity of assets; the history of earnings and of the retention thereof; the quality and character of ownership; the burden of meeting occupancy expenses; potential volatility of the bank's deposit structure, the quality of operating procedures and bank's capacity to meet present and future financial needs of its trade area, considering the competition it faces" (Van Horn, 1972). Also in 1972, the Federal Reserve Board proposed revisions to the ABC Form to make it reflect more recent credit risk and deposit volatility experience. Shortly thereafter, the Board dropped the form altogether.

Ironically, the deemphasis of capital ratios by the regulatory agencies preceded by only a year or so the difficulties encountered by several relatively large banks in the mid-1970s. Within a period of about five years, the U.S. National Bank of San Diego, the Franklin National Bank of New York, the Commonwealth Bank of Detroit, and the Herstatt Bank of West Germany failed, while the First Pennsylvania Bank of Philadelphia survived only because of generous liquidity assistance from the Federal Reserve discount window. Economically, if not legally, the Continental Illinois National Bank and Trust Company of Chicago failed in 1984. In the last half of the 1980s only one major Texas bank escaped insolvency and similar problems have emerged in New England. Throughout the 1980s several large money center banks repeatedly saw their capital depleted by the repeated emergence of problems in their loan portfolios.

Concern over the low capital ratios of most money-center banks led the federal bank regulatory agencies to adopt minimum acceptable ratios for banks and bank holding companies in 1981. Initially, the minimum ratio of primary capital (equity, mandatory convertible instruments, reserves for loan and lease losses, and minority interests in consolidated subsidiaries minus equity commitment notes and intangible assets) to assets was set at 5.5%, and the minimum ratio of total capital (primary capital plus limited life preferred stock, subordinated notes and debentures, and mandatory convertible instruments not eligible for primary capital) to assets was set at 6%. For the first time in 1983, the International Lending and Supervision Act of 1983 provided a statutory basis for such requirements. In early 1985, a Treasury Department study group and the FDIC suggested a minimum total capital/assets ratio of 9%. It was estimated at the time that, for the banking system as a whole, either total capital would have to be increased by 29% or assets would have to shrink by more than 20% to meet the new standard (Gilbert, Stone, and Trebing, 1985).

In their concern over the possible systemic effects of large bank failures in the wake of the failures of Franklin National and the Herstatt Bank, the G10 industrial countries had formed the Basle Committee on Banking

Regulations and Supervisory Practices in 1975. In the words of its chairman, the committee "has tried to concentrate on those common features in each country's banking system that derive from banks' international activities, with a view to focusing on potentially dangerous systemic pressures" (Cooke, 1987). By 1987, the countries represented on the Committee had reached agreement in principle on the adoption of risk-based capital guidelines. The three federal bank regulatory agencies have now adopted the guidelines, with some modifications, and are phasing them in over a transition period ending December 31, 1992.

The guidelines establish four risk categories with weights of 0%, 20%, 50%, and 100%. The dollar amounts of the various items are multiplied by their weights and summed to obtain a measure of the bank's risk-adjusted assets. When the standards are fully implemented, each bank should have a minimum ratio of total capital to risk-adjusted assets of 8% and a minimum ratio of Tier 1 (primary) capital to risk-adjusted assets of 4%. The Financial Institutions Reform, Recovery and Enforcement Act of 1989 required that risk-based capital standards be developed for thrift institutions that are at least as strict as those for banks. However, it should be noted that prior to this legislation, capital regulation in the thrift industry had become progressively more lax (Barth, 1990).

6.3. Interest-Rate Regulation and Deregulation

The interest-rate ceilings on deposits imposed by the Federal Reserve in 1933 became meaningless as market rates fell below the ceilings and stayed there for the next 20 years. Through World War II and into the late 1940s, banks continued to hold large amounts of excess reserves and to operate in a generally conservative manner.

However, as the economy and loan demand continued to recover, banks' loan-to-deposit ratios increased and their reservoirs of liquidity were eventually depleted to the point that they again became active in competing for funds. In 1953, for the first time since 1934, the market interest rates on passbook savings accounts pressed against the legal ceilings. At that time, absent any sign of excessive competition, the Federal Reserve raised the ceiling. It did so on at least three other occasions prior to the mid-1960s. However, in 1966, faced by accelerating inflation and rapidly growing loan demand, the Federal Reserve refused to raise the ceilings when market rates rose sharply late in the year. Unable to roll over maturing certificates of deposit, banks were wracked by the first major postwar episode of disintermediation as borrowers turned to commercial paper and other sources of direct financing. Ironically, Congress chose this occasion to enact the Interest Rate Adjustment Act of 1966, which extended interest-rate ceilings to deposits at savings and loan associations.

Thus began a decade and a half of "regulatory dialectic" between banks increasingly constricted by regulation but willing and able to find ways to circumvent it and regulators who, at least inititally, were determined to plug each new loophole that appeared (Kane, 1977). During the later 1960s and the 1970s, the ingenuity of the banks in escaping regulation, competition from new products such as Merrill Lynch's Money Management Account, and the entry of new, unregulated competitors such as the money market mutual fund increasingly undermined the effectiveness of interest-rate ceilings.

By the mid-1970s regulators had begun to accommodate change, rather than to resist it (Kaufman, Mote, and Rosenblum, 1983). Thus, state and federal regulators authorized the issue by thrift institutions of NOW accounts—interest-bearing checking accounts—in Massachusetts and New Hampshire in 1972 and 1973, the issue of NOW accounts by all banks and thrift institutions in New England in 1974, the payment of market-related interest rates on so-called money market deposits in 1977, and the automatic transfer of funds from savings to checking accounts in 1979. Eventually, in the summer of 1979, a federal court held that NOW accounts constituted the illegal payment of interest on demand deposits and gave Congress six months to change the law or suffer the disruptive effects of terminating these accounts. However, by then a major constituency had developed demanding the retention of NOW accounts and their extension to other areas of the country. In conjunction with the sharp rise in interest rates in early 1980 to the highest levels since 1929, which put banks under enormous pressure to raise their deposit rates, this support was enough to bring about passage of the Depository Institutions Deregulation and Monetary Control Act of 1980, which phased out interest-rate ceilings on deposits over a six-year period and, in the interest of reducing their vulnerability to interest-rate risk, broadened the asset powers of thrift institutions.

6.4. Powers of Depository Institutions

The 1980s have witnessed major changes in the powers of depository institutions. For banking organizations the change has been a gradual one. For thrift institutions the changes have been more rapid, more dramatic, and in some cases, less beneficial.

6.4.1. Banking Organizations. The activities of banking organizations are governed by the provisions of commercial bank charters, the National Bank Act, the Glass–Steagall Act, and the Bank Holding Company Act. The "incidental powers" clause of the National Bank Act empowers national banks to "carry on the business of banking by obtaining and issuing circulating notes . . . ; by discounting bills, notes, and other evidences of debt; . . . by receiving deposits; by buying and selling gold and silver bullion, foreign coins, and bills of exchange; by loaning money on real and personal security . . . and by exercising such incidental powers as shall be necessary to carry on such business . . . ." Section 20 of the Glass–Steagall Act prohibits members of the Federal Reserve System from being affiliated with "any corporation . . . engaged principally in the issue, flotation, underwriting, public sale, or distribution . . . of stocks, bonds, debentures, notes, or other securities." Section 4(c)(8) of the Bank Holding Company Act restricts subsidiaries of bank holding companies to activities that are "so closely related to banking or managing or controlling banks as to be a proper incident thereto . . ." and directs the Federal Reserve Board in determining whether an activity should be permissible to consider ". . . whether its performance by an affiliate of a holding company can reasonably be expected to produce benefits to the public, such as greater convenience, increased competition, or gains in efficiency, that outweigh possible adverse effects, such as undue concentration of resources, decreased or unfair competition, conflicts of interests, or unsound banking practices."

The Glass–Steagall Act's prohibition of investment banking activities was never absolute. It always permitted banks to engage in private placements; to provide trust services; to underwrite, distribute, and deal in U.S. Treasury securities, general obligation municipal bonds, and bank loans; and to engage in full service investment banking overseas. The types of securities explicitly exempted by Glass–Steagall are known as *bank-eligible* securities. However, through a series of controversial decisions by the Federal Reserve Board in the 1980s, bank holding companies gained the power to underwrite, distribute, and deal in commercial paper, asset-backed securities, corporate bonds, and corporate equities (Kaufman and Mote, 1990). A chronology of this deregulation is presented in table 10-5.

How have banks fared with their investment banking activities? As table 10-6 indicates, banks command a sizeable share of the market in the two areas—private placements and general obligation municipal securities—where they traditionally have been permitted to compete. However, banking's share of underwriting activity in the general obligation market declined dramatically during the 1970s from a high of 70% (Dale, 1988). U.S. commercial banks also failed to make significant inroads into the London securities markets following the "Big Bang" of October 1986, when most restrictions on banks' securities activities in London were removed. Indeed, in 1989 and 1990, several major U.S. banks reduced their presence in the London markets. In a similar vein, several banks have been pulling back from brokerage activity in the United States. Indeed, the one true success of commercial banks has been in the area of private placements, where they greatly increased their share of the market during the 1970s and 1980s. These bits of evidence suggest that, even if they are freed of legal restraints, commercial banks are unlikely to become the dominant force in U.S. investment banking except through the acquisition of existing investment banks.

Table 10-5. Securities Activities of Domestic Commercial Banks,[a] April 1991

Activities	Year Started[b]
Permissible	
Underwriting, distributing, and dealing	Always
U.S. Treasury securities	Always
U.S. federal agency securities	Various years
Commercial paper	1987
Mortgage and other asset-backed securities	
Collateral originated by other banks	1987
Collateral originated by issuing bank	1989
Municipal securities	
General obligation	Nearly always
Some revenue bonds	1968
All revenue bonds	1987
Corporate bonds	1989
Corporate equities	1989
Financial and precious-metal futures brokerage and dealing	1983[c]
Private placement (agency capacity)	Always
Sponsor closed-end funds	1974
Underwrite deposits with returns tied partially to stock market performance	1987
Offshore dealing in Eurodollar securities	Always
Mergers and acquisitions	Always
Trust investments	
Individual accounts	Nearly always
IRA commingled accounts	1982
Automatic investment service	1974
Dividend investment service	Always

Table 10-5. Securities Activities of Domestic Commercial Banks,[a] April 1991

Activities	Year Started[b]
Financial advising and managing	
Closed-end funds	1974
Mutual funds	1974
Restricted	Always
Brokerage	
Limited customer	Always
Public retail (discount)	1982
Securities swapping	Always
Research advice to investors	
Separate from brokerage	1983
Combined with brokerage	
Institutional	1986
Retail	1987
Nonpermissible	
Mutual funds underwriting and distributing	

[a] Federal Reserve member banks or nonbank affiliates of bank holding companies.

[b] After the Civil War. Different dates may apply to national and state banks and among state banks. With some exceptions, the earliest date is shown. Regulatory rulings frequently concluded that a specific activity was permissible before the date of ruling. If the activity was halted by enactment of the Glass–Steagall Act, the date of renewed activity is given.

[c] Restricted to futures contracts for which banks may hold the underlying security or that are settled only in cash.

6.4.2. Thrift Organizations. During the early 1980s savings and loan associations and mutual savings banks gained many new powers as well as greater freedom to use existing powers granted by state authorities. The Depository Institutions Deregulation and Monetary Control Act of 1980 (DIDMCA) permitted thrifts to hold up to 20% of their assets in consumer loans and 20% of their assets in first mortgages on commercial real estate. The Garn-St. Germain Depository Institutions Act of 1982 raised the limits on consumer and commercial real estate loans to 30% and 40% respectively. In addition, it granted thrifts the power to make unsecured commercial loans up to 5% of assets. In May 1983, the Federal Home Loan Bank Board permitted federally chartered savings and loan associations (S&Ls) to invest up to 11% of their assets in junk bonds.

During the same period, many state governments enacted statutes that granted even broader asset powers to state-chartered thrifts. In several

Table 10-6. Banking's Share of Selected Domestic Investment Banking Activities, 1988 (percent)

Activity	Percentage
Private placements	25
Mergers and acquisitions	3
Municipal securities	7
general obligation bonds	24
Corporate underwriting	3
Mortgage-backed securities	2
Asset-backed securities	26

states, state-chartered S&Ls were permitted to invest a considerable portion of their assets in real estate, corporate equities, and subsidiaries known as service corporations. A summary of state provisions can be found in Olin (1987). In some states, direct investments in real estate became extremely important. In Texas, for instance, direct investments accounted for 16.4% of S&L assets at year-end 1988 (Brewer, 1989a). The power to make direct investments was misused by many poorly capitalized thrifts. Thrifts that were insolvent at year-end 1988 had 8.9% of their assets in direct investments vs. an industry average of 2.8% (Brewer, 1989a).

Alarmed by the apparent link between direct investments and insolvency, Congress chose to restrict direct investments and junk-bond holdings when it reorganized the thrift industry with the passage of the Financial Institutions Reform, Recovery and Enforcement Act of 1989 (FIRREA). FIRREA restricts commercial real estate loans to 400% of an institution's capital, limits institutions to investment-grade corporate debt, prohibits state-chartered institutions from acquiring or retaining any equity investment that would not be permissible for federally chartered S&Ls, and limits investments in commercial loans and commercial real estate loans to 20% of residential real estate and consumer lending.

6.4.3. Expanded Powers and Risk. The thrift experience with nontraditional activities has led some to argue that these activities are inherently inappropriate for depository institutions. However, a careful examination of the historical record suggests that the problems in the thrift industry were the result of permitting undercapitalized and insolvent thrifts to continue operating without supervisory restraint. Permitting insolvent institutions to have access to government-subsidized, insured deposits gave these firms an incentive to increase expected profits by taking additional risk. Benston and Koehn (1989) found that increased emphasis on riskier nontraditional activities resulted in greater stock price volatility. In contrast, shifts toward nontraditional activities by healthy thrifts reduced stock price volatility. Brewer (1990) found that shareholders of sick thrifts rewarded risk-taking while shareholders of healthy institutions did not. These findings suggest that the problem has to do with the condition of the firm rather than the inherent riskiness of nontraditional activities.

This conclusion is supported by a study of the impact of nontraditional activities on bank holding companies. In contrast to the thrift experience, Brewer (1989b) found that nontraditional activities were risk-reducing for all bank holding companies and were most beneficial for those that initially had the greatest risk of failure. Why the difference between the two industries? One reason is that, while S&L depositors are insured, creditors of BHCs are not. Because BHCs' creditors are at risk, their subsidiaries will not be able to fund themselves unless they make prudent investments. The lesson is clear. With creditor discipline or adequate capital, expanded powers are beneficial; without one or the other they are a disaster.

6.5. Geographic Restrictions

The establishment of branch offices by state-chartered banks is regulated by the laws of the respective states. Under the McFadden Act of 1927, as amended by the Banking Act of 1933, national banks are subject to the branching laws of the state in which their head office is located and interstate branching is permitted only by agreement between the states. However, many states have liberalized their branching laws in recent decades, and the number of states permitting some form of statewide banking rose from 15 in 1941 to 36 in 1989.

The Bank Holding Company Act of 1956 also leaves it to the individual state to determine whether domestic bank holding companies are to be permitted. The so-called Douglas Amendment to the act empowers the individual state to decide whether holding companies headquartered in other states may acquire banks within its boundaries. Today, 47 states permit some form of interstate banking, virtually all via the holding company route rather than branching. Twenty-six of these states permit acquisitions, either on an unlimited or reciprocal basis, by bank holding companies located anywhere in the United States. Another 17 states, primarily in the Midwest and Southeast, permit acquisitions, generally on a reciprocal basis, only by holding companies based within a particular region. The reliance on compacts between the states to achieve regional interstate banking, rather than revising the McFadden Act to permit full nationwide branching, has protected some institutions from competition and will limit the level of diversification that can be achieved.

Although interstate banking as it has evolved over the past decade involves the ownership by a bank holding company of independently incorporated banks in more than one state rather than branching by a single bank across state lines, provisions of the Financial Institutions Reform, Recovery and Enforcement Act of 1989 make the capital of all banking affiliates available to cover depositor losses anywhere in the holding company. Thus, from the limited perspective of loss allocation, nationwide branching is now effectively a reality.

The legacy of restrictive branching legislation is reflected in the size distribution of commercial banks. In 1988, banks with assets of less than $50 million accounted for 57% of U.S. commercial banks but only 7% of domestic assets (see table 10-7). At the other extreme, the 361 banks with more than $1 billion of domestic assets accounted for only 3% of all U.S. banks but 65% of domestic assets.

The liberalization of state branching restrictions has begun to reduce the number of banks in the United States (see figure 10-1). From 1960 to 1980, the number of commercial banks rose from 13,126 to 14,836. However, from 1980 to 1989, the number of commercial banks fell to 12,706, the first major decline since the depression of the 1930s. Of even

Table 10-7A. Sizes of U.S. Commercial Banks as of December 31, 1988

Category	Number	Assets (billions $)
< $10 Million	897	6.3
$10 M to < $50 M	6,603	178.2
$50 M to < $100 M	2,786	194.3
$100 M to < $300 M	1,903	307.5
$300 M to < $500 M	343	130.9
$500 M to < $750 M	141	85.1
$750 M to < $1 B	74	64.5
$1 B to < $5 B	263	564.1
$5 B to < $10 B	60	408.9
>= $10 B	38	820.2
Total	13,108	2,760.0

Table 10-7B. Sizes of U.S. Commercial Banks as of December 31, 1988 (Percent)

Asset Size Category	Number (percent)	Assets (percent)
< $10 Million	6.8	0.2
$10 M to < $50 M	50.4	6.5
$50 M to < $100 M	21.3	7.0
$100 M to < $300 M	14.5	11.1
$300 M to < $500 M	2.6	4.7
$500 M to < $750 M	1.1	3.1
$750 M to < $1 B	0.6	2.3
$1 B to < $5 B	2.0	20.4
$5 B to < $10 B	0.5	14.8
>= $10 B	0.3	29.7
Total	100.0	100.0

greater economic significance has been the reduction in the number of independent banking organizations, defined as the number of independent banks plus the number of bank holding companies. The number of banking organizations, which had risen from 12,747 in 1960 to 12,760 in 1970 and remained virtually unchanged during the 1970s, fell sharply to 9640 by 1989—a 25% reduction in only 10 years. Indeed, if the banking structure of the state of California is any indication, the number of independent organizations in the U.S. will decline from the current level to approximately 5000 two decades from now.

The passage of regional interstate banking legislation by most states during the 1980s also contributed to the decline in the number of independent banking organizations and is likely to have an even greater impact during the 1990s. So far, the primary beneficiaries of interstate banking legislation have been the 39 largest regional organizations, which increased their share of domestic deposits from 17.4% in 1980 to 28.2% in 1989. In contrast, the 11 money center organizations saw their share of domestic deposits fall from 19.4% to 15.2%, largely as a consequence of heavy losses on lending in the Southwest and Latin American, which left them with much lower levels of capital than their regional competitors, and the restrictions in regional interstate banking laws that prevented them from making acquisitions in the Southeast and Midwest. This latter factor will become less important as an increasing number of states shift from regional to nationwide interstate banking.

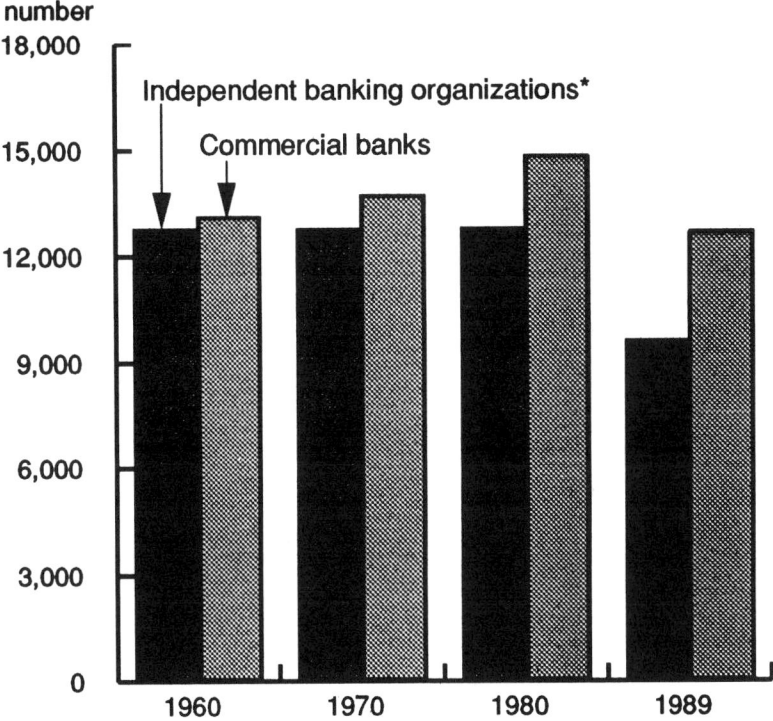

Figure 10-1. Number of Commercial Banks and Independent Commercial Banking Organizations. Total commercial banks less bank subsidiaries of bank holding companies plus bank holding companies.

6.6. Antitrust Regulation

The United States has a long history of concern over concentration and monopoly. The American legal system, continued many of the common law's proscriptions of activities viewed as hindering the free operation of the competitive process. Congress enacted the Sherman Act of 1890 and the Clayton Act of 1914 in response to the wave of industrial mergers in the late nineteenth century. Another wave of mergers in the 1950s led Congress to amend section 7 of the Clayton Act to cover mergers effectuated through acquisitions of assets, which had proven to be a major loophole in the original act. Because the banking industry was one of those experiencing heavy merger activity and because it had long been assumed that bank mergers were not subject to the antitrust laws (Berle, 1949), Congress also enacted the Bank Holding Company Act of 1956 and the Bank Merger Act of 1960. Although both acts made the competitive effects of the merger or acquisition one of the criteria to be considered in approving the transaction, it was widely believed that they provided an alternative standard that was more lenient than that of the antitrust laws.

Ironically, it was only three years after the enactment of the Bank Merger Act of 1960 that the long-standing assumption that bank mergers were not subject to the antitrust laws was overturned by the decision of the Supreme Court in the *Philadelphia National Bank* case (Mote, 1987). Revisions to the Bank Holding Company Act and the Bank Merger Act in 1966 reaffirmed the applicability of the antitrust laws to bank acquisitions by giving the Antitrust Division the weapon of an automatic injunction to stop temporarily any merger that they challenged on competitive grounds, while grandfathering several mergers that had already been consummated (Goodman, 1967).

From the time of enactment of the Bank Merger Act until the late 1970s, enforcement of competitive criteria in bank merger and acquisition cases became progressively more sophisticated and, on balance, more stringent. During the 1980s, bank merger enforcement was gradually weakened by changing views within the economics profession on the value and appropriate role of antitrust policy (Brozen, 1982), greater emphasis on regulation as a determinant of banking performance (Greenbaum, 1967b; Phillips, 1970), changes in banking regulation and industry practice that had the effect of broadening markets and moderating the impact of increases in concentration (Kaufman, Mote, and Rosenblum, 1982), and the election of new administrations that were hostile or indifferent to antitrust enforcement.

6.7. The Deregulation Decade: An Assessment

The 1980s saw major changes in the assets that depository institutions were permitted to hold, the rates they could pay on retail deposits, and their ability to expand geographically. Has deregulation lived up to its billing? The answer would appear to be a qualified yes. Expanded powers have reduced the risk of bank holding companies. As a result of interest-rate deregulation, the velocity of bank deposits has declined markedly—a sure sign that consumers find such deposits more attractive. The removal of restrictions on intrastate branching restrictions has led to decreased concentration in local banking markets (Evanoff and Fortier, 1986). The removal of restrictions on interstate banking has given banks that are efficient and well capitalized an opportunity to expand more rapidly. And, indeed, the banks that have been growing most rapidly during the 1980s are those that are well capitalized and, according to a recent study, highly efficient (FMCG Capital Strategies and the Bank Administration Institute, 1989).

However, the acid test of deregulation is whether the wedge between rates on loans and deposits narrows—in short, has deregulation caused profitability to decline? While the process is far from complete, the preliminary answer appears to be that it has. For all but the largest banks, profitability fell dramatically between 1982 and 1988 (see figure 10-2). The decline was most dramatic for small banks, precisely the banks that benefited most from the old regulatory regime. Large banks appear to be the major beneficiaries of deregulation, a logical outcome given the presence of moderate economies of scale in banking. However, as inefficient firms exit the industry, competition may well begin to erode the profits of large firms as well.

If there was a dark side to the deregulation movement, it was the failure of its advocates to understand fully the interactions between deregulation and deposit insurance. Removal of interest-rate ceilings

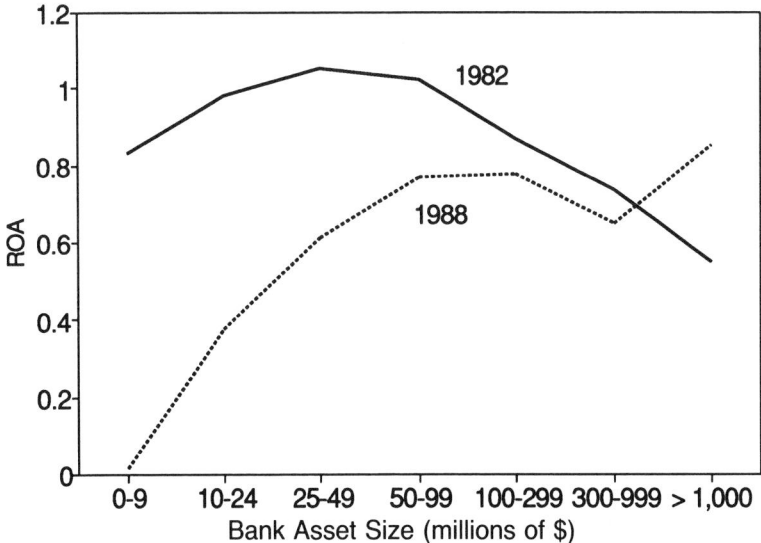

Figure 10-2. Net Income as a Percentage of Total Assets for U.S. Banks.

allowed risk-seeking insolvent institutions nearly unlimited access to the brokered deposit market and enabled them to compete with solvent institutions for deposits. In Texas, this drove rates 75 basis points above the national average (Short and Gunther, 1988). And, while expanded powers for thrifts cannot be blamed for the thrift crisis, permitting insolvent institutions to undertake nontraditional activities made a bad situation worse.

7. Current Problems

During the 1980s, the U.S. financial system made considerable progress toward eliminating anticompetitive regulations in the banking industry. In the 1990s, the U.S. financial system faces three major challenges: the reform of deposit insurance, adjusting to the elimination of barriers between banking and commerce, and the continued shift of credit intermediation from banks to other intermediaries.

7.1. The Deposit Insurance Problem

The 1980s proved to be a crucial decade for the nation's federal and state deposit insurance schemes. The number of bank failures, which had averaged fewer than 10 per year for several decades, jumped from 10 to 200 between 1980 and 1988 and the number of thrift failures from 11 to 205, and losses quickly mounted. Faced with mounting losses brought on by excessive interest-rate risk, credit risk, misregulation, and fraud, the Federal Savings and Loan Insurance Corporation (FSLIC) became insolvent and was reconstituted in 1989 as the Savings Association Insurance Fund (SAIF) under the management of the Federal Deposit Insurance Corporation (FDIC). The job of cleaning up the thrift debacle was delegated to the Resolution Trust Corporation (RTC), which was to be managed by the FDIC under the supervision of an Oversight Committee consisting of leading officials of the FDIC, the Treasury, and the Federal Reserve. While the ultimate present-value cost of the thrift debacle will not be known for some time, estimates range from $150 billion to $250 billion.

The FSLIC was not the only insurance fund to face rough sledding in the 1980s. Several state-sponsored insurance funds became insolvent (Kane, 1987) and the FDIC suffered losses of $25 billion, finishing the decade in a weakened state with its ratio of reserves to deposits at an all-time low (Brumbaugh, 1990).

Why has federal deposit insurance proven so costly? On paper, the system would seem to have substantial safeguards to limit losses. Since deposit insurance is limited to deposits of less than $100,000, runs by uninsured depositors should serve to discipline institutions taking excessive risks and to close institutions that are clearly insolvent. Even with runs absent, the courts have typically given regulators substantial discretion in determining whether or not a bank is solvent. So, it is necessary to explain why the deposit insurance system began to break down in the late 1970s.

It appears that this breakdown can be traced to three major developments in U.S. banking. The first of these was that bank and thrift capital was permitted to decline steadily throughout the 1960s and 1970s. When economic volatility increased and interest rates rose abruptly from 1979 through 1981, institutions were not adequately capitalized to weather the resulting losses in asset values (Kane, 1989).

The second development was the growing tendency of the FDIC and the FSLIC to circumvent the legal limits on deposit insurance by selling the bank as a going concern or recapitalizing the bank without first closing it. In the former process, known as purchase and assumption (P&A), the FDIC asks potential buyers to bid on a package of cash, earning assets, and deposits (including uninsured deposits). In the latter process, known as open bank assistance, the FDIC injects capital directly into the bank without first closing it. The rationale for adopting these approaches has been that they are cheaper or that they eliminate destabilizing depositor runs (Bovenzi and Muldoon, 1990). The use of P&A transactions to deal with the failures of the U.S. National Bank of San Diego in 1973 and the Franklin National Bank in 1974 helped to establish the belief in the market for large, nominally uninsured certificates of deposit that regulators would prefer not to impose losses on depositors. The unprecedented action taken by the three federal bank regulatory agencies in 1984 to guarantee all the obligations of Continental Illinois National Bank of Chicago further suggested that the regulators considered some banks to be "too large to fail" (Kaufman, 1990).

Frequent use of P&A and open bank assistance has substantially eroded depositor discipline. Since depositors are unlikely to incur losses, they have little incentive to worry about the risk or solvency of their banks or to demand higher interest rates to compensate them for that risk. This permits institutions to take substantial risks without facing any constraint on funding. As the conviction that all deposits are de facto insured has grown, an increasing proportion of the burden of risk control has shifted from the market to the regulators.

This shift has been unfortunate because it has occurred at the same time that the deposit insurance funds were being weakened by a series of adverse events, including the sharp run-up in interest rates during the early 1980s, the collapse in oil prices beginning in 1982, the restructuring of heavy industry and agriculture in the Midwest, the collapse in Southwest real estate between 1985 and 1989, the collapse of the junk-bond market in 1989, the emergence of real estate problems in the Northeast in 1989, and the more or less steady erosion in the value of loans to less developed countries in bank portfolios throughout the decade.

The third development contributing to the breakdown of the deposit insurance system was the delay in liquidating or recapitalizing failed institutions. A desire to conserve scarce cash, combined in some instances with intense political pressure, led regulators to delay closing institutions that were clearly insolvent. James Barth et al. (1989) estimated that 45% of the thrift institutions closed in 1988 had been insolvent for four or more years. Freed of discipline from regulators or depositors, the management of insolvent institutions frequently chose to take high-stakes risks in the hopes of returning to solvency. This was most evident in the savings and loan industry but also appears to have occurred in the banking industry (Brewer, 1990; Gajewski, 1989).

The net result has been a failure rate that is at a post-depression high, a rate of loss per dollar of deposits that *exceeds* that experienced during the Depression (see figure 10-3), and an insurance system that gives

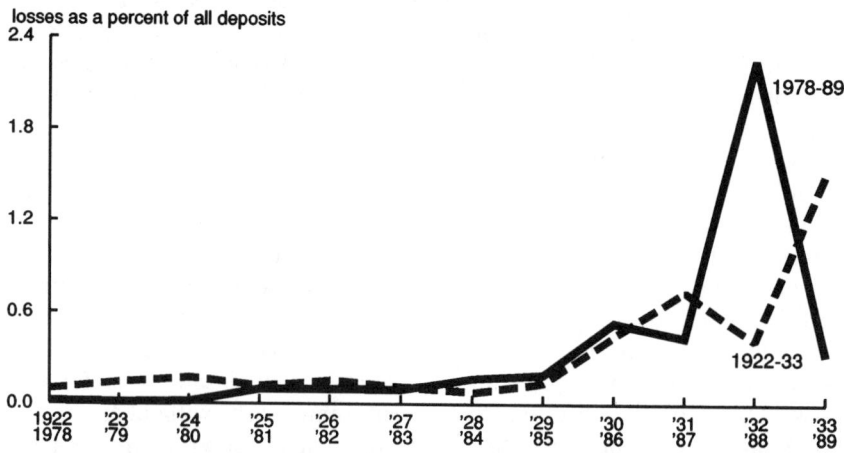

Figure 10-3. Depositor and Insurance Fund Losses. *Source*: Bert Ely, Ely and Company., Inc.

institutions incentives to take excessive risks. The challenge of the 1990s will be to reform U.S. deposit insurance by creating a system of failure resolution that is compatible with the incentives of bankers *and* regulators. This will require changes that make regulators liquidate or auction off insolvent institutions in a way that forces the private sector, rather than the insurance funds, to bear the majority of the losses.

Several proposals clearly seem capable of doing this, including those that call for early closure (see Benston et al., 1986) and those that would require banks to carry a cushion of subordinated debt (Keehn, 1989a; Parry, 1990; and Wall, 1989). Other proposals, for example those calling for a rollback in insurance coverage, pass the market incentive test but fail to deal adequately with regulatory incentives. Finally, those proposals that rely on bureaucracies to set risk-related deposit insurance premiums are likely to fail the market incentive test precisely because regulatory incentives are likely to prevent the premiums from being set in an actuarily sound way.

7.2. Expanded Powers

Banks first breached the barriers between traditional commercial banking and investment banking during the 1980s. During the 1990s Congress is likely to largely eliminate these barriers and to begin dismantling the barriers between banking and commerce. However, the question of how best to structure and regulate corporations engaged in a wide range of banking and nonbanking activities has yet to be decided. Some advocate a holding-company approach with substantial financial (and sometimes informational) barriers, or "firewalls," between the bank and the rest of the holding company (Johnson, 1989). At the other extreme, some advocate the adoption of universal banking as practiced in Germany or Switzerland (Weatherstone, 1989). Each system has its advantages and disadvantages.

Universal banking permits an organization to maximize its operational efficiency by allowing the free flow of information and capital throughout the organization (Saunders, 1990). However, universal banking may create situations in which government decisions to support a firm's banking activities have the effect of spreading the safety net beyond banking to other areas of the economy. This is of special concern as long as there is deposit insurance and it is mispriced. Adoption of universal banking in the United States would also require an overhaul of the mechanism for regulating financial transactions, since the current capital requirements and regulatory philosophies of bank regulators on the one hand and futures and securities regulators on the other are glaringly inconsistent (Craine and Nelson, 1990). Futures and securities firms rely on mark-to-market accounting and risk-based capital schemes that take account of differences in asset price volatility—techniques eschewed by bank regulators. On the other hand, the capital requirements applicable to futures and securities firms treat nonmarketable assets in a way that could not and should not be carried over to commercial bank loans, many of which are not marketable but are subject to examination.

A holding company approach with effective firewalls has the potential to confine the effects of the bank safety net to the banking sector. It would also permit regulators to avoid dealing with the incompatibilities in their regulatory approaches. However, the firewall approach can be effective in compartmentalizing risk only if regulators enforce and respect the firewalls they have sought to create. Moreover, even if regulators are willing to make firewalls work, the benefits of the firewall approach must be balanced against the possible loss in efficiency arising from operational and financial restrictions.

7.3. The Continuing Disintermediation of Traditional Bank Lending

Throughout the 1970s and 1980s, the role of banks in the financial system has been subject to continuous change as the funding of consumer and commercial credit has shifted from the banking industry to the capital markets. This process of disintermediation is being driven by three factors: regulations that place banks at a disadvantage in intermediating low-risk credits; relatively low levels of market capitalization at some of the nation's largest banks; and broader availability of financial information (Baer and Pavel, 1988). While many of these factors are difficult to quantify, it is possible to estimate the regulatory tax on the intermediation of low-risk assets by commercial banks. Based on the approach developed by Baer and Pavel (1988), it would appear that in 1989 banks faced a cost disadvantage of 56 basis points when intermediating these assets. Projected increases in deposit insurance premiums would raise this to 62 basis points.

This process of disintermediation can be broken down into four phases: the growth of the commercial paper market, the securitization of consumer credit, the creation of a market for bank commercial loans, and the securitization of commercial loans.

Banks' share of short-term lending to large corporations was the first area to feel the pressure of disintermediation. Between 1975 and 1988, banking's share of short-term borrowings by these large corporations fell from 49% to 26%. Most of this decline was directly attributable to the growing importance of commercial paper, which accounted for 36% of large firms' short-term borrowing in 1975 and 57% in 1988. However, the shift toward commercial paper has served to change rather than eliminate the role of commercial banks. Instead of funding short-term borrowings, banks now provide backup liquidity through loan commitments and credit enhancement through the issuance of standby letters of credit to commercial paper purchased by third parties.

Loans are securitized by creating securities backed by a pool of loans (see Pavel, 1989, for a detailed discussion). The securitization of consumer receivables began in 1970 with the issuance of the first mortgage-backed securities by Ginnie Mae (the Government National Mortgage Association). Government-sponsored agencies have played an important role in the securitization of residential mortgages by supplying explicit or implicit credit enhancements. Since their inauguration, mortgage-backed securities have steadily increased their role in the mortgage market. In 1989, 35% of all residential mortgages were held as mortgage-backed securities.

During the 1980s securitization spread to other types of consumer credit. The most popular instruments are credit card lending, where 10% of outstanding loans are securitized, and auto lending, where 5% of outstanding loans have been securitized. In contrast to its key role in developing mortgage-backed securities, the federal government has played no role in the securitization of auto and credit card receivables. To combat the moral hazard inherent in such arrangements, purchasers rely on third-party guarantees, the subordination of the originator's servicing fee, and the reputations of the originator, the underwriter, and the rating agency.

The 1980s also witnessed the birth of a market for commercial loans. In the loan sales market, loans are sold without any legal recourse to the originator (Pavel and Phillis, 1986). Purchasers rely on their own credit evaluations, the reputation of the originator, and the fact that the originator usually retains a portion of the loan to control the moral hazard inherent in such a transaction. Loans sold and outstanding have grown from 3% of commercial lending in 1985 to 13% in 1989. Initially, most loans sold were still held by other banks. However, by 1989, 12% of loans sold were being held outside the banking industry.

The most recent development in the disintermediation process has been the securitization of commercial lending. Despite the failures of several early attempts to securitize commercial loans and the doubts of many observers that commercial loans could ever be successfully securitized, recent events suggest that they can. The securitization of commercial loans is being accomplished in two ways—the creation of mutual funds that hold loans and the creation of loan-backed debt instruments. Commercial-loan mutual funds began operation in 1988 and currently hold $7 billion in commercial loans—about 1% of total commercial loans outstanding. Commercial loan-backed securities were first issued in 1989. Credit enhancement is generally achieved by creating senior and subordinated claims against the cash flows. The senior claims are sold to outside investors while the subordinated claims are retained by the originator. It is estimated that in 1990 there were $8 billion in loan-backed securities backed by commercial loans and $32 billion of asset-backed commercial paper.

Commercial banks and thrifts have long played a dominant role in the U.S. financial system. However, the progressive disintermediation of the credit function raises the possibility that their future role will be more limited. Only time will tell whether the process of securitization is simply the market's response to a banking system that is overregulated and undercapitalized or whether it is the consequence of a reduction in information costs and an increase in the efficiency of financial markets.

8. Implications of Globalization

The integration of formerly distinct financial markets, both within countries and across national boundaries, is a process that has been going on for a long time. But the integration of financial markets across national boundaries has proceeded at an accelerating rate over the past several decades. It is this development that has given rise to the term *globalization* and called widespread attention to its implications for heretofore domestically oriented financial institutions and their regulators.

8.1. Foreign Competition in U.S. Banking Markets

Today, the global inegration of the world's banking markets is clearly an inevitability if not an already accomplished fact. However, the accommodations that global integration will force upon U.S. banks may well be more disruptive and anxiety-producing than those experienced in other sectors of the U.S. economy that have been integrated into the global marketplace (Keehn, 1989b).

8.1.1. Banking in Perspective. Most sectors of the U.S. economy have been free to sell their products in nationally integrated markets and, despite tariff protection, many have been subject to foreign competition for years or decades. In contrast, for most of its history, the American banking system has been simply a collection of local banking markets tied together by a correspondent banking network and the existence of large nationwide corporate customers. For many customers, interstate competition, let alone international competition, was rare. Indeed, only 25 years ago, foreign and U.S. branches of foreign banks accounted for only 1.5% of total commercial lending by banks to U.S. customers. In contrast, at that same time, imports of manufactured and semi-manufactured goods accounted for about 7% of the supply of U.S. manufactures.

The fragmented nature of U.S. banking is likely to place U.S. banks in a weak position as they compete for market share in a globally integrated market for banking services. Indeed, by 1988 foreign banking organizations accounted for 28.3% of wholesale banking in the United States, up from 14.2% in 1980 (see figure 10-4). Thus, foreign penetration of U.S. wholesale banking markets exceeds the level achieved in primary metals, electronic equipment, and transportation equipment. Higher levels of foreign penetration have been achieved in only one major industry group—leather goods. In short, U.S. wholesale banking has gone from an extremely protected position in the 1960s to a relatively exposed position in the 1990s.

8.1.2. Accessing the U.S. Market. Foreign banks can provide services to U.S. customers through branches located in the United States, through subsidiary banks chartered in the United States, and through offices outside the United States. Foreign-owned banks chartered in the United States are subject to exactly the same regulations as domestically owned banks. If the owner of the bank is a bank or some other corporation, then the owner is generally treated as a bank holding company for regulatory purposes.

Prior to 1978, foreign banking organizations enjoyed some advantages over domestic organizations—in particular, they were permitted to acquire banks and establish branches in more than one state. The International Banking Act of 1978 was designed to equalize the restrictions on foreign and domestic banking organizations. However, some attempt is made to accommodate differences in banking practices. For instance,

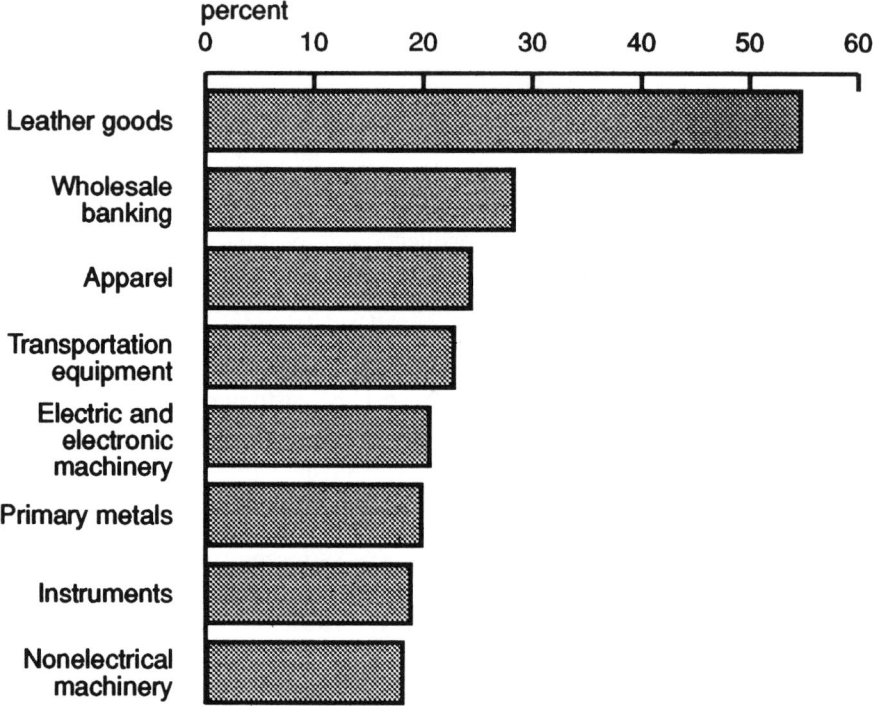

Figure 10-4. Foreign Penetration of U.S. Markets. Imports plus value-added by foreign-owned U.S. firms as a percent of new supply. *Source: Statistical Abstract of the United States*, 1989, p. 734; and "U.S. Affiliates of Foreign Companies: Benchmark Survey Results," *Survey of Current Business*, July 1989.

some foreign banks with controlling interests in commercial firms are permitted to own bank subsidiaries in the United States. At the other extreme, banks lending to U.S. customers from overseas offices are entirely free of U.S. regulation. Foreign-owned banks can also serve U.S. customers using a third approach—setting up a branch in the United States. The branch's assets and liabilities are commingled with those of the rest of the bank. Capital requirements and lending limits are set by regulators in the bank's home country. However, the branch is subject to examination by the licensing state.

8.1.3. Market Shares. Foreign banking organizations play virtually no role in the retail segment of the U.S. banking market. However, they are playing an increasingly important role in the wholesale banking market. As indicated in figure 10-5, the share of outstanding commercial and industrial (C&I) loans held by U.S. branches of foreign banks rose from 8.6% in 1980 to 14.4% in 1988. All of this increase was accounted for by branches of Japanese banks, whose share of C&I loans rose from 2.7% in 1980 to 8.5% in 1988. Over the same period, the market share of the U.S. branches of other foreign banks remained steady at 5.9%. The growth in C&I loans held by foreign-owned banks chartered in the United States has been less dramatic, rising from 4.4% in 1980 to 6.3% in 1988. In contrast to the striking inroads made by branches of Japanese banks, the share of C&I loans held by Japanese-owned U.S. banks has remained relatively small, rising from 0.1% in 1980 to 2.4% in 1988.

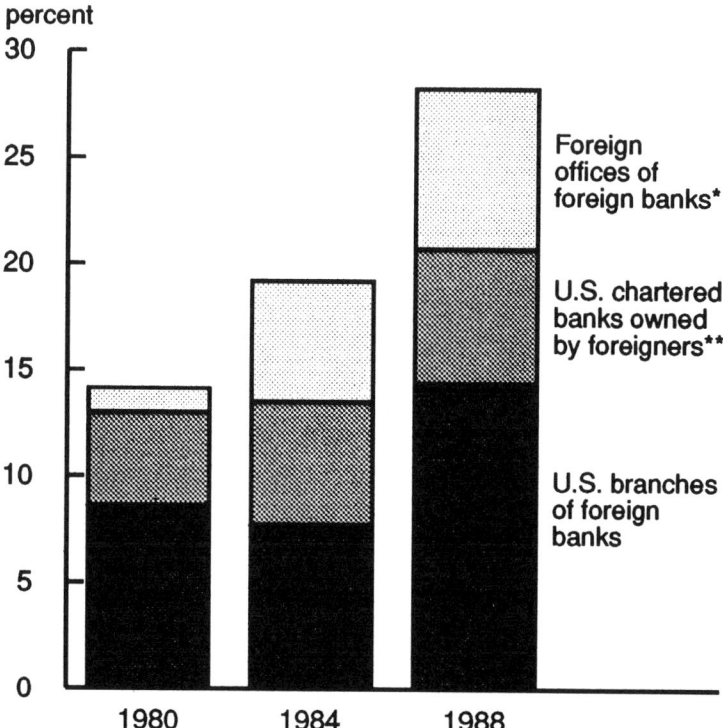

Figure 10-5. Foreign Share of Commercial Lending in the U.S. *Indicates estimates based on foreign borrowings of U.S. nonfinancial corporations as reported by Board of Governors, 1989 (includes lending by nonbank entities). **Indicates banks with greater than 50% foreign ownership.

Although the volume of C&I lending to U.S. firms through banking offices located outside the United States is more difficult to come by, Federal Reserve numbers, which include borrowings from both banks and nonbanks, indicate that the share of outstanding C&I loans held by offshore offices rose sixfold from 1.2% in 1980 to 7.6% in 1988.

Guarantees in the form of standby letters of credit (SLOC) represent another important wholesale banking product. As of December 1988, there were $288 billion in SLOCs outstanding to U.S. customers compared with $660 billion in commercial loans. Growth in SLOCs issued by foreign banking organizations has been explosive. In 1989 U.S. branches of foreign banks accounted for only 10% of all SLOCs issued to U.S. customers. By 1988, they accounted for 53%. In contrast to the market for C&I loans, branches of Japanese banks have been responsible for only a third of this increase. Market shares of banks based in Switzerland, West Germany, France, Italy, and the United Kingdom have all grown dramatically.

8.1.4. Factors Promoting Increased Foreign Competition. What explains the rapid growth in competition from foreign banking organizations? One obvious factor is the continued integration of the nonfinancial portion of the U.S. economy through greater trade and increased foreign direct investment in the United States. However, this increase is capable of explaining only a portion of the observed increase in the market shares of foreign banking organizations.

Sales of domestic C&I loans by U.S. commercial banks account for a significant portion of the competitive inroads being achieved by foreign banking organizations. Banks voluntarily sell loans to other institutions (including foreign banks) to avoid violating lending limits, to achieve a more diversified loan portfolio, to reduce capital requirements, or to take advantage of lower funding costs available at other institutions. Loans are bought by other banks because they wish to diversify their portfolios, because their ability to raise deposits exceeds their ability to generate loans directly, because they are attempting to develop banking relationships with particular customers, or because they are able to raise funds at a lower rate than the seller. By all accounts, loan sales were relatively unimportant prior to the early 1980s. By 1985, when the first formal figures are available, loans sold to foreign banking organizations accounted for 1.9% of total C&I loans outstanding and 24% of total loans held by U.S. branches of foreign banks. By 1988, they accounted for 2.5% of total C&I loans. Thus, sales of loans originated by U.S. banks have been directly responsible for over two fifths of the 5.8 percentage point increase in the market share of foreign banking organizations that occurred between 1980 and 1988.

Others have pointed to differences in regulation as the principal reason for the rapid growth in foreign banking. Excessive regulation of banks in their home markets has certainly played a role in the growth of the Eurodollar activities of U.S. banks (Baer and Pavel, 1988) and the Eurodollar and Euroyen activities of Japanese banks (Terrell, Dohner, and Lowrey, 1989). However, the impact of lax regulation in foreign banks' home markets on their competitive position in the domestic U.S. market is another matter. It ultimately boils down to the assertion that foreign banks are able to hold less capital per dollar of risk or pay less for the capital that they raise. If this complaint is correct, those banks that have made the greatest inroads into the U.S. market, the large Japanese banks (known as "city" banks), would be the least capitalized of the major international banks.

Yet, as figure 10-6 shows, the large Japanese city banks, as a group, have the highest ratio of market capitalization (share price times number of shares outstanding) to assets of all the major international banks. The lowest figure for a Japanese bank is about 16%, while two have ratios over 20%. The major U.S. money center banks, in contrast, have much lower market capitalization ratios. The highest market capitalization ratio for a U.S. money center bank is about 9.5%, while three money center banks have market capitalization ratios of under 3%. The capitalization

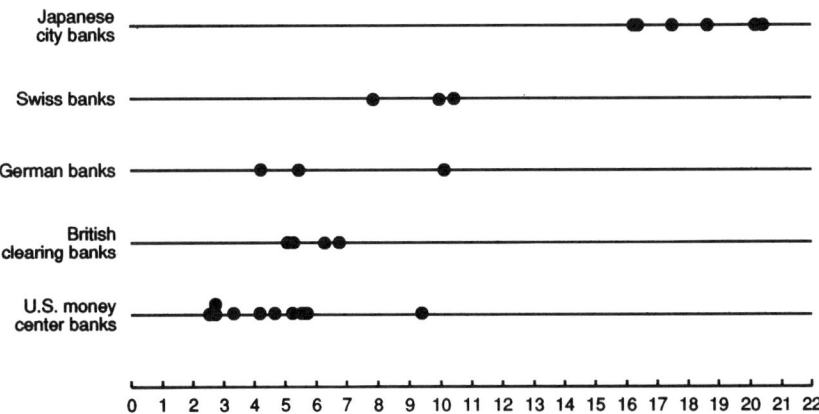

Figure 10-6. Market Capitalization of U.S. Banks and Foreign Banks (Percent of Assets). *Source*: Salomon Brothers *Bank Stock Weekly*, January 12, 1990; and *International Bank Biweekly*, January 11, 1990.

ratios of banks based in Switzerland, West Germany, and the United Kingdom lie between the extremes of the U.S. and Japanese banks.

8.1.5. Too Much of a Good Thing? If the rapid growth of Japanese banks in the United States cannot be explained by too little capital, perhaps it is worth considering whether it can be explained by too much capital. Figure 10-7 plots the growth in international assets and market capitalization ratios for banks in Japan, Switzerland, the United Kingdom, the United States, and West Germany. Banks from France and Italy are excluded because their ownership by a national government makes it difficult to measure their true capital. Figure 10-7 suggests that the success of Japanese banks is only the most dramatic example of a more general principle—namely, that banks with high market-capitalization ratios have made greater inroads in foreign markets than have banks with relatively low market-capitalization ratios. Interestingly enough, Swiss and German banks, which also have relatively high market-capitalization ratios due to unrecognized gains on equity portfolios, have also been expanding into foreign markets at a relatively rapid rate.

One possible response to such high capitalization ratios would be to

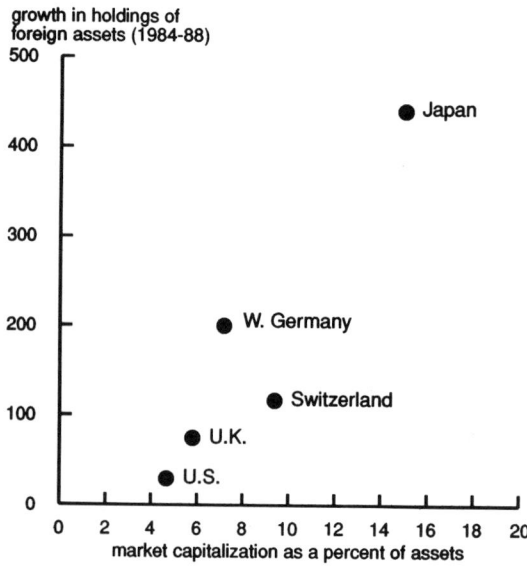

Figure 10-7. Impact of Market Capitalization on Growth in Foreign Bank Activity.
Source: Bank for International Settlements and Salomon Brothers.

realize some of the unrecognized gains and to pay the proceeds to the bank's shareholders through a special dividend. However, tax laws may make this unattractive. If this leads the bank to retain its capital gains (realized or unrealized), the bank will find itself in the position of having "too much" capital. Assuming that the bank's portfolio was previously in equilibrium, the bank would now be able to issue uninsured liabilities at a lower rate than before and to take larger exposures to borrowers while maintaining the same level of overall risk. The sharp increase in highly leveraged transactions by large U.S. and British firms in the latter half of the 1980s has made this latter effect particularly important and surely explains a significant portion of the rapid growth of Japanese banks in the United States.

Even if the bank is forced to raise book capital, it will still have strong incentives to grow. It can increase book equity either by realizing capital gains or by simply issuing additional securities. In contrast to banks with relatively low market capitalization, it will find securities issuance relatively inexpensive, in large part because the issuance of additional securities does not generate an offsetting loss of value of the subsidy implicit in government deposit insurance. As Edward Kane (1990) has pointed out, this factor explains why the adoption of risk-based capital has not resulted in a noticeable decline in the Japanese banks' share of the U.S. banking market. According to this view, inroads by foreign banks will cease only if further asset growth or a decline in the value of their equity portfolios brings the market capitalization ratios of Japanese banks back to the level of the early 1980s or if the market capitalization ratios of major U.S. banks rise significantly.

8.2. The Globalization of U.S. Financial Markets

Globalization has also increased foreign participation in U.S. securities, futures, and options markets while at the same time exposing these markets to greater foreign competition. However, the overall impact on U.S. firms operating in these markets has not been dramatic.

8.2.1. Trading in Derivative Products. The United States is home to the world's leading futures and options exchanges. Much of the growth experienced by these exchanges during the 1980s was in trading contracts with an international client base. Between 1984 and 1987, the volume of trading in foreign currency futures and options grew by 50%. During the same period, trading volume grew by 400% in Eurodollar CD contracts and by 300% in Treasury bond contracts. While no formal estimates are available, it is commonly accepted that about 30% of derivative product trading in the United States is done for the accounts of foreign customers.

While futures and options products were once the exclusive preserve of the American exchanges, the increasing international demand to trade such instruments has led to the rapid growth of foreign exchanges. Between 1985 and 1988, overseas exchanges' share of trading in Treasury bond futures contracts grew from 1.5% to 3%. Overseas trading held steady at 15% of total volume in Eurodollar futures, and overseas trading rose from 1% to nearly 50% of total volume in yen futures.

At the same time that foreign exchanges have been increasing their share of trading in contracts originally developed by U.S. exchanges, they have also been creating a broad array of new contracts designed to serve their home markets. The combination of direct competition through the creation of contracts that duplicate those already offered by U.S. exchanges and indirect competition through the creation of new contracts by foreign exchanges caused the share of worldwide trading volume executed on U.S. futures and options exchanges to fall from 98% in 1983 to 80% in 1988. The growing importance of overseas exchanges is derived in part from their proximity to domestic markets, in part from the fact that they are open when U.S. exchanges are closed, and in part from regulatory differences.

U.S. exchanges have experimented with three approaches for meeting the demand for trading outside of traditional business hours. The first attempt came in 1984 when the Chicago Mercantile Exchange (CME) entered into an agreement with the Singapore International Monetary Exchange (SIMEX) that permitted contracts purchased on one exchange to be offset by trading on the other exchange. The second attempt came in 1987 when the Chicago Board of Trade decided to extend its trading hours for its Treasury bond contract. The third and most recent approach to expanding trading hours consisted of developing electronic trade matching systems that can be accessed by traders located around the globe. The first of these systems to become operational, the GLOBEX system developed by the Chicago Mercantile Exchange, will permit exchanges to shift to electronic trade matching when the exchange floor is closed. The Chicago Board of Trade and MATIF have already agreed to join, and negotiations are underway with exchanges in New York, Singapore, Sydney, and Osaka. Because GLOBEX gives participants access to the order book, traders will have more information than they do at present, with the likely result that the prices generated by GLOBEX will be superior to those currently provided through floor trading (Domowitz, 1990). The introduction of nighttime trading will also increase the demand for extending the hours of operation of the payments system to facilitate nighttime margin calls, further improving the efficiency of the system (Baer and Evanoff, 1991).

U.S. exchanges have also sought, with limited success, to compete with the growing array of domestic contracts being introduced by foreign exchanges. The Chicago Mercantile Exchange has received approval to offer a futures contract on the Nikkei index and is currently trading sterling, deutschemark, and yen short-term interest-rate futures. The Chicago Board of Trade has received authorization to trade futures contracts tied to Japanese government bonds and index options tied to the TOPIX index of Japanese stocks. However, at this writing the only true success in competing with products offered by foreign exchanges has been achieved by the American Stock Exchange, which lists several warrants that are tied to the Nikkei index of Japanese stock prices.

The stock market crash of 1987 and the "minicrash" of 1989 have stimulated extensive debate about the regulation of derivative product markets in the United States. In the aftermath of the 1987 crash, price limits were instituted on stock index futures, and the Securities and Exchange Commission (SEC), among others, has sought the authority to regulate and increase margins on these contracts. The key question is what the impact of such a move will be, given the growing importance of foreign derivative product markets. Further tightening of U.S. regulations will leave U.S. derivative product markets more heavily regulated than many overseas markets. Whether U.S. regulation can be significantly tightened without driving trading activity overseas is an open question. However, the Japanese experience with introducing derivative products in a highly restrictive regulatory framework suggests that large investors will avoid markets that are subject to excessive regulation.

8.2.2. Trading in Securities. Globalization has also increased the role of foreign investors in U.S. securities markets and the importance of foreign securities in U.S. portfolios. Trading in U.S. domestic securities by foreign investors is less important in the United States than in many other countries, but has been growing at a rapid rate (see table 10-8). Between 1985 and 1988, trading of U.S. bonds by foreigners grew from 19% of total trading to 29%. The greatest part of this increase was due to foreign trading in U.S. government securities. Over the same period, the share of foreign transactions in U.S. equity markets increased from 9.7% to 13.1%.

U.S. securities are increasingly being traded overseas. This shift in

Table 10-8. The Changing Importance of Foreign Transactions in Domestic Markets

	Percent of total domestic trading	
	1985	1988
Bonds		
Canada	16	28
Germany	17	53
Japan	5	4
United States	19	29
Equities		
Canada	29	21
France	38	43
Germany	30	8
Japan	8	6
Switzerland	4	6
United States	10	13
United Kingdom	37	20

Source: Various central bank statistical releases for bonds and Salomon Brothers for equities.

trading is being driven by increased foreign holdings of U.S. securities and differences in regulation. Among the more restrictive U.S. regulations that tend to push trading offshore are issuance requirements that effectively prohibit resale of securities in U.S. markets and restrictions on short sales (U.S. Securities and Exchange Commission, 1987). Most overseas trading in U.S. securities occurs in London. While recent data are not available, the SEC reported in 1987 that daily volume of trading in U.S. stocks in London averaged about $200 million a day—roughly 2.5% of total volume on U.S. exchanges. The growing interest in trading U.S. securities outside of traditional business hours has led the New York Stock Exchange and the National Association of Securities Dealers to announce the development of electronic trading systems to permit such trading.

Trading of foreign securities by U.S. residents has also become more active. Between 1982 and 1989, the dollar value of shares traded on the New York Stock Exchange increased 215% while trading in foreign equities by U.S. citizens grew 660%. U.S. markets have captured some of this business through American Depository Receipts (ADRs) and by direct listing of foreign securities. Between 1983 and 1989 the number of

ADRs listed on the American Stock Exchange, the New York Stock Exchange, and the National Association of Securities Dealers Automated Quotation System (NASDAQ) increased 70%. Trading in foreign shares and ADRs listed on the New York Stock Exchange accounted for 7.4% of NYSE volume in 1989. Trading in ADRs and listed foreign securities accounted for 8% of the shares traded on NASDAQ in 1988, up from 5.9% in 1984. Several ADRs are among the volume leaders on NASDAQ (National Association of Securities Dealers, 1989). The ADRs for firms listed on U.K exchanges often trade twice as actively in the United States as in the United Kingdom. Trading in Canadian shares in the United States is also very active (U.S. Securities and Exchange Commission, 1987).

The strictness of U.S. laws governing the issuance and trading of securities has been both a boon and a burden for U.S. securities markets. Their presence has made U.S. markets extremely attractive for investors who value disclosure and for firms that do not find disclosure and registration unduly costly. However, firms that find U.S. disclosure, registration, and listing requirements to be costly are forced to choose between the domestic private placement market and the Euromarkets. Restrictions on the trading of unregistered privately placed securities have led many firms to choose the Euromarkets. In an attempt to capture some of this business for domestic markets, the SEC announced in 1990 that it would relax restrictions on the trading of privately placed securities. Many observers expect that this action will further increase the U.S. role in international securities markets.

9. Outlook

Intelligent regulation holds the key to the fate of the U.S. financial system. Only countries that are adept at balancing the need for free competition against depositor and taxpayer demands for an effective regulatory system will maintain a dominant position. Countries that over- or underregulate their markets will lose customers. For countries that attempt to gain share by subsidizing financial activity, international arbitrage will drive the cost of the subsidy up to prohibitively high levels. With intelligent regulatory policies, the United States can maintain its lead in the provision of nonbank financial services and remedy its now obvious weaknesses in the provision of banking services.

During the 1980s, the U.S. financial system was buffeted by many shocks, including the globalization of financial markets, the stock market crash of October 1987, the interest rate run-up in 1980–1982, the collapse in oil prices in 1982, and the poor performance of Third World borrowers. Those parts of the system that have been subject to reasonable regulation have dealt with these changes fairly well.

Other parts of the system—particularly banks and thrifts—have fared less well. The decapitalization of the bank and thrift industries has not only created opportunities for well-capitalized financial intermediaries, domestic or foreign, but also has encouraged credit markets to minimize the role of banks and thrifts in funding many types of credit that were formerly their domain.

Of course, a healthy *and* competitive banking system will require that the structural reforms implemented in the 1980s be permitted to run their course, particularly the elimination of restrictions on geographic expansion. The benefits of the 1980s deregulation movement are already being realized. Elimination of restrictions on deposit rates and the lowering of barriers to geographic expansion have raised deposit rates paid by consumers, accelerated consolidation in the industry, reduced the number of undiversified banks, lowered rates of return in banking, and made relative operating efficiency the major determinant of profitability.

Policymakers will have to accept that significant consolidation in banking will and must be the order of the day. Indeed, by the end of the decade, the number of independent banking entities will have fallen from the current level of 9,600 to perhaps 6,000 or 7,000. Although much of this exit from the industry will be voluntary, some will occur through failure. Policymakers must also recognize that, in combination, the increased competitiveness of wholesale banking markets and the growing importance of securities issuance as a source of capital will make the artificial separation of investment banking and commercial banking more costly for the public and a greater burden for bank shareholders.

However, deregulation alone will not ensure that the U.S. banking system will regain its health. Drastic changes are also required in the failure resolution and deposit insurance policies followed during the 1980s. One key change would be a shift toward early regulatory intervention to force recapitalization of banks that are solvent but capital-deficient. A second key change would be the reintroduction of creditor discipline. This will ensure that insolvent banks will not be able to continue operation.

If deregulation is allowed to continue and policies on failure resolution and deposit insurance are altered, U.S. banks will begin the next century considerably more diversified and better capitalized than they are today. This will permit them to regain much of the wholesale business lost to foreign bank competitors. Whether U.S. banks can regain business lost to other types of financial intermediaries, particularly money market mutual funds and prime rate funds, remains unclear. To the extent that the growth of these competitiors was a consequence of changes in the cost of information, the prospects are not good, because these changes are likely to be irreversible. However, to the extent that the growth was a consequence of bad banking regulation, there is some hope. A more intelligent policy towards failure resolution will reduce deposit insurance premiums, one of the most important sources of competitive disadvantage for banks in the funding of low-risk assets. Payment of interest on reserves or a reduction in reserve requirements would eliminate another unnecessary restraint on banks.

The health of other parts of the U.S. financial system depends less on the correction of existing misregulation than on the avoidance of well-intentioned but inappropriate proposals for new regulations. The costs of a regulatory misstep in these markets are rising as foreign marketplaces increasingly come to be viewed as alternatives to the domestic marketplace. Possible missteps include the indiscriminate use of trading halts in futures, options, and stock markets; the introduction of transactions taxes on financial trading; intervention to prevent the failure of nonbank financial firms; and hasty and ill-considered moves to regulate the margins on futures contracts, the private placement market, and the emerging financial clearing houses. In the absence of such missteps, the outlook for the future growth, stability, and efficient functioning of the U.S. financial system could be much brighter than at any time in recent decades.

Note

1. Unless otherwise indicated, statistics on the U.S. banking system are derived from *Flow of Funds Accounts: Financial Assets and Liabilities. Year-End, 1965–1988* (Washington DC: The Board of Governors of the Federal Reserve System, September 1989).

References

Alhadeff, David A. "A Reconsideration of Restrictions on Bank Entry," *Quarterly Journal of Economics* 76. (May 1962), 246–263.

Alhadeff, David A. *Monopoly and Competition in Banking*. Berkeley, CA: University of California Press, 1954.

Angermueller, Hans J. "The Customer Is Always Right: The Case for Functional Regulation of Financial Services," in *Merging Commercial and Investment Banking*, Proceedings of a Conference on Bank Structure and Competition. Chicago: Federal Reserve Bank of Chicago, 1987, pp. 1–10.

Apilado, Vincent R. and Thomas G. Gies. "Capital Adequacy and Commercial

Bank Failure," *The Bankers Magazine* 155 (Summer 1972), 24–30.

Aspinwall, Richard C. "Market Structure and Commercial Bank Mortgage Interest Rates," *Southern Economic Journal* 36 (April 1970), 376–384.

Baer, Herbert L., and Douglas D. Evanoff. "Payments System Issues in a 24-Hour Global Economy," forthcoming in George G. Kaufman (ed.), *Research in Financial Services*, Vol. 4. Greenwich, CT: JAI Press, 1991.

Baer, Herbert L. and Christine A. Pavel. "Does Regulation Drive Innovation?" Federal Reserve Bank of Chicago, *Economic Perspectives* 12 (March/April 1988), 3–15.

Bank Administration Institute. "International Convergence of Capital Measurement and Capital Standards," *Issues in Bank Regulation* 12 (Fall 1988), 3–4.

Barth, James R. "Post-FIRREA: The Need to Reform the Federal Deposit Insurance System," paper presented at the 26th Conference on Bank Structure and Competition, Federal Reserve Bank of Chicago, May 9–11, 1990.

Barth, James R., Philip F. Bartholomew, and Carol J. Labich. "Moral Hazard and the Thrift Crisis: An Analysis of 1988 Resolutions," in *Banking System Risk: Charting a New Course*, Proceedings of a Conference on Bank Structure and Competition. Chicago: Federal Reserve Bank of Chicago, 1989, pp. 344–384.

Beighley, H. Prescott and Allan S. McCall. "Market Power and Structure in Commercial Bank Installment Lending," *Journal of Money, Credit and Banking* 7 (November 1975), 449–467.

Bell, Frederick W. and Neil B. Murphy. *Costs in Commercial Banking: A Quantitative Analysis of Bank Behavior and Its Relation to Bank Regulation*. Research Report to the Federal Reserve Bank of Boston No. 41. Boston: Federal Reserve Bank of Boston, April 1968.

Benston, George J., Robert A. Eisenbeis, Paul M. Horvitz, Edward J. Kane, and George G. Kaufman. *Perspectives on Safe and Sound Banking: Past Present, and Future*. Cambridge, MA: The MIT Press, 1986.

Benston, George J., Allen N. Berger, Gerald A. Hanweck, and David B. Humphrey. "Economies of Scale and Scope in Banking," Research Papers in Banking and Financial Economics, Board of Governors of the Federal Reserve System, June 1983.

Benston, George J., Gerald A. Hanweck, and David B. Humphrey. "Scale Economies in Banking: A Restructuring and Reassessment," *Journal of Money, Credit and Banking* 14 (November 1982), 435–456.

Benston, George J. and Michael F. Koehn. "Capital Dissipation, Deregulation, and the Insolvency of Thrifts," unpublished paper, June 1989.

Berle, Adolph A., Jr. "Banking Under the Antitrust Laws," *Columbia Law Review* 49 (1949), 589–606.

Board of Governors of the Federal Reserve System. *The Bank Holding Company Movement to 1978: A Compendium*. Washington, DC: Board of Governors of the Federal Reserve System, 1978.

Bovenzi, John F. and Maureen E. Muldoon. "Large Bank Failure Resolution Methods and Policy Considerations," paper presented at the annual meeting of the Western Economic Association International, San Diego, CA, July 2, 1990.

Brewer, Elijah III. "Full-blown Crisis, Half-measure Cure," Federal Reserve Bank of Chicago, *Economic Perspectives*, 13 (November/December 1989), 2–17.

Brewer, Elijah III. "The Risk of Existing Nonbank Activities," in *Banking System Risk: Charting a New Course*, Proceedings of a Conference on Bank Structure and Competition. Chicago: Federal Reserve Bank of Chicago, 1989, pp. 401–423.

Brewer, Elijah III. "The Impact of Deposit Insurance on S&L Shareholders' Risk/Return Trade-offs," paper presented at the 26th Conference on Bank Structure and Competition, Federal Reserve Bank of Chicago, May 9–11, 1990.

Brimmer, Andrew W. "Central Banking and the Availability of Residential Mortgage Credit," remarks before the 76th annual convention of the U.S. Savings and Loan League, Miami Beach, Florida, November 12, 1968.

Brozen, Yale. *Concentration, Mergers, and Public Policy*. New York: Macmillan Publishing Co. Inc., 1982.

Brumbaugh, R. Daniel, Jr. "FIRREA: Ignoring Economic Analysis," paper presented at the annual meetings of the Western Economic Association International, San Diego, California, June 30, 1990.

Calomiris, Charles W. and Larry Schweikart, "The Panic of 1857: Origin, Transmission and Containment," Journal of Economic History (December 1991).

Carron, Andrew S. *The Plight of the Thrift Institutions*. Washington: The Brookings Institution, 1982.

Chandler, Lester V. "Monopolistic Elements in Commercial Banking," *Journal of Political Economy* 46 (February 1938), 7–10.

Chandler, Lester V. *Benjamin Strong: Central Banker*. Washington: The Brookings Institution, 1958.

Commission on Money and Credit. *Money and Credit: Their Influence on Jobs, Prices, and Growth*. Englewood Cliffs, NJ: Prentice-Hall, Inc., 1961.

Committee on Financial Institutions. *Report*. Washington, DC: USGPO, 1963.

Cooke, W. Peter. "Comments on Expanding Bank Powers: An International Perspective," in *Merging Commercial and Investment Banking*, Proceedings of a Conference on Bank Structure and Competition. Chicago: Federal Reserve Bank of Chicago, 1987, pp. 62–69.

Cotter, Richard V. "Capital Ratios and Capital Adequacy," *National Banking Review* 3 (March 1966), 333–346.

Cox, Albert H., Jr. *Regulation of Interest Rates on Deposits*. Michigan Business Studies, Vol. 17, No. 4. Ann Arbor, MI: The University of Michigan, 1966.

Craine, Roger and Richard W. Nelson. "Can Depository Institutions Be Regulated as if They Were Margin Accounts?" Paper presented at the 26th Conference on Bank Structure and Competition, Federal Reserve Bank of Chicago, May 9–11, 1990.

Dale, Betsy. "The Grass May Not Be.Greener: Commercial Banks and Investment Banking," Federal Reserve Bank of Chicago, *Economic Perspectives* 12 (November/December 1988), 3–15.

Dince, Robert E. and James C. Fortson. "The Use of Discriminant Analysis to Predict the Capital Adequacy of Commercial Banks," *Journal of Bank Research* 3 (Spring 1972), 54–62.

Domowitz, Ian. "The Mechanics of Automated Trade Execution Systems," paper presented at the 26th annual Conference on Bank Structure and Competition, Federal Reserve Bank of Chicago, May 9, 1990.

Edwards, Franklin R. "Concentration in Banking and Its Effects on Business Loan Rates," *Review of Economics and Statistics* 46 (August 1964), pp. 294–300.

Evanoff, Douglas D. "Branch Banking and Service Accessibility," *Journal of Money, Credit and Banking* 20 (May 1988), 191–202.

Evanoff, Douglas D. and Diana Fortier. "The Impact of Geographic Expansion in Banking: Some Axioms to Grind," Federal Reserve Bank of Chicago, *Economic Perspectives* 10 (May/June 1986), 24–38.

Flannery, Mark J. "An Economic Evaluation of Bank Securities Activities Before 1933," in Ingo Walter. (ed.), *Deregulating Wall Street: Commercial Bank Penetration of the Corporate Securities Market*. New York: John Wiley & Sons, 1985, pp. 67–87.

FMCG Capital Strategies and Bank Administration Institute. *Analyzing Success and Failure in Banking Consolidation: The Implications for Bank Acquisition Strategies*. Rolling Meadows, IL: Bank Administration Institute, 1990.

Fraser, Donald R. and Peter S. Rose. "Bank Entry and Bank Performance," *Journal of Finance* 27 (March 1972), 65–78.

Frieder, Larry A. "The Interstate Landscape: Trends and Projections," in *Toward Nationwide Banking*. Chicago: Federal Reserve Bank of Chicago, 1986, pp. 1–16.

Friedman, Milton and Anna Jacobson Schwartz. *A Monetary History of the United States, 1867–1960*. Princeton, NJ: Princeton University Press, 1963.

Gajewski, Gregory R. "Assessing the Risk of Bank Failure," in *Banking System Risk: Charting a New Course*, Proceedings of a Conference on Bank Structure and Competition. Chicago: Federal Reserve Bank of Chicago, 1989, pp. 432–456.

Galbraith, John A. *The Economics of Banking Operations: A Canadian Study*. Montreal: McGill University Press, 1963.

Gilbert, R. Alton and Geoffrey E. Wood. "Coping with Bank Failures: Some Lessons from the United States and the United Kingdom." Federal Reserve Bank of St. Louis, *Review* 68 (December 1986), 5–14.

Gilbert, R. Alton, Courtenay C. Stone, and Michael E. Trebing. "The New Bank Capital Adequacy Standards." Federal Reserve Bank of St. Louis, *Review* 67 (May 1985), 12–20.

Gilligan, Thomas W., Michael Smirlock, and William Marshall. "Scale and Scope Economies in the Multiproduct Banking Firm," *Journal of Monetary Economics* 13 (May 1984), 393–405.

Goldberg, Lawrence G., Gerald A. Hanweck, Michael Keenan, and Allan Young. "Economies of Scale and Scope in the Securities Industry: A Model Using Survey Data from New York Securities Firms," in *The Financial Services Industry in the Year 2000: Risk and Efficiency*, Proceedings of a Conference on Bank Structure and Competition. Chicago: Federal Reserve Bank of Chicago, 1988, pp. 372–396.

Goodman, Laurie S., Christine M. Cumming, and Joanne Kumekawa. "Product Line Regulations for Financial Institutions: A Cross Country Comparison," in *Proceedings of a Conference on Bank Structure and Competition*. Chicago: Federal Reserve Bank of Chicago, 1984, pp. 79–108.

Goodman, Oscar R. "A Review of Recent Legislative and Judicial Trends Affecting Banking Structure," in *Bank Structure and Competition*, a summary of discussion and selected papers presented at a conference at the Federal Reserve Bank of Chicago. Chicago: Federal Reserve Bank of Chicago, 1967, pp. 48–77.

Gorton, Gary. "Banking Panics and Business Cycles," *Oxford Economic Papers* 40 (December 1988), 751–781.

Greenbaum, Stuart I. "A Study of Bank Costs," *National Banking Review* 4 (June 1967), 415–434.

Greenbaum, Stuart I. "Competition and Efficiency in the Banking System—Empirical Research and its Policy Implications," *Journal of Political Economy* 75 (August 1967, Part 2), 461–479.

Hackley, Howard H. "Our Baffling Banking System," *Virginia Law Review*. 52 (May 1966), 605–620; and (June 1966), 771–830.

Hall, George R. and Charles F. Phillips, Jr. *Bank Mergers and the Regulatory Agencies*. Washington, DC: Board of Governors of the Federal Reserve System, 1964.

Heggestad, Arnold A. and John J. Mingo. "Prices, Nonprices and Concentration in Commercial Banking," *Journal of Money, Credit and Banking* 8 (February 1976), 107–117.

Hodgman, Donald R. "The Deposit Relationship and Commercial Bank Investment Behavior." *Review of Economics and Statistics* 43 (August 1961), 257–268.

Horvitz, Paul M. and Bernard Shull. "The Impact of Branch Banking on Bank Performance," *National Banking Review* 2 (December 1964), 143–188.

Hoskins, W. Lee and J. Fred Weston. "The Changing Nature of Banking Competition," in *Proceedings of a Conference on Bank Structure and Competition*. Chicago: Federal Reserve Bank of Chicago, 1970, pp. 97–111.

Johnson, Manuel. "Altering Incentives in an Evolving Depository System: Safe Banking for the 1990s," in *Banking System Risk: Charting a New Course*, Proceedings of a Conference on Bank Structure and Competition. Chicago: Federal Reserve Bank of Chicago, 1989, pp. 19–26.

Kane, Edward J. "Short-Changing the Small Saver: Federal Government Discrimination against Small Savers During the Vietnam War: A Comment," *Journal of Money, Credit and Banking* 2 (November 1970), 513–522.

Kane, Edward J. "Good Intentions and Unintended Evil: The Case Against Selective Credit Allocation," *Journal of Money, Credit and Banking* 9 (February 1977), 55–69.

Kane, Edward J. *The Gathering Crisis in Deposit Insurance.* Cambridge, MA: MIT Press, 1985.

Kane, Edward J. "Who Should Learn What from the Failure and Delayed Bailout of the ODGF?" In *Merging Commercial and Investment Banking*, Proceedings of a Conference on Bank Structure and Competition. Chicago: Federal Reserve Bank of Chicago, 1987, pp. 306–326.

Kane, Edward J. *The S & L Insurance Mess: How Did it Happen?* Washington: The Urban Institute Press, 1989.

Kane, Edward J. "Incentive Conflict in the International Risk-Based Capital Agreement," Federal Reserve Bank of Chicago, *Economic Perspectives*, 14 (May/June 1990), 33–36.

Kaufman, George G. "Bank Market Structure and Performance: The Evidence from Iowa," *Southern Economic Journal* 32 (April 1966), 429–439.

Kaufman, George G. "Banking Risk in Historical Perspective," in *Proceedings of a Conference on Bank Structure and Competition*. Chicago: Federal Reserve Bank of Chicago, 1986, pp. 231–249.

Kaufman, George G. "Are Some Banks Too Large to Fail?" *Contemporary Policy Issues*, forthcoming, 1990.

Kaufman, George G. and Larry R. Mote. "The Securities Activities of Banks: What Remains of Glass-Steagall?" Unpublished paper, February 1990.

Kaufman, George G., Larry R. Mote, and Harvey Rosenblum. "Implications of Deregulation for Product Lines and Geographical Markets of Financial Institutions," Staff Memoranda 82-2. Federal Reserve Bank of Chicago, 1982.

Kaufman, George G., Larry R. Mote, and Harvey Rosenblum. "The Future of Commercial Banks in the Financial Services Industry," Staff Memoranda 83–5. Federal Reserve Bank of Chicago, 1983.

Keehn, Silas. *Banking on the Balance—Powers and the Safety Net: A Proposal.* Chicago: Federal Reserve Bank of Chicago, 1989.

Keehn, Silas. "Global Financial Integration," speech at the Conference on the Future of Canadian and U.S. Financial Services in the Global Context, Centre for Canadian-American Studies, University of Windsor, Windsor, Ontario, Canada, March 1, 1989.

Klebaner, Benjamin J. *Commercial Banking in the United States: A History.* Hinsdale, IL: The Dryden Press, 1974.

Krooss, Herman E. and Martin R. Blyn. *A History of Financial Intermediaries.* New York: Random House, 1971.

Langohr, Herwig and Anthony M. Santomero. "The Impact of Equity in Bank Portfolios," in *Proceedings of a Conference on Bank Structure and Competition*. Chicago: Federal Reserve Bank of Chicago, 1984, pp. 109–133.

Lawrence, Robert J. *The Performance of Bank Holding Companies.* Washington, DC: Board of Governors of the Federal Reserve System, 1967.

Lindow, Wesley. "Bank Capital and Risk Assets," *National Banking Review* 1 (September 1963), 29–46.

Linke, Charles. M. "The Evolution of Interest Rate Regulation on Commercial Bank Deposits in the United States," *National Banking Review* 3 (June 1966),

Meyer, Paul A. and Howard W. Pifer. "Prediction of Bank Failures," *Journal of Finance* 27 (September 1970), 853–868.

Miller, Merton H. "Margins and the Future of the Markets," in *The Financial Services Industry in the Year 2000: Risk and Efficiency*, Proceedings of a Conference on Bank Structure and Competition. Chicago: Federal Reserve Bank of Chicago, 1988, pp. 73–78.

Mints, Lloyd W. *A History of Banking Theory in Great Britain and the United States*. Chicago: University of Chicago Press, 1945.

Morrison, George R. *Liquidity Preferences of Commercial Banks*. Chicago: University of Chicago Press, 1966.

Mote, Larry R. "The Philadelphia National Bank Case in Retrospect," *Business and Society* 26 (Spring 1986), 27–38.

Mote, Larry R. "The Perennial Issue: Branch Banking," Federal Reserve Bank of Chicago, *Business Conditions*. (February 1974), 3–23.

Motter, David C. and Deane Carson. "Bank Entry and the Public Interest," *National Banking Review* 1 (June 1964), 469–512.

Murphy, Neil B. and Steven J. Weiss. "The Effect of Concentration on Performance: Evaluating Statistical Studies," *The Magazine of Bank Administration* 45 (November 1969), 34–36, 61–64.

National Commission on Social Security Reform. *Report*. Washington, DC: USGPO, 1983.

Olin, Harold. "The Thrift Institutions' Experience with Service Corporations," in *Merging Commercial and Investment Banking*, Proceedings of a Conference on Bank Structure and Competition. Chicago: Federal Reserve Bank of Chicago, 1987, pp. 101–117.

Parkinson, Patrick M. "Innovations in Clearing Arrangements: A Framework for Analysis," In *Game Plans for the 90's*, Proceedings of a Conference on Bank Structure and Competition, Federal Reserve Bank of Chicago, May 9–11, 1990.

Parry, Robert. "Deposit Insurance Reform: A Personal View," Federal Reserve Bank of San Francisco (March 1990).

Pavel, Christine A. *Securitization: The Analysis and Development of the Loan-Based Asset-Backed Securities Markets*. Chicago: Probus Publishing, 1989.

Pavel, Christine and David Phillis. "Why Commercial Banks Sell Loans: An Empirical Analysis," in *Merging Commercial and Investment Banking*, Proceedings of a Conference on Bank Structure and Competition. Chicago: Federal Reserve Bank of Chicago, 1987, pp. 145–165.

Phillips, Almarin. "Structure, Conduct, and Performance—and Performance, Conduct, and Structure?" In Jesse W. Markham and Gustav F. Papanek. (eds.) *Industrial Organization and Economic Development*. Boston: Houghton Mifflin Company, 1970, pp. 26–37.

Presidential Task Force on Market Mechanisms. *Report*. Washington, DC: U.S. Government Printing Office, 1988.

President's Commission on Financial Structure and Regulation. *Report*. Washington, DC: USGPO, 1971.

Pringle, John. "The Capital Decision in Commercial Banks," *Journal of Finance* 29 (June 1974), 779–795.

Rhoades, Stephen A. "Structure-Performance Studies in Banking: A Summary and Evaluation," *Staff Economic Studies* No. 92, Board of Governors of the Federal Reserve System, 1977.

Rhoades, Stephen A. "Nonbank Thrift Institutions as Determinants of Performance in Banking Markets," *Journal of Economics and Business* (Fall 1979), 66–72.

Robertson, Ross M. *The Comptroller and Bank Supervision: A Historical Appraisal*. Washington, DC: The Office of the Comptroller of the Currency, 1968.

Robinson, Roland I. and Richard H. Pettway. *Policies for Optimum Bank Capital*. A Study Prepared for the Trustees of the Banking Research Fund. Chicago: Association of Reserve City Bankers, 1967.

Rolnick, Arthur I. and Warren E. Weber. "Free Banking, Wildcat Banking, and Shinplasters," Federal Reserve Bank of Minneapolis, *Quarterly Review* 6 (Fall 1982), 10–19.

Rose, Sanford. "The Future Competitive Environment: Strategic Planning for the 1990s," in *Proceedings of a Conference on Bank Structure and Competition*. Chicago: Federal Reserve Bank of Chicago, 1982, pp. 22–26.

Saunders, Anthony. "Universal Banking in the U.S.: The Implications for Bank Risk and the Federal Safety Net," unpublished paper, May 2, 1990.

Savage, Donald T. and David B. Humphrey. "Branching Laws and Banking Offices," *Journal of Money, Credit and Banking* 11 (May 1979), 227–230.

Short, Genie D. and Jeffery W. Gunther. *The Texas Thrift Situation: Implications for the Texas Financial Industry*. Dallas, TX: Federal Reserve Bank of Dallas, 1988.

Shull, Bernard. "The Separation of Banking and Commerce: Origin, Development, and Implications for Antitrust," *The Antitrust Bulletin* 27 (Spring 1983), 255–279.

Shull, Bernard and Paul M. Horvitz. "Branch Banking and the Structure of Competition," *National Banking Review* 1 (March 1964), 301–341.

Smith, Adam. *An Inquiry into the Nature and Causes of the Wealth of Nations*. New York: The Modern Library, 1937.

Soldofsky, Robert W. *Institutional Holdings of Common Stock, 1900–2000: History, Projections, and Interpretation*. Michigan Business Studies, Vol. 18, No. 3. Ann Arbor, MI: University of Michigan, 1971.

Temin, Peter. *Did Monetary Forces Cause the Great Depression?* New York: Norton, 1976.

Terrell, Henry S., Robert S. Dohner, and Barbara R. Lowrey. "The U.S. and U.K. Activities of Japanese Banks, 1980–1988." Board of Governors of the

Federal Reserve System. *International Finance Discussion Papers*, No. 361, September 1989.
Trescott, Paul B. *Financing American Enterprise: The Story of Commercial Banking*. New York: Harper & Row, 1963.
Tussing, A. Dale. "Bank Failure: A Meaningful Competitive Force?" In *Proceedings of a Conference on Bank Structure and Competition*. Chicago: Federal Reserve Bank of Chicago, 1968, pp. 99–109.
U.S. Securities and Exchange Commission. *Internationalization of the Securities Markets*. Washington, DC: U.S. Government Printing Office, 1987.
Vandenbrink, Donna Craig. "The Effects of Usury Ceilings: the Economic Evidence," Working Paper Series on Regional Economic Issues 82-1, Federal Reserve Bank of Chicago, 1982.
Van Horn, Charles. "Banks with Good Earnings Can Perform Better in Five Areas," *American Banker* August 2, 1972.
Vice President's Task Group on Regulation of Financial Services. *Blueprint for Reform*. Washington, DC: USGPO, 1984.
Wall, Larry D. "A Plan for Reducing Future Deposit Insurance Losses: Puttable Subordinated Debt," Federal Reserve Bank of Atlanta, *Economic Review* (July/August 1989), 2–17.
Warburg, Paul M. *The Federal Reserve System: Its Origin and Growth* (two volumes). New York: Macmillan Company, 1930.
Weatherstone, Dennis. "Firewalls and the Structure of the Future," in *Banking System Risk: Charting a New Course*, Proceedings of a Conference on Bank Structure and Competition. Chicago: Federal Reserve Bank of Chicago, 1989, pp. 27–32.
Wheelock, David C. "The Fed's Failure to Act as Lender of Last Resort During the Great Depression, 1929–1933," in *Banking System Risk: Charting a New Course*, Proceedings of a Conference on Bank Structure and Competition. Chicago: Federal Reserve Bank of Chicago, 1989, pp. 154–176.
White, Eugene Nelson. "Before the Glass–Steagall Act: An Analysis of the Investment Banking Activities of National Banks," *Explorations in Economic History* 23 (January 1986), 33–55.
White, Lawrence H. *Free Banking in Britain: Theory, Experience, and Debate, 1800–1845*. Cambridge: Cambridge University Press, 1984.
Woods, Jack H. "Branch Banking and the Adequacy of Banking Facilities," unpublished paper, 1970.
Wriston, Walter B. "Maintaining Comparative Advantage in an Information Society," in *Proceedings of a Conference on Bank Structure and Competition*. Chicago: Federal Reserve Bank of Chicago, 1986, pp. 1–8.

11 BANK STRUCTURE IN WEST GERMANY

Randall Johnston Pozdena and Volbert Alexander

1. Introduction

The banking system of the German Federal Republic (West Germany) is distinguished from many other modern banking systems by its structural complexity and the breadth of powers afforded banks. In addition, the supervisory, regulatory, and monetary environment in which German banks and financial markets operate differs significantly from that of banking systems in many other countries. These differences result in important distinctions in the role played by banks in intermediating between savers and investors, and in the incentives faced by bank management.

In section 2 of this chapter, we present a sketch of the industrial structure of German banking and describe the functions of the key features of the banking industry, the financial markets, and the payments system. In section 3, we analyze the implications of German bank structure on the efficient provision of financial services and examine the potential advantages and problems posed by the present structure. In section 4, we discuss the supervisory and regulatory environment in which German banks operate. We conclude, in section 5, with some observations on current issues in German banking and its potential in an environment of internationally coordinated regulation and globalized financial markets.

2. The Structure of German Banking

The business of banking in Germany is defined in the Banking Act of 1961.[1] The Act defines a credit institution engaged in banking as any enterprise engaged in the following activities: 1) accepting deposits; 2) making loans; 3) discounting bills; 4) providing securities brokerage services; 5) providing trust (safe custody) services; 6) operating investment funds; 7) factoring; 8) providing financial guarantees; and 9) providing funds transfer (giro) services.

By this definition, as of 1988, there were approximately 4700 banking institutions in Germany, with 45,000 banking offices. The total number of banks has been declining for at least 30 years, and there are today only about one third the number of banks there were in the mid-1950s. The number of banking offices, in contrast, has nearly doubled in that same period.

The large number of banking offices makes the German economy one of the most heavily "banked" economies in the world, on a per capita basis. Only in Switzerland is the banking industry as prominent in the industrial landscape as it is in the German Federal Republic. By comparison, the United States has fewer than one third the number of banking offices on a per capita basis.

Overlaying this broad pattern is a complex organizational structure. The ownership of banking organizations is a mixture of private, cooperative, and public forms. In addition, while most of these organizations have broad, "universal" powers to provide financial services, there also are specialist banks chartered to perform a narrower range of services. Finally, there is a regional pattern to the presence of the various banking organizations. This regional pattern is a carryover from an earlier period during which some banks' operations were restricted to specific regions. There are, at present, however, no restrictions on the location of these banks' activities. Figure 11-1 illustrates the variety of distinct banking institutions in Germany.[2]

2.1. Universal Banks

The vast majority of banks in Germany are of the universal or fully empowered type (Universalbanken). As of 1988, they represented about

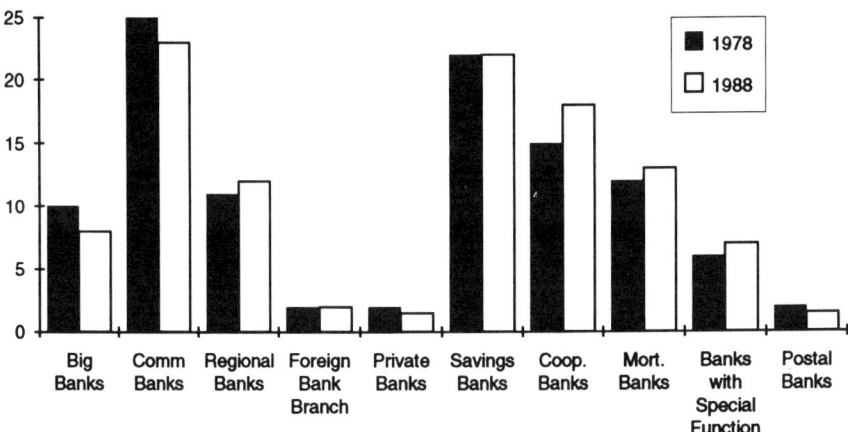

Figure 11-1. Asset Shares of German Banks (percent).

94% of the incorporated banks, 99% of the offices, and 73% of the assets. These institutions have extremely broad legal authority to provide banking services. In addition, they may invest directly in nonfinancial enterprises and also may be owned by nonfinancial institutions.

All three forms of ownership may be found in the universal banking sphere. There are private commercial banks, cooperative banks, and publicly owned banks with universal powers authority. In practice, however, full use of universal power is practiced only by the large, private commercial and some publicly owned banks.

2.1.1. Private Commercial Banks. Only about 300 of Germany's banks (6% of the total) are private commercial banks, but they maintain about 15% of the total offices and represent over 22% of total assets. In addition, they hold about 55% of all nongovernment deposits, and dominate the securities trading and safekeeping business.

Most bonds, stocks, and other investment certificates are held on deposit at the commercial banks, and the banks routinely vote the proxies of these shares on behalf of their customers.[3] The commercial banks also have a dominant role in the new issues market as investment bankers. In addition, the banks themselves hold substantial interests in commercial enterprises, as well as other financial institutions providing specialized or mortgage banking services.[4] These roles and relationships elevate considerably the importance of the private, commercial banking sector.

The three big branch banks (Deutsche Bank, Dresdner Bank, and

Table 11-1. The Structure of German Banking, 1988

Type of Bank	No. of Banks[a]	No. of Offices[a]	Concentration Ratio, 3-Firm[b]	Total Assets DM Billion
Universal banks	4,513	44,362	0.11	3,098
Private commercial banks	308	6,691	0.38	940
Big banks + Berlin subs.	6	3,124	1.00	353
Regional banks	148	3,060	0.62	455
Private banks	92	409	0.34	59
Foreign bank branches	62	98	0.21	73
Cooperative banks	3,604	19,587	0.24	672
Credit cooperatives	3,597	19,532	0.03	491
Central cooperative banks	7	55	0.88	181
Public law banks	601	18,084	0.17	1,486
Savings banks	589	17,837	0.06	864
Central savings banks	12	247	0.42	622
Specialist banks	219	356	N/A	952
Private institutions	167	214	0.21	473
Mortgage banks	25	48	0.28	358
Housing loan societies	17	37	N/A	107
Investment companies	34	36	N/A	140
Securities deposit corps.	8	8	0.55	6
Ship mortgage, guarantee banks, others	83	85	N/A	2
Public law banks	56	146	N/A	573
Mortgage banks	12	18	0.52	196
Housing loan societies	13	17	N/A	51
Banks w. special functions	16	96	N/A	265
Postal banks	15	15	N/A	61

[a] Data from 1986
[b] Calculated as share of assets; estimated due to effects of consolidation.
Source: Deutsche Bundesbank; Bank-Verlag, Cologne

Commerzbank) dominate the German banking landscape, although a publicly owned institution (the Central Giro of the Westdeutche Landesbank) ranks third nationally in assets after Deutsche Bank and Dresdner Bank AG. (Indeed, five of the ten largest banking institutions in Germany, on an asset basis, are publicly or cooperatively owned. This is a feature of German banking structure to which we will return later.)

2.1.2. Regional and Other Commercial Banks. The remainder of the private, commercial banking group consists of regional banks, private banks, and the branches of foreign commercial banks. The 100 or so regional banks have about 10% of total banking assets in Germany and have over 3000 offices. As a group, they have a somewhat larger market share than the big branch banks, although their national and international significance is less. Since most new banks begin with a regional presence, the regional bank grouping also has shown growth in its ranks and market share in the last 30 years or so, increasing in number by about 50% in that period.

The largest of the regional banks is Bayerische Vereinsbank AG, headquartered in Munich, and similar in size to Commerzbank. It is a blend of a German commercial bank and a mortgage bank, empowered by the Mortgage Banking Act to engage not only in general banking business, but also to issue mortgage and municipal bonds. (The big branch banks provide mortgage banking services through subsidiaries.) In general, however, regional banks are simply smaller, private universal banks than the big branch banks.

As was indicated earlier, designation as a regional bank is historical, and no significant restrictions exist on the ability of a regional bank to branch elsewhere. The Bank für Gemeinwirtschaft (BfG), for example, has over 250 offices throughout Germany. In addition, mergers of regional banks have occurred. The BHF Bank, for example, was formed by the combination of two regional banks.

The ownership structure of regional banks is quite varied. Unlike the big branch banks, which are all stock corporations (AG), regional banks are organized as limited-share partnerships (KGaA) or a limited liability private company (GmbH). In addition, the share ownership structure blurs some of the distinctions in organizational form in German banking. The large BfG organization, for example, was owned by trade unions and cooperatives and is now owned by a large insurance company.

The third type of institution in the private, commercial banking sector is represented by the private banks (Privatbanken). Private banks are sole proprietorships (since 1965, on a grandfathered basis only) or partnership organizations. They raise their equity privately, but as universal banks may offer demand liabilities and myriad other services. Their share of total banking assets is on the order of 1.2% and the 92 private banks today have approximately 400 offices.

Private banking was the original form of German banking, and the family names Oppenheim, Warburg, Berenberg, and Hauck remain associated with German private banking. However, the significance of private banking has declined sharply since the eighteenth and nineteenth centuries, when it was the dominant organizational form. In just the past 30 years, about two thirds of all private banks have disappeared. Their comparative advantage in banking lay in the networks of private contacts that were important to prudent lending in earlier times. Today, the legal, tax, and regulatory advantages that are enjoyed by stock corporations have diminished the viability of private banks.

The private banks that remain typically specialize in the financing of a particular industrial sector or provision of selected services. Foreign-trade financing, investment banking, trust services, real estate management, and portfolio management are all important areas of emphasis. The largest private banking firm, founded in 1789, is Sal. Oppenheim Jr. & Cie. This firm is less than one tenth the size of Commerzbank, and is four times as large as the next biggest private bank.

The fourth, and final, major component of the private commercial banking business in Germany is the foreign commercial banks. Germany places no significant, special restrictions on foreign banks operating in the country. Despite the highly developed state of German banking, therefore, the number of foreign banks operating in Germany has grown significantly in recent years to 70 institutions, but with an asset share of the total German banking market of only about 2%. U.S. banks account for about 30% of that total, followed by Japanese banks. Another 100 or so German banks with an additional 2% market share have majority foreign ownership and may be considered under foreign control. Around 170 other foreign banks have representative offices (Repräsentanzen) in Germany, which means that they cannot make transactions on their own account.

The foreign banks tend to emphasize credit services associated with trade, as well as services to the German subsidiaries of home commercial firms. With some exceptions in the lead underwriting of DM securities, foreign banks have been able to participate to the extent of their ability in domestic markets. The ubiquitousness of the supply of domestic banking services, however, has limited effective foreign penetration of German domestic markets. The large German commercial banks, however, have important affiliations with other European banks through consortia such as EBIC, ABECOR, and Europartners. Through these groups, and the joint subsidiaries, joint ventures, and other participations they support, there likely are other avenues for involvement in German banking markets by foreign banks.

2.1.3. Public Law Banks. The German banking system is distinguished sharply from the American and British systems by the prominence of banks and other credit institutions owned by the public sector. Cities, states, and districts in Germany operate a variety of institutions providing banking services to the public. Another set of public law institutions ("central" institutions) operate as wholesalers of services of the main groups of public law credit institutions.

There are approximately 600 public institutions operating as universal-type banks (about 13% of the total). Their number has declined over the last 30 years or so, but the number of their offices and their market share has grown. Today, they constitute about 36% of total assets in German banking and operate fully 40% of all banking offices.

Privatization of publicly owned banks is discussed periodically primarily because of the concerns over the public costs of the capital needs of these banks. In 1984, for example, the privatization of Landesbank Rheinland-Pfalz was discussed seriously by the state government. In most cases, however, the political pressure to maintain the traditional role and status of public banking in Germany derails privatization efforts.

The two main groups of public law institutions are the Savings Banks (Sparkassen) and the Central Giro institutions. The savings banks were established in the early nineteenth century as an element of social reforms. They were intended to provide financial services to the socially disadvantaged in their communities. The laws establishing the institutions were promulgated at the state (Länder) level, and considerable variation in the laws affecting savings banks persists today. Their day-to-day business is directed by management committees (Vorstand) operating under a board of administrators (Aufsichtsrat or Verwaltungsrat) comprised of local business and government officials.

This structure creates serious problems: the most important task of the board of administrators is to supervise major activities of the management committee. This cannot be done effectively by government officials having no knowledge and experience in banking. The president of the board of administrators of the different Central Giro institutions, for example, is by law the governor of the respective state. In the 1970s, some serious mismanagement could be observed in these institutions, leading to losses of several billion DM and even to political pressure on state governments up to the resignation of a governor. The ability of such institutions to receive support from the states prevents them from closing their doors.

Public law institutions have evolved from providing simple deposit and real estate lending services to the provision of a wide range of banking services. Real estate loans and mortgages, however, remain a significant part of their portfolios. Savings deposits and certificates also remain the dominant source of financing. The savings banks are perceived by Germans to be most like American mutual savings banks or savings and loan associations, but with greater potential powers and with public ownership.

The Central Giro Banks (Girozentralen) are the major second group of public credit institution. They operate to provide services to the savings bank sector, operating clearing houses and holding the savings banks' excess liquidity reserves. They also provide syndication services, foreign-trade financing, and foreign-exchange services—services that the savings banks themselves are too small to provide or are (in the case of foreign exchange) prohibited from providing. The largest of the Central Giro Banks, Wesdeutsche Landesbank-Girozentrale (WestLB) in Duesseldorf, and some others too, operate as full-fledged universal banks, with branches and representative offices worldwide.

There are 11 Central Giro Banks, and a twelfth bank, Deutsche Girozentrale-Deutsche Kommunalbank, that operates as the central wholesale institution for the savings bank sector. They are owned either by state governments or by regional savings bank associations. As a result of these local government affiliations, they often operate as the banker for regional governments. WestLB, for example, is the bank for the state of Northrhine-Westphalia.

2.1.4. The Cooperative Banking System. Cooperative banking systems worldwide have their origins in the German cooperative banks. These banks were set up in the last half of the nineteenth century in towns and in the countryside to cooperatively serve the financial needs of local households. They operate as "shareholder-owned" enterprises, and the deposits are technically shares (equity liabilities) rather than demand debt liabilities. They are called variously *people's banks* (*Volksbanken*) or *Raiffeisen banks* (after the movement's founder, Friedrich Raiffesen). The latter operate primarily as rural or agriculture-oriented banks.

The organizational structure of the cooperative banking system is complex, with a system of central banks under the overall leadership of an organization called Deutsche Genossenschaftsbank (DG Bank). DG Bank is a public corporation, but operates as a full-fledged universal bank, providing wholesale services to other cooperative and central co-operative banks, as well operating as universal bank in its own right.

The central cooperative banks, in turn, provide services to local and regional cooperative banks loosely organized around the nature of the cooperative organizations. In particular, there is a central cooperative bank for agricultural, industrial, consumer, and credit cooperative banks. Altogether, there are about 3500 cooperative banks today, operating 16,000 offices (about 35% of all German banking offices). Their assets represent only about 16% of total German banking assets, however, and in recent years, growth of this sector has been only slight. Many of the cooperative banks are very small, and there are efforts underway to improve the efficiency of the cooperative system through merger. In addition, some of the banks in the cooperative banking sector have experienced serious financial difficulty, usually linked to concentrated lending activity. This, too, has provided impetus for further consolidation in this sector.

2.2. Specialist Banks

Although the German banking marketplace is dominated by universal banks, banks with narrow powers play an important role in providing credit services. There are about 200 nonuniversal banking institutions, representing about 25% of German banking assets. They consist primarily of banks providing mortgage- and housing-related credit services, although investment companies and purveyors of specialized business services also are important. As in the universal banking sector, there are both private and public law institutions. Only the major groups of specialist banks are discussed in this section.

2.2.1. Mortgage Banks. About half of all specialist banks (on an asset basis) are mortgage banks (Hypothekenbanken). There are 25 private mortgage banks and another 12 incorporated under public law. They specialize in long-term mortgage lending in residential, industrial, and agricultural real estate markets and in the finance of shipbuilding. The lending is financed by the issuance of mortgage bonds secured by the general portfolio of the mortgage banks.

The existence of specialized mortgage lenders in a country of universal banking is largely a consequence of law and regulation. Although universal banks may make mortgage loans, the Mortgage Banking Act of 1963[6] does not allow them to issue bonds to finance these assets; section 5a of the Act restricts the issuance of mortgage bonds to mortgage banks. Universal banks desiring to participate in this activity thus must do so by operating a mortgage banking subsidiary. As a result, most private mortgage banks are wholly owned by universal banks.

There are 12 public law mortgage banks, owned by state governments. They are derived from eighteenth-century rural lending societies (Landgemeinschaften) and specialize primarily in the finance of low-income housing. The public sector mortgage banks perform the same basic functions as their private counterparts and are about half as large, in the aggregate, as the private mortgage banks. Mortgage lending to the public sector is performed by both the private and public mortgage banks, and has been a growing line of business in recent years.

2.2.2. Housing Loan Societies. There are 30 housing loan societies (Bausparkassen) in Germany, 17 privately owned and 13 incorporated under public law. Their assets represent about 4% of total German banking assets, or about 20% of the specialist bank total.

The primary business of the housing loan society is the financing of owner-occupied housing through special saving contracts. Specifically, would-be borrowers must maintain a saving deposit for a certain period of time, after which they receive a fixed-rate, long-term mortgage contract of a size related to their deposit amount with an interest rate far below the market interest rate. About 80% of the funding of the housing loan societies is represented by such saving contracts, and there are about 26 million such contracts in place in Germany as a whole.

Deposits into housing loan societies enjoy favorable treatment under German tax law. These deposits are tax-deductible in most cases and, if a depositor's income meets a certain means test, there is modest matching of the depositor's funds by public funds. This special treatment of deposit funds contributes to the role played by this class of credit institution in Germany.

2.2.3. Postal Giro and Postal Savings. The postal service in Germany (Deutsche Bundespost) operates two savings banks (Postsparkassen) and 13 giro banks (Postscheckkassen). The savings banks provide saving account services in the form of interest-earning accounts, while the giro provides transactions services to the public, offering accounts in the form of noninterest-earning demand liabilities.

The assets of the postal banks (mainly loans to the postal service) represent only about 1% of total banking assets. Because the postal service operates about 18,000 offices in Germany, however, the postal giro and savings banks represent a convenient source of savings and transactions services for German households. There are about 25 million postal saving accounts and 5 million postal giro accounts.

2.2.4. Special-Purpose Banks. There exist in Germany 20 or so "special purpose" banks, with assets equal to about 20% of all specialist banks. They are engaged in the provision of such things as export credit, financing German reconstruction and development, provision of acceptance services, agricultural credit, industrial credit, small business credit, and the financing of transportation facilities.

The special-purpose banks are both private and public in form, and have been established by governments or business associations to centralize and facilitate certain types of credit flows. Often their viability is explained by special tax advantages they enjoy (as in the case of the industrial lending activities of the Berliner Industriebank AG) or access to special central bank rediscount facilities (as in the case of the export credit activities of the ADA Ausfuhrkredit-GmbH.)

Two of the special purpose banks deserve more detailed reference. One, the Liquiditaets-Konsortialbank GmbH (the "Liko-Bank"), is a liquidity consortium financed by share capital provided by the central bank and various banking sectors (public and private). It was founded in 1974 after the collapse of the Bankhaus I. D. Herstatt caused settlement problems for other, solvent banks whose transactions were entangled with Herstatt.

The total size of the facility (in the form of paid in shares plus contingent liabilities) is about 1 billion DM. (By way of reference, this is about 0.04% of the assets of the universal banks.) Its purpose is to provide liquidity to the payments system by providing interim credit to providers of domestic and foreign payments services. The Liko-Bank is interesting because it serves as an example of a liquidity or lender-of-last-resort facility outside of a central bank. However, it is not considered an important source of liquidity by German bankers.

A second institution worth noting is the GZS (Gesellschaft für Zahlungssysteme mbH or "Payments Company"). It issues the EUROCARD for German credit institutions and handles the settlement of Eurochecks written abroad by Germans in other currencies. The Payments Company is owned by private commercial, savings, and co-operative banks.

The Payments Company is of interest because it is the main developer of credit card, retail electronic payments, and point-of-sale systems in Germany. These systems are highly developed and check writing is used far less in Germany than in the United States.

2.3. German Financial Markets

The markets for primary securities in Germany are less well developed than the financial intermediation markets. The German stock market is the fourth largest equity market in the world (in terms of market capitalization, after the U.S., Japan, and the U.K.), but is relatively small given the size of the German economy. In addition, the German bond markets, while very large, are not completely distinct from the financial intermediation industry; the influence of the banks pervades these markets because of their broad securities powers. The five largest members of the German exchanges are banks, with Deutsche Bank alone accounting for almost 50% of bond trading activity, for example.

2.3.1. The Stock Market. Stock trading remains regionalized in Germany, with seven regional exchanges in Frankfurt, Duesseldorf, Munich, Stuttgart, West Berlin, Hanover, and Bremen. Frankfurt and Duesseldorf are by far the largest of the exchanges, with about 75% of total turnover, but overly strong regionalism continues to hamper development of German equities market.[7]

The exchanges span three markets, the official (amtlicher) market, the semiofficial market (geregelter freiverkehr), and the over-the-counter market (Telefonverkehr). The semiofficial market was established in 1987 to provide a market for smaller volume issues. It offers simpler, less expensive listing procedures and condensed prospectus requirements.

The undeveloped state of the German stock exchanges is illustrated in the simple statistics. Across all of the exchanges, only 400 companies are publicly traded. Turnover on the stock exchanges, on a comparative basis, is currently about 7% of German GNP compared to about 25% for the U.S.

In addition, the effective, traded float is reduced by the fact that share ownership is heavily concentrated in holdings by families, banks, and other institutions. Consequently, public ownership and participation in the stock market is slight (only 5% of German households own stock), and private investors are said to be uncomfortable holding equity positions.[8]

All quoted companies, foreign securities, and government agency securities trade in the official market. Floor trading occurs for only two hours a day, but off-the-floor trading occurs for an additional four hours a day. These trades are not disclosed, however, and the fact that the transactions in these hours are primarily among banks is a further indication of the prominence of banks in the primary securities markets.

The relatively nascent state of German primary securities markets is manifested particularly in the weakness of futures and options activity. There is no tradition of a traded futures market in Germany. (The Deutsche Termin-Bourse, Germany's first futures and options exchange, opened in January 1990.) Trading in options began in 1986, but is of little practical significance. In addition, short selling and margining of securities is restricted, limiting further the range of financial strategies that may be pursued in the primary market.

2.3.2. The Bond Market. The bond market is more significant in Germany than the stock market, having over eight times the new issue volume. There are five main categories of bonds in the German markets. The largest single component consists of the so-called communal bonds (Kommunalobligationen), representing about 36% of outstanding bond debt. These bonds are issued by banks and backed by public sector loans. Thus, they represent indirect debt placement by public entities.[9]

The second largest component consists of the direct placements of public authorities (state and federal governments and agencies). These bonds represent about 31% of the DM 1.2 trillion of outstanding bonds.

Third in importance are mortgage bonds (Pfandbriefe), representing about 17% of outstanding bond debt. As discussed earlier, these bonds may not be issued by commercial banks, and are issued instead by mortgage banks. Real estate, shipping, and other mortgages are the collateral for these bonds.

Sonstige Bankschuldverschreibungen is the fourth category, made up of noncommunal and nonmortgage bank bonds that make up about 10% of the total bonds outstanding. These represent mainly the unsecured issue of debt by banks in the form of bearer bonds (Inhaberschuldverschreibungen). Bearer bonds have historically had the advantage that they were not subject to the high reserve requirements of registered bonds.

The fifth category consists of the bonds of the special-purpose banks. Representing about 6% of total bonds outstanding, these bonds consist of mortgage bonds, unsecured bearer bonds, and communal bonds. They are issued by the special function banks described earlier.

Finally, a conspicuously small component of the bond market is the industrial bond. Domestic borrowing by German corporations or companies in the bond markets represents less than 0.5% of all German bonds outstanding. Euro-DM borrowings by corporations, while larger (equivalent of 2% of all domestic outstandings) are still small by international standards. This is vivid testimony to the importance of bank loans (as opposed to direct floatations) in the raising of funds by German corporations. Indeed, even in the Euro-DM bond market itself, outstanding bond issues by banks are twice as large as those for corporations.

Banks also figure prominently in the underwriting of the bonds of the German government. A fixed syndicate of banks must subscribe an entire new public issue. This syndicate, the Konsortialgesellschaft, presently consists of 95 banks (including, since 1986, foreign banks).

2.3.3. The Schuldscheine Market. Of almost equal importance to the bond market in Germany is the market in "certificates of indebtedness" or Schuldscheinedarlehen. Schuldscheine are negotiable promissory note or loan certificates. They are not securities, but can be traded by transfer or assignment of title to all or part of the loan. Simple letters of reassignment are created to effect transfers. In essence, they are negotiable private placement promissory notes.

They represent a very significant component of outstanding debt instruments in Germany. Outstanding Schuldscheine are, in relative terms, about two fifths the size of the domestic German bond market. Schuldscheine are issued mainly by the public sector, and banks and other credit intermediaries. Their term is variable (up to about 15 years) and they generally are issued at a fixed interest rate. While issued in a pri-

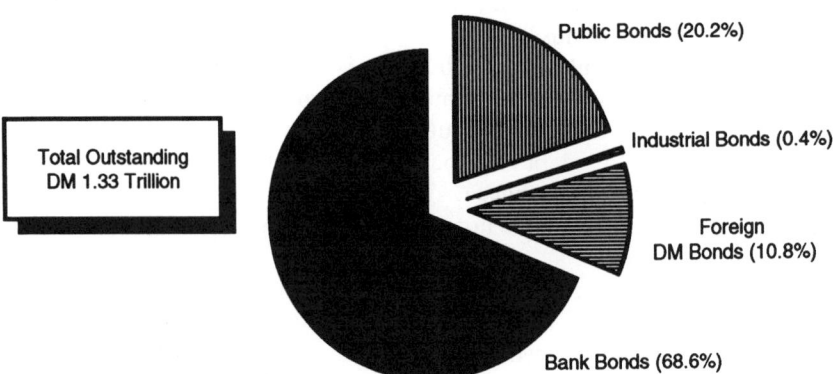

Figure 11-2. Share of DM Bonds Outstanding By Issuer, 1988.

vate placement market, there is an active over-the-counter market in Schuldscheine. The main participants are institutions, since the minimum denomination is DM 1 million.

The existence and prominence of Schuldscheine are testimony to the burden of regulation and other underwriting costs on traditional bond issuance. Because Schuldscheine are loans, rather than securities, they are exempt from registration and documentation requirements of listed securities. In addition, they do not need approval (as do registered securities) of the Ministry of Finance.

It is estimated that the legal and documentary expenses associated with bond issuance in Germany result in the unusually high underwriting fees of 2% to 2.5%. By comparison, the Schuldscheine can be issued for about one quarter of that.[10] In addition, elimination of the Ministry of Finance approval delay means that Schuldscheine can be issued more rapidly than straight bond debt.

It is tempting, but inappropriate, to attribute the weakness of these primary markets entirely to the dominance of financial intermediaries. A number of features of German law, tax policy, and regulation have contributed to the nascency of primary instrument markets. German law, for example, treats options and futures contracts as "gambling" contracts, limiting their enforceability. In addition, whole classes of potential writers and holders of derivative securities (such as insurance companies and mutual funds) are prohibited from engaging in options and futures activity. Tax policy also limits the attractiveness of high-value, high-turnover, short-term financial assets. Germany levies a Stock Exchange Turnover Tax (Boersenumsatzsteuer) of between 0.1% and 0.25% of the market value of traded securities. Finally, the lack of basic consumer protections (such as the absence of sanctions against insider trading) reduces public confidence in the stock markets.

These considerations undoubtedly are important in shaping German financial markets. Indeed, the fact that some DM-denominated financial contracts are traded outside of Germany, but not inside, attests to their importance. (In 1988, for example, a futures contract on German government bonds was introduced on a London futures exchange.) Nonetheless, the fact that significant reform of primary securities markets in Germany has not occurred suggests that financial intermediaries are able to service adequately the instrumentation needs of Germany's financial markets. Thus, the state of German primary security markets may illustrate, to a minor extent at least, a potential side effect of universally empowered banking.

2.4. The Payments System

The payment system in Germany also differs in important ways from many other western banking systems. The distinctions are both in the retail aspects of the payment system and at the wholesale, or interbank level.

2.4.1. Retail Payments Technology. The most distinctive feature of retail payments patterns is the lack of reliance on paper check transactions. In Germany, paper checks account for less than 9% of all retail funds transfers. In the United States, in contrast, paper checks account for over 90% of all retail funds transfers. Germans rely, instead, on the credit transfer, by which a customer gives an order to his bank to credit the account of a payee. Credit transfers account for about 55% of total retail payments volume (by number). About half of these, in turn, are in paperless form, and about half involve written transfer orders.[11]

Credit transfers evolved out of conventions employed in the savings bank and postal giro sectors. They appear to have dominated check-based transfers because of their superior cost-effectiveness in the German institutional environment. In particular, the German central banking authorities did not create, early on, a centralized, multilateral check-clearing and settlement system. (Such a system was not introduced by the Bundesbank, in fact, until 1950.) Absent such a system, banks needed a transfer mechanism that minimized the burden as regards failed or returned items. A credit transfer system does this because credit transfers do not proceed unless the payer's account balance is sufficient to support the transfer. (Credit transfers in Germany are irrevocable.) Thus, except in unusual circumstances, there is no "return item" in a credit transfer system.

The use of checks has increased somewhat in recent years with the introduction of check guarantee cards (which give check transfers the same irrevocable quality offered by credit transfers). However, the ease of automation of the credit transfer system and the relatively unimportant value of check float to the payer has kept the check from being an important transfer medium. The system lends itself to further automation and the use of debit and credit card at point-of-sale terminals. At the retail level, fully 60% of all transactions are already paperless (versus less than 10% in the United States), and this percentage is likely to grow.

2.4.2. Interbank Funds Transfer. Interbank transfers occur in a number of ways. The large banks, the savings bank and cooperative bank associations, and the postal giro systems operate internal funds transfer systems.

Other transfers can use the facilities of the Bundesbank of clearing and settling interbank obligations. Credit transfers, checks, and direct debits can be handled by the central bank's giro network. Once paid to the account of the payee, the transfer is irrevocable. In sharp contrast to the U.S. policy in this area, however, the Bundesbank does not take any risks on interbank transfers; it only executes payments if the requisite cover exists. Partly as a result of these considerations, the total value of interbank transfers in Germany (about $35 trillion) is very small compared to the U.S. total (about $300 trillion).

2.4.3. Securities Transfer. Securities transfer in Germany occurs predominantly in registered (noncertificate) form. The credit institutions jointly operate collective securities deposit banks or security-clearing associations to process securities transactions. Settlement and delivery occurs two days after the transaction. The security-clearing associations present settlement position sheets to the local Bundesbank branch for settlement. Securities settlement receives the same credit treatment by the central bank as do other interbank funds transfers.

3. The Role of Banks in the German Economy

The German banks are much more prominent features of their economy than are banks in most other Western industrialized countries. This springs partly from historical accident, and partly from the regulatory environment in which banks in Germany have operated over the last century or so. The implications of this prominence on the efficiency of the financial sector, on the efficiency of the German economy, and on the concentration of economic and political power has been debated in recent years. In this section, we discuss the elements of these debates.

3.1. Universal Banking and Economic Development

Prior to 1848, German banking houses were organized as proprietorships or private partnerships. These private banks had no ability to raise equity funds from other than private sources.

An economic crisis in that year prompted the Prussian government to issue the first of many corporate bank charters (to A. Schaafhausen'scher Bankverein). These so-called joint-stock banks not only had the ability to float shares to acquire new capital, but also enjoyed both investment and commercial banking powers.

Having been founded partly to perform a commercial development role, the Kreditbanken were permitted to develop intimate relationships with German industry—an intimacy that continues today. In particular, there were no antitrust laws against interlocking directorates: German banks were permitted to require representation on supervisory boards of firms to whom they lent funds. In addition, a lead bank or consortium of banks could demand that all of the borrower's business be conducted through the lead lender. These features gave the lenders both information and control, both of which were valuable in the risky investment environment that prevailed in the early days of German industrialization.

In return, the borrowers obtained very flexible, current-account-type credit. Specifically, on the security of the real or financial assets of the firm, the banks offered lines of credit combined with interest-earning deposit accounts. The loan rates and the deposit rates were linked by a simple interest-rate spread. The industrial loan customers of the banks used these flexible sources funds to finance fixed and working-capital investments.

In general, the relationship between Germany's banks and her industry proved a productive one, although overexuberant lending is sometimes blamed for the so-called Company Promotion crisis that started in Vienna in 1873 (and propagated to Germany, the U.S., and the U.K.). Although many failures occurred among Germany's young banks in this period, the rationale of the joint stock company or the basic relationship between banks and industry was not questioned. Indeed, although the ground was laid for the consolidation of German banking that persists today in the Big Three, there were more banks after the crisis than before 1870.[12]

The German economy grew very rapidly throughout the turn of the century and up to the First World War. Historians and economists such as Riesser, Gerschenkron, and Schumpeter have attributed the rapidity of German growth in large measure to intermediation services provided by the Kreditbanken. In recent years, this assumption has been challenged (most notably by Neuberger and Stokes) by examining the statistical link between the use of current-account credit and macroeconomic growth. At best, however, the models and data employed in these tests are weak, and the conventional wisdom that the universal banks played an important role in economic development seems intact.

3.2. Universal Banking and Financial Market Efficiency

The relationship between German universal banking and the efficiency of financial markets also has been debated over the years. One concern is that the dominance of the banking sector has resulted in poorly developed direct placement and nonbank venture-capital markets. In Germany, for example, banks provide 60% of external corporate financing, as against only about 30% in the United States. Similarly, banks in Germany supply about 45% of all venture capital, whereas the figure is only about 10% or so in the United States.

A related concern is that universal banking has resulted in a too-powerful nexus of relationships among the largest German industrial corporations and the banking sector. In contrast to the United States, ownership by banks of the shares of nonbank corporations is permitted in Germany. (Ownership of banks by nonbank companies is also permitted, but this appears to be unattractive in practice.)

There are limits, linked to bank capital, of the equity investment that a bank may have in a commercial firm. However, among Western banking systems, only Luxembourg has more liberal policies regarding ownership of nonbank corporations. Moreover, in addition to direct holdings of voting shares, German banks also exercise proxies on behalf of their customers, about half of whom keep their shares "on deposit" at banks (Depotstimmrecht). The result is particularly intimate interrelationships among banks and corporations.

A 1979 report by the Monopoly Commission, for example, found that banks had representatives on the boards of two thirds of the top 100 corporations, far more than their shareholdings would justify on a pro rata basis. Although direct holdings of voting shares made up only about 5% of the total for the large firms, when proxy powers are considered, banks vote nearly 40% of the outstanding shares of these large firms. In addition, although the commercial banks, in the aggregate, only hold about 5% of their assets in the form of corporation equity, the ownership is highly concentrated, with the top five banks holding over 50% of all nonbank equity.[13]

These patterns of ownership and control have raised the political-economic concern that the German banking system may function primary for the benefit of a few large corporations, to the surfeit of smaller firms seeking financing. It should also be pointed out, however, that when the German banks exercise their considerable authority over corporate customers by removing management or pressing for other changes, they also are criticized for excessive power over the industrial sector. An earlier report of the Monopoly Commission (the Gessler Report) had recommended, for these reasons, that the participation by banks in industrial companies be limited to 25%. At this time, however, these recommendations have not been implemented.

Accumulation of political power aside, it seems unlikely that the German banking market is inefficiently structured as a result of universal banking per se; entry into German banking is relatively unconstrained, and credit institutions of all types obtain the same access to universal powers. This entry is likely to restrain exploitation of economic power by the large banks. Indeed, many of the cooperative and public-sector banking systems exist, arguably, to provide services to areas shunned by the large commercial banks.

In contrast to the view that broad bank powers lead to inefficient allocation of credit, Pozdena has recently argued that there are important theoretical reasons to expect universal banking, in fact, to improve credit allocation.[14] This follows from the argument that bank lending can be superior to open-market financing for certain types of projects because banks can economically monitor those projects on an ongoing basis, whereas credit markets cannot. This argument implies that if banks can improve their monitoring—as German banks have done by gaining entrance to the internal decision-making processes of the firm—they can better identify and finance projects.

It may also be the case that by simultaneously lending to and owning the equity of a corporation, German banks can help control inefficiency arising from "agency" problems in corporations. Specifically, if the various liabilities of a firm are held by separate investors, the only mechanism for controlling inefficient management behavior would be for liability holders to remove incompetent management through proxy fights. These mechanisms are cumbersome, and debt and equity holders may have conflicting interests in effecting such change. If, instead, a bank were to own the full range of classes of the firm's debt and equity, the bank would be in a position to gain progressively greater authority to intercede in the management of the firm as dividend and interest payment performance deteriorated. Moreover, because the debt holder is also the equity holder, there are no conflicts between holders of debt and equity securities to impede a needed reorganization.

It is consistent with this rationale for universal banking that bank loans are the major source of industrial credit in Germany. The purely "open" form of corporate financing seems unable to compete with firms financed with the help of universal banks; indeed, Cable has found that universal bank affiliations are correlated with better financial performance of industrial firms. It is also expected that banks' most durable relationships would be with larger firms, since agency problems are more serious and complex for such organizations. Finally, this theory is consistent with the relative rarity of corporate takeovers in Germany. This would be expected to follow from the role of universal banking as a channel for resolving corporate control problems.

3.3. The German Central Bank System

To understand fully the role of banks in the German economy, it is also important to understand the role of the central bank (the Deutsche Bundesbank) with respect to the private banking system. In contrast to other countries, Germany has no treasury distinct from the central bank; the Deutsche Bundesbank, therefore, is the only monetary authority and federal fiscal agent in the German economy.

3.3.1. Origins and Basic Characteristics. Until the middle of the nineteenth century, more than 30 monetary authorities were in existence in Germany, issuing more than 140 different notes and coins. With the formation of the German Reich in 1871, the various banks and currencies were unified. The Central Bank of Prussia was changed to the Deutsche Reichsbank, the first central bank of Germany. Originally, the Reichsbank was strictly under government control. It became independent in 1924 after the "Great Inflation." In 1939, once again, the bank was brought under total government control.

In 1945, after the cessation of hostilities, the Allies closed the Deutsche Reichsbank and prohibited central banking. From 1945 to 1948, Germany was under the control of the Allies, and separated into four zones. In the three zones of the Western Allies, state-level central banks were established and the Bank Deutscher Länder (literally, Bank of German States) as a central facility for the state banks and for the issuance of notes was formed. This so-called two-stage central bank system gave considerable independence to the state central banks, on the model of the U.S. Federal Reserve System.

In 1957, the Central Bank Law was passed, founding the Deutsche Bundesbank (literally, German Central Bank) to replace the Bank Deutscher Länder. The state central banks lost their independence, and became pure branches of the Bundesbank. The present Deutsche Bundesbank system consists of the central facility in Frankfurt and 11 state central banks with 200 branches. The Bundesbank regained independence over government control, and under the Central Bank Law, must only support economic policy in general, and maintain a stable DM value. As the government's bank, the Bundesbank provides the usual deposit services, as well as providing agency services relating to government bonds, foreign currencies, and other similar transactions. Germane to the topic at hand, it also serves as a lender-of-last-resort to the banking system.

3.3.2. Banks and Monetary Control. Unlike in the U.S., where open-market operations provide the main channel of monetary control, the German central bank relies more heavily on rediscount and reserve requirement policies.[15]

This creates a very visible link between monetary policy and bank portfolio performance. In Germany, the rediscount facility permitted by section 19 the Central Bank Law gives German banks the right to sell special bills to the Bundesbank up to a limit fixed by the Bundesbank. These bills are mainly trade bills, of three months or less of maturity, of solvent payees, or collateralized loans of three-month maturity. The quotas are linked to banks' nonborrowed reserves. Manipulation of these rediscount quotas, the qualitative characteristics of rediscountable bills, and the rate of rediscount is an important means of monetary control.

The second, very important channel of monetary control is via regulation of reserve requirements. German banks are required to hold noninterest-earning balances at the Bundesbank. The required reserve ratios are very high, and vary by type of deposit (demand, time, and savings), place of deposit (being generally higher for central or branch deposits), and by the amount of bank deposits. In addition, during some periods, there are different (generally higher) reserve requirements on the deposits of nonresidents or on increases of these deposits. This latter regulation is employed by the Bundesbank to sterilize the inflationary effects of foreign capital inflows via an expansion of German base money.

The effect of high reserve requirements, not surprisingly, has been to stimulate holding of idle household balances in nonreservable accounts. Thus, shifts into longer-term savings deposits, investment funds, and other alternative investment vehicles can be observed in reaction to tightening of reserve requirements. The focus of German monetary policy on required reserves ratios thus has important market-share implications for German banks and other credit intermediaries.

From 1957 up to now, the most important objective of the Bundesbank's monetary policy was to keep inflation rates down. Except for some short periods in the 1970s, it was able to achieve the economic goal of stable prices better than nearly all industrial countries (except Switzerland). This credible and generally accepted anti-inflationary policy had, beside others, one important effect for the liability structure of

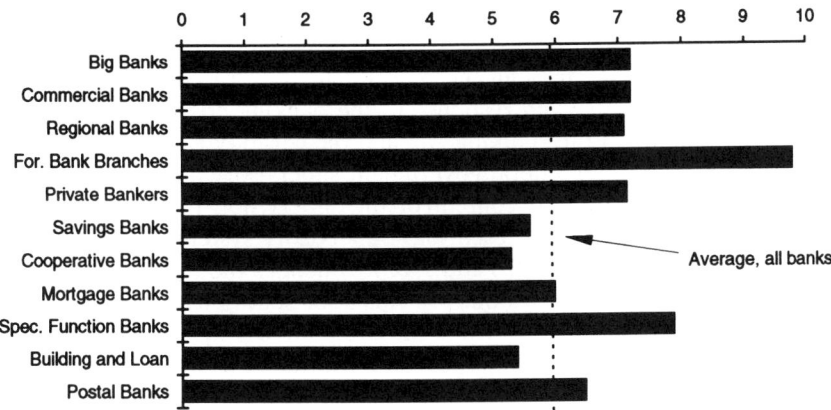

Figure 11-3. Effective Reserve Ratios, January 1989 (as Percent of Reservable Liabilities).

German banks: most of German households keep their savings in the form of savings deposits at German banks, not as stocks or bonds. Interest rates for savings deposits are lower and more stable over time than bond rates. As a consequence, the banking system is supported by a cheap supply of financial funds and, therefore, is able to meet loan demand at competitive conditions—another reason for the minor importance of stock and bond activities in Germany.

4. The Supervision of Banks

Despite its size and diversity, the postwar German system has been reasonably free of episodes of bank failures. There likely are many explanations for this, including the relatively consistent and robust growth of the German economy, the geographical diversification enjoyed by German lenders, and the intimate relations enjoyed between bankers and their commercial customers. In addition, however, German banking policy appears to have been designed to mobilize market disciplinary forces as well as the forces of a firmly administered supervisory system.

In this section, we discuss the role of the supervisory system, the central bank, and debt and equity holders in supervising the safety and soundness of the German banking system.

4.1. The Supervisory Environment

The basic legislation enabling the present supervisory system was established in the early 1930s in response to the banking crisis of the time. It was at that time that the Banking Act and the Custody Business Act were passed, first giving the federal government supervisory authority.

The legal structure and content of the supervision has changed over time. At the heart of the present-day supervisory system is the Banking Act of 1961 (amended in 1976 and 1985). It defines the organizations that constitute "banks," and lays out principles for setting banking ratios and standards. Articles 10 and 10a of the Act, for example, point out the basic principles for establishing adequate capital, and provide definitions of capital for the various legal bank forms. Similarly, articles 13 to 20 present rules for limited credit exposure.

4.1.1. The Federal Banking Supervisory Authority. Also laid out in the Banking Act is the supervisory structure itself. Today, the locus of supervisory authority for all banks is the Federal Banking Supervisory Authority (Bundesaufsichtsamt für das Kreditwesen) or FBSA. The FBSA was established in 1961, when the Banking Act was passed, as an independent government authority, nominally within the Ministry of Finance.

The functions granted the FBSA by the Banking Act are fourfold. First, the Banking Act requires that all institutions doing banking business be licensed. The FBSA is the sole issuer of those licenses and has the authority to determine the adequacy of capital, managerial, and other resources of would-be licensees, including foreign banks. It also has the authority to remove licenses.

Second, the FBSA promulgates standards relating to capital and liquidity adequacy, foreign-exchange exposure, and credit exposure. While the Banking Act lays out specific standards with respect to some ratios and requirements, the FBSA has some latitude to establish other standards. The power to regulate interest rates on deposit rates or loans, however, was eliminated in 1967.

The third function of the FBSA is to collect timely financial information and conduct periodic audits of credit institutions. The same reports, in general, are required of all credit institutions and are weekly, monthly, quarterly, or annual in frequency. Weekly reports, for example, are required on foreign short-term credits and liabilities. Loan commitment reports, balance sheet reports indicating compliance with banking ratios, and reports on the condition of foreign assets and liabilities are required monthly. Reports on the condition of domestic loans, sovereign debt, and other loans are required quarterly. Overall financial and statistical summaries are required to be reported annually.

The final role of the FBSA is to intervene in the event of a capital inadequacy and endangerment of deposits. Its powers are quite broad in this respect. In addition to the authority to withdraw a banking license, the FBSA can conduct surprise audits, require activities to be suspended or limited, appoint substitute managers to take control, and force liquidation of a bank.

4.1.2. Financial and Accounting Standards.

There is a strong emphasis on capital adequacy in the German banking system, both from a regulatory and accounting viewpoint. The Banking Act (the so-called principle 1 of section 10) requires, specifically, that all banks maintain a maximum ratio of loans and investments to equity of 18 to 1. In addition, the aggregate book value of equity participations in real estate, shares, and other forms may not exceed the bank's equity capital.

Until 1985, principle 1 was applicable legally only on an unconsolidated basis. After the failure of Schröder, Münchmeyer, Hengst, and Company in 1983, however, the Banking Act was amended to recognize the burden that nonbanking activities can place on capital. Presently (with a transition period ending 1991), banks must consolidate all banking and nonbanking activities in which they have control for the purposes of meeting principle 1.[16] This has been an important burden on the larger, integrated universal banks, a burden reflected in the significant growth in capital that has occurred since 1985.[17]

Germany's response to the recent Basil agreement on risk-based capital requirements also is typical of their orientation toward strong capital. This international agreement on bank capital standards employs asset risk classifications that require greater or lesser capital to be held against those assets depending upon the risk potential of that type of asset. The weighting scheme formally embraces only credit risk. The German Finance Ministry, however, has taken those standards one step further, requiring capital to be held against price risks and interest-rate risk. The Germans began implementing the standard in October 1989.

The financial standards imposed by the FBSA are quite specific. For example, at the present time (before implementation of international risk-based capital standards), the minimum capital-to-asset ratio is 5.6%. Liquidity standards are similarly very specific, attempting to avoid serious cash-flow mismatches between long-term assets and long-term liabilities. And foreign exchange exposure at the close of each business day may not exceed 30% to 40% of equity (depending upon the maturity of the asset).

Finally, FBSA regulations on loan concentration link loans to specific equity ratios. A single large credit (a loan exceeding 15% of equity), for example, may not exceed 50% of total equity, with other restrictions on the total number of large credits.

4.1.3. Entry Conditions. Entry into the business of banking in Germany is relatively unrestricted. The Banking Act permits minimum capital standards, as well as minimum standards regarding the owners' personal and professional qualifications and management staffing. At the present time, the official minimum capital requirement is about $3 million ($1.5 million if deposits are not to be taken). In practice, however, new banks are not permitted without at least $5 million in capital.

Entry from abroad is similarly unrestricted. The few restrictions that existed historically on the participation of foreign banks and branches (in the securities markets, in particular) have been largely eliminated. Once licensed, foreign banks and branches enjoy the full range of universal powers in Germany. In addition, as was stated earlier, there are no restrictions on the geography of banking activity within Germany.

4.2. The Central Bank Role

The central bank of Germany (Deutsche Bundesbank) is involved in, but not central to, bank supervision and regulation. The FBSA determines and implements the system of supervisory controls, such as the reporting requirements and compliance standards. The Bundesbank, for its part, assists in the evaluation of these reports, but leaves implementation of sanctions to the FBSA. The Bundesbank also operates the Central Risks Office, which receives information on large loans (1 million DM or larger) which it shares with the FBSA to permit surveillance of large loan concentration.

The role of the Deutsche Bundesbank as a lender of last resort to banks with liquidity problems generally is quite similar to the role played by other central banks in this respect. That is, banks with eligible collateral may seek to resolve liquidity problems by obtaining credit at the central bank. Granting of discount window credit is subject to a stringent quota system. If a bank encounters financial conditions that cause it to breach these quotas, therefore, it must resort to the Lombard credit facility of the Bundesbank. Lombard credits are restricted in supply and available only at a 1 to 2 percentage-point penalty rate above the discount rate.

The stringency of the rediscount and Lombard credit systems likely imposes useful discipline on German banks; in effect, the central bank cannot be expected to provide significant or long-term credit, and banks must take prudent steps to preserve their liquidity in the face of adverse circumstances. After the failure of Bankhaus I. D. Herstatt in 1974, however, many German bankers felt that the central bank's lender-of-last-resort facility had failed to be flexible enough to deal with the cascade of liquidity problems that followed.

The Liko-Bank liquidity facility mentioned earlier was established as a consequence of the Herstatt failure. Over 150 million DM in Liko-Bank credit was used to avoid a calamitous collapse of Schröder, Münchmeyer, Hengst and Company (SMH) in 1983. It is unclear from this first major use of the Liko-Bank whether it is serving its intended purpose of bridging liquidity problems; SMH had deeply negative net worth as the result of an excessive (and apparently illegal) concentration of nonperforming loans to a single borrower.

4.3. Market and Depositor Surveillance

German banking policy reflects the desire to rely on market forces, where possible. When the Herstatt Bank failed in 1974, the German banking authorities did not intervene to compensate the bank's creditors. Even payments sent by Herstatt that had cleared, but not settled, were allowed to default. This relatively consistent policy of providing little ex post public support likely enhances the role of market and depositor discipline in restraining risk-taking at German banks.

The Herstatt incident, nonetheless, raised concern among German banking policy makers that some confidence in the banking system had been lost, and reliance on market-oriented discipline has declined somewhat in recent years. The deposit guarantee systems, for example, were purely private enterprises or consortia before 1976. Partly in reaction to Herstatt, the Banking Act amendments in 1976 brought these funds under public regulation, although they are still administered as by the private sector.

The German deposit protection fund, begun in 1966, is an industry-sponsored organization that provides insurance against depositor losses. The Federal Association of German Commercial Banks is the sponsoring organization. Both domestic deposits and deposits at the foreign branches of domestic banks are insured, although interbank deposits are not. The premium is assessed at a rate of 0.03% of total deposits.

The deposit insurance scheme, though private in origin, is intended to recognize the mutual dependency of banks on each other's financial condition. Maintenance of banking system stability is one of the stated functions of the deposit protection scheme,[18] and examination of banks for compliance with insurance-fund standards is done by the Association. This provides the industry with an opportunity to perform a limited degree of self-examination, since the insuring institution is a mutual-type organization.

It is difficult to assess the relative strength of market disciplinary forces in German banking. On the one hand, the German practice of maintaining hidden reserves (stille Reserven) might be seen as an attempt to present a stable equity structure to maintain investor confidence. (By this logic, hidden reserves are used to buffer published capital from the effects of risks taken in the portfolio, thereby communicating a stable financial picture to a presumably wary investment community.) This, in turn, suggests that German banks are disciplined to some degree by investor and/or depositor surveillance.

On the other hand, however, others report a perception that the large German banks would never be permitted to fail. This poses a potentially serious moral hazard problem that is held in check partly by the supervisory process and partly by the severity of legal sanctions against bank management. The 1976 amendments to the Banking Act increased the supervisory power of the FBSA; and under German law, violation of banking principles can be punishable by criminal penalties levied against management. Nonetheless, faced with competitive pressures from elsewhere in the world, the moral hazard problem remains, and may pose future, if not current, problems.

5. Current Issues in German Banking

The German banking system has not suffered extremely disruptive changes in its structure or performance for many years. German banks have enjoyed their broad product powers for many years, and regulations affecting pricing and entry conditions have been similarly liberal, particularly for the last two decades. Significant changes have occurred in the market shares and activities of the various credit intermediaries. However, these changes mainly have been in response to changing economic, technological, and competitive conditions, rather than sweeping regulatory changes, as in the United States.

5.1. The Power of German Banks

There appear to be several major issues confronting domestic German banking. One, alluded to above, concerns the close links between German banks and industry. Outsiders to the German banking system long have expressed concern about the potential for conflicts of interest and anticompetitive behavior in German banking as a result of the closeness of German banks and German industry. Moreover, the dominance of the banks and the consequent underdevelopment of the venture capital market in Germany is blamed for Germany's low rate of business start-ups.[19]

Interest in restricting the power of German banks has come and gone a number of times with changes in political climate. In 1987, the opposition Social Democrats proposed a number of curbs on banks' control of industrial corporations. Pressure also has come from the European Economic Community to regularize German antitrust treatment of banks. The Economics Ministry, in 1987, drafted a proposal to end the exemption that banks currently enjoy from antitrust law, for example.[20] In addition, in 1986, the Public Monopolies Commission proposed limiting outside directorships held by bankers, and limiting bank ownership of industrial companies to 5%. These proposals, reminiscent of those that followed the Gessler Commission in 1976, are idle politically at the moment. If implemented, however, they might crucially alter the monitoring advantages of universal-type banking.

5.1.1. Banks and Corporate Control. One aspect of the debate concerns the processes by which corporate control is exerted in Germany in contrast to the U.S. and most other European countries. In the U.S. and the U.K. in particular, active share trading and active takeover markets are seen as bringing important discipline to the corporate sector. In Germany, in contrast, true takeovers are relatively rare, and there has been only one hostile takeover (the takeover of Feldmuehle Nobel in 1989 by Flick). Management buy-outs and buy-ins are similarly less common in Germany than the U.S. and the U.K.[21]

The paucity of takeovers can be attributed to a number of factors, but central in the explanation is the fact that banks play a greater role in stock ownership and management of German corporations than do their counterparts in the U.S., the U.K., and elsewhere in Europe. Banks not only have representatives on the supervisory boards of corporations, but in some cases serve as board chairmen. This raises the natural question whether the German model is more or less successful than the U.S. or

U.K. model in encouraging efficient corporate behavior. The question has become more than academic, with the attention of the European Community (EC) presently focused on whether to "harmonize" its policy toward takeovers.

Recent studies of control changes in German corporations find that executive dismissals, changes in controlling ownership, and other indicators of the vigor of corporate discipline processes are weaker in Germany than in the U.K. or France. On the other hand, the strong performance of the German economy certainly suggests that the corporate control exerted by banks has not been entirely dysfunctional. Moreover, it is possible that fewer instances of control and management disturbance are observed because fewer are necessary to stimulate good managerial performance.

5.2. Changes in Competition

A second issue of considerable importance in Germany concerns the increasing competition faced by the commercial banks, both from foreign competition and from other types of credit institutions in Germany. Germany's entry barriers traditionally have been low, and many credit institutions—foreign and domestic—enjoy access to universal powers. Insurance companies also have been recent entrants into conventional banking and vice versa. The Big Three, for example, each have an affiliation with an insurer; Dresdner Bank is affiliated with Allianz, Europe's largest insurer. Meanwhile, dedicated special-purpose sectors—such as the building and loan sector—have grown less quickly than integrated enterprises.[22]

As exploitation of universal powers proceeds, some of the distinctions among the various banking sectors in Germany have begun to blur, and competition for the traditional business of the commercial banks has increased. This, in turn, has resulted in sharp squeezes on the profitability of the large German banks, and a reduction in their portfolio market share. Indeed, the big banks' deposit market share fell from 12.6% in 1978 to 10.1% in 1988.

In contrast, the credit cooperative sector experienced increases in deposit market share from 17.1% to 20.5%, as a result of newly aggressive participation in interbank lending and securities investment. Similarly, the mortgage banking sector increased its market share from 7.2% to 10% by more aggressive investment in money markets in addition to traditional mortgage assets. (Other relatively strong sectors were the regional banks, while the savings banks and foreign banks maintained their positions, and the regional giro institutions suffered below-average business growth.)[23]

To some extent, these changes in portfolio market shares overstate the deterioration in the importance of the commercial banks, since these banks remain premier in the investment banking and bond markets. However, Germany's capital markets recently have opened up to foreign participation as the few remaining constraints on foreign commercial and investment banks have gradually disappeared. In May 1985, for example, foreign banks were permitted to be lead managers of new DM bond issues. In April 1986, the federal debt underwriting syndicate was expanded to include foreign banks. These changes have had the effect of increasing the level of effective foreign competition in German banking markets.

Recent public policy seems to have proceeded oblivious to the increased sensitivity of German financial markets to international competition. When withholding of tax on domestic interest income was introduced in 1988, for example, borrowing in domestic DM bond markets declined by one half, while DM-denominated foreign securities (free from the withholding tax) soared.[24] Although the unpopularity and perverse effects of the tax prompted a rapid reversal of policy (the tax was removed in July 1989), some observers of German banking express concern that German banking markets suffer too much interference from regulators and policymakers. Burdensome securities registration procedures also are argued to be responsible for the current weakness of domestic issuance of industrial bonds.[25]

Despite these setbacks, universal banking remains an important sector of the German economy, employing 25% more of the labor force in 1988 than it did ten years earlier. Its total contribution to German value-added is also estimated to have grown about 15% in the same period. Activity in Germany by foreign-owned banks, while important, remains a relatively low 5% of total banking assets.[26]

This mixed picture of the state of competitiveness of German banking is nicely summarized in a recent editorial in the International Financing Review:

> ...The German financial system is in fetters: it is perceived to be underdeveloped and anachronistic. This view, held by many, is truly a paradox, given the significant contribution of Germany to the global economy. There are reasons for Germany's financial services hysteresis; much of the blame for the lack of progress is laid at the door-step of the German regulatory auth-

orities. That said, the German authorities have overhauled the system in a series of moves that has been both modernizing and liberalizing....[27]

5.3. German Banks in a Globalized Banking Environment

A third contemporary issue for German banks is their role in the global banking community. It seems clear that the German banks stand handsomely poised to participate in the continuing internationalization of financial markets, both in a European, and broader international, context. In 1992, the members of the EC will implement a far-reaching integration of European financial markets. The German banks are uniquely positioned to take advantage of the new opportunities posed by the liberalization of European financial markets. The basic banking model adopted by the EC is the very universal banking with which Germans, more than any other Europeans, have long-standing experience.

The Home Rule and Reciprocity principles governing the EC integration plan work significantly to the advantage of Germany. The Home Rule principle states that branches of EC-country banks may provide abroad the same services they are empowered to provide at home. Clearly, this principle is advantageous to the most broadly empowered banks as in Germany; indeed, these banks may lead the cutting edge of banking reform outside of Germany.

The Reciprocity principle, meanwhile, states that banking systems outside the EC will be treated as they, reciprocally, treat EC-member banks. Thus, European banking markets may enjoy some protection from strong Japanese and American banks until those banking systems embrace expanded powers. This may reduce, temporarily at least, the competition from other entrants faced by German bank expansions.

5.3.1. Financial Strength. German banks also are financially poised to take advantage of global opportunities and to survive application of more stringent capital standards. First, German banks have very strong capital positions. Deutsche Bank, Bayerische Vereinsbank, Frankfurther Hypothekenbank, and Landeskreditbank Banden-Württemberg all enjoy AAA Standard and Poors ratings. Indeed, as a group, there are more German banks enjoying this rating than any other banking group in the world.

In addition, traditionally high German capital standards, coupled with the fact that subordinated debt has not been included in German bank capital, apparently leave the German banks able to easily meet the 8% B.I.S. capital adequacy standard. This leaves German banks free to consider expansion or acquisition opportunities while other banks must pause to build up capital. Their financial strength was underscored by recent revelations of the scale of their hidden reserves. Dresdner Bank, for example, revealed hidden reserves equal to about 30% of capital in 1989. Deutsche Bank's hidden reserves totalled about 56% of shareholder equity.[28]

Their holdings of Third World debt also are light; German banks in the aggregate, hold only 6% of the outstanding total to the five biggest Latin American debtors, for example, versus fully 36% in the hands of U.S. banks and 13% in Japanese banks. German banks also are said to have reserved extensively against the debt. Deutsche Bank, for example, is now 77% provisioned against its LDC exposure, and could provision the remaining amount on only three months earnings.[29] U.S. banks, in comparison, have reserved less than one third of their total exposure.

Second, German banks have extensive experience in establishing and maintaining a foreign presence. The 110 or so foreign branches of German banks currently are equivalent in size to about 10% of total commercial bank assets. The Germans also have been leading proponents of joint ventures of the European banking consortia such as ABECOR, EBIC, and Europartners. Combined with strong financial resources, this experience has resulted in bold recent moves, such as Deutsche Banks's acquisition of Bank of America's Italian retail banking operations in 1986.

Against these advantages must be weighed the disadvantages of the nascent state of German securities markets. U.S., British, and Japanese investment banking firms have far superior experience in nonbanking markets than do their German universal bank counterparts. This will continue to be a major handicap to the Germans' taking the lead in the continuing globalization of financial markets.

5.4. The Challenge of Unification

These limitations may be accentuated by the recent moves toward reunification of West and East Germany. Revitalizing East German housing and industrial capital, and restructuring East German public sector obligations (such as pension funds and welfare programs) is estimated to require between DM 250 billion ($150 million) and DM 1 trillion ($590 billion) in the next decade. As was made clear in the May 16, 1990, announcement of the DM 115 billion German Unity Fund, it is the intention of the German goverment to finance the costs of reunification via existing budget surpluses and funds raised in the capital market—not taxes or monetary expansion.[28]

German financial institutions are likely to enjoy some comparative advantage in monitoring the obligations associated with these reforms. Deutsche Bank and others already have begun multibranch operations in East Germany, far ahead of non-German institutions. However, the sheer scale of the restructuring required poses significant challenges for the German banking and securities markets. Only about $5 billion a year is raised today in German equity markets, and another $30 to $40 billion in the bond markets. The rest (between 60% and 70% of the total, historically) is raised via the German banking system. German banks clearly will be challenged to provide the financing involved, and there may be further stimulus to increased international outreach of the big German banks, and further pressure to deregulate German securities markets.

Given the historical conservatism of the German central bank, it is unlikely that any West German budgetary deficits will be financed by monetary expansion. More likely, the increased credit demands will be permitted to drive up German interest rates and the exchange value of the DM. The result may cause difficulties for some classes of German financial institutions, such as the mortgage intermediaries, with fixed interest obligation assets. In addition, the reduced competitiveness of German business (because of the DM appreciation), may cause selected difficulties for some banks in this strongly export-oriented economy.

Notes

1. Kreditwesengesetz, amended 1976 and 1985.

2. The organizational taxonomy is the one employed by the German Banking Association, Cologne, in their publication *The Banking System in Germany*, Bank-Verlag GmbH, Köln, 1987. This section of this chapter draws heavily on that publication. Other major sources of information for this section include: "The Universal Banks of West Germany: Competitive Strategies Begin to Emerge," Salomon Brothers, New York, 1987; "Country Report, German Banking," International Bank Credit Analysis, Ltd., London, various dates; "Banking in Germany," Peat Marwick Mitchell & Co., Frankfurt, various dates; and "Selected Financial Centres, Summary of Banking and Tax Regulation," Price Waterhouse, 1988.

3. Banks must be authorized by individual shareholders to engage in proxy voting (Depotstimmrecht). According to the Monopoly Commission, the voting of proxies is common only among the largest banks. See Monopolkommission, Fortschreitende Konzentration bei Grossunternehmen, Baden-Baden, 1978.

4. Notable holdings include, for example, Deutsche Bank's 75% ownership in Horten AG, a retail chain, and Dresdner Bank's 25% share in Hapag-Lloyd shipping.
5. "Partly Private?" *The Banker*, May 1984, p. 15.
6. Hypothekenbankengesetz, 1963, amended 1968, 1974, and 1988.
7. "Equities: Bellicose Exchanges," *International Financing Review*, May 1989, p. 22.
8. *Ibid.*
9. This discussion of German bond markets draws heavily on Fage, P. and T. Hannigan, *The Deutsche Mark Bond Markets*, London: Credit Suisse First Boston, October 1988.
10. Fage, P. and T. Hannigan, *op cit.*, part V.
11. Bank for International Settlements, *Payment Systems in Eleven Developed Countries*, New York: Bank Administration Institute, May 1989.
12. Pohl, M., "The Deutsche Bank During the Company Promotion Crisis," in M. Pohl (ed.), *Studies in Economic and Monetary Problems and on Banking History*, nos. 1–22. Mainz: Hase and Koehler, 1988, pp. 277–296.
13. Grundsatzfragen der Kreditwirtschaft, Bonn: Schriftenreihe des Bundesministeriums der Finanzen, May 1979.
14. Pozdena, R., "Commerce and Banking: The German Case," *Weekly Letter* (Federal Reserve Bank of San Francisco: San Francisco), December 18, 1987.
15. The reason for the relatively unimportant role of open-market operations in German monetary policy is primarily a historical one. German financing of World War II expenditures had been through print money rather than selling bonds, and in the currency reform of 1948, all of the liabilities of the central government were devalued to zero. The result was that no government bonds were available for open-market operations of the central bank (although some of the instruments of the currency reform were converted to Mobilization Paper, which was used for open market operations). Although the supply of government debt has changed since then, the emphasis on rediscounting of private debt remains.
16. The amended section 10 of the Banking Act requires consolidation if the bank has an interest of 40% or more, or an otherwise controlling influence.
17. Data from the Deutsche Bundesbank suggest that the published capital-to-asset ratio for the big commercial banks has increased from about 5.2% in 1984 to almost 6.5%. The regional banks have increased their capital from 4.2% to 4.8% in the same period.
18. Section 2 of the Bylaws of the Deposit Protection Fund states that the fund's purpose includes preventing ". . . impairment of confidence in private banks."
19. "Why Germany's Growth is Slow," *New York Times*, December 31, 1987, p. 25.
20. The exemption is contained in paragraph 102 of the Cartel Act.
21. J. Franks and C. Mayer, "Capital Markets and Corporate Control: A Study of France, Germany and the U,K.," *Economic Policy*, April 1990, pp. 191–231.
22. This trend toward one-stop financial enterprises is referred to as the *all-finance argument* in Germany.
23. Report of the Deutsche Bundesbank, 1988.
24. *Ibid.*
25. Sections 795 and 808a of the Civi Code require extensive information and lengthy steps in securities registration.
26. "Longer Term Trends in the Banking Sector and Market Position of the Individual Categories of Banks," Monthly Report of the Deutsche Bundesbank, April 1989.
27. "German Banking and Finance: Banking in Shackles," *International Financial Review*, May 1989, p. 1.
28. Salomon Brothers, European Equity Research reports, May 31, 1990, and October 31, 1990.

29. "German Banks Avoid Worst of Debt Crisis," *The Wall Street Journal*, September 18, 1987, p. 22, and "U.S. Banks Pressed to Lift LDC Reserves," *American Banker*, February 26, 1990.

30. Hang-Sheng Cheng, "German Economic Unification," *Weekly Letter* (Federal Reserve Bank of San Francisco: San Francisco), June 29, 1990.

ADDENDUM TO CHAPTER 7: THE EVOLUTION OF JAPANESE BANKING AND FINANCE

Thomas F. Cargill and Shoichi Royama

1987

Feb.	Qualification standards relaxed for unsecured (without collateral) corporate debentures.	3
Apr.	Minimum large-denominated time deposit reduced from 300 million to 100 million yen.	6
Apr.	Minimum denomination of MMCs reduced from 30 million to 20 million yen.	6
Apr.	Upper maturity limit of MMCs raised from one year to two years, and ceiling on issuance enlarged from 250 to 300 percent of bank's net worth.	6
Apr.	Ceiling on issuance of CDs enlarged from 250 to 300 percent of bank's net worth.	6
May	Transactions at foreign futures market liberalized for financial institutions.	5
Oct.	Ceiling on issuance of CDs abolished.	6
Oct.	Lower majority limit of large-denominated time deposit lowered from three months to one month.	6
Oct.	Minimum denomination of MMCs reduced from 20 million to ten million yen.	6

Nov.	CP market established.	1
Nov.	Restrictions on nonresidents' Euroyen CP transactions removed.	3, 5
Dec.	BOJ initiated gensaki open-market operations in bonds.	7

1988

Jan.	Restrictions on nonresidents' CP transaction removed.	3, 5
Mar.	Option transactions abroad permitted for financial institutions.	5
Apr.	Minimum large-denominated time deposit reduced from 100 million to 50 million yen.	6
Apr.	Maturity limit of CDs enlarged from one month – one year to two weeks – two years.	6
Apr.	Minimum denomination of CDs reduced from 100 million to ten million yen.	6
Apr.	The tax exemption system for interest income from small savings abolished.	1
Apr.	Upper maturity limit at Euroyen CDs extended from one year to two years.	1, 5
May	The Financial Future Transaction Law proclaimed.	1, 3
	Amendments made to the Securities and Exchange Law.	1, 3
May	Some foreign securities companies received membership in the Tokyo Stock Exchange.	3, 5
July	Future Transactions for 20-year term government bonds initiated.	3
Aug.	Nichigin Net (Interbank on line system) initiated.	1, 7
Sept.	The futures transactions of stock price index initiated at the Tokyo Stock Exchange and Osaka Stock Exchange.	3
Nov.	Minimum large-denominated time deposit reduced from 50 million to 30 million yen.	6
Nov.	BOJ introduced the New Credit Control System. Shorter term transactions from one week to one month initiated in the Bill Market. Longer term transactions from one month to six months initiated in the Unsecured Call Market.	1, 2, 7

1989

Jan.	City banks introduced the New Prime Rate System.	1, 6
Feb.	Some Sogo banks were permitted to change to ordinary banks and organized the Secondary Association of Regional Banks.	1, 3
Apr.	Minimum large-denominated time deposit reduced from 30 million to 20 million yen.	6
Apr.	The competitive bidding system for 10-year term government bonds initiated.	3, 6
May	Medium and long term Euroyen loans for residents permitted.	1, 4, 5
June	Small-denominated MMCs initiated with more than 3 million yen and six months and one year maturity.	6
June	The futures transactions of money rates (Eurodollar and Euroyen 3-month rates) and foreign exchange initiated at the Tokyo Financial Future Market.	6
June	Restrictions on nonresidents' Euroyen bonds transactions removed.	1, 4, 5
Oct.	Minimum large-denominated time deposit reduced from 20 million to 10 million yen.	6
Oct.	Maturity limit of small-denominated MMCs extended to three months, six months, one year, two years, and three years.	6
Oct.	The option transactions of stock price index initiated at the Tokyo Stock Exchange and Osaka Stock Exchange.	3
Dec.	The Pre-paid Card Law proclaimed.	1, 3, 4, 6
Dec.	BOJ initiated open market operation in TBs.	1, 7

1990

Feb.	City bank cash dispenser system (BANCS) and regional bank cash dispenser system (ACS) jointed into one service network (MILES).	1, 4
Feb.	Rules on issuance of CPs revised.	3, 4
Apr.	Minimum denomination of small-denominated MMCs reduced from 3 million to 1 million yen.	6

Index

ABECOR, 560–561, 587
AFB Banks (France), 246, 255, 270, 276
  market share trends of foreign banks in activities, 292
African Development Bank, 137
Agencias de Valores (Chile), 60, 64, 67, 74, 90, 93
Agricultural Bank of China (ABC), 116–117, 128, 134, 142, 147, 148
Aldrich-Vreeland Act (U.S., 1908), 501
Alexander, Volbert, 555–588
Aliber, R.Z., 213, 214, 215
Allende government (Chile), 72, 84
American Depository Receipts (ADRs), 542–543
American Express Company, 48
American Stock Exchange (ASE), 28, 541, 542–543
Amex Bank of Canada, 48
Amsterdam Stock Exchange, 303
Anti-Monopoly Law (Japan, 1947), 352
Antitrust Division, Department of Justice (U.S.), 509, 524
Asia, French banks' presence, 254
Asian Development Bank, 122, 137–138, 154
Association of Swiss Stock Exchanges, 421
Associazione Bancaria Italiana (ABI), 300
Australia, 116, 151
  CITIC subsidiary, 125

Baer, Herbert L., 469–545
Bahamas, 49
Baker, Hugh C., 26
Baltensperger, 452
Banca d'America e d'Italia (BAI), 300
Bancassurance (France), 277
Banco del Estado (Chile), 64, 68–69, 72–73, 99, 101
Bank Act (Canada), 5, 13, 42
  enacted in 1871, 31
  1954 revision, 33
  1967 revision, 16, 18, 34
  1980 revision, 16, 31, 34, 35, 47, 48, 52n
  1990 revision, 35
Bank-eligible securities, 516
Bank for International Settlements (BIS), 44, 410
  capital adequacy, 274, 326, 372, 586–587
Bankhaus I.D. Herstatt (Germany), 565, 581
Bank holding companies, 520
Bank Holding Company Act of 1956 (U.S.), 516, 520, 524
Banking Act (France, 1984), 245, 280n, 290
  credit institution regulation, 256–259, 264, 266, 272
  Section 11 (insurance companies), 250
  Section 99 (securities houses), 248–249
Banking Act (Germany, 1961), 556, 578–582

595

Banking Act of 1933 (U.S.), 352, 354, 470, 503–504, 520
Banking Act of 1935 (U.S.), 503–504
Banking Law (Chile), 101
  enacted in 1860, 68
  SBIF authorization of opening or closing branch offices, 92
Banking Law (Japan), 346
Banking Law of 1936 (Italy), 296, 305, 320, 321, 323
Bank Insurance Fund (BIF), 510
Bank Law (Japan, 1890), 348
Bank Merger Act (U.S., 1960), 509, 524
Bank of America, 152, 463, 587
  Italian subsidiary, 187, 300
Bank of Canada, 19, 39, 41, 42, 44
Bank of China (BOC), 115–116, 138, 145, 148, 150, 151, 153
Bank of Communications of China (BCC), 116, 118–119
Bank of England, 216, 217, 437, 438, 457, 459, 496
Bank of Italy, 312, 315–324, 326–331
Bank of Japan (BOJ), 333, 345, 347–349, 351–352, 368, 370–371
  financial liberalization, 362, 364, 366
  Policy Board and collateralization, 357
Bank of Japan Act (1942), 351
Bank of Montreal (BOM), 10–16, 26, 29
  globalization, 49, 50
  income tax rate, 51
  retrenchment in Europe, 49
Bank of Nova Scotia (BNS), 10–16, 38
  globalization, 49, 50
  income tax rate, 51
  retrenchment in Europe, 49
Bank of Tokyo, 152, 373n
Bankruptcy Law, reform in 1983 (Chile), 74
Banks. *See* Chartered commercial banks
Banque de France, 251
Banque Nationale de Paris, 152
Barbados, 49
Barclays Bank, 152
Barth, James, 528
Basle Committee on Banking Regulations and Supervisory Practices (U.S., 1975), 513–514
Basle Concordat, 415, 416–417, 579

Basle Supervisors Bank Capital Standards, 215
BAT company, 441
Bayerische Vereinsbank AG, 559, 586
BCE Inc., 39
Beckhart, B.H., 33
Belgium, banking structure, 151
  banking concentration ratios, 325
  bank mergers, 463
  capital market, 172
  commercial banks, 181–185, 187–189, 192, 200
  deposit insurance system coverage, 219
  financial product price impacts, EC internal market, 210
  financial services price decline, 210–213
  interest rates, 207
  joint participation agreement, 214
  nonfinancial group bank control, 222
  price differentials in banking products, 209
  reserve requirements, 204–205
  taxes, 173, 203
Belize, 49
Benston, George J., 32, 520
Biddle, Nicholas, 497
"Big Bang" (England, 1986), 176, 192, 217, 451, 453, 517
  securities industry, 444–445, 449
Birchler, Urs W., 389–426
Bisignano, Joseph, 155–224
Black Monday (1989), 541
Blue Paper, 36
Bolsa de Comercio (Chile, stock exchange), 61
"Bordered Hessian" landholding, 52n
Boyd, J.H., 433
Brewer, Elijah, III, 520
Brimmer, Andrew, 483
Britannia, 438
Broker, G., 207–208
Brokerage firms, in France, 248–249
Building Societies Act (1986), 450
Bundesbank (Germany), 173, 191, 206, 215, 570–571, 575–577, 580–581
Bush, George, 510

Cable, J., 186, 574
Caisse des Dépôts et Consignations

INDEX 597

(CDC), 247
Calomiris, Charles, 498
CAMEL criteria, 43
Canada, bank structure, 1–52
  Amex bank chartered, 30
  bank failures, 31–33, 35, 41, 45, 53n
  Big Six banks, 10–16, 35, 42, 44, 51
  branching, 10–11, 32, 47–48
  caisses populaires, 2–3, 4, 10, 17–18, 30, 36
  chartered (commercial) banks, 1–14, 16, 18–19, 23, 29–31, 35–39, 42
  chartered (commercial) banks and Third World loans, 50–51
  CITIC subsidiary, 125
  credit unions, 1–5, 10, 13, 16–18, 30, 34, 36
  deposit insurance, 30, 32, 35, 44–46, 219
  domestic assets of financial institutions, 4
  domestic trading, 542
  federal and provincial views on regulatory change, 37
  finance companies, 34, 36
  financial institutions and regulatory milestone founding dates, 30
  financial markets, 28–30, 40, 47–50
  financial services industry, 1
  foreign trade of shares in U.S., 543
  futures traded, 29
  general insurance companies, 1–3, 5, 18, 23–28, 30, 35–36
  globalization, 47–52
  Great Depression's effect, 32
  gross national product share, 1, 30, 32, 37
  history, 29–35
  holding companies, 10, 46
  insurance companies, 38
  investment dealers, 1–3, 19–22, 29, 30, 36
  legislation regulating selected financial institutions, 36
  leverage ratios, 34–35
  life insurance companies, 1–3, 23–26, 30, 34, 36, 50
  merchant banking, 22–23
  mergers of banks, 33
  mortgage loan companies, 2–3, 4, 36
  pension funds, 4, 10, 27, 28, 30, 36
  reciprocity principle in banking, 201
  regulation, 35–47
  regulatory differences among financial institutions, 2–3
  safety and competitive equilibrium, 44–47
  savings banks, 17, 30
  Schedule One banks, 5, 10, 29
  Schedule Two banks, 5, 10, 22, 30, 34, 47
  Superintendent of Financial Institutions, 42–45, 47
  Superintendent of Insurance, 26
  top financial institutions based on total assets (1988), 6–10
  trust companies, 1–5, 12–17, 26, 30, 34, 35
Canada Deposit Insurance Corporation (CDIC), 16, 39, 41, 42, 45
Canada Life, 24, 26
Canada Mortgage and Housing Corporation (CMHC), 29
Canada Payments system, 34
Canada Trustco Mortgage Company, 39
Canadian Bankers Association, 45, 53n
Canadian Business Corporations Act, 47
Canadian Imperial Bank of Commerce (CIBC), 10–16, 22–23
  globalization, 49, 50
  income tax rate, 51
  nonaccrual loans, 51
Capital accumulation certificates (France), 250
Capital adequacy ratio, 274
Capital-dimension ratio, 326
Capital markets
  in France, 249, 252, 260, 262, 272–273, 275–276, 279
  in Germany, 585
  in Italy, 303–315
  in Japan, 364–365
  in Switzerland, 392, 403–407, 410, 412, 419–422
  in United Kingdom, 432, 439, 441–442
  in United States, 530
Capital-to-asset ratio, 579
CAPS, 439
Cargill, Thomas F., 333–388
Caribbean, 409, 410

"Cassis de Dijon" judgment, 196, 198–199, 229n
Caymen, 151
Central Bank Law (Germany, 1957), 575, 576
Centrobanca (Italy), 303
Chartered (commercial) banks
  in Belgium, 181–185, 187–189, 192, 200
  in Canada, 1–16, 18–19, 23, 29–31, 35–39, 42, 50–51
  in Chile, 60, 64–65, 69, 71–78, 80–82, 85, 87–88
  in China, 115–125, 131–133, 137, 139–141, 144–145, 148–149
  in Denmark, 181, 183–185, 201
  in France, 181–194, 200–201, 245–247, 253–258, 264, 272, 290–292
  in France, bank competition, 276–279
  in France, treasury classification in national accounts and monetary statistics, 284–286
  in Germany, 180–194, 200–201, 278–279, 557–561, 567–568, 572–575, 578–588
  in Greece, 181, 183–185
  in Ireland, 181–185, 201
  in Italy, 181–191, 194, 200–201, 279, 293–300, 304–307, 326–327
  in Italy, capital markets, 171–172
  in Japan, 202, 334, 341–344, 348–354, 371
  in Luxembourg, 181, 183–185, 200, 278
  in Netherlands, 181–185, 187–189, 200, 202
  in Portugal, 181, 183–185
  in Spain, 181–185, 187–191, 200, 201
  in Switzerland, 189–192, 201, 389–403, 408–413, 417, 420–421, 423
  in United Kingdom, 278–279, 429–430, 438–439, 442, 445–459, 462–464
  in United Kingdom, as European Economic Community member, 180–193, 200–202
  in United States, 202, 470–481, 485, 492, 505, 517–536, 544–545
  in United States, regulation, 508–509, 512–514
  regulation, 90–99, 105, 108–109
Chase Manhattan Bank, 152, 463

Chicago Board of Trade, 540, 541
Chicago Mercantile Exchange (CME), 29, 540, 541
Chile, bank structure, 59–109
  bank capitalization by creditors, 102, 103–104
  bank failures, 68, 71, 73–74, 77–87, 100–102
  Central Bank, 61, 64–67, 75, 78, 81–85, 88–92, 95–109
  chartered banks, 60, 64–65, 69–82, 85–99, 105, 108–109
  copper price falling sharply, 76
  debt crisis of 1981–1983, 60
  deposit insurance, 60, 82, 84, 99–100, 102–103
  financial intermediary insolvencies, 73, 74, 76, 78
  financial markets, 60–61, 90–104
  financial system, 1952–1988, 69–70
  foreign banks having branches or subsidiaries in Chile, 110n
  globalization, 106–107
  gross domestic product, 61–64, 66, 69–70, 80, 82, 90, 109
  history, 68–90
  inflation, 71
  insurance companies, 60, 67–68, 70, 71, 90–91
  leasing companies, 60
  life insurance companies, 60, 66–67, 70, 90, 105, 108
  monetization and financial deepening, 61–64
  mutual funds, 60, 67, 90, 93, 108
  open corporations, 90
  pension funds, 60, 61, 66, 69, 90–92, 97, 105
  recovery from 1980s international debt crisis, 59
  reforms to the banking law (1986–1989), 60
  regulation, 71, 75–79, 83, 90–105
  rehabilitation and privatization of failed banks, 83–87
  shell companies, 79, 82, 84
  stabilization of banking, 87–90
  stock exchanges, 61, 67, 70–72, 93, 108
  taxes, 98

INDEX 599

China, bank structure, 113–154
 abbreviations for China's financial institutions, 116
 Bank Control Regulation, 138, 148
 banking development, 146–151
 bonds, 134, 153
 central bank (People's Bank of China), 113–120, 123, 126–141, 143–146, 148–150, 152
 city credit cooperatives, 128–131, 133
 commercial banks, 115–125, 131–133, 137, 139–141, 144–145, 148–149
 commercial bills, 133
 credit cooperatives, 127–131, 133
 finance companies affiliated with industrial groups, 126
 financial markets, 132–136
 foreign exchange markets, 135–136, 145–146
 foreign financial institutions, 152–154
 foreign trade, 150–151
 globalization, 116, 119–120, 122–125, 130–131, 150–154
 housing, banks for, 122–123
 insurance companies, 130–131, 151–152, 154
 international trust and investment corporations, 123–125
 leasing companies, 130, 145
 Ministry of Finance, 113, 121, 134
 money markets' interbank rates, 143
 mutual funds, 131
 overview of chapter, 113–114
 postal savings, 131
 regulation, 138–146, 148, 152–153
 rural credit cooperatives, 127–128, 131, 133
 securities market, 134, 135
 State Council, 115, 117–121, 124, 133, 137–138, 141, 145–148
 State Science Commission, 123
 treasury bills, 134, 135
 trust and investment corporations, 125–126, 133, 140, 145, 148
China Investment Bank (CIB), 116, 122
China Venturetech Investment Corporation (CVIC), 116, 123
Chinese International Trust and Investment Corporation (CITIC), 116, 119, 120, 124–125
 subsidiaries, 124
"Chinese Walls," 46
Ciampi, C.A., 222, 330
CICR. *See* International Committee for Credit and Savings
Citibank, 225n
 Chilean subsidiary, 106, 110n
 in Italy, 300
CITIC Industrial Bank (CITIC IB), 116, 119–120, 124
Clark, J.A., 433
Clayton Act (U.S., 1914), 523
COLLARS, 439
Comfort letters, 201
Commercial banks. *See* Chartered commercial banks
Commercial loan theory of banking (U.S.), 476
Commercial paper
 Canadian banks underwriting in a global environment, 51–52
 in France, 251
Commerzbank, 557–558, 560
Commission on Reorganization of the Federal Government (U.S.), 509
Commodities Futures Trading Commission (U.S.), 494
Companies and Stock Exchange Commission (Italy), 171
Comptroller of the Currency (U.S.), 499–500
Confederation (Canada), 26, 29–30, 31
CONSOB. *See* National Commission for Corporation and Exchange
Continental Illinois National Bank of Chicago, 527
Cooke ratio, 272, 274, 275
Cooperative Banks (France), 246–247
CORFO (Chilean state industrial holding company), 72, 85–88
Corrigan, E.G., 436
Corrigan, G.E., 177
Coupon taxes, 173
Crash of 1987, 541, 543
Crédit Agricole (France), 182
Crediop (Italy), 302–303
Credit institutions
 in France, 247–249

in Japan, 353
Credit Lyonnais (France), 463
Credit Suisse, 390, 393, 403
Credit Union National Association (U.S.), 508
Credit unions
  in Canada, 1–5, 10, 13, 16–18, 30, 34, 36
  in China, 127–130
  in U.S., 18, 474, 475, 484, 508
Custody Business Act (Germany), 578

Dai Ichi Kangyo Bank, 334
Decision on Reform of Economic System (China), 136
De la Cuadra F., Sergio, 59–109
Delors Law (France, 1983), 166–167
Denmark, bank structure
  commercial banks, 181, 183–185, 201
  deposit insurance system coverage, 219
  financial services price decline, 210–213
  increased competition pressure from foreign banks, 210
  money market instruments, 208
  nonfinancial group bank control, 222
  reserve requirements, 204–205
  taxes, 173, 203
Deposit Insurance Corporation (DIC, Japan), 370
Depository Institutions Deregulation and Monetary Control Act of 1980 (DIDMCA, U.S.), 515, 518
Dermine, 452
Desjardins, Alphonse, 17, 18
Deutsche Bank, 463, 557–558, 566, 586, 587, 588
Dominica, 49
Dominion Republic, 49
Douglas Amendment (U.S.), 520
Dresdner Bank (Germany), 557–558, 584, 587
Ducruezet, L. Beduc F., 245–292
"Dutch action" method, 267

Eastern Europe, 150
EBIC, 560–561, 587
Economic Council of Canada, 46

Economies of scope, 215
Efibanca (Italy), 303
Eisenbeis, R.A., 431, 439
Elimination of Excessive Concentration of Economic Power Law (Japan, 1947), 352
Employee Retirement Income Security Act (ERISA, U.S., 1974), 490
Endowment capital, 196
Estey, Willard Z., 42
Estey Commission report, 36, 43
Eurobonds, 173, 191–192, 444–445
EUROCARD, 565
Euromoney, 11, 13
Europartners, 560–561, 587
European capital adequacy ratio, 272
European Economic Community (EEC), 155–224
  bank failures, 177–178, 221
  bank gross and net margins, 188
  banking activities subject to mutual recognition, 198
  banking concentration of five largest banks, 182
  Banking Federation, 202
  banking integration 1992 initiative, 195–206
  banking services, 189–195
  bank number and total assets, 325
  bank ownership by nonfinancial firms, 187
  bank ownership statistical summary, 179
  bank profitability comparative measures, 190
  bank profit before taxes, 189
  bank role, 177–189
  bank sector distribution of 100 largest, 180
  bank structure and performance, 184–185
  capital/asset ratios of banks, 180
  capital market role, 162–177, 328
  "commercial banking" market saturation data, 183
  Competition Commission (1989), 194
  corporate separateness, 161
  corporate takeovers, 202
  cross-country bank mergers and acquisitions, 330

INDEX 601

deposit guarantee schemes (insurance), 159–160, 177–178, 196–197, 220–223, 225n, 233n
deposit insurance systems comparison, 219
European Commission documents, 195–200, 202, 206, 216, 231n
exchange controls, 200
financial services price decline potential, 210–212
harmonization of policy toward takeovers, 584
home country control, 197
Home Rule and Reciprocity principles, 586
information trade, 157–158
integration of banking markets as goal, 155–156
liabilities of nonfinancial companies and bank lending, 164–165
negotiable money market instruments, 207–208
1992 financial integration, 107
1992 integration effect on United Kingdom, 459–467
payments system, 157, 161
post-1992 regulatory principles forcing integration, 329–330
price differentials in banking products, 209
price reductions of financial products from EC internal market, 210
public policy and the single market in banking services, 216–224
public policy role in banking, 157–162
Q-ratios, 214
reciprocity principle in financial services, 50
reciprocity privileges, 201–202
reserve requirements, 204–205
Second Banking Coordination Directive (1988), 156, 157
securities markets, 208
single banking market effect, 207–216
solvency ratio, 274
stock exchanges, 330
Swiss banks, 422–423
taxation, 203
European Free Trade Association, 425

Factors (U.S.), 486
Federal Association of German Commercial Banks, 581–582
Federal Banking Commission (FBC, Switzerland), 413–415, 418, 419, 421
Federal Banking Supervisory Authority (FBSA, Germany), 578–580, 582
Federal Deposit Insurance Corporation (FDIC, U.S.), 221, 508–510, 512, 513, 526–527
Federal Financial Institutions Examination Council, 509
Federal Home Loan Act (U.S.), 482
Federal Home Loan Bank Board (U.S.), 510, 518
Federal Home Loan Banks (U.S.), 482, 483
Federal Home Loan Mortgage Corporation (U.S.), 477
Federal Housing Authority (U.S.), 477
Federal National Mortgage Association (U.S.), 477
Federal Open Market Committee, 504
Federal Reserve Act (U.S., 1913), 476, 501, 502
Federal Reserve Board (U.S.), 493–494, 501, 503–504, 513, 514, 516
  deposit insurance, 33
  investment dealers (Canada) and U.S. securities subsidiaries, 22
Federal Reserve System, 161, 345, 501–504, 508–510, 512, 516, 526
Federal Savings and Loan Insurance Corporation (FSLIC), 526–527
Finance Act (Canada), 33
Finance companies
  in Canada, 34, 36
  in France, 248, 255–256, 258, 264–265, 284–286, 290
  in Switzerland, 389, 392, 397, 400–401, 412–413, 417
  in U.S., 474–476, 484–486, 491
Financial Institutions Reform, Recovery and Enforcement Act of 1989 (FIRREA), 510, 514, 519, 521
Financial Services Act (United Kingdom, 1986), 201–202, 216
Financieras, 60, 64, 73–77, 81, 90–91, 99

First European Directive (Dec. 12, 1977), 264
Foreign Exchange and Foreign Trade Control Law (Japan, 1980 amendment), 365
Foreign Exchange Control Law (1949), 354
Form for Analyzing Bank Capital (ABC Form), 512, 513
France, bank structure, 54n, 151, 152, 245–292
  bank absorption trend, 277
  banking concentration ratios, 325
  banking integration 1992 initiative, 195
  banking trends, 274–280
  bank mergers, 463
  bond futures and options markets, 172–173
  bonds and shares, 167
  brokerage firms, 255–256, 260, 261, 271
  capital/assets ratio, 275
  capital markets, 163–169, 173, 194, 222, 249, 252, 260–262
  capital markets and globalization, 272–276, 279
  commercial banks, 181–194, 200–201, 245–247, 253–258, 264, 272, 290–292
  commercial banks and insurance companies, 276–279
  commercial banks, treasury classification and monetary statistics, 284–286
  commercial paper, 167–168
  Commission Bancaire study, 274
  competitive money, 168
  concentration of banks, 276
  credit institutions, 247–249, 253–254, 257–259, 261, 263–265, 270–271
  credit institutions subject to Banking Act, 290
  deposit insurance, 219, 266
  domestic trading, 542
  exchange controls, 200
  finance companies, 248, 255–256, 258, 264–265, 284–286, 290
  financial product price impacts, EC internal market, 210
  financial services price decline, 210–213
  foreign banks, 275–276, 292
  foreign financial institution presence, 255–256
  French Securities and Exchange Commission (COB), 262–263
  futures market, 261, 271
  geographical analysis of foreign investment by French banks, 291
  globalization (internationalization), 253–256, 272–277, 291–292
  government bond futures market, 168
  history, 256–258, 270
  insurance companies, 194–195, 250–252, 261, 273, 276–280
  interbank market, 251
  interest rates, 207, 208
  investment funds (SICAVs and FCPs), 168, 194
  liabilities of nonfinancial companies and bank lending, 164–165
  life insurance companies, 250
  liquidity ratio, 268
  money market instruments, 208, 251
  mortgage market, 252
  mutual companies, 247, 250
  options contracts, 168
  pension funds, 247, 252
  price differentials in banking products, 209
  Q-ratios, 214
  regulation, 256–271
  savings institutions, 247
  second marche', 167
  securities houses and brokerage firms, 248–249
  securities markets, 248–249, 251–252, 262, 266, 269, 270
  securitization, 252
  taxation, 202–204
  treasury bills, 167–168, 267–268
  treasury classification in national accounts of financial institutions, 284–286
Free Banking Era (U.S.), 497–499
Free Trade Agreement (Canada-U.S., 1989), 48
French Bankers' Association (AFB), 245
French Insurance Code, 250
Friedman, Milton, 504
Fukuda, S., 368

G-10 countries, 178–180, 205, 372
Garn-St. Germain Depository Institutions

INDEX

Act of 1982 (U.S.), 518
Gearing ratios, 201, 205, 268
General Accident (Insurance Company), 436
General Banking Law (Chile), 89, 92–93, 101
General Motors Acceptance Corporation, 485
Germany, bank structure, 54n, 116, 151, 555–588
  bank failures, 565, 579, 581, 582
  banking concentration ratios, 325
  bank role, 571–577
  banks and corporate control, 583–584
  bond market, 167, 567–569, 588
  capital market, 163, 168–169, 172, 177, 585
  central bank (Bundesbank), 173, 191, 206, 215, 570–571, 575–577, 580–581
  Central Giro institutions, 561–562
  commercial banks, 180–191, 193–194, 200–201, 278–279, 557–561, 567–568, 572–588
  concentration of banks, 276
  cooperative banks, 562–563, 570, 577
  credit transfers, 570, 571
  deposit insurance, 219, 582
  domestic trading, 542
  equity market capitalization, 169, 194
  financial assets and liabilities of domestic nonfinancial sectors, 166
  financial product price impacts, EC internal market, 210
  financial services price decline, 210, 213
  financing of corporate sector, 163
  foreign banks, 538, 560–561, 577–578, 584–585
  globalization, 586–587
  government bond futures, 193
  history, 571–573, 575, 589n
  housing loan societies, 564
  insurance companies, 166, 193, 280, 584
  interest rates, 207, 208
  joint participation agreement, 215
  liabilities of nonfinancial companies and bank lending, 164–165
  market capitalization ratios, 537–538
  mortgage banks, 563–564, 567, 577, 584–585
  nonbank corporation ownership by a bank, 573–575, 583
  nonfinancial group bank control, 222, 223
  organizational structure, 556
  payments system, 570–571
  Postal Giro banks, 564–565, 570, 577
  Postal Savings banks, 564–565, 577
  price differentials in banking products, 209
  private banks, 559–561, 577
  public law banks, 561–562
  Q-ratios, 214
  regional, 559–561, 577, 584–585
  reunification costs financed, 587–588
  savings banks, 561–562, 570, 577, 584–585
  Schuldscheine market, 568–569
  securities markets, 166, 193, 566–567, 569, 571, 588
  single banking market effect, 207
  special-purpose banks, 565–566, 577
  stock exchanges, 193–194, 566, 569
  supervision of banks, 577–582
  taxes, 173, 203
  universal banking, 529, 556–564, 572–575, 585
Gerschenkron, 572
Gessler Commission (Germany), 583
Gessler Report (Germany), 187, 573–574
Giddy, I.H., 215–216
Gilbart, R.A., 433
Gilibert, P.L., 210
Glass–Steagall Act (Banking Act of 1933, U.S.), 22, 352, 507, 516
GLOBEX system, 540–541
Golembe, C.H., 178
Gordon Investment Corporation (GIC), 22–23
Government National Mortgage Association (Ginnie Mae, U.S.), 477, 531
Government of Canada securities, 19
Government Securities Clearing Corporation (U.S., 1986), 494
Graham, S.L., 433
Great Depression, 318, 412, 493, 503–504, 528–529
Greece, bank structure
  commercial banks, 181, 183–185
  deposit insurance system coverage, 219

interest rates, 207
money market instruments, 208
taxation, 203
Green Paper (Canada), 36, 46
Guaranteed Investment Certificates (GICs), 41
Gurley, John G., 338
Guttentag, J.M., 223
Guyana, 49

Haiti, 49
Hamilton, Alexander, 496
Herring, R.J., 223
Holding companies
in Canada, 10, 46
in United Kingdom, 192
Hong Kong, 116, 118–119, 125, 151–152
Horiuchi, Akiyoshi, 368
Humphrey, D.B., 277

IG, 41
Imasco Ltd., 39
IMF, 137, 154
Income Tax Act (Canada), 28
Incumbency rents, 232
India, 49
Industrial and Commercial Bank of China (ICBC), 116–118, 134–135, 138, 142–143, 147–148
Industrial banks, in U.S., 484
Institute of Industrial Conversion (IRI, Italy), 296
Insurance companies
in Canada, 1–3, 5, 18, 23–28, 30, 35–36, 38
in Chile, 60, 67–68, 70–71, 90–91
in China, 130–131, 151–152, 154
in France, 194–195, 250–252, 261, 273, 276–280
in Germany, 166, 193, 280, 584
in Italy, 280, 307, 329
in The Netherlands, 280
in Spain, 280
in Switzerland, 401–403, 411
in United Kingdom, 280, 436–438, 441
in United States, 473–475, 486–488, 509
Insurance Companies Law (Chile), 89

Interbanca (Italy), 303
Interest Rate Adjustment Act of 1966 (U.S.), 514–515
International Banking Act of 1978 (U.S.), 533
International Committee for Credit and Savings (CICR, Italy), 321, 328–329
International Convergence of Capital Measurement and Capital Standards, 205
International Fund for Agricultural Development, 117
International Lending and Supervision Act of 1983 (U.S.), 511, 513
International Securities Regulatory Organization, 444–445
International Stock Exchange (U.K.), 444–445
Investment banks, in U.S., 491–493
Investment dealers, in Canada, 1–3, 19–22, 29, 30, 36
Ireland, bank structure
banking concentration ratios, 325
commercial banks, 181–185, 201
deposit insurance system coverage, 219
taxation, 203
Istituto Mobiliare Italiano (IMI), 302
Italy, bank structure, 54n, 293–331
bank absorption trend, 277
bank failures, 317–318, 327
banking associations, 300–301
banking concentration ratios, 325
banking integration 1992 initiative, 195
Banking System, 294–300
bank mergers, 463
Bank of America retail banking operations, 587
Bank of Italy, 300, 305
bonds and government securities, 170
capital/assets ratio, 275
capital markets, 170–172, 303–315
commercial bank branching, 297
commercial banks, 171–172, 181–191, 194, 200–201, 293–300, 304–307, 326–327
commercial banks, strengths and weaknesses, 279
commercial paper, 171
concentration of banks, 276

INDEX

coverage of Italian public-sector deficit, 313
credit institutions, 301–303
cross-ownership between banks and industry, 328–329
deposit insurance, 219, 300, 318, 327
equity markets, 171–172
exchange controls, 200
financial product price impacts, EC internal market, 210
financial services price decline, 210–213
foreign banks, 296, 299–300
growth ratios (%), 295
history, 293–294, 316–321
insurance companies, 280, 307, 329
interest rates, 207, 229n
joint participation agreement, 215
liabilities of nonfinancial companies and bank lending, 164–165
life insurance companies, 194
merchant banking, 172
money market instruments, 208
mutual funds, 315–316
nonfinancial group bank control, 221–222
option contracts, 311–312
portfolio constraint, 320
price differentials in banking products, 209
regulation, 293–294, 321–327
reserve requirements, 204–205
securities market, 309–314, 319
stock exchanges, 303–316, 322–323
taxation, 203
Treasury bills, 312

Jackson, Andrew, 497
Jamieson, A.B., 32
Japan, bank structure, 54n, 151, 152, 333–388
  bank failures, 348, 349–350
  bank profitability comparative measures, 190
  borrowing country of Switzerland, 405
  Canadian bank branches, 47–48, 49
  capital market, 364–365
  central bank, 333
  collateralization, 357
  commercial banks, 202, 334, 341–344, 348–354, 371
  credit associations, 353
  deposit insurance, 219, 346, 370
  Dodge line, 357
  domestic trading, 542
  earthquake (9/1/23) and its effect, 349
  earthquake bills, 349, 357
  equity market, 365
  financial liberalization, 361–372
  financial strength of banks, 587
  Financial System Research Council, 368, 369
  flow of funds, 335–341, 361
  foreign banks, 342, 344
  gensaki market, 362, 364
  German branches of banks, 560
  globalization, 370–372
  government financial institutions, 343–345
  gross national product, 336
  High Growth Period (HGP), 334–335, 353, 358–362
  history, 333–335, 348–357
  history, chronology of major changes 1975–1986, 376–388
  indirect finance ratio, 338–339
  intermediation finance institutions, 341–345
  investment companies, 365
  liabilities of nonfinancial companies and bank lending, 164–165
  life insurance companies, 280, 342
  market capitalization ratios, 538
  Ministry of Finance (MOF), 343–347, 352, 356–357, 362–363, 368–371
  money market, 364–366
  net external asset position, 334
  offshore market, 365–366, 371
  private financial institutions, 342
  protection for European banking markets, 586
  Q-ratios, 214
  regulation, 345–347, 355–357, 359, 364, 366
  securities market, 352, 367, 371
  securitization, 367–372, 373n
  specialization, 368–369
  stock exchanges, 352, 365

Swiss banks, 422–423
trade credit, 361
uniqueness prior to financial liberalization, 358–361
U.S. bank branches, 535, 537, 539
U.S. Occupation, 351–355
zaibatsu, 350–355

Kalymon, Basil A., 29
Kane, E.J., 215–216
Kane, Edward, 539
Klebaner, Benjamin, 496
Klein, 452
Koehn, Michael F., 520
Kryzanowski, Lawrence, 1–52

Lamont, Ann, 37n
Latin America, 409, 410, 587
  Canadian bank trade finance, 49
Leasing companies
  in Chile, 60
  in China, 130, 145
Less developed countries (LDCs), Canadian banks financing debt, 51
Life insurance companies
  in Canada, 1–3, 23–26, 30, 34, 36, 50
  in Chile, 60, 66–67, 70, 90, 105, 108
  in France, 250
  in Italy, 194
  in Japan, 280, 342
  in Switzerland, 402
  in United Kingdom, 192, 193
  in United States, 474–476, 486–488, 491
Liko-Bank (Germany), 565, 581
Lin, Zhou, 113–154
"Little Bang in 1987," 38
Llewellyn, David, 429–467
Loans at risk (Chile), 94
Loehnis, A., 437, 438, 459
London, City of, 440
London International Financial Futures Exchange (LIFFE), 193
London Stock Exchange (LSE), 208, 303, 444, 445, 451
Luxembourg, bank structure, 372
  bank capital standards, 205
  capital market, 173

commercial banks, 181, 183–185, 200, 278
deposit insurance system coverage, 219
financial product price impacts, EC internal market, 210
financial services price decline, 210–212
nonbank corporation ownership by a bank, 573
price differentials in banking products, 209
reserve requirements, 204–205
taxation, 203

Macao, 116, 151–152
McCulloch v. Maryland, 497
McFadden Act (U.S., 1927), 470, 507, 520, 521
McKinnon, Ronald, 73
Malaysia 49
Marks and Spencer, 436, 437, 441
MATIF (France), 168, 249, 252, 255, 261, 540
Mediobanca (Italy), 172, 302
Mercato Ristretto, 305–306, 308, 310
Merchant banking, in Canada, 22–23
Merrill Lynch, 492, 515
Merrill Lynch Canada, 48
Middle East, 409, 410
Midland Bank, 463
Milan Stock Exchange, 303, 306, 312, 315
Mints, Lloyd, 476
Molyneux, P., 182, 213
Monaco, Principality of, 246, 290
MONEP (Paris traded-options market), 255, 280n
Monory Law of 1978 (France), 166
Montetitoli S.p.A. (Italy, public corporation), 305
Monti, 452
Montreal Exchange (ME), 28, 36
Montreal Trustco Inc., 39
Morris, Robert, 496
Morris Plan Associations (U.S.), 484
Mortgage Banking Act, 559
Mortgage Banking Act of 1963 (Germany), 564
Mortgage banks, in U.S., 486–487
Mortgage loan companies, in Canada, 2–3, 4, 36

INDEX 607

Mote, Larry R., 469–545
Mutual banks (France), 246–247
Mutual companies, in France, 247, 250
Mutual funds, 515
   in Chile, 60, 67, 90, 93, 108
   in China, 131
   in Italy, 315–316
   in United Kingdom, 193
   in United States, 473, 483, 490–491, 532, 544–545
Mutual savings banks, in U.S., 474–475, 481–483, 508, 518–520, 532, 544

NASDAQ. *See* National Association of Securities Dealers Automated Quotation System
National Association of Securities Dealers (U.S.), 492, 542
National Association of Securities Dealers Automated Quotation System (NASDAQ), 167, 542–543
National Bank Act (formerly National Banking Act, U.S., 1864), 499–500, 502, 516
National Banking Act of 1864 (U.S.), 348, 477
National Bank of Canada, 10–16, 23
   globalization, 49
   income tax rate, 51
National Claridge Inc., 23
National Commission for Corporation and Exchange (CONSOB), 304–305, 307–308, 310–311, 322–323
National Currency Act (U.S., 1863), 348, 499
National Fund for Credit to Trade and Industry (Belgium), 172
National Housing Act (Canada), 33
National Industrial Credit Company (Belgium), 172
National Mobilization Act of 1938 (Japan), 351
National Monetary Commission (U.S.), 501
National Provincial Building Society, 436
Netherlands, bank structure
   banking concentration ratios, 325
   bank mergers, 463
   capital markets, 169
   commercial banks, 181–182, 200, 202–203
   deposit insurance system coverage, 219
   equity market capitalization, 169
   financial product price impacts, EC internal market, 210
   financial services price decline, 210–212
   insurance companies, 280
   interest rates, 207, 208
   joint participation agreement, 214
   long-term business financing, 169
   money market instruments, 208
   pension funds, 169
   price differentials in banking products, 209
   taxation, 173, 203–204
Neuberger, 572
Neufeld, E.P., 26, 31
New York Federal Reserve Bank, 503
New York's International Banking Facility, 371
New York Stock Exchange (NYSE), 28, 132, 449, 451, 492–493, 540, 542–543
NIFs, 439
Nikkei index, 541
Nonbanking financial services, 192
Normative capital (Chile), 95
NOW accounts (U.S.), 515

ODA, 154
OECD
   permissible banking activities, 206
   study of obstacles to international trade in banking services, 201
Official Public Offering of New Shares (OPS, Italy), 308
Old Age, Survivors, and Disability Insurance (OASDI). *See* Social Security
Open bank assistance, 527
Open-end investment companies. *See* Mutual funds
Osaka Stock Exchange, 540

Packer, F., 368
Padoa-Schioppa, T., 215–216

Panama, 106–107, 116
Papadacci, P., 245–292
Paris Bourse, 303
Pavel, Christine A., 530
Payments Company (Germany), 565–566
Pecchioli, R.M., 206
Pension Benefit Guaranty Corporation (U.S., 1985), 490
Pension funds
  in Canada, 4, 10, 27–28, 30, 36
  in Chile, 60–61, 66, 69, 90–92, 97, 105
  in France, 247, 252
  in Netherlands, 169
  in Switzerland, 401–403
  in United States, 473, 486, 488–491
People's Bank of China (PBC), 113–120, 123, 126–128, 130–132, 134, 136–141, 143–152
People's Construction Bank of China (PCBC), 116, 121–122, 148
People's Insurance Company of China (PICC), 116, 130–131, 151–152
Pettway, Richard H., 369
Phelan, John, 132
Philadelphia National Bank case (U.S.), 524
Portugal, bank structure
  capital markets, 176
  commercial banks, 181, 183–185
  deposit insurance system coverage, 219
  interest rates, 207
  money market instruments, 208
  taxation, 203
Postal savings system (PSS), 345, 347, 348
Pozdena, Randall Johnston, 555–588
Preferential exchange rate, 83
President's National Commission on Social Security Reform (U.S., 1983), 489
Price Waterhouse, 200, 208
Provident Funds (France), 247
Provisional Fund Control Act of 1937 (Japan), 351
Public Companies Law (Chile), 74
Public Finance Law (Japan, 1947), 352, 357
Purchase and assumption (P&A), 527
Pyle, David, 177

Q-ratios, 213–214

Rates of return on assets (ROA), 454–456
Rates of return on equity (ROE), 454–457
Real Bills Doctrine (1776), 475, 502
Real estate lending (U.S.), 477
Resolution Trust Corporation (RTC, U.S.), 526
Revell, J., 218
Rich, Georg, 389–426
Riesser, 572
Risk-asset ratios, 254, 269, 271
Risk distribution ratio, 269, 271
Risk ratio, 326
Roberts, Gordon S., 1–52
Robertson, Ross, 500
Rolnick, Arthur, 505
Roosevelt, Franklin D., 488–489, 503
Royal Bank of Canada, 10–16, 22, 48
  globalization, 49
  income tax rate, 51
  nonaccrual loans, 51
  retrenchment in Europe, 49–50
Royal Trustco Ltd., 39
Royama, Shoichi, 333–388
RTPC (U.K.), 445
Russell Sage Foundation (U.S.), 484–485

St. Francis Xavier University (Nova Scotia), community credit unions as result of cooperative education programs, 18
Salomon Brothers, 187, 208, 231n
Santomero, A.M., 177
Sanwa Bank of Japan, 152
Savings and loan associations, in U.S., 474–477, 481–484, 508, 515, 518–520, 532, 544
Savings Association Insurance Fund (SAIF, U.S.), 510, 526
Savings banks advance fund (Italy), 300
Schwartz, Anna, 504
Schumpeter, 572
Scotland, joint participation agreement, 214
Sears Roebuck, 436
Securities and Exchange Commission (SEC, U.S.), 493–495, 509, 541–543
Securities and Exchange Law (Article 65, 1947), 352, 354

INDEX

Securities houses, in France, 248–249
Securities Industry Association (U.S.), 492
Securities Law (Chile), 99
Shanghai Investment and Trust Corporation (SITCO), 116, 125
Shanghai Municipal People's Government (SMPG), 125
Shaw, Edward S., 73, 338
Sherman Act (U.S., 1890), 523
Simons, Henry, 102
SINAP (savings and loan industry, Chile), 64, 69, 71–76, 109n
Singapore, 151–152
Singapore International Monetary Exchange (SIMEX), 540
Singapore Stock Exchange, 540
Single European Act (EEC), 204, 227n, 230n
"The Single European Market," 217
Smith, Adam, 475
Social Security (U.S.), 489
Societa' d'Intermediazione Mobiliare (SIM), 305
SOFFEX. *See* Swiss Options and Financial Futures Exchange
South Africa, restriction of capital exports by Switzerland, 406
Soviet Union, 150
  Chinese banking principles adopted from, 146, 148
Spain, bank structure
  bank absorption trend, 277
  banking concentration ratios, 325
  bank mergers, 463
  commercial banks, 181–185, 187–191, 200, 201
  concentration of banks, 276
  deposit insurance system coverage, 219
  exchange controls, 200
  financial product price impacts, EC internal market, 210
  financial services price decline, 210–213
  insurance companies, 280
  joint participation agreement, 215
  money market instruments, 208
  price differentials in banking products, 209
  Q-ratios, 214
  taxation, 203

Standby letters of credit (SLOC), 536
State General Administration of Foreign Exchange Control (SGAEC), 116, 126, 145
Steinherr, A., 210
Stiglitz, 452
Stock-adjustment factors, 454
Stock Exchange Clearing House, 304
Stokes, 572
Strong, Benjamin, 503
Sun Life Assurance (U.K.), 463
Suzuki, Yoshio, 358–359
Sweden, banking concentration ratios, 325
Swiss Admissions Board, 420
Swiss Bank Act (1934), 396, 398, 400–401, 412–413, 415–416
Swiss Bank Corporation, 390, 393, 403
Swiss Bankers' Association (SBA), 414, 418, 419
Swiss Cantobank, 398–399
Swiss Cartel Commission, 417
Swiss Corporation for International Securities (Intersettle), 419
Swiss Market Index, 407
Swiss National Bank (SNB), 401, 403–404, 406, 411, 420
  authority limited, 413–416
Swiss Options and Financial Futures Exchange (SOFFEX), 407–408, 419, 420
Swiss Securities Clearing Corporation (SEGA), 419
Switzerland, bank structure, 54n, 389–426
  bank capital standards, 205
  bank composition of assets and liabilities, 393
  bank failures, 411–412
  banking concentration ratios, 325
  banking industry as prominent as Germany's, 556
  banking services, 189–192, 201, 231n
  bank market shares in total assets, 394, 395
  cantonal banks, 389–392, 394–395, 397–399, 403, 411, 415
  capital exports, 405, 406–407, 410
  capital markets, 392, 403–407, 410, 412, 419–422

central bank. *See* Swiss National Bank
commercial banks, 389–403, 408–410, 412–413, 417, 420–421, 423
deposit insurance, 398, 414–415
description of financial institutions and markets, 389–410
domestic trading, 542
European integration, 423–425
fiduciary funds, 392, 396, 423
finance companies, 389, 392, 397, 400–401, 412–413, 417, 422
financial market competition, 425–426
foreign banks, 389–394, 397, 401, 408–412, 415, 422, 538
globalization, 392, 394, 395, 408–410, 422–425
history, 410–413
insider trading, 418
insurance companies, 401–403, 411
interest rates, 207, 208
joint participation agreement, 215
joint-stock companies, 398
largest banks (in assets), 390–391
life insurance companies, 402
market capitalization ratios, 537–538
medium-term bonds, 396
money laundering, 418–419
money market, 403–404
pension funds, 401–403
private banks, 389, 396–398
Q-ratios, 214
Raiffeisenkassen, 389–390, 392, 394–395, 400, 403
regional banks, 389, 391–392, 394–395, 397, 399–400, 403, 411
regulation, 413–422
savings banks, 389, 394, 395, 397, 399–400, 411
secrecy and funds from criminal sources, 418–419, 426
securities market, 398, 407–408, 412, 419–423
stock exchanges, 407–408, 411, 419–421, 426
taxes, 173
universal banking, 529
Sydney Stock Exchange, 540
Systemic risk potential, 220

Tapley, T. Craig, 369
Temporary Interest Rate Adjustment Law (Japan, 1947), 352, 356
Teranishi, Juro, 349
Terra Con Capital Corporation, 22
Third Market (Italy), 305, 306, 308
Third World loans, Canadian banks affected, 50–51
Tobin, J., 218
Too-big-to-fail doctrine, 221, 225n, 233n
Tokyo International Banking Facility, 365
Tokyo Stock Exchange, 365, 368
TOPIX index (Japan), 541
Toronto-Dominion Bank (TD), 10–16
 globalization, 49
 income tax rate, 51
 retrenchment in Europe, 49
Toronto Futures Exchange, 36
Toronto Stock Exchange (TSE), 11, 28, 29
TransCanada Options Exchange, 36
Treasury bills
 in France, 251, 267–268
 in Italy, 312
Trescott, Paul B., 499
Trinidad, 49
Trust companies, in Canada, 1–5, 12–17, 26, 30, 34–36, 38, 40
Trustee Savings Bank, 438

UAP (France, insurance group), 463
Undertakings for collective investment in transferable securities (UCITS, France), 252, 278
Uniform Small Loan Law (U.S.), 484–485
Union Bank of Switzerland, 390, 393, 403
United Kingdom, bank structure, 54n, 151–152, 429–467
 bank excess capacity and profitability, 453–458
 building societies, 440–441, 447–452, 454–455, 466
 capital/assets ratio, 275
 capital markets, 173–176, 192, 432, 439, 441–442
 commercial banks, 180–193, 200–202, 278–279, 429–430, 438–439, 442, 445–459

INDEX   611

commercial banks and retail banking, 462–464
competition and its effects, 446–454, 457, 462–465
concentration of banks, 276
cross-subsidizing, 448–450, 453
deposit insurance, 219, 432
diversification, 432–438, 440–441, 452–453, 456, 458–459
domestic trading, 542
equity market, 176
finance companies, 459
financial conglomerates, 458–459
financial innovation, 438–440, 442
financial markets, 216
financial product price impacts, EC internal market, 210
financial services price decline, 210–213
financial strength, 587
foreign banks, 429, 464
globalization, 460
history, 439–441
industrial and commercial companies borrowing and financing, 174–175
insurance companies, 280, 436–438, 441
joint participation agreement, 215
liabilities of nonfinancial companies and bank lending, 164–165
life insurance companies, 192, 193
market capitalization ratios, 537–538
money market instruments, 208
mutual funds, 193
1992 integration effect, 459–467
price differentials in banking products, 209
Q-ratios, 214
regulation, 431–432, 440
retail banking, 441–444
risk-return tradeoff, 432–435
securities market, 192, 441, 444–445, 448–449
stock exchanges, 192, 444–445, 449, 543
structural change, 430–445
taxation, 176, 203
United States, bank structure, 469–545
  antitrust regulation, 523–524
  Banco de Chile New York branch, 107
  bank failures, 54n, 227n, 498–506, 512–513, 526–529
  Bank Holding Company, 506
  banking services, 191
  Bank Merger Acts, 506
  bank operations permitted, 161
  bank profitability comparative measures, 190
  building and loan associations, 482
  capital adequacy, 511–514
  capital/assets ratio, 275
  capital markets, 530
  CITIC subsidiaries, 125
  commercial banks, 202, 470–481, 485, 492, 505, 517–536, 544–545
  commercial banks and regulation, 508–509, 512–514
  competition, 506–507
  Comptroller of the Currency, 499–500, 508–512
  credit unions, 18, 474–475, 484, 508
  deposit insurance, 178, 221, 504, 508, 512, 525–530, 544–545
  deposit insurance premiums, 478–479, 483
  deposit insurance system coverage, 219
  disintermediation of bank lending, 530–532
  diversification, 506, 521
  diversity characteristic, 471
  domestic trading, 542
  equity markets, 541
  finance companies, 471, 474–476, 484–486, 491
  financial strength of banks, 587
  foreign banks, 532–539
  foreign-exchange trades, 479–480
  fragmentation characteristic, 470–471
  futures market, 493–495, 530, 539–541
  German bank branches, 560
  globalization, 532–543
  history, 495–507
  holding companies, 520–522, 524, 529–530
  industrial banks, 484
  insurance companies, 473–475, 486–488, 509
  investment banks, 491–493
  joint participation agreement, 215

612 INDEX

liabilities of nonfinancial companies and bank lending, 164–165
life insurance companies, 474–476, 486–488, 491
market capitalization ratios, 537–538
mortgage banks, 486–487
mutual funds, 473, 483, 490–491, 515, 518–519, 532, 544–545
mutual savings banks, 474–475, 481–483, 508, 518–520, 532, 544
net external liability, 334
nonbanking financial services, 192
options market, 493–495, 539, 540
pension funds, 473, 486, 488–491
portfolio restrictions, 511
protection for European banking markets, 586
Q-ratios, 214
regulation, 494–495, 504–527, 529–530, 537, 541, 543
relative importance of direct finance, 472–473
savings and loans, 474–477, 481–484, 508, 515, 518–520, 532, 544
securities markets, 472–475, 488, 491–495, 511, 516–519, 530–532, 541–544
securities markets enlarged, 500
securities markets globalization, 539
securitization, 530–532
stock exchanges, 492, 542

thrift industry crisis, 218, 220, 226n, 233n
U.S. Treasury Department, 513, 526
Unrestricted banking, 191
Uruguay, 107

Vancouver Stock Exchange (VSE), 28
Venezuela, 51
Voldés-Prieto, Solvodor, 59–109

Wallich, Henry C., 358
Wallich, Mable I., 358
Weber, Warren, 505
Weighted risk-asset ratio, 205
Weis, 452
Westinghouse Credit Corporation, 485
White Paper (1985), 196, 198, 201, 229n
Williamson, O.E., 337
Wilson, Woodrow, 501
World Bank, 117, 122, 137, 154, 404
Wriston, Walter, 225n
Wyman Report, 36

Yamada, Takeshi, 369

Zero percent bills, 82
Ziyang, Zhao, 118